Mobil
Travel Guide®

# SOUTHWEST

## ACKNOWLEDGEMENTS

We gratefully acknowledge the help of our representatives for their efficient and perceptive inspections of the lodging and dining establishments listed, the establishments' proprietors for their cooperation in showing their facilities and providing information about them, and the many users of previous editions who have taken the time to share their experiences. Mobil Travel Guide is also grateful to all the talented writers who contributed entries to this book.

Front cover photos:
Sunset behind giant saguaro catcus:
Copyright © 2007 Corel Corp.
Convention Center: Denver Metro
Convention & Visitors Bureau
Red Rocks Amphitheater: Denver Metro
Convention & Visitors Bureau
Echo Lake: Denver Metro Convention &
Visitors Bureau

ISBN: 0-8416-0320-0 or 978-0-8416-0320-2
Manufactured in the Canada.

10 9 8 7 6 5 4 3 2 1

# CONTENTS

## MAPS

## SOUTHWEST

## CELEBRATING 50 YEARS

Because time is precious and the travel industry is ever-changing, having accurate, reliable travel information at your has fingertips is essential. Mobil Travel Guide provided invaluable insight to travelers for 50 years, and we are committed to continuing this service into the future.

The Mobil Corporation (known as Exxon Mobil Corporation since a 1999 merger) began producing the Mobil Travel Guide books in 1958 following the introduction of the U.S.-interstate highway system in 1956. The first edition covered only five Southwestern states. Since then, our books have become the premier travel guides in North America, covering all 50 states and Canada.

Since its founding, Mobil Travel Guide has served as an advocate for travelers seeking knowledge about hotels, restaurants and places to visit. Based on an objective process, we make recommendations to our customers that we believe will enhance the quality and value of their travel experiences. Our trusted Mobil One- to Five-Star rating system is the oldest and most respected lodging and restaurant inspection and rating program in North America. Most hoteliers, restaurateurs and industry observers favorably regard the rigor of our inspection program and understand the prestige and benefits that come with receiving a Mobil Star rating.

The Mobil Travel Guide process of rating each establishment includes:
★ Unannouced facility inspections
★ Incognito service evaluations for
★ A review of unsolicited comments from the general public
★ Senior management oversight

For each property, more than 450 attributes, including cleanliness, physical facilities and employee attitude and courtesy, are measured and evaluated to produce a mathematically derived score, which is then blended with the other elements to form an overall score. These scores form the basis that we use to assign our Mobil One- to Five-Star ratings.

This process focuses on guest expectations, guest experience and consistency of service, not just physical facilities and amenities. It's fundamentally a rating system that rewards those properties that continually strive for and achieve excellence each year. The very best properties are consistently raising the bar for those that wish to compete with them.

Only facilities that meet Mobil Travel Guide's standards earn the privilege of being listed in the guide. Deteriorating, poorly managed establishments are deleted. A Mobil Travel Guide listing constitutes a positive quality recommendation. Every listing is an accolade, a recognition of achievement.

★★★★★The Mobil Five-Star Award indicates that a property is one of the very best in the country and consistently provides gracious and courteous service, superlative quality in its facility and a unique ambience. The lodgings and restaurants at the Mobil Five-Star level consistently continues their commitment to excellence, doing so with grace and perseverance.

★★★★The Mobil Four-Star Award honors properties for outstanding achievement in overall facility and for providing very strong service levels in all areas. These award winners provide a distinctive experience for the ever-demanding and sophisticated consumer.

★★★The Mobil Three-Star Award recognizes an excellent property that provides full services and amenities. This category ranges from exceptional hotels with limited services to elegant restaurants with a less-formal atmosphere.

★★The Mobil Two-Star property is a clean and comfortable establishment that has expanded amenities or a distinctive environment. These properties are an excellent place to stay or dine.

★The Mobil One-Star property is limited in its amenities and services but provides a value experience while meeting travelers' expectations. Expect the properties to be clean, comfortable and convenient.

We do not charge establishments for inclusion in our guides. We have no relationship with any of the businesses and attractions we list and act only as a consumer advocate. We do the investigative legwork so that you won't have to.

Restaurants and hotels—particularly small chains and stand-alone establishments—change management or even go out of business with surprising quickness. Although we make every effort to update continuously information, we recommend that you call ahead to make sure the place you've selected is still open.

We hope that your travels are enjoyable and relaxing and that our books help you get the most out of every trip you take. If any aspect of your accommodation, dining, spa or sightseeing experience motivates you to comment, please contact us. Mobil Travel Guide, 200 W. Madison St., Suite 3950, Chicago, IL 60611, or send an e-mail to info@mobiltravelguide.com.

Happy travels.

# HOW TO USE THIS BOOK

The Mobil Travel Guide Regional Travel Planners are designed for convenience. Each state has its own chapter, beginning with a general introduction that provides a geographical and historical orientation to the state and gives basic statewide tourist information. The remainder of each chapter is devoted to travel destinations within the state—mainly cities and towns, but also national parks and tourist areas—which, like the states, are arranged in alphabetical order.

## MAPS

We have provided state maps as well as maps of selected larger cities to help you find your way.

## DESTINATION INFORMATION

We list addresses, phone number and web sites for travel information resources—usually the local chamber of commerce or office of tourism—and a brief introduction to the area. Information about airports, ground transportation and suburbs is included for large cities.

## DRIVING TOURS AND WALKING TOURS

The driving tours that we include for many states are usually day trips that make for interesting side excursions. They offer you a way to get off the beaten path. These trips frequently cover areas of natural beauty or historical significance.

## WHAT TO SEE AND DO

Mobil Travel Guide offers information about thousands of museums, art galleries, amusement parks, historic sites, national and state parks, ski areas and many other attractions.

Following an attraction's description, you'll find the months, days and, in some cases, hours of operation, address, telephone number and web site (if there is one).

## SPECIAL EVENTS

Special events are either annual events that last only a short time, such as festivals and fairs or longer, seasonal events such as horse racing, theater and summer concerts. Our Special Events listings also include infrequently occurring occasions that mark certain dates or events, such as a centennial or other commemorative celebration.

## LISTINGS

Hotels, restaurants and spas are usually listed under the city or town in which they're located. Make sure to check the nearby cities and towns for additional options, especially if you're traveling to a major metropolitan area that includes many suburbs. If a property is located in a town that doesn't have its own heading, the listing appears under the town nearest it. In large cities, hotels located within 5 miles of major commercial airports may be listed under a separate Airport Area heading that follows the city section.

## THE STAR RATINGS
### MOBIL RATED HOTELS

Travelers have different needs when it comes to accommodations. To help you pinpoint properties that meet your particular needs, Mobil Travel Guide classifies each lodging by type according to the following characteristics.

★★★★★The Mobil Five-Star hotel provides consistently superlative service in an exceptionally distinctive luxury environment, with expanded services. Attention to detail is evident throughout the hotel, resort or inn, from bed linens to staff uniforms.

★★★★The Mobil Four-Star hotel provides a luxury experience with expanded amenities in a distinctive environment. Services may include automatic turndown service, 24-hour room service and valet parking.

★★★The Mobil Three-Star hotel is well appointed, with a full-service restaurant and expanded amenities, such as a fitness center, golf course, tennis courts, 24-hour room service and optional turndown service.

★★The Mobil Two-Star hotel is considered a clean, comfortable and reliable establishment that has expanded amenities, such as a full-service restaurant on the premises.

★The Mobil One-Star lodging is a limited-service hotel, motel or inn that is considered a clean, comfortable and reliable establishment

For every property, we also provide pricing information. The pricing categories break down as follows:

★    **$** = Up to $150
★    **$$** = $151-$250
★    **$$$** = $251-$350
★    **$$$$** = $351 and up

All prices quoted are accurate at the time of publication, however prices cannot be guaranteed. In some locations, special events, holidays or seasons can affect prices. Some resorts have complicated rate structures that vary with the time of year, so confirm rates when making your plans.

### SPECIALITY LODGINGS

A Speciality Lodging is a unique inn, bed and breakfast or guest ranch with limited service, but appealing, attractive facilities that make the property worth a visit.

## MOBIL RATED RESTAURANTS

All Mobil Star-rated dining establishments listed in this book have a full kitchen and most offer table service.

★★★★★The Mobil Five-Star restaurant offers one of few flawless dining experiences in the country. These establishments consistently provide their guests with exceptional food, superlative service, elegant décor and exquisite presentations of each detail surrounding a meal.

★★★★The Mobil Four-Star restaurant provides professional service, distinctive presentations and wonderful food.

★★★The Mobil Three-Star restaurant has good food, warm and skillful service and enjoyable décor.

★★The Mobil Two-Star restaurant serves fresh food in a clean setting with efficient service. Value is considered in this category, as is family friendliness.

★The Mobil One-Star restaurant provides a distinctive experience through culinary specialty, local flair or individual atmosphere.

Each restaurant listing gives the cuisine type, street address, phone and website, meals served, days of operation (if not open daily year-round) and pricing category. Information about appropriate attire is provided, although it's always a good idea to call ahead and ask if you're unsure; the meaning of "casual" or "business casual" varies widely in different parts of the country. We also indicate whether the restaurant has a bar, whether a children's menu is offered and whether outdoor seating is available. If reservations are recommended, we note that fact in the listing. When valet parking is available, it is noted in the description. Because menu prices can fluctuate, we list a pricing category rather than specific prices. The pricing categories are defined as follows, per diner, and assume that you order an appetizer or dessert, an entrée and one drink:

★  **$** = $15 and under
★  **$$** = $16-$35
★  **$$$** = $36-$85
★  **$$$$** = $86 and up

All prices quoted are accurate at the time of publication, but prices cannot be guaranteed.

## MOBIL RATED SPAS

Mobil Travel Guide is pleased to announce its newest category, hotel and resort spas. Until now, hotel and resort spas have not been formally rated or inspected by any organization. Every spa selected for inclusion in this book underwent a rigorous inspection process similar to the one Mobil Travel Guide has been applying to lodgings and restaurants for five decades. After researching more than 300 spas and performing exhaustive incognito inspections of more than 200 properties, we narrowed our list to the best spas in the United States and Canada.

Mobil Travel Guide's spa ratings are based on objective evaluations of more than 450 attributes. Approximately half of these criteria assess basic expectations, such as staff courtesy, the technical proficiency and skill of the employees and whether the facility is maintained properly and hygienically. Several standards address issues that impact a guest's physical comfort and convenience, as well as the staff's ability to impart a sense of personalized service and anticipate clients' needs. Additional criteria measure the spa's ability to create a completely calming ambience.

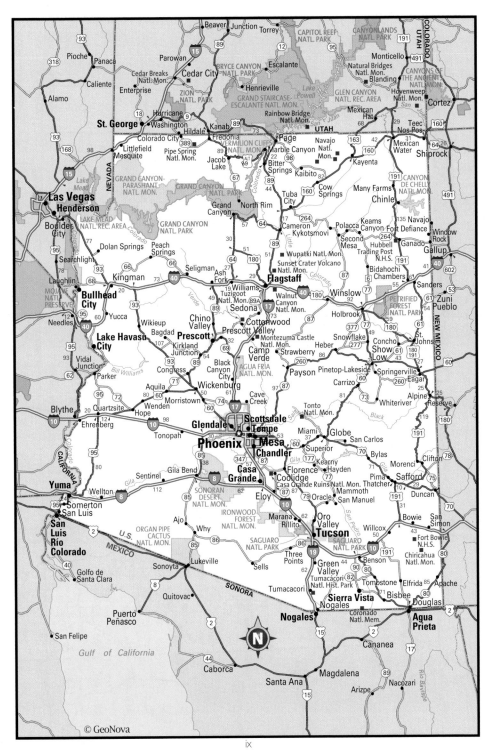

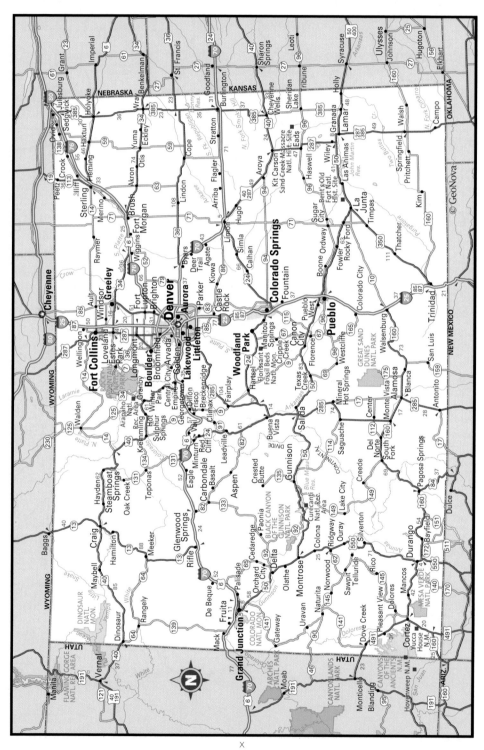

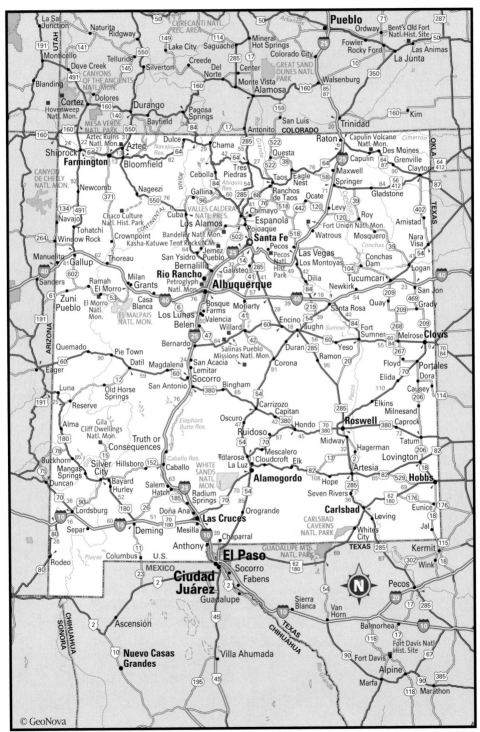

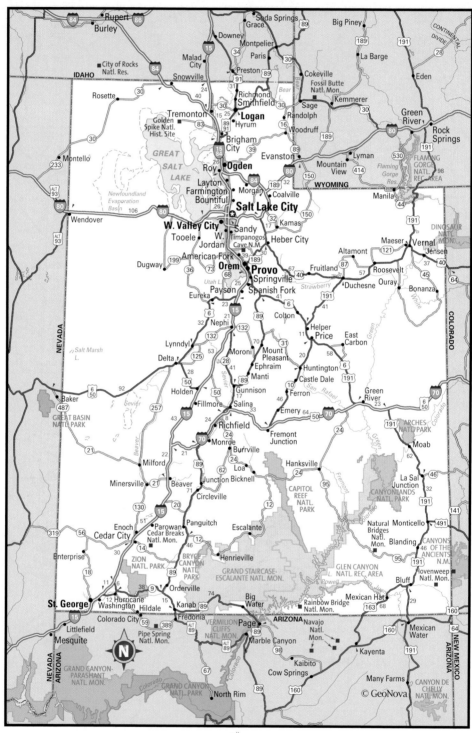

The Mobil Star ratings focus on much more than the facilities available at a spa and the treatments it offers. Each Mobil Star rating is a cumulative score achieved from multiple inspections that reflects the spa management's attention to detail and commitment to consumers' needs.

★★★★★The Mobil Five-Star spa provides consistently superlative service in an exceptionally distinctive luxury environment with extensive amenities. The staff at a Mobil Five-Star spa provides extraordinary service beyond the traditional spa experience, allowing guests to achieve the highest level of relaxation and pampering. A Mobil Five-Star spa offers an extensive array of treatments, often incorporating international themes and products. Attention to detail is evident throughout the spa, from arrival to departure.

★★★★The Mobil Four-Star spa provides a luxurious experience with expanded amenities in an elegant and serene environment. Throughout the spa facility, guests experience personalized service. Amenities might include, but are not limited to, single-sex relaxation rooms where guests wait for their treatments, plunge pools and whirlpools in both men's and women's locker rooms, and an array of treatments, including a selection of massages, body therapies, facials and a variety of salon services.

★★★The Mobil Three-Star spa is physically well appointed and has a full complement of staff.

# ★CELEBRATING★
## 50 YEARS OF MOBIL TRAVEL GUIDE

**1962** — **1964** — **1968** — **1971**

**1973** — **1976** — **1978** — **1979**

**← 1986 ——————— 1988 ——————— 1989 ——————— 1992 →**

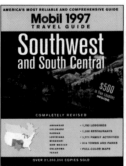

**← 1994 ——————— 1997 ——————— 1998 ——————— 2003 →**

# ARIZONA

HIKE THE GRAND CANYON. RELAX AT A SPA. HIT THE LINKS. THIS RAPIDLY GROWING STATE— it has more than tripled its population since 1940—offers all of this and much more.

Arizona is known for its hot summers, mild winters and desert landscape. But the northern mountains, cool forests, spectacular canyons and lakes offer a variety of vacation activities, including fishing, white water rafting, hiking and camping. The northern, central part of the state is on a plateau at higher altitudes than the desert in the southern region of the state and has a cooler climate.

There are also meadows filled with wildflowers, ghost and mining towns, dude ranches and intriguing ancient American Indian villages. The state has 23 reservations and one of the largest Native American populations in the United States. More than half of that population is Navajo. Visitors can scoop up craft specialties including basketry, pottery, weaving, jewelry and kachina dolls.

Arizona has scores of water parks, interesting museums, zoos and wildlife exhibits. And who says it doesn't snow in Arizona? There are several places for downhill skiing, including the Arizona Snowball in northern Arizona, Mt. Lemmon Ski Valley near Tucson and Sunrise Ski Resort in the east.

Of course, there is also plenty of what people have come to expect here. There are more than 300 golf courses across the state, making it home to several stops on the PGA Tour, most notably the Phoenix Open. You'll also find some of the best spas in the country. Enjoy.

**Information: www.arizonaguide.com**

## ★ SPOTLIGHT

★ Arizona does not observe Daylight Saving Time, except on the Navajo reservation, which stretches over three states.

★ The state is home to 22 tribal nations.

## BEYOND THE GRAND CANYON

This loop drive, a side trip for visitors to the South Rim of Grand Canyon National Park, combines scenic beauty with archeological, historical, geologic and scientific sites. It can be done in one full day or divided into a day and a half with an overnight stop in Flagstaff.

From Grand Canyon Village, head south on Hwy. 64/Hwy. 180, turning southeast on Hwy. 180 at Valle for a drive through the San Francisco Mountains. Those interested in the history of the area, including prehistoric peoples and more recent Native Americans, will want to stop at the Museum of Northern Arizona (3101 N. Ft. Valley Rd., Flagstaff). Continue along Hwy. 180 to the turnoff to Lowell Observatory (1400 W. Mars Hill Rd., Flagstaff), which has been the site of many important astronomical discoveries since its founding in 1894. Guided tours of the facilities are offered, and there's a public observatory.

You are now on the north edge of Flagstaff. From the city, go east on I-40, and take the turnoff to Walnut Canyon National Monument to see dozens of small cliff dwellings built by the Sinagua people some 700 years ago. The monument can be explored on two trails. One is a fairly easy walk along a mesa-top; the other is a bit more strenuous but provides a much closer look at the cliff dwellings as it drops about 185 feet into Walnut Canyon.

Leaving the monument, head back toward Flagstaff on I-40 and go north on Hwy. 89 to the Sunset Crater Volcano/Wupatki national monuments loop road, where there is an extinct volcano, fields of lava rock and ruins of prehistoric stone pueblos. Wupatki National Monument's main attraction is Wupatki Pueblo, a 100-room dwelling built in the 12th century by the Sinaguans. This handsome apartment house was constructed of red sandstone slabs, blocks of pale beige limestone and chunks of brown basalt and cemented together with clay. Nearby, Sunset Crater Volcano National Monument offers an intimate look at a dormant volcano, with its rugged landscape of jet-black basalt, twisted into myriad shapes. Sunset Crater's primary eruption was in the winter of 1065.

After rejoining U.S. 89, continue north into the Navajo Reservation and the community of Cameron, with the historic but still operating Cameron Trading Post, which sells museum-quality items as well as more affordable rugs, baskets, jewelry and other American Indian crafts. From Cameron, head west on Hwy. 64 back into the national park. Approximately 215 miles.

# AJO

Once a copper-mining hub, Ajo is located about 40 miles from the Mexico border. It's a prime spot to stop while visiting nearby Organ Pipe Cactus National Monument.
Information: www.ajochamber.com

## WHAT TO SEE AND DO

### Organ Pipe Cactus National Monument
Hw. 85, Ajo, 520-387-6849;
www.nps.gov/orpi

This 516-square-mile Sonoran desert area on the Mexican border is Arizona's largest national monument. The organ pipe cactus grows as high as 20 feet and has 30 or more arms, which resemble organ pipes. The plant blooms in May and June, and the blossoms are white with pink or lavender. During February and March, depending on rainfall, parts of the area may be covered with Mexican gold poppy, magenta owl clover, blue lupine and bright orange mallow. Many desert plants thrive here, including mesquite, saguaro, several species of cholla, barrel cacti, paloverde trees, creosote bush and ocotillo.

You can take two scenic drives, both self-guided: the 53-mile Puerto Blanco and the 21-mile Ajo Mountain drives. There is a 208-site campground near headquarters May-mid-January, 30-day limit; mid-January-April, 14-day limit.

## SPECIALTY LODGINGS

### Guest House Inn
700 Guest House Rd., Ajo, 520-387-6133;
www.guesthouseinn.biz
4 rooms. Complimentary full breakfast. $

# BISBEE

Located in the foothills of the Mule Mountains of southeastern Arizona, Bisbee was a tough mining town known as "Queen of the Copper Camps." Today, it's rich in architecture and culture with many art galleries, period hotels and bed-and-breakfasts.
Information: Greater Bisbee Chamber of Commerce, 1 Main St., 520-432-5421; www.bisbeearizona.com

## WHAT TO SEE AND DO

### Bisbee Mining and Historical Museum

5 Copper Queen Plaza, Bisbee, 520-432-7071; www.bisbeemuseum.org
Housed in the 1897 office building of the Copper Queen Consolidated Mining Company, this museum depicts early development of this urban center through displays on mining, historical photographs and more.

### Bisbee Restoration Association & Historical Museum

37 Main St., Bisbee, 520-432-4106
Local historical and pioneer artifacts; Mining relics. Tuesday-Saturday 10 a.m.-3 p.m.

### Queen Mine

118 Arizona St., Bisbee, 520-432-2071, 866-432-2071
This one-hour guided tour on a mine train takes you 1,800 feet into mine tunnel. Daily 9 a.m., 10:30 a.m., noon, 2 p.m., 3:30 p.m.

## HOTELS

### ★★Copper Queen Hotel

11 Howell Ave., Bisbee, 520-432-2216; www.copperqueen.com
48 rooms. Restaurant, bar. Pool. $

### Calumet and Arizona Guest House

608 Powell St., Bisbee, 520-432-4815; www.calumetaz.com
6 rooms. Complimentary full breakfast. Pets accepted. $

**3**

# BULLHEAD CITY

Bullhead City was established in 1945 as a construction camp for Davis Dam, a reclamation facility located three miles to the north. The name is derived from its proximity to Bull's Head Rock, now largely concealed by the waters of Lake Mohave. Bullhead City is across the Colorado River from Laughlin, Nevada, and its casinos.
Information: Chamber of Commerce, 1251 Hwy. 95, 928-754-4121; www.bullheadcity.com

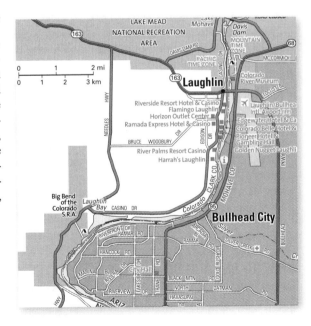

**ARIZONA**

## WHAT TO SEE AND DO
### Davis Dam and Power Plant
Bullhead City, 928-754-3620
This dam has a surface area of 28,500 acres and reaches 67 miles upstream to Hoover Dam.

## HOTELS
### ★Best Western Bullhead City Inn
1126 Hwy. 95, Bullhead City,
928-754-3000, 800-780-7234;
www.bestwestern.com
88 rooms. Complimentary continental breakfast. Pets accepted. Pool. $

### ★★Lake Mohave Resort
2690 E Katherine Spur Rd.,
Bullhead City, 928-754-3245;
www.sevencrown.com
51 rooms. Restaurant, bar. Pets accepted. $

## RESTAURANTS
### ★El Encanto
125 Long Ave., Bullhead City,
928-754-5100
Mexican menu. Breakfast, lunch, dinner. Bar. Children's menu. Outdoor seating. $

**4**

**ARIZONA**

## CANYON DE CHELLY NATIONAL MONUMENT
The smooth red sandstone walls of the canyon extend straight up as much as 1,000 feet from the nearly flat sand bottom. When William of Normandy defeated the English at the Battle of Hastings in 1066, the Pueblo had already built apartment houses in these walls. Many ruins are still here.

The Navajo came long after the original tenants had abandoned these structures. In 1864, Kit Carson's men drove nearly all the Navajo out of the area, marching them on foot 300 miles to the Bosque Redondo in eastern New Mexico. Since 1868, Navajo have returned to farming, cultivating the orchards and grazing their sheep in the canyon. In 1931, Canyon de Chelly and its tributaries, Canyon del Muerto and Monument Canyon, were designated a national monument.

There are more than 60 major ruins—some dating from circa A.D. 300—in these canyons. White House, Antelope House and Mummy Cave are among the most picturesque. Most ruins are inaccessible but can be seen from either the canyon bottom or from the road along the top of the precipitous walls. Two spectacular, 16-mile rim drives can be made by car in any season. Lookout points—sometimes a short distance from the road—are clearly marked. The only self-guided trail (2 1/2 miles round-trip) leads to the canyon floor and White House ruin from White House Overlook. Other hikes can be made only with a National Park Service permit and an authorized Navajo guide. Only four-wheel drive vehicles are allowed in the canyons—and each vehicle must be accompanied by an authorized Navajo guide and requires a National Park Service permit obtainable from a ranger at the visitor center. Information: Hwy. 191, Window Rock, 928-674-5500; www.nps.gov/cach

## WHAT TO SEE AND DO
### Canyon Tours
Hwy. 191 and RR 7, Chinle,
928-674-5841, 800-679-2473
Personnel from Thunderbird Lodge conduct jeep tours into the canyons; half-day (daily) and full-day (April-October, daily) trips.

## HOTELS
### ★★Best Western Canyon De Chelly Inn
100 Main St., Chinle,
928-674-5874, 800-327-0354;
www.bestwestern.com
102 rooms. Restaurant. Pets accepted. Pool. $

## ★★Thunderbird Lodge
Hwy. 191 and Rte. 7, Chinle,
928-674-5841, 800-679-2473;
www.tbirdlodge.com
73 rooms. Restaurant. Pets accepted. **$**

# CAREFREE

The immense Tonto National Forest stretches to the north and east. In the center of town is the largest and most accurate sundial in the Western Hemisphere.

Information: Carefree/Cave Creek Chamber of Commerce, 748 Easy St., 480-488-3381; www.carefree.org

## SPECIAL EVENTS

### Carefree Fine Art and Wine Festivals
Easy and Ho Hum Streets,
Carefree, 480-837-5637;
www.thunderbirdartists.com

At each of these pleasant outdoor festivals, more than 150 booths feature the work of nationally recognized artists. You'll find a wide range of mediums from paintings and pottery to sculptures and stained glass, in all price ranges. In the wine pavilion, host to Arizona's largest wine-tasting event, visitors can sample vintages from around the world. The popular festivals draw more than 180,000 art lovers each year. Late October, early November, mid-January, early March: Friday-Sunday 10 a.m.-5 p.m.

### Fiesta Days
28th St. and New River Rd.,
Memorial Arena, Carefree,
480-488-3381

This three-day event features a rodeo, family entertainment and a parade. Usually the second weekend in April.

## HOTELS

### ★★★★The Boulders Resort and Golden Door Spa
34631 N. Tom Darlington Dr., Carefree,
480-488-9009, 866-397-6520;
www.theboulders.com

Located in the foothills of the Sonoran Desert just north of Scottsdale, the Boulders Resort and Golden Door Spa blends perfectly with the surrounding rock outcroppings, ancient boulders and saguaro cactus plants. The adobe casitas are distinguished by overstuffed leather chairs, exposed beams, and Mexican tiles, while one-, two- and three-bedroom Pueblo Villas are ideal for families or for those on longer visits. The resort boasts a first-rate tennis facility and an 18-hole championship golf course. There's also rock climbing, hiking and tours of Native American cave dwellings and ruins. Guided night hikes using night vision equipment are especially fun. The Golden Door Spa, an outpost of the famous California spa, is divine.

215 rooms. Pets accepted, some restrictions; fee. High-speed Internet access. Five restaurants, three bars. Children's activity center. Fitness room, fitness classes available, spa. Three outdoor pools, whirlpool. Golf, 36 holes. Tennis. Business center. **$$$$**

## SPAS

### ★★★Golden Door Spa at the Boulders
34631 N. Tom Darlington Dr., Carefree,
480-595-3500, 800-553-1717;
www.theboulders.com

This branch of the original California spa is the jewel in the crown at the Boulders Resort. Many treatments are a nod to the region's Native American history. Ancient Ayurvedic principles are revived in the mystical treatments of *bindi* balancing, where crushed herbs exfoliate and light oils moisturize your skin, and *shirodhara*, which begins with massaging warm oil into your scalp and concludes with a mini facial massage and a heated hand and foot treatment. The 33,000-square-foot spa also includes a meditation labyrinth inspired by Hopi medicine wheels and a movement studio, which offers yoga, tai chi, Pilates, kickboxing and more. **$$**

**5**

**ARIZONA**

★
★
★
★
★

## RESTAURANTS

### ★★★The Latilla

34631 N. Tom Darlington Dr., Carefree, 480-488-9009, 866-397-6520; www.theboulders.com

The cuisine at this glass-enclosed restaurant in the Boulders Resort and Spa focuses on fresh, organic produce, free-range meats and poultry and responsibly caught seafood from clean waters. Most of the wines are also organic. The rustic, cozy dining room is decorated with Ocotillo branches (called *latilla*, which means little sticks in Spanish). The outdoor patio, warmed by a blazing fire, is an ideal spot to have a drink before or after dinner. California menu. Dinner. Bar. Business casual attire. Reservations recommended. Valet parking. Outdoor seating. $$$

# CASA GRANDE

Named for the Hohokam ruins 20 miles northeast of town, Casa Grande is situated in an agricultural and industrial area.

Information: Chamber of Commerce, 575 N. Marshall St., 520-836-2125, 800-916-1515; www.casagrandechamber.org

## WHAT TO SEE AND DO

### Casa Grande Valley Historical Society and Museum

110 W Florence Blvd., Casa Grande, 520-836-2223; www.cgvhs.org

Exhibits trace the growth of the Casa Grande Valley from prehistoric times to the present, with an emphasis on farm, ranch, mining and domestic life. September-May: Monday-Saturday 1-5 p.m.; closed summer.

### Picacho Peak State Park

15520 Picacho Peak Rd., Picacho, 520-466-3183; www.pr.state.az.us/Parks/parkhtml/picacho.html

This 3,400-acre park includes a sheer-sided peak rising 1,500 feet above the desert floor that was a landmark for early travelers. The only Civil War battle in Arizona was fought near here. Colorful spring wildflowers; desert nature study. Hiking, picnicking. Daily 8 a.m.-10 p.m.

## SPECIAL EVENTS

### O'Odham Tash-Casa Grande's Indian Days

Casa Grande, 520-836-4723

Rodeo, parades, ceremonial dances, arts and crafts, barbecue and more. Reservations advised. Mid-February.

---

### CASA GRANDE RUINS NATIONAL MONUMENT

The four-story Casa Grande was built during the 14th century. It was constructed of caliche-bearing soil (a crust of calcium carbonate on stony soil) and is covered by a large protective roof, making it the only structure of its type and size in southern Arizona. After being occupied for some 100 years, Casa Grande was abandoned. Father Kino, the Jesuit missionary and explorer, sighted and named it Big House in 1694. Museum with archaeological exhibits; self-guided tours.

Information: 1100 Ruins Dr., Coolidge, 520-723-3172; www.nps.gov/cagr

---

# CHANDLER

Chandler is one of the major suburbs of Phoenix. A growing number of high-technology companies have facilities here, including Intel, Motorola and Microchip Technologies.

Information: Chandler Chamber of Commerce, 25 S. Arizona Place, 480-963-4571, 800-963-4571; www.chandleraz.org

## WHAT TO SEE AND DO

### Casa Paloma

7131 W. Ray Rd., Chandler, 480-777-2272
It's worth stopping at this upscale strip mall
with 35 shops. After shopping, pamper
yourself at Rolfs Salon and Spa or dine at
one of seven restaurants. Daily.

### Chandler Center for the Arts

250 N. Arizona Ave., Chandler,
480-782-2680; www.chandlercenter.org
This 64,000-square-foot performance center is known for its superb acoustics. The
London City Opera, Jay Leno, Anne Mur-
ray, Rita Moreno, Bob Newhart and the
Phoenix Boys Choir are among those who
have helped the center earn its reputation
for staging shows that bring audiences to
their feet. The main auditorium seats 1,550
but can be subdivided into three separate
halls holding 1,000, 350, and 250 people,
respectively.

### Wild Horse Pass Casino

5550 W. Wild Horse Pass, Chandler,
800-946-4452; www.wingilariver.com
With nearly 170,000 square feet of gaming action, this casino offers lots of
options. The card room is decked out
with 19 poker tables, while the bingo hall
has 1,200 seats. There's also a 24-hour
live keno section and more than 500 slot
machines.

## SPECIAL EVENTS

### Chandler Jazz Festival

Chandler, 480-782-2735;
www.chandleraz.gov
More than 20 bands perform mostly swing
music. The two-day event attracts about
6,000 jazz lovers. Late April.

### Chandler Ostrich Festival

Tumbleweed Park, 2250 S. McQueen Rd.,
Chandler, 480-963-4571;
www.ostrichfestival.com
Features ostrich racing, food, entertainment,
arts and crafts, carnival with rides and other
amusements such as a petting zoo and pony
rides. Early March.

## HOTELS

### ★Fairfield Inn

7425 W. Chandler Blvd., Chandler,
480-940-0099, 800-228-2800;
www.fairfieldinn.com
66 rooms. Complimentary continental
breakfast. Pool. $

### ★★Radisson Hotel Phoenix-Chandler

7475 W. Chandler Blvd., Chandler,
480-961-4444, 888-201-1718;
www.radisson.com/chandleraz
159 rooms. High-speed Internet access.
Restaurant, bar. Airport transportation
available. Pets accepted. Pool. $

### ★★★Crowne Plaza San Marcos Golf Resort

1 San Marcos Place, Chandler,
480-812-0900, 800-528-8071;
www.sanmarcosresort.com
Built in 1912, this was the first golf course
in Arizona. Located just a few miles from
companies like Motorola and Intel, it's a
great choice for business travelers. Families can enjoy tennis and horseback riding. Guest rooms include eye pillows, ear
plugs, lavender spray and sleep CDs.
307 rooms. Restaurant, bar. Pets accepted.
Pool. Golf. Tennis. Business center. $

### ★★★Sheraton Wild Horse Pass Resort and Spa

5594 W. Wild Horse Pass Blvd., Chandler,
602-225-0100, 800-325-3535;
www.wildhorsepassresort.com
This unique resort on Gila River tribal
land blends the décor and traditions of the
area with the convenience and services of
a modern hotel. Each detail of the interior
has been included for its significance to
Native American Indian traditions, from
the design of the title to the petroglyph-
engraved furniture. The destination resort
also features two 18-hole golf courses, a
17,500-square-foot spa, equestrian center
for riding lessons and trail rides, jogging
paths and tennis courts. A two-mile replica of the Gila River runs through the
property and offers boat rides to the Wild

ARIZONA

Horse Pass Casino or the Whirlwind Golf Club.

500 rooms. High-speed Internet access. Three restaurants, three bars. Spa. Airport transportation available. Pets accepted. Golf. Tennis. **$$$**

## RESTAURANTS

### ★★C-Fu Gourmet
2051 W Warner Rd., Chandler, 480-899-3888; www.cfugourmet.com
Chinese, dim sum, sushi. Lunch, dinner. Bar. Casual attire. Reservations recommended. **$$**

### ★El Sol Bakery
760 N. Arizona Ave., Chandler, 480-786-0811
Mexican menu. Breakfast, lunch, dinner. Closed Sunday. Casual attire. **$**

### ★★★★Kai
5594 W. Wild Horse Pass Blvd., Chandler, 602-385-5726; www.wildhorsepassresort.com
Lodged in the Sheraton Wild Horse Pass, this sophisticated eatery showcases locally grown produce and a surprisingly rich Arizona-made olive oil in recipes that merge contemporary tastes and time-honored Native American techniques. (Kai means "seed" in Pima.) The results include lobster tail, corn and avocado atop fry bread, and rack of lamb sauced with a mole made from American Indian seeds. Southwestern menu. Dinner. Closed Sunday-Monday. Bar. Business casual attire. Outdoor seating. **$$$**

### ★Soul in the Hole
601 N. Arizona Ave., Chandler, 480-963-7787
American menu. Lunch, dinner. Closed Monday. Casual attire. **$**

# COTTONWOOD

This town is in the beautiful Verde Valley, an area offering many opportunities for exploration.
Information: Chamber of Commerce, 1010 S. Main St., Cottonwood, 928-634-7593; www.cottonwoodarizona.com.

## WHAT TO SEE AND DO
### Dead Horse Ranch State Park
675 Dead Horse Ranch Rd., Cottonwood, 928-634-5283; www.azparks.gov/Parks/parkhtml/deadhorse.html
This 423-acre park offers fishing, nature trails, hiking, picnicking, camping . Visitor center. Daily from 8 a.m.

## SPECIAL EVENTS
### Verde Valley Fair
Fairgrounds, 800 E. Cherry St., Cottonwood, 928-634-3290; www.verdevalleyfair.com

This annual fair features live music, arts and crafts, racing and swimming swines, novelty shows, food and contests. First weekend in May.

## HOTELS
### ★★Best Western Cottonwood Inn
993 S. Main St., Cottonwood, 928-634-5575, 800-350-0025; www.bestwestern.com
77 rooms. Complimentary continental breakfast. Pool. **$**

# FLAGSTAFF

In 1876, the Boston Party, a group of pioneers made camp in a mountain valley on the Fourth of July. They stripped a pine tree of its branches and hung a flag at its top. Afterward, the tree was used as a marker for travelers who referred to the place as the spring by the flag staff. In

1882, Flagstaff became a railroad town when the Atlantic and Pacific Railroad (now the Santa Fe) was built.

Today, Flagstaff, home of Northern Arizona University, is an educational and cultural center. And tourism is the main industry—the city is a good place to see the Navajo country, Oak Creek Canyon, the Grand Canyon and Humphreys Peak (12,670 feet), the tallest mountain in Arizona. Tall pine forests fill the surrounding area.
**Information: Chamber of Commerce, 101 W. Rte. 66, 928-774-4505; www.flagstaff.az.gov**

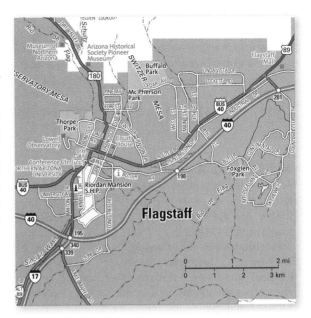

## SUNSET CRATER VOLCANO NATIONAL MONUMENT

Between the growing seasons of 1064 and 1065, violent volcanic eruptions built a large cone-shaped mountain of cinders and ash called a cinder cone volcano. Around the base of the cinder cone, lava flowed from cracks, creating the Bonito Lava Flow on the west side of the cone and the Kana'a Lava Flow on the east side. The approximate date of the initial eruption was determined by examining tree rings of timber found in the remains of American Indian pueblos at Wupatki National Monument.

This cinder cone, now called Sunset Crater, stands about 1,000 feet above the surrounding terrain. Mineral deposits around the rim stained the cinders, giving the summit a perpetual sunset hue.

Park rangers are on duty all year. Do not attempt to drive off the roads; the cinders are soft and the surrounding landscape is very fragile. The U.S. Forest Service maintains a campground (May-mid-September) opposite the visitor center. Guided tours and naturalist activities are offered during the summer. Visitor center daily. A 20-mile paved road leads to Wupatki National Monument. Information: 7133 N. US 89, Flagstaff, 928-526-0502; www.nps.gov/sucr

**9**

**ARIZONA**

## WUPATKI NATIONAL MONUMENT

The nearly 2,600 archeological sites of the Sinagua and Anasazi cultures were occupied between A.D. 1100-1250. The largest of them, Wupatki Pueblo, was three stories high, with about 100 rooms. The eruption of nearby Sunset Crater spread volcanic ash over an 800-square-mile area and for a time, made this an active farming center.

The half-mile ruins trail is self-guided. Books are available at its starting point. The visitor center and main ruin are open daily. Wupatki National Monument and Sunset Crater Volcano National Monument are located on a 35-mile paved loop off of Hwy 89. The nearest camping is at Bonito Campground (May-October; 520-526-0866).

Information: 6400 N. Hwy. 89, Flagstaff, 928-679-2365; www.nps.gov/wupa

## WHAT TO SEE AND DO

### Arizona Historical Society Pioneer Museum
2340 N. Fort Valley Rd.,
Flagstaff, 928-774-6272;
www.arizonahistoricalsociety.org
This museum highlights the history of Flagstaff and northern Arizona. There are changing exhibits throughout the year. Monday-Saturday.

### Arizona Snowbowl Ski & Summer Resort
6355 Hwy. 180, Flagstaff, 928-779-1951;
www.arizonasnowbowl.com
The 50-acre resort has two triple, two double chairlifts; patrol, school, rentals; restaurants, bars, lounge; lodges. Thirty-two trails, longest run more than two miles; vertical drop 2,300 feet. Mid-December-mid-April, daily. Skyride (Memorial Day-Labor Day) takes riders to 11,500 feet.

### Coconino National Forest
1824 S. Thompson St., Flagstaff,
928-527-3600;
www.fs.fed.us/r3/coconino
This national forest surrounds the city of Flagstaff and the community of Sedona. Outstanding scenic areas include Humphreys Peak—Arizona's highest point—as well as parts of the Mogollon Rim and the Verde River Valley, the red rock country of Sedona; Oak Creek Canyon (where Zane Grey wrote *Call of the Canyon*) and the San Francisco Peaks. Includes extinct volcanoes and high country lakes. Fishing, hunting, winter sports, camping.

### Lowell Observatory
1400 Mars Hill Rd., Flagstaff,
928-774-3358; www.lowell.edu
The planet Pluto was discovered from this observatory in 1930. Guided tours, slide presentations, telescope viewing. Telescope domes are unheated so appropriate clothing is advised. November-Februray: daily noon-5 p.m.; March-October: daily 9 a.m.-5 p.m.; September-May Wednesday, Friday, Saturday 5:30-9:30 p.m.; June-August Monday-Saturday 5:30-10:00 p.m.

### Mormon Lake Ski Center
5075 N. Hwy. 89, Flagstaff, 928-354-2240
This terrain includes snowy meadows, huge stands of pine, oak and aspen, old logging roads and turn-of-the-century railroad grades. Plus, more than 20 miles of marked, groomed trails. School, rentals, ski shop. Guided tours (including moonlight tours on full moon weekends). Restaurant, bar, motel, cabins. Daily 8 a.m.- 5 p.m.

### Museum of Northern Arizona
3101 N. Fort Valley Rd., Flagstaff,
928-774-5213; www.musnaz.org
Exhibits on the archaeology, geology, biology, paleontology and fine arts of the Colorado Plateau. Daily 8 a.m.-5 p.m.

### Oak Creek Canyon
Slide Rock State Park, 6871 N. Hwy. 89A,
Sedona, 928-282-3034;
www.azparks.gov/parks/parkhtml/sliderock.html
This spectacular gorge may look familiar to you—it's a favorite location for western movies. The northern end of the road starts with a lookout point atop the walls and descends nearly 2,000 feet to the stream bed. The creek has excellent trout fishing. At the southern mouth of the canyon is Sedona.

### Riordan Mansion State Historic Park

409 Riordan Rd., Flagstaff, 928-779-4395;
www.azparks.gov/parks/parkhtml/
riordan.html

This six-acre park features an Arts and Crafts-style mansion built in 1904 by Michael and Timothy Riordan, two brothers who played a significant role in the development of Flagstaff and northern Arizona. Original artifacts, handcrafted furniture, mementos. Picnic area. Guided tours (reservations recommended). May-October: daily 8:30 a.m.-5 p.m.; November-April: daily 10:30 a.m.-5 p.m.

### Walnut Canyon National Monument

Walnut Canyon Rd., Flagstaff,
928-526-3367;
www.nps.gov/waca

A spectacular, rugged 400-foot-deep canyon with 300 small cliff dwellings dating back to around AD 1100. The dwellings are well preserved because they are under protective ledges in the canyon's limestone walls. There are two self-guided trails and an educational museum in the visitor center. Picnic grounds. Daily.

## SPECIAL EVENTS

### Coconino County Fair

Flagstaff, 928-774-5139;
www.coconino.az.gov/parks.aspx

This annual fair in Coconino County features livestock auctions, contests, entertainment, fine arts and food. Labor Day weekend.

### Hopi Artists' Exhibition

Museum of Northern Arizona,
3101 N. Fort Valley Rd., Flagstaff,
928-774-5213; www.musnaz.org

Exhibition and sale of Hopi artwork. Late June-early July.

### Navajo Artists' Exhibition

Museum of Northern Arizona,
3101 N. Fort Valley Rd., Flagstaff,
928-774-5213; www.musnaz.org

Last weekend in July-first weekend in August.

### Winterfest

Flagstaff, 928-774-4505;
www.flagstaffchamber.com

Features theater performances, sled dog and other races, games, entertainment and more. February.

## HOTELS

### ★★Embassy Suites

706 S. Milton Rd., Flagstaff,
928-774-4333, 800-774-4333;
www.embassysuites.com

119 rooms, all suites. Complimentary full breakfast. High-speed wireless Internet access. Bar. Pool. $

### ★Fairfield Inn

2005 S. Milton Rd., Flagstaff,
928-773-1300, 800-574-6395;
www.fairfieldinn.com

131 rooms. Complimentary continental breakfast. High-speed wireless Internet access. Pool. $

### ★Hampton Inn

2400 S Beulah Blvd., Flagstaff,
928-913-0900, 800-426-7866;
www.hampton.com

126 rooms. Complimentary continental breakfast. High-speed Internet access, wireless Internet access. Airport transportation available. Pool. $

### ★★★Little America Hotel

2515 E. Butler Ave., Flagstaff,
928-779-7900, 800-865-1401;
www.littleamerica.com/flagstaff

Located on 500 acres of beautiful pine forest, this hotel includes private hiking trails. The outdoor pool offers views of the mountains. The spacious guest rooms include floor to ceiling windows and flat screen TVs. Complimentary hors d'oeuvres are served nightly. 247 rooms. High-speed Internet access. Restaurant, bar. Children's activity center. Airport transportation available. $

### ★★★Inn at 410 Bed & Breakfast

410 N. Leroux St., Flagstaff,
928-774-0088, 800-774-2008;
www.inn410.com

**11**

**ARIZONA**

★
★
★
★
★

Known as the place with the personal touch, this charming 1894 Craftsman home offers fresh-baked cookies in the evenings. Each room has its own individual theme and is decorated with charming antiques.

Nine rooms. Children over five permitted. Complimentary full breakfast. Wireless Internet access. Airport transportation available. $$

## RESTAURANTS

### ★Kachina Downtown
522 E. Rte. 66, Flagstaff,
928-779-1944, 877-397-2743;
www.kachinarestaurant.com
Mexican menu. Lunch, dinner. Bar. Children's menu. Reservations recommended. $$

### ★★Mamma Luisa
2710 N. Steves Blvd., Flagstaff,
928-526-6809
Italian menu. Dinner. Children's menu. Casual attire. Reservations recommended. $$

# FOUNTAIN HILLS

An affluent community not far from Scottsdale in the Valley of the Sun, Fountain Hills offers distinct beauty and lots of opportunities for outdoor recreation.

Information: Chamber of Commerce, 16837 Palisades Blvd., Fountain Hills, 480-837-1654; www.fountainhillschamber.com

## WHAT TO SEE AND DO

### Fort McDowell Casino
Fort McDowell Rd. and Beeline Hwy., Fountain Hills, 800-843-3678;
www.fortmcdowellcasino.com
This casino boasts the state's largest card room, a 1,400-seat bingo hall with jackpots as high as $50,000, a keno lounge with million-dollar payouts and 475 slot machines that keep the decibel level high night and day. Spend some of your winnings in one of four restaurants or at the lounge, which offers live entertainment daily. Only those 21 and older can come and play. Daily.

## HOTELS

### ★★★CopperWynd Resort and Club
13225 N. Eagle Ridge Dr., Fountain Hills, 480-333-1900, 877-707-7760;
www.copperwynd.com
This elegant full-service resort, located on a mountain ridge overlooking Scottsdale, provides views of the Sonoran Desert and the surrounding mountain ranges. The spacious European-inspired guest rooms feature gas fireplaces, private balconies, granite counters and Italian linens. Play tennis on one of the nine courts, or golf at one of the nearby courses.

42 rooms. Wireless Internet access. Two restaurants, three bars. Pool. Tennis. $$$

### ★★★Inn at Eagle Mountain
9800 N. Summer Hill Blvd., Fountain Hills, 480-816-3000, 800-992-8083;
www.innateaglemountain.com
This small boutique hotel is located on the 18th fairway with views of Red Mountain, overlooking Scottsdale and Arizona. The suites have kiva fireplaces, sitting areas and whirlpool tubs. Six of them have a theme, ranging from the Frank Lloyd Wright inspired décor in the Prairie Suite to the cowboy items in the Wild West suite.

42 rooms, all mini suites. Restaurant, bar. Pool. $$

# GLENDALE

Located just west of Phoenix in the beautiful and scenic Valley of the Sun, Glendale shares all of the urban advantages of the area. Luke Air Force Base is located here.

Information: Chamber of Commerce, 7105 N. 59th Ave., 623-937-4754, 800-437-8669; www.glendaleaz.com

★
★
★
★
★

## WHAT TO SEE AND DO
### Arizona's Antique Capital
Glendale, 623-930-4500, 877-800-2601;
www.visitglendale.com
This shopping area in downtown Glendale includes antique stores, specialty shops and a candy factory. Most stores open Monday-Saturday.

### Bo's Funky Stuff
5605 W. Glendale Ave., Glendale,
623-842-0220
This offbeat emporium proves the old adage that one man's junk is another man's treasure. Two rooms are crammed with old advertising signs, housewares and '50s furniture. Prices range from under a dollar to several thousand. September-May: Monday-Saturday noon-5 p.m.; June-August: Saturday 11 a.m.-6 p.m.

### Cerreta Candy Company
5345 W. Glendale Ave., Glendale,
623-930-9000; www.cerreta.com
It doesn't getter any sweeter than this old-fashioned factory, where the Cerreta family has been cooking up mouthwatering confections for more than 30 years. Guided tours are offered at 10 a.m. and 1 p.m. Monday through Friday, but the kitchens are visible to customers, so you can get a flavor for how things are made anytime. Monday-Saturday 8 a.m.-6 p.m.

### Glendale Arena
9400 W Maryland Ave., Glendale,
623-772-3200; www.glendalearenaaz.com
Glendale Arena is home to the Phoenix Coyotes NHL ice hockey team. It also hosts concerts, family shows and more.

### Waterworld Safari
4243 W. Pinnacle Peak Rd., Glendale,
623-581-8446; www.phoenix.golfland.com
Despite its desert location, there's no shortage of water at this wildly fun aquatic play land with an African theme. Ride the big ones at the Serengeti Surf wave pool, zoom down the Cobra and Black Mamba slides, squeeze into an inner tube and float down the Zambezi River and more. May 24-August 13: Monday-Thursday 10 a.m.-8 p.m., Friday-Saturday to 9 p.m., Sunday 11 a.m.-7 p.m.

## HOTELS
### ★Hampton Inn
8408 W Paradise Lane, Peoria,
623-486-9918, 800-445-8667;
www.hamptoninn.com
112 rooms. Complimentary continental breakfast. High-speed Internet access. Pool. $

### ★La Quinta Phoenix Inn and Suites Peoria
16321 N. 83rd Ave., Peoria,
623-487-1900, 800-642-4271;
www.laquinta.com

# GRAND CANYON NATIONAL PARK
Look out over the great expanse of the Grand Canyon and the awe-inspiring vistas reveal a spectacular desert landscape. Rocks in this great chasm change colors from sunrise to sunset and hide an ecosystem of wildlife. It's no wonder millions of visitors pay a visit to this world wonder every year.

Visitors come here to hike the trails, travel down by mule, camp at the base, raft the river or simply stare in awe from the rim. The entire park is 1,904 square miles in size, with 277 miles of the Colorado River running through it. At its widest point, the north and south rims are 18 miles across, with average elevations of 8,000 feet and 7,000 feet, respectively. The canyon averages a depth of one mile. At its base, 2 billion-year-old rocks are exposed.

The South Rim, open all year, has the greater number of services, including day and overnight mule trips through Xanterra Parks & Resorts, horseback riding through Apache Stables (928-638-2891) and air tours (both fixed-wing and helicopter) through several local companies.

In addition to these tours, there are a variety of museums and facilities on the South Rim. The Kolb Studio in the Village Historic District at the Bright Angel Trailhead features art displays and a bookstore. It was once the home and business of the Kolb brothers, who were pioneering photographers here. The Yavapai Observation Station, one mile east of Market Plaza, contains temporary exhibits about the fossil record at Grand Canyon.

The North Rim, blocked by heavy snows in winter, is open from mid-May to mid-October. Due to the higher elevation, mule trips from the North Rim do not go to the river. Trips range in length from one hour to a full day. For more information, contact Grand Canyon Trail Rides at 435-679-8665.

Fall and spring are the best times for to trek into the canyon, when it's less crowded. Don't plan to hike to the base and back up in one day—changing elevations and temperatures can exhaust hikers quickly. It's best to camp in the canyon overnight (plan on an additional night if hiking from the North Rim). Fifteen main trails provide access to the inner canyon. Make reservations for camping or lodging facilities early.

Rafting the Colorado River through Grand Canyon National Park also requires reservations far in advance of your intended visit. Trips vary in length from three to 21 days and can be made through a commercial outfitter, a private river trip or a one-day trip (which may or may not be in Grand Canyon National Park). For one-day whitewater raft trips, contact Hualapai River Runners, 928-769-2119. Half-day smooth-water raft trips are provided by Wilderness River Adventures, 800-992-8022.

Information: Grand Canyon, approximately 50 miles north on Hwy. 180 (Hwy. 64) to the South Rim, 928-638-7888; www.nps.gov/grca

**ARIZONA**

113 rooms. Complimentary continental breakfast. Pets accepted. Pool. **$**

## WHAT TO SEE AND DO

### Drive to Cape Royal
North Rim (Grand Canyon National Park), about 23 miles from Bright Angel Point over paved road

You'll encounter several good viewpoints along the way—many visitors say the view from here is better than from the South Rim. Archaeology and geology talks are given in summer and fall.

## HOTELS

### ★★Grand Canyon Lodge
Hwy. 67, Grand Canyon, 928-638-2611; www.grandcanyonnorthrim.com
214 rooms. Closed mid-October-mid-May. Restaurant, bar. **$**

## RESTAURANTS

### ★★Arizona Room
South Rim, Grand Canyon Village, 928-638-2631; www.grandcanyonlodges.com
American. Southwestern menu. Lunch, dinner. **$$**

### ★★Grand Canyon Lodge
AZ 67, Grand Canyon, 928-638-2611; www.grandcanyonnorthrim.com
American menu. Breakfast, lunch, dinner. Reservations required for dinner. Closed November-April. **$**

### ★Jacob Lake Inn
Hwy. 89A and AZ 67, Jacob Lake, 928-643-7232; www.jacoblake.com
American menu. Breakfast, lunch, dinner. **$**

# GRAND CANYON NATIONAL PARK (SOUTH RIM)

Information: Grand Canyon National Park, approximately 80 miles northwest of Flagstaff via US 180, 928-638-7888; www.nps.gov/grca

## WHAT TO SEE AND DO

### Drives to viewpoints

1 Main St., South Rim (Grand Canyon National Park)

The West Rim and East Rim drives out from Grand Canyon Village are both rewarding. Grandview Point and Desert View on the East Rim Drive are especially magnificent. West Rim Drive is closed to private vehicles from early April to early October. Free shuttle buses serve the West Rim and Village area during this period.

### Grand Canyon IMAX Theatre

Hwys. 64 and 180, Tusayan, 928-638-2468; www.explorethecanyon.com

Large screen film (35 minutes) highlighting features of the Grand Canyon. March-October: 8:30 a.m.-8:30 p.m.; November-February: 10:30 a.m.-6:30 p.m.; movie is shown hourly on the half hour.

### Kaibab National Forest

Hwy. 64, Grand Canyon, 928-638-2443; www.fs.fed.us/r3/kai

More than 1.6 million acres; one area surrounds Williams and includes Sycamore Canyon and Kendrick Mountain wilderness areas and part of National Historic Route 66. A second area is 42 miles north on Highway 180 (Hwy. 64) near the South Rim of the Grand Canyon; a third area lies north of the Grand Canyon (outstanding views of the canyon from seldom-visited vista points in this area) and includes Kanab Creek and Saddle Mountain wilderness areas, the Kaibab Plateau and the North Rim Parkway National Scenic Byway.

### Williams Ski Area

Fourth St., Williams, 928-635-9330

Pomalift, rope tow; patrol, school, rentals; snack bar. Vertical drop 600 feet. Mid-December-Easter: Thursday-Monday. Sledding slopes and cross-country trails nearby.

### Mule trips into the canyon

1 Main St., South Rim (Grand Canyon National Park), 928-638-3283; www.grandcanyonlodges.com

A number of trips are scheduled, all with guides. There are some limitations. Trips take one, two or three days. Reservations should be made several months in advance (preferably one year prior).

### Tusayan Museum

Desert View Rd., South Rim (Grand Canyon National Park); www.nps.gov/grca

Exhibits on prehistoric man in the Southwest. Excavated pueblo ruin (circa 1185) nearby. Daily 9 a.m.-5 p.m., weather permitting. Ranger-led tours daily 11 a.m.-1:30 p.m.

### Yavapai Observation Station

South Rim (Grand Canyon National Park); www.nps.gov/grca

The station features a small museum, scenic views, geological exhibits and a bookstore. Daily 8 a.m.-8 p.m.

## HOTELS

### ★★Best Western Grand Canyon Squire Inn

100 Hwy. 64, Grand Canyon, 928-638-2681, 800-622-6966; www.grandcanyonsquire.com

250 rooms. Complimentary continental breakfast. Three restaurants, two bars. Children's activity center. Airport transportation available. Pool. Tennis. $

### ★★Bright Angel Lodge

Hwy. 64, Grand Canyon, 928-638-2631, 888-297-2757; www.grandcanyonlodges.com

89 rooms. Restaurant, bar. Canyon tour service. $

### ★★Grand Hotel

Hwy. 64, Grand Canyon, 928-638-3333, 888-634-7263; www.visitgrandcanyon.com

121 rooms. Restaurant, bar. Indoor pool, whirlpool. $

**15**

**ARIZONA**

### ★★Quality Inn

Hwy. 64, Grand Canyon,
928-638-2673, 877-424-6423;
www.QualityInn.com
232 rooms. Complimentary continental breakfast. Restaurant, bar. Airport transportation available. Pets accepted. Pool. **$**

### ★Thunderbird Lodge

On the Canyon rim,
928-638-2631, 888-297-2757;
www.grandcanyonlodges.com
55 rooms. Canyon tour service. **$**

### ★★Yavapai Lodge

Half-mile from the Canyon Rim,
928-638-2631, 888-297-2757;
www.grandcanyonlodges.com
358 rooms. Closed two weeks in mid-November, three weeks in early December., also January-February. Restaurant. **$**

### ★★★El Tovar

On the Canyon rim,
928-638-2631, 888-297-2757;
www.grandcanyonlodges.com
The premier lodging facility at the Grand Canyon, El Tovar Hotel—named in honor of the Spanish explorer Don Pedro de Tovar, who reported the existence of the Grand Canyon to fellow explorers—opened its doors in 1905 and was said to be the most expensive log house in America. Just 20 feet from the edge of the Canyon's South Rim, the building is charming and rustic. The hotel features a fine dining room, lounge and a gift shop highlighting Native American Indian artists. With so much to do right at your doorstep—hiking, mule rides, train excursions, interpretive walks, cultural activities—El Tovar offers the best of the Grand Canyon, combining turn-of-the-century lodge ambience with the highest standard of service. Advance reservations are recommended, especially for the summer season, which is usually booked up a year in advance.
78 rooms. Restaurant, bar. Airport transportation available. **$**

## RESTAURANTS

### ★★★El Tovar Dining Room

1 Main St., South Rim, 928-638-2631;
www.grandcanyonlodges.com
Considered the premier dining establishment at the Grand Canyon, this restaurant provides a memorable experience, thanks to the spicy regional cuisine and spectacular Canyon views. The atmosphere is casually elegant with native stone fireplaces, Oregon pine vaulted ceilings, American Indian artwork and Mission-style accents. Diners can select from a well-rounded menu that blends regional flavors and contemporary techniques and offers many vegetarian options. The wine list extensive.
Southwestern menu. Breakfast, lunch, dinner. Children's menu. Reservations recommended. **$$**

### ★Yippee-ei-o Steakhouse

Hwy. 64 and Hwy. 180, Grand Canyon,
928-638-2780
American, Steak menu. Lunch, dinner. Bar. Children's menu. **$$**

# GOLD CANYON

At the foot of the Superstition Mountains, Gold Canyon is a tiny town with golf courses, cacti and craggy rocks. The community is a popular area for second homes.
Information: www.goldcanyon.net

## HOTELS

### ★★★Gold Canyon Golf Resort

6100 S Kings Ranch Rd., Gold Canyon,
480-982-9090, 800-827-5281;
www.gcgr.com
Located in the foothills of the Superstition Mountains on 3,300 acres, this is a good choice for golfers who don't want to spend a fortune. The resort features a golf school and many scenic holes. The accommodations include suites and private casitas, some with fireplaces or whirlpools.
101 rooms. Two restaurants, bar. Spa. Airport transportation available. Pets accepted. Golf. **$**

**16**

**ARIZONA**

# HOLBROOK

This small town has a lot to offer, especially when it comes to the histories of the Navajo, Hopi, Zuni and White Mountain Apache Indian tribes. Stop here on your way to Petrified Forest National Park to learn about these unique tribes.

Information: Chamber of Commerce, 100 E. Arizona St., 928-524-6558, 800-524-2459; www.ci.holbrook.az.us

## PETRIFIED FOREST NATIONAL PARK

These 93,532 acres include one of the most spectacular displays of petrified wood in the world. The trees of the original forest may have grown in upland areas and then been washed down onto a floodplain by rivers. Subsequently, the trees were buried under sediment and volcanic ash, causing the organic wood to be filled gradually with mineral compounds, especially quartz. The grain, now multicolored by the compounds, is still visible in some specimens.

The visitor center is located at the entrance off I-40. The Rainbow Forest Museum (off US 180) depicts the paleontology and geology of the Triassic Era Daily. Service stations and cafeteria at the north entrance. Prehistoric Pueblo inhabitants left countless petroglyphs of animals, figures and symbols carved on sandstone throughout the park.

The park contains a portion of the Painted Desert, a colorful area extending 200 miles along the north bank of the Little Colorado River. This highly eroded area of mesas, pinnacles, washes and canyons is part of the Chinle formation, a soft shale, clay and sandstone stratum of the Triassic age. The sunlight and clouds passing over this spectacular scenery create an effect of constant, kaleidoscopic change. There are very good viewpoints along the park road.

Picnicking facilities at Rainbow Forest and at Chinle Point on the rim of the Painted Desert; no campgrounds. It is forbidden to take even the smallest piece of petrified wood or any other object from the park. Nearby curio shops sell wood taken from areas outside the park. Daily.

Information: Petrified Forest National Park, 1 Park Rd., Holbrook, 928-524-6228; www.nps.gov/pefo

ARIZONA

## WHAT TO SEE AND DO

### Navajo County Historical Museum

100 E. Arizona, Holbrook, 928-524-6558; www.ci.holbrook.az.us

Exhibits on Navajo, Apache, Hopi and Hispanic cultures. Includes petrified forest and dinosaurs. Monday-Friday 8 a.m.-5 p.m., Saturday-Sunday to 4 p.m.

## SPECIAL EVENTS

### Navajo County Fair and Rodeo

Navajo County Fairgrounds, 404 E. Hopi Dr., Holbrook, 928-524-4757; www.navajocountyfair.org

Includes livestock judging, a 4-H competition and exhibitors. Mid-September.

### Old West Celebration

Navajo County Historic Courthouse, 100 E. Arizona St., Holbrook, 928-524-6558; www.ci.holbrook.az.us

Running, swimming and biking races, a quilt auction, arts and crafts and more. Mid-September.

## HOTELS

### ★★Best Western Arizonian Inn

2508 Navajo Blvd., Holbrook, 928-524-2611, 877-280-7300; www.bestwestern.com

70 rooms. Complimentary continental breakfast. Restaurant. Pets accepted. Pool. $

**★Holiday Inn Express**
1308 E. Navajo Blvd., Holbrook,
928-524-1466, 888-465-4329;
www.holiday-inn.com
59 rooms. Complimentary continental breakfast. Pets accepted. Pool. **$**

# RESTAURANTS
**★★Mesa Italiana**
2318 N. Navajo Blvd., Holbrook,
928-524-6696
Italian menu. Lunch, dinner. Bar. Children's menu. **$$**

## HOPI INDIAN RESERVATION

Inside the Navajo Indian Reservation is the 1.5 million-acre Hopi Indian Reservation. The Hopi are pueblo people of Shoshonean ancestry who have lived here for more than 2,000 years in some of the continent's most intriguing towns.

Excellent farmers, the Hopi also herd sheep, as well as craft pottery, silver jewelry, kachina dolls and baskets. Both the Navajo and Hopi are singers and dancers—each in their own style. The Hopi are most famous for their Snake Dance, which may not be viewed by visitors, but there are dozens of other beautiful ceremonies that visitors are allowed to watch. (The photographing, recording or sketching of any events on the reservation is prohibited.)

The Hopi towns are located, for the most part, on three mesas. On the first mesa is Walpi, founded around 1680, one of the most beautiful Hopi pueblos. It is built on the tip of a narrow, steep-walled mesa, along with its companion villages, Sichomovi and Hano, which are inhabited by the Tewa and the Hano. Hanoans speak a Tewa language as well as Hopi. You can drive to Sichomovi and walk along a narrow connecting mesa to Walpi. Only passenger cars are allowed on the mesa; no RVs or trailers. Individuals of Walpi and First Mesa Villages offer Hopi pottery and kachina dolls for sale; inquire locally.

The second mesa has three towns: Mishongnovi, Sipaulovi, and Shungopavi, each fascinating in its own way. The Hopi Cultural Center, located on the second mesa, includes a museum and craft shops, a restaurant serving both Hopi and American food and a motel. Reservations (928-734-2401) for May through August should be made at least three months in advance. Near the Cultural Center is a primitive campground.

The third mesa has Oraibi, the oldest Hopi town, and its three offshoots, Bacavi, Kyakotsmovi and Hotevilla, a town of considerable interest. A restaurant, a small motel and tent and trailer sites can be found at Keams Canyon. There are not many places to stay, so plan your trip carefully. All major roads leading into and across the Navajo and Hopi Reservations are paved.

Information: 928-734-3283; www.hopi.nsn.us

**18**

**ARIZONA**

# NAVAJO NATIONAL MONUMENT

This monument comprises three scattered areas totaling 600 acres and is surrounded by the Navajo Nation. Each area is the location of a large and remarkable prehistoric cliff dwelling. Two of the ruins are accessible by guided tour.

Headquarters for the monument and the visitor center are near Betatakin, the most accessible of the three cliff dwellings. Guided tours, limited to 25 people (Betatakin tour), are arranged on a first-come, first-served basis (May-September; tours sometimes possible earlier in spring and late in fall; phone for schedule). Hiking distance is five miles round-trip, including a steep 700-foot trail and takes five to six hours. Betatakin may also be viewed from the Sandal Trail overlook—a 1/2-mile, one-way, self-guided trail. Daily.

The largest and best-preserved ruin, Keet Seel (Memorial Day-Labor Day, phone for schedule), is 8 1/2 miles one-way by foot or horseback from headquarters. A permit is required either way, and reservations can be made up to two months in advance. A primitive campground is available for overnight hikers. The horseback trip takes all day. Horses should be reserved when making reservations (no children under 12 without previous riding experience).

The visitor center has a museum and film program. Daily,
Information: Kayenta, 19 miles southwest of Kayenta on Hwy. 163, then nine miles north on paved road Hwy. 564 to visitor center, 928-672-2700; www.nps.gov/nava

# KAYENTA

Located in the spectacular Monument Valley, Kayenta's surrounding area offers some of the most memorable sightseeing in the state, including the great tinted monoliths.
Information: Kayenta, 928-697-8451; www.kayentatownship.com

## WHAT TO SEE AND DO

### Crawley's Monument Valley Tours
Kayenta, 928-697-3463;
www.crawleytours.com
Guided tours in backcountry vehicles to Monument Valley, Mystery Valley and Hunt's Mesa. Half- and full-day rates. Sunset tours are also available. Daily.

## HOTELS

### ★★Goulding's Lodge
1000 Main St., Monument Valley, 435-727-3231; www.gouldings.com
62 rooms. Restaurant. Pets accepted. Pool. $$

### ★★Holiday Inn
Highways 160 and 163, Kayenta, 928-697-3221, 888-465-4329; www.holiday-inn.com
162 rooms. Restaurant. Pool. $

★
★
★
★
★

# KINGMAN

Kingman lies at the heart of historic Route 66 and is a convenient stop on the way to the Grand Canyon. Several lakes are nearby with year-round swimming, waterskiing, fishing and boating. To the south are the beautiful Hualapai Mountains. Kingman was once a rich silver and gold mining area and several ghost towns are nearby.
Information: Chamber of Commerce, 120 W. Andy Devine, 928-753-6253; www.kingmanchamber.org

## WHAT TO SEE AND DO

### Bonelli House
430 E. Spring St., Kingman, 928-753-3175;
www.kingmantourism.org
One of the earliest permanent structures in the city, this restored home is furnished with many original pieces. Monday-Friday 11 a.m.-3 p.m.

### Mohave Museum of History and Art
400 W Beale St., Kingman, 928-753-3195;
www.ctaz.com/~mocohist/museum
See a portrait collection of U.S. presidents and first ladies at this museum that traces local and state history. Also featured is a turquoise display, rebuilt 1926 pipe organ, local artists' gallery and more. Monday-Friday 9 a.m.-5 p.m., Saturday-Sunday 1-5 p.m.

### Oatman
Hwy. 66, Oatman, 928-768-6222;
www.oatmangoldroad.com
In the 1930s, this was the last stop in Arizona before entering the Mojave Desert in California. Created in 1906 as a tent camp, it flourished as a gold mining center until 1942, when Congress declared that gold mining was no longer essential to the war effort. The ghost town has been kept as authentic as possible and several motion pictures have been filmed here. Turquoise and antique shops. Gunfights staged on weekends.

### Powerhouse Visitor Center
120 W. Rte. 66, Kingman,
928-753-6106, 866-427-7866;
www.kingmantourism.org
Houses the Historic Route 66 Association of Arizona, Tourist Information Center, Carlos Elmer Memorial Photo Gallery and more. Model railroad shop, gift shop, deli. March-November: daily 9 a.m.-6 p.m.; December-February: daily 9 a.m.-5 p.m.

## SPECIAL EVENTS

### Andy Devine Days & PRCA Rodeo
Mohave County Fairgrounds,
2600 Fairgrounds Blvd., Kingman,
928-757-7919; www.kingmantourism.org
Sports tournaments, parade and more. Two days in late September.

### Mohave County Fair
Mohave County Fairgrounds,
2600 Fairgrounds Blvd., Kingman,
928-753-2636; www.mcfafairgrounds.org
Annual event featuring a carnival, livestock auctions, 4-H competition and food. First weekend after Labor Day.

## HOTELS

### ★Best Western A Wayfarer's Inn
2815 E. Andy Devine Ave., Kingman,
928-753-6271, 800-548-5695;
www.bestwestern.com
101 rooms. Pets accepted. Pool. **$**

# LAKE HAVASU CITY

This is the center of a year-round resort area on the shores of 45-mile-long Lake Havasu. The London Bridge, imported from England and reassembled here in 1968 as part of a recreational area, connects the mainland city with a three-square-mile island that has a marina, golf course, tennis courts, campgrounds and other recreational facilities.
Information: Lake Havasu City Convention & Visitors Bureau, 314 London Bridge Rd., 928-453-3444, 800-242-8278; www.golakehavasu.com

## WHAT TO SEE AND DO

### Lake Havasu State Park
699 London Bridge Rd., Lake Havasu City,
928-855-2784;
www.pr.state.az.us/Parks/parkhtml/havasu.html
This park occupies 13,000 acres along 23 miles of shoreline. Windsor Beach Unit, two miles north on old Hwy. 95 (London Bridge Rd.) has swimming, fishing, boating), hiking and camping; 928-855-2784. Cattail Cove Unit, 15 miles south and 1/2 mile west of Hwy. 95, has swimming, fishing, boating and camping; 928-855-1223. Sunrise-10 p.m.

**London Bridge Resort & English Village**
1477 Queens Bay, Lake Havasu City,
928-855-0888, 866-331-9231;
www.londonbridgeresort.com
This English-style village on 110 acres is
home to the world-famous London Bridge.
Specialty shops, restaurants, boat rides,
nine-hole golf course, accommodations.
Village. Daily.

**Topock Gorge**
Lake Havasu City
Scenic (and steep) volcanic banks along
the Colorado River. Migratory birds spend
winters here, while herons, cormorants and
egrets nest in April and May. Fishing, picnicking.

## HOTELS
★★Hampton Inn
245 London Bridge Rd., Lake Havasu,
928-855-4071, 800-426-7866;
www.hamptoninn.com
162 rooms. Restaurant, bar. Pets accepted.
Pool. $

## RESTAURANTS
★★Shugrue's
1425 McCulloch Blvd., Lake Havasu City,
928-453-1400; www.shugrues.com
Seafood, steak menu. Lunch, dinner. Bar.
Children's menu. $$

# LITCHFIELD PARK

## WHAT TO SEE AND DO
**Wildlife World Zoo**
16501 W. Northern Ave., Litchfield Park,
623-935-9453; www.wildlifeworld.com
You'll see white tigers, African lions, cam-
els and rhinos at this zoo boasting the largest
collection of exotic animals (about 2,400,
representing nearly 400 species). Daily
9 a.m.-5 p.m.

## SPECIAL EVENTS
**West Valley Invitational American Indian
Arts Festival**
The West Valley Fine Arts Council,
200 W. Fairway Dr., Litchfield Park,
623-935-6384; www.wvfac.org
Approximately 200 American Indian craft
vendors display their goods. Also includes
American Indian dancing and other enter-
tainment. Mid-January.

## HOTELS
★★★The Wigwam Resort and Golf Club
300 Wigwam Blvd., Litchfield Park,
623-935-3811, 800-327-0396;
www.wigwamresort.com
Once a private club for executives of the
Goodyear Tire Company, the Wigwam
Resort is one of Arizona's best. The rooms
and suites highlight authentic regional
design with whitewashed wood furniture,
slate floors and Mexican ceramic tiles.
The property includes award-winning golf
courses, nine tennis courts, two pools with
a water slide and a spa. Five restaurants and
bars have something for everyone.
331 rooms. Three restaurants, 2 bars.
Children's activity center. Spa. Airport
transportation available. Pets accepted.
Golf. Tennis. Business center. $$$

## RESTAURANTS
★★★Arizona Kitchen
300 Wigwam E. Blvd., Litchfield Park,
623-535-2598; www.wigwamresort.com
This always-packed Southwestern restaurant is a showcase for the fiery culinary
techniques and flavors of the region. Using
herbs grown on the premises, the kitchen
pays homage to local ingredients with signature dishes like smoked corn chowder,
grilled sirloin of buffalo with sweet potato
pudding and mesquite-dusted Chilean sea
bass. The dining room with adobe fireplace,
red brick floors, wood-beamed ceilings and
an open kitchen featuring a mesquite wood-
fired hearth and grill, is the perfect setting
to enjoy it.
Southwestern menu. Breakfast, lunch, dinner. Bar. Children's menu. Business casual
attire. Reservations recommended. Valet
parking. Outdoor seating. $$$

**21**

**ARIZONA**

★
★
★
★
★

# MARBLE CANYON

This section of Grand Canyon National Park has some of the nation's best camping and most captivating scenery. Pitch your tent here and enjoy the view.

## WHAT TO SEE AND DO
### Marble Canyon
Marble Canyon, 928-638-7888;
www.nps.gov/grca
Part of Grand Canyon National Park.

## HOTELS
### ★★Cliff Dwellers Lodge
HC. 67, Marble Canyon,
928-355-2261, 800-962-9755;
www.leesferry.com
20 rooms. Restaurant, bar. Pets accepted. **$**

# MCNARY

McNary is in the northeastern section of the Fort Apache Indian Reservation. The White Mountain Apaches have a number of recreation areas on their reservation. Trout fishing, exploring and camping are available.

Information: White Mountain Recreation Enterprise, Whiteriver, 928-338-4385

## WHAT TO SEE AND DO
### Hawley Lake
White Mountain Apache Indian Reservation, McNary, 12 miles east on Hwy. 260, then 11 miles south on Hwy. 473, 928-335-7511
With an elevation of 8,200 feet, Hawley Lake is one of the highest lakes in Arizona. Summer activities include fishing, hiking and camping. Cabin rentals are also available. Ice fishing is a popular winter activity.

### Sunrise Park Resort
Fort Apache Indian Reservation, Hwy. 273, Greer, 928-735-7669, 800-772-7669;
www.sunriseskipark.com
Resort has two quad, four triple, double chairlift, three rope tows; patrol, school, rentals; cafeteria, restaurants, bars. Sixty-five runs. Snowboarding. November-mid-April, daily. Summer activities include swimming, fishing, canoeing, hiking, horseback riding and tennis. Camping.

**ARIZONA**

# MESA

Mesa, Spanish for "table," sits atop a plateau overlooking the Valley of the Sun and is one of the state's largest and fastest-growing cities. Mesa offers year-round golf, tennis, hiking and water sports. It also provides easy access to other Arizona and Southwest attractions, and is the home of Arizona State University-Polytechnic Campus.

Information: Convention & Visitors Bureau, 120 N. Center, 480-827-4700, 800-283-6372; www.mesacvb.com

## WHAT TO SEE AND DO
### Arizona Museum for Youth
35 N. Robson St., Mesa, 480-644-2468;
www.arizonamuseumforyouth.com
Fine arts museum with changing hands-on exhibits for children. Tuesday-Saturday 10 a.m.-4 p.m., Sunday noon-4 p.m.

### Boyce Thompson Southwestern Arboretum
37615 Hwy. 60, Superior, 520-689-2723;
www.ag.arizona.edu/bta
See a large collection of plants from arid parts of the world. Visitor center features biological and historical displays. September-April daily 8 a.m.-4 p.m.; May-August daily 6 a.m.-3 p.m.

### Dolly Steamboat Cruises

Apache Junction, 480-827-9144;
www.dollysteamboat.com

Narrated tours and twilight dinner cruises of Canyon Lake follow the original path of the Salt River. Nature Cruise: daily at noon, 2 p m. by reservation only, arrangements can be made for 10 a.m. or 4 p.m.; Twilight Dinner Cruise: weekends, call for schedule.

### Factory Stores of America

2050 S. Roslyn Place, Mesa, 480-984-0697
Look for deals at the 25 stores here. Monday-Saturday 10 a.m.-8 p.m., Sunday 12 p.m.-5 p.m.

### Lost Dutchman State Park

6109 N. Apache Trail, Apache Junction, 480-982-4485;
www.pr.state.az.us/Parks/parkhtml/dutchman.html

This 300-acre park in the Superstition Mountains area offers hiking, picnicking and improved camping. Interpretive trails and access to nearby forest service wilderness area. Daily sunrise-10 p.m.

### Mesa Southwest Museum

53 N MacDonald St., Mesa, 480-644-2230;
www.ci.mesa.az.us/swmuseum

Learn about the Native Americans who lived here, see a replica of a Spanish mission and more as you explore this 80,000-square-foot regional resource. Interactive center for kids. Tuesday-Friday 10 a.m.-5 p.m., Saturday 11 a.m.-5 p.m., Sunday 1-5 p.m.

### River tubing, Salt River Recreation Inc

Tonto National Forest, 1320 N. Bush Hwy., Mesa, www.saltrivertubing.com

Go tubing down the Salt River—the fee includes tube rental, parking and shuttle bus service to various points on the river. Early May-September, daily 9 a.m.-7 p.m.

## SPECIAL EVENTS

### Chicago Cubs Spring Training

Hohokam Park, 1235 N. Center St., Mesa, 480-964-4467;
www.cactus-league.com/cubs.html

Watch the Cubs during spring training at exhibition games. Early March-early April.

### Mesa Territorial Day Festival

Sirrine House, 160 N. Center, Mesa, 480-644-3428;
www.mesasouthwestmuseum.com

Come celebrate Arizona's birthday in Old West style. This festival features Western arts and crafts, music, food, games and activities, and historical re-enactments. Second Saturday in February.

## HOTELS

### ★★Best Western Dobson Ranch Inn

1666 S. Dobson Rd., Mesa, 480-831-7000, 800-528-1356;
www.dobsonranchinn.com

213 rooms. Complimentary full breakfast. Restaurant, bar. Pets accepted. Pool. **$**

### ★Best Western Superstition Springs Inn

1342 S. Power Rd., Mesa, 480-641-1164, 800-780-7234;
www.bestwestern.com

57 rooms. Complimentary continental breakfast. Pets accepted. Pool. **$**

### ★La Quinta Inn

6530 E. Superstition Springs Blvd., Mesa, 480-654-1970, 800-642-4271;
www.lq.com

107 rooms. Complimentary continental breakfast. High-speed Internet access, wireless Internet access. Pets accepted. Pool. **$**

### ★★★Hilton Phoenix East/Mesa

1011 W. Holmes Ave., Mesa, 480-833-5555, 800-445-8667;
www.phoenixeastmesa.hilton.com

This newly renovated hotel is centrally located in the East Valley, allowing for easy freeway access to many attractions and business in all directions. Phoenix Sky Harbor airport is 12 miles away. Guest rooms are arranged around the large atrium lobby and are decorated in rich autumn colors with velvety textures. French doors lead to a balcony. Relax by the pool, go horseback riding or a hit the links at one of the nearby courses. The Zuni Bar & Grill serves a breakfast buffet and Sunday brunch. The bar is a good spot to meet friends for one of the micro-brewed beers or tasty margaritas.

263 rooms. High-speed Internet access. Restaurant, two bars. Pool. Business Center. **$**

★★★**Arizona Golf Resort & Conference Center**
425 S. Power Rd., Mesa,
480-832-3202, 800-528-8282;
www.azgolfresort.com

Tropical palms and beautiful lakes surround this East Valley resort occupying 150 acres. Guest suites are arranged in clusters with courtyards, barbecue grills and heated spas.

The resort has a golf school and the 14th hole of the championship course requires a 175 yard-shot through the trees and over the water.

187 rooms. High-speed wireless Internet access. Two restaurants, bar. Pets accepted. Pool. Golf. Business center.**$**

## RESTAURANTS

★★**Landmark**
809 W. Main St., Mesa, 480-962-4652;
www.lmrk.com

American menu. Lunch, dinner. Children's menu. Casual attire. **$$**

# NAVAJO INDIAN RESERVATION

The Navajo Nation is the largest Native American tribe and reservation in the United States. The reservation covers more than 25,000 square miles within three states—with the largest portion in northeastern Arizona and the rest in New Mexico and Utah.

More than 400 years ago, the Navajo people (the Dineh) moved into the arid southwestern region of the United States and carved out a way of life that was in harmony with the natural beauty of Arizona, New Mexico and Utah. In the 1800s, westward-moving settlers interrupted this harmonious life. For the Navajo, this conflict resulted in their forced removal from their ancestral land and the "Long Walk" to Fort Sumner, New Mexico. The plan was judged a failure and in 1868, they were allowed to return to their homeland. Coal, oil and uranium have been discovered on the reservation. The income from these, which is handled democratically by the tribe, has helped improve its economic and educational situation.

The Navajo continue to practice many of their ancient ceremonies, including the Navajo Fire Dance and the Yei-bi-chei (winter) and Enemy Way Dances (summer). Many ceremonies are associated with curing the sick and are primarily religious in nature. Visitors must obtain permission to view these events—photography, recording and sketching are prohibited.

There are a number of paved roads across the Navajo and Hopi Reservations, as well as some unpaved gravel and dirt roads. During the rainy season (mostly August to September), the unpaved roads are difficult or impassable.

Some of the most spectacular areas in Navajoland are Canyon de Chelly National Monument, Navajo National Monument, Monument Valley Navajo Tribal Park (north of Kayenta) and Four Corners Monument. Accommodations on the reservation are limited; reservations are recommended months in advance. Information: www.explorenavajo.com

# PAGE

Page is at the east end of the Glen Canyon Dam, on the Colorado River. The dam, 710 feet high, forms Lake Powell, a part of the Glen Canyon National Recreation Area. The lake, 186 miles long with 1,900 miles of shoreline, is the second-largest man-made lake in the United States. The lake is named for John Wesley Powell, the intrepid and brilliant geologist who lost an arm at the Battle of Shiloh. Powell led an expedition down the Colorado in 1869 and was later director of the United States Geological Survey.

Information: Page/Lake Powell Chamber of Commerce, 608 Elm St., 928-645-2741, 888-261-7243; www.cityofpage.org

## WHAT TO SEE AND DO

### Boat trips on Lake Powell

Lake Powell Resorts & Marinas,
100 Lakeshore Dr., Page,
928-645-2433, 888-896-3829;
www.lakepowell.com
One-hour to one-day trips, some include Rainbow Bridge National Monument. Houseboat and powerboat rentals. Reservations advised.

### Glen Canyon National Recreation Area

Hwy. 89, Page, 928-608-6200;
www.nps.gov/glca
More than one million acres, including Lake Powell. Campfire program (Memorial Day-Labor Day). Swimming, water-skiing, fishing, boating, hiking, picnicking, restaurants, lodge, camping. The visitor center on canyon rim, adjacent to Glen Canyon Bridge on Hwy 89, has historical exhibits. Ranger station, seven miles north of the dam at Wahweap. Daily.

### John Wesley Powell Memorial Museum

6 N. Lake Powell Blvd., Page,
928-645-9496, 888-597-6873;
www.powellmuseum.org
See a replica of Powell's boat, plus a fluorescent rock collection, Native American artifacts and more. Monday-Friday 9 a.m.-5 p.m.

### Rainbow Bridge National Monument

Page, approximately 60 miles northeast in Utah, northwest of Navajo Mountain,
928-608-6200; www.nps.gov/rabr
See the world's largest known natural bridge, a breathtaking phenomenon that attracts more than 300,000 visitors a year.

### Wilderness River Adventures

2040 E. Frontage Rd., Page,
928-645-3296, 800-992-8022;
www.riveradventures.com
Specializes in multi-day trips on the Colorado River in Glen Canyon in raft-like neoprene boats. Reservations are required. April-October.

## HOTELS

### ★Best Western Lake Powell

208 N. Lake Powell Blvd., Page,
928-645-5988, 888-794-2888;
www.bestwesternatlakepowell.com
132 rooms. Complimentary continental breakfast. High-speed wireless Internet access. Airport transportation available. **$**

### ★Travelodge

207 N. Lake Powell Blvd., Page,
928-645-2451, 800-578-7878;
www.travelodge.com
132 rooms. Complimentary continental breakfast. Pets accepted. Pool. **$**

## RESTAURANTS

### ★★Bella Napoli

810 N. Navajo Dr., Page, 928-645-2706;
www.italiasbuffet.com
Italian menu. Dinner. Closed January. Casual attire. Reservations recommended. Outdoor seating. **$$**

### ★Ken's Old West

718 Vista Ave., Page, 928-645-5160;
www.kensoldwest.net
Steak menu. Dinner. Closed Sunday-Tuesday December-February. Bar. Children's menu. Casual attire. Reservations recommended. **$$**

# PARADISE VALLEY

A dozen resorts make this small town one of Arizona' hottest tourist destinations.
Information: www.ci.paradise-valley.az.us

## HOTELS

### ★★★Sanctuary on Camelback Mountain
5700 E. McDonald Dr., Paradise Valley,
480-948-2100, 800-245-2051;
www.sanctuaryoncamelback.com

This boutique hotel overlooking the valley from Camelback Mountain truly is a sanctuary. You won't find typical Southwestern décor here. Casitas are the very essence of desert chic with their spectacular contemporary design. Mountain casitas have wood block floors, glass-tiled dry bars and luxurious bathrooms with travertine marble. The multi-level spa casitas boast floor-to-ceiling windows and walk-in closets, while the spa suites have outdoor soaking tubs in case you just can't bring yourself to walk the short distance to the large infinity-edge pool. Elements restaurant offers new American fare with an Asian influence, served in a contemporary, elegant setting.
98 rooms. Pets accepted. Pool. Fitness room. Tennis. Business center. **$$$**

### ★★★The Hermosa Inn
5532 N. Palo Cristi Rd., Paradise Valley,
602-955-8614, 800-241-1210;
www.hermosainn.com

Built by cowboy artist Lon Megargee as his home and studio, this inn, and its acclaimed on-site restaurant LON's, is situated on a half acre marked by olive and mesquite trees, towering palms and brilliant flowers, and is a nice alternative to the bigger resorts. The accommodations range from cozy casitas to huge villas. Rooms feature authentic furnishings and original artwork painted by Megargee some 70 years ago.
35 rooms. Complimentary continental breakfast. Restaurant, bar. Pets accepted Pool. Tennis. **$$**

## RESTAURANTS

### ★★El Chorro Lodge
5550 E. Lincoln Dr., Paradise Valley,
480-948-5170; www.elchorro.com

American menu. Dinner, Sunday brunch. Bar. Casual attire. Valet parking. Outdoor seating. **$$$**

### ★★★elements
5700 E. McDonald Rd., Paradise Valley,
480-607-2300, 800-298-9766;
www.elementsrestaurant.com

Situated on the grounds of the Sanctuary at Camelback Mountain, Elements is a sleek spot that adds a touch of sophistication to leisurely breakfasts, power lunches and romantic dinners. Its clean, minimalist décor features stone and wood accents and expansive floor-to-ceiling windows that offer spectacular views of the sunset over Paradise Valley. The kitchen uses fresh, seasonal ingredients to create the menu of Asian-influenced New American cuisine, which has included dishes such as chilled sesame and lime noodle salad, chili-cured duck breas and braised short ribs with citrus-scented mushrooms. The Jade Bar is a great spot for a drink.
American menu. Breakfast, lunch, dinner, Sunday brunch. Bar. Casual attire. Outdoor seating. **$$$**

### ★★★Lon's
5532 N. Palo Cristi Rd., Paradise Valley,
602-955-7878; www.lons.com

Built by Southwestern artist Lon Megargee in the 1930s, the inn's adobe design and rustic furnishings are a fitting setting for some of the best American comfort food in Phoenix. The chef grows many herbs, heirloom fruits and vegetables and grains in the onsite garden to use in fresh seasonal specials such as pork tenderloin with prickly pear braised cabbage, green beans and mashed potatoes and roasted lamb with goat cheese herb grits.
American menu. Lunch, dinner, Sunday brunch. Bar. Children's menu. Casual attire. Reservations recommended. Outdoor seating. **$$$**

**ARIZONA**

## SPAS

### ★★★★The Sanctuary Spa at Sanctuary on Camelback Mountain

5700 E. McDonald Dr., Paradise Valley, 480-607-2330, 800-245-2051; www.sanctuaryoncamelback.com

Originally designed as a tennis club in the 1950s by Frank Lloyd Wright protégé Hiram Hudson Benedict, the resort was completely renovated in 2001. The understated elegance first defined by Benedict is still here. The resort's spa was expanded and seems to include practically every treatment under the sun, from standard facials to acupuncture and numerology. The spa menu includes several Asian-inspired treatments including Thai massage and shiatsu. The resort retains its commitment to the championship tennis courts that defined it from the start, but the grounds are also ideal for Yoga and meditation. Guided desert hikes are also available. **$$**

# PARKER

Parker is located on the east bank of the Colorado River, about 16 miles south of Parker Dam, which forms Lake Havasu. Popular recreational activities in the area include fishing, boating, jet and water skiing, golfing, rock hunting and camping.

Information: Chamber of Commerce, 1217 California Ave., 928-669-2174; www.ci.parker.az.us

## WHAT TO SEE AND DO

### Buckskin Mountain State Park

5476 Hwy. 95, Parker, 928-667-3231; www.pr.state.az.us/Parks/parkhtml/buckskin.html

On 1,676 acres, this park features scenic bluffs overlooking the Colorado River. Swimming, fishing, boating; nature trails, hiking; picnicking, camping, riverside cabanas. River Island Unit has boating, picnicking, camping. Daily.

### Colorado River Indian Tribes Museum

Rte. 1, Parker, 928-669-9211; www.museum of man.org

Exhibits interpret the history of the four Colorado River Tribes: Mohave, Chemehuevi, Navajo and Hopi. You'll find authentic Native American arts and crafts on sale here.

### BlueWater Resort & Casino

11300 Resort Dr., 928-669-9211, 888-243-3360; www.bluewaterfun.com

Bluewater Casino is open 24 hours and includes slots, poker and bingo.

### Colorado River Indian Tribes Reservation

Rte. 1, Parker, 928-669-6757

This reservation spans 278,000 acres in Arizona and California, and offers fishing, boating, waterskiing, hunting (tribal permit required) and camping.

### La Paz County Park

7350 Riverside Dr., Parker, 928-667-2069; www.co.la-paz.az.us

A 540-acre park with 4,000 feet of Colorado River beach front. Swimming, water-skiing, fishing, boating, tennis court, golf course, driving range, picnicking (shelter), playground, camping.

### Parker Dam & Power Plant

Parker, 17 miles north via Hwy. 95, 760-663-3712

One of the deepest dams in the world—73 percent of its structural height of 320 feet is below the riverbed. Daily.

## SPECIAL EVENTS

### Holiday Lighted Boat Parade

Colorado River, Parker

Decorated boats parade on the 11-mile strip to a selected site for trophy presentation; viewing from both sides of the Parker River. Late November.

### La Paz County Fair

Fairgrounds at Four Corners, 13991 Second Ave., Parker, 928-669-8100

**27**

Carnival, livestock auction, entertainment and more. Mid-March.

### Parker 400 Off Road Race
1217 S. California Ave., Parker
Four hundred miles of desert racing. Late January.

### Parker Enduro Weekend
One Park Dr., Parker
Longest and oldest boat racing event in the country. May.

## HOTELS
### ★Kofa Inn
1700 S. California Ave., Parker, 928-669-2101, 800-742-6072; 41 rooms. Pool. **$**

# PAYSON
Payson, in the heart of the Tonto National Forest, provides many outdoor recreational activities in a mild climate.
Information: Chamber of Commerce, 100 W Main St., 928-474-4515; www.ci.payson.az.us

## WHAT TO SEE AND DO
### Tonto National Forest
2324 E. McDowell Rd., Phoenix, 602-225-5200; www.fs.fed.us/r3/tonto
This area includes almost three million acres of desert and mountain landscape. Six lakes along the Salt and Verde rivers offer opportunities for fishing, boating, hiking and camping. Seven wilderness areas are located within the forest's boundaries, providing hiking and bridle trails. The forest also features Tonto Natural Bridge, the largest natural travertine bridge in the world. Scenic attractions include the Apache Trail, Four Peaks, the Mogollon Rim and Sonoran Desert country.

## SPECIAL EVENTS
### Old-Time Fiddlers Contest & Festival
Rumsey Park, Payson, 928-970-1760

Fiddling contest, storytellers, Irish step-dancers, entertainment, food, arts and crafts, and more. Late September.

### World's Oldest Continuous PRCA Rodeo
Multi-Event Center, Payson, 800-672-9766
The rodeo features calf roping, bull riding and barrel racing. Third weekend in August.

## HOTELS
### ★★Best Western Payson Inn
801 N. Beeline Hwy., Payson, 928-474-3241, 800-247-9477; www.bestwestern.com
99 rooms. Complimentary continental breakfast. Restaurant, bar. Pets accepted. Pool. **$**

# PEORIA
One of Phoenix's largest suburbs, Peoria is home to the Challenger Space Center of Arizona, a brand new performing arts hall and other cultural and educational facilities.
Information: City of Peoria, 8401 W. Monroe St., Peoria, 623-773-7000; www.peoriaaz.com

**28**

**ARIZONA**

## WHAT TO SEE AND DO

**Lake Pleasant Regional Park**

41835 N. Castle Hot Springs Rd.,
Morristown, 602-372-7460;
www.maricopa.gov/parks/lake_pleasant

Go coastal 30 miles north of Phoenix at this manmade reservoir with 114 miles of sunday-drenched shoreline. The park has campgrounds for RVs and tents, boat ramps, plenty of picnic tables with grills. Daily.

# PHOENIX

The capital of Arizona lies on flat desert, surrounded by mountains. People come to the Valley of the Sun for the golf, mega-resorts and spas. Phoenix has been getting bigger and better in recent years, with an influx of retirees and new industry. The resorts have grown more contemporary, the spas have constantly made themselves over and the restaurants serve a lot more then Southwestern cuisine these days.

Information: Greater Phoenix Convention & Visitors Bureau, 50 N. Second St., 602-254-6500, 877-225-5749; www.visitphoenix.com

## SPOT★LIGHT

★IT IS ILLEGAL IN PHOENIX TO WALK THROUGH A HOTEL LOBBY WEARING SPURS.

★PHOENIX IS THE COUNTRY'S FIFTH LARGEST CITY.

## WHAT TO SEE AND DO

**Antique Gallery/Central Antiques**

5037 N. Central Ave., Phoenix,
602-241-1174

More than 150 dealers showcase heirloom-quality antiques in this 30,000 square foot space. Shop for period furniture, American and English silver, European porcelain and much more. Monday-Saturday 10 a.m.-5:30 p.m., Sunday noon-5 p.m.

**Arizona Center**

400 E. Van Buren St., 602-271-4000;
www.arizonacenter.com

This park-like plaza situated among palm trees, gardens and pools, includes 15 stores

and kiosks. Restaurants, bars, 24-screen theater. Daily.

**Arizona Diamondbacks (MLB)**

Bank One Ballpark, 401 E. Jefferson,
Phoenix, 602-462-6000;
arizona.diamondbacks.mlb.com

Professional baseball team.

**Arizona Mining and Mineral Museum**

1502 W. Washington, Phoenix,
602-771-1600, 800-446-4259;
www.admmr.state.az.us/musgen.htm

This museum showcases minerals and gems as well as petrified wood. Mining exhibits. Monday-Friday 8 a.m.-5 p.m., Saturday 11 a.m.-4 p.m.

### Arizona Science Center

600 E. Washington St., Phoenix,
602-716-2000; www.azscience.org

More than 300 hands-on exhibits on topics ranging from geology to healing make learning fun. Gaze up at the stars in the planetarium and stare wide-eyed at science films in the theater with a five-story screen. Daily 10 a.m.-5 p.m.

### Arizona Capitol Museum

1700 W. Washington St., Phoenix,
602-926-3620; www.lib.az.us/museum

Built in 1899, this stately building first served as the capitol for the territorial government, then as the state capitol after Arizona was admitted to the Union in 1912. The state moved to adjacent office building in the 1970s for more space, and the original structure has operated as a museum since its restoration in 1981. See the House and Senate chambers exactly as they looked in early statehood. Guided tours are offered daily at 10 a.m. and 2 p.m. A landscaped area includes a variety of native trees, shrubs and cacti. Museum Monday-Friday 8 a.m.-5 p.m. Saturday 11 a.m.-4 p.m.

### Biltmore Fashion Park

2502 E. Camelback Rd., Phoenix,
602-955-1963; www.shopbiltmore.com

Bring your oversized designer handbag to this outdoor shopping area with brick walkways and retailers such as Cartier, Escada and Saks Fifth Avenue. Monday-Wednesday, 10 a.m.-7 p.m.; Thursday-Friday 10 a.m.-8 p.m.; Saturday 10 a.m.-6 p.m., Sunday noon-6 p.m.

### Camelback Mountain

E. McDonald at Tatum Blvd., Phoenix,
www.ci.phoenix.az.us/PARKS/
hikecmlb.html

Its distinctive hump makes this mountain a very visible local landmark—and a popular spot for hiking. Trails wind through desert flora and fauna. The two strenuous summit trails (each approximately 1 1/2 miles) gain more than 1,200 feet in elevation. Two shorter ones at the base provide much easier trekking, with elevation gains of only 100 and 200 feet. Daily dawn-dusk.

### Celebrity Theatre

440 N. 32nd St., Phoenix, 602-267-1600;
www.celebritytheatre.com

Some of the entertainment industry's biggest names bring their music and comedy to this theater, where no seat is more than 75 feet from the revolving center stage.

### Char's Has the Blues

4631 N. Seventh Ave., Phoenix,
602-230-0205;
www.charshastheblues.com

Bands sing the blues every night at this small, no-frills joint. A diverse crowd spans all ages. Daily, doors open at 7:30 p.m.

### Desert Botanical Garden

Papago Park, 1201 N. Galvin Pkwy.,
Phoenix, 480-941-1225; www.dbg.org

Walk along the peaceful trails of this 150-acre botanical oasis, home to one of the world's foremost collections of desert plants. Thousands of plants line the one-third mile main trail, including more than half the world's cactus, century plant and aloe species. Music in the Gardens features performances by local bands on Friday evenings from February through June, and Saturday evenings from October through mid-November.     October-April: daily 8 a.m.-8 p.m.; May-September: daily 7 a.m.-8 p.m.

### Encanto Park and Recreation Area

2605 N. 15th Ave., Phoenix, 602-261-8991;
www.enchantedisland.com

Pack up the family and head to this 222-acre park just minutes from downtown. Kids can fish in a small lake, feed ducks in a pond, ride in boats, cool off in the swimming pool, hop aboard a train and eight other rides geared toward 2- to 10-year-olds at the Enchanted Island amusement park. Two public golf courses (18 holes and 9 holes) appeal to an older crowd. Daily.

★
★
★
★
★

### Hall of Flame Firefighting Museum
6101 E. Van Buren St., Phoenix,
602-275-3473; www.hallofflame.org
Believed to be the largest of its kind in the world, the five galleries at this museum are packed with more than 100 pieces of awe-inspiring firefighting equipment, from antique, hand-drawn pumps dating as far back as the 1700s to snazzy, motorized fire engines. Monday-Saturday 9 a.m.-5 p.m., Sunday noon-4 p.m.

### Heard Museum
2301 N. Central Ave., Phoenix,
602-252-8848; www.heard.org
Immerse yourself in the culture and art of the Southwest at this internationally-acclaimed Native American museum. The 130,000-square-foot museum boasts 10 galleries (and a working-artist studio), all packed with items that attract nearly 250,000 visitors each year. Works include contemporary American Indian fine art, historic Hopi katsina dolls, important Navajo and Zuni jewelry and prize-winning documented Navajo textiles. The Heard also offers artist demonstrations, music and dance performances. Daily 9:30 a.m.-5 p.m.

### Heritage Square
Heritage & Science Park, 115 N. Sixth St.,
Phoenix, 602-262-5071;
www.ci.phoenix.az.us/parks/heritage.html
Heritage Square is one of three sites that make up Heritage & Science Park. (The other two sites are the Arizona Science Center and Phoenix Museum of History.) Historic Heritage Park has eight turn-of-the-century houses, including the restored 1895 Victorian Rosson House (docent-guided tours: Wednesday-Saturday 10 a.m.-4 p.m., Sunday noon-4 p.m.; closed mid-August-Labor Day; fee) and Arizona Doll & Toy Museum (The Stevens House, Tuesday-Saturday 10 a.m.-4 p.m., Sunday noon-4 p.m.; closed early August-Labor Day). You'll also find the open-air Lath House Pavilion here. Daily.

### Mystery Castle
800 E. Mineral Rd., Phoenix, 602-268-1581
This quirky, imaginative 18-room castle made of native stone and found objects was built by Boyce Luther Gulley for his daughter Mary Lou, who often leads tours. October-May, Thursday-Sunday 11 a.m.-4 p.m.

### Papago Park
625 N. Galvan Pkwy., Phoenix,
602-261-8318;
www.phoenix.gov/PARKS/hikepapa.html
This 1,200-acre park with sandstone buttes is flatter than many others in the area, appealing to novice hikers and mountain-bikers. (There are more than 10 miles of trails.) Families often come to enjoy its many picnic areas and fishing lagoon, while the golf course lures duffers. The park offers good views of the city, especially at sunset from the Hole-in-the-Rock Archaeological Site, a naturally eroded rock formation. Daily 5 a.m.-11 p.m.

### Phoenix Art Museum
1625 N. Central Ave., Phoenix,
602-257-1222; www.phxart.org
At more than 160,000 square feet, this is one of the largest art museums in the Southwest. There are more than 17,000 works here—about 1,000 of which are on display at any given time, in addition to major traveling exhibits. The museum sponsors Family Sundays every third Sunday of the month for children ages 5-12, which includes imaginative art projects and self-guided explorations of the galleries. Wednesday-Sunday 10 a.m.-5 p.m.; Tuesday 10 a.m.-9 p.m. Free admission Tuesday 3 p.m.-9 p.m.

### Phoenix Coyotes (NHL)
Glendale Arena, 9400 W. Maryland Ave.,
Glendale, 486-563-7825;
www.phoenixcoyotes.com
Professional hockey team.

### Phoenix International Raceway
7602 S. Avondale Blvd., Avondale,
602-252-2227;
www.phoenixintlraceway.com
If you've seen *Days of Thunder* with Tom Cruise, you've seen this high-octane speedway. Big-name drivers fire up their

**31**

**ARIZONA**

★
★
★
★
★

engines on six weekends spread throughout the year. More than 100,000 spectators pack the raceway for NASCAR Weekend in late fall. Other events include the Rolex Grand American Sports Car Series and the IRL Indy Car Series. No other speedway in Arizona opens to so many different classes of cars. IRL also hosts plenty of non-racing event, including a large Fourth of July celebration.

### Phoenix Mercury (WNBA)
America West Arena, 201 E. Jefferson St., Phoenix, 602-252-9622;
www.wnba.com/mercury
Women's professional basketball team.

### Phoenix Mountains Park
2701 E. Squaw Peak Lane, Phoenix,
602-262-6861;
www.ci.phoenix.az.us/parks/hikephx.html
The parks offer more than 7,000 acres of unique desert mountain recreational activities. Hiking, horseback riding and picnicking. Daily 5 a.m.-11 p.m. Echo Canyon, located in the park offers several hiking trails.

### Phoenix Museum of History
Heritage & Science Park, 105 N. Fifth St., Phoenix, 602-253-2734; www.pmoh.org
Celebrates more than 2,000 years of Arizona history. Tuesday-Saturday 10 a.m.-5 p.m.

### Phoenix Suns (NBA)
America West Arena, 201 E. Jefferson, Phoenix, 602-379-7867;
www.nba.com/suns
Professional basketball team.

### Phoenix Zoo
Papago Park, 455 N. Galvin Pkwy.,
Phoenix, 602-273-1341;
www.phoenixzoo.org
See more than 400 mammals, 500 birds and 500 reptiles and amphibians. Especially popular are the Arabian oryx and desert bighorn sheep. The zoo holds special events, educational programs and outdoor recreational activities. Walk, bike (rentals) or take a train ride around the park.

September-May: daily 9 a.m.-5 p.m.; June-August: Monday-Friday 7 a.m.-1 p.m., Saturday-Sunday until 4 p.m.

### Pioneer Living History Museum
3901 W. Pioneer Rd., Phoenix,
623-465-1052; www.pioneer-arizona.com
Experience city life as pioneers in the Old West did. On these 90 acres celebrating the 1800s, you can belly up to the bar in the saloon, check out the chiseling in the blacksmith shop, eye the vintage fashions in the dress store, say a little prayer in the community church and more. October-May: Wednesday-Sunday 9 a.m.-5 p.m.; June-September: Friday-Sunday 8 a.m.-2 p.m.

### Pueblo Grande Museum and Archaeological Park
4619 E Washington St., Phoenix,
602-495-0901, 877-706-4408;
www.ci.phoenix.az.us/parks/pueblo.html
At the ruins of a Hohokam village, revisit the past and learn how these prehistoric people lived in Arizona 1,500 years ago. You'll see an old platform mound that the Hohokam probably used for ceremonies or as an administrative center, an excavated ball court, reproductions of adobe homes and irrigation canals used for farming. Make the rounds of this 102-acre park on your own, or take a guided tour on Saturday at 11 a.m. or 1 p.m. or on Sunday at 1:30 p.m. Monday-Saturday 9 a.m.-4:45 p.m., Sunday 1-4:45 p.m. Free admission Sunday.

### Roadrunner Park Farmers' Market
3501 Cactus Rd., Phoenix, 623-848-1234
Thousands of people come to this outdoor market to stock up on fresh produce grown in the Arizona desert. As many as 60 vendors sell melons, onions, peppers, squash, tomatoes and other fresh-from-the-farm crops. A few sell arts and crafts. Saturday 8 a.m.-noon.

### Squaw Peak Park
Phoenix, 602-262-7901
The views—and the hiking—will take your breath away. The demanding, 1.2-mile trek up the Summit Trail will test you every step

of the way. For an easier route, opt for the Circumference Trail. Daily.

### Vans Skatepark
**9617 N. Metro Pkwy. W., Phoenix, 602-870-8727**
Riding areas and obstacles include a street course with birch ramps and a wooden bowl with swimming-pool tiles and coping. The park accommodates all skill levels. Sessions for BMX bikers are offered on certain days. Daily 10 a.m.-10 p.m.

## SPECIAL EVENTS

### Arizona Opera
**4600 N. 12th, Phoenix, 602-266-7464; www.azopera.com**
Five operas are held each year at the Phoenix Symphony Hall. October-March, Friday-Sunday.

### Arizona State Fair
**1826 W. McDowell Rd., Phoenix, 602-252-6771; www.azstatefair.com**
This annual event attracts big crowds. It has everything you'd expect of a good state fair: a busy midway packed with exciting rides and games, high-decibel concerts, gooey cotton candy and other carnival fare, rodeo action, cooking contests and much more. Mid-October-early November.

### Arizona Theatre Company
**Herberger Theater Center, 222 E. Monroe St., Phoenix, 520-622-2823; www.aztheatreco.org**
Professional regional company performs both classic and contemporary works. October-May.

### Cowboy Artists of America Sale and Exhibition
**Phoenix Art Museum, 1625 N. Central Ave., Phoenix, 602-307-2007; www.phxart.org**
Members of Cowboy Artists of America—a select group who produce fine Western American art—are considered the most prestigious in this genre. And at this annual event, they offer more than 100 of their new, never-before-viewed works for sale—some of which command six figures. If that's more than you can wrangle, all the painting, drawings and sculptures remain on exhibit for several weeks so everyone can enjoy them before buyers claim them. Late October-mid-November.

### Firecracker Sports Festival
**Rose Mofford, Papago and Desert West Complexes, Phoenix, 602-262-6485**
About 140 teams from throughout Arizona come to play ball during this annual event, the state's largest and longest-running softball tournament. The action features adult slow pitch and youth (girls) fast pitch in up to 13 divisions. The opening-night party includes a fireworks display. Last weekend in June.

### Indian Fair and Market
**The Heard Museum, 2301 N. Central Ave., Phoenix, 602-252-8848; www.heard.org/fair.php**
American Indian artisans, demonstrations, dances, native foods. First weekend in March.

### New Works Festival
**Phoenix Theatre's Little Theatre, 100 E. McDowell Rd., Phoenix, 602-258-1974**
See plays and musicals staged in their early phases. Actors perform works-in-progress with books in hand and with minimal set decorations. Some get produced as part of Phoenix Theatre's regular season. Late July-mid-August.

### Phoenix Symphony
**Symphony Hall, 75 N. Second St., Phoenix, 602-495-1999, 800-776-9080; www.phoenixsymphony.org**
Annual programming includes classics, chamber orchestra, symphonic pops and family and holiday events.

### Yaqui Indian Easter Ceremonies
**Avenida del Yaqui, Yaqui Temple and Ceremonial Grounds, Guadalupe, 520-883-2838; www.guadalupeaz.org**

**33**

**ARIZONA**

These Lenten celebrations are still a sacred obligation of the Yaqui and represent a unique combination of traditional Yaqui and Catholic customs. Friday-Sunday afternoons from Ash Wednesday to Easter.

# HOTELS

### ★★★Arizona Biltmore Resort and Spa
2400 E. Missouri Rd., Phoenix,
602-955-6600, 800-950-2575;
www.arizonabiltmore.com
The Arizona Biltmore Resort and Spa opened to great fanfare in 1929. The nice thing about it today is that it's not trying to remain great—it just is. The Frank Lloyd Wright-inspired architecture, as well as the photos of all the presidents and famous people who have stayed here, take you back to another time. Spend your days lounging at one of the eight pools, playing the adjacent golf course or relaxing in the 22,000-square-foot spa. The comfortable rooms have Mission-style furnishings and textiles in calming dessert tones and fluffy beds.
738 rooms. High-speed Internet access. Restaurant, bar. Children. Spa. Airport transportation available. Pets accepted. Pool. Tennis. $$$

### ★★Doubletree Guest Suites Phoenix Gateway Center
320 N. 44th St., Phoenix,
602-225-0500, 800-800-3098;
www.doubletree.com
242 rooms, all suites. Complimentary full breakfast. High-speed wireless Internet access. Restaurant, bar. Airport transportation available. Pool. Business Center. $

### ★★Embassy Suites Hotel Phoenix-Biltmore
2630 E. Camelback Rd., Phoenix,
602-955-3992, 800-362-2779;
www.phoenixbiltmore.embassysuites.com
232 rooms, all suites. Complimentary full breakfast. Wireless Internet access. Restaurant, bar. Pets accepted. Pool. $$

### ★★Embassy Suites Hotel Phoenix-North
2577 W. Greenway Rd., Phoenix,
602-375-1777; www.embassysuites.com

314 rooms, all suites. Complimentary full breakfast. Restaurant, bar. Pets accepted. Pool. Tennis. $

### ★★Hilton Phoenix Airport
2435 S. 47th St., Phoenix,
408-894-1600, 800-445-8667;
www.hilton.com
255 rooms. High-speed Internet access. Restaurant, bar. Airport transportation available. Pool. Business center. $

### ★★★JW Marriott Desert Ridge Resort and Spa
5350 E. Marriott Dr., Phoenix,
480-293-5000, 800-835-6206;
www.jwdesertridgeresort.com
This resort has it all: four sun-kissed pools, two 18-hole golf courses designed by Arnold Palmer and Tom Fazio, an eight-court tennis center, miles of hiking trails, a renowned spa and five restaurants. The rooms have balconies and patios. In summer, families can watch favorite movies like *Charlotte's Web* at the pool.
950 rooms. Restaurant, bar. Children's activity center. Spa. Pool. Golf. Tennis. $$$

### ★★The Legacy Golf Resort
6808 S. 32nd St., Phoenix,
602-305-5500, 888-828-3673;
www.legacygolfresort.com
328 rooms, all suites. High-speed Internet access. Restaurant, bar. Children's activity center. Pool. Golf. Tennis. $$$

### ★★Maricopa Manor Bed & Breakfast
15 W. Pasadena Ave., Phoenix,
602-274-6302, 800-292-6403;
www.maricopamanor.com
7 rooms, all suites. Complimentary continental breakfast. High-speed wireless Internet access. Airport transportation available. Pool. $

### ★★★Pointe Hilton Squaw Peak Resort
7677 N. 16th St., Phoenix,
602-997-2626, 800-947-9784;
www.pointehilton.com

This sprawling all-suite resort at the base of Squaw Peak is great for families. The nine-acre recreational area includes swimming pools with waterfalls and a huge slide and an 18-hole miniature golf course. Kids will think they're in heaven after spending a day here and then hitting the old-fashioned ice cream parlor. For adults there's a spa with salon and fitness center, tennis courts, shopping and hikes in the adjacent Phoenix Mountain Preserve. Accommodations range from two-bedroom suites to three-bedroom casitas.

563 rooms, all suites. High-speed Internet access. Two restaurants, three bars. Children's activity center. Spa. Airport transportation available. **$$**

### ★★★Pointe Hilton Tapatio Cliffs Resort
11111 N. Seventh St., Phoenix,
602-866-7500, 800-947-9784;
www.pointehilton.com

This resort is situated among the peaks of the Phoenix North Mountains, offering dramatic views of the city and valley below. The resort boasts its own water playground and a total of eight swimming pools, some with waterfalls. The Lookout Mountain Golf Club is an 18-hole championship course set along the border of an 8,000-acre Sonoran desert park. A full-service spa offers a variety of pampering treatments. The two-room suites all have living rooms and two TVs.

585 rooms, all suites. High-speed Internet access. Restaurant, bar. Children's activity center. Spa. Airport transportation available. Pets accepted. Golf. Tennis. **$$**

### ★★★Pointe South Mountain Resort
7777 S. Pointe Pkwy., Phoenix,
602-438-9000, 877-267-1321;
www.pointesouthmtn.com

This upscale and well-maintained resort offers spacious rooms with high-quality furnishings and an endless list of things to do. The on-site water park is Arizona's largest, boasting an eight-story water slide, wave pool and "river" for tubing. There are also six swimming pools, lighted tennis courts, water and sand volleyball courts, racquet-ball and croquet, an 18-hole golf course and horseback riding. When you exhaust all that, there's hiking and biking in South Mountain Park next door.

640 rooms. Restaurant, bar. Children's activity center. Spa. Business center. Golf. Tennis. **$$$**

### ★★★★The Ritz-Carlton, Phoenix
2401 E. Camelback, Phoenix,
602-468-0700, 800-241-3333;
www.ritzcarlton.com

The hotel is smack in the middle of the Camelback Corridor, the exclusive shopping, dining and financial district of Phoenix. The rooms, classically decorated with beds topped with luxury linens, all have views of the skyline or the Squaw Peak Mountain Range—and of course, there's the Ritz level of service. Concierges will offers tips on everything from the area's best golf courses to the tastiest cocktail to sip in the lobby lounge. You'll find modern takes on French classics (think steak au poivre with crisp frites) at the hotel's festive Bistro 24. The outdoor pool sparkles and the sundeck area is cooled with hydro-misters.

281 rooms. High-speed Internet access, wireless Internet access. Restaurant, two bars. Airport transportation available. Exercise. Swim. Busn. Center. **$$$**

### ★★★Royal Palms Resort and Spa
5200 E. Camelback Rd., Phoenix,
602-840-3610, 800-672-6011;
www.royalpalmsresortandspa.com

Constructed in the late 1920s as a private mansion, this hotel brings a bit of the Mediterranean to the Sonoran Desert. Palm trees line the entrance to this hideaway surrounded by fountains and citrus trees, where lavish casitas and guest rooms have fireplaces and balconies. The dreamy open-air spa has treatment rooms with garden areas and a villa with stone heated tables under overhead showers. T. Cooks is an award-winning restaurant.

119 rooms. High-speed Internet access, wireless Internet access. Two restaurants, two bars. Spa. Airport transportation available. Pets accepted. **$$$**

**35**

**ARIZONA**

★
★
★
☆

# RESTAURANTS

### ★★★Avanti of Phoenix
2728 E. Thomas Rd., Phoenix,
602-956-0900; www.avanti-az.com
A stark Art Deco-inspired interior of black and white is the backdrop for this romantic restaurant specializing in fresh pasta with rich sauces. Enjoy piano music in the lounge area Thursday through Saturday.
Italian menu. Lunch, dinner. Bar. Business casual attire. Reservations recommended. Valet parking. Outdoor seating. **$$$**

### ★Baby Kay's Cajun Kitchen
2119 E. Camelback Rd., Phoenix,
602-955-0011;
www.babykayscajunkitchen.com
Cajun/Creole menu. Lunch, dinner. Closed Sunday. Bar. Casual attire. Outdoor seating. **$$**

### ★★Barrio Cafe
2814 N. 16th St., Phoenix, 602-636-0240;
www.barriocafe.com
Mexican menu. Lunch, dinner, Sunday bunch. Closed Monday. Bar. Casual attire. Valet parking. **$$$**

### ★★★Bistro 24
2401 E. Camelback Rd., Phoenix,
602-468-0700; www.ritzcarlton.com
Located within the Ritz-Carlton, Bistro 24 serves classic dishes like steak *au poivre* and grilled seafood like butter-poached halibut. The restaurant is spacious and unpretentious with colorful murals and an outdoor patio, and the service is impeccable. Come for happy hour for half-priced martinis and appetizers.
French bistro menu. Breakfast, lunch, dinner, Sunday brunch. Bar. Children's menu. Business casual attire. Reservations recommended. Valet parking. Outdoor seating. **$$$**

### ★★Convivo
7000 N. 16th St., Phoenix, 602-997-7676
Mediterranean menu. Lunch, dinner. Closed Sunday-Monday. Casual attire. Reservations recommended. **$$**

### ★Coronado Cafe
2201 N. Seventh St., Phoenix,
602-258-5149; www.coronadocafe.com
American menu. Lunch, dinner. Closed Sunday. Casual attire. Reservations recommended. **$**

### ★★Coup des Tartes
4626 N. 16th St., Phoenix, 602-212-1082;
www.nicetartes.com
American menu. Dinner. Closed Sunday-Monday, also Tuesday in June-August. Casual attire. Reservations recommended. **$$**

### ★★Fish Market
1720 E. Camelback Rd., Phoenix,
602-277-3474; www.thefishmarket.com
Seafood menu. Lunch, dinner. Bar. Children's menu. Casual attire. Reservations recommended. Outdoor seating. **$$**

### ★The Fry Bread House
4140 N. Seventh Ave., Phoenix,
602-351-2345
Southwestern menu. Lunch, dinner. Closed Sunday. Children's menu. Casual attire. **$**

### ★★Havana Cafe
4225 E. Camelback Rd., Phoenix,
602-952-1991; www.havanacafe-az.com
Cuban menu. Lunch, dinner. Bar. Children's menu. Casual attire. Valet parking. Outdoor seating. **$$**

### ★★★La Fontanella
4231 E. Indian School Rd., Phoenix,
602-955-1213
The Italian husband and wife team who run this Phoenix gem serve up hearty recipes from their homeland, including fresh pastas and grilled meats.
Italian menu. Dinner. Closed two weeks in July. Bar. Casual attire. Reservations recommended. **$$$**

### ★Mi Cocina, Mi Pais
4221 W. Bell Rd., Phoenix, 602-548-7900
Latin American menu. Lunch, dinner. Closed Monday. Children's menu. Casual attire. **$$**

### ★★Persian Garden
1335 W. Thomas Rd., Phoenix,
602-263-1915;
www.persiangardencafe.com
Mediterranean, Middle Eastern menu. Lunch, dinner. Closed Sunday, Monday; also late June-early July. Casual attire. **$$**

### ★★Rustler's Rooste
8383 S. 48th St., Phoenix, 602-431-6474;
www.rustlersrooste.com
Steak menu. Dinner. Bar. Children's menu. Casual attire. Valet parking. Outdoor seating. **$$**

### ★★★Ruth's Chris Steak House
2201 E. Camelback Rd., Phoenix,
602-957-9600; www.ruthschris.com
Born from a single New Orleans restaurant, the chain is a favorite among steak lovers. Aged prime midwestern beef is broiled at 1,800 degrees and served on a heated plate sizzling in butter with sides like creamed spinach and au gratin potatoes.
Steak menu. Dinner. Bar. Reservations recommended. Valet parking. Outdoor seating. **$$$**

### ★★Soma Cafe
10810 N. Tatum Blvd., Phoenix,
602-867-2175; www.somacafe.com
Vegetarian menu. Breakfast, lunch, dinner. Children's menu. Casual attire. Outdoor seating. **$**

### ★★Sophie's Bistro
2320 E. Osborn Rd., Phoenix,
602-956-8897; www.sophies bistro.com
French menu. Lunch, dinner. Closed Sunday. Bar. Casual attire. Reservations recommended. **$$**

### ★★Steamers Genuine Seafood
2576 E. Camelback Rd., Phoenix,
602-956-3631;
www.steamersgenuineseafood.com
Seafood menu. Lunch, dinner. Bar. Children's menu. Valet parking. Outdoor seating. **$$$**

### ★★★T. Cook's
5200 E. Camelback Rd., Phoenix,
602-808-0766, 866-579-3636;
www.royalpalmsresortandspa.com
Located in the Royal Palms Hotel and Spa, this stylish restaurant has deep cherry wood floors, hand-painted Italian frescoes and floor-to-ceiling windows with views of Camelback Mountain. The Mediterranean menu includes dishes such as roast duck with preserved apricots and spiced yogurt and grilled veal flank steak with warm potato salad. Some dishes are made in the restaurant's fireplace.
Mediterranean menu. Breakfast, lunch, dinner, Sunday brunch. Bar. Business casual attire. Reservations recommended. Valet parking. Outdoor seating. **$$$**

### ★★★Tarbell's
3213 E. Camelback Rd., Phoenix,
602-955-8100; www.tarbells.com
Celebrated chef Marc Tarbell—he recently appeared on *Iron Chef*—continues to dazzle with fresh seasonal dishes such as hand cut pasta with locally-made chicken fennel sausage, organic tomatoes and English peas, and double-cut pork chop with Wisconsin cheddar grills, collard greens and wild boar bacon. The sophisticated restaurant features blond wood, white tablecloths and an exhibition kitchen—and somehow maintains a friendly neighborhood feel, perhaps thanks to the large curved bar that's a focal point.
American menu. Dinner. Bar. Business casual attire. Reservations recommended. Valet parking. **$$$**

### ★★Tomaso's
3225 E. Camelback Rd., Phoenix,
602-956-0836; www.tomasos.com
Italian menu. Lunch, dinner. **$$$**

### ★★★Vincent Guerithault on Camelback
3930 E. Camelback Rd., Phoenix,
602-224-0225;
www.vincentsoncamelback.com
This intimate restaurant, which combines hearty Southwest flavors with elegant French cuisine, spawned Phoenix's culinary reputation. The flawless wait staff and

★

★

★

★

★

enduring menu continue to impress diners. On Friday and Saturday evenings, a pianist performs .

French menu. Lunch, dinner. Closed Sunday. Bar. Business casual attire. Reservations recommended. Valet parking. $$$

### ★★The Wild Thaiger

2631 N. Central Ave., Phoenix, 602-241-8995; www.wildthaiger.com
Thai menu. Lunch, dinner. Bar. Children's menu. Casual attire. Outdoor seating. $$

### ★★★Wright's

2400 Missouri Rd., Phoenix, 602-381-7632; www.arizonabiltmore.com
A homage to Frank Lloyd Wright, this restaurant off the lobby of the Arizona Biltmore reflects the architect's penchant for stark angles and contrasts. Muted Southwestern colors fill the comfortable room and a large-paneled window lets in the views. The American cuisine features the freshest ingredients from boutique farms across the country. The menu changes weekly and includes dishes such aged buffalo with white cheddar and Yukon purée. Be sure to sample one of the delectable chocolate desserts.

American menu. Dinner, Sunday brunch. Bar. Business casual attire. Reservations recommended. Valet parking. Outdoor seating. $$$

### ★★Zen 32

3160 E. Camelback Rd., Phoenix, 602-954-8700; www.zen32.com
Japanese menu. Lunch, dinner. Casual attire. $$

# SPAS

### ★★★★Alvadora Spa at Royal Palms

5200 E. Camelback Rd., Phoenix, 602-977-6400, 800-672-6011; www.royalpalmsresortandspa.com
Inspired by that region's native flowers, herbs and oils, this Mediterranean-style spa brings the outdoors in through its open-air design and plant-inspired therapies. The healing properties of water are a focal point here, whether you're soaking in a bath of grape seeds and herbs or floating in the Watsu pool. Indulge in the Fango mud wrap, a traditional therapy that uses volcanic mud from Italy's northern regions to purify and cleanse skin. The vino therapy facial uses grape leaf extract for intense moisturizing. Enjoy yoga, tai chi, meditation and mat Pilate's classes in the 24-hour fitness center. $$

### ★★★Revive Spa at JW Marriott Desert Ridge Resort

5350 E. Marriott Dr., Phoenix, 480-293-3700, 866-738-4834; www.jwdesertridgeresort.com
The serenity and beauty of the desert are the true inspirations at this spa, where outside celestial showers for men and women, private balconies—ideal for outdoor massages—and a rooftop garden with flowing water add to the atmosphere. Indigenous botanicals influence most of Revive's body treatments. Mesquite clay and desert algae body wraps detoxify and purify. Prickly pear and lime-salt body scrubs soften skin. Recharge with a workout in the spacious and well-equipped fitness center. In addition to cardio machines and free weights, this facility offers several classes, including tai chi, water fitness, golf conditioning, flexibility, yoga and mat Pilates. After a workout, dine on calorie-conscious meals at Revive's Spa Bistro. $$

★
★
★
★
★

## PIPE SPRING NATIONAL MONUMENT

Located on the Kaibab-Paiute Indian Reservation, the focal point of this monument is a beautifully built sandstone Mormon fort dating to 1870. Several years earlier, Brigham Young had ordered the exploration of this region north of the Grand Canyon. According to legend, rifleman William "Gunlock Bill" Hamblin gave the place its name by shooting the bottom out of a smoking pipe at 50 paces.

The fort, actually a fortified ranch house, was built under the direction of Bishop Anson P. Winsor to protect the families caring for the church's cattle. Cattle drives, headed for the railroad in Cedar City, Utah, began here.

Guide service daily; living history demonstrations June-September. Kaibab Paiute Campground, 1/2 mile north of access road to visitor center.

Information: HC 65, Fredonia, 14 miles west on a spur off Hwy. 389, 928-643-7105; www.nps.gov/pisp

# PRESCOTT

When President Lincoln established the territory of Arizona, Prescott became the capital. In 1867, the capital was moved to Tucson and then back to Prescott in 1877. After much wrangling, it was finally moved to Phoenix in 1889.

Tourism and manufacturing are now Prescott's principal occupations. The climate is mild during summer and winter. The Prescott National Forest surrounds the city.

Information: Chamber of Commerce, 117 W. Goodwin St., 928-445-2000, 800-266-7534; www.prescott.org

## WHAT TO SEE AND DO

### Prescott National Forest
344 S. Cortez St., Prescott, 928-443-8000; www.fs.fed.us/r3/prescott

Minerals and varied vegetation abound in this forest of more than one million acres. Within the forest are Juniper Mesa, Apache Creek, Granite Mountain, Castle Creek, Woodchute and Cedar Bench wilderness areas, as well as parts of Sycamore Canyon and Pine Mountain wilderness areas. Fishing (Granite Basin, Lynx lakes); hunting, picnicking, camping.

### Sharlot Hall Museum
415 W. Gurley St., Prescott, 928-445-3122; www.sharlot.org

Period houses include the Territorial Governor's Mansion (1864), restored in 1929 by poet-historian Sharlot Hall; Fort Misery (1864); William Bashford house (1877); and John C. Fremont house (1875). Period furnishings. Museum, library, archives. Also on the grounds is the grave of Pauline Weaver. Rose and herb garden. Pioneer schoolhouse. All buildings May-September: Monday-Saturday 10 a.m.-5 p.m., Sunday noon-4 p.m.; October-April: Monday-Saturday 10 a.m.-4 p.m., Sunday noon-4 p.m.

### Smoki Museum
147 N. Arizona St., Prescott, 928-445-1230; www.smokimuseum.org

Native American artifacts, ancient and modern. Tuesday-Saturday 10 a.m.-4 p.m., Sunday 1-4 p.m.

## SPECIAL EVENTS

### Bluegrass Festival
Courthouse Plaza, 130 N. Cortez St., Prescott, 928-445-2000; www.prescottbluegrassfestival.com

Features performances from local bluegrass artists. Late June.

### Phippen Museum Western Art Show and Sale
Courthouse Plaza, 130 N. Cortez St., Prescott, 928-778-1385; www.phippenartmuseum.org

More than 50 artists participate in this event, displaying works of several different media, including watercolor, sculpture, acrylic and more. Memorial Day weekend.

### Prescott Frontier Days Rodeo
848 Rodeo Dr., Prescott, 928-445-3103, 800-358-1888; www.worldsoldestrodeo.com

Spend a couple of days at the "world's oldest rodeo." Festivities and events are held throughout the city. There is also a parade and laser show. Late June-July 4.

### Territorial Prescott Days
Courthouse Plaza, 130 N. Cortez St., Prescott,
928-445-2000
This citywide celebration features an art show, craft demonstrations, old-fashioned contests and home tours. Early June.

## HOTELS
### ★Days Inn
7875 E. Hwy. 69,
Prescott Valley,
928-772-8600, 800-329-7466;
www.daysinn.com
59 rooms. Complimentary continental breakfast. Pets accepted. Pool. $

### ★★Forest Villas Hotel
3645 Lee Circle, Prescott,
928-717-1200, 800-223-3449;
www.forestvillas.com
62 rooms. Complimentary continental breakfast. Pool. $

### ★★Hassayampa Inn
122 E. Gurley St., Prescott,
928-778-9434, 800-322-1927;
www.hassayampainn.com

67 rooms. Complimentary full breakfast. Restaurant, bar. $

## SPECIALTY LODGINGS
### Pleasant Street Inn Bed & Breakfast
142 S. Pleasant St., Prescott,
928-445-4774, 877-226-7128;
www.pleasantbandb.com
6 rooms. Complimentary full breakfast. $

## RESTAURANTS
### ★★Gurley Street Grill
230 W. Gurley St., Prescott, 928-445-3388;
www.murphysrestaurants.com
American menu. Lunch, dinner. Bar. Children's menu. Casual attire. Outdoor seating. $$

### ★★Murphy's
201 N. Cortez, Prescott, 928-445-4044;
www.murphysrestaurants.com
American menu. Lunch, dinner, Sunday brunch. Bar. Children's menu. Business casual attire. Reservations recommended. $$$

### ★★Pine Cone Inn Supper Club
1245 White Spar Rd., Prescott,
928-445-2970; www.pcisupperclub.com
American menu. Dinner Wednesday-Sunday. Closed Monday-Tuesday. Bar. Children's menu. Business casual attire. Reservations recommended. $$

## SAFFORD
This small town has no shortage of places to play: Opt for a trek up nearby Mount Graham, a hike along Bonita Creek or a day of fishing at Roper Lake.
Information: Graham County Chamber of Commerce, 1111 Thatcher Blvd., Safford, 928-428-2511, 888-837-1841; www.visitgrahamcounty.com

## WHAT TO SEE AND DO
### Roper Lake State Park
101 E. Roper Lake Rd., Safford,
928-428-6760;
www.pr.state.az.us/parks/parkhtml/
roper.html
This 320-acre park includes a small artificial lake, swimming beach and natural hot springs with tubs for public use. Fishing, boat launch (no gas-powered motors); nature

trails, hiking; picnicking (shelter), camping, tent and trailer sites. Daily 6 a.m.-10 p.m.

### The Swift Trail
504 S. Fifth Ave., Safford, 928-428-4150;
www.fs.fed.us/r3/coronado/forest/
recreation/scenic_drives/
pinaleno_swift.shtml
Hwy 366 snakes its way 36 miles southwest from Safford to the high elevations of the

Pinaleo Mountains in Coronado National Forest. Five developed campgrounds (mid-April-mid-November, weather permitting); trout fishing at Riggs Flat Lake and in the streams. The upper elevations of Hwy. 366 are closed mid-November-mid-April.

## SPECIAL EVENTS
### Cinco de Mayo Bash
311 S. Central Ave., Safford, 928-428-4920
Mexican-American commemoration of Cinco de Mayo (May Fifth). Entertainment, dancing, world's longest tequila shot chain, games. First weekend in May.

### Graham County Fair
527 E. Armory Rd., Safford, 85546, 928-428-7180;
www.casinocity.com/us/az/safford/grahamfa
Horse racing, quarter horse racing, race book. The complex also hosts the annual rodeo, Old Time Fiddlers Contest and other events. Mid-October.

## HOTELS
### ★Comfort Inn
1578 W. Thatcher Blvd., Safford, 928-428-5851; www.comfortinn.com
44 rooms. Complimentary continental breakfast. Pool. $

# SAN CARLOS
The San Carlos Apache Indian Reservation covers almost two million acres ranging from desert to pine forests. Many lakes, rivers and ponds offer fishing year-round for trout, bass and catfish. Hunting for small game, large game and waterfowl is also year-round. Apache guides may be hired to lead visitors into the wilderness portions of the reservation. Sunrise ceremonial dances are held from time to time.
Information: San Carlos Recreation & Wildlife Department, San Carlos, 928-475-2343, 888-475-2344; www.sancarlosrecreationandwildlife.com

# SCOTTSDALE
Scottsdale is a popular resort destination located on the eastern border of Phoenix. It is renowned for outstanding art galleries, excellent shopping and dining, lush golf courses, and abundant recreational activities.
Information: Chamber of Commerce, 4725 N. Scottsdale Rd., 480-355-2700; www.scottsdalecvb.com

## WHAT TO SEE AND DO
### Antique Trove
2020 N. Scottsdale Rd., Scottsdale, 480-947-6074; www.antiquetrove.com
More than 150 dealers sell everything from vintage mink jackets to colonial rockers from the 1940s to claw-foot bathtubs. Prices range from $1 to several thousand. Daily.

### Casino Arizona at Salt River
524 N. 92nd St., Scottsdale; www.casinoaz.com
The Salt River Pima-Maricopa Indian Community hit the jackpot when it opened this casino in a prime location off the 101 Freeway on the Valley's east side. They promptly opened a second location just a few miles north, off the same freeway (9700 E Indian Bend Rd.). The original funhouse is larger and a notch more upscale with five restaurants—the best being the elegant Cholla Prime Steakhouse. The 250-seat cabaret-style showroom rocks with name entertainers. Daily.

### Cosanti Foundation
6433 Doubletree Ranch Rd.,
Paradise Valley,
480-948-6145, 800-752-3187;
www.cosanti.com

The famous Paolo Soleri wind-bells are made and sold here. Self-guided tours daily. Guided tours by reservation only. Daily 9 a.m.-5 p.m.

### Cruise Night at Scottsdale Pavilions
9175 E. Indian Bend Rd.,
Scottsdale,
480-905-9111;
www.scottsdalepavilions.com

While Scottsdale Pavilions may be one of the largest and most attractive shopping centers in the country, Saturday nights bring more people to the parking lot than the shops. They come for the hot rods: muscle cars, custom cars, street rods, antique roadsters, vintage trucks, motorcycles and even a few finely tuned imports. Starts about 4 p.m., generally winds down around 8:30 p.m.

### Desert Course at The Phoenician
6000 E. Camelback Rd.,
Scottsdale,
480-941-8200, 800-888-8234;
www.thephoenician.com

This nine-hole wonder joins two other nine-hole courses (aptly named the "Oasis" and the "Canyon") to earn the swanky Phoenician some major accolades.

### Grayhawk Golf Club
8620 E. Thompson Peak Pkwy.,
Scottsdale,
480-502-1800;
www.grayhawk.com

Grayhawk has two courses: Talon (designed by David Graham and Gary Panks) and Raptor (designed by Tom Fazio). Both are nice, but Talon deserves more attention. Built in the Sonoran Desert, the course features many shots over desert brush or sand, with some water worked in for good measure. The course is good enough to host international-caliber tournaments such as the World Championship of Golf. If your game needs work, schedule some time at the Kostis

McCord Learning Center, whose instructors include the two CBS commentators.

### Ironwood Course at The Westin Kierland Golf Resort & Spa
15636 Clubgate Dr., Scottsdale,
480-922-9283, 888-625-5144;
www.kierlandresort.com/golf

Designed by Scott Miller (once a designer for Jack Nicklaus), the Ironwood, like the other two nine-hole courses at this resort, offers a beautiful setting for birdies, bogies and maybe even a hole-in-one.

### Kierland Commons
Scottsdale Rd. and Greenway Pkwy.,
Scottsdale,
480-348-1577;
www.kierlandcommons.com

This 38-acre urban village bills itself as "today's version of yesterday," given its Main Street feel and pedestrian-friendly layout. The well-landscaped streets are lined with more than 50 upscale retailers, iRestaurants include Morton's Steak House, News Cafe and P.F. Chang's China Bistro. Monday-Saturday 10 a.m.-9 p.m., Sunday noon-6 p.m.

### Legend Trail Golf Club
9462 E. Legendary Lane, Scottsdale,
480-488-7434;
www.legendtrailgc.com

Drive, chip and putt your way through the Sonoran Desert on this picturesque course. Even if you don't quite shoot par, you'll enjoy the gorgeous vistas and desert landscape.

### McCormick-Stillman Railroad Park
7301 E. Indian Bend Rd., Scottsdale,
480-312-2312; www.therailroadpark.com

Kids will enjoy circling around this 30-acre city park aboard the Paradise and Pacific Railroad, a miniature reproduction of a Colorado narrow-gauge railroad. There's also a 1950s carousel and well-equipped playgrounds. Be sure to also tour the Roald Amundsen Pullman Car, used by Herbert Hoover, Franklin Roosevelt, Harry Truman and Dwight Eisenhower. Daily.

★
★
★
☆

### Mesquite Course at The Westin Kierland Golf Resort & Spa

15636 Clubgate Dr., Scottsdale,
480-922-9283, 888-625-5144;
www.kierlandresort.com/golf

Like its two nine-hole counterparts, this course was designed by Scott Miller (former designer for Jack Nicklaus). The resort offers three 18-hole combinations to challenge and delight duffers of all skill levels.

### Monument Course at Troon North Golf Club

10320 E. Dynamite Blvd., Scottsdale,
480-585-5300;
www.troonnorthgolf.com

Test your skills in the shadow of Pinnacle Peak at this beautiful desert course.

### North Course at Talking Stick Golf Club

9998 E. Indian Bend Rd., Scottsdale,
480-860-2221;
www.talkingstickgolfclub.com

This Scottish links course stands ready to challenge golfers with its fairway bunkers, so don't let the gorgeous setting distract you too much.

### Oasis Course at The Phoenician

6000 E. Camelback Rd.,
Scottsdale,
480-423-2450, 800-888-8234;
www.thephoenician.com

The Phoenician has earned praise national critics and local fans alike. Don't miss an opportunity to swing your clubs at one of three 18-hole combinations, of which the Oasis makes up nine holes.

### The Phoenician-Canyon Course

6000 E. Camelback Rd.,
Scottsdale,
480-941-8200, 800-888-8234;
www.thephoenician.com

The Canyon is the last in the triumvirate of courses that make the Phoenician a celebrated resort. This nine-hole course can be combined with either of the other two courses (Oasis or Desert) to make a challenging and enjoyable 18-hole trek through the picturesque desert.

### Pinnacle Course at Troon North Golf Club

10320 E. Dynamite Blvd., Scottsdale,
480-585-5300; www.troonnorthgolf.com

Named for Pinnacle Peak, the course is one of two you'll find at the Troon North Golf Club. After swinging your heart out on the green—and admiring the view—dine at the club's Grille.

### Rawhide Wild West Town

5700 W. North Loop Rd., Chandler,
480-502-5600, 800-527-1880;
www.rawhide.com

Gallop into the Old West at Arizona's largest Western-themed attraction. Roam the range on the stagecoach or train, test your aim in the shooting gallery, ride the mechanical bull, pan for gold, go horseback riding and take in the shows—from stuntmen throwing punches and squaring off in gunfights to performances by American Indian and Mexican dancers. The Steakhouse serves up mesquite-grilled steaks. Browse through the 15 shops. Daily.

### Scottsdale Center for the Arts

7380 E. Second St., Scottsdale,
480-994-2787; www.scottsdalearts.org

Offers theater, dance and music. Lectures, outdoor festivals and concerts. Sculpture garden; art exhibits. Daily.

### Scottsdale Fashion Square

7014-590 E. Camelback Rd., Scottsdale,
480-941-2140; www.fashionsquare.com

The largest shopping destination in the Southwest features more than 225 retailers, including Neiman Marcus, Nordstrom, Louis Vuitton, Sephora and Tiffany & Co. Ten restaurants, food court, movies. Daily.

### Taliesin West

12621 N. Frank Lloyd Wright Blvd.,
Scottsdale, 480-860-2700;
www.franklloydwright.org

Take a guided tour of this amazing compound and see Frank Lloyd Wright's passion for organic architecture. In the late 1930s, Wright and his apprentices literally built this winter camp out of the Sonoran desert, using rocks and sand they gathered

**43**

**ARIZONA**

★
★
★
★
★

from the rugged terrain. In true Wright fashion, the architect designed the various buildings with terraces, gardens and walkways that link the outdoors with the indoors. Taliesin West still functions as a school for more than 20 architectural students. Daily.

### Talking Stick Golf Club-South Course
9998 E. Indian Bend Rd., Scottsdale, 480-860-2221;
www.talkingstickgolfclub.com
Unlike its counterpart, which is a Scottish links course, the South Course is a traditional American-style golf course, punctuated with cottonwood and sycamore trees, creeks and lakes.

### Tournament Players Club of Scottsdale
17020 N. Hayden Rd., Scottsdale, 480-585-4334;
www.tpc.com
Follow in the footsteps of Tiger Woods, Vijay Singh and other big-name golfers and swing into action on the TPCs greens—home of the Phoenix Open. The club has two options: the Stadium Course (the one the pros shoot) and the Desert Course, both open for daily-play.

### The Westin Kierland Golf Resort and Spa-Acacia Course
15636 Clubgate Dr., Scottsdale, 480-922-9285;
www.kierlandresort.com/golf
Part of the resort's 27 perfectly manicured holes, the Acacia was created by Scott Miller, who once designed for Jack Nicklaus. Combine these nine holes with Ironwood or Mesquite's nine holes for 18 holes of great golf in one of Arizona's most beautiful resorts.

### WestWorld of Scottsdale
16601 N. Pima Rd., Scottsdale, 480-312-6802;
www.scottsdaleaz.gov/westworld
A 360-acre recreation park, equestrian center, and event facility at the base of the McDowell Mountains. Concerts, sports competitions, special events. Daily.

### Wild West Jeep Tours
7127 E. Becker Lane, Scottsdale, 480-922-0144;
www.wildwestjeeptours.com
Three to four hour guided desert tour. Explore an ancient ruin. Daily.

## SPECIAL EVENTS
### Arabian Horse Show
WestWorld, 16601 N. Pima Rd., Scottsdale, 480-515-1500;
www.scottsdaleshow.com
Arabian horse owners come from all over the world to show their horses. Two weeks in mid-February.

### ArtWalk
Downtown Scottsdale, 480-990-3939;
www.scottsdalegalleries.com
Locals brag that Scottsdale has more art galleries per capita than most any other U.S. city. To get a taste of this thriving scene, stroll the downtown streets during ArtWalk, a weekly Thursday night tradition for more than 20 years. For two hours, galleries host special exhibits, demonstrations and meet-the-artist receptions complete with wine, champagne and hors d'oeuvres. Thursday evenings.

### Parada del Sol & Rodeo
Scottsdale, 480-990-3179;
www.scottsdalejaycees.com/paradadelsol/art.html
This annual festival is sponsored by the Scottsdale Jaycees and includes a parade, rodeo and live music. Mid-February.

### Safeway International at Superstition Mountain
Superstition Mountain Golf & Country Club, 3976 S. Ponderosa Dr., Superstition Mountain, 877-983-3300;
www.superstitionmountain.com
Major LPGA Tour golf tournament. Late March.

### San Francisco Giants Spring Training
Scottsdale Stadium, 7408 E. Osborn Rd., Scottsdale, 480-312-2586, 800-225-2277;
www.cactus-league.com/giants.html

**44**

ARIZONA

San Francisco Giants baseball spring training, exhibition games. Early March-early April.

### Scottsdale Culinary Festival
7309 E. Evans, Scottsdale, 480-945-7193; www.scottsdaleculinaryfestival.org
Indulge in some of the tastiest dishes at this culinary adventure that brings the Southwest's best chefs together. Choose from any of nine individual events ranging from casual to black-tie-only. Proceeds benefit area charities. Mid-March and mid-April.

# HOTELS
### ★★Chaparral Suites Resort
5001 N. Scottsdale Rd., Scottsdale, 480-949-1414, 800-528-1456; www.chaparralsuites.com
311 rooms, all suites. Complimentary full breakfast. High-speed Internet access. Restaurant, bar. Airport transportation available. Pet. Exercise. Swim. Tennis. Busn. Center. **$$**

### ★Country Inn & Suites by Carlson
10801 N. 89th Place, Scottsdale, 480-314-1200, 888-201-1746; www.countryinns.com
163 rooms. Complimentary continental breakfast. Pets accepted. Pool. **$**

### ★Gainey Suites
7300 E. Gainey Suites Dr., Scottsdale, 480-922-6969, 800-970-4666; www.gaineysuiteshotel.com
162 rooms, all suites. Complimentary continental breakfast. High-speed Internet access. Pool. **$$**

### ★★Hilton Garden Inn
7324 E. Indian School Rd., Scottsdale, 480-481-0400, 877-782-9444; www.scottsdale.gardeninn.com
199 rooms. High-speed Internet access. Restaurant, bar. Pool. Business center. **$$**

### ★La Quinta Inn
8888 E. Shea Blvd., Scottsdale, 480-614-5300, 800-642-4271; www.laquinta.com
140 rooms. Complimentary continental breakfast. Pets accepted. Pool. **$**

### ★Summerfield Suites
4245 N. Drinkwater Blvd., Scottsdale, 480-946-7700, 800-889-6829; www.hyatt.com
164 rooms, all suites. Complimentary full breakfast. High-speed Internet access. Pets accepted. Pool. **$$**

### ★★★Marriott Suites Scottsdale Old Town
7325 E. Third Ave., Scottsdale, 480-945-1550, 888-236-2427; www.marriott.com
Catering mainly to business travelers, this Old Town hotel is close to Scottsdale Road and a large shopping mall. Its 251 suites come equipped with the latest in amenities, and it has plenty of recreational facilities, including a pool and fitness center, to help guests wind down at the end of the day.
251 rooms, all suites. High-speed wireless Internet access. Restaurant, bar. Airport transportation available. Pool. Business Center. **$$$**

### ★★★Mondrian Hotel
7353 E. Indian School Rd., Scottsdale, 480-308-1100, 800-697-1791; www.mondrianscottsdale.com
This sleek, modern hotel has crisp, white rooms with flat-screen TVs and glass-tiled showers in the bathrooms, but you might choose to stay here for the chic Skybar and the unique fusion fare at Asia de Cuba (which originated in New York). The serenity pool is a nice place to relax, and the Aqua spa offers a variety of treatments. (You can also get treatments in poolside cabanas.) Be sure to call ahead to let the staff know how to customize the goods in your mini-bar.
194 rooms. High-speed Internet access, wireless Internet access. Restaurant, two bars. Pool. **$$**

### ★★★Scottsdale Marriott at McDowell Mountains
16770 N. Perimeter Dr., Scottsdale, 480-502-3836, 800-288-6127; www.scottsdalemarriott.com

**ARIZONA**

This all-suites hotel is located in north Scottsdale. The colorful, attractive public areas and well-furnished guest rooms are designed for both families and the business traveler. Some rooms have views of the TPC-Scottsdale golf course.

270 rooms, all suites. High-speed Internet access. Restaurant, bar. Pets accepted. Pool. Business center. **$**

### ★★★Fire Sky Resort and Spa
4925 N. Scottsdale Rd., Scottsdale, 480-945-7666, 800-528-7867; www.fireskyresort.com

A three-story sandstone fireplace flanked by hand-painted adobe walls is the centerpiece of this romantic resort's lobby. A traditional Western theme is reflected in the décor, while the grounds include a sandy-beach pool surrounded by palm trees and flowers, as well as cozy fire pits. The convenient location is near restaurants and sports venues and a short drive from the airport.

204 rooms. High-speed wireless Internet access. Restaurant, bar. Spa. Beach. Airport transportation available. Pets accepted. **$$**

### ★★★★Four Seasons Resort Scottsdale at Troon North
10600 E. Crescent Moon Dr., Scottsdale, 480-515-5700, 888-207-9696; www.fourseasons.com

Located on a 40-acre nature preserve, rooms are spread across 25 Southwestern-style casitas, with views of the stunning desert. Spring for a suite if you can—you'll get a plunge pool, alfresco garden shower and outdoor kiva fireplace. A veritable mecca for golfers, the resort grants priority tee times at Troon North's two courses, considered among the best in the world. The spa offers desert nectar facials and moonlight massages, plus salon services and a fitness center. Three restaurants reflect the resort's casual elegance.

210 rooms. High-speed Internet access. Restaurant, bar. Children's activity center. Spa. Pets accepted. Pool. Golf. Tennis. **$$$$**

### ★★★Hilton Scottsdale Resort and Villas
6333 N. Scottsdale Rd., Scottsdale,

480-948-7750, 800-528-3119; www.scottsdaleresort.hilton.com

Warm shades of gold, blue and apricot complement the natural wood décor, creating a warm and welcoming atmosphere. The villas here just received a total makeover. Galleries, shops and restaurants of Old Town Scottsdale are within easy walking distance, or you can take advantage of the hotel's bike rental facility. The resort has three distinct eateries, and Griff's is a nice spot for cocktails and live entertainment.

187 rooms. Three restaurants, three bars. Pets accepted. Pool. Business center. **$**

### ★★★Hotel Valley Ho
6850 E. Main St., Scottsdale, 480-248-2000, 866-882-4484, www.hotelvalleyho.com

A mid-century modern masterpiece, this quirky hotel received a facelift in 2005, which took the property and furnishings back to their 50s-era Jetsonian glory. Rooms now have plasma TVs, luxury bedding, CD players and Red Flower bath products. The huge outdoor pool has private cabanas for al fresco massages or simply sipping cocktails in private, while the VH Spa offers a full menu of 21st century treatments, from lomi lomi massages to Tibetan yoginic bodywork (a mix of acupressure and massage). Onsite restaurants include the retro-chic Trader Vic's, comfort-food themed Café ZuZu and Oh poolbar.

194 rooms. Restaurant, bar. Pool. Spa. Fitness center. Business center. High speed Internet wireless. Pets accepted. **$$**

### ★★★Hyatt Regency Scottsdale Resort and Spa at Gainey Ranch
7500 E. Doubletree Ranch Rd., Scottsdale, 480-444-1234, 800-554-9288; www.scottsdale.hyatt.com

Set against the backdrop of the McDowell Mountains, the resort is nestled on 560 acres filled with shimmering pools, trickling fountains and cascading waterfalls. Desert tones and regional furnishings create serene havens in the rooms and suites. The grounds feature championship golf,

ARIZONA

tennis, water playground and camp for kids.

500 rooms. Restaurant, bar. Children's activity center. Spa. Beach. Golf. Tennis. Business center. **$$$$**

### ★★★Marriott Camelback Inn Resort Golf Club & Spa

5402 E. Lincoln Dr., Scottsdale,
480-948-1700, 800-242-2635;
www.camelbackinn.com

Since the 1930s, the Camelback Inn has appealed to travelers seeking the best of the Southwest. This special hideaway is situated on 125 acres in the Sonoran Desert. The pueblo-style casitas feature wood-beamed ceilings, private patios and kitchenettes. Suites have private pools. Set at the base of Mummy Mountain, the spa is a peaceful retreat. Five restaurants satisfy every craving.

453 rooms. High-speed Internet access. Five restaurants, four bars. Children's activity center. Spa. Airport transportation available. Pets accepted. Pool. Golf. Tennis. **$$$**

### ★★★Millennium Resort Scottsdale, McCormick Ranch

7401 N. Scottsdale Rd., Scottsdale,
480-948-5050, 800-243-1332;
www.millennium-hotels.com

Situated on a 40-acre lake in the midst of the McCormick Ranch, the setting at this hotel attracts couples on romantic getaways, business travelers making the most of the amenities and vacationers looking for a full-service resort experience. Proximity to the lake means easy access to paddle boats and sailboats. The resort also offers volleyball, tennis and swimming. The individually decorated villas include gas fireplaces, laundry facilities and private patios with grills.

175 rooms. Restaurant, two bars. Airport transportation available. Pets accepted. Pool. Tennis. **$$**

### ★★★Renaissance Scottsdale Resort

6160 N. Scottsdale Rd., Scottsdale,
480-991-1414, 800-309-8138;

www.renaissancehotels.com

The lobby, with its Spanish colonial Monk's Tower, is both the entrance to the resort's many amenities and a buffer against the commotion of busy Scottsdale Road next to Borgata Shopping Center. Lush landscaping with plenty of grass and flowers separates the lobby from the single-story guest rooms and suites. Head to one of the two pools for a relaxing swim, play shuffleboard or volleyball, make use of the putting green or jog with your pooch along a trail that includes workout stations.

171 rooms. High-speed Internet access. Restaurant, bar. Pets accepted. Pool. Tennis. Business center. **$$**

### ★★★The Fairmont Scottsdale Princess

7575 E. Princess Dr., Scottsdale,
480-585-4848, 800-257-7544;
www.fairmont.com

The pink Spanish colonial buildings are spread out over 450 lush acres overlooking Scottsdale and the majestic McDowell Mountains. Golfers come here to play the two championship courses—one of which hosts the PGA Tours Phoenix Open. The Willow Stream Spa is also a big draw. Kids will love the aquatic recreation area with two water slides. The spacious rooms and suites are a blend of Mediterranean design with Southwestern accents, and offer fantastic views.

650 rooms. Six restaurants, bars. Children's activity center. Spa. Pets accepted. Pool Golf. Tennis. **$$$**

### ★★★★The Phoenician

6000 E. Camelback Rd., Scottsdale,
480-941-8200, 800-888-8234;
www.thephoenician.com

This world-class resort, located at the base of Camelback Mountain, is hyperluxurious. Everywhere you look you see crystal, rich fabrics and leather-topped furniture. The rooms and suites feature imported Irish linens and oversized bathrooms with Italian marble. But there is no attitude here. Someone is always around to help or steer you toward one of a number of recreational opportunities, includ-

**ARIZONA**

ing desert hikes. A resort within a resort, the Canyon Suites at the Phoenician offer sprawling, luxuriously decorated rooms and a separate pool with private cabanas. Guests are assigned to ambassadors who arrange everything from in-room aromatherapy baths to chauffered trips into town in the resort Mercedes. There's little reason to leave the elegant, comfortable suites (which have DVD players, flat screen TVs and Italian linen-swathed beds), but the resort's golf courses and full-service spa serve as primary temptations.

647 rooms. High-speed Internet access, wireless Internet access. Restaurant, bar. Children's activity center. Spa. Airport transportation available. Pets accepted. Pool. Golf. Tennis. Business center. **$$$**

### ★★★The Westin Kierland Resort And Spa
6902 E. Greenway Pkwy., Scottsdale,
480-624-1000, 800-937-8461;
www.westin.com/kierlandresort

Located in northeast Phoenix, this handsome boutique-style resort is adjacent to the 38-acre Kierland Commons, where specialty shops and restaurants attract serious shoppers and diners. The spacious rooms and suites feature soothing earth tones and regional furnishings. Everything is at hand here, including two 18-hole golf courses, tennis courts, multiple pools (including a flowing river pool with landscaped waterfall), beach and volleyball courts and six restaurants. The expansive Agave Spa looks to the traditional therapies used by American Indians for inspiration.

732 rooms. Restaurant, bar. Children's activity center. Spa. Beach. Pets accepted. Pool. Golf Tennis. **$$$**

## SPAS
### ★★★★The Centre for Well Being
6000 E. Camelback Rd., Scottsdale,
480-941-8200, 800-843-2392;
www.centreforwellbeing.com

This spa is always thinking big, which means services here are on the cutting edge. Want to be more Zen in the real world? Sign up for a private meditation session, where you can learn visualization and other stress-reducing techniques. Have to work 100 hours just to take a week off? The *jin shin jyutsu* utilizes a series of holding techniques to alleviate tension blocked in the body. Tend to overdo it on the golf course? The neuromuscular treatment offers spot relief for injuries. Of course, you'll want to go home looking as great as you feel, and for that there's no shortage of wraps, facials and scrubs. Even the state-of-the-art gym is inviting. **$$**

### ★★★The Spa at Camelback Inn
5402 E. Lincoln Dr., Scottsdale,
480-948-1700; www.camelbackinn.com

Following an $8 million facelift, the Spa at Camelback Inn has swapped its old Southwest-style décor for sophisticated chocolate brown woods, flagstone walls and expansive windows to create an inviting, placid retreat. If the gas fireplace in the main relaxation room doesn't soothe your spirit, head outside to the solarium and let the sound of rippling water from a flowing fountain do the trick. Relax in your own private casita, while you choose from the menu of massages, facials and body treatments—many of which draw from Native American techniques and indigenous ingredients. **$$**

### ★★★★Spa at Four Seasons Resort Scottsdale at Troon North
10600 E. Crescent Moon Dr., Scottsdale,
480-513-5145, 888-207-9696;
www.fourseasons.com

You're guaranteed to relax at this 12,000-square-foot spa. The resort's signature moonlight massage is the perfect way to end the day. You'll also find hot stone massage and facials that feature local, seasonal ingredients, including saguaro blossom, the state flower, as well as the more common green tea and honey. Half-day and full-day packages are available. Full-service salon and fitness center. **$$**

### ★★★★Willow Stream Spa
7575 E. Princess Dr., Scottsdale,
480-585-2732, 800-908-9540;
www.fairmont.com

★

★

★

★

★

The facilities at the Fairmont Scottsdale Princess are top-notch—from championship golf courses to award-winning restaurants—and the spa is no exception. Many of the treatments make use of the Havasupai Waterfall (inspired by the oasis of waterfalls in the Grand Canyon) located on the spa's first floor. The Havasupai Body Oasis treatment combines warm eucalyptus and herbal baths with the healing power of the waterfalls. Other treatments also reflect local surroundings. The Desert Purification features a body mask of cornmeal, clay and oats. An *Ayate* cloth (made from the cactus plant) is then used to exfoliate skin. Or keep it simple with a facial or massage—and hit the beauty salon for a spa pedicure. **$$**

# RESTAURANTS

### ★★Acapulco Bay Company
3030 N. 68th St., Scottsdale,
480-429-1990
Mexican menu. Lunch, dinner. Bar. Children's menu. Casual attire. Reservations recommended. Outdoor seating. **$$**

### ★★Ajo Al's Mexican Cafe
9393 N. 90th St., Scottsdale,
480-860-2611; www.ajoals.com
Southwestern menu. Lunch, dinner. Bar. Children's menu. Casual attire. **$$**

### ★★Atlas Bistro
2515 N. Scottsdale Rd., Scottsdale,
480-990-2433; www.atlasbistro.com
International menu. Dinner. Closed Sunday-Tuesday. Casual attire. Reservations recommended. **$$$**

### ★★Bloom
8877 N. Scottsdale Rd., Scottsdale,
480-922-5666; www.foxrc.com
American menu. Lunch, dinner. Bar. Casual attire. Reservations recommended. Outdoor seating. **$$$**

### ★★Blue Wasabi Sushi & Martini Bar
20751 N. Pima Rd., Scottsdale,
480-538-5161; www.bluewasabi.net
Japanese menu. Dinner, late-night. Bar. Casual attire. Outdoor seating. **$$**

### ★The Breakfast Club
4400 N. Scottsdale Rd., Scottsdale,
480-222-2582; www.thebreakfastclub.us
American menu. Breakfast, lunch. Casual attire. Outdoor seating. **$**

### ★★Callaloo
7051 E. Fifth Ave., Scottsdale,
480-941-1111
Caribbean menu. Dinner. Closed Sunday. Bar. Casual attire. Reservations recommended. **$$**

### ★★Chart House
7255 McCormick Pkwy., Scottsdale,
480-951-2250; www.chart-house.com
Seafood menu. Dinner. Bar. Children's menu. Casual attire. Outdoor seating. **$$$**

### ★Chompie's
9301 E. Shea Blvd., Scottsdale,
480-860-0475; www.chompies.com
Deli menu. Breakfast, lunch, dinner. Closed holidays. Bar. Children's menu. Casual attire. Outdoor seating. **$$**

### ★★★deseo
6902 E. Greenway Pkwy., Scottsdale,
480-624-1030, 888-625-5144;
www.kierlandresort.com
The open display kitchen is the focal point of this restaurant located in Scottsdale's Westin Keirland Resort. Choose from a variety of mojitos and be sure to order one of the signature ceviches. Other items include foie gras empanadas and Muscovy duck breast with Asian pear and mango.
Latin American menu. Dinner. Closed Monday in summer. Bar. Business casual attire. Reservations recommended. Valet parking. Outdoor seating. **$$$**

### ★★Drift
4341 N. 75th St., Scottsdale,
480-949-8454; www.driftlounge.com
Polynesian menu. Lunch, dinner. Bar. Casual attire. Outdoor seating. **$$**

### ★★★Eddie V's Edgewater Grille
20715 N. Pima Rd., Scottsdale,
480-538-8468; www.eddiev.com

**ARIZONA**

The relaxed lodge-themed interior features murals, black leather chairs, crisp white table linens and brick walls. Diners are entertained nightly by a band or a vocalist. But the main draw here is the food. The Maryland-style all-lump crab cakes are a must for an appetizer, and the bananas Foster makes a memorable end to a meal.
Seafood menu. Dinner. Bar. Business casual attire. Reservations recommended. Valet parking. Outdoor seating. **$$$**

### ★★Farrelli's Cinema & Supper Club
14202 N. Scottsdale Rd., Scottsdale, 480-905-7200; www.farrellis.com
Continental menu. Dinner. Bar. Children's menu. Casual attire. Reservations recommended. **$$**

### ★★Fusion
4441 N. Buckboard Trail, Scottsdale, 480-423-9043; www.restaurantfusion.com
International menu. Lunch, dinner. Children's menu. Casual attire. **$$**

### ★Grazie Pizzeria & Wine Bar
6952 E. Main St., Scottsdale, 480-663-9797; www.grazie.us
Italian menu. Lunch, dinner. Bar. Casual attire. Reservations recommended. Outdoor seating. **$$**

### ★★Jewel of the Crown
7373 E. Scottsdale Mall, Scottsdale, 480-949-8000; www.jewelofthecrown.com
Indian menu. Lunch, dinner. Bar. Casual attire. Reservations recommended. Outdoor seating. **$$**

### ★★★L'Ecole
8100 E. Camelback Rd., Scottsdale, 480-990-3773; www.chefs.edu/about.asp
You can be sure that the food is top-of-the-line at this training ground for the Scottsdale Culinary Institute. The student-operated, full-service restaurant is set in a lovely dining room that is booked weeks in advance. The menu changes based on the student curriculum, but it always offers a nice variety. The outdoor patio has colorful awnings and views of a golf course.

French menu. Lunch, dinner. Closed Saturday-Sunday; also two weeks in early July and two weeks in end of December. Business casual attire. Reservations recommended. Outdoor seating. **$$**

### ★★★La Hacienda
7575 E. Princess Dr., Scottsdale, 480-585-4848; www.fairmont.com
Located in a turn-of-the-century Mexican ranch house on the lush grounds of the Fairmont Scottsdale Princess, La Hacienda offers traditional Mexican specialties, prepared with the care and the technique of generations past. Signatures include *filete a la parrilla* (grilled filet mignon poblano salsa and cascabel glaze) and *cochinillo asadoa* (barbeque-style suckling pig that is spit-roasted and stuffed with homemade chorizo sausage and carved tableside). Strolling mariachis, flagstone flooring, tapestry-upholstered seating and magnificent views make this an alluring spot to dine and watch the sun go down. Like any respectable authentic Mexican eatery, La Hacienda makes killer margaritas, served with crisp, golden tortilla chips to keep you thirsting for more.
Mexican menu. Dinner. Closed Wednesday; also Monday-Tuesday in summer. Bar. Children's menu. Casual attire. Reservations recommended. Valet parking. Outdoor seating. **$$$**

### ★★Leccabaffi Ristorante
9717 N. Hayden Rd., Scottsdale, 480-609-0429; www.leccabaffi.com
Italian menu. Dinner. Closed Sunday in summer. Bar. Casual attire. Reservations recommended. **$$$**

### ★Los Sombreros
2534 N. Scottsdale Rd., Scottsdale, 480-994-1799
Mexican menu. Dinner. Closed Monday. Bar. Casual attire. Outdoor seating. **$$**

### ★★★★Mary Elaine's
6000 E. Camelback Rd., Scottsdale, 480-423-2530; www.thephoenician.com

Special occasions practically beg to be celebrated at Mary Elaine's. This upscale restaurant's rooftop location in the posh Phoenician resort features dramatic views of Camelback Mountain and the surrounding valley, although you may find yourself staring up at the glittering ceiling of 24-karat gold and the hand-painted murals inside. The modern French cuisine is a triumph, and the cheese course has up to 20 varieties of cheese and includes house-baked breads. The wine cellar is diverse, with more than 45,000 bottles available, and five sommeliers are on hand to assist with selections. To top off the experience, live jazz is performed nightly.

French menu. Dinner. Closed Sunday-Monday; also the month of August. Bar. Business casual attire. Reservations recommended. Valet parking. Outdoor seating. $$$

### ★★★Mosaic
10600 E. Jomax Rd., Scottsdale, 480-563-9600;
www.mosaic-restaurant.com
Chef/owner Deborah Knight uses ingredients and cooking techniques from around the world to create her own brand of eclectic cuisine, which has included dishes such as Louisiana spiced prawns, Thai shrimp and coconut soup, and fennel and pesto risotto. Three types of five-course tasting menus are available to suit all tastes (Mosaic, Ocean and Vegetable). Local artwork punctuates the earth-toned dining room with color, and a beautiful, custom-made mosaic floor adds sparkle.

International/Fusion menu. Dinner. Closed Sunday-Monday; mid-August-late September. Bar. Business casual attire. Reservations recommended. Outdoor seating. $$$

### ★★North
15024 N. Scottsdale Rd., Scottsdale, 480-948-2055;
www.foxrestaurantconcepts.com/north.html
Italian menu. Lunch, dinner. Bar. Casual attire. Reservations recommended. Outdoor seating. $$

### ★★★Palm Court
7700 E. McCormick Pkwy., Scottsdale, 480-991-9000, 800-528-0293;
www.thescottsdaleresort.com
Although this restaurant is located on the third floor of the main building at the Scottsdale Conference Resort, you'd never know it once you enter the elegant candlelit dinning room, where tuxedo-clad waiters serve lavish French fare. A classical guitarist provides lovely background music during dinner and Sunday brunch sittings.

French menu. Breakfast, lunch, dinner, Sunday brunch. Bar. Business casual attire. Reservations recommended. Valet parking. $$$

### ★★Pepin
7363 Scottsdale Mall, Scottsdale, 480-990-9026; www.pepinrestaurant.com
Spanish, tapas menu. Lunch, dinner. Closed Monday. Bar. Casual attire. $$$

### ★Pischke's Paradise
7217 E. First St., Scottsdale, 480-481-0067; www.pischkes.com
American menu. Breakfast, lunch, dinner. Bar. Casual attire. Outdoor seating. $$

### ★Quilted Bear
6316 N. Scottsdale Rd., Scottsdale, 480-948-7760; www.quiltedbearaz.com
American menu. Breakfast, lunch, dinner. Bar. Children's menu. Casual attire. Outdoor seating. $$

### ★★RA Sushi Bar & Restaurant
3815 N. Scottsdale Rd., Scottsdale, 480-990-9256; www.rasushi.com
Japanese, sushi menu. Lunch, dinner. Bar. Casual attire. Valet parking. Outdoor seating. $$

### ★★★Rancho Pinot Grill
6208 N. Scottsdale Blvd., Scottsdale, 480-367-8030; www.ranchopinot.com
Situated within the Lincoln Village Shops, Rancho Pinot Grill offers American cuisine using the best ingredients, many of them

**ARIZONA**

from local farms. You might find dishes like handmade pasta with summer squash, scallions, mint and Parmesan cheese on the menu. Art and Southwestern décor adorn the walls, and an open kitchen allows guests to watch the chef at work.

American menu. Dinner. Closed Sunday-Monday in mid-April-mid-October. Bar. Business casual attire. Reservations recommended. Outdoor seating. $$$

### ★Reata Pass Steak House

27500 N. Alma School Pkwy., Scottsdale, 480-585-7277;
www.reatapass.com

American, Steak menu. Lunch, dinner. Bar. Children's menu. Casual attire. Outdoor seating. $$

### ★★★Remington's

7200 N. Scottsdale Rd., Scottsdale, 480-951-5101; www.scottsdaleplaza.com

Steak menu. Lunch, dinner. Bar. Business casual attire. Reservations recommended. Valet parking. Outdoor seating. $$$

### ★★★Roaring Fork

4800 N. Scottsdale Rd., Scottsdale, 480-947-0795; www.roaringfork.com

One of the founders of Southwestern cuisine, chef Robert McGrath turns out Western American cooking at this rustic yet refined dining room filled with exposed brick and blond wood. An open display kitchen is featured, with some booths situated across the aisle for great viewing. The adjacent J-Bar is a fun place to congregate for a drink.

American menu. Dinner. Bar. Children's menu. Casual attire. Reservations recommended. Valet parking Friday-Saturday. Outdoor seating. $$$

### ★★Salt Cellar

550 N. Hayden Rd., Scottsdale, 480-947-1963;
www.saltcellarrestaurant.com

Seafood menu. Dinner, late-night. Bar. Casual attire. Reservations recommended. $$

### ★★★Sassi

10455 E. Pinnacle Peak Pkwy., Scottsdale, 480-502-9095; www.sassi.biz

New York's famed chef Wade Moises prepared authentic Italian cuisine at this restaurant resembling a Tuscan villa. The extensive wine list offers many delicious complements. A live pianist entertains diners Wednesday through Sunday and is joined by a bass player on the weekends.

Italian menu. Dinner. Closed Monday. Bar. Business casual attire. Reservations recommended. Valet parking. Outdoor seating. $$$

### ★★★Sea Saw

7133 E. Stetson Dr., Scottsdale, 480-481-9463; www.seasaw.net

Japanese, sushi menu. Dinner. Casual attire. Reservations recommended. Valet parking. $$$

### ★★Sushi on Shea

7000 E. Shea Blvd., Scottsdale, 480-483-7799; www.sushionshea.com

Japanese menu. Lunch, dinner. Bar. Casual attire. Reservations recommended. Valet parking. Outdoor seating. $$

### ★★★Terrace Dining Room

6000 E. Camelback Rd., Scottsdale, 480-941-8200; www.thephoenician.com

Situated on the ground floor of the main lobby building at the Phoenician, this restaurant offers a variety of steak and seafood specialties. Guests can enjoy the live jazz music played nightly and at the Sunday and holiday brunches.

Steak menu. Breakfast, lunch, dinner, brunch. Bar. Children's menu. Casual attire. Reservations recommended. Valet parking. Outdoor seating. $$$

### ★★Thaifoon

8777 N. Scottsdale Rd., Scottsdale, 480-998-0011;
www.thaifoon.com

Pacific-Rim/Pan-Asian, Thai menu. Lunch, dinner. Bar. Casual attire. Reservations recommended. $$

### ★★★Trader Vic's
6850 E. Main St., Scottsdale,
480-248-2000, 866-882-4484,
www.hotelvalleyho.com
This branch of the classic 50s Polynesian-themed restaurant serves up potent punches in bamboo coolers (and perfect Mai Tais, which they purport to have invented in 1944) plus pu pu platters of eggrolls and crab Rangoon. Entrées include wok-fried Szechuan prawns and ginger beef, or crispy duck with moo shu pancakes. The décor takes its cue from the tiki bars of the past (plenty of rattan, a totem here or there), but is updated for the new millennium.
Asian Pacific Rim. Brunch, dinner. Outdoor seating. Valet parking. $$

### ★★Village Tavern
8787 N. Scottsdale Rd., Scottsdale,
480-951-6445; www.villagetavern.com
International menu. Lunch, dinner, Sunday brunch. Bar. Children's menu. Casual attire. Reservations recommended. Outdoor seating. $$

### ★★★Windows on the Green
6000 E. Camelback Rd., Scottsdale,
480-941-8200; www.thephoenician.com
Windows on the Green, located near the golf shop at the Phoenician, offers great views from the large picture windows. Dig into grilled Indian bread Portobello tacos and tortilla-encrusted ahi tuna—or try one of the chef's tapas tastings. Guacamole is prepared tableside. Guests can relax to the sounds of a Spanish guitarist who performs live in the dining room. The bar boasts some unique tequilas and signature margaritas.
Southwestern menu. Dinner. Closed Tuesday-Wednesday. Bar. Children's menu. Business casual attire. Reservations recommended. Valet parking. Outdoor seating. $$$

### ★★★Zinc Bistro
15034 N. Scottsdale Rd., Scottsdale,
480-603-0920; www.zincbistroaz.com
A high-energy spot, Zinc Bistro is located in the Kierland Commons shopping center. The Parisian-style space, decorated with a tin ceiling and solid zinc bar, serves up crepes, omelets, steaks, onion soup and more.
French bistro menu. Lunch, dinner. Bar. Casual attire. Outdoor seating. $$

### ★★ZuZu
6850 E. Main St.,
480-248-2000, 866-882-4484,
www.hotelvalleyho.com
American. Breakfast, lunch, dinner. Reservations recommended. Outdoor seating. $$

# SEDONA
Known worldwide for the beauty of the red rocks surrounding the town, Sedona has grown from a pioneer settlement into a favorite film location. This is a resort area with numerous outdoor activities, including hiking, fishing and biking, which can be enjoyed all year. Also an art and shopping destination, Sedona boasts Tlaquepaque, a 4 1/2-acre area of gardens, courtyards, fountains, galleries, shops and restaurants.
Information: Sedona-Oak Creek Canyon Chamber of Commerce, 331 Forest Rd., Sedona, 928-282-7722, 800-288-7336; www.sedonachamber.com

## WHAT TO SEE AND DO
### Chapel of the Holy Cross
780 Chapel Rd., Sedona,
928-282-4069;
www.sjvsedona.org/Chapel of the Holy Cross.htm
Chapel perched between two pinnacles of uniquely colored red sandstone. Daily 9 a.m.-5 p.m.

### Oak Creek Canyon
Sedona, 800-288-7336;
www.visitsedona.com
A beautiful drive along a spectacular fishing stream, north toward Flagstaff.

### Slide Rock State Park
6871 N. Hwy. 89A, Sedona, 928-282-3034;
www.aaparks.gov/Parks/parkhtml/Sliderock.html

A 43-acre day-use park on Oak Creek. Swimming, natural sandstone waterslide, fishing, hiking, picnicking. Summer: daily 8 a.m.-7 p.m.; winter: daily 8 a.m.-5 p.m.; fall and spring: daily 8 a.m.-6 p.m.

### Red Rock Jeep tours
270 N. Hwy. 89A, Sedona,
928-282-6826, 800-848-7728;
www.redrockjeep.com
Two-hour back country trips. Daily. Other tours also available.

### Tlaquepaque
336 Hwy. 179, Sedona, 928-282-4838;
www.tlaq.com
Consists of 40 art galleries and stores set in a Spanish-style courtyard. Daily 10 a.m.-5 p.m.

## SPECIAL EVENTS

### Red Rock Fantasy of Lights
Los Abrigados Resort & Spa,
160 Portal Lane, Sedona,
928-282-1777, 800-521-3131;
www.redrockfantasy.com
This annual event features kids' activities, concerts, carriage rides and special events. Late November-mid-January.

### Sedona Film Festival
Harkins Theatre, 2081 W. Highway 89A, Sedona, 928-282-1177;
www.sedonafilmfestival.com
Features independent films and film workshops. Late February.

### Sedona Jazz on the Rocks
1487 W. Hwy. 89A, Sedona, 928-282-1985;
www.sedonajazz.com
This extended weekend of entertainment features both local and national jazz acts, and it draws more than 7,500 visitors and music lovers to scenic Sedona each year. Late September.

## HOTELS

### ★★★Amara Creekside Resort
310 N. Hwy. 89A, Sedona,
928-282-4828, 866-455-6610;
www.amararesort.com

Located along the banks of Oak Creek, this chic, contemporary resort features well-appointed rooms and tranquil surroundings with a heated saltwater pool and fire pit. Rooms have pillow-top mattresses, Italian linens and sleek work desks. The new 4,000 square foot spa offers a wide variety of pampering treatments.
100 rooms. High-speed wireless Internet access. Restaurant, bar. Airport transportation available. **$$**

### ★Best Western Arroyo Roble Hotel & Creekside Villas
400 N. Hwy. 89A, Sedona,
928-282-4001, 800-773-3662;
www.bestwesternsedona.com
65 rooms. Complimentary continental breakfast. High-speed Internet access. Airport transportation available. Tennis. **$**

### ★Best Western Inn of Sedona
1200 W. Hwy. 89A, Sedona,
928-282-3072, 800-292-6344;
www.innofsedona.com
110 rooms. Complimentary continental breakfast. High-speed wireless Internet access. Airport transportation available. Pets accepted. Pool. **$**

### ★★★El Portal Sedona
95 Portal Lane, Sedona,
928-203-9405, 800-313-0017;
www.innsedona.com
This secluded hacienda-style inn is conveniently located in the heart of Sedona near more than 50 shops and restaurants. The 12 luxurious rooms feature Arts and Crafts furnishings, high-beam ceilings, stained glass, whirlpool tubs, cashmere blankets and Egyptian cotton sheets. After a busy day exploring the area, relax with a delicious meal at the inn's dining room. On Wednesday nights there's a barbecue cookout in the courtyard.
12 rooms. High-speed wireless Internet access. Restaurant. Pets accepted. **$$$$**

### ★★★Enchantment Resort
525 Boynton Canyon Rd., Sedona,
928-282-2900, 800-826-4180;
www.enchantmentresort.com

ARIZONA

★
★
☆
★
☆

Located within Boynton Canyon, this resort offers spectacular views of the rugged landscape from just about everywhere. This resort is full of Southwestern charm, from the Native American furnishings and decorative accents in the rooms to the regional kick of the sensational dining. Tennis, croquet, swimming and pitch-and-putt golf are some of the activities available for adults, while Camp Coyote entertains young guests with arts and crafts and special programs. The Mii Amo Spa is a destination unto itself with 16 casitas used for treatments.

220 rooms. High-speed Internet access. Restaurant, bar. Children. Spa. Airport transportation available. Tennis. Business center. **$$$**

### ★Hampton Inn

1800 W. Hwy. 89A, Sedona,
928-282-4700, 800-426-7866;
www.hamptoninn.com

56 rooms. Complimentary continental breakfast. High-speed wireless Internet access. Airport transportation available. Pool. **$**

### ★★★Hilton Sedona Resort and Spa

90 Ridge Trail Dr., Sedona,
928-284-4040, 877-273-3763;
www.hiltonsedona.com

This Southwestern-style resort is located amid the Coconino National Forest. The spacious guest rooms and suites are decorated have gas fireplaces, wet bars, sleeper sofas and patios or balconies with views of the Red Rock vistas. There are three pools to choose from, a full-service fitness center, tennis and racquetball and the nearby Sedona Golf Resort, featuring a 71-par championship course. The spa is located steps from the hotel's main building. The property's Grille at ShadowRock features a Southwestern menu, and with its earth tones and soft lighting, is the perfect spot for a romantic dinner. During the day, the restaurant's outdoor patio is a great place to have a hearty breakfast or a light lunch.

219 rooms. High-speed Internet access. Restaurant, bar. Spa. Pets accepted. **$$**

### ★★★L'Auberge de Sedona

301 L'Auberge Lane, Sedona,
928-282-1661, 800-905-5745;
www.lauberge.com

This secluded resort offers views of the Red Rock Canyon and Magenta Cliffs. Accommodations include cozy cottages with fireplaces (the staff light a juniper-infused fire nightly) and an inviting lodge. Gourmet dining is an integral part of the experience. L'Auberge Restaurant is noted for its fine French food, special five-course tasting menu and award-winning wine list. The world-class spa will banish every last drop of tension. Enjoy a massage in one of the poolside cabanas.

56 rooms. Wireless Internet access. Restaurant, bar. Airport transportation available. Pool. **$$$**

### ★★★Los Abrigados Resort and Spa

160 Portal Lane, Sedona,
928-282-1777, 800-521-3131;
www.ilxresorts.com

This Spanish-style stucco and tile-roofed hotel is set among the buttes of Oak Creek Canyon. Rooms are spacious with kitchen facilities and pullout sofas. Activities such as Jeep tours, hiking, biking and helicopter rides are nearby.

182 rooms, all suites. Three restaurants, three bars. Airport transportation available. Pool. Tennis. **$$$**

### ★★Radisson Poco Diablo Resort

1752 S. Hwy. 179, Sedona,
928-282-7333, 888-201-1718;
www.radisson.com/sedonaaz

138 rooms. High-speed Internet access, wireless Internet access. Restaurant, bar. Airport transportation available. Pool. Golf. Tennis. Business center. **$$**

### ★Sedona Real Inn

95 Arroyo Pinon Dr., Sedona,
928-282-1414, 877-299-6016;
www.sedonareal.com

89 rooms. Complimentary continental breakfast. High-speed Internet access. Airport transportation available. Pets accepted. Pool. **$$**

### ★Southwest Inn at Sedona
3250 W. Hwy. 89A, Sedona,
928-282-3344, 800-483-7422;
www.swinn.com
28 rooms. Complimentary continental breakfast. Pool. **$$**

### ★★Territorial House Bed and Breakfast
65 Piki Dr., Sedona,
928-204-2737, 800-801-2737;
www.territorialhousebb.com
4 rooms. Complimentary full breakfast. High-speed wireless Internet access. Whirlpool. Airport transportation available. **$$**

## SPECIALTY LODGINGS
### Adobe Village Graham Inn
150 Canyon Circle Dr., Sedona,
928-284-1425, 800-228-1425;
www.sedonasfinest.com
Relax in your own private casita with a king bed and a waterfall shower.
11 rooms. Complimentary full breakfast. Pool. **$$$**

### Alma De Sedona Inn
50 Hozoni Dr., Sedona,
928-282-2737, 800-923-2282;
www.almadesedona.com
12 rooms. **$$**

### Apple Orchard Inn
656 Jordan Rd., Sedona,
928-282-5328, 800-663-6968;
www.appleorchardbb.com
Personal service awaits guests at this inn with a charming Southwestern atmosphere. It has easily accessible hiking trails with views of Wilson Mountain and Steamboat Rock.
7 rooms. Children over 16 years only. Complimentary full breakfast. Pool. **$$**

### Canyon Villa Inn of Sedona
40 Canyon Circle Dr., Sedona,
928-284-1226, 800-453-1166;
www.canyonvilla.com

Charming and intimate, this inn offers views of Sedona's renowned red rock formations. Nearly all of the guest rooms frame unparalleled vistas, with French doors opening onto private patios or decks for even better viewing. Rooms features four-poster beds and floral patterns.
11 rooms. Children over 11 years only. Complimentary full breakfast. Pool. **$$$**

### Casa Sedona Bed and Breakfast
55 Hozoni Dr., Sedona,
928-282-2938, 800-525-3756;
www.casasedona.com
16 rooms. Children over 12 years only. Complimentary full breakfast. **$$$**

### The Inn on Oak Creek
556 Hwy. 179, Sedona,
928-282-7896, 800-499-7896;
www.innonoakcreek.com
This exquisite inn was formerly an art gallery. Family designed and built, it sits on Oak Creek, near reservations and fantastic shopping. A professional cooking staff prepares different breakfasts and hors d'oeuvres daily.
11 rooms. Children over 10 years only. Complimentary full breakfast. **$$$**

### The Lodge at Sedona
125 Kallof Place, Sedona,
928-204-1942, 800-619-4467;
www.lodgeatsedona.com
This lodge is situated on 2 1/2 wooded acres with rustic timber and red sandstone décor. A labyrinth of rocks on a clearing of red earth creates a quiet place to meditate.
14 rooms. Complimentary full breakfast. Pets accepted. Business center. **$$$**

## RESTAURANTS
### ★★Cowboy Club
241 N. Hwy. 89A, Sedona, 928-282-4200;
www.cowboyclub.com
American menu. Lunch, dinner. Bar. Children's menu. Casual attire. Reservations recommended. **$$$**

### ★★★Heartline Cafe
1610 W. Hwy. 89A, Sedona, 928-282-0785;
www.heartlinecafe.com

**56**

**ARIZONA**

This intimate, cozy restaurant in a cottage is surrounded by an English garden and showcases unique daily specials. The menu is creative, with a variety of culinary influences and vegetarian options. Dishes include smoked mozzarella ravioli and pistachio crusted chicken breasts with pomegranate sauce.

International menu. Lunch, dinner. Closed Tuesday in summer. Bar. Casual attire. Reservations recommended. Outdoor seating. $$$

### ★★★L'Auberge
301 L'Auberge, Sedona, 928-282-1667l; www.lauberge.com

Several separate dining rooms are decorated with imported fabrics, fine china and walls of green or mocha. A covered porch with large windows offers views of the creek, and an outdoor patio area is a relaxing choice in good weather. Dine on roasted pheasant with tomato polenta or silver snapper with coconut bamboo rice.

California menu. Breakfast, lunch, dinner, Sunday brunch. Bar. Business casual attire. Reservations recommended. Outdoor seating. $$$

### ★★★Ren at Tlaquepaque
336 Hwy. 179, Sedona, 928-282-9225; www.rene-sedona.com

Located in the Tlaquepaque shopping area, this local favorite has been a mainstay in Sedona since 1977. The menu is varied, offering selections such as tenderloin of venison, grilled ahi tuna salad, sweet potato ravioli and the signature dish, Colorado rack of lamb. Dine in one of two separate dining areas, where tables are topped with green and white tablecloths and flower-filled vases. Friday and Saturday entertainment includes the sounds of guitar, piano, saxophone and Native American flutes.

French menu. Lunch, dinner. Bar. Children's menu. Casual attire. Reservations recommended. Outdoor seating. $$$

### ★★★Shugrue's Hillside Grill
671 Hwy. 179, Sedona, 928-282-5300; www.shugrues.com

Great views of the Red Rocks can be seen from the large windows of this modernized Old-World restaurant. Flame-broiled shrimp scampi, whiskey-barbecued duck and herb-grilled rib eye are among the specialty dishes. Light jazz entertainment is offered nightly, with a pianist and guitarist performing on alternate nights. A nice outdoor seating area offers guests a picturesque dining experience.

American menu. Lunch, dinner. Bar. Children's menu. Casual attire. Reservations recommended. Outdoor seating. $$

# SELIGMAN

Arizona's historic Route 66 begins here, and the tiny town (population about 450) has more Route 66 kitsch than you can imagine. Stop by on your way to the Grand Canyon (about two hours north of here) for a taste of Americana.

Information: Chamber of Commerce, 217 W. Chino Ave., 928-422-3939; www.seligmanarizona.org

## WHAT TO SEE AND DO
### Grand Canyon Caverns
Old Rte. 66, Peach Springs, 928-422-3223; www.gccaverns.com

This natural limestone cavern is 210 feet underground and is the largest dry cavern in the U.S. Take an elevator down (the temperature is around 55 degrees, so bring a sweater). 50-minute guided tours. A 48-room motel is located at the entrance. Restaurant. Summer: daily 9 a.m.-5 p.m.; winter: 10 a.m.-5 p.m.

# SIERRA VISTA

About 75 miles southeast of Tuscon, Sierra Vista is surrounded by mountains—appropriate for a city whose name means "mountain view" in Spanish.

Information: Chamber of Commerce, 21 E Wilcox, 520-458-6940; www.visitsierravista.com

## WHAT TO SEE AND DO

### Coronado National Forest
300 W. Congress St., Sierra Vista, 520-388-8300; www.fs.fed.us/r3/coronado
One of the larger sections of the forest lies to the south and west of Fort Huachuca Military Reservation. Picnicking, camping.

### Coronado National Memorial
4101 E. Montezuma Canyon Rd., Hereford, 520-366-5515; www.nps.gov/coro
Commemorates Francisco Vasquez de Coronado's expedition in 1540 through 1542, when hundreds of soldiers came in search of gold and brought rich Spanish traditions into the area. Daily 8 a.m.-5 p.m.

### Fort Huachuca
Hwy. 90, Sierra Vista, 520-538-7111; huachuca-www.army.mil
Founded by the U.S. Army in 1877 to protect settlers and travelers from hostile Apache raids, the fort is now the home of the U.S. Army Intelligence Center, the Information Systems Command and the Electronic Proving Ground. A historical museum is on the "Old Post," Boyd and Grierson Avenues (Monday-Friday 9 a.m.-4 p.m., Saturday-Sunday 1-4 p.m.). The historic Old Post area (1885-1895) is typical of frontier post construction and is home to the post's ceremonial cavalry unit; open to public. Directions and visitor's pass at main gate, just west of Sierra Vista. Bronze statue of buffalo soldier.

## SPECIALTY LODGINGS

### Ramsey Canyon Inn
29 E. Ramsey Canyon Rd., Hereford, 520-378-3010; www.ramseycanyoninn.com
9 rooms. Children under 16 years cottages only. Complimentary full breakfast. $$

## RESTAURANTS

### ★★Mesquite Tree
Hwy. 92 S. and Carr Canyon Rd., Sierra Vista, 520-378-2758; www.mesquitetreerestaurant.com
American, Steak menu. Dinner. Closed Monday. Bar. Children's menu. Outdoor seating. $$

# TEMPE

Founded as a trading post by the father of former Senator Carl Hayden, this city is now the site of Arizona State University, the state's oldest institution of higher learning.

Information: Chamber of Commerce, 909 E. Apache Blvd., Tempe, 480-967-7891; www.tempecvb.com

## WHAT TO SEE AND DO

### Arizona Historical Society Museum
Papago Park, 1300 N. College Ave., Tempe, 480-929-0292; www.arizonahistoricalsociety.org
Wander through this regional museum to learn more about 20th-century life in the Salt River Valley. The 28,000 items in its collection include about 14,000 pieces in a country store and 2,800 stage props and sets from the 37-year run of the *Wallace and Ladmo* Show on KPHO Television. Another exhibit focuses on the many ways World War II transformed Arizona. Tuesday-Saturday 10 a.m.-4 p.m., Sunday noon-4 p.m.

### Arizona Mills
5000 S Arizona Mills Circle, Tempe, 480-491-7300; www.arizonamills.com
More than 150 stores offer tempting markdowns. Shopping diversions include a large

food court, five restaurants, a 24-screen cinema and an IMAX theater. Daily.

### Arizona State University
University Dr., and Mill Ave., Tempe,
480-965-9011; www.asu.edu
Established in1885; 52,000 students. Divided into 13 colleges. Included on the 700-acre main campus are several museums and collections featuring meteorites; anthropology and geology exhibits; the Charles Trumbull Hayden Library; the Walter Cronkite School of Journalism; and the Daniel Noble Science and Engineering Library. Also on campus is the Grady Gammage Memorial Auditorium, the last major work designed by Frank Lloyd Wright, and the Nelson Fine Arts Center, which features exhibits of American paintings and sculpture.

### Big Surf
1500 N. McClintock, Tempe,
480-947-2477; www.tempe.golfland.com
Check out America's original water park, a 20-acre desert oasis with a Polynesian theme. Ride some big ones in the wave pool, whoosh down 16 slippery water slides and more. June-mid-August, daily; late May and mid-late August, weekends; closed rest of year.

### Niels Petersen House Museum
1414 W. Southern Ave., Tempe,
480-350-5151;
www.tempe.gov/petersenhouse
Built in 1892 and remodeled in the 1930s. Restoration retains characteristics of both the Victorian era and the 1930s. Half-hour, docent-guided tours available. Tuesday-Thursday, Saturday 10 a.m.-2 p.m.)

### Phoenix Rock Gym
1353 E. University, Tempe, 480-921-8322;
www.phoenixrockgym.com
Scale 30-foot walls at Arizona's largest climbing gym. Beginners receive brief video training and a hands-on orientation. Gear is available to rent. Daily.

### Tempe Bicycle Program
Tempe, 480-350-2775;
www.tempe.gov/tim
This bicycle-friendly city has more than 150 miles of bikeways and most major destinations provide bicycle racks (including some particularly eye-catching ones designed by local artists). City buses are also equipped with racks. Several bicycle shops offer rentals for as little as $15 per day and give free bikeway maps.

### Tempe Historical Museum
809 E. Southern Ave., Tempe,
480-350-5100; www.tempe.gov/museum
Exhibits relate the history of Tempe from the prehistoric Hohokam to the present, with artifacts, videos and interactive exhibits. Monday-Thursday, Saturday 10 a.m.-5 p.m., Sunday 1-5 p.m.

### Tempe Improvisation Comedy Theatre
930 E. University Dr., Tempe,
480-921-9877;
www.symfonee.com/improv/tempe
Check out some of the country's best stand-up comedians. An optional dinner precedes the 8 p.m. shows. Thursday-Sunday.

### Tempe Town Lake
620 N. Mill Ave., Tempe,
480-350-8625;
www.tempegov/lake
Tempe Town Lake on the Rio Salado, near the Mill Avenue shopping and dining district, is a 224-acre, two-mile waterway that charters cruises and offers rowboats, pedal boats, kayaks and canoes for rent. The nicely renovated 1931 Tempe Beach Park has shaded picnic groves, sandy play areas, a grassy amphitheater and the popular Splash Playground water park (late April-late September). Take the tour, or simply enjoy the shoreline.

## SPECIAL EVENTS
### Anaheim Angels Spring Training
Tempe Diablo Stadium,
2200 W. Alameda Dr., Tempe,
602-438-9300;
www.cactus-league.com/angels.html
Anaheim Angels baseball spring training, exhibition games. Early March-early April.

### Tempe Festival of the Arts
Tempe, 480-355-6069;
www.tempefestivalofthearts.com
When a three-day event attracts nearly a quarter-million people, you know you need to get there. Mill Avenue in downtown Tempe closes to traffic—and this street party is a blast. Buy handmade goods from more than 500 artisans, chow down on tasty food from around the world, quench your thirst with ice-cold beer and rock to live bands. Activities for kids include arts and crafts. It's so fun—the party gets crankin' twice a year. Late March and early December.

### Tostitos Fiesta Bowl
University of Phoenix Stadium,
Cardinals Dr., Glendale, 480-350-0911;
www.tostitosfiestabowl.com
College football game. Early January.

### Tostitos Fiesta Bowl Block Party
Tempe Beach Park and Mill Ave., Tempe,
480-350-0911;
www.tostitosfiestabowl.com
Includes games, rides, entertainment, pep rally, fireworks, food. December 31.

**ARIZONA**

## HOTELS

### ★★★The Buttes, A Marriott Resort
2000 Westcourt Way, Tempe,
602-225-9000, 888-867-7492;
www.marriott.com/phxtm
This secluded resort sits atop a bluff overlooking Phoenix and the surrounding mountains. Take a dip in the pool or enjoy one of the four hot tubs carved out of the mountainside, relax in the spa, play some sand volleyball or horseshoes, or get in a game of tennis on the resort's eight courts. The Top of the Rock restaurant is a great spot for dining. This hotel is non-smoking. 353 rooms. High-speed wireless Internet access. Three restaurants, three bars. Spa. Airport transportation available. $$

### ★Country Inn & Suites
1660 W. Elliot Rd., Tempe,
480-345-8585, 888-201-1746;
www.countryinns.com

138 rooms. Complimentary full breakfast. High-speed Internet access. Airport transportation available. Pets accepted. $

### ★★Embassy Suites
4400 S. Rural Rd., Tempe,
480-897-7444, 800-362-2779;
www.embassysuitestempe.com
224 rooms, all suites. Complimentary full breakfast. Wireless Internet access. Restaurant, bar. Children's activity center. Airport transportation available. Pool. $

### ★★Fiesta Inn Resort
2100 S. Priest Dr., Tempe,
480-967-1441, 800-501-7590;
www.fiestainnresort.com
270 rooms. High-speed wireless Internet access. Restaurant, bar. Airport transportation available. $

### ★Holiday Inn Express
1520 W. Baseline Rd., Tempe,
480-831-9800, 800-972-3574;
www.hiexpress.com/tempeaz
128 rooms. Complimentary continental breakfast. High-speed Internet access. Airport transportation available. Pets accepted. Pool. $

### ★★Sheraton Phoenix Airport Hotel Tempe
1600 S. 52nd St., Tempe,
480-967-6600, 800-325-3535;
www.sheraton.com/phoenixairport
210 rooms. High-speed Internet access, wireless Internet access. Restaurant, bar. Airport transportation available. Airport transportation available. Pets accepted. $

### ★★Tempe Mission Palms Hotel
60 E. Fifth St., Tempe,
480-894-1400, 800-547-8705;
www.missionpalms.com
303 rooms. High-speed Internet access. Restaurant, bar. Airport transportation available. Pets accepted. $$

## RESTAURANTS

### ★Blue Nile Ethiopian Cuisine
933 E. University Dr., Tempe,

480-377-1113
Ethiopian/African menu. Lunch, dinner. Closed Monday. Casual attire. Reservations recommended. $

### ★★Byblos
3332 S. Mill Ave., Tempe, 480-894-1945;
www.amdest.com/az/tempe/br/byblos.html
Mediterranean menu. Lunch, dinner. Closed Monday. Bar. Casual attire. $$

### ★★House of Tricks
114 E. Seventh St., Tempe,
480-968-1114;
www.houseoftricks.com
American menu. Lunch, dinner. Closed Sunday; also the last two weeks in July. Bar. Children's menu. Casual attire. Outdoor seating. $$

### ★Macayo Depot Cantina
300 S. Ash Ave., Tempe,
480-966-6677;
www.macayo.com

Mexican menu. Lunch, dinner, late-night. Bar. Children's menu. Casual attire. Outdoor seating. $

### ★★Marcello's Pasta Grill
1701 E. Warner Rd., Tempe, 480-831-0800;
www.marcellospastagrill.com
Italian menu. Lunch, dinner. Closed Sunday. Bar. Children's menu. Casual attire. Outdoor seating. $$

### ★★Michael Monti's La Casa Vieja
100 S. Mill Ave., Tempe, 480-967-7594;
www.montis.com
American menu. Lunch, dinner. Bar. Children's menu. Casual attire. Outdoor seating. $$

### ★Siamese Cat
5034 S. Price Rd., Tempe, 480-820-0406;
www.thesiamesecat.com
Thai menu. Lunch, dinner. Casual attire. Reservations recommended. $$

# TOMBSTONE

Shortly after Ed Schieffelin discovered silver, Tombstone became a rough-and-tumble town with saloons, bawdyhouses and lots of gunfighting. Tombstone's most famous battle was that of the O.K. Corral, between the Earps and the Clantons in 1881. Later, water rose in the mines and could not be pumped out. Fires and other catastrophes occurred, but Tombstone was "the town too tough to die." Now a health and winter resort, it is also a living museum of Arizona frontier life. In 1962, the town was designated a National Historic Landmark.
Information: Tombstone Chamber of Commerce, Tombstone, 888-457-3929; www.tombstone.org

## GUNFIGHTS AND SALOONS
Begin exploring the town on Toughnut Street. At the corner of Third, explore the gorgeous Cochise County Courthouse, now a museum and state historic park. Built in 1882, it's a beautiful example of Victorian Neoclassical architecture. Check out the town gallows in the courtyard and browse the bookshop. To the east one block, the Rose Tree Inn Museum at Fourth and Toughnut occupies a 1880s home. Inside its courtyard is a century-old rose tree that blooms every April and covers an 8,000-square-foot space. At Fifth and Toughnut Streets, stop in to Nellie Cashman's, the oldest restaurant in town (homemade pies are the specialty).
    Follow Third Street north one block to Allen Street, essentially the main drag of historic Tombstone. Stop at the Historama and then next door, see life-size figures

in the O.K. Corral, the alleged site of the legendary gunfight between the Earp and Clanton brothers and Doc Holliday.

On the corner of Allen and Fifth Streets, the Crystal Palace Saloon has been restored to its 1879 glory, looking every bit the lusty watering hole and gambling den of legend. On the block of Allen between Fifth and Sixth Streets, the Prickly Pear Museum is chock-full of military history; on Allen at Sixth, find the famous old Bird Cage Theater Museum. The Pioneer Home Museum, between Eighth and Ninth streets, continues telling the rowdy-days story. From Fifth and Allen, walk north a half-block to the Tombstone Epitaph Museum to see a 1880s printing press and newsroom equipment and buy a copy of the 1881 Epitaph report of the O.K. Corral shoot-out.

## WHAT TO SEE AND DO

### Arizona-Sonora Desert Museum
2021 N. Kinney Rd., Tucson,
520-883-2702;
www.desertmuseum.org
Live desert creatures: mountain lions, beavers, bighorn sheep, birds, tarantulas, prairie dogs, snakes, otters and many others. Nature trails through labeled desert botanical gardens. Underground earth sciences center with limestone caves; geological, mineral and mining exhibits. Orientation room provides information on natural history of deserts. June-August 7:30 a.m.-10 p.m.; March-May, September: 7:30 a.m.-5 p.m.; October-February: 8:30 a.m.-5 p.m.

### Bird Cage Theatre
517 E. Allen, Tombstone,
520-457-3421, 800-457-3423;
www.tombstoneaz.net
Formerly a frontier cabaret (1880s), this landmark was known in its heyday as "the wildest and wickedest nightspot between Basin Street and the Barbary Coast." The upstairs "cages" where feathered girls plied their trade, inspired the refrain "only a bird in a gilded cage." Original fixtures and furnishings. Daily 8 a.m.-6 p.m.

### Boothill Graveyard
Hwy. 80, Tombstone,
520-457-3300
About 250 marked graves, some with unusual epitaphs and many of famous characters.

### Crystal Palace Saloon
420 Allen St., Tombstone,
520-457-3611;
www.crystalpalacesaloon.com
Restored. Dancing Friday-Sunday evenings. Daily.

### O.K. Corral
308 Allen St. E.,
Tombstone,
520-457-3456;
www.ok-corral.com
Restored stagecoach office and buildings surrounding the gunfight site; life-size figures; Fly's Photography Gallery (adjacent) has early photos. Daily; 9 a.m.-5 p.m.

### Rose Tree Inn Museum
116 S. Fourth St.,
Tombstone,
520-457-3326
Largest rose bush in the world, spreading more than 8,000 square feet; blooms in April. The museum is housed in an 1880 boarding house (the oldest house in town); original furniture, documents. Daily 9 a.m.-5 p.m.

### St. Paul's Episcopal Church
19 N. Third St., Tombstone,
520-255-3435;
www.1882.org
Oldest Protestant church still in use in the state, built in 1882; original fixtures. Services 10:30 a.m. every Sunday.

### Tombstone Courthouse State Historic Park

223 Toughnut St., Tombstone,
520-457-3311;
www.pr.state.az.us/Parks/parkhtml/
tombstone.html

Victorian building (1882) houses exhibits that recall Tombstone in the turbulent 1880s. Tombstone and Cochise County history. Daily 8 a.m.-5 p.m.

### Tombstone Epitaph Museum

9 S. Fifth St., Tombstone,
520-457-2211;
www.tombstone-epitaph.com

The oldest continuously published newspaper in Arizona, founded in 1880; it is now a monthly journal of Western history. Office houses a collection of early printing equipment. Daily 9:30 a.m.-5 p.m.

### Tombstone Historama

308 Allen St. E.,
Tombstone,
520-457-3456

A film narrated by Vincent Price tells the story of Tombstone. Daily 9:30 a.m.-4:30 p.m.; half-hourly showings.

### Tombstone Western Heritage Museum

Sixth St., and Fremont,
Tombstone,
520-457-3800

This new museum has a great collection of Wyatt Earp memorabilia along with lots of Old West artifacts and cowboy photos. Thursday-Tuesday 9 a.m.-6 p.m.

## SPECIAL EVENTS

### Helldorado

Tombstone,
520-457-3291;
www.tombstonevigilantes.com

Three days of Old West re-enactments of Tombstone events of the 1880s. Third full weekend in October.

### Territorial Days

Fourth and Fremont Streets, Tombstone,
520-457-9317, 888-457-3929;
www.tombstone.org

Commemorates formal founding of the town. Fire-hose cart races and other events typical of a celebration in Arizona's early days. Second weekend in March.

### Wild West Days and Rendezvous of Gunfighters

O.K. Corral, 308 Allen St. E.,
Tombstone,
520-457-9465

This annual event showcases different gunfight re-enactment groups from throughout the United States. Activities include costume contests and a parade. Labor Day weekend.

### Wyatt Earp Days

O.K. Corral, 108 W. Allen St. E.,
Tombstone,
520-457-3434;
www.tombstonevigilantes.com

This annual festival is held in honor of the famous lawman. The festivities include a barbecue, gunfights, street entertainment, dances, chili cook-off and more. Memorial Day weekend.

## RESTAURANTS

### ★Longhorn

501 E. Allen St., Tombstone,
520-457-3107;
www.bignosekate.com

American menu. Breakfast, lunch, dinner. Casual attire. **$**

### ★Nellie Cashman's

117 S. Fifth St., Tombstone,
520-457-2212;
www.nelliecashman.freeservers.com

American menu. Breakfast, lunch, dinner. Casual attire. Outdoor seating. **$$**

**ARIZONA**

# TUCSON

Tucson offers a rare combination of delightful Western living, colorful desert, mountain scenery and cosmopolitan culture. It is one of several U.S. cities that developed under four flags. The Spanish standard flew first over the Presidio of Tucson, built to withstand Apache attacks in 1776. Later, Tucson flew the flags of Mexico, the Confederate States and finally, the United States. Today, Tucson is a resort area, an educational and copper center, a cotton and cattle market, headquarters for the Coronado National Forest and a place of business for several large industries.

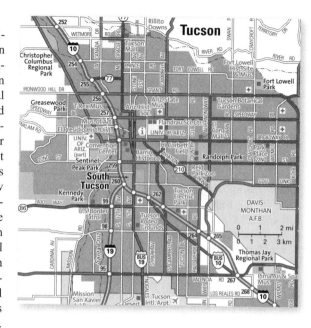

The city has many shops, restaurants, resorts and attractions.

Information: Metropolitan Tucson Convention & Visitors Bureau, 100 S. Church Ave., Tucson, 520-624-1817, 800-638-8350; www.visittucson.org

ARIZONA

## SAGUARO NATIONAL PARK

The saguaro cactus that gives this park its name may grow as high as 50 feet and live to be 200 years old. The fluted columns with sharp, tough needles sometimes branch into fantastic shapes. During the rainy season, large saguaros can absorb enough water to sustain themselves during the dry season.

The saguaro's waxy, white blossoms (Arizona's state flower), which open at night and close the following afternoon, bloom in May and June, and the red fruit ripens in July. The Tohono O'Odham people eat this fruit fresh and dried or use it to make jellies, jams and wines.

Wildlife in the park is abundant. Gila woodpeckers and gilded flickers drill nest holes in the saguaro trunks. Once vacated, these holes become home to many other species of birds, including the tiny elf owl. Peccaries (pig-like mammals), coyotes, mule deer and other animals are often seen. Yuccas, agaves, prickly pears, mesquite, paloverde trees and many other desert plants grow here.

The Rincon Mountain District offers nature trails, guided nature walks (winter), eight-mile self-guided drive, mountain hiking, bridle trails, picnicking (no water) and backcountry camping. Stop by the visitor center to check out the museum and see an orientation film.

The Tucson Mountain District offers nature trails, a six-mile self-guided drive, and hiking and bridle trails. Five picnic areas (no water). Visitor center; exhibits, slide program daily.

Information: Rincon Mountain District, 17 miles east of Tucson via Broadway and Old Spanish Trail; Tucson Mountain District, 16 miles west of Tucson via Speedway and Gates Pass Rd.; 520-733-5153; www.nps.gov/sagu

## WHAT TO SEE AND DO

### Arizona Historical Society Fort Lowell Museum

2900 N. Craycroft Rd.,
Tucson,
520-885-3832;
www.arizonahistoricalsociety.org
Reconstruction of commanding officer's quarters. Exhibits, period furniture. Wednesday-Saturday 10 a.m.-4 p.m.

### Arizona Historical Society Fremont House Museum

151 S. Granada Ave., Tucson,
520-622-0956;
www.arizonahistoricalsociety.org
This adobe 19th century house, once occupied by John C. Fremont's daughter, Elizabeth, when he was territorial governor (1878-1881), has been restored. Special programs all year, including slide shows on Arizona history (Saturday) and walking tours of historic sites (November-March, Saturday; registration in advance). Museum Wednesday-Saturday 10 a.m.-4 p.m.

### Arizona Historical Society Museum, Library, and Archives

949 E. Second St., Tucson,
520-628-5774;
www.arizonahistoricalsociety.org
Exhibits depicting state history from the Spanish colonial period to present; Arizona mining hall; photography gallery. Research library Monday-Friday 10 a.m.-3 p.m., Saturday 10 a.m.-1 p.m.

### Biosphere 2

32540 Biosphere Rd., Oracle,
520-838-6200;
www.bio2.com
An ambitious attempt to learn more about our planet's ecosystems began in September 1991 with the first of a series of missions in this 3 1/2-acre, glass-enclosed, self-sustaining model of Earth. (The crew of researchers rely entirely on the air, water and food generated and recycled within the structure.) It contains more than 3,500 species of plants and animals in multiple ecosystems, including a tropical rain forest with an 85-foot-high mountain. Visitors are permitted within the biospherian living areas of the enclosure. Because of variance in research schedule, the biospherian crew may not always be present. Walking tours include multimedia introduction to Biosphere 2. Daily 9 a.m.-4 p.m.

### Catalina State Park

11570 N. Oracle Rd., Tucson,
520-628-5798;
www.pr.state.az.us/parks/parkhtml/catalina.html
A 5,500-acre desert park with a vast array of plants and wildlife; bird area (nearly 170 species). Nature and horseback riding trails, hiking, trail access to adjacent Coronado National Forest.

### Center for Creative Photography

University of Arizona,
1030 N. Olive Rd., Tucson,
520-621-7968;
www.creativephotography.org
This collection of art by more than 2,000 photographers includes the archives of Ansel Adams and Richard Avedon. Gallery Monday-Friday 9 a.m.-5 p.m., Saturday-Sunday noon-5 p.m.

### Coronado National Forest

300 W. Congress St., Tucson,
520-388-8300;
www.fs.fed.us/r3/coronado
Mount Lemmon Recreation Area, part of this two-million-acre forest, offers fishing, bird watching, hiking, horseback riding, picnicking, skiing and camping. Madera Canyon offers recreation facilities and a lodge. Pea Blanca Lake and Recreation Area and the Chiricahua Wilderness area in the southeast corner of the state are part of the 12 areas that make up the forest. The Santa Catalina Ranger District, located in Tucson (520-749-8700), has its headquarters at Sabino Canyon, 12 miles northeast on Sabino Canyon Rd; a 1/4-mile nature trail begins at the headquarters, as does a shuttle ride almost four miles into Sabino Canyon. Northeast, east and south of the city.

**65**

**ARIZONA**

### Flandrau Science Center & Planetarium

University of Arizona,
1601 E. University Blvd., Tucson,
520-621-7827;
www.gotuasciencecenter.org

Interactive, hands-on science exhibits. Monday-Wednesday 9 a.m.-5 p.m.; Thursday-Saturday 9 a.m.-5 p.m., 7-9 p.m.; Sunday 1-5 p.m.; planetarium shows (limited hours). Nightly telescope viewing. Mid-August-mid-May: Wednesday-Saturday 6:40-10 p.m.; mid-May-mid-August: Wednesday-Saturday 7:30-10 p.m.

### International Wildlife Museum

4800 W. Gates Pass Rd., Tucson,
520-629-0100;
www.thewildlifemuseum.org

Includes hundreds of wildlife exhibits from around the world; hands-on, interactive computer displays; videos; cafe. Monday-Friday 9 a.m.-5 p.m., Saturday-Sunday 9 a.m.-6 p.m.

### Mount Lemmon Ski Valley

10300 Ski Run Rd., Mount Lemmon,
520-576-1400;
www.fs.fed.us/r3/coronado

Double chairlift, two tows; patrol, school, rentals; snack bar, restaurant. Twenty-one runs, longest run one mile; vertical drop 900 feet. Late December-mid-April, daily. Chairlift operates the rest of the year. Nature trails.

### Old Town Artisans

201 N. Court Ave., Tucson,
520-623-6024, 800-782-8072;
www.oldtownartisans.com

Restored adobe buildings (circa 1850s) in the historic El Presidio neighborhood serve as shops for handcrafted Southwestern and Latin American art. September-May: Monday-Saturday 9:30 a.m.-5:30 p.m., Sunday 11 a.m.-5 p.m.; June-August: Monday-Saturday 10 a.m.-4 p.m., Sunday 11 a.m.-4 p.m.

### Pima Air & Space Museum

6000 E. Valencia Rd., Tucson,
520-574-0462;
www.pimaair.org

Aviation history exhibits with an outstanding collection of more than 250 aircraft, both military and civilian. Walking tours. Daily 9 a.m.-5 p.m.

### Reid Park Zoo

1030 S. Randolph Way, Tucson,
520-881-4753;
www.tucsonzoo.org

Picnicking; zoo; rose garden; outdoor performance center. Daily 9 a.m.-4 p.m.

### Titan Missile Museum

1580 W. Duval Mine Rd., Sahuarita,
520-625-7736;
www.titanmissilemuseum.org

Deactivated Titan II missile on display; UH1F helicopter; other exhibits. A one-hour guided tour begins with a briefing and includes a visit down into the missile silo. The silo may also be viewed from a glass observation area located at the museum level. Daily 9 a.m.-5 p.m.

### Tohono Chul Park

7366 N. Paseo del Norte, Tucson,
520-742-6455;
www.tohonochulpark.org

A 37-acre preserve with more than 400 species of arid climate plants; nature trails; demonstration garden; geology wall; ethno botanical garden. Many varieties of wild birds visit the park. Exhibits, galleries, tearoom and gift shops in restored adobe house. Walking tours. Daily 8 a.m.-5 p.m.

### Tucson Botanical Gardens

2150 N. Alvernon Way, Tucson,
520-326-9686; www.tucsonbotanical.org

Gardens include Mediterranean and landscaping plants; native wildflowers; tropical greenhouse; xeriscape/solar demonstration garden. Tours, special events. Picnic area. Daily 8:30 a.m.-4:30 p.m.

### Tucson Mountain Park

Ajo Way & Kinney Rd., Tucson,
520-883-4200; www.co.pima.az.us

Includes more than 18,000 acres of saguaro cactus and mountain scenery. Picnic facilities.

**66**

**ARIZONA**

★
★
★
✮
✩

### Tucson Museum of Art
140 N. Main Ave., Tucson, 520-624-2333;
www.tucsonarts.com
Housed in six renovated buildings within the boundaries of El Presidio Historic District (circa 1800). Pre-Columbian, Spanish Colonial and Western artifacts; decorative arts and paintings; art of the Americas; contemporary art and crafts; changing exhibits. Mexican heritage museum; historic presidio room; 6,000-volume art resource library; art school. Tuesday-Saturday 10 a.m.-4 p.m., Sunday noon-4 p.m. Free admission first Sunday of month.

### University of Arizona
Campbell Ave. and Sixth St., Tucson, 520-621-5130; www.arizona.edu
Established in 1885; 35,000 students. The 343-acre campus is beautifully landscaped and has handsome buildings. The visitor center, located at University Boulevard and Cherry Avenue, has campus maps and information on attractions and activities. Tours Monday-Saturday.

## SPECIAL EVENTS
### Arizona Opera
3501 Mountain Ave., Tucson, 520-293-4336; www.azopera.com
Five operas are produced each season. October-March: Friday-Sunday.

### Arizona Theatre Company
The Temple of Music and Art, 330 S. Scott Ave., Tucson, 520-622-2823; www.aztheatreco.org
The State Theatre of Arizona performs both classic and contemporary works. Evening performances Tuesday-Sunday; matinees Wednesday, Saturday-Sunday. September-May.

### Baseball
Hi Corbett Field, Tucson Electric Park, 2500 E. Ajo Way, Tucson, 520-434-1000, 866-672-1343; www.cactus-league.com
Tucson Electric Park. Chicago White Sox and Arizona Diamondbacks baseball spring training, exhibition games; late February-late March. Also the home of the minor league Tucson Sidewinders; April-September.

### Chrysler Classic of Tucson
Omni Tucson National Golf Resort & Spa, 2727 W. Club Dr., Tucson, 520-571-0400; www.pgatour.com/tournaments/r001
This $3-million tournament features top pros. Late February-early March.

### Gem & Mineral Show
Tucson Convention Center, 260 S. Church Ave., Tucson, 520-322-5773, 800-638-8350; www.tgms.org
Displays of minerals; jewelry; lapidary skills; Smithsonian Institution collection. Mid-Februray.

### Tucson Meet Yourself Festival
El Presidio Park, Tucson, 520-792-4806; www.tucsonmeetyourself.org
Commemorates Tucson's cultural and historic heritage with a torchlight pageant, American Indian dances, children's parade, Mexican fiesta, frontier encampment and other events. October.

### Tucson Symphony Orchestra
Tucson Symphony Center, 2175 N. Sixth Ave., Tucson, 520-882-8585; www.tucsonsymphony.org
The symphony's eight-month season includes classic ensembles, performances by guest artists and special events such as BeatleMania! September-May.

## HOTELS
### ★★★Arizona Inn
2200 E. Elm St., Tucson, 520-325-1541, 800-933-1093; www.arizonainn.com
This inn was built in 1930 by Arizona Congresswoman Isabella Greenway and is still owned by her family today. Guests who stay here are treated to quiet comfort with spacious, individually decorated rooms and 15 acres of beautifully landscaped lawns and gardens.

ARIZONA

95 rooms. High-speed wireless Internet access. Restaurant, bar. Airport transportation available. Pool. Tennis. **$$**

### ★Best Western Continental Inn
8425 N. Cracker Barrel Rd., Marana,
520-579-1099, 800-780-7234;
www.bestwestern.com
65 rooms. Complimentary continental breakfast. Pool. **$**

### ★★Best Western Royal Sun Inn and Suites
1015 N. Stone Ave., Tucson,
866-293-9454;
www.bwroyalsun.com
79 rooms. Complimentary full breakfast. High-speed wireless Internet access. Restaurant, bar. Airport transportation available. Pool. **$**

### ★Country Inn & Suites By Carlson
7411 N. Oracle Rd., Tucson,
520-575-9255, 800-456-4000;
www.countryinns.com
156 rooms. Complimentary continental breakfast. Airport transportation available. Pets accepted. Pool. **$**

### ★★Courtyard Tucson Airport
2505 E. Executive Dr., Tucson,
520-573-0000, 800-321-2211;
www.courtyard.com
149 rooms. High-speed Internet access. Restaurant, bar. Airport transportation available. Pool. **$**

### ★★Doubletree Hotel
445 S. Alvernon Way, Tucson,
520-881-4200, 800-222-8733;
www.doubletreehotels.com
295 rooms High-speed Internet access. Two restaurants, two bars. Airport transportation available. Pets accepted. Pool. **$**

### ★★Embassy Suites Hotel Tucson-Williams Center
5335 E. Broadway Blvd., Tucson,
520-745-2700, 800-362-2779;
www.embassysuites.com

142 rooms, all suites. Complimentary full breakfast. High-speed wireless Internet access. Pool. **$**

### ★Hampton Inn
6971 S. Tucson Blvd., Tucson,
520-889-5789, 800-426-7866;
www.hamptoninn.com
126 rooms. Complimentary continental breakfast. High-speed wireless Internet access. Airport transportation available. Pool. **$**

### ★★★Hilton Tucson El Conquistador Golf and Tennis Resort
10000 N. Oracle Rd., Tucson,
520-544-5000, 800-325-7832;
www.hiltonelconquistador.com
This resort and country club lures visitors with its extensive golf and tennis facilities. The resort offers 45 holes of golf on three championship courses. There are 16 lighted tennis courts. Each of the newly remodeled rooms has a patio and balcony. The spa offers a full range of treatments.
428 rooms. High-speed Internet access, wireless Internet access. Restaurant, bar. Children's activity center. Spa. Airport transportation available. Pets accepted. Pool. Golf. Tennis. Business center. **$$**

### ★★★Lodge At Ventana Canyon
6200 N. Clubhouse Lane, Tucson,
520-577-1400, 800-828-5701;
www.thelodgeatventanacanyon.com
Located in the foothills of the Santa Catalina Mountains on a 600-acre desert preserve, the Lodge is a peaceful getaway for tennis players, golfers and those in pursuit of nothing more than a day at the pool. Two 18-hole Tom Fazio-designed golf courses wind their way through the landscape of wild brush and giant saguaros, while the tennis champ can help you master your serve on the 12 hard courts. Rooms have Mission-style furniture, fully-stocked kitchens and old-fashioned freestanding bathtubs.
50 rooms. Restaurant, bar. Pets accepted. Pool. Golf. Tennis. **$$$$**

**68**

ARIZONA

### ★★★Loews Ventana Canyon Resort

7000 N. Resort Dr., Tucson, 520-299-2020; www.loewshotels.com

Set on 93 acres in the Sonoran Desert, this resort just completed a multi-million dollar room renovation. The new décor offers modern comfort with a Southwestern twist. The two award-winning Tom Fazio-designed 18-hole golf courses challenge duffers. The Spa and Tennis Center offers a full range of treatments as well as a fitness center. Five restaurants and lounges give a taste of every kind of cuisine in a variety of settings, from poolside cafés to refined dining rooms. The Ventana Room delivers artfully presented, elegant cuisine. This intimate and romantic restaurant has floor to ceiling windows which makes the perfect setting for dinner at sunset.

398 rooms. Pets accepted. Four restaurants, bars. Children's activity center. Fitness room, spa. Outdoor pool, whirlpool. Golf, 36 holes. Tennis. Business center. **$$$**

### ★★★Marriott Tucson University Park

880 E. Second St., Tucson, 520-792-4100; www.marriott.com

This hotel is a good choice for those visiting the University of Arizona's campus. It's located right at the front gate and features rooms that are specifically designed for business travelers. This hotel is non-smoking.

267 rooms. Restaurant, bar. Pool. Business center. **$**

### ★★★Omni Tucson National Golf Resort and Spa

2727 W. Club Dr., Tucson, 520-297-2271, 888-444-6664; www.omnihotels.com

Located in the foothills of the Santa Catalina Mountains, the Omni Tucson National Golf Resort and Spa has been the home to countless PGA Tours. But there's more than just golf here. There are two pools, four tennis courts, sand volleyball, lots of biking trails and the spa, which boasts 13,000 pleasure-pursuing square feet. Sign up for the terzetto massage, where two therapists perform choreographed massage. The comfortable rooms have a Southwest décor

and feature views of the course or mountains. Some rooms also have full kitchens, although most people leave the cooking up to the resort's talented chefs.

167 rooms. Restaurant, bar. Spa. Pets accepted. Pool. Golf. Tennis. Business center. **$**

### ★★Sheraton Tucson Hotel And Suites

5151 E. Grant Rd., Tucson, 520-323-6262, 800-325-3535; www.sheraton.com

216 rooms. Complimentary continental breakfast. Restaurant, bar. Pets accepted. Pool. **$**

### ★Windmill Suites At St., Phillips Plaza

4250 N. Campbell Ave., Tucson, 520-577-0007, 800-547-4747; www.windmillinns.com

122 rooms, all suites. Complimentary continental breakfast. Pets accepted. Pool. **$**

### ★★★The Westin La Paloma Resort and Spa

3800 E. Sunrise Dr., Tucson, 520-742-6000, 800-937-8461; www.westin.com/lapaloma

The large rooms here have warm, golden color schemes and feature patios or balconies and bathrooms with granite countertops and dual sinks. Golfers are drawn to the 27-hole Jack Nicklaus-designed course adjoining the resort. You'll also find tennis, three shimmering pools—one with a 177-foot waterslide—and the Elizabeth Arden Red Door Spa on site, as well as five restaurants.

487 rooms. Five restaurants, bars. Children's activity center. Spa. Pets accepted. Golf. Tennis. Business center. **$$**

### ★★★Westward Look Resort

245 E. Ina Rd., Tucson, 520-297-1151, 800-722-2500; www.westwardlook.com

The newly renovated Westward Look Resort combines top-notch facilities, gourmet dining and sumptuous spa treatments in a naturally beautiful setting. Set on 80 acres filled with giant cacti and blooming

**ARIZONA**

★

★

★

★

★

wildflowers, this resort is home to a variety of birds and wildlife. Enjoy horseback riding, on-site tennis, nearby golf—or just the peace and quiet.

244 rooms. High-speed wireless Internet access. Two restaurants, bar. Spa. Airport transportation available. Pets accepted. Tennis. $$$

## SPECIALTY LODGINGS

### Adobe Rose Inn Bed And Breakfast
940 N. Olsen Ave., Tucson,
520-318-4644, 800-328-4122;
www.aroseinn.com
7 rooms. Children over 10 years only. Complimentary full breakfast. Pool. $

### Catalina Park Inn
309 E. First St., Tucson,
520-792-4541, 800-792-4885;
www.catalinaparkinn.com
6 rooms. Closed mid June-August. Children over 10 years only. Complimentary full breakfast. $

**ARIZONA**

### Tanque Verde Guest Ranch
14301 E. Speedway Blvd., Tucson,
520-296-6275, 800-234-3833;
www.tanqueverderanch.com
74 rooms. Complimentary full breakfast. High-speed Internet access. Restaurant. Children's activity center. Airport transportation available. Pool. Tennis. $$

### White Stallion Ranch
9251 W. Twin Peaks Rd., Tucson,
520-297-0252, 888-977-2624;
www.wsranch.com
41 rooms. Closed June-August. Complimentary full breakfast. Restaurant, bar. Airport transportation available. Pool. Tennis. $$$

★
★
★
★
★

## RESTAURANTS

### ★★Cafe Poca Cosa
110 E. Pennington, Tucson,
520-622-6400
Mexican menu. Lunch, dinner. Closed Sunday-Monday; mid-July-mid-August. Bar. Casual attire. Reservations recommended. Outdoor seating. $$

### ★★Chad's Steakhouse
3001 N. Swan, Tucson, 520-881-1802;
www.chadssteakhouse.com
Steak menu. Lunch, dinner. Bar. Children's menu. Casual attire. Reservations recommended. $$

### ★Delectables
533 N. Fourth Ave., Tucson, 520-884-9289;
www.delectables.com
French bistro menu. Lunch, dinner. Bar. Children's menu. Casual attire. Reservations recommended. Outdoor seating. $$

### ★★El Parador Tucson
2744 E. Broadway Blvd., Tucson,
520-881-2744, 800-964-5908;
www.elparadortucson.com
Mexican menu. Lunch, dinner, late night, Sunday brunch. Bar. Children's menu. Casual attire. Reservations recommended. Outdoor seating. $$

### ★★★Fuego
6958 E. Tanque Verde Rd., Tucson,
520-886-1745; www.fuegorestaurant.com
Chef and owner Alan Zeman serves up ostrich, beef, game and vegetarian dishes. And the oysters are considered the best in town. The contemporary Southwestern décor includes lots of brick and wood flooring. A large picture window offers views of the mountain.

Southwestern menu. Dinner. Bar. Children's menu. Casual attire. Reservations recommended. Outdoor seating. $$

### ★★★The Gold Room
245 E. Ina Rd., Tucson, 520-297-1151;
www.westwardlook.com
Set at the base of the Catalina Mountains in north central Tucson, the Gold Room features both regional Southwestern fare and traditional American cuisine. Assorted chilies, beans, squash and other produce are cultivated in the chef's on-site garden and are winningly blended into entrées like mesquite-grilled buffalo sirloin with chipotle maple glaze and mesquite-grilled lamb, ostrich and venison with green chile mashed potatoes. Wraparound windows afford spectacular

views of the mountains, desert and city. A jazz brunch on Sundays features a weekly changing menu of inspired regional dishes like blue corn pancakes with prickly pear syrup and Sonoran Caesar salad with smoked duck. American menu. Breakfast, lunch, dinner, brunch. Children's menu. Casual attire. Reservations recommended. Valet parking. Outdoor seating. **$$$**

### ★★★The Grill at Hacienda del Sol
5601 N. Hacienda del Sol Rd., Tucson, 520-299-1501; www.haciendadelsol.com
Rustic Spanish colonial architecture, fine pottery and Mexican art adorn this beautifully restored Tucson landmark. The New American cuisine is complemented by a spectacular wine list and excellent service. The creative menu, which includes dishes like roasted tomato and basil soup with garlic and chevre croustade, makes this one of Tucson's favorite dining destinations. Jazz musicians perform every Thursday through Sunday.
American menu. Dinner, Sunday brunch. Bar. Children's menu. Business casual attire. Reservations recommended. Valet parking. Outdoor seating. **$$$**

### ★★★Janos Restaurant
3770 E. Sunrise Dr., Tucson, 520-615-6100; www.janos.com
The legendary Janos Wilder presides over this French-inspired Southwestern masterpiece located inside the Westin La Paloma Resort & Spa. The restaurant features both tasting and la carte menus, which are constantly changing and are inspired by influences from around the world. The emphasis is on ingredients from the region, utilizing an established network of local farmers. The romantic setting features original artwork and views of the valley.
Southwestern menu. Dinner. Closed Sunday. Bar. Business casual attire. Reservations recommended. Valet parking. Outdoor seating. **$$$**

### ★★★Kingfisher
2564 E. Grant, Tucson, 520-323-7739; www.kingfisherbarandgrill.com

The popular spot serves up dishes like pan-seared Atlantic salmon, spinach tagliatelle and barbecued chicken pasta. There's also a full oyster bar with 15 varieties of oysters. On Mondays and Saturdays, the sounds of jazz and blues can be heard until midnight. American menu. Lunch, dinner, late night. Bar. Casual attire. Reservations recommended. **$$**

### ★★La Fuente
1749 N. Oracle Rd., Tucson, 520-623-8659; www.lafuenterestaurant.com
Mexican menu. Lunch, dinner, brunch. Bar. Children's menu. Casual attire. Reservations recommended. **$$**

### ★★La Parrilla Suiza
2720 N. Oracle Rd., Tucson, 520-624-4300; www.laparrillasuiza.com
Mexican menu. Lunch, dinner. Bar. Children's menu. Casual attire. Reservations recommended. **$**

### ★La Placita Cafe
2950 N. Swan Rd., Tucson, 520-881-1150
Mexican menu. Lunch, dinner. Casual attire. Reservations recommended. Outdoor seating. **$$**

### ★★★McMahon's Prime Steakhouse
2959 N. Swan Rd., Tucson, 520-327-7463; www.metrorestaurants.com
This local favorite is a perfect spot for a romantic evening or that special occasion. Original local artwork adorns the walls and a pianist performs nightly. Entrées include filet mignon with Portobello mushrooms, garlic and aged Romano cheese, and New York Sirloin with onions, mushrooms, garlic and cracked black pepper.
Steak menu. Lunch, dinner. Bar. Children's menu. Business casual attire. Reservations recommended. Valet parking. Outdoor seating. **$$$**

### ★Mi Nidito
1813 S. Fourth Ave., Tucson, 520-622-5081; www.minidito.net
Mexican menu. Lunch, dinner. Closed Monday-Tuesday. Casual attire. **$$**

**ARIZONA**

### ★★★Olive Tree

7000 E. Tanque Verde Rd., Tucson,
520-298-1845

A family-owned and-operated restaurant, Olive Tree is a local favorite that serves the freshest Greek food in town. The interior is decorated with blue banquettes, floral curtains and wood paneling; tables are set with double white cloths and nautical blue napkins in the shape of sails. Enjoy mousaka, souvlaki and other Greek favorites.

Mediterranean menu. Lunch, dinner. Bar. Business casual attire. Reservations recommended. Outdoor seating. **$$**

### ★Pinnacle Peak

6541 E. Tanque Verde Rd.,
Tucson,
520-296-0911;
www.traildusttown.com

Steak menu. Dinner. Bar. Children's menu. Casual attire. Outdoor seating. **$$**

### ★Seri Melaka

6133 E. Broadway, Tucson,
520-747-7811;
www.serimelaka.com

Pacific-Rim, Malaysian menu. Lunch, dinner. Casual attire. Reservations recommended. **$$**

### ★★★Soleil

3001 E. Skyline Dr., Tucson,
520-299-3345

Soleil is a great spot for dining, thanks to the contemporary cuisine and awesome views. Dishes include herb roasted free-range chicken, scallops with truffle oil and lamb shake. Guests can enjoy entertainment, which includes an invisible theater during summer months (mid-June-early July) and Friday night jazz. The décor here is contemporary, with lots of windows, offering panoramic views of the city and mountains.

Mediterranean menu. Lunch, dinner, Sunday brunch. Closed Monday; also one week in summer. Bar. Business casual attire. Reservations recommended. Outdoor seating. **$$$**

### ★Tohono Chul Tea Room

7366 N. Paseo del Norte, Tucson,
520-797-1222;
www.tohonochulpark.org

American menu. Breakfast, lunch. Children's menu. Casual attire. Outdoor seating. **$**

### ★★★★The Ventana Room

7000 N. Resort Dr., Tucson,
520-615-5494;
www.ventanaroom.com

Located in the Loews Ventana Canyon Resort, the Ventana Room is the place to go for panoramic views of the city lights and mountain ranges. The contemporary American cuisine features wild cuts of game, as well as lamb and seafood. A three-, four- or five-course prix fixe menu is offered, and there's a four-course Farmland Degustation, with dishes such as partridge with black truffle or Niman Ranch leg of lamb confit. Maitre'd Kevin Brady oversees the substantial wine list. A chef's table for six is available.

French menu. Dinner. Closed Sunday-Monday; also mid-August-mid-September. Bar. Business casual attire. Reservations recommended. Valet parking. **$$$$**

## SPAS

### ★★★★The Spa at Omni Tucson National

2727 West Club Dr., Tucson,
520-575-7559;
www.tucsonnational.com

The Spa at Omni Tucson National has a tranquil and picturesque location in the foothills of the Santa Catalina Mountains. Whether you have half an hour or an entire day, this spa has something to offer. In 25 minutes, the tension reliever massage works its magic where you are most tense, while the business facial cleanses, tones, exfoliates and hydrates in just under 30 minutes. Other tfacials include aromatherapy, deep-cleansing, antiaging and deluxe hydration. Body masks smooth rough skin with a variety of ingredients, including seaweed, desert rose clay, rich mud from the Dead Sea, shea butter and aspara, a plant that grows by the beach and is recognized for its calming properties. **$$**

# WICKENBURG

Early Hispanic families who established ranches in the area and traded with the local American Indians first settled Wickenburg. The town was relatively unpopulated until a Prussian named Henry Wickenburg picked up a rock to throw at a stubborn burro and stumbled onto the richest gold find in Arizona, the Vulture Mine. His discovery began a $30-million boom and the birth of a town. Today, Wickenburg is the oldest town north of Tucson and is well known for its area dude ranches.
Information: Chamber of Commerce, Santa Fe Depot, 216 N. Frontier St., 928-684-5479, 800-942-5242; www.wickenburgchamber.com

## WHAT TO SEE AND DO

### Desert Caballeros Western Museum
21 N. Frontier St., Wickenburg,
928-684-2272;
www.westernmuseum.org
This museum houses a Western art gallery, diorama room, street scene (circa 1915), period rooms, mineral display and Native American exhibit. Monday-Saturday 10 a.m.-5 p.m., Sunday noon-4 p.m.

### Frontier Street
Wickenburg,
928-684-5479;
www.wickenburgchamber.com
Preserved in early 1900s style. Train depot (houses the Chamber of Commerce), brick Hassayampa building (former hotel) and many other historic buildings.

### Garcia Little Red Schoolhouse
245 N. Tegner St., Wickenburg,
928-684-7473;
www.wco.org
This pioneer schoolhouse is on the National Register of Historic Places.

### Old 761 Santa Fe Steam Locomotive
Apache and Tegner, Wickenburg,
928-684-5479;
www.wickenburgchamber.com
This engine and tender ran the track between Chicago and the West.

### The Jail Tree
Tegner and Wickenburg Way,
Wickenburg,
928-684-5479
This tree was used from 1863 to 1890 (until the first jail was built) to chain rowdy prisoners. Friends and relatives visited the prisoners and brought picnic lunches.

## SPECIAL EVENTS

### Bluegrass Music Festival
Hwy. 60, Everett Bowman Rodeo Grounds, Wickenburg,
928-684-5479;
www.wickenburgchamber.com
Four-Corner States Championship. Contests include mandolin, violin, guitar and banjo. Second full weekend in November.

### Gold Rush Days
Wickenburg
Bonanza days are revived during this large festival, with a chance to pan for gold and keep all you find. Rodeo, contests, food, parade. Second full weekend in February.

### Septiembre Fiesta
Wickenburg Community Center,
160 N. Valentine St., Wickenburg,
928-684-5479;
www.wickenburgchamber.com
This celebration of Hispanic heritage featuring exhibits, arts and crafts, food, dancers and mariachi bands. First Saturday in September.

## HOTELS

### ★★Best Western Rancho Grande
293 E. Wickenburg Way,
Wickenburg,
928-684-5445, 800-854-7235;
www.bwranchogrande.com
80 rooms. Airport transportation available. Pets accepted. Pool. Tennis. **$**

**ARIZONA**

## SPECIALTY LODGINGS

**Flying E Ranch**
2801 W. Wickenburg Way, Wickenburg,
928-684-2690, 888-684-2650;
www.flyingeranch.com
Located on a 20,000-acre cattle ranch in the shadow of Vulture Peak, this property offers breakfast cookouts, family-style meals and chuck wagon dinners.
17 rooms. Closed March-October. Pool. Tennis. $$

**Rancho De Los Caballeros**
1551 S. Vulture Mine Rd., Wickenburg,
928-684-5484, 800-684-5030;
www.sunc.com
Experience the Old West at this historic guest ranch and golf club. Dine by campfire.
79 rooms. Closed mid-May-mid-October. Restaurant, bar. Children's activity center. Airport transportation available. Pool. Golf. Tennis. $$$$

# WILLCOX

Visit historic downtown Willcox to see the state's oldest operating store amid antique shops, restaurants, boutiques and museums. This little town will give you a flavor of the Old West.

Information: Chamber of Commerce, Cochise Information Center, 1500 N. Circle I Rd., Willcox, 520-384-2272, 800-200-2272; www.willcoxchamber.com

## CHIRICAHUA NATIONAL MONUMENT

This national monument features 20 square miles of picturesque natural rock sculptures and deep twisting canyons. The Chiricahua (Cheer-a-CAH-wah) Apaches—Geronimo was one—hunted in this region in the 1870s and 1880s.
A visitor center, about two miles from the entrance, has geological, zoological and historical displays. Daily. At Massai Point Overlook, geologic exhibits explain the volcanic origin of the monument. The road up Bonita Canyon leads to a number of other outlook points. There are also 18 miles of excellent day-use trails to points of special interest. Picnicking and camping sites are located within the national monument. Daily 8 a.m.-4:30 p.m.
Information: 32 miles southeast of Willcox on Hwy. 186, then three miles east on Hwy. 181, 520-824-3560; www.nps.gov/chir

## WHAT TO SEE AND DO

**Amerind Foundation**
2100 N. Amerind Rd., Dragoon,
520-586-3666;
www.amerind.org
Amerind (short for American Indian) Museum contains one of the finest collections of archaeological and ethnological artifacts in the country. Paintings by Anglo and American Indian artists are on display in the gallery. Picnic area, museum shop. Tuesday-Sunday 10 a.m.-4 p.m.

**Cochise Stronghold**
Coronada National Forest,
1500 N. Circle I Rd., Willcox,
520-364-3468;
www.cochisestronghold.com
This rugged canyon once sheltered Chiricahua Apache. Unique rock formations provided protection and vantage points. Camping, picnicking, hifking, horseback and history trails. Daily.

**Fort Bowie National Historic Site**
3203 S. Old Fort Bowie Rd., Bowie,
520-847-2500; www.nps.gov/fobo

On the way to the ruins, you'll see a stage station, post cemetery, Apache Spring. Visitor center daily 8 a.m.-4:30 p.m.

**Rex Allen Arizona Cowboy Museum and Cowboy Hall of Fame**
150 N. Railroad Ave., Willcox,
520-384-4583, 877-234-4111;
www.rexallenmuseum.org
This museum is dedicated to Willcox native Rex Allen, the "last of the Silver Screen Cowboys." It details his life from ranch living in Willcox to his radio, TV and movie days. It also has special exhibits on pioneer settlers and ranchers. The Cowboy Hall of Fame pays tribute to real cattle industry heroes. Daily 10 a.m.-4 p.m.

## SPECIAL EVENTS
**Rex Allen Days**
Rex Allen Arizona Cowboy Museum and Cowboy Hall of Fame,
150 N. Railroad Ave., Willcox,
520-384-2272;
www.willcoxchamber.com

PRCA Rodeo, concert by Rex Allen Jr., parade, country fair, Western dances, softball tournament. First weekend in October.

**Wings Over Willcox/Sandhill Crane Celebration**
1500 N. Circle I Rd., Willcox,
520-384-2272, 800-200-2272;
www.wingsoverwillcox.com
Tours of bird-watching areas, trade shows, seminars, workshops. Third weekend in January.

## HOTELS
**★★Best Western Plaza Inn**
1100 W. Rex Allen Dr., Willcox,
520-384-3556, 800-262-2649;
www.bestwestern.com
91 rooms. Complimentary full breakfast. Restaurant, bar. Pets accepted. Pool. $

# WILLIAMS

This town lies at the foot of Bill Williams Mountain (named for an early trapper and guide) and is the principal entrance to the Grand Canyon. It is a resort town in the midst of Kaibab National Forest, which has its headquarters here. There are seven small fishing lakes in the surrounding area.
Information: Williams-Grand Canyon Chamber of Commerce, 200 W. Railroad Ave., Williams, 928-635-4061; www.williamschamber.com

## WHAT TO SEE AND DO
**Grand Canyon Railway**
233 N. Grand Canyon Blvd.,
Williams,
800-843-8724;
www.thetrain.com
First operated by the Santa Fe Railroad in 1901 as an alternative to the stagecoach, this restored line carries passengers northward aboard authentically refurbished steam locomotives and coaches. Full-day round trips include a 3 1/2-hour layover at the canyon. Museum of railroad history at William's Depot.

## SPECIAL EVENTS
**Bill Williams Rendezvous Days**
Buckskinner's Park, 204 W. Railroad Ave.,
Williams, 928-635-1418;
www.williamschamber.com
Black powder shoot, carnival, street dances, pioneer arts and crafts. Memorial Day weekend.

**Labor Day Rodeo**
200 W. Railroad, Williams, 928-635-1418;
www.williamschamber.com
Professional rodeo and Western celebration. Labor Day weekend.

## HOTELS

### ★Best Western Inn Of Williams
2600 W. Rte. 66, Williams,
928-635-4400, 800-635-4445;
www.bestwestern.com
80 rooms. Complimentary full breakfast.
Pool. **$**

### ★★Grand Canyon Railway & Resort
233 N. Grand Canyon Blvd., Williams,
800-843-8724; www.thetrain.com
196 rooms. Restaurant, bar. **$**

### ★★Grand Canyon Railway Hotel
235 N. Grand Canyon Blvd., Williams,
928-635-4010, 800-843-8724;
www.thetrain.com
297 rooms. Restaurant, bar. **$**

### ★★Holiday Inn
950 N. Grand Canyon Blvd., Williams,
928-635-4114, 888-465-4329;
www.holiday-inn.com
120 rooms. Restaurant, bar. Pets accepted.
Pool. **$**

## RESTAURANTS

### ★Rod's Steak House
301 E. Rte. 66, Williams, 928-635-2671;
www.rods-steakhouse.com
Steak menu. Lunch, dinner. Closed Sunday;
also first two weeks of January. Bar. Children's menu. Casual attire. Reservations
recommended. **$$**

# WINDOW ROCK

This is the headquarters of the Navajo Nation. The 88-member tribal council, democratically elected, meets in an octagonal council building; tribal officials conduct tribal business from Window Rock. Behind the town is a natural bridge that looks like a window. It is in the midst of a colorful group of sandstone formations called "the Window Rock."

Information: Navajoland Tourism Department, Window Rock, 928-810-8501;
discovernavajo.com

**ARIZONA**

★
★
★
★

## WHAT TO SEE AND DO
### Canyon de Chelly National Monument
Hwy. 191, Window Rock, 928-674-5500;
www.nps.gov/cach
The smooth red sandstone walls of the canyon extend straight up as much as 1,000 feet from the nearly flat sand bottom. When William of Normandy defeated the English at the Battle of Hastings in 1066, the Pueblo had already built apartment houses in these walls. Many ruins are still here. The Navajo came long after the original tenants had abandoned these structures. In 1864, Kit Carson's men drove nearly all the Navajo out of the area, marching them on foot 300 miles to the Bosque Redondo in eastern New Mexico. Since 1868, Navajo have returned to farming, cultivating the orchards and grazing their sheep in the canyon. In 1931, Canyon de Chelly and its tributaries, Canyon del Muerto and Monument Canyon, were designated a national monument. There are more than 60 major ruins—some dating from circa A.D. 300—in these canyons. White House, Antelope House and Mummy Cave are among the most picturesque. Most ruins are inaccessible but can be seen from either the canyon bottom or from the road along the top of the precipitous walls. Two spectacular, 16-mile rim drives can be made by car in any season. Lookout points—sometimes a short distance from the road—are clearly marked. The only self-guided trail (2 1/2 miles round-trip) leads to the canyon floor and White House ruin from White House Overlook. Other hikes can be made only with a National Park Service permit and an authorized Navajo guide. Only four-wheel drive vehicles are allowed in the canyons—and each vehicle must be accompanied by an authorized Navajo guide and requires a National Park Service permit obtainable from a ranger at the visitor center. The visitor center has an archaeological museum and restrooms. Daily.

### Guided tours of Navajoland

Window Rock, 928-674-5500

Various organizations and individuals offer walking and driving tours of the area. Fees and tours vary; phone for information.

### Navajo Nation Museum

Hwy. 64 and Loup Rd., Window Rock, 928-871-7941

Established in 1961 to preserve Navajo history, art, culture and natural history; permanent and temporary exhibits. Literature and Navajo information available. Monday-Tuesday, Thursday-Friday 8 a.m.-5 p.m., Wednesday 8 a.m.-8 p.m., Saturday 9 a.m.-5 p.m.; closed on tribal and other holidays.

### Navajo Nation Zoological and Botanical Park

Tse Bonito Tribal Park, Window Rock. 928-871-6573; www.explorenavajo.com

Features a representative collection of animals and plants of historical or cultural importance to the Navajo people. Daily 8 a.m.-5 p.m.

### St. Michael's

Hwy. 264, Window Rock, 928-871-4171

This Catholic mission, established in 1898, has done much for the education and health of the tribe. The original mission building now serves as a museum depicting the history of the area. Memorial Day-Labor Day, Monday-Friday 9 a.m.-5 p.m.

## SPECIAL EVENTS

### Navajo Nation Fair

Navajo Nation Fairgrounds, Hwy. 264, Window Rock, 928-871-6478; www.navajonationfair.com

Dances, ceremonials, rodeo, arts and crafts, educational and commercial exhibits, food, traditional events. Week after Labor Day.

### Powwow and PRCA Rodeo

Navajo Nations Fairgrounds, Hwy. 264, Window Rock, 928-871-6478; www.navajonationfair.com

Rodeo, carnival, fireworks, and entertainment. July 4.

# WINSLOW

A railroad town, Winslow is also a trade center and convenient stopping point in the midst of a colorful and intriguing area; a miniature painted desert lies to the northeast. The Apache-Sitgreaves National Forests, with the world's largest stand of ponderosa pine, lie about 25 miles to the south.

Information: Chamber of Commerce, 101 E. Second St., Winslow, 928-289-2434; www.winslowarizona.org

## WHAT TO SEE AND DO

### Homolovi Ruins State Park

HCR 63, Winslow, 928-289-4106; www.pr.state.az.us/parks/parkhtml/homolovi.html

This park contains six major Anasazi ruins dating from A.D. 1250-1450. The Arizona State Museum conducts occasional excavations in June and July. The park also has trails, a visitor center and interpretive programs. Daily.

### Meteor Crater

Winslow, 20 miles west on I-40, then five miles south on Meteor Crater Rd., 928-289-5898, 800-289-5898; www.meteorcrater.com

Crater is one mile from rim to rim and 560 feet deep. The world's best-preserved meteorite crater was used as a training site for astronauts. Museum, lecture; Astronaut Wall of Fame; telescope on highest point of the crater's rim offers excellent view of surrounding area. Memorial Day-Labor Day: 7 a.m.-7 p.m.; rest of year: 8 a.m.-5 p.m.

### Old Trails Museum

212 N. Kinsley Ave., Winslow, 928-289-5861

Operated by the Navajo County Historical Society; exhibits and displays of local history, Native American artifacts and early Americana. March-October: Tuesday-Saturday 1-5 p.m.; rest of year: Tuesday, Thursday-Saturday.

★
★
★
★
★

# YUMA

The Yuma Crossing, where the Colorado River narrows between the Yuma Territorial Prison and Fort Yuma (one of Arizona's oldest military posts), was made a historic landmark in recognition of its long service as a river crossing. If the scenery looks familiar, it may be because movie producers have used the dunes and desert for location shots. A Marine Corps Air Station and an army proving ground are adjacent to the town.

Information: Convention & Visitors Bureau, 377 Main St., Yuma, 800-293-0071; www.visityuma.com

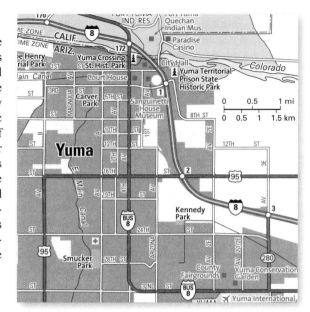

## WHAT TO SEE AND DO

### Arizona Historical Society Sanguinetti House

240 Madison Ave., Yuma, 928-782-1841; www.arizonahistoricalsociety.org

This former home of E. F. Sanguinetti, pioneer merchant, is now a division of the Arizona Historical Society, where you can see artifacts from the Arizona Territory, including documents, photographs, furniture and clothing. Gardens and exotic birds surround museum. Historical library open by appointment. Tuesday-Saturday 10 a.m.-4 p.m.

### Fort Yuma-Quechan Museum

350 Picacho Rd., Yuma, 928-572-0661

Part of one of the oldest military posts (1855) associated with the Arizona Territory. Museum houses tribal relics of southwestern Colorado River Yuman groups. Daily 8 a.m.-noon, 1-5p.m.

### Imperial National Wildlife Refuge

100 Red Cloud Mine Rd., Yuma, 928-783-3371; www.southwest.fws.gov/refuges/arizona/imperial.html

Bird watching; photography. Fishing, hunting, hiking.

### Yuma River Tours

1920 Arizona Ave., Yuma, 928-783-4400; www.yumarivertours.com

Narrated historical tours on the Colorado River; half- and full-day trips. Sunset dinner cruises. Also jeep tours to sand dunes. Monday-Friday.

### Yuma Territorial Prison State Historic Park

1 Prison Hill Rd., Yuma, 928-783-4771; www.pr.state.az.us/Parks/parkhtml/yuma.html

Remains of 1876 prison; original cellblocks. Southwest artifacts and prison relics. Daily 8 a.m.-5 p.m.

### Yuma Valley Railway

980 S. Palm Ave., Yuma, 928-783-3456

Tracks run 12 miles through fields along the Colorado River levee and Morelos Dam. Two-hour trips; dinner trips. November-March, Saturday-Sunday; April-May, October, Saturday only; June by appointment only; closed July-September.

## SPECIAL EVENTS

### Midnight at the Oasis Festival
The Ray Kroc Complex,
Desert Sun Stadium,
3500 S. Ave. A, Yuma;
www.caballeros.org/midnight.html
This annual event features classic cars and concerts. First full weekend in March.

### Yuma County Fair
2520 E. 32nd St., Yuma, 928-726-4420;
www.yumafair.com
Features carnival rides, live entertainment, food booths and a variety of exhibits. Five days in early April.

## HOTELS

### ★★Quality Inn
711 E. 32nd St., Yuma,
928-726-4721, 877-424-6423;
www.qualityinn.com

80 rooms. Complimentary full breakfast. Restaurant, bar. Pets accepted. Pool. **$**

### ★★Shilo Inn
1550 S. Castle Dome Ave., Yuma,
928-782-9511, 800-222-2244;
www.shiloinns.com
134 rooms. Complimentary full breakfast. Restaurant, bar. Airport transportation available. Pets accepted. Pool. **$**

## RESTAURANTS

### ★Hunter Steakhouse
2355 S. Fourth Ave., Yuma, 928-782-3637
Steak menu. Lunch, dinner. Bar. Children's menu. Casual attire. **$$**

### ★The Crossing
2690 S. Fourth Ave., Yuma, 928-726-5551
American menu. Lunch, dinner. Children's menu. Casual attire. Outdoor seating. **$$**

ARIZONA

# COLORADO

COLORADO'S TERRAIN IS DIVERSE AND SPECTACULARLY BEAUTIFUL—AND ATTRACTS THOSE who want to venture outdoors. Throughout the state there are deep gorges, rainbow-colored canyons, beautiful landmass variations carved by ancient glaciers and erosion, grassy plains and breathtaking alpine mountains. Colorado is the highest state in the Union, with an average elevation of 6,800 feet. It has 53 peaks above 14,000 feet.

Whether you're visiting one of Colorado's booming big cities—Denver, Boulder, Colorado Springs—or heading for the glitz of Vail or Aspen, Colorado beckons people to spend more time outdoors. Hit the slopes, take a river rafting trip or drive up to the famous Pikes Peak. In between, take a trip back in time by visiting historic homes, railroad depots and ghost towns. Colorado has a rich history. When gold was discovered near present-day Denver in 1858, an avalanche of settlers poured into the state. Then, when silver was discovered soon afterward, a new flood came. Mining camps—usually crude tent cities on the rugged slopes of the Rockies—contributed to Colorado's colorful, robust history. Some of these mines still operate, but most of the early mining camps are ghost towns today.

**Information: www.colorado.com**

 **SPOTLIGHT**

★ Denver lays claim to the invention of the cheeseburger. The trademark for the name cheeseburger was awarded to Louis Ballast in 1935.

**80**

## ALAMOSA

The settlers who came to the center of the vast San Luis Valley were pleased to find a protected area on the Rio Grande shaded by cottonwood trees, so they named their new home Alamosa, Spanish for "cottonwood." The little town quickly became a rail, agricultural, mining and educational center.

**Information: Alamosa County Chamber of Commerce, 300 Chamber Dr., Alamosa, 719-589-3681, 800-258-7597; www.alamosa.org**

### WHAT TO SEE AND DO

**Cole Park**

425 Fourth St., Alamosa, 719-589-3681
See Old Denver and Rio Grande Western narrow-gauge trains on display. Chamber of Commerce located in old train station. Tennis, bicycle trails, picnicking, playgrounds.

**Cumbres & Toltec Scenic Railroad, *Colorado Limited***

500 S. Terrace Ave., Antonito,
719-376-5483 , 888-286-2737;
www.cumbrestoltec.com

Take a round-trip excursion to Osier on a 1880s narrow-gauge steam railroad. The route passes through backwoods country and mountain scenery, including the Phantom Canyon and the Toltec Gorge. Warm clothing is advised due to sudden weather changes. Memorial Day-mid-October, daily. Also trips to Chama, New Mexico, via the *New Mexico Express* with van return. Reservations advised.

### Fort Garland Museum
29477 Hwy. 159, Fort Garland,
719-379-3512;
www.coloradohistory.org/hist_sites/ft_
Garland/ft_garland.htm
Army post (1858-1883) where Kit Carson held his last command. Restored officers' quarters; collection of Hispanic folk art. April-October: daily 9 a.m.-5 p.m.; rest of year: Monday, Thursday-Sunday 8 a.m.-4 p.m.

### SPECIAL EVENTS
**Early Iron Festival**
Cole Park, 425 Fourth St., Alamosa,
719-589-9170, 888-589-9170;
www.earlyironclub.com
This annual auto show attracts lovers of antique cars and hot rods. Labor Day weekend.

**Sunshine Festival**
Cole Park, 425 Fifth St., Alamosa,
719-589-3681
Arts, crafts, food booths, bands, horse rides, parade, pancake breakfast, contests. First full weekend in June.

### HOTELS
**★★Best Western Alamosa Inn**
2005 Main St., Alamosa,
719-589-2567, 800-459-5123;
www.bestwestern.com/alamosainn
53 rooms. Complimentary continental breakfast. Restaurant, bar. Airport transportation available. Pets accepted. Pool. **$**

**★★Inn of the Rio Grande**
333 Santa Fe Ave., Alamosa,
719-589-5833, 800-669-1658;
www.innoftherio.com
125 rooms. Restaurant, bar. Airport transportation available. Pets accepted. **$**

### RESTAURANTS
**★True Grits Steakhouse**
100 Santa Fe Ave., Alamosa,
719-589-9954
Steak menu. Lunch, dinner. Bar. Children's menu. Casual attire. **$$**

★
★
★
★
★

# ASPEN
The first settlers came here in 1878 in pursuit of silver and named the town for the abundance of aspen trees in the area. They enjoyed prosperity until the silver market crashed in 1893. By World War I, most of the local mining operations had gone bust. Aspen was practically a ghost town for decades—until 1946, when developer Walter Paepcke founded the Aspen Skiing Company with the vision of a cerebral, arts-oriented community. In 1950, Aspen hosted the Alpine Skiing World Championship, and the rest is history. Today, Aspen is home to some of the most expensive real estate in the world and draws in the rich and famous with immaculate ski slopes, spectacular shopping and fine dining.
Information: Aspen Chamber Resort Association, 425 Rio Grande Place, Aspen, 970-925-1940, 800-670-0792; www.aspenchamber.org

### WHAT TO SEE AND DO
**Ashcroft Ghost Town**
Castle Creek Rd., Aspen, 970-925-3721;
www.aspenhistory.org/ac.html
This partially restored ghost town and mining camp features 1880s buildings and a hotel. Guided tours mid-June-early September: daily 11 a.m., 1 p.m. and 3 p.m. Self-guided tours available daily.

**Aspen Highlands**
76 Boomerang Rd., Aspen,
970-925-1220, 800-525-6200;
www.aspensnowmass/highlands
Three quads, two triple chairlifts; patrol, school, rentals, snowmaking; five restaurants, bar. One hundred twenty-five runs; longest run 3 1/2 miles; vertical drop 3,635 feet. Snowboarding. Shuttle bus service to and from Aspen. Half-day rates. Mid-December-early April, daily.

## Aspen Mountain

601 E. Dean, Aspen,
970-925-1220, 800-525-6200;
www.aspensnowmass.com/aspenmountain
Three quad, four double chairlifts; gondola; patrol, school, snowmaking; restaurants, bar. Seventy-six runs; longest run 3 miles; vertical drop 3,267 feet. Mid-November-mid-April, daily. Shuttle bus service to Buttermilk, Aspen Highlands and Snowmass.

## Blazing Adventures

407 E. Hyman Ave., Aspen,
970-923-4544, 800-282-7238;
www.blazingadventures.com
Half-day, full-day and overnight river rafting trips on the Arkansas, Roaring Fork, Colorado and Gunnison rivers. Trips range from scenic floats for beginners to exciting runs for experienced rafters. Whitewater rafting. May-October; reservations required. Transportation to site. Bicycle, jeep and hiking tours are also available.

## Buttermilk Mountain

806 W. Hallam, Aspen,
970-925-1220, 800-525-6200;
www.aspensnowmass.com/buttermilk
Two quad, three double chairlifts, surface lift; patrol, school, rentals, snowmaking; cafeteria, restaurants, bar, nursery. Forty-four runs; longest run three miles; vertical drop 2,030 feet. Snowboarding. December-early April: daily 9 a.m.-3:30 p.m. Shuttle bus service from Ajax and Snowmass.

## HeritageAspen

620 W. Bleeker St., Aspen,
970-925-3721, 800-925-3721;
www.aspenhistory.org
Learn all about Aspen's history. Early June-September and mid-December-mid-April: Tuesday-Friday; rest of year: by appointment.

## Independence Pass

Aspen, Hwy. 82 from Hwy. 24;
www.independence-pass.com
Highway 82 through Independence Pass is a spectacular visual treat, not to mention an adrenaline rush—if you're afraid of heights,

opt for another route. The winding road between Highway 24 and Aspen is among the nation's highest, reaching 12,095 feet at its rocky summit—and offers beautiful vistas of Colorado's majestic forests and snow-covered peaks at every turn. Stop at the top for the views and a short trail hike. The pass is closed between November and May.

## SPECIAL EVENTS

### Aspen Music Festival

2 Music School Rd., Aspen, 970-925-3254;
www.aspenmusicfestival.com
Symphonies, chamber music concerts, opera and jazz. June-August.

### Aspen Theater in the Park

110 E. Hallam, Aspen, 970-925-9313;
www.theatreaspen.org
Performances nightly and afternoons. June-August.

### Winterskol Carnival

Aspen, 800-670-0792
Also known as the Festival of Snow, this annual four-day event features a parade, torchlight ski procession, contests and more. Mid-January.

## HOTELS

### ★★★Aspen Meadows

845 Meadows Rd., Aspen,
970-925-4240, 800-452-4240;
www.aspenmeadowsresort.dolce.com
This 40-acre mountain retreat with its famous Bauhaus design is made of up six buildings, and has hosted leaders from around the world since 1949 thanks to its state-of-the art conference facilities. The spacious guest suites include study areas, wet bars and floor-to-ceiling windows with views of the mountains or Roaring Fork River.
98 rooms. Restaurant. Airport transportation available. Pets accepted. Pool. Tennis. Business center. $$$

### ★Aspen Mountain Lodge

311 W. Main St., Aspen,
970-925-7650, 800-362-7736;
www.aspenmountainlodge.com

38 rooms. Closed late April-late May. Complimentary continental breakfast. Pets accepted. Pool. **$$**

### ★Hotel Aspen
**110 W. Main St., Aspen,**
**970-925-3441, 800-527-7369;**
**www.hotelaspen.com**
45 rooms. Complimentary continental breakfast. High-speed Internet access, wireless Internet access. Pets accepted. Pool. Business Center. **$$**

### ★★★Hotel Jerome
**330 E. Main St., Aspen,**
**970-920-1000, 800-412-7625;**
**www.hoteljerome.com**
This downtown hotel was built in 1889 by Jerome B. Wheeler, co-owner of Macy's Department Store, and was one of the first buildings west of the Mississippi River to be fully lit by electricity. The boutique-style rooms here are magnificent, reflecting the hotel's Victorian heritage with carved armoires and beautiful beds. The service is superb: the ski concierge will take care of your every need, and guests are driven to the slopes in luxury SUVs. You also get access to the Aspen Club and Spa, a 77,000-square-foot exercise facility and spa. The dashing J Bar is still one of the hottest places in town.
92 rooms. High-speed Internet access. Two restaurants, two bars. Airport transportation available. Pets accepted. Fitness center. Pool. Business center. **$$$$**

### ★★★Hotel Lenado
**200 S. Aspen St., Aspen,**
**970-925-6246, 800-321-3457;**
**www.hotellenado.com**
Located in the heart of Aspen, this small inn is a comfortable year-round retreat. Four-poster beds with down comforters adorn each room. You'll also find Bose stereos and plush terry robes. Enjoy a gourmet breakfast and complimentary hors d'oeuvres and hot cider (or lemonade in the summer) in the afternoon. There's also a rooftop pool, hot tub and heated boot lockers.

19 rooms. Complimentary full breakfast. Bar. Whirlpool. Pets accepted. **$$$$**

### ★★★★★The Little Nell
**675 E. Durant Ave., Aspen, 970-920-4600;**
**www.thelittlenell.com**
Tucked away at the base of a mountain, the Little Nell provides a perfect location either to hit the slopes or roam the streets in search of Aspen's latest fashions. The rooms and suites are heavenly cocoons with fireplaces, overstuffed furniture and luxurious bathrooms. Some suites feature vaulted ceilings showcasing glorious mountainside views, while others overlook the charming former mining town. Enjoy the well-equipped fitness and outdoor pool and Jacuzzi. Montagna restaurant is one of the most popular spots in town with its inventive reinterpretation of American cuisine.
92 rooms. Closed late April-mid-May. High-speed Internet access. Three restaurants, two bars. Airport transportation available. Pets accepted. Pool. Business center. **$$$$**

### ★Molly Gibson Lodge
**101 W. Main St., Aspen,**
**970-925-3434, 888-271-2304;**
**www.mollygibson.com**
58 rooms. Complimentary continental breakfast. Pool. **$$**

### ★★★Sky Hotel
**709 E. Durant Ave., Aspen,**
**970-925-6760, 800-882-2582;**
**www.theskyhotel.com**
This sleek hotel is the place to stay for those who want to see and be seen. After a day on the slopes—there's ski-in access from the base of Aspen Mountain—hit the "Altitude Adjustment" cocktail reception in the lobby bar. Rooms feature white quilted headboards, faux fur throws, l'Occitane bath products, iHome clock radios and Nintendo. Complimentary morning coffee and Wi-Fi access throughout the hotel are also nice perks.

**83**

**COLORADO**

90 rooms. Restaurant, bar. Airport transportation available. Pets accepted. Pool. **$$$**

### ★★★★The St. Regis Aspen
315 E. Dean St., Aspen,
970-920-3300, 888-454-9005;
www.stregis.com/aspen

Located at the base of Aspen Mountain between the gondola and lift, this hotel's upscale Western atmosphere is the perfect respite from skiing, shopping and warm weather activities such as fly-fishing and white water rafting. The outdoor pool and accompanying lounge are ideal for whiling away warm afternoons, or you can relax in the lavish spa. Rooms are richly decorated in muted colors with bursts of color and oversized leather furniture. (Expect complimentary water bottle service and a humidifier at turndown.) The Club Floor offers its own concierge and five complimentary meals throughout the day. Olives Aspen serves Mediterranean-inspired cuisine from renowned chef Todd English, and Whiskey Rocks is a popular gathering place.
253 rooms. Closed late October-mid-November. High-speed Internet access. Restaurant, two bars. Airport transportation available. **$$$$**

## SPECIALTY LODGINGS

### Hearthstone House
134 E. Hyman Ave., Aspen,
970-925-7632, 888-925-7632;
www.hearthstonehouse.com
15 rooms. **$$**

### The Independence Square
404 S. Galena, Aspen,
970-920-2313, 800-633-0336;
www.indysquare.com
28 rooms. **$$**

### Little Red Ski Haus
118 E. Cooper Ave., Aspen,
970-925-3333, 866-630-6119;
www.littleredskihaus.com
13 rooms. Complimentary full breakfast. **$$**

## RESTAURANTS

### ★Boogie's Diner
534 E. Cooper Ave., Aspen, 970-925-6610
American menu. Lunch, dinner. Closed mid-April-mid-June. Bar. Children's menu. Casual attire. **$$**

### ★★Cantina
411 E. Main St., Aspen, 970-925-3663
Mexican menu. Lunch, dinner. Bar. Children's menu. Casual attire. Outdoor seating. **$$**

### ★★★Jimmy's An American Restaurant
205 S. Mill St., Aspen, 970-925-6020;
www.jimmysaspen.com
Known for both the lively bar and seriously good food, such as the dry-aged rib eye on the bone, Chesapeake Bay crab cakes and center cut ahi tuna with herbed rice. The chocolate volcano cake is also a favorite.
American menu. Dinner. Bar. Children's menu. Casual attire. Outdoor seating. **$$$**

### ★★L'Hostaria
620 E. Hyman Ave., Aspen, 970-925-9022;
www.hostaria.com
Italian menu. Dinner. Closed mid-April-mid-May. Bar. Children's menu. Casual attire. Reservations recommended. Outdoor seating. **$$**

### ★★La Cocina
308 E. Hopkins, Aspen, 970-925-9714
Mexican menu. Dinner. Closed mid-April-mid-June. Bar. Children's menu. Outdoor seating. **$**

### ★★★Matsuhisa
303 E. Main St., Aspen, 970-544-6628;
www.nobumatsuhisa.com
Renowned chef Nobu Matsuhisa, who has built a mini-empire of restaurants from New York to L.A., gives Aspen a taste of his outstanding heartfelt Japanese cuisine in this sleek restaurant located 9,000 feet above sea level. The service is polished and prompt, making for a superb experience.
Japanese menu. Dinner. Bar. Casual attire. **$$$$**

### ★★Mezzaluna
624 E. Cooper Ave., Aspen, 970-925-5882;
www.mezzalunaaspen.com
Italian menu. Lunch, dinner. Casual attire.
$$$

### ★★★★Montagna
675 E. Durant Ave., Aspen, 970-920-4600;
www.thelittlenell.com
Located in the Little Nell hotel, Montagna
is one of the top dining spots in Aspen.
With its buttery walls, iron chandeliers
and deep picture windows, the restaurant
has the feeling of a chic Swiss chalet. The
menu is outstanding (from the pasta with
wild boar to the lemon roasted chicken),
and the sommelier oversees a 15,000-bottle
wine cellar.
American menu. Dinner. Sunday brunch.
Closed late April-mid-May. Bar. Children's
menu. Casual attire. Valet parking. Outdoor
seating. $$$$

### ★★★Olives
315 E. Dean St., Aspen, 970-920-3300;
www.toddenglish.com
Olives, located in the St. Regis and under
the direction of star chef Todd English,
delivers American cuisine with strong
Mediterranean influences. The seasonal
menu incorporates local ingredients to
create such favorites as pan braised Prince
Edward Island mussels, brick-oven-fired
oyster flatbread, skillet-seared Rocky
Mountain trout and goat cheese gnocchi.
The warm dining room with pinewood
floors, antique furniture and Tuscan-
influenced exhibition kitchen strikes just
the right tone.
Mediterranean menu. Lunch, dinner. Chil-
dren's menu. $$$

### ★★Pacifica
307 S. Mill St., Aspen, 970-920-9775
American, seafood menu. Lunch, dinner.
Bar. Children's menu. Outdoor seating. $$

### ★★★Pinon's
105 S. Mill St., Aspen, 970-920-2021
This is one of the most sought-after
reservations in town. Hidden away on the
second floor of a shop in downtown Aspen,
the contemporary restaurant is decorated
in a tropical theme and the atmosphere is
upbeat and festive. The service is warm
and the innovative, seasonal menu delights
diners.
American menu. Dinner. Closed early
April-early June, October-November. Bar.
Casual attire. $$$

### ★★★Pine Creek Cookhouse
3145 Second St., Aspen, 970-925-1044;
www.pinecreekcookhouse.com
Dine on warm duck breast salad and wild
game kabobs in this cozy cabin located in a
scenic valley in the Elk Mountains. Locals
like to cycle up Castle Creek road for lunch
at the cookhouse.
American menu. Lunch, dinner. Closed
mid-April-mid-June, mid-September-mid-
November. Bar. Casual attire. Reservations
recommended. Outdoor seating. $$$

### ★★★Syzygy
520 E. Hyman Ave., Aspen, 970-925-3700;
www.syzygyrestaurant.com
You might spot a celebrity or two dining
at this romantic spot that serves modern
American food. Signature dishes include
elk tenderloin and vintage beef. The din-
ing room upfront boasts spectacular views
of Aspen Mountain, while the jazz room in
the back features eight intimate booths.
American menu. Dinner. Closed mid-April-
May. Bar. Children's menu. Casual attire.
$$$

### ★★Takah Sushi
420 E. Hyman Ave., Aspen, 970-925-8588;
www.takahsushi.com
Japanese, sushi menu. Dinner. Closed mid-
April-May, late October-late November.
Bar. Casual attire. $$

### ★★The Tavern
685 E. Durant, Aspen, 970-920-9333
Italian menu. Lunch, dinner. Closed mid-
April-mid-May. Bar. Casual attire. Valet
parking. Outdoor seating. $$$

★

★

★

★

★

★★Wienerstube
633 E. Hyman Ave., Aspen, 970-925-3357
Continental menu. Breakfast, lunch. Closed
Monday. Bar. Children's menu. Outdoor
seating. $$

# AURORA

This Denver suburb, Colorado's third largest city, offers plenty of opportunities to bask in
Colorado's sunny days. Visitors will enjoy Aurora's golf courses, hiking and biking trails,
and Aurora Reservoir, where locals fish, swim and even scuba dive.
**Information: Aurora Chamber of Commerce, 562 Sable Blvd., Aurora, 303-344-1500;
www.aurorachamber.org**

## HOTELS
★★Doubletree Hotel
13696 E. Iliff Place, Aurora,
303-337-2800, 800-528-0444;
www.doubletree.com
248 rooms. Restaurant, bar. Pool. Business
center. $

★★Radisson Hotel Denver Southeast
3200 S. Parker Rd., Aurora,
303-695-1700, 888-201-1718;
www.radisson.com/auroraco
477 rooms. High-speed Internet access,
wireless Internet access. Restaurant, bar.
Airport transportation available. Pets
accepted. Business center. $

## RESTAURANT
★★La Cueva
9742 E. Colfax Ave., Aurora, 303-367-1422;
www.lacueva.net
Mexican menu. Lunch, dinner. Closed
Sunday. Bar. Children's menu. Casual
attire. $$

COLORADO

# AVON

Avon is the gateway to Beaver Creek Resort, located about two miles south of the town.
**Information: 970-748-4060; www.avon.org**

## WHAT TO SEE AND DO
**Beaver Creek/Arrowhead Resort**
137 Benchmark Rd.,
Avon, 970-949-5750;
www.beavercreek.com
Ten quad, two triple, three double chairlifts; patrol, rentals, snowmaking; cafeteria, restaurants, bar, nursery. Longest run
2 3/4 miles; vertical drop 4,040 ft. Late
November-mid-April, daily. Cross-country trails and rentals, November-April; ice
skating, snowmobiling, sleigh rides. Chairlift rides, July-August, daily; September,
weekends.

**Colorado River Runs**
Rancho del Rio, 28 miles northwest
off Hwy. 131; 800-826-1081, 970-653-4292;
www.coloradoriverruns.com

Raft down the Colorado River. Tours
depart from Rancho del Rio (just outside
State Bridge) and last two and a half to
three hours.

## HOTELS
★★★Beaver Creek Lodge
26 Avondale Lane, Beaver Creek,
970-845-9800, 800-525-7280;
www.beavercreeklodge.net
Located at the base of the Beaver Creek
Resort, this European-style boutique hotel
is close to the Centennial and Strawberry
Park chairlifts. Curl up on the leather couch
in front of the fireplace in your two-room
suite, which feature kitchenettes. Condos have state-of-the-art kitchens, laundry
facilities and master bedrooms with whirlpool baths.

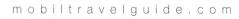

72 rooms, all suites. Closed mid-April-mid-May, two weeks in November. Wireless Internet access. Restaurant, bar. Ski in/ski out. **$$**

### ★★★The Inn at Beaver Creek
10 Elk Track Rd., Avon,
970-845-5990, 888-485-4317;
www.innatbeavercreek.com

It's all about location here: this ski-in/ski-out is just steps away from the Strawberry Park Express chairlift and is within walking distance of shops and eateries. The cozy guest rooms and suites have mountain lodge décor and offer an array of amenities, including high speed Internet access, plush robes and ski boot heaters. A complimentary hot breakfast buffet fuels you up for your day on the slopes.

42 rooms. Closed May & October. Complimentary full breakfast. High-speed Internet access. Bar. Ski in/ski out. **$$$**

### ★★★Park Hyatt Beaver Creek Resort and Spa
50 W. Thomas Place, Avon,
970-949-1234, 800-233-1234;
www.beavercreekhyatt.com

This resort is Western-country style at its best. Located at the base of the Gore Mountains, in the heart of the Beaver Creek Village, the ski-in/ski-out resort is a classic mountain lodge, with rooms featuring oversized furniture, comfy quilts and marble bathrooms. Enjoy great service—warmed boots await you in the morning, while chocolate chip cookies are available after your run. The Performance Skiing Program helps guests improve their skiing within days. Afterward, visit the newly redesigned spa that focuses on water-based treatments. In the summer, hit the links on the championship golf course. Five restaurants cover all the bases, with family dining places and intimate bars.

190 rooms. High-speed wireless Internet access. Restaurant, bar. Ski in/ski out. Golf. Tennis. Business center. **$$$**

### ★★★The Pines Lodge
141 Scott Hill Rd., Avon,
970-845-7900, 866-605-7625;
www.rockresorts.com

Nestled among towering pines, this resort offers views of slopes of Beaver Creek Resort. The spacious rooms include refrigerators, marble bathrooms and ski boot heaters. Enjoy the use of a complimentary Volvo during your stay—there's heated underground parking. Other freebies include Internet access and Starbucks coffee in the guest rooms. The friendly service makes this a great place to stay year-round. 60 rooms. High-speed Internet access. Restaurant, bar. **$$$**

### ★★★★The Ritz-Carlton Bachelor Gulch
130 Daybreak Ridge, Avon, 970-748-6200;
www.ritzcarlton.com

Rugged meets refined at this resort, located at the base of the mountain at Beaver Creek. From the 10-gallon hat-clad doorman who greets you to the rustic great room, this resort captures the spirit of the Old West while incorporating polished style. The rooms and suites are comfortable and stylish, with leather chairs, dark wood furniture and wood beamed ceilings. Iron chandeliers and twig furnishings adorn the public spaces. This family-friendly resort offers an abundance of activities, including fly fishing, a horseshoe pit, two children's play areas, an outdoor pool, golf and of course, skiing.

237 rooms. High-speed Internet access, wireless Internet access. Two restaurants, bar. Spa. Ski in/ski out. Pets accepted. Golf. Tennis. Business center. **$$$$**

## SPECIALTY LODGINGS
West Beaver Creek Lodge
220 W. Beaver Creek Blvd., Avon,
970-949-9073, 888-795-1061;
www.wbclodge.com

This cozy bed and breakfast is a budget-friendly alternative to the area's pricey resorts. All rooms feature rustic beamed

ceilings, and larger rooms and condos are available for families and groups. Door-to-door shuttles to Beaver Creek and Vail, on-site ski storage and discounted lift tickets and equipment rentals make this lodge a good choice for families and ski enthusiasts.
9 rooms. Complimentary full breakfast. **$$**

## SPAS

### ★★★Allegria Spa at Park Hyatt Beaver Creek
50 W. Thomas Place, Avon,
970-748-7500, 888-591-1234;
www.allegriaspa.com
Aged copper fountains and a crackling fireplace set the mood at this spa inside the Park Hyatt Beaver Creek, which offers a blend of local-flavored and Eastern-inspired therapies. A three-layer hydration facial is a lifesaver for parched, wind-burned skin. Three feng shui-inspired body treatments incorporate gentle exfoliation, a nourishing body wrap and a rewarding massage into one blissful experience. The body scrubs take their inspiration from the garden, with a wild berry and honey scrub, sweet orange and citrus salt glow, and ginger-peach polish rendering supple skin. The lavender, lemon and Japanese mint hot oil wraps are luxurious ways to hydrate skin. After a day on the slopes, treat your toes to the hot stone and mineral pedicure. **$$**

### ★★★★The Bachelor Gulch Spa at RitzCarlton
130 Daybreak Ridge, Avon,
970-343-1138, 800-576-5582;
www.ritzcarlton.com

The Bachelor Gulch Spa captures the essence of its alpine surroundings with polished rock, stout wood and flowing water in its interiors. The rock grotto with a lazy river hot tub is a defining feature, and the fitness rooms have majestic mountain views. The beauty of the outdoors also extends to treatments that utilize ingredients indigenous to the region. Alpine berries, Douglas fir and blue spruce sap are just some of the natural components of the exceptional signature treatments. After a rigorous day on the slopes, there are also plenty of massage options, from the Roaring Rapids, which uses hydrotherapy, or the Four-Hands, where two therapists work out knots. **$$**

## RESTAURANTS

### ★★★Grouse Mountain Grill
141 Scott Hill Rd., Avon, 970-949-0600;
www.grousemountaingrill.com
Located in the Pines Lodge, this elegant, European-style restaurant is the perfect choice for breakfast, lunch or a quiet dinner. The dark wood furnishings, nightly piano music and tables topped with crisp white linens create a warm and cozy atmosphere. The dinner menu focuses on rustic American dishes such as grilled Yukon River salmon with crab bread pudding and cracked mustard sauce, and pretzel-crusted pork chops with orange mustard sauce and balsamic syrup. The warm apple bread pudding is a perfect finish.
American menu. Dinner. Closed mid-April-mid-May. Bar. Casual attire. Valet parking. Outdoor seating. **$$$**

# BEAVER CREEK

Beaver Creek's slogan is "not exactly roughing it," a perfect description for this resort town. If you're searching for great skiing, fine dining and luxury in a pristine setting, head to Beaver Creek.
Information: www.beavercreek.snow.com

## HOTELS

### ★★★The Charter At Beaver Creek
120 Offerson Rd., Beaver Creek,
970-949-6660, 800-525-2139;
www.thecharter.com

This lodge features hotel rooms (as well as one- to five-bedroom condos) that offer guests fine hotel amenities like plush robes, Aveda bath products and high-speed Internet access. Each condo also includes a fully equipped kitchen, wood-burning fireplace, private bath and TV for each bedroom as well as maid service.

80 rooms. High-speed Internet access. Restaurant, bar. Spa. Ski in/ski out. **$$**

## RESTAURANTS

### ★★★Beano's Cabin
Beaver Creek, 970-949-9090
This log cabin restaurant is located amid the aspen trees on Beaver Creek Mountain. There are a few ways to get here: sleigh, horse-drawn wagon, van or horseback. Regardless of your mode of transport, Beano's is worth the trip. Enjoy a five-course meal (think: barbecue-glazed boneless veal baby back ribs and gingerbread crusted Colorado rack of lamb) by the cracking fire while listening to live music. American menu. Dinner. Closed early April-late June, late September-mid-December. Bar. Children's menu. Casual attire. Reservations recommended. **$$$$**

### ★★★★Mirabelle at Beaver Creek
55 Village Rd., Beaver Creek, 970-949-7728;
www.mirabelle1.com
Love is in the air at this charming 19th-century cottage in the mountains. Each of the spacious, bright rooms is cozy and warm, while the outdoor porch, lined with colorful potted flowers, is the perfect spot for outdoor dining. The food is just as magical. The kitchen offers sophisticated French food prepared with a modern sensibility. Signature dishes include Colorado lamb chops and roasted elk medallions with fruit compote. The house-made ice cream is the perfect finish.
French menu. Dinner. Closed Sunday; also May, November. Bar. Children's menu. Casual attire. Outdoor seating. **$$$**

### ★★★Splendido at the Chateau
17 Chateau Lane, Beaver Creek, 970-845-8808;
www.splendidobeavercreek.com
Locals come to this picturesque, chalet-style dining room tucked into the hills of Beaver Creek to celebrate special occasions and for the wonderful piano music offered nightly. The food is splendid, too. The menu changes nightly, but seasonal signatures have included dishes like sesame-crusted Atlantic salmon with coconut basmati rice and cilantro-lemongrass sauce, and grilled elk loin with braised elk osso bucco.
American menu. Dinner. Closed mid-April-mid-June, mid-October-mid-November. Bar. Children's menu. Reservations recommended. Valet parking. **$$$**

# BLACK HAWK
Established as a gold mining town, Black Hawk still attracts visitors in search of gold—at its local casino.
Information: www.cityofblackhawk.org

## WHAT TO SEE AND DO
### Black Hawk Casino by Hyatt
111 Richman St., Black Hawk, 303-567-1234
Once a boom-to-bust mining town, Black Hawk is experiencing a new rush of fortune-seekers thanks to the introduction of limited-stakes gambling in Colorado in 1990. Of the 25 casinos in Black Hawk and nearby Central City, the 55,000-square-foot Black Hawk by Hyatt is by far the largest and most elaborate. The casino boasts more than 1,000 slot machines, 22 poker and blackjack game tables, and three restaurants. Daily 8-2 a.m.

# BOULDER

Dubbed "the city between the mountains and reality," Boulder has a combination of great beauty and great weather that makes the area ideal for outdoor activity. Its location between the base of the Rocky Mountains and the head of a rich agricultural valley provides an ideal year-round climate, with 300 sunny days annually. More than 30,000 acres of open, unspoiled land and 200 miles of hiking and biking paths make the city an outdoor lover's paradise.

Home to several high-tech companies, the University of Colorado, the National Institute of Standards and Technology and the National Center for Atmospheric Research, Boulder is sophisticated and artsy with a wealth of cultural activities, from music to dance, art to one-of-a-kind shops.

Information Convention & Visitors Bureau, 2440 Pearl St., 303-442-2911, 800-444-0447; www.bouldercvb.com

## WHAT TO SEE AND DO

### Boulder Creek Path
Boulder, from 55th St. and Pearl Pkwy. to Boulder Canyon, 303-413-7200
This nature and exercise trail runs some 16 miles through the city and into the adjacent mountains, leading past a sculpture garden, restored steam locomotive and several parks. Daily.

### Boulder History Museum
Harbeck Bergheim House,
1206 Euclid Ave., Boulder, 303-449-3464;
www.boulderhistorymuseum.org
Learn about the history of Boulder from 1858 to the present. This museum includes 20,000 artifacts, 111,000 photographs and 486,000 documents. Permanent and rotating interpretive exhibits and educational programs. Tuesday-Friday 10 a.m.-5 p.m., Saturday-Sunday noon-4 p.m.

### Boulder Museum of Contemporary Art
1750 13th St., Boulder, 303-443-2122;
www.bmoca.org
See exhibits of contemporary and regional painting, sculpture, and other media, and changing exhibits with local, domestic and international artists. Check out the experimental performance series (Thursday). Also: lectures, workshops and special events. Tuesday-Friday 11 a.m.-5 p.m., Saturday 9 a.m.-4 p.m., Sunday noon-3 p.m.

### Boulder Reservoir
5565 N. 51 St., Boulder, 303-441-3468;
www.bouldercolorado.gov
Swimming beach, Memorial Day-Labor Day, daily; water-skiing, fishing. Boating daily; get a power boat permit at the main gate; boat rentals Memorial Day-Labor Day, daily.

### Celestial Seasonings Factory Tour
4600 Sleepytime Dr., Boulder,
303-581-1202;
www.celestialseasonings.com
This 45-minute tour takes visitors through beautiful gardens that produce the herbs and botanicals used in the teas (with a stop in the sinus-clearing Mint Room) and into the production area, where eight million tea bags are made every day. You can also check out the company's art gallery of original paintings from tea boxes and be among the first to sample some of the company's newest blends. Children must be over five to enter the factory. Hourly. Monday-Saturday 9 a.m.-5 p.m., Sunday 11 a.m.-5 p.m.

### Eldora Mountain Resort
2861 Eldora Ski Rd., Nederland,
303-440-8700; www.eldora.com
Two quad, two triple, four double chairlifts; four surface lifts; patrol, school, rentals, snowmaking; cafeteria, bar, nursery. Fifty-three runs; longest run three miles; vertical drop 1,400 feet. Cross-country skiing (27 miles). Mid-November-early April.

### Leanin' Tree Museum of Western Art
6055 Longbow Dr., Boulder,
303-530-1442, 800-777-8716;
www.leanintreemuseum.com

Check out the original works of art used in many of the greeting cards produced by Leanin' Tree, a major greeting card publisher. The museum also features the private collection of paintings and sculptures from Edward P. Trumble, the chairman and founder of Leanin' Tree Inc. Monday-Friday 8 a.m.-5 p.m., Saturday-Sunday 10 a.m. -5 p.m.

### Macky Auditorium Concert Hall
1Seventh St., and University Ave., Boulder, 303-492-8423;
www.colorado.edu/macky
This 2,047-seat auditorium hosts the Boulder Philharmonic Orchestra. Concerts during the academic year.

### National Center for Atmospheric Research
1850 Table Mesa Dr., Boulder, 303-497-1000; www.ncar.ucar.edu/ncar
Designed by I. M. Pei, the center includes exhibits on global warming, weather, the sun, aviation hazards and supercomputing. There's also a 400-acre nature preserve on-site. Guided tours. Visitor center Monday-Friday 8 a.m.-5 p.m.; Saturday-Sunday, holidays 9 a.m.-4 p.m.

### Pearl Street Mall
900 to 1500 Pearl St., Boulder, 303-449-3774
Open year-round, this retail and restaurant district is particularly appealing in the summer with its brick walkways, Victorian storefronts, lush landscaping and parade of colorful personalities. Offering four blocks of mostly upscale restaurants, galleries, bars, and boutiques, the mall beckons visitors to conclude a day of shopping with a meal at one of its many European-style cafes while taking in the impromptu performances of street musicians, jugglers, artists and mimes.

### Sommers-Bausch Observatory
2475 Kittridge Loop Dr., Boulder, 303-492-6732;
www.lyra.colorado.edu/sbo

Come here for an evening of stargazing. Weather permitting, school year; closed school holidays. Reservations required on Fridays.

### University of Colorado
914 Broadway St., Boulder, 303-492-1411; www.colorado.edu
Established in 1876; 25,000 students. Tours of campus. Many of the buildings on this 786-acre campus feature distinctive native sandstone and red-tile.

### University of Colorado Museum
Henderson Building, 15th St. and Broadway St., Boulder, 303-492-6892;
www.cumuseum.colorado.edu
See relics and artifacts of early human life in the area, plus regional geological, zoological and botanical collections. Changing exhibits. Monday-Friday 9 a.m.-5 p.m., Saturday 9 a.m.-4 p.m., Sunday 10 a.m.-4 p.m.; closed school holidays.

### Vista Ridge Golf Club
2700 Vista Pkwy., Erie, 303-665-1723; www.vistaridgegc.com
This 18-hole Jay Morrish-designed course, occupying more than 200 acres, offers golfers a lot of space to test their skills. The course's gently rolling hills and views of the Rockies take the edge off even the worst shots, while generous fairways make up for ample water hazards.

## SPECIAL EVENTS
### Bolder Boulder 10K Race
5500 Centrd Ave., Boulder, 303-444-7223; www.bolderboulder.com
Join one of the largest road races in the world, with 45,000 runners and more than 100,000 spectators. Live music and entertainment along the route add to the enjoyment of this family-centered celebration. Races begin at 7 a.m., awards at 2:30 p.m.

### Boulder Bach Festival
University of Colorado, Boulder, Grusin Concert Hall, Boulder, 303-776-9666; www.boulderbachfest.org

COLORADO

Listen to the music of Johann Sebastian Bach. Late January.

### Colorado Music Festival
Chautauqua Auditorium, 900 Baseline Rd., Boulder, 303-449-1397;
www.coloradomusicfest.org
Classical music concerts featuring the CMF Chamber Orchestra. Eight weeks in June-August.

### Colorado Shakespeare Festival
University of Colorado,
Mary Rippon Outdoor Theatre, Boulder, 303-492-0554; www.coloradoshakes.org
See three Shakespeare plays in repertory. June-August.

### Kinetic Conveyance Sculpture Challenge
Boulder Reservoir, Boulder, 303-444-5600
People-powered sculpture race across land, mud and water. Early May.

## HOTELS

### ★★Courtyard Boulder
4710 Pearl East Circle, Boulder, 303-440-4700, 800-321-2211;
www.courtyard.com
149 rooms. High-speed Internet access. Restaurant. Airport transportation available. Pool. $

### ★Hampton Inn
912 W. Dillon Rd., Louisville, 303-666-7700, 800-426-7866;
www.stonebridgecompanies.com
80 rooms. Complimentary continental breakfast. Airport transportation available. $

### ★★★Hotel Boulderado
2115 13th St., Boulder, 303-442-4344, 800-433-4344;
www.boulderado.com
Boulder was a sleepy little town of 11,000 back in 1905, when the city's fathers decided they could move things along by providing the comfort of a first-class hotel. Back then, men worked 24 hours a day stoking the huge coal furnace to keep the hotel evenly heated, and rooms went for $1 per night. Today the hotel has been

restored to its original grandeur. You'll feel like you've stepped back in time when you enter the lobby with its stained-glass ceiling, cherry staircase, plush velvet furniture and swirling ceilings fans.
160 rooms. High-speed wireless Internet access. Two restaurants, bar. Airport transportation available. Business center. $$

### ★★★Marriott Boulder
2660 Canyon Blvd., Boulder, 303-440-8877, 888-238-2178;
www.marriott.com
This newly renovated hotel is located at the base on the Flatiron Mountains in downtown Boulder. Rooms feature free Internet and fitness kits. Opting for the Concierge level will get you access to two private rooftop terraces, and includes complimentary continental breakfast and evening appetizers. Take a dip in the outdoor pool or hit the spa. This hotel is non-smoking.
155 rooms. Restaurant, bar. $$

### ★Quality Inn & Suites
2020 Arapahoe Ave., Boulder, 303-449-7550, 888-449-7550;
www.qualityinnboulder.com
46 rooms. Pets accepted. $

### ★★★St. Julien Boulder's Hotel And Spa
900 Walnut St., Boulder, 720-406-9696, 877-303-0900;
www.stjulien.com
Relax at this luxurious yet casual hotel with a 10,000-square-foot spa and fitness center, two-lane infinity pool and outdoor terrace. The elegant rooms feature custom pillow-top beds with fluffy duvets and oversized slate bathrooms with separate showers. They also include complimentary high-speed Internet access, Direct TV and organic coffee. The martini bar, T-Zero, is an intimate spot for a drink.
201 rooms. Restaurant, bar. $$

## SPECIALTY LODGINGS
### Alps Boulder Canyon Inn
38619 Boulder Canyon Dr., Boulder, 303-444-5445, 800-414-2577;
www.alpsinn.com

**92**

COLORADO

A cross between a luxurious country inn and a cozy bed and breakfast, the Alps caters to those who want to be within 10 minutes of the city but feel a million miles away. Each of the 12 rooms has a wood-burning fireplace, sitting area and some have claw-foot tubs or double Jacuzzis.

12 rooms. Complimentary full breakfast. High-speed Internet access. **$$**

### Briar Rose Bed & Breakfast
2151 Arapahoe Ave., Boulder,
303-442-3007, 888-786-8440;
www.briarrosebb.com

This Victorian-style 1896 house offers cozy rooms with organic cotton sheets and natural bath products. There is also an extended-stay suite with a full kitchen that is rented by the week or the month. The afternoon tea tray, with herbal and black teas, iced tea, lemonade, cider and special short-bread cookies, is a treat. So is the organic breakfast.

10 rooms. Complimentary full breakfast. High-speed Internet access. Airport transportation available. **$**

# RESTAURANTS

### ★★Antica Roma Caffe
1308 Pearl St., Boulder, 303-449-1787;
www.anticaroma.com

Italian menu. Lunch, dinner. Bar. Children's menu. Outdoor seating. **$$**

### ★★★★Flagstaff House Restaurant
1138 Flagstaff Rd., Boulder, 303-442-4640;
www.flagstaffhouse.com

From its location on Flagstaff Mountain, this is easily one of the most amazing spots to watch the sunset. And the food here rivals the amazing setting. The upscale and inspired menu changes daily, with plates like beef wellington dressed up with black truffle sauce and Hawaiian ono with ginger, scallions and soft-shell crabs. The wine list is massive (the restaurant has a 20,000-bottle wine cellar), so enlist the assistance of the attentive sommelier for guidance. The restaurant is owned by the Monette family, which means that you'll be treated to refined

service and homegrown hospitality, making dining here a delight from start to finish. If you can, arrive early and have a seat at the stunning mahogany bar for a pre-dinner cocktail.

American menu. Dinner. Bar. Business casual attire. Reservations recommended. Valet parking. Outdoor seating. **$$$$**

### ★★★The Greenbriar Inn
8735 N. Foothills Hwy., Boulder,
303-440-7979, 800-253-1474;
www.greenbriarinn.com

Originally built in 1893, this Boulder landmark sits on 20 acres at the mouth of Left Hand Canyon. The atrium room has French doors that open up to south garden and lawn. The mouthwatering food includes blue crab crusted beef tournedos and maple cured duck breasts. A Champagne brunch is served on Saturday and Sunday.

American menu. Dinner, Sunday brunch. Closed Monday. Bar. Outdoor seating. **$$$**

### ★★★John's Restaurant
2328 Pearl St., Boulder, 303-444-5232;
www.johnsrestaurantboulder.com

You'll feel like you're stepping into someone's home when you enter this century-old cottage with lace curtains and white tablecloths. In the spring and summer, windows open to courtyards filled with bright flowers. On the menu, you'll find contemporary dishes from France, Italy, Spain and Scotland, with specialties like smoked Scottish salmon, filet mignon with Stilton and ale sauce, and Italian-style gelato.

International menu. Dinner. Closed Sunday-Monday. **$$$**

### ★★Laudisio
1710 29th St., Boulder, 303-442-1300;
www.laudisio.com

Italian menu. Lunch, dinner. Bar. Outdoor seating. **$$$**

### ★★The Mediterranean
1002 Walnut St., Boulder, 303-444-5335;
www.themedboulder.com

**COLORADO**

Mediterranean menu. Lunch, dinner. Closed holidays. Bar. Children's menu. Outdoor seating. **$$**

### ★★★Q's
2115 13th St., Boulder, 303-442-4880;
www.qsboulder.com

This welcoming, bistro-style restaurant in the Hotel Boulderado offers a spectacular selection of seafood, meat and game. The international wine collection is eclectic and includes small barrel and boutique selections as well as a proprietor's reserve list. The service is delightful and efficient, making dining a pleasure.

American menu. Breakfast, lunch, dinner, brunch. Bar. Children's menu. Casual attire. Valet parking. **$$$**

### ★★Rhumba
950 Pearl St., Boulder, 303-442-7771;
www.rhumbarestaurant.com

Caribbean menu. Lunch, dinner. Children's menu. **$$**

### ★Royal Peacock
5290 Arapahoe Ave., Boulder,
303-447-1409;
www.royalpeacocklounge.com

Indian menu. Lunch , dinner. Outdoor seating. **$$**

# BRECKENRIDGE

Born as a mining camp when gold was discovered along the Blue River in 1859, modern Breckenridge wears its rough-and-tumble past like a badge. With 350 historic structures, the town is the largest historic district in Colorado. The population peaked at near 10,000 in the 1880s but dwindled to less than 400 in 1960, the year before the town's ski resort opened. Breckenridge now sees more than one million skier-visits annually. Located on four interconnected mountains named Peaks 7, 8, 9 and 10, the ski terrain is revered by skiers but is especially popular with snowboarders. It's more affordable—and rowdier—than Aspen and Vail. During the summer months, outdoor enthusiasts love hiking, mountain biking, fly-fishing, white water rafting and horseback riding in surrounding area. The Jack Nicklaus designed Breckenridge Golf Club offers 27 holes of world-class championship play.

Information: Breckenridge Resort Chamber, 311 S. Ridge St., 970-453-2913, 888-251-2417; www.breckenridge.com

## WHAT TO SEE AND DO
★ **Breckenridge Ski Area**
Ski Hill Rd., Breckenridge,
★ 970-453-5000, 800-789-7669;
www.breckenridge.snow.com
★ Seven high-speed quad, triple, six double chairlifts; four surface lifts, eight carpet
★ lifts; school, rentals, snowmaking; four cafeterias, five restaurants on mountain, picnic
area; four nurseries (from two months old). One hundred twelve runs on three interconnected mountains; longest run 3 1/2 miles; vertical drop 3,398 feet. Ski mid-November-early May, daily. Cross-country skiing (23 kilometers), heliskiing, ice-skating, snowboarding and sleigh rides. Shuttle bus service. Multiday, half-day and off-season

rates. Chairlift and alpine slide operate in summer, mid-June-mid-September.

**Summit Historical Society walking tours**
111 N. Ridge St., Breckenridge,
970-453-9022;
www.summithistorical.org

Tour the historic district, which includes trips to abandoned mines. Late June-August: Tuesday-Saturday 10 a.m.

## SPECIAL EVENTS
**Backstage Theatre**
121 S. Ridge St., Breckenridge,
970-453-0199; www.backstagetheatre.org
Melodramas, musicals, comedies. July-Labor Day, mid-December-March.

### Breckenridge Music Festival
150 W. Adams, Breckenridge,
970-453-9142;
www.breckenridgemusicfestival.com
This eight-week summer celebration includes regular full orchestra performances by Breckenridge's own highly acclaimed National Repertory Orchestra. Performances are held at Riverwalk Center in the heart of downtown Breckenridge, an 800-seat, tented amphitheater opening in back to allow lawn seating for an additional 1,500-2,000 symphony lovers who come to picnic and enjoy music under the stars. Most concerts begin at 7:30 p.m. Late June-mid-August.

### International Snow Sculpture Championships
Breckenridge, 800-936-5573
Sixteen teams from around the world create works of art from 12-foot-tall, 20-ton blocks of artificial snow. Late January-early February.

### No Man's Land Day Celebration
Breckenridge, 970-453-6018
Breckenridge was mistakenly forgotten in historic treaties when Colorado joined the Union. It became part of Colorado and the United States at a later date. This celebration emphasizes Breckenridge life in the 1880s with a parade, dance and games. Second weekend in August.

### Ullr Fest & World Cup Freestyle
Breckenridge, 970-453-6018
Honors the Norse god of snow with parades, fireworks and a ski comPetsition. Seven days in late January.

## HOTELS

### ★★★Allaire Timbers Inn
9511 Hwy. 9, Breckenridge,
970-453-7530, 800-624-4904;
www.allairetimbers.com
This charming log cabin bed-and-breakfast at the south end of Main Street is made from local pine. The innkeepers welcome guests with hearty homemade breakfasts, afternoon snacks and warm

hospitality. Take the free shuttle from the inn to several chair lifts. After a day of activity, relax in the sunroom or retreat to the reading loft.
10 rooms. Children over 13 years only. Complimentary full breakfast. **$$**

### ★★★Beaver Run Resort And Conference Center
620 Village Rd., Breckenridge,
970-453-6000, 800-265-3560;
www.beaverrun.com
This large resort is popular with families in both winter and summer. The suites feature full kitchens and the largest ones sleep up to 10 people. The property includes eight hot tubs and indoor/outdoor pool, tennis courts, and a spa with facials by Dermalogica. There's also a ski school for the kids, as well as miniature golf and a video arcade.
567 rooms. Restaurant, bar. Ski in/ski out. Exercise. **$$**

### ★★★Great Divide Lodge
550 Village Rd., Breckenridge,
970-547-5550, 888-906-5698;
www.greatdividelodge.com
Located just 50 yards from the base of Peak 9 and two blocks from Main Street, this lodge is excellent for winter or summer vacationing. The large guest rooms come with a wet bar, Starbucks coffee, Nintendo and wireless Internet. Get around on the free hotel shuttle.
208 rooms. Restaurant, bar. Airport transportation available. Pool. **$$**

### ★★★Hunt Placer Inn
275 Ski Hill Rd., Breckenridge,
970-457-4777, 877-647-4777;
www.huntplacerinn.com
Individually designed rooms with mountain views and hearty, homemade breakfasts distinguish this Bavarian-style chalet located just blocks from Main Street. The inn offers ski in/ski out access.
Nine rooms. Children over 10 years only. Complimentary full breakfast. **$**

**COLORADO**

## SPECIALTY LODGINGS

**Bed & Breakfast on North Main St**
303 N. Main St., Breckenridge,
970-453-2975, 800-795-2975;
www.breckenridge-inn.com
Innkeepers Fred Kinat and Diane Jaynes welcome guests to one of the three historic inns that compose this bed and breakfast. The individually decorated rooms are pleasant and include high-speed wireless Internet, TVs and private balconies or patios.
12 rooms. Closed three weeks in May, last week in October, first two weeks in November. Complimentary full breakfast. Check-in by appointment. **$**

## RESTAURANTS

**★Breckenridge Brewery**
600 S. Main St., Breckenridge,
970-453-1550;
www.breckenridgebrewery.com
American menu. Lunch, dinner, late-night. Bar. Children's menu. Casual attire. Outdoor seating. **$$**

**★★Cafe Alpine**
106 E. Adams, Breckenridge,
970-453-8218; www.cafealpine.com
International/Fusion menu. Lunch, dinner. Closed late May. Bar. Children's menu. Casual attire. Reservations recommended. Outdoor seating. **$$$**

**★★Hearthstone Restaurant**
130 S. Ridge St., Breckenridge,
970-453-1148; www.stormrestaurants.com
American menu. Dinner. Bar. Children's menu. Casual attire. Reservations recommended. Outdoor seating. **$$$**

**★Horseshoe 2**
115 S. Main, Breckenridge, 970-453-7463

American menu. Breakfast, lunch, dinner. Closed mid-April-mid-May. Bar. Children's menu. Casual attire. Outdoor seating. **$$$**

**★★Mi Casa Mexican Cantina**
600 S. Park Ave., Breckenridge,
970-453-2071;
www.stormrestaurants.com
Mexican menu. Lunch, dinner. Bar. Children's menu. Casual attire. Outdoor seating. **$$**

**★★Salt Creek**
110 E. Lincoln Ave., Breckenridge,
970-453-4949
Steak menu. Breakfast, lunch, dinner. Closed May. Bar. Children's menu. Casual attire. Outdoor seating. **$$**

**★St. Bernard Inn**
103 S. Main St., Breckenridge,
970-453-2572
Italian menu. Lunch, dinner. Closed two weeks in May and October. Bar. Casual attire. Reservations recommended. Outdoor seating. **$$**

**★★Swan Mountain Inn**
16172 Hwy. 9, Breckenridge,
970-453-7903
American menu. Breakfast, dinner. Closed Monday-Tuesday. Bar. Children's menu. Casual attire. Reservations recommended. Outdoor seating. **$$**

**★★Top of the World**
112 Overlook Dr., Breckenridge,
970-453-9300, 800-736-1607;
www.thelodgeatbreck.com
American menu. Breakfast, dinner. Closed Monday-Tuesday; also May. Bar. Casual attire. Reservations recommended. **$$$**

# BROOMFIELD

Broomfield is midway between Denver and Boulder in what is referred to as the technology corridor. The area experienced tremendous growth in the 1990s, much of it focused on technology. The biggest employers include IBM and Sun Microsystems.
Information: www.broomfield.org

★
★
★
★
★

## WHAT TO SEE AND DO

### FlatIron Crossing

1 W. FlatIron Circle, Broomfield, 720-887-7467, 866-352-8476; www.flatironcrossing.com

This architecturally innovative, 1.5 million-square-foot retail and entertainment complex located between Denver and Boulder was designed to reflect the natural flatirons, canyons and prairies of its surroundings. The result is a one-of-a-kind visual and shopping experience, with more than 200 stores and numerous restaurants for both indoor and outdoor dining. Daily; closed Easter, December 25.

## HOTELS

### ★★★Omni Interlocken Resort

500 Interlocken Blvd., Broomfield, 303-438-6600, 888-444-6664; www.omnihotels.com

Set against the backdrop of the Rocky Mountains, this 300-acre resort has something for everyone. Golfers needing to brush up on their game head for the L.A.W.s Academy of Golf for its celebrated instruction before hitting the three nine-hole courses. There's a well-equipped fitness center and pool, and a full-service spa that offers a variety of treatments. The guest rooms are comfortable and elegant and include amenities like WebTV and high-speed Internet connections. Three restaurants run the gamut from traditional to pub style.

390 rooms. Three restaurants, bar. Spa. Airport transportation available. Pets accepted. **$$**

# BUENA VISTA

Lying at the eastern edge of the Collegiate Range and the central Colorado mountain region, Buena Vista is a natural point of departure for treks into the mountains. Within 20 miles you'll find four rivers, 12 peaks with elevations above 14,000 feet, and more than 500 mountain lakes and streams.

Information: Chamber of Commerce, 343 S. US 24, 719-395-6612; www.buenavistacolorado.org

## WHAT TO SEE AND DO

### Arkansas River Tours

126 S. Main St., Buena, Vista, 719-942-4362, 800-321-4352; www.arkansasrivertours.com

The upper Arkansas River in south central Colorado offers some of the most beautiful and challenging rafting experiences. With its long, placid stretches of scenic wilderness punctuated by plunges through dramatic whitewater canyons, it accommodates all levels of river-rafting thrill-seekers. Experienced rafters won't want to miss an adrenaline-pumping ride through the magnificent Royal George Canyon. Families will love a scenic float through the gently rolling Cottonwood Rapid. Arkansas River Tours is one of several rafting outfitters along Highway

50 offering a variety of outings, from 1/4-day trips to multiple-day high-adventure expeditions. Daily; weather permitting.

### Noah's Ark Whitewater Rafting Company

23910 Hwy. 285 S, Buena Vista, 719-395-2158; www.noahsark.com

Half-day to three-day trips on the Arkansas River. Mid-May-late August.

### Wilderness Aware

12600 Hwy. 24/285, Buena Vista, 719-395-2112, 800-462-7238; www.inaraft.com

Half-day to 10-day river rafting trips on the Arkansas, Colorado, Dolores, North Platte and Gunnison rivers. May-September.

**COLORADO**

## HOTELS

**★Best Western Vista Inn**
733 Hwy. 24 N., Buena Vista,
719-395-8009, 800-809-3495;
www.bestwestern.com
52 rooms. Three hot springs whirlpools.
Pets accepted. **$**

## RESTAURANTS

**★★Buffalo Bar & Grill**
710 Hwy. 24 N., Buena Vista,
719-395-6472

American menu. Dinner. Closed Sunday.
Bar. Children's menu. **$$**

**★Casa Del Sol**
333 Hwy. 24 N., Buena Vista,
719-395-8810
Mexican menu. Lunch, dinner. Closed late
May-Labor Day. Children's menu. Casual
attire. Outdoor seating. **$**

# BURLINGTON

On the eastern edge of Colorado, Burlington is a small town dedicated to preserving its part of the West's history.
Information: Chamber of Commerce, 415 15th St., Burlington, 719-346-8652; www.burlingtoncolo.com

## WHAT TO SEE AND DO

**Kit Carson County Carousel**
Fairgrounds, Colorado Ave. and 15th St.,
Burlington; www.burlingtoncolo.com
Built in 1905, this restored carousel houses
a 1912 Wurlitzer Monster Military Band
organ—and rides are only a quarter. Memorial Day-Labor Day: daily 1-8 p.m.

**Old Town**
420 S. 14th St., Burlington,
719-346-7382, 800-288-1334;
www.burlingtoncolo.com
This historical village includes 20 buildings
that reflect Colorado prairie heritage, plus
cancan shows, gunfights and melodramas

(summer). A two-day hoedown takes place
on Labor Day. Tours. Memorial Day-Labor
Day: Monday-Saturday 9 a.m.-5 p.m.,
Sunday noon-5 p.m.

## SPECIAL EVENTS

**Kit Carson County Fair & Rodeo**
Fairgrounds, Burlington, 719-346-0111
Early August.

## HOTELS

**★Best Value Inn-Burlington**
2100 Fay St., Burlington, 719-346-5627;
www.bestvalueinn.com
39 rooms. Pool. **$**

# CANON CITY

Lieutenant Zebulon Pike, in 1807, was one of the first white men to camp on this site, which was long a favored spot of the Ute Indians. Canon City is located at the mouth of the Royal Gorge, ringed by mountains.
Information: Chamber of Commerce, 403 Royal Gorge Blvd., Canon City, 719-275-2331, 800-876-7922; www.canoncitychamber.com

## WHAT TO SEE AND DO

**Buckskin Joe Frontier Town & Railway**
1193 Fremont County Rd., Canon City,
719-275-5149; www.buckskinjoes.com

This Old West theme park includes an old
Western town with 30 authentic buildings.
Daily gunfights, horse-drawn trolley ride,
magic shows and entertainment, plus a

30-minute train ride to the rim of Royal Gorge Railway. March-October: daily 8 a.m.-7 p.m., November-December: weekends. Park May-September: daily 9 a.m.-6:30 p.m.

### Canon City Municipal Museum
612 Royal Gorge Blvd., Canon City, 719-276-5279
The complex includes Rudd Cabin, a pioneer log cabin constructed in 1860, and Stone House, built in 1881. Galleries display minerals and rocks, artifacts from the settlement of the Fremont County region and guns. Early May-Labor Day, Tuesday-Sunday; rest of year, Tuesday-Saturday.

### Dinosaur Depot Museum
330 Royal Gorge Blvd., Canon City, 719-269-7150, 800-987-6379; www.dinosaurdepot.com
Check out an entire Stegosaurus skeleton that was discovered less than 10 miles away. Open daily 9 a.m.-6 p.m. summer; Wednesday-Sunday 10 a.m.-5 p.m. winter.

### Fremont Center for the Arts
505 Macon Ave., Canon City, 719-275-2790; www.fremontarts.org
This community art center features visual art exhibits and cultural programs. Tuesday-Saturday. 10 a.m.-4 p.m.

### Garden Park Fossil Area
3170 E. Main St., Canon City, 719-269-7150; www.dinosaurdepot.com/exhibits.htm
Fossils of well-known species of large dinosaurs have been discovered at this site over the last 120 years, many of which are on exhibit at museums around the country, including the Smithsonian. Fossils of dinosaurs, dinosaur eggs and dinosaur tracks have also been discovered in the Garden Park Fossil Area, along with fossils of rare plants. Daily.

### Royal Gorge
4218 County Rd., Canon City, 719-275-7507, 888-333-5597; www.royalgorgebridge.com

This magnificent canyon has cliffs rising more than 1,000 feet above the Arkansas River. The Royal Gorge Suspension Bridge, 1,053 feet above the river, is the highest in the world. The Royal Gorge Incline Railway, the world's steepest, takes passengers 1,550 feet to the bottom of the canyon. A 2,200-foot aerial tramway glides across the spectacular canyon. Daily 10 a.m.-4:30 p.m.

### Royal Gorge Route
401 Water St., Canon City, 303-569-1000, 888-724-5748; www.royalgorgeroute.com
Travel by train through the Royal Gorge on two-hour round-trips departing from Canon City. Summer; daily; call for schedule.

## SPECIAL EVENTS
### Blossom & Music Festival
Depot Park, Canon City, 719-275-2331; www.ccblossomfestival.com
This celebration of springtime features arts and crafts, a parade and a carnival. First weekend in May.

### Royal Gorge Rodeo
1436 S. Fourth St., Canon City, 719-275-4784; www.horsestop.net/royalgorgerodeoevents.htm
In addition to the rodeo, the weekend features a Friday night barbecue and Sunday morning pancake breakfast. Late April-Early May.

## HOTELS
★★Best Western Royal Gorge
1925 Fremont Dr., Canon City, 719-275-3377, 800-231-7317; www.bestwestern.com
67 rooms. Restaurant, bar. Pool. $

## RESTAURANTS
★★Le Petsit Chablis
512 Royal Gorge Blvd., Canon City, 719-269-3333
French menu. Lunch, dinner. Closed Sunday-Monday. $

**COLORADO**

# CASCADE

Named for the many waterfalls nearby, Cascade hosts visitors who arrive to visit the popular Pikes Peak.

Information: www.colorado.com/city151

## SPECIALTY LODGINGS

**Black Bear Inn of Pikes Peak**
5250 Pikes Peak Hwy., Cascade,
719-684-0151, 877-732-5232;
www.blackbearinnpikespeak.com
9 rooms. Children over 8 years only. Complimentary full breakfast. Whirlpool. **$**

**Eastholme in the Rockies**
4445 Haggerman Ave., Cascade,
719-684-9901, 800-487-6420;
www.eastholme.com
8 rooms. Complimentary full breakfast. **$**

# COLORADO SPRINGS

Areas containing fantastic rock formations surround Colorado Springs, at the foot of Pikes Peak. General William J. Palmer founded the city as a summer playground and health resort. The headquarters of Pike National Forest is in Colorado Springs.
Information: Convention & Visitor Bureau,
515 S. Cascade,
719-635-7506,
877-745-3773; www. coloradosprings-travel.com

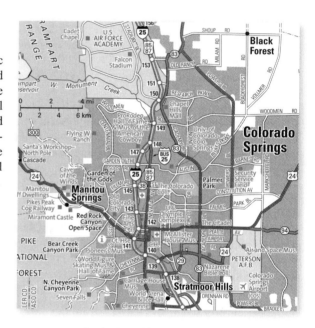

## ★ WHAT TO SEE AND DO

**Broadmoor-Cheyenne Mountain Area**
1 Lake Ave., Colorado Springs
Broadmoor-Cheyenne Mountain Highway zigzags up the east face of Cheyenne Mountain with view of plains to the east. Round-trip to Shrine of the Sunday is six miles. Daily; weather permitting.

**Cheyenne Mountain Zoological Park**
4250 Cheyenne Mountain Zoo Rd.,
Colorado Springs 719-633-9925;
www.cmzoo.org
This little gem located on the side of the Cheyenne Mountains in Colorado Springs is known for its beautiful setting and for the diversity of its animal collection. There are more than 650 animals here, including many endangered species. Feed the giraffes and check out the monkeys. Admission includes access to the Will Rogers Shrine of the Sunday. Memorial Day-Labor Day: daily 9 a.m.-6 p.m.; Labor Day-Memorial Day: daily 9 a.m.-5 p.m.

**El Pomar Carriage Museum**
16 Lake Circle, Colorado Springs,
719-577-7000; www.elpomar.org
Collection of fine carriages, vehicles, Western articles of 1890s. Monday-Saturday 10 a.m.-5 p.m., Sunday 1-5 p.m.

## Shrine of the Sun

4250 Cheyenne Mountain Zoo Rd.,
Colorado Springs, 719-577-7000;
www.elpomar.org

This memorial to Will Rogers, who was killed in a plane crash in 1935, is built of Colorado gray-pink granite and steel. Contains memorabilia. Fee for visit is included in zoo admission price. Memorial Day-Labor Day: daily 9 a.m.-5 p.m.; Labor Day-Memorial Day: daily 9 a.m.-4 p.m.

## Colorado Springs Fine Arts Center

30 W. Dale St., Colorado Springs,
719-634-5581;
www.csfineartscenter.org

Permanent collections include American Indian and Hispanic art, Guatemalan textiles, 19th- and 20th-century American Western paintings, graphics, and sculpture by Charles M. Russell and other American artists. Tuesday-wednesday 10 a.m.-5 p.m., Thursday-Saturday 10 a.m.-8 p.m., Sunday 10 a.m.-5 p.m.

## Colorado Springs Pioneers Museum

Former El Paso County Courthouse,
215 S. Tejon St., Colorado Springs,
719-385-5990; www.cspm.org

Learn about the history of the Pikes Peak region. Tuesday-Saturday 10 a.m.-5 p.m., Sunday 1-5 p.m. May-October.

## Flying W. Ranch

3330 Chuckwagon Rd., Colorado Springs,
719-598-4000, 800-232-3599;
www.flyingw.com

A working cattle and horse ranch with chuck wagon suppers and Western stage show. More than 12 restored buildings with period furniture. Reservations required. Mid-May-September: daily; rest of year: Friday-Saturday; closed December 25-February.

## Garden of the Gods

1805 N. 30th St., Colorado Springs,
719-634-6666; www.gardenofgods.com

This 1,350-acre park at the base of Pikes Peak is a showcase of geological wonders. It's best known for its outstanding red sandstone formations, including the famous Balanced Rock and Kissing Camels. The park offers eight miles of well-groomed trails to view the geological treasures, plants and wildlife. Take a free guided walking tour or hop on a bus to experience the garden. Other activities include horseback riding (Academy Riding Stables, 719-633-5667) and rock climbing (by permit only). Try to plan a visit at sunrise or sunset, when you'll get a true understanding of where the area gets its name. Memorial Day-Labor Day: daily 8 a.m.-8 p.m.; rest of year: daily 9 a.m.-5 p.m.

## Lake George (Eleven Mile State Park)

4229 Hwy. Rd., 92, Lake George,
719-748-3401;
www.parks.state.co.us/parks/elevenmile

Offering 3,400 surface acres, the reservoir is fully stocked with hungry kokanee salmon, carp, trout and northern pike. A number of local outfitters, such as 11 Mile Sports, Inc. (877-725-3172) can supply the necessary equipment as well as a guide. Daily. Ice fishing in winter.

## May Natural History Museum

710 Rock Creek Canyon Rd.,
Colorado Springs, 719-576-0450;
www.maymuseum-camp-rvpark.com

See a collection of more than 8,000 invertebrates from the tropics. Then, check out the Museum of Space Exploration, which includes NASA space photos and movies. May-October: daily; rest or year: by appointment.

## McAllister House Museum

423 N. Cascade Ave., Colorado Springs,
719-635-7925

Six-room, 1873 Gothic-style cottage with Victorian furnishings. Carriage house. Guided tours. September-April: Thursday-Saturday 10 a.m.-4 p.m.; May-August: Wednesday-Saturday noon-4 p.m.

★
★
★
★

### Museum of the American Numismatic Association

818 N. Cascade Ave., Colorado Springs, 719-632-2646, 800-367-9723; www.money.org/moneymus.html
Learn all about the study of currency through the collections of coins, tokens, medals and paper money here. Changing exhibits; library. Tuesday-Friday 9 a.m.-5 p.m., Saturday 10 a.m.-5 p.m., Sunday noon-5 p.m.

### Old Colorado City

2400 block of Colorado Ave., Colorado Springs, 719-577-4112
This renovated historic district features more than 100 quaint shops, art galleries and restaurants. Daily.

### Palmer Park

Colorado Springs, on Maizeland Rd. off N. Academy Blvd., 719-578-6640
Occupying 710 acres on Austin Bluffs, this park boasts magnificent views from scenic roads and trails. Picnic areas.

### Petserson Air & Space Museum

150 E. Ent Ave., 21st Space Wing/MU, Petserson Air Force Base, 719-556-4915; www.Petsemuseum.org
Display of 17 historic aircraft from World War I to present, plus exhibits on the history of the Air Force base. Open on restricted basis, call for times.

### Pike National Forest

1920 Valley Dr., Pueblo, 719-545-8737
The more than 1.1 million acres north and west of town via Highway 24 include world-famous Pikes Peak; Wilkerson Pass (9,507 feet), 45 miles west on Highway 24, with visitor information center, Memorial Day-Labor Day; Lost Creek Wilderness, northwest of Lake George; Mount Evans Wilderness, northwest of Bailey.

### Pikes Peak

Pikes Peak Hwy., Cascade, 719-385-7325, 800-318-9505; www.pikespeakcolorado.com
Soaring 14,110 feet, Pikes Peak is the second most visited mountain in the world (behind Mt. Fuji). To reach the peak, you can undertake an eight-hour hike or drive an hour up the 19-mile road, the last half of which is unpaved, has no guardrails and contains steep drops (a four-by-four vehicle isn't necessary but weather causes road closures even in summer). Daily; weather permitting. Closed during annual Hill Climb in July.

### Pikes Peak Cog Railway

515 Ruxton Ave., Manitou Springs, 719-685-5401; www.cograilway.com
The surest bet to the summit of Pikes Peak is the cog railway. Trains usually depart five times daily, rain or shine, but make reservations early. Whenever you go, bundle up: temperatures are 30-40 degrees cooler at the top. Water and aspirin help alleviate altitude sickness. April-December daily.

### Pikes Peak Auto Hill Climb Educational Museum

135 Manitou Ave., Manitou Springs, 719-685-4400; www.ppihc.com
More than two dozen racecars, plus numerous exhibits on the Pikes Peak race, considered America's second-oldest auto race. Daily, shorter hours in winter.

### Pikes Peak ghost town

400 S. 21st St., Colorado Springs, 719-634-0696; www.ghosttownmuseum.com
This authentic Old West town is housed in an 1899 railroad building. Includes a general store, jail, saloon, re-created Victorian home, horseless carriages and buggies and a 1903 Cadillac—plus, old-time nickelodeons, player pianos, arcade "movies" and a shooting gallery. Daily.

### Pikes Peak Mountain Bike Tours

306 S. 25th St., Colorado Springs, 888-593-3062; www.bikepikespeak.com
Tours vary in length and endurance level, and professional guides provide all necessary

equipment to make your ride safe, comfortable, and most of all, fun. Tour schedules vary; call or visit Web site for schedule.

### ProRodeo Hall of Fame and Museum of the American Cowboy

101 ProRodeo Dr., Colorado Springs, 719-528-4764;
www.prorodeohalloffame.com

The Hall of Fame pays tribute to giants like nine-time world champion Casey Tibbs, while the museum will help you appreciate the life of the cowboy—try roping one of the dummy steer. The outdoor exhibits include live rodeo animals and a replica rodeo arena. Daily 9 a.m.-5 p.m.

### Rock Ledge Ranch Historic Site

1401 Recreation Way, Colorado Springs, 719-578-6777; www.rockledgeranch.com

A living history program demonstrating everyday life in the region, including a working ranch. Braille nature trail. June-Labor Day: Wednesday-Sunday 10 a.m.-5 p.m.; Labor Day-December: Saturday 10 a.m.-4 p.m., Sunday noon-4 p.m.

### Seven Falls

2850 S. Cheyenne Canyon Rd., Colorado Springs, 719-632-0765;
www.sevenfalls.com

The only completely lighted canyon and waterfall in the world. Best seen from Eagle's Nest, reached by mountain elevator. Native American dance interpretations (summer, daily). Night lighting (summer).

### U.S. Air Force Academy

2346 Academy Dr., Colorado Springs, 719-333-2025, 800-955-4438;
www.usafa.af.mil

Established in 1955; 4,200 cadets. Located on the grounds of the academy is Cadet Chapel, the city's most famous architectural landmark, with its striking combination of stained glass and 150-foot aluminum spires. Stop by the visitor's center for a free self-guided tour map or to view films and informative exhibits about the Air Force. Also check out the planetarium, which may be

offering a special program, and don't miss a chance to see a T-38 and B-52 bomber up close. Call before visiting—the chapel closes for special events, and security events may close the base unexpectedly. Visitors Center: daily 9 a.m.-5 p.m.; Chapel: Monday-Saturday 9 a.m.-5 p.m.

### U.S. Olympic Training Center

1 Olympic Plaza, Colorado Springs, 719-632-5551, 888-659-8687;
www.usoc.org

Tours offers an insider's view of how Olympic-level athletes train. And for most of us, the closest we'll get to a medal are the replicas available in the gift shop. Monday-Saturday 9 a.m.-5 p.m., last tour at 4 p.m.; gift shop and visitor center: Sunday 11 a.m.-6 p.m.

### World Figure Skating Hall of Fame and Museum

20 First St., Colorado Springs, 719-635-5200; www.usfsa.org

Exhibits on the history of figure skating. Includes a skate gallery and video collection. Monday-Friday 10 a.m.-4 p.m.; November-April: Saturday 10 a.m.-4 p.m.; May-October: Saturday 10 a.m.-5 p.m.

## SPECIAL EVENTS

### Colorado Springs Balloon Classic

Memorial Park, Colorado Springs, 719-471-4833; www.balloonclassic.com

An annual event featuring more than 100 balloons and entertainment. Labor Day weekend.

### Little Britches Rodeo

Colorado Springs, Fairgrounds, 719-389-0333

Late May.

### Pikes Peak International Hill Climb

Colorado Springs, last 12 miles of Pikes Peak Hwy., 719-685-4400; www.ppihc.com

The Race to the Clouds has been a part of Colorado Spring's July 4 celebration since 1916. Spectators of all ages marvel at those who dare speed their racecars, trucks and motorcycles along the final 12.4 miles of Pikes Peak Highway, a gravel route with 156 turns and a 5,000-foot rise in elevation. Vehicles can reach more than 130 mph on straightaways. (There isn't a guardrail in sight.) You need to be on the mountain at the crack of dawn to catch the action. Those who don't take advantage of the overnight parking the evening before the race can arrive as early as 4 a.m. to stake out a good spot. The road closes to additional spectators at 8 a.m., so plan to spend the day here. Those who park above the start line won't be able to leave until late afternoon when the race is over. The best views are above the tree line, so dress warmly. Late June, 9:30 a.m.-late afternoon.

### Pikes Peak Marathon
Colorado Springs, race starts at Memorial Park and ends at Ruxton and Manitou Avenues in Manitou Springs, 719-473-2625; www.pikespeakmarathon.org
Late August.

### Pikes Peak or Bust Rodeo
Morris-Penrose Events Center, 945 W. Rio Grande St., Colorado Springs, 719-635-3547; www.pikespeakorbustrodeo.org
Bareback riding, bull riding, calf roping, steer wrestling and more. Mid-August.

## ★ HOTELS

### ★★The Academy Hotel
8110 N. Academy Blvd., Colorado Springs, 719-598-5770, 800-766-8524; www.theacademyhotel.com
200 rooms. Complimentary full breakfast. High-speed Internet access. Restaurant, bar. Airport transportation available. Pets accepted. Pool. $

### ★★Antlers Hilton Colorado Springs
4 S. Cascade, Ave., Colorado Springs, 719-955-5600; www.antlers.com
292 rooms. High-speed Internet access. Two restaurants, two bars. $

### ★★★★★The Broadmoor
1 Lake Ave., Colorado Springs, 719-634-7711; www.broadmoor.com
Located at the foot of the Rocky Mountains and surrounded by beautiful Cheyenne Lake, the Broadmoor has been one of America's favorite resorts since 1918. This all-season paradise is close to Colorado Springs, yet feels a million miles away. The opulent accommodations include rooms with views of the mountains or lake. Activities include a tennis club, three championship golf courses, paddleboating on the lake and horseback riding. Kids will love the "mountain" waterslide. And the world-class spa incorporates indigenous botanicals and pure spring water. The resort includes 15 restaurants, cafes and lounges, and several shops.
700 rooms, all suites. High-speed Internet access. Restaurants, bars. Spa. Airport transportation available. Pets accepted. Pool. Golf. Tennis. Business center. $$$

### ★★Doubletree Hotel
1775 E. Cheyenne Mountain Blvd., Colorado Springs, 719-576-8900, 800-222-8733; www.doubletree.com
299 rooms. High-speed Internet access. Restaurant, bar. Airport transportation available. Pets accepted. Pool. $

### ★Drury Inn
8155 N. Academy Blvd., Colorado Springs, 719-598-2500, 800-325-8300; www.druryhotels.com
118 rooms. Complimentary continental breakfast. High-speed Internet access. Pets accepted. Pool. $

### ★★Embassy Suites
7290 Commerce Center Dr., Colorado Springs, 719-599-9100; www.embassysuites.com
206 rooms, all suites. Complimentary full breakfast. High-speed Internet access, wireless Internet access. Restaurant, bar. Children's activity center. Pool. $

**104**

**COLORADO**

### ★Fairfield Inn
2725 Geyser Dr., Colorado Springs,
719-576-1717, 800-228-2800;
www.fairfieldinn.com
85 rooms. Complimentary continental breakfast. Wireless Internet access. Pets accepted. Pool. **$**

### ★Holiday Inn Express
1815 Aeroplaza Dr., Colorado Springs,
719-591-6000, 888-465-4329;
www.hiexpress.com/cos-airport
94 rooms. Complimentary continental breakfast. High-speed Internet access. Airport transportation available. Airport. **$**

## SPECIALTY LODGINGS

### Cheyenne Canon Inn
2030 W. Cheyenne Blvd.,
Colorado Springs,
719-633-0625, 800-633-0625;
www.cheyennecanoninn.com
This mission-style mansion, with views of the mountains, offers access to some of the area's best hiking and driving tours. The warm, professional service will ensure your stay is cozy.
10 rooms. Complimentary full breakfast. Whirlpool. **$$**

### Holden House 1902 Bed & Breakfast
1102 W. Pikes Peak Ave.,
Colorado Springs,
719-471-3980, 888-565-3980;
www.holdenhouse.com
Located in a historic home and carriage house dating to 1902, this inn has modern guest rooms with Victorian charm. Enjoy a gourmet breakfast and afternoon wine social.
5 rooms. No children allowed. Complimentary full breakfast. **$**

### Old Town Guest House
115 S. 26th St., Colorado Springs,
719-632-9194, 888-375-4210;
www.oldtown-guesthouse.com
This bed and breakfast located in Old Colorado City has all the amenities of a modern hotel, including an elevator to whisk you to your room, where you'll find a TV/DVD

player, coffee machine and desk with voice mail.
8 rooms. Children over 12 years only. Complimentary full breakfast. High-speed wireless Internet access. Airport transportation available. **$**

## SPAS

### ★★★★The Spa at the Broadmoor
1 Lake Ave., Colorado Springs,
719-577-5770, 866-686-3965;
www.broadmoor.com
With the beautiful scenery of the Rocky Mountains as a backdrop, the Spa at the Broadmoor already has an advantage over other luxury spas. But even without these surroundings, an experience at this two-level lakefront spa is pure bliss. With Venetian chandeliers, earth tones and an overall feeling of serenity, the treatment rooms perfectly set the scene for the spa's luxurious massage therapies and skin treatments. If your Rocky Mountain adventures have left you with aching muscles, a variety of massage therapies will make you feel like new again, while facial therapies such as the calming chamomile facial will get skin glowing. The Junior Ice Cream manicure and pedicure is reserved for those guests ages 11 and under. **$$**

## RESTAURANTS

### ★★★Charles Court
1 Lake Ave., Colorado Springs,
719-577-5733, 806-634-7711;
www.broadmoor.com
One of the many restaurants at the luxurious Broadmoor Hotel, Charles Court offers progressive American fare in a relaxed and contemporary setting. In warm weather, you can dine outdoors with lakeside views. The menu features regional Rocky Mountain fare such as Colorado rack of lamb and the signature Charles Court Game Grill. The wine list boasts more than 600 selections from all around the world. For special occasions, opt for the Chef's Table in the kitchen (four guests minimum). American menu. Breakfast, dinner, Sunday brunch. Bar. Business casual attire. Reservations recommended. Valet parking. Outdoor seating. **$$$**

**105**

**COLORADO**

★
★
★
☆
☆

### ★★Edelweiss
34 E. Ramona Ave., Colorado Springs,
719-633-2220; www.edelweissrest.com
German, Continental menu. Lunch, dinner.
Bar. Children's menu. Casual attire. Reservations recommended. Outdoor seating. **$$**

### ★★Famous Steakhouse
31 N. Tejon St., Colorado Springs,
719-227-7333;
www.restauranteur.com/famous
Steak menu. Lunch, dinner. Bar. Casual
attire. Reservations recommended. **$$$**

### ★★Giuseppe's Old Depot
10 S. Sierra Madre, Colorado Springs,
719-635-3111; www.giuseppes-depot.com
American menu. Lunch, dinner. Bar. Children's menu. Casual attire. Reservations
recommended. **$$**

### ★Il Vicino
11 S. Tejon St., Colorado Springs,
719-475-9224; www.ilvicino.com
Italian menu. Lunch, dinner, late-night. Bar.
Casual attire. Outdoor seating. **$**

### ★★Jake and Telly's Greek Dining
2616 W. Colorado Ave., Colorado Springs,
719-633-0406; www.greekdining.com
Greek menu. Lunch, dinner. Bar. Children's
menu. Casual attire. Reservations recommended. Outdoor seating. **$$**

### ★La Creperie Bistro
204 N. Tejon, Colorado Springs,
719-632-0984
French menu. Breakfast, lunch, dinner.
Casual attire. Reservations recommended.
Outdoor seating. **$$**

### ★★La Petite Maison
1015 W. Colorado Ave., Colorado Springs,
719-632-4887;
www.restauranteur.com/maison
French American menu. Lunch, dinner.
Closed Monday. Business casual attire.

Reservations recommended. Outdoor
seating. **$$$**

### ★★MacKenzie's Chop House
128 S. Tejon, Colorado Springs,
719-635-3536;
www.mackenzieschophouse.com
American, seafood, steak menu. Lunch,
dinner. Bar. Children's menu. Casual
attire. Reservations recommended. Outdoor
seating. **$$$**

### ★Old Chicago Pasta & Pizza
118 N. Tejon, Colorado Springs,
719-634-8812; www.oldchicago.com
American, pizza menu. Lunch, dinner, late-night. Bar. Children's menu. Casual attire.
Outdoor seating. **$**

### ★★★★Penrose Room
1 Lake Ave., Colorado Springs,
719-577-5733, 800-634-7711;
www.broadmoor.com
Located within the Broadmoor is the sophisticated and recently renovated Penrose
Room, which offers a spectacular dining
experience set against the magnificent views
of Colorado Springs and Cheyenne Mountain. Chef Bertrand Bouquin serves up contemporary, continental cuisine featuring the
influences of Italy, Spain, Africa and France.
The menu changes often and offers prix
fixe meals of three, four and seven courses.
Favorite appetizers include pistachio-laden
warm goat cheese salad, five herbs ravioli and chilled Peekytoe crab with cherry
relish salad. Entrées feature choices such as
roasted loin of Colorado lamb with purple
mustard and slowly cooked halibut in black
olive oil. After dinner, enjoy live music and
dancing.
French menu. Dinner. Closed Sunday. Bar.
Children's menu. Jacket required. Reservations recommended. Valet parking. **$$$$**

★

★

★

★

★

# CORTEZ

Originally a trading center for sheep and cattle ranchers, Cortez now accommodates travelers visiting Mesa Verde National Park and oil workers whose business takes them to the nearby Aneth Oil Field. The semi-desert area 38 miles southwest of Cortez is the only spot in the nation where one can stand in four states (Colorado, Utah, Arizona, New Mexico) and two Native American nations (Navajo and Ute) at one time. A simple marker located approximately 100 yards from the Four Corners Highway (Hwy. 160) indicates the exact place where these areas meet. There are many opportunities for hunting and fishing in the Dolores River valley. Information: Cortez/Mesa Verde Visitor Info Bureau, 928 E. Main, Cortez, 970-565-3414; www.cortezchamber.org

## WHAT TO SEE AND DO

### Anasazi Heritage Center and Escalante
27501 Hwy. 184, Dolores, 970-882-5600; www.co.blm.gov/ahc/index.htm
This is a museum of the Anasazi and other Native American cultures. See exhibits on archaeology and local history. The Escalante site, discovered by a Franciscan friar in 1776, is within a half mile of the center. This is also the starting point for visits to the Canyons of the Ancients National Monument. March-October: daily 9 a.m.-5 p.m.; November-February: daily 9 a.m.-4 p.m.

### Hovenweep National Monument
McElmo Rte., Cortez, 970-562-4282; www.nps.gov/hove
This monument consists of six units of prehistoric ruins—the best preserved is at Square Tower, which includes the remains of pueblos and towers. Self-guided trail (park ranger on duty); visitor area. Daily 8 a.m.-5 p.m.

### Lowry Pueblo
County Rd. CC, Cortez, 970-882-5600
Part of the Canyons of the Ancients National Monument, the Lowry Pueblo was constructed by the Anasazi (circa 1075) and includes forty excavated rooms. Picnic facilities. No camping. Daily, weather and road conditions permitting.

### Ute Mountain Tribal Park
Hwy. 666, Cortez, 970-749-1452; www.utemountainute.com/tribalpark.htm
The Ute Mountain Tribe developed this 125,000-acre park on their tribal lands, opening hundreds of largely unexplored 800-year-old Anasazi ruins to the public. Tours begin at the Ute Mountain Visitor Center/Museum, 19 miles south via Highway 666 (Daily); reservations required. Backpacking trips in summer. Primitive camping available.

## SPECIAL EVENTS

### Montezuma County Fair
Montezuma County Fairgrounds, 30100 Hwy. 160, Cortez, 970-565-1000; www.co.montezuma.co.us
The fair includes an antique tractor parade, barbecue and carnival. First week in August.

### Ute Mountain Round-Up Rodeo
Montezuma County Fairgrounds, 30100 Hwy. 160, Cortez, 970-565-8151; www.utemountainroundup.com
The weeklong extravaganza includes rodeo events as well as a children's "parade"— kids march to businesses downtown and receive treats. Early-mid-June.

## HOTELS

### ★Best Western Turquoise Inn & Suites
535 E. Main St., Cortez, 970-565-3778, 800-547-3376; www.cortezbestwestern.com
77 rooms. Complimentary continental breakfast. Airport transportation available. Pets accepted. Pool. $

### ★Holiday Inn Express
2121 E. Main St., Cortez, 970-565-6000, 800-626-5652; www.coloradoholiday.com

**107**

**COLORADO**

100 rooms. Complimentary continental breakfast. Airport transportation available. Pets accepted. Pool. **$**

# CRAIG

Craig is known for excellent big-game hunting for elk, deer and antelope, as well as bass fishing in Elkhead Reservoir. The Yampa River area draws float-boaters, hikers and wildlife photographers in summer and cross-country skiers in winter.

**Information: Greater Craig Area Chamber of Commerce, 360 E. Victory Way, Craig, 970-824-5689, 800-864-4405; www.craig-chamber.com**

## WHAT TO SEE AND DO

**Marcia**

**Craig City Park, 341 E. Victory Way, Craig, 970-824-5689**

See the private, luxury Pullman railroad car of David Moffat—an important financier and industrialist in late 19th-century Colorado who built many railroads. The car, named for his daughter, is listed on the National Register of Historic Places. Tours are available through the Moffat County Visitors Center.

**Museum of Northwest Colorado**

**590 Yampa Ave., Craig, 970-824-6360; www.museumnwco.org**

Learn about local history and see wildlife photography. Includes a cowboy and gunfighter collection. Memorabilia from Edwin C. Johnson, governor of Colorado and a U.S. senator, are also on display. Monday-Saturday 9 a.m.-5 p.m.

**Save Our Sandrocks Nature Trail**

**900 Alta Vista Dr., Craig, 970-824-5689**

This sloped, 3/4-mile trail provides a view of American Indian Petsroglyphs on the sandrocks.

## HOTELS

**★★Holiday Inn**

**300 S. Hwy. 13, Craig, 970-824-4000, 888-465-4329; www.holiday-inn.com**

152 rooms. Restaurant. Pets accepted. Pool. **$**

# CRESTED BUTTE

Crested Butte is a picturesque mining town in the midst of magnificent mountain country. Inquire locally for information on horseback pack trips to Aspen through the West Elk Wilderness. Guided fishing trips are also available on the more than 1,000 miles of streams and rivers within a two-hour drive of Crested Butte.

**Information: Crested Butte Visitor Center: Crested Butte 81224, 800-544-4505; www.crestedbutteresort.com**

## WHAT TO SEE AND DO

**Crested Butte Mountain Resort Ski Area**

**12 Snowmass Rd., Crested Butte, 800-810-7669; www.skicb.com**

Four high-speed quad, two triple, three double chairlifts, three surface lifts, two magic car-Petss; patrol, school, rentals, snowmaking. Longest run 2 1/2 miles; vertical drop 3,062 feet. Multi-day, half-day rates. Late November-mid-April, daily. Nineteen miles of groomed cross-country trails, 100 miles of wilderness trails; snowmobiling, sleigh rides.

## SPECIALTY LODGINGS

**The Nordic Inn**

**14 Treasury Rd., Crested Butte, 970-349-5542, 800-542-7669; www.nordicinncb.com**

27 rooms. Closed May. Complimentary continental breakfast. Whirlpool. **$**

## RESTAURANTS

**★Donita's Cantina**
332 Elk Ave., Crested Butte, 970-349-6674
Mexican menu. Dinner. Bar. Children's menu. Casual attire. **$$**

**★★Le Bosquet**
Sixth and Belleview, Crested Butte, 970-349-5808
French menu. Dinner. Closed mid-April-mid-May. Bar. Outdoor seating. **$$**

# CRIPPLE CREEK

At its height, Cripple Creek and the surrounding area produced as much as $25 million in gold in a single year. It was nearly a ghost town when voters allowed legalized gambling in the 1990s. Today it is mostly a gambling and tourist town and has managed to preserve some of its Old West charm.
Information: Chamber of Commerce, 719-689-2169, 877-858-4653; www.visitcripplecreek.com

## WHAT TO SEE AND DO

**Cripple Creek Casinos**
Cripple Creek, 877-858-4653; www.visitcripple-creek.com
Cripple Creek has nearly 20 limited-stakes (**$5** bet limit) casinos along its Victorian storefront main street area. Daily.

**Cripple Creek District Museum**
Fifth and Bennett, Cripple Creek, 719-689-2634; www.cripple-creek.org
See artifacts of Cripple Creek's glory including pioneer relics, mining and railroad displays. June-September: daily 10 a.m.-5 p.m.; October-May: Friday-Sunday 10 a.m. 4 p.m.

**Cripple Creek-Victor Narrow Gauge Railroad**
Fifth and Bennet, Cripple Creek, 719-689-2640; www.cripplecreekrailroad.com
Authentic locomotive and coaches depart from Cripple Creek District Museum. Four-mile round-trip past many historic mines. Late May-early October: daily, departs every 45 minutes.

**Imperial Casino Hotel**
123 N. Third St., Cripple Creek, 719-689-7777, 800-235-2922; www.imperialcasinohotel.com
This 1896 hotel was constructed shortly after the town's great fire.

**Mollie Kathleen Gold Mine**
Hwy. 67, Cripple Creek, 719-689-2466, 888-291-5689; www.goldminetours.com
Descend 1,000 feet on a one-hour guided tour through a gold mine. April-October: daily; tours depart every 10 minutes.

**Victor**
Cripple Creek, five miles south on Hwy. 67, on the southwest side of Pikes Peak, 719-689-2284; www.victorcolorado.com
This "city of mines" actually has streets paved with gold (low-grade ore was used to surface streets in the early days).

## SPECIAL EVENTS

**Donkey Derby Days**
City Park and Bennett, Cripple Creek, 719-689-3315
Donkey races. Last full weekend in June.

**Veteran's Memorial Rally**
City Park, Cripple Creek, 719-487-8005
Four-day event honoring veterans. Mid-August.

## HOTELS

**★★Double Eagle Hotel & Casino**
442 E. Bennett Ave., Cripple Creek, 719-689-5000, 800-711-7234; www.decasino.com
158 rooms. Complimentary full breakfast. Wireless Internet access. Restaurant, two bars. Casino. **$**

**109**

**COLORADO**

**★★Imperial Casino Hotel**
123 N. Third St., Cripple Creek,
719-689-7777, 800-235-2922;
www.imperialcasinohotel.com
26 rooms. Restaurant, bar. **$**

**★★★Carr Manor**
350 E. Carr Ave., Cripple Creek,
719-689-3709; www.carrmanor.com
This boutique hotel housed in a former
1890's schoolhouse includes a full breakfast
served in the original high school cafeteria.
Rooms feature original chalkboards for
messages. There's also a small fitness spa.
15 rooms. Closed January-February; also
weekdays March-April. Children over 12

years only. Complimentary full breakfast.
Wireless Internet access. **$**

## SPECIALTY LODGINGS
**Victor Hotel**
Fourth St. and Victor Ave., Victor,
719-689-3553, 800-713-4595;
www.victorhotelcolorado.com
20 rooms. Complimentary continental breakfast. Restaurant. Pets accepted. **$**

## RESTAURANT
**★★Stratton Dining Room**
123 N. Third St., Cripple Creek,
719-689-7777
Breakfast, lunch, dinner. Bar. Valet parking. **$$**

# DENVER

The capital of Colorado, nick-
named the Mile High City
because its official elevation
is exactly one mile above sea
level, began as a settlement of
gold seekers, many of them
unsuccessful. In its early
years, Denver almost lost out
to several booming mountain
mining centers in becoming
the state's major city. In 1858,
the community consisted of
some 60 raffish cabins, plus
Colorado's first saloon. With
the onset of the silver rush in
the 1870s, Denver came into
its own. By 1890, the popu-
lation had topped 100,000.
Bolstered by the wealth that
poured in from the rich mines in the Rockies, Denver rapidly became Colorado's economic
and cultural center. It boomed again after World War II and in the 1990s.

Today, with the Great Plains sweeping away to the east, the foothills of the Rocky
Mountains immediately to the west, and a dry, mild climate (where you'll find 300 days
of sunshine), Denver is a growing city with 2.5 million people in the metropolitan area.
A building boom in the 1990s resulted in a new airport, a downtown baseball park sur-
rounded by a lively nightlife district dubbed LoDo (lower downtown), new football, bas-
ketball and hockey stadiums, and a redeveloped river valley just west of downtown with
an aquarium, amusement park and shopping district. Once economically tied to Colorado's
natural resources, Denver now boasts one of the most diverse economies in the United
States and is a hub for the cable and telecom industries.

Parks have long been a point of civic pride in Denver. The Denver Mountain Park System
covers 13,448 acres, scattered over 380 square miles. The chain begins 15 miles west of the

**110**

**COLORADO**

city at Red Rocks Park (the site of a renowned musical venue) and extends to Summit Lake (perched 12,740 feet above sea level), 60 miles to the west.
Information: Denver Metro Convention & Visitors Bureau, 1555 California St., 303-892-1112, 800-233-6837; www.denver.org

# WHAT TO SEE AND DO

## 16th Street Mall
16th St., Denver, 303-534-6161
This tree-lined pedestrian promenade of red and gray granite runs through the center of Denver's downtown shopping district—outdoor cafés, shops, restaurants, hotels, fountains and plazas line its mile-long walk. European-built shuttle buses offer transportation from either end of the promenade. Along the mall you'll find Laramer Square. This restoration of the first street in Denver includes a collection of shops, galleries, nightclubs and restaurants set among Victorian courtyards, gaslights, arcades and buildings. Carriage rides around square. Daily.

## Antique Row
400-2000 S. Broadway, Denver, 303-765-1372
More than 400 shops along a 14-block stretch of South Broadway sell everything from books to music to vintage Western wear to museum-quality furniture. Take the light rail to Broadway and Interstate 25 to begin your tour. Most dealers are located between the 400 and 2000 blocks of South Broadway and 25 and 27 blocks of East Dakota Avenue. Daily.

## Arvada Center for the Arts & Humanities
6901 Wadsworth Blvd., Arvada, 720-898-7200; www.arvadacenter.org
Performing arts center with concerts, plays, classes, demonstrations, art galleries and banquet hall. Amphitheater seats 1,200 (June-early September). Historical museum with old cabin and pioneer artifacts. Museum and gallery. Monday-Friday 9 a.m.-6 p.m., Saturday 9 a.m.-5 p.m., Sunday 1-5 p.m.

## Auditorium Theatre
Denver, 303-893-4100
This 1908 theater, which has hosted operas, political conventions, revivalist meetings and more—is now the stage for Broadway productions and the Colorado Ballet. It's also the home of Colorado Contemporary Dance.

## Boettcher Concert Hall
Denver, 720-865-4220
The first fully "surround" symphonic hall in the U.S.—all of its 2,630 seats are within 75 feet of the stage. Home of the Colorado Symphony Orchestra (September-early June) and Opera Colorado with performances in the round (May).

## Byers-Evans House Museum
1310 Bannock St., Denver, 303-620-4933; www.coloradohistory.org
Restored Victorian house featuring the history of two noted Colorado pioneer families. Guided tours available. Tuesday-Sunday 11 a.m.-3 p.m.

## Charles C. Gates Planetarium
2001 Colorado Blvd., Denver, 303-322-7009
A variety of star and laser light shows are shown here daily. The Phipps IMAX Theater has an immense motion picture system projecting images on screen 4 1/2 stories tall and 6 1/2 stories wide. Located in the Denver Museum of Nature and Science. Daily showings.

**111**

**COLORADO**

### Cheesman Park
E. Eighth Ave. and Franklin St., Denver
This park has excellent views of nearby mountain peaks with aid of dial and pointers. The Congress Park swimming pool is next to it. The Denver Botanical Gardens are also nearby.

### The Children's Museum of Denver
2121 Children's Museum Dr.,
Denver, 303-433-7444;
www.cmdenver.org
This 24,000-square-foot, two-story hands-on museum allows children to learn and explore the world around them. Exhibits include a year-round ski slope, science center and grocery store. Monday-Friday 9 a.m.-4 p.m., Saturday-Sunday 10 a.m.-5 p.m.

### Colorado Avalanche (NHL)
Pepsi Center, 1000 Chopper Circle,
Denver, 303-405-1100;
www.coloradoavalanche.com
Professional hockey team.

### Colorado History Museum
1300 Broadway, Denver, 303-866-3682;
www.coloradohistory.org
Permanent and rotating exhibits on people and history of the Colorado including full-scale mining equipment, American Indian artifacts and photographs, and a sod house. Monday-Saturday 10 a.m.-5 p.m., Sunday noon-5 p.m.

### Colorado Rapids (MLS)
Dick's Sporting Goods Park
6000 Victory Way, Commerce City,
303-727-3500; www.coloradorapids.com
Professional soccer team. Tours. Thursday-Saturday 10 a.m.-3 p.m., every 30 minutes.

### Colorado Rockies (MLB)
Coors Field, 2001 Blake St., Denver,
303-762-5437, 800-388-7625;
www.colorado.rockies.mlb.com
Professional baseball team. Tours of Coors Field available; call for fees and schedule.

### Colorado's Ocean Journey
700 Water St., Denver,
303-561-4450, 888-561-4450
This world-class, 106,500-square-foot aquarium brings visitors face to face with more than 300 species of fish, birds, mammals and invertebrates from around the world. Check out the pool stocked with stingrays. Sunday-Thursday 10 a.m.-10 p.m., Friday-Saturday 10 a.m.-11 p.m.

### Comanche Crossing Museum
56060 E. Colfax Ave., Strasburg,
303-622-4322
Experience what is was like to travel via the railway in the late 1800s. This museum includes memorabilia of the completion of the transcontinental railway and includes two buildings on landscaped grounds with period rooms, a restored schoolhouse (circa 1891) and wood-vaned windmill (circa 1880). May-August: daily 1-4 p.m.

### Denver Art Museum
100 W. 14th Ave. Pkwy., Denver,
720-865-5000; www.denverartmuseum.org
Houses a collection of art objects representing almost every culture and period, including a fine collection of American Indian arts; changing exhibits. Free admission first Saturday of the month. Tuesday-Saturday 10 a.m.-5 p.m., Sunday noon-5 p.m.

### Denver Botanic Gardens
1005 York St., Denver, 720-865-3500;
www.botanicgardens.org
This tropical paradise occupying 23 acres about 10 minutes east of downtown is home to more than 15,000 plant species from around the world. The Conservatory, with more than 850 tropical and subtropical plants in an enclosed rain forest setting, is a soothing retreat for midwinter guests. A recent exhibit is the Cloud Forest Tree covered with hundreds of orchids and rare tropical plants. Other gardens include alpine, herb, Japanese and wildflower. Children particularly enjoy navigating the mazes in the Secret Path garden and climbing the resident banyan tree. Mid-September-April: daily 9 a.m.-5 p.m.; May-mid-September: Saturday-Tuesday 9 a.m.-8 p.m., Wednesday-Friday 9 a.m.-5 p.m.

**112**

**COLORADO**

★ ★ ★ ★ ★ ★

### Denver Broncos (NFL)
Invesco Field at Mile High, 1701 Bryant St., Denver, 720-258-3888; www.denverbroncos.com
Professional football team. Tours are available; call for fees and schedule.

### Denver Firefighters Museum
1326 Tremont Place, Denver, 303-892-1436; www.denverfirefightersmuseum.org
Housed in Fire House No. 1, this museum maintains the atmosphere of a working firehouse, with firefighting equipment from the mid-1800s. Monday-Saturday 10 a.m.-4 p.m.

### Denver Museum of Nature and Science
City Park, 2001 Colorado Blvd., Denver, 303-322-7009, 800-925-2250; www.dmns.org
Ninety habitat exhibits from four continents are displayed against natural backgrounds. The Prehistoric Journey exhibit displays dinosaurs in re-created environments. There's also an earth sciences lab, gems and minerals, and a Native American collection. Daily 9 a.m.-5 p.m.

### Denver Nuggets (NBA)
Pepsi Center, 1000 Chopper Circle, Denver, 803-405-1100; www.nba.com/nuggets
Professional basketball team. Tours of the arena are available.

### Denver Performing Arts Complexv
Speer and Arapahoe Denver, 720-865-4220; www.artscomplex.com
One of the most innovative and comprehensive performing arts centers in the county and with the addition of the Temple Hoyne Buell Theatre, it's also one of the largest under one roof. The complex also contains shops and restaurants.

### Denver Public Library
10 W. 14th Ave. Pkwy., Denver, 720-865-1111; www.denverlibrary.org

This is the largest public library in the Rocky Mountain region with nearly four million items, including an outstanding Western History collection and Patent Depository Library. Programs, exhibits. Monday-Tuesday 10 a.m.-8 p.m., Thursday-Friday. 10 a.m.-6 p.m., Saturday 9 a.m.-5 p.m., Sunday 1-5 p.m.

### Denver Zoo
City Park, 2300 Steele St., Denver, 303-376-4800; www.denverzoo.org
Located in City Park just east of downtown, this 80-acre zoological wonderland is home to more than 4,000 animals representing 700 species. Founded in 1896, the zoo has evolved into one of the nation's premiere animal exhibits, noted for its beautiful grounds, innovative combination of outdoor and enclosed habitats and world-class conservation and breeding programs. Don't miss the Primate Panorama, a seven-acre showcase of rare monkeys and apes. Visit the 22,000-square-foot, glass-enclosed Tropical Discovery and feel what its like to walk into a tropical rain forest complete with caves, cliffs, waterfalls and some of the zoos most exotic (and dangerous) creatures. The Northern Shores Arctic wildlife habitat provides a nose-to-nose underwater look at swimming polar bears and sea lions. Be sure to check out the feeding schedule posted just inside the zoos entrance. During evenings throughout December, millions of sparkling lights and holiday music transform the zoo as part of the traditional Wonderlights festival. April-September: daily 9 a.m.-6 p.m.; October-March: daily 10 a.m.-5 p.m.

### Elitch Gardens
2000 Elitch Circle, Denver, 303-595-4386; www.elitchgarderns.com
Located in downtown Denver, this park is best known for its extreme roller coaster rides. Other favorites include a 22-story freefall in the Tower of Doom, whitewater rafting and the new Flying Coaster, which simulates the experience of flying. Includes a kiddie park for younger children, the popular Island Kingdom water park and live entertainment nightly. June-August

**113**

COLORADO

10 a.m.-10 p.m.; limited and weekend hours May and September.

## Forney Museum of Transportation
4303 Brighton Blvd., Denver,
303-297-1113; www.forneymuseum.com
This museum houses more than 300 antique cars, carriages, cycles, sleighs, steam locomotives and coaches. One of the most notable permanent exhibits is that of Union Pacific "Big Boy" locomotive X4005, which was involved in a horrific crash in 1953, but has been restored and sits on the museum's grounds. You can also see the "Gold Bug" Kissel automobile owned by Amelia Earhart and Crown Prince Aly Khan's Rolls Royce. Monday-Saturday 9 a.m.-5 p.m.

## Four Mile Historic Park
715 S. Forest St., Denver, 720-865-0800;
www.fourmilehistoricpark.org
Once a stage stop, this 14-acre living history museum encompasses the oldest house still standing in Denver (circa 1859), plus other outbuildings and farm equipment from the late 1800s. Guides in period costume reenact life on a farmstead. And it's a great place for a picnic. April-September: Wednesday-Friday noon-4 p.m., Saturday-Sunday 10 a.m.-4 p.m.; October-March: Wednesday-Sunday noon-4 p.m.

## Hall of Life
2001 Colorado Blvd., Denver,
303-370-6453
This health education center has permanent exhibits on genetics, fitness, nutrition and the five senses. Daily 9 a.m.-5 p.m.

## The Helen Bonfils Theatre Complex
Denver, 303-572-4466
Home of the Denver Center Theatre Company. Contains three theaters: the Stage, seating 547 in a circle around a thrust platform; the Space, a theater-in-the-round seating 450; and the Source, a small theater presenting plays by American playwrights. Also contains the Frank Ricketson Theatre, a 195-seat theater available for rental for community activities, classes and festivals.

## Hyland Hills Water World
1800 W. 89th Ave., Federal Heights,
303-427-7873;
www.waterworldcolorado.com
Ranked among the nation's largest water parks, this 64-acre aquatic extravaganza is a great time for all ages. Water World's beautifully landscaped grounds include a wave pool the size of a football field, 16 water slides, nine inner-tube rides and a splash pool for tots. Hours vary according to season and weather, so be sure to call ahead. Late May-early September: daily 10 a.m.-6 p.m.

## Molly Brown House Museum
1340 Pennsylvania St., Denver,
303-832-4092; www.mollybrown.org
This museum stands as an enduring tribute to Margaret Molly Brown, the "unsinkable survivor" of the *Titanic*. A spectacular example of Colorado Victorian design, the fully restored 1880s sandstone and lava stone mansion, designed by one of Denver's most famous architects, William Lang, is filled with many of the lavish furnishings and personal possessions of its famous occupant. September-May: Monday-Saturday 10 a.m.-3:30 p.m.; Sunday noon-3:30 p.m. June-August: Monday-Saturday 9 a.m.-4 p.m.; Sunday noon-4 p.m.

## Pearce-McAllister Cottage
1880 Gaylord St., Denver, 303-322-1053
This 1899 Dutch Colonial Revival house contains original furnishings. The second floor houses the Denver Museum of Dolls, Toys and Miniatures. Tuesday-Saturday 10 a.m.-4 p.m., Sunday 1-4 p.m.

## Sakura Square
Between 19th and 20th Streets, Denver
Denver's Japanese Cultural and Trade Center features Asian restaurants, shops, businesses and authentic Japanese gardens. This is also the site of a famed Buddhist Temple.

**COLORADO**

## Ski Train

**Union Station, 555 1Seventh St., Denver, 303-296-4754; www.skitrain.com**

A ride on the Ski Train from downtown Denver to Winter Mountain Ski Resort in Winter Park has been a favorite day trip for skiers, hikers, bikers and family vacationers since 1940. Operating on weekends year-round, the 14-car train takes you on a spectacular 60-mile wilderness ride through the Rockies and across the Continental Divide, climbing 4,000 feet and passing through 28 tunnels before dropping you off at the front entrance of beautiful Winter Park Resort. Tickets are for round-trip, same-day rides only, and reservations are highly recommended. Winter: Saturday-Sunday; June-August: Saturday.

## State Capitol

**200 E. Colfax Ave., Denver, 303-866-2604; www.milehighcity.com/capitol**

This magnificent edifice overlooking Civic Center Park is a glorious reminder of Denver's opulent past. Designed by architect Elijah Myers in the classical Corinthian style, it was 18 years in the making before its official dedication in 1908. The building is renowned for its exquisite interior details and use of native materials such as gray granite, white marble, pink Colorado onyx and of course, the gold that covers its dome. Tours include a climb to the dome, 272 feet up, for a spectacular view of the surrounding mountains. Look for the special marker on the steps outside noting that you are, indeed, a mile high. Monday-Friday 7 a.m.-5:30 p.m.

## University of Denver

**S. University Blvd. and E. Evans Ave., Denver, 303-871-2000; www.du.edu**

Established in 1864; 8,500 students. Handsome 125-acre main campus with historic buildings dating from the 1800s. The 33-acre Park Hill campus at Montview Boulevard and Quebec Street is the site of the University of Denver Law School (Lowell Thomas Law Building) and the Lamont School of Music (Houston Fine Arts Center). For a schedule of performances, 303-871-6400. Campus tours. The University also includes the Chamberlin Observatory, which houses a 20-inch aperture Clark-Saegmuller refractor in use since 1894.

## Washington Park

**Denver, 303-698-4962**

This 165-acre park features a large recreation center with an indoor pool and floral displays include a replica of George Washington's gardens at Mount Vernon.

# SPECIAL EVENTS

## Cherry Creek Arts Festival

**Cherry Creek North, on Second and Third Avenues between Clayton and Steele Streets; www.cherryarts.org**

Features works by 200 national artists, plus culinary and performing arts. July 4 weekend.

## Denver Film Festival

**Starz FilmCenter at the Tivoli, 900 Auraria Pkwy., Denver, 303-595-3456; www.denverfilm.org**

Movie junkies will get more than their fill of flicks at this 10-day festival, which showcases 175 films, including international feature releases, independent fiction and documentaries, experimental productions and children's programs. All films are shown at the Starz FilmCenter at the Tivoli. Fall.

## Denver Lights and Parade of Lights

**Denver, downtown starting at Civic Center Park in front of the City and County Building, 303-478-7878; www.denverparadeoflights.com**

From early December through January, downtown Denver is ablaze with what is possibly the largest holiday light show in the world. Locals and tourists drift down to Civic Center Park after dark to view the incredible rainbow display covering the buildings. A spectacular Parade of Lights that winds for two miles through Denver's downtown kicks off the holiday season.

**115**

**COLORADO**

### National Western Livestock Show, Horse Show, & Rodeo
National Western Complex,
4655 Humboldt St., Denver,
303-297-1166, 888-551-5004;
www.nationalwestern.com

This two-week extravaganza—which includes 600,000 exhibitors and spectators—is packed with nonstop shows and demonstrations, from sheep shearing to steer wrestling. Daily rodeos showcase the horse and bull-riding skills of some of the best riders in the country before cheering, sellout crowds in the National Western Complex. Other favorites include barrel races, show-horse contests, a junior rodeo (where some of the riders are as young as three years old), Wild West shows and the colorful Mexican Rodeo Extravaganza. Take a break from the action and tour the exhibition hall for demonstrations in wool spinning and goat milking, or walk the grounds to see what a yak looks like up close. Mid-Janaury.

### The International at Castle Pines Golf Club
1000 Hummingbird Lane,
Castle Rock, 303-688-6000;
www.golfintl.com

The International is a week-long, world-class golf event that attracts some of the top professional golfers. The Jack Nicklaus-designed course is renowned for the beauty of its pine-strewn mountain setting and the challenge of its terrain. The tournament begins in earnest on Thursday, but spectators are welcome to watch practice rounds as well as the junior and pro-am tournaments held earlier in the week. One week in August.

## HOTELS

### ★★★★The Brown Palace Hotel
321 17th St., Denver,
303-297-3511, 800-321-2599;
www.brownpalace.com

Denver's most celebrated and historic hotel, the Brown Palace has hosted presidents, royalty and celebrities since 1892. The elegant lobby features a magnificent stained-glass ceiling that tops off six levels

of cast-iron balconies. The luxurious guest rooms have two styles—Victorian or Art Deco. The award-winning Palace Arms restaurant features signature favorites like rack of lamb and pan-roasted veal. Cigar aficionados take to the library-like ambience of the Churchill Bar. Afternoon tea is accompanied by live harp music. And Ellygnton's Sunday brunch is legendary. After a busy day of exploring nearby attractions like the 16th Street Mall and the Museum of Natural History, the full-service spa is the perfect place to unwind with a deep massage, body treatment or facial.

241 rooms. High-speed wireless Internet access. Three restaurants, bar. Spa. Pets accepted. **$$$**

### ★Comfort Inn Downtown
401 17th St., Denver,
303-296-0400, 877-424-6423;
www.comfortinn.com

231 rooms. Complimentary full breakfast. High-speed Internet access, wireless Internet access. Airport transportation available. Pets accepted. **$$**

### ★★★Grand Hyatt
1750 Welton St., Denver,
303-295-1234, 888-591-1234;
grandhyattdenver.com

The beautiful lobby of this centrally located hotel has a 20-foot sandstone fireplace and cozy seating areas with touches of mahogany, granite and wrought iron. Stay fit with the rooftop tennis courts surrounded by a jogging track, indoor pool and health club. The hotel's restaurant, 1876 (which is the year Colorado became a state) is a nice spot for dinner.

512 rooms. Complimentary continental breakfast. High-speed wireless Internet access. Restaurant, bar. Exercise. Pool. Business center. **$$$**

### ★★Historic Castle Marne Inn
1572 Race St., Denver,
303-331-0621, 800-926-2763;
www.castlemarne.com

9 rooms. Complimentary full breakfast. Wireless Internet access. **$$**

### ★★★Hotel Monaco Denver
1717 Champa St., Denver,
303-296-1717, 800-990-1303;
www.monaco-denver.com

The lobby feels like an elegant, somewhat exotic living room with cushy couches, recessed bookshelves and potted palms. But the scene stealer at this hotel is the domed ceiling, described as a Russian Circus Tent, with diamond shapes in blue and green and gold. The punchy décor carries through to the hallways and guest rooms, with bold colorful stripes on the walls and very glam black and white ottomans. The rooms also include plush duvet covers, bathroom phones and terrycloth shower curtains. The 24-hour room service is like the cherry on top.
189 rooms. Pets accepted. High-speed wireless Internet access. Restaurant. $$$

### ★★★Hotel Teatro
1100 14th St., Denver,
303-228-1100, 888-727-1200;
www.hotelteatro.com

Located across from the Denver Center for the Performing Arts, the Hotel Teatro inspires its guests with creative design and contemporary flair. Down comforters, Frette linens, Aveda bath products and Starbucks coffee keep you feeling relaxed, while the staff attends to your every whim. Want someone to draw you an aromatherapy bath? This is the place. Even Fido gets the VIP treatment, with a doggie dish with his name on it and Fiji water. Chef Kevin Taylor, who oversees two restaurants here, is something of a local sensation.
110 rooms. High-speed wireless Internet access. Two restaurants, bar. Pets accepted. $$$

### ★★★Jet Hotel
1612 Wazee St., Denver,
303-572-3300, 877-418-2462;
www.thejethotel.com

The dimly lit lobby gives you an idea of what you can expect from this ultra-modern boutique hotel. To the right is the open counter of Velocity, where you can get crepes and organic coffee each morning.

To the left, stretching almost the entire length of the lobby, is the futuristic Flow Bar, backlit in soft colors that change every few minutes. Step around a handful of tall, round cocktail tables to get to the inconspicuous reception desk. There are just 19 rooms here, in which standard amenities are anything but. No coffeemakers—just French plunge pots. No ice buckets—only funky insulated pitchers. No clock radios, either. Instead, there's a CD alarm clock with a library of CDs.
19 rooms. No children allowed. Complimentary continental breakfast. High-speed wireless Internet access. Restaurant, two bars. $$$

### ★★★JW Marriott Denver At Cherry Creek
150 Clayton Lane, Denver, 303-316-2700;
www.jwmarriottdenver.com

There is plenty to do right outside the doors of this property located just a few miles east of downtown in Cherry Creek. The area is filled with high-end boutiques, art galleries and trendy restaurants. The luxury boutique hotel has modern décor and features comfortable guest rooms with 32-inch flat-screen TVs and minibars—though you may find yourself hanging out in the lobby, which has a waterfall, fireplace and live jazz. Pets are welcomed with sheepskin beds, their own dining menus and designer bowls.
196 rooms. High-speed wireless Internet access. Restaurant, bar. Spa. Whirlpool. $$$

### ★★★Loews Denver Hotel
4150 E. Mississippi Ave., Denver,
303-782-9300, 800-563-9712;
www.loewshotels.com

Saying this hotel caters to the entire family is an understatement. Kids get Frisbees, backpacks and games. The hotel also offers a variety of amenities for babies, including tubs, electric bottle warmers and invisible outlet plugs. For mom and dad, there's a menu of comfort items like chenille throws, a pillow menu and CDs. And everyone will appreciate the fitness room and restaurant.

★
★
★
★
★

183 rooms. High-speed wireless Internet access. Restaurant, bar. Children's activity center. **$$**

### ★★★The Magnolia Hotel
818 17th St., Denver,
303-607-9000, 888-915-1110;
www.magnoliahoteldenver.com
Many visitors to Denver make the Magnolia their home for extended stays. It's easy to see why. Set back from busy 17th Street, the Magnolia says cozy, from the wing-back chairs and fireplace in its lobby to the full-size kitchens in its suites. Access to a snazzy health club is included with your stay. Upgrading to the Magnolia Club gets you wireless Internet access, access to a nightly cocktail reception and continental breakfast and late-night milk and cookies. Petss are welcome and receive a goodie bag at check-in.
246 rooms. Complimentary continental breakfast. High-speed wireless Internet access. Restaurant, bar. Airport transportation available. **$$$**

### ★★★Marriott Denver City Center
1701 California St., Denver,
303-297-1300, 800-228-9290;
www.denvermarriott.com
You'd be hard pressed to find a better health club in an urban hotel than this one. There is a wide variety of equipment, personal trainers, massage therapy, body treatments and a pool and whirlpool—all of which will come in very handy if you're staying here on business. Located on the first 20 floors of an office building in downtown Denver, this property is within walking distance of Coors Field, as well as several restaurants and shops.
615 rooms. High-speed wireless Internet access. Restaurant, bar. Business Center. **$$$**

### ★★★Oxford Hotel
1600 17th St., Denver,
303-628-5400, 866-654-6376;
www.theoxfordhotel.com
Built in 1891, this restored hotel is touted as the city's "oldest grand hotel." The luxurious property is filled with antiques, marble floors, stained glass and beautiful paintings. It's also near many attractions, including Coors Field, the 16th Street Mall, Larimer Square and many shops and galleries. Spend the day getting pampered at the hotel's full-service spa.
80 rooms. High-speed wireless Internet access. Restaurant, bar. Spa. Airport transportation available. Pets accepted. **$$$**

### ★★Queen Anne Bed and Breakfast
2147-51 Tremont Place, Denver,
303-296-6666, 800-432-4667;
www.queenannebnb.com
14 rooms. Complimentary full breakfast. Wireless Internet access. **$$**

### ★★★Renaissance Denver Hotel
3801 Quebec St., Denver, 303-399-7500;
www.denverrenaissance.com
This atrium hotel has Rocky Mountain views and large rooms with mini-refrigerators, free laundry and porches, making it a good choice for families looking for a full-service hotel while trying to stay within a budget, or business travelers who prefer to stay near the airport. (Downtown Denver is about a 10-minute drive.) There's also a pool and exercise facility.
400 rooms. Complimentary continental breakfast. High-speed wireless Internet access. Two restaurants, bar. Airport transportation available. **$$**

### ★★★The Westin Tabor Center
1672 Lawrence St., Denver,
303-572-9100, 800-937-8461;
www.starwoodhotels.com
Located in downtown Denver, adjacent to the 16th Street Mall, this hotel boasts some of the largest guest rooms in the city, many with panoramic views of the Rocky Mountains. The signature Heavenly Beds and Baths and nightly wine service ensure a relaxing stay. Get a massage, hit the rooftop pool or whirlpool, work out in the

**118**

**COLORADO**

outstanding fitness center (with a personal flat-screen TV on each piece of cardio equipment) or get in a game at the indoor half-basketball court. Afterward, relax in the lobby with Starbucks coffee.
430 rooms. Wireless Internet access. Two restaurants, bar. Pets accepted. **$$$**

## SPECIALTY LODGINGS

### Capitol Hill Mansion Bed & Breakfast
1207 Pennsylvania St., Denver,
303-839-5221, 800-839-9329;
www.capitolhillmansion.com
With its ruby sandstone exterior and dramatic entrance, this charming 1891 mansion offers a romantic getaway for couples. The richly decorated inn features rooms with fresh flowers and antique furniture, as well as refrigerators stocked with complimentary water and soft drinks (there's an open kitchen policy, too).
8 rooms. Complimentary full breakfast. **$**

### The Lumber Baron Inn
2555 W. 37th Ave., Denver, 303-477-8205;
www.lumberbaron.com
This place is huge—and there are only five guest rooms. The ground floor consists of a parlor, large dining room and kitchen. Each guest room has a different theme, but they all have separate showers and whirlpool tubs. The entire third-floor is an old ballroom, with 20-foot vaulted ceiling, small kitchen and bathroom, and is used for anything from a romantic dinner for two to the weekly murder mystery dinner hosted by the inn.
5 rooms. Petss accepted, some restrictions. Complimentary full breakfast. Pets accepted. **$$**

## RESTAURANTS

### ★Annie's Cafe
4012 E. Eighth Ave., Denver,
303-355-8197
American menu. Breakfast, lunch, dinner. Children's menu. Casual attire. **$**

### ★★★Barolo Grill
3030 E. Sixth Ave., Denver, 303-393-1040;
barologrilldenver.com

This upscale Italian farmhouse, named after the famous wine, serves authentic Northern Italian food. The interior is rustic and romantic, with grapevines covering one corner and hand-painted porcelain on display throughout, and the fireplace casts a warm glow. Be sure to ask about the daily tasting menu. And yes, the extensive wine list includes more than Barolo, but why bother?
Italian menu. Dinner. Closed Sunday-Monday. Bar. Business casual attire. Reservations recommended. Valet parking. **$$$**

### ★★Benny's
301 E. Seventh Ave., Denver,
303-894-0788; www.bennysrestaurant.com
Mexican menu. Breakfast, lunch, dinner. Bar. Children's menu. Casual attire. Outdoor seating. **$**

### ★★★The Broker Restaurant
821 17th St., Denver, 303-292-5065;
www.thebrokerrestaurant.com
Located in downtown Denver in what was once the Denver National Bank, the Broker is a fun place to dine. Private parties can take over one of the old boardrooms. The restaurant's centerpiece is a huge bank vault, now a dining room. Go down some stairs and through what seems like it might have been a secret passageway, and you find yourself in the restaurant's massive wine cellar, which has a dining table that can seat up to 20—or just two, if you're feeling romantic.
Steak menu. Lunch, dinner. Bar. Children's menu. Business casual attire. Reservations recommended. Valet parking. **$$$**

### ★★Buckhorn Exchange
1000 Osage St., Denver, 303-534-9505;
www.buckhorn.com
Steak menu. Lunch, dinner. Bar. Children's menu. Casual attire. Reservations recommended. Outdoor seating. **$$$**

### ★★Denver Chophouse & Brewery
1735 19th St., Denver, 303-296-0800;
www.chophouse.com
Steak and seafood menu. Microbrewery. Lunch, dinner. Bar. Outdoor seating. **$$**

**COLORADO**

### ★Empress Seafood
2825 W. Alameda Ave., Denver,
303-922-2822
Chinese menu. Lunch, dinner. Bar. **$$**

### ★★★Highlands Garden Cafe
3927 W. 32nd Ave., Denver, 303-458-5920;
www.highlandsgardencafe.com
This unique Denver mainstay is actually two converted Victorian houses from about 1890. The main dining room is all exposed brick, polished hardwood floors and crisp white tablecloths, but other rooms have a different feel. The country room is painted white and has double French doors leading out to the gardens. The eclectic American menu takes advantage of seasonal ingredients.
American menu. Lunch, dinner, Sunday brunch. Closed Monday. Outdoor seating. **$$$**

### ★★★Imperial Chinese
431 S. Broadway, Denver, 303-698-2800;
www.imperialchinese.com
From the giant fish tank at the entrance to the inventive Szechwan, Cantonese and Mandarin menu, this restaurant dazzles. The large dining room is segmented with partitions that provide a sense of privacy. The service is unobtrusive, and the dishes are as eye catching as they are delicious.
Chinese menu. Lunch, dinner. Bar. Casual attire. Reservations recommended. **$$**

### ★★India's Restaurant
3333 S. Tamarac, Denver, 303-755-4284;
www.indiasrestaurant.com
Indian menu. Lunch, dinner. Bar. **$$**

### ★Japon Restaurant
1028 S. Gaylord St., Denver, 303-744-0330;
www.japonsushi.com
Japanese menu. Lunch, dinner. **$$**

### ★Las Delicias
439 E. 19th Ave., Denver, 303-839-5675;
www.lasdeliciasmexicanrestaurant.com
Mexican menu. Breakfast, lunch, dinner. **$**

### ★★Le Central
112 E. Eighth Ave., Denver, 303-863-8094;
www.lecentral.com
French menu. Lunch, dinner, brunch. Casual attire. Reservations recommended. **$$**

### ★★★Morton's, The Steakhouse
1710 Wynkoop St., Denver, 303-825-3353;
www.mortons.com
One of the few places left where you can light up a cigar, this national chain fits right into the upscale Denver meat-and-potatoes scene. It's very simple here: order a martini, listen to the server recite the menu, dig in. Go home stuffed.
Steak menu. Dinner. Bar. Valet parking. **$$$**

### ★★★Palace Arms
321 17th St., Denver,
303-297-3111, 800-321-2599;
www.brownpalace.com
The Palace Arms opened its doors in 1892—and has carried on a tradition of culinary excellence ever since. Located on the ground level of the Brown Palace Hotel, the majestic Palace Arms' dining room has a unique Western charisma, with rich wood, brocade-upholstered seating, wood shutters and antiques. The delicious International cuisine is prepared with regional accents. Taste the oldest known blended cognac, which dates back to Napoleonic times.
International menu. Dinner. Bar. Children's menu. Business casual attire. Reservations recommended. Valet parking. **$$$**

### ★★★★Restaurant Kevin Taylor
1106 14th St., Denver, 303-640-1012;
www.ktrg.net
Located inside the stylish Hotel Teatro and across from the Denver Center for Performing Arts, this 70-seat restaurant brings French style to downtown Denver. Vaulted ceilings are offset with Versailles mirrors and alabaster chandeliers. Chairs are covered in green-and-yellow-striped silk fabric, and tables are topped with yellow Frette linens, Bernadaud china and Christofle silver.

**120**

**COLORADO**

Chef Kevin Taylor earns applause for his unpretentious contemporary cuisine. Start with seared Grade A French foie gras, and then try one of the signature dishes such as butter-poached Atlantic salmon, pancetta-roasted pork loin, and Colorado lamb sirloin. Top it off with a killer dessert like caramelized pineapple Napoleon. The restaurant features seasonal menus that change every two months, four- and five-course tasting menus and a prix fixe pre-theatre menu. There are also 900 vintages here— ask for a private table in the wine cellar. American, French menu. Dinner. Closed Sunday. Bar. Business casual attire. Reservations recommended. Valet parking. **$$$**

### ★Rocky Mountain Diner
800 18th St., Denver, 303-293-8383; www.rockymountaindiner.com
American menu. Lunch, dinner. Bar. Children's menu. Outdoor seating. **$$**

### ★★★Strings
1700 Humboldt St., Denver, 303-831-7310; www.stringsrestaurant.com
Strings is like no other restaurant in Denver. The locals know it—and so do the scores of celebrities and politicians who have dined here, many of whom have left autographed pictures on the wall. Some love it for the unusual eclectic cuisine served in the light and airy dining room with an open kitchen. Others are admirers of owner Noel Cunningham, a well-known humanitarian who constantly holds fundraisers at the restaurant to help fight illiteracy and hunger. International menu. Lunch, dinner. Bar. Business casual attire. Reservations recommended. Valet parking. Outdoor seating. **$$$**

### ★★Three Sons
2915 W. 44th Ave., Denver, 303-455-4366; www.threesons.net
Italian menu. Lunch, dinner. Closed Monday. Bar. Children's menu. **$$**

### ★★★Tuscany
4150 E. Mississippi Ave., Denver, 303-639-1600; www.loewshotels.com

Located in the Loews Denver Hotel, Tuscany is decorated in creamy earth tones and luxurious fabrics with soft lighting. Pen-and-ink drawings and paintings of the Tuscan countryside dot the walls, and a central, marble fireplace serves to divide the room. The feeling is contemporary and comfortable, and the restaurant uses only the freshest ingredients to create its outstanding fare paired with wines from the exceptional list. Live music is performed on Wednesday and Thursday evenings.
Italian menu. Breakfast, lunch, dinner. Bar. Children's menu. Casual attire. Reservations recommended. Valet parking. **$$$**

### ★Wazee Supper Club
1600 15th St., Denver, 303-623-9518; www.wazeesupperclub.com
American menu. Lunch, dinner, late-night. Bar. Children's menu. Casual attire. **$**

### ★★★Wellshire Inn
3333 S. Colorado Blvd., Denver, 303-759-3333; www.wellshireinn.com
The tables at this restaurant are topped with crisp white linens and beautiful china that was created exclusively for the Wellshire and based on the Tudor period, a theme that is richly executed here. Built in 1926 as a clubhouse for the exclusive Wellshire Country Club, the castle-like building fell into disrepair. Today, it has four intimate dining rooms. Classics like shrimp cocktail and Maryland crab cakes are featured as appetizers, while entrées include steak Oscar, pan-roasted Cornish game hen and grilled North Atlantic salmon.
American menu. Lunch, dinner, Sunday brunch. Bar. Children's menu. Business casual attire. Reservations recommended. Outdoor seating. **$$$**

### ★Zaidy's Deli
121 Adams St., Denver, 303-333-5336; www.zaidysdeli.com
American, deli menu. Breakfast, lunch, dinner. Children's menu. Casual attire. Valet parking. Outdoor seating. **$**

**COLORADO**

★
★
★
★
★
★

## SPAS

### ★★★★The Spa at the Brown Palace
321 17th St., Denver,
303-312-8940, 800-321-2599;
www.brownpalace.com

An artesian well has supplied the Brown Palace Hotel since it opened in 1892. The soothing natural rock waterfall at its spa's entrance speaks to this history. The Spa at the Brown Palace's six massage, facial and water treatment rooms, separate men's and women's lounges, and private couples' suite are spread over two floors. The facility also has a full-service hair and nail salon. This commitment to guest pampering isn't new—the spa occupies the same space as a spa that opened with the hotel more than a century ago. The treatment menu offers five distinct soaks, and the artesian plunge is 20 minutes of tub time followed by a sea algae masque. **$$**

# DILLON

After the entire town was moved in the early 1960s to make way for Dillon Lake, a reservoir for the Denver water system, this planned community became a popular resort area in the midst of wonderful mountain scenery.

Information: Summit County Chamber of Commerce, 246 Rainbow Dr., Silverthorne, 800-530-3099; www.summitnet.com

## WHAT TO SEE AND DO

### Copper Mountain Resort Ski Area
I-70 and Hwy. 91, Dillon, 866-841-2481;
www.coppercolorado.com

Six-person, four high-speed quad, five triple, five double chairlifts; six surface lifts; patrol, school, rentals, snowmaking; 125 runs; longest run approximately three miles; vertical drop 2,601 feet. November-April, daily. Cross-country skiing. Half-day rates. Athletic club. Summer activities include boating, sailing, rafting, hiking, bicycling, horseback riding, golf. Jeep tours. Chairlift also operates to the summit of the mountain (late June-September, daily).

### Summit County Biking Tour
Silverthorne; www.summitbiketours.com

The Summit County region in northwest Colorado is a mountain biker's dream with its diverse terrain, spectacular scenery and Wild West heritage. Hundreds of miles of wilderness roads and trails—many left over from the days when miners crisscrossed the land in search of gold and silver—draw cyclists into an unforgettable exploration of Colorado's high country. A ride over the Argentine Pass, at an elevation of more than 13,207 feet, is the ultimate conquest for experienced bikers. Those who want to take it all in without all the huffing and puffing can opt to ride a ski lift up the mountain for some awe-inspiring views of the Ten Mile Range, followed by a breathtaking, one-way plunge back to the valley below. Check out area visitor centers, bike shops and ski resorts for tips and trail maps. March-November.

## HOTELS

### ★Best Western Ptarmigan Lodge
652 Lake Dillon Dr., Dillon,
970-468-2341, 800-842-5939;
www.bestwestern.com

69 rooms. Complimentary continental breakfast. Bar. Whirlpool. Pets accepted. **$**

**122**

**COLORADO**

## DINOSAUR NATIONAL MONUMENT

This 325-square-mile monument on the Utah/Colorado border holds one of the largest concentrations of fossilized Jurassic-era dinosaur bones in the world. Visitors can get a close-up view of a quarry wall containing at least 1,500 fossil bones dating back 150 million years. The wall was once part of an ancient riverbed.

The monument itself is distinguished by its beautiful landscape of high plateaus and river-carved canyons. Access to the Colorado backcountry section, a land of deeply eroded canyons of the Green and Yampa Rivers, is via the Harper's Corner Road, starting at monument headquarters on Highway 40 (two miles east of Dinosaur). At the end of this 32-mile surfaced road, a one-mile foot trail leads to a promontory overlooking the Green and Yampa rivers.

The entrance to the Dinosaur Quarry section in Utah is at the junction of Highways 40 and 149 in Jensen, Utah (13 miles east of Vernal). Dinosaur Quarry is seven miles north on Highway 149. The Green River campground is about five miles from there. No lodgings are available other than at campgrounds. The visitor's centers and one quarry-section campground are open all year; the remainder are often closed by snow from mid-November to mid-April.

Information: 4545 E Hwy. 40, Dinosaur, 435-781-7700; www.nps.gov/dino

# DURANGO

Will Rogers once said of Durango, "It's out of the way and glad of it." For more than 100 years, this small Western city has profited from its secluded location at the base of the San Juan Mountains. Durango has been the gateway to Colorado's riches for Native Americans, fur traders, miners, prospectors, ranchers and engineers.

Founded by the Denver & Rio Grande Railroad, Durango was a rowdy community during its early days. The notorious Stockton-Eskridge gang once engaged local vigilantes in an hour-long gun battle in the main street. In the 1890s, the Durango *Herald-Democrat* was noted for the stinging, often profane, wit of pioneer editor "Dave" Day, who once had 42 libel suits pending against him.

Information: Durango Area Tourism office, 111 S. Camino Del Rio, Durango, 800-525-8855; www.durango.org

**123**

## COLORADO'S GOLD MINES

The San Juan Skyway is a scenic 236-mile loop out of Durango that ranges over five mountain passes as it wanders through the San Juan Mountains. From Durango, head west on Highway 160 to Hesperus, where you can take a side trip into La Plata Canyon to see mining ruins and a few ghost towns. Continuing west, you'll pass Mesa Verde National Park and come to Highway 145 shortly before Cortez. Head north to the town of Dolores and the Anasazi Heritage Center, which features a large display of artifacts, most more than 1,000 years old. The road now follows the Dolores River, a favorite of trout anglers, and climbs the 10,222-foot Lizard Head Pass, named for the imposing rock spire looming overhead.

Descending from the pass, take a short side trip into Telluride, a historic mining town and ski resort nestled in a beautiful box canyon. Follow the San Miguel River valley to Highway 62, and turn north to cross the 8,970-foot Dallas Divide. After the historic railroad town of Ridgway and Ridgway State Park, where you might stop for a swim or picnic, turn south on Highway 550 and drive to Ouray, a picturesque old mining town. Continue over the 11,008-foot Red Mountain Pass—there is a monument here dedicated to snowplow operators who died while trying to keep the road open during winter storms. Next stop is Silverton, a small mining town and the northern terminus of the Durango and Silverton Narrow Gauge Railroad. South of Silverton is the 10,910-foot Molas Divide, after which the road almost parallels the rails as they follow the Animas River back to Durango. This tour can be done in one long day by those who want to see only the mountain scenery, but is better over two or three days, with stops at Mesa Verde National Park and the historic towns along the way. Approximately 236 miles.

## WHAT TO SEE AND DO

### Diamond Circle Theatre

Durango Arts Center, Eighth and Second Avenues, Durango, 970-247-3400; www.diamondcirclemelodrama.com
Professional turn-of-the-century melodrama and vaudeville performances June-September, nightly; closed Sunday. Advance reservations advised.

### Durango & Silverton Narrow Gauge Railroad

479 Main Ave., Durango, 970-247-2733, 877-872-4607; www.durangotrain.com
This historic Narrow Gauge Railroad, in operation since 1881, links Durango in southwest Colorado with the Victorian-era mining town of Silverton, 45 miles away. A journey on this coal-fired, steam-powered locomotive up the Animas River and through the mountainous wilderness of the San Juan National Forest gives you the chance to relive history while taking in some of the most breathtaking scenery Colorado has to offer. Round-trip travel takes approximately nine hours. Same-day travelers may opt to return by bus; others can stay overnight in historic Silverton with a return train ride the next day. During the winter season, the train makes a shorter, round-trip journey to and from Cascade Canyon. May-October; shorter routes during the winter months.

### Durango & Silverton Narrow Gauge Railroad Museum

479 Main Ave., Durango, 970-247-2733, 877-872-4607
Climb aboard a restored railroad car and locomotive, and see exhibits on steam trains,

historic photos and railroad art. Hours correspond to the train depot hours.

### Durango Mountain Resort (also known as Purgatory)

1 Skier Place, Durango, 970-247-9000, 800-982-6103; www.ski-purg.com
Quad, four triple, three double chairlifts; patrol, school, rentals; five restaurants, five bars, nursery, lodge, specialty stores. 85 runs; longest run two miles; vertical drop 2,029 feet. Late November-early April. Cross-country skiing. Multi-day, half-day rates. Chairlift and alpine slide also operate mid-June-Labor Day.

### San Juan National Forest

15 Burnett Court, Durango, 970-247-4874; www.fs.fed.us/r2/sanjuan
This forest consists of nearly two million acres and includes the Weminuche Wilderness, Colorado's largest designated wilderness, with several peaks topping 14,000 feet. The Colorado Trail begins in Durango and traverses the backcountry all the way to Denver. Recreation includes fishing in high mountain lakes and streams, boating, whitewater rafting, hiking, biking and camping. The San Juan Skyway is a 232-mile auto loop through many of these scenic areas. Daily.

### Southern Ute Indian Cultural Museum

Southern Ute Indian Reservation, Ignacio, 23 miles southeast via Highways 160 and 172, 970-563-9583; www.southernutemuseum.org
This historical museum contains archival photos, turn-of-the-century Ute clothing, tools, and accessories. Multimedia presentation. Daily.

**124**

**COLORADO**

## SPECIAL EVENTS

### Durango Cowboy Gathering

Stater Hotel, 699 Main Ave., Durango,
970-382-7494;
www.durangocowboygathering.org
This celebration of the American cowboy features several poetry and vocal performances. First weekend in October.

### Iron Horse Bicycle Classic

346 S. Camino Del Rio, Durango,
970-259-4621;
www.ironhorsebicycleclassic.com
Cyclists race the Silverton narrow-gauge train (47 miles). Late May.

### Snowdown Winter Carnival

Durango, 970-247-8163;
www.snowdown.org
Winter festival with entertainment, contests, food and more. Late January-early February.

## HOTELS

### ★★★Apple Orchard Inn

7758 County Rd. 203, Durango,
970-247-0751, 800-426-0751;
www.appleorchardinn.com
This lovely inn is just 15 minutes from town and a 20-minute drive to Durango Mountain Resort. The property includes beautiful gardens, trout ponds, waterfalls and streams. All rooms feature featherbeds. Homemade baked goods and jam at breakfast—as well as fresh chocolate chip cookies any time—make visits extra sweet. Gourmet dinners are also available with a reservation.
10 rooms. Complimentary full breakfast. $$

### ★Best Western Durango Inn And Suites

21382 US Hwy. 160, Durango,
970-247-3251, 800-547-9090;
www.durangoinn.com
71 rooms. Restaurant, bar. Pool. $

### ★★Doubletree Hotel

501 Camino Del Rio, Durango,
970-259-6580, 800-222-8733;
www.doubletree.com

159 rooms. Restaurant, bar. Airport transportation available. Airport. Pets. Exercise. Swim. $

### ★★Historic Strater Hotel

699 Main Ave., Durango, 800-247-4431;
www.strater.com
93 rooms. Complimentary full breakfast. Restaurant, bar. Whirlpool. $

### ★★★Tamarron Resort

40292 Hwy. 550 N., Durango,
970-259-2000, 800-982-6103;
www.lodgeattamarron.com
Pine trees surround this scenic resort, located on a 750-acre site in the San Juan Mountains. The property is just a short drive or shuttle from Durango and Purgatory Village and the chairlifts. Accommodations range from studios and lofts to suites, and amenities include golf, tennis and indoor/outdoor pools.
210 rooms. Restaurant, bar. Children's activity center. Spa. Airport transportation available. Pets accepted. Golf. $

### ★★★Lightner Creek Inn

999 County Rd. 207, Durango,
970-259-1226, 800-268-9804;
www.lightnercreekinn.com
This inn, built in 1903, resembles a French country manor and offers finely decorated rooms. The mountain getaway feels very secluded but is only five minutes from downtown. Guests are encouraged to make themselves at home here—grab a drink from the kitchen and watch a movie in the living room.
9 rooms. $$

### ★★★New Rochester Hotel

721 E. Second Ave., Durango,
970-385-1920, 800-664-1920;
www.rochesterhotel.com
Built in 1892, this Victorian hotel has been authentically restored and evokes the Old West, and it's only one block from downtown Durango. It bills itself as a "green" hotel—Electra Cruiser bikes are available

COLORADO

for guests to get around and all-natural Aveda products are provided.

15 rooms. Complimentary continental breakfast. Pets accepted. **$$**

### Colorado Trails Ranch

12161 County Rd. 240, Durango,
970-247-5055, 877-711-7843;
www.coloradotrails.com

This ranch is on 450 acres adjacent to San Juan National Forest.

15 rooms. Closed October-May. Restaurant. Children's activity center. Airport transportation available. Pool. **$$**

### Country Sunshine Bed & Breakfast

35130 Hwy. 550 N., Durango,
970-247-2853, 800-383-2853;
www.countrysunshine.com

6 rooms. Complimentary continental breakfast. Whirlpool. **$**

### General Palmer Hotel

567 Main Ave., Durango,
970-247-4747, 800-523-3358;
www.generalpalmerhotel.com
39 rooms. **$$**

### Jarvis Suite Hotel

125 W. 10th St., Durango,
970-259-6190, 800-824-1024;
www.jarvishoteldurango.com

This restored historic hotel was built in 1888.

21 rooms. Complimentary continental breakfast. Whirlpool. **$**

### Leland House Bed & Breakfast Suites

721 E. Second Ave., Durango,
970-385-1920, 800-664-1920;
www.leland-house.com

Restored apartment building (1927) with many antiques.

10 rooms. Complimentary full breakfast. Pets accepted. **$$**

### Tall Timber Resort

1 Silverton Star Rte., Durango,
970-259-4813; www.talltimberresort.com

Accessible exclusively by train or helicopter, Tall Timber Resort is a true getaway.

This unique resort rests on 180 private acres rimmed by the San Juan National Forest. There are no televisions, radios or phones to distract from the majestic beauty of crashing waterfalls, majestic evergreens and mesmerizing canyons. Only 30 guests are treated to this singular experience at one time. The resort's two-story, ski condo-like accommodations feature simple, rustic décor with stone fireplaces and faux wood paneling.

10 rooms. Closed late October-May. Restaurant. Pool. **$$$$**

### Wit's End Guest Ranch and Resort

254 County Rd. 500, Bayfield,
970-884-4113, 800-236-9483;
www.witsendranch.com

In a valley on 550 acres. All cabins are adjacent to a river or pond.

19 rooms. Restaurant, bar. Children's activity center. Spa. **$$$$**

# RESTAURANTS

### ★★Ariano's Italian Restaurant

150 E. College Dr., Durango,
970-247-8146

Italian menu. Dinner. Bar. Children's menu. Casual attire. **$$**

### ★Carver Brewing Co.

1022 Main Ave., Durango, 970-259-2545

American, Southwestern menu. Breakfast, lunch, dinner. Bar. Children's menu. Casual attire. **$**

### ★★★Chez Grand-Mere

Three Depot Place, Durango, 970-247-7979;
www.chezgrand-mere.com

This restaurant offers a six-course prix fixe French menu that changes nightly. The largest wine list in the region is available here, with bottles from around the world.

French menu. Lunch, dinner. **$$$**

### ★★Francisco's

619 Main Ave., Durango, 970-247-4098;
www.franciscosrestuarante.com

Mexican, American menu. Lunch, dinner. Bar. Children's menu. Casual attire. **$$**

**126**

### ★★Palace
505 Main Ave., Durango, 970-247-2018;
www.palacedurango.com
American menu. Lunch, dinner. Closed
Sunday November-May. Bar. Casual attire.
Outdoor seating. **$$**

### ★★Red Snapper
144 E. Ninth St., Durango, 970-259-3417;
www.redsnapperdurango.com
Seafood, steak menu. Dinner. Bar. Children's
menu. Casual attire. **$$**

# EDWARDS

Not far from tony Vail Valley and Beaver Creek, Edwards has all of the resorts' beauty
without the hype. With a charming shopping and dining district, proximity to ski resorts
and plenty of Colorado's natural beauty, Edwards is a good option for visitors looking to
spend some time on a Rocky Mountain high.
Information: www.visitedwards.com

## HOTELS

### ★★The Inn And Suites At Riverwalk
27 Main St., Edwards,
970-926-0606, 888-926-0606;
www.innandsuitesatriverwalk.com
59 rooms. Two restaurants, bar. **$**

### ★★★The Lodge and Spa at Cordillera
2205 Cordillera Way, Edwards,
970-926-2200, 866-650-7625;
www.cordillera.rockresorts.com
The French-chateau architecture and
beautiful mountaintop location make this
one of the most exclusive resorts in the
area. A lovely rustic style dominates the
accommodations, where wood-burning
or gas fireplaces add warmth and terraces
offer views of the Vail Valley. The lodge
also includes award-winning golf and a
full-service spa. Four restaurants feature
everything from steaks and seafood to
the traditional Irish fare at Grouse-on-
the-Green, where even the interiors were
constructed in Ireland.
    56 rooms. Restaurant, bar. Pool. Golf.
Tennis. Business center. **$$**

## RESTAURANTS

### ★★★Mirador
2205 Cordillera Way, Edwards,
970-926-2200;
www.cordillera-rockresorts.com
Located in the luxurious Lodge and Spa
at Cordillera, Mirador features breathtak-
ing views of the Rocky Mountains and an
elegant atmosphere. Its innovate menu of
regional Colorado fare has won cricial
acclaim. It's complemented by an impres-
sive wine list. If you'd like to dine pri-
vately with a group, you can reserve the
24-seat private dining area or the 12-seat
family table in the wine cellar.
French menu. Dinner. Bar. Valet parking.
Outdoor seating. **$$$**

# ENGLEWOOD

Englewood is located in Denver's south metro area, which is home to the Denver Technological Center.
Information: Greater Englewood Chamber of Commerce, 3501 S. Broadway,
303-789-4473; www.ci.englewood.co.us

## WHAT TO SEE AND DO

### Castle Rock Factory Shops
5050 Factory Shops Blvd.,
Castle Rock, 303-688-4494
More than 40 outlet stores; food court.
Daily.

### Coors Amphitheatre
6350 Greenwood Plaza Blvd.,
Greenwood Village, 303-220-7000
Coors Amphitheatre is located 15 minutes
south of downtown Denver. The park-
like setting is an inviting venue for a wide

**127**

COLORADO

variety of musical performances during the summer months, from marquee names to classical orchestras. Come early to enjoy the mountain sunset. Bring a blanket or tarp (no lawn chairs are allowed) and a picnic. Or reserve an indoor seat, purchase dinner from one of the many vendors and watch the acts up close. June-August.

### The Museum of Outdoor Arts
1000 Englewood Pkwy., Englewood, 303-806-0444; www.moaonline.org
Outdoor sculpture garden on 400 acres. Guided tours available. Lunchtime summer performance series (Wednesday). Daily.

## HOTELS

### ★★Embassy Suites
10250 E. Costilla Ave., Centennial, 303-792-0433, 800-654-4810; www.embassysuites.com
236 rooms, all suites. Complimentary full breakfast. Restaurant, bar. Pool. $

### ★Hampton Inn
9231 E. Arapahoe Rd., Greenwood Village, 303-792-9999, 800-426-7866; www.hamptoninn.com
150 rooms. Complimentary continental breakfast. Pets accepted. Pool. $

### ★★★Sheraton Denver Tech Center Hotel
7007 S. Clinton, Greenwood Village, 303-799-6200, 800-325-3535; www.sheraton.com
The spacious guest rooms at this hotel will appeal to both business and leisure travelers. Nearby attractions include the Denver Museum of Natural History, the Denver Zoo and the Coors Brewery. Complimentary shuttle service is provided within a five-mile radius.
262 rooms. Restaurant, bar. Airport transportation available. Pets accepted. Pool. $

### ★★★Inverness Hotel And Golf Club
200 Inverness Dr. W., Englewood, 303-799-5800, 800-832-9053; www.invernesshotel.com
This hotel and conference center, with 60,000 square feet of function space, is the perfect choice for corporate retreats, thanks to naturally lit boardrooms, "fatigue-free" chairs, built-in audiovisual equipment and more. All rooms feature views of the golf course or Rocky Mountains and suites on the Club Floor have sunken living rooms. The spa offers a variety of treatments.
302 rooms. Restaurant, bar. Airport transportation available. Pool. Golf. Tennis. Business center. $$

# ESTES PARK

Estes Park occupies an enviable swath of land at the eastern edge of the Rockies. Many claim that Estes Park offers the quintessential Colorado experience. History certainly would support this. The area has been a vacation destination for thousands of years. Archaeological evidence indicates that Native Americans were drawn here to escape the summer heat. Situated 7,500 feet above sea level, the town's elevation manages to keep summertime temperatures comfortably cool—and also brings an average of 63 inches of snow during the winter months. The snowfall draws hordes of skiers and snowboarders to the area, with a season that typically lasts from November until April. During the warmer months, Estes Park becomes even more crowded.

The city's downtown area features an array of shops, restaurants and accommodations, including the Stanley Hotel, constructed nearly 100 years ago in the neoclassical Georgian style—and where Stephen King stayed while he was writing *The Shining* in 1973.
Information: Center at the Chamber of Commerce, 500 Big Thompson Ave., 970-586-4431, 800-378-3708; www.estesparkresort.com

COLORADO

# WHAT TO SEE AND DO

## Aerial Tramway

420 Riverside Dr., Estes Park,
970-586-3675

Two cabins suspended from steel cables move up or down Prospect Mountain at 1,400 feet per minute. You get a superb view of Continental Divide during trip. Picnic facilities at 8,896-foot summit; panoramic dome shelter; snack bar. Mid-May-mid-September, daily.

## Big Thompson Canyon

Estes Park, east on Hwy. 34

One of the most beautiful canyon drives in the state.

## Enos Mills Original Cabin

6760 Hwy. 7, Estes Park, 970-586-4706

On this family-owned 200-acre nature preserve stands the 1885 cabin of Enos Mills, regarded as the "father of Rocky Mountain National Park." In the shadow of Longs Peak, the cabin contains photos, notes and documents of the famed naturalist. Nature guide and self-guided nature trails. Memorial Day-Labor Day: Wednesday-Friday 10 a.m.-3 p.m.; rest of year by appointment.

## Estes Park Area Historical Museum

200 Fourth St., Estes Park, 970-586-6256;
www.estesnet.com/Museum

Three facilities including a building that served as headquarters of Rocky Mountain National Park from 1915 to 1923. See exhibits on the history of the park and surrounding area. Gallery May-October: Monday-Saturday 10 a.m.-5 p.m., Sunday 1-5 p.m.; November-April: Friday-Saturday 10 a.m.-5 p.m., Sunday 1-5 p.m.

## Fun City Amusement Park

455 Prospect Village Dr., Estes Park,
970-586-2828; www.funcityofestes.com

There's plenty of fun here—bumper cars, 15-lane giant slide and spiral slide, arcade, miniature golf, two 18-hole golf courses and go-karts. Mid-May-mid-September, daily.

## Roosevelt National Forest

240 W. Prospect Rd., Fort Collins,
970-498-1100; www.fs.fed.us/r2/arnf

More than 780,000 acres of icy streams, mountains and beautiful scenery. Trout fishing, hiking trails, winter sports area, picnicking, camping. Includes the Cache la Poudre River, five wilderness areas and the Peak-to-Peak Scenic Byway.

# SPECIAL EVENTS

## Estes Park Music Festival

Performance Park Pavilion,
Estes Park, 970-586-9519;
www.estesparkmusicfestival.org

Chamber, symphonic and choral concerts. Early June-late August.

## Horse shows

Estes Park, 800-443-7837;
www.estes-park.com

Includes an Arabian and Hunter-Jumper horse shows. July-August.

## Longs Peak Scottish-Irish Highland Festival

Estes Park, 970-586-6308, 800-903-7837;
www.scotfest.com

Athletic and dance competitions, arts and crafts shows, magic shows, folk dancing. Weekend after Labor Day.

## Rooftop Rodeo

Stanley Park Fairgrounds, Estes Park,
970-586-6104; www.estesnet.com/events/
rooftoprodeo.htm

Rodeo parade, nightly dances, kids jamboree, steer wrestling, bull riding. Five days in mid-July.

# HOTELS

## ★Best Western Silver Saddle

1260 Big Thompson Ave., Estes Park,
970-586-4476, 800-780-7234;
www.bestwestern.com

55 rooms. Complimentary continental breakfast. Pool. $

## ★Boulder Brook on Fall River

1900 Fall River Rd., Estes Park,
970-586-0910, 800-238-0910;
www.boulderbrook.com

16 rooms. Airport transportation available. $

**129**

COLORADO

### ★Comfort Inn

1450 Big Thompson Ave., Estes Park,
970-586-2358, 877-424-6423;
www.comfortinn.com

75 rooms. Closed November-April. Complimentary continental breakfast. Pool. **$**

### ★★Holiday Inn

101 S. St. Vrain, Estes Park,
970-586-2332, 888-465-4329;
www.holiday-inn.com

150 rooms. Restaurant, bar. Airport transportation available. Pets accepted. Pool. **$**

### ★Ponderosa Lodge

1820 Fall River Rd., Estes Park,
970-586-4233, 800-628-0512;
www.ponderosa-lodge.com

23 rooms. **$**

### ★★★Stanley Hotel

333 Wonderview, Estes Park,
970-586-3371, 800-976-1377;
www.stanleyhotel.com

The inspiration behind *The Shining*, the Stanley Hotel was built in 1909 by automaker F. O. Stanley and is only six miles from Rocky Mountain National Park. Multi-million dollar renovations have restored the gorgeous white hotel, which occupies 35 acres surrounded by the Rocky Mountains, to its original grandeur. The cozy rooms are classically styled and feature pillow-top mattresses and free wireless Internet.

135 rooms. Restaurant, bar. Pool. Tennis. **$**

## SPECIALTY LODGINGS

### Aspen Lodge Ranch

6120 Hwy. 7, Estes Park,
970-586-8133, 800-332-6867;
www.aspenlodge.net

59 rooms. Restaurant (open to the public by reservation), bar. Children's activity center. Airport transportation available. Pool. Tennis. Business center. **$$**

### Romantic Riversong Inn

1766 Lower Broadview Rd., Estes Park,
970-586-4666;
www.romanticriversong.com

A gurgling trout stream, gazebo and pond add to the charm of this 1928 bed-and-breakfast. (All rooms are named after wildflowers.) Located on 27 acres adjacent to Rocky Mountain National Park, the property offers impressive views.

16 rooms. Children over 12 years only. Complimentary full breakfast. Airport transportation available. **$$**

## RESTAURANTS

### ★Mama Rose's

338 E. Elkhorn Ave., Estes Park,
970-586-3330, 877-586-3330;
mamarosesrestaurant.com

Italian menu. Breakfast, dinner. Closed January-February; also Monday-Wednesday (winter). Bar. Children's menu. Outdoor seating. **$$**

### ★★Nicky's

1360 Fall River Rd., Estes Park,
970-586-5377, 866-464-2597;
www.nickysresort.com

American menu. Breakfast, lunch, dinner. Bar. Children's menu. Outdoor seating. **$$**

### ★★Twin Owls Steakhouse

800 MacGregor Ave., Estes Park,
970-586-9344; www.twinowls.net

Steak menu. Dinner. Bar. Children's menu. Casual attire. Reservations recommended. **$$**

## EVERGREEN

This small town, about 45 minutes from downtown Denver, has real mountain charm. At an elevation of about 7,200 feet, Evergreen has cooler summers than Denver and mild winters. Evergreen is home to several beautiful designated open spaces, great for hiking. At Evergreen Lake you can rent canoes and paddleboats in summer and go ice skating or ice fishing in winter.

Information: Evergreen Area Chamber of Commerce, 28065 Hwy 74, Evergreen,
303-674-3412; www.evergreenchamber.org

**130**

COLORADO

## FLORISSANT FOSSIL BEDS NATIONAL MONUMENT

Florissant Fossil Beds National Monument consists of 6,000 acres once partially covered by a prehistoric lake. Thirty-five million years ago, ash and mudflows from volcanoes in the area buried a forest of redwoods, filling the lake and fossilizing its living organisms. Insects, seeds and leaves of the Eocene Epoch are preserved in perfect detail, along with remarkable samples of standing petrified sequoia stumps. You'll also find nature trails, picnic areas and a restored 19th-century homestead. Guided tours are available. The visitor center is two miles south on Teller County Road 1. Daily.

Information: Florissant, 22 miles west of Manitou Springs on Hwy. 24; www.nps.gov/flfo

# FORT COLLINS

Founded as a military post in 1864, Fort Collins is a large college town—home to Colorado State University. It's a thriving community these days because of great schools, low crime, jobs in the high-tech field and great outdoor living. Many high-tech companies have moved here, and there are three microbreweries and Anheuser-Busch. Old Town is a historic shopping district with red brick pedestrian walkways and street lamps.

The headquarters for the Roosevelt National Forest and the Arapaho National Forest are also located in Fort Collins.

Information: Fort Collins Convention & Visitors Bureau, 19 Old Town Square, 970-232-3840, 800-274-3678; www.ftcollins.com

## WHAT TO SEE AND DO

### Anheuser-Busch Brewery Tour

2351 Busch Dr., Fort Collins, 970-490-4691; www.budweisertours.com

The Anheuser-Busch Brewery in Fort Collins produces 2.6 million cans of beer a day. The tour includes an overview of the company's history (which dates back to the mid-1800s), a walking tour of the brewing and control rooms and a visit with the famous Budweiser Clydesdales, housed with their Dalmatian companions in picturesque stables on the beautiful Busch estate. Enjoy complimentary beer tasting at the end of the tour. October-May: Thursday-Monday 10 a.m.-4 p.m.; June-August: daily 9:30 a.m.-4.30 p.m.; September: daily 10 a.m.-4 p.m.

## Colorado State University

Fort Collins, W. Laurel and Howes Streets, 970-491-4636;
www.welcome.colostate.edu

Established in 1870; 24,500 students. Land-grant institution with an 833-acre campus. Pingree Park, adjacent to Rocky Mountain National Park, is the summer campus for the natural resource science education and forestry program.

## Discovery Science Center

703 E. Prospect Rd., Fort Collins, 970-472-3990; www.dcsm.org

This hands-on science and technology museum features more than 100 educational exhibits. Tuesday-Saturday 10 a.m.-5 p.m., Sunday noon-5 p.m.

## Fort Collins Museum

Library Park, 200 Mathews St., Fort Collins, 970-221-6738;
www.ci.fort-collins.co.us/museum

Exhibits include a model of the army post, a fine collection of Folsom points and American Indian beadwork, plus displays of historic household, farm, and business items and three historic cabins. Tuesday-Saturday 10 a.m.-5 p.m., Sunday noon-5 p.m.

## Lincoln Center

417 W. Magnolia, Fort Collins, 970-221-6735

Includes a theater for the performing arts, concert hall, sculpture garden, art gallery and display areas with changing exhibits. Daily.

## Lory State Park

708 Lodgepole Dr., Bellvue, 970-493-1623; parks.state.co.us/Parks/lory

Approximately 2,500 acres near Horsetooth Reservoir. Water-skiing, boating, nature trails, hiking, stables, picnicking. Daily.

## HOTELS

### ★Best Western Kiva Inn

1638 E. Mulberry St., Fort Collins, 970-484-2444, 888-299-5482;
www.bestwestern.com

62 rooms. Complimentary continental breakfast. Pets accepted. Pool. $

### ★★Ramada Inn

3836 E. Mulberry St., Fort Collins, 970-484-4660, 800-272-6232;
www.ramada.com

197 rooms. Restaurant, bar. Children's activity center. Pets accepted. Pool. $

### ★★★Marriott Fort Collins

350 E. Horsetooth Rd., Fort Collins, 970-226-5200, 800-342-4398;
www.marriott.com

Located just three miles from Colorado State University, this hotel is a great place to stay during CSU parents' weekend. Rooms feature new luxury bedding with down comforters and fluffier pillows. Take a swim in the indoor or outdoor pool and hit the gym for a workout. This hotel is non-smoking. 230 rooms. Restaurant, bar. Pool. Business center. $

## SPECIALTY LODGINGS

### Porter House B&B Inn

530 Main St., Windsor, 970-686-5793, 888-686-5793;
www.porterhouseinn.com

4 rooms. Children over 12 years only. Complimentary full breakfast. Whirlpool. Business center. $

# FORT MORGAN

The original fort was built in the mid 1860s by "galvanized rebels," former Confederate soldiers who were released from prison on the condition that they move west and fight against Native Americans. The fort protected mail delivery and immigrants traveling along the Overland Trail. About 80 miles from Denver, Fort Morgan today offers opportunities to fish, golf and learn about the nation's westward expansion in the 19th century.

Information: Fort Morgan Area Chamber of Commerce, 300 Main St., 970-867-6702, 800-354-8660; www.fortmorganchamber.org

132

COLORADO

# GEORGETOWN

Georgetown is named for George Griffith, who discovered gold in this valley in 1859 and opened up the area to other gold seekers. The area around Georgetown has produced almost $200 million worth of gold, silver, copper, lead and zinc. Numerous 19th-century structures remain standing.
Information: Town of Georgetown Visitor Information, 800-472-8230; www.georgetowncolorado.com

## WHAT TO SEE AND DO

### Georgetown Loop Historic Mining and Railroad Park
Georgetown, 888-456-6777;
www.georgetownlooprr.com
The reconstructed Georgetown Loop Railroad was used in the late 1800s for shipping ore and was hailed as an engineering marvel. It now carries visitors on a scenic 6-1/2-mile trip, which includes a stop at the mine area for tours. The train leaves from Devil's Gate Viaduct (west on 1-70 to exit 228, then half mile south on Old US 6) or Silver Plume (1-70, exit 226). Five or six round-trips per day. Late May-early October, daily.

### Hamill House Museum
305 Argentine St., Georgetown,
303-569-2840;
www.historicgeorgetown.org/houses/
hamill.htm
Early Gothic Revival house acquired by William A. Hamill, Colorado silver magnate and state senator with period furnishings. Partially restored carriage house and office. Late May-September, daily; rest of year, by appointment.

### Hotel de Paris Museum
409 Sixth St., Georgetown, 303-569-2311;
www.hoteldeparismuseum.org
This internationally known hostelry was built in 1875 and is elaborately decorated with original furnishings. Memorial Day-Labor Day: daily 10 a.m.-4:30 p.m.; May, September-December: Saturday-Sunday noon-4 p.m.

### Loveland Ski Area
Loveland Pass, Georgetown,
303-569-3203, 800-736-3754;
www.skiloveland.com
Three quad, two triple, four double chairlifts, Pomalift, Mighty-mite; patrol, school, rentals, snowmaking; cafeteria, restaurants, bars; nursery; 60 runs; longest run two miles; vertical drop 2,410 feet. Mid-October-mid-May: Monday-Friday 9 a.m.-4 p.m., Saturday-Sunday 8:30 a.m.-4 p.m.

## SPECIAL EVENTS

### Georgetown Christmas Market
Sixth St., Georgetown,
303-569-2405, 303-569-2888;
www.georgetowncolorado.com
For a delightful old-fashioned Christmas experience, visit the little Victorian hamlet of Georgetown during the first two weekends in December. The streets and shops come alive with holiday lights, music, dancing and strolling carolers. Early December.

## SPECIALTY LODGINGS

### North Fork
55395 Hwy. 285, Shawnee,
303-838-9873, 800-843-7895;
www.northforkranch.com
6 rooms. Closed mid-September-mid-May. Restaurant. Children's activity center. Airport transportation available. Pool. **$$**

## RESTAURANTS

### ★Happy Cooker
412 Sixth St., Georgetown, 303-569-3166
American menu. Breakfast, lunch. Children's menu. Outdoor seating. **$**

COLORADO

★
★
★
☆

# GLENWOOD SPRINGS

Doc Holliday, the famous gunman, died here in 1887. Today, Glenwood Springs is a popular year-round health spa destination, thanks to its famous hot springs. The town is located between Aspen and Vail on the forested banks of the Colorado River, and is the gateway to White River National Forest. Excellent game and fishing country surrounds Glenwood Springs, and camping areas are sprinkled throughout the region. The nearby town offers museums, art galleries, specialty shops and restaurants in a relaxed, Western-style setting. Information: Chamber Resort Association, 1102 Grand Ave., 970-945-6589; 888-445-3696; www.glenscape.com

## WHAT TO SEE AND DO

### Glenwood Hot Springs Pool
Hot Springs Lodge and Pool,
415 Sixth St., Glenwood Springs,
970-945-6571, 800-537-7946;
www.hotspringspool.com
For centuries, visitors have traveled to the hot springs in Colorado to soak in their soothing—and many say healing—mineral-rich waters. Today, those same legendary springs feed this hot spring pool—the world's largest. The main pool, more than two blocks long, circulates 3.5 million gallons of naturally heated, spring-fed water each day. The complex includes lap lanes, a shallow play area, diving area, two water slides (summer only) and a therapy pool. Late May-early September: daily 7:30 a.m.-10 p.m.; early September-late May: daily 9 a.m.-10 p.m.

### Scenic drives
Glenwood Springs, on Hwy. 133,
visit Redstone, Marble and Maroon peaks;
I-70 provides access to Lookout Mountain and Glenwood Canyon
Just a two-mile hike from the road, you'll find beautiful Hanging Lake and Bridal Veil Falls. The marble quarries in the Crystal River Valley are the source of stones for the Lincoln Memorial in Washington, D.C. and the Tomb of the Unknown Soldier in Arlington National Cemetery.

### Sunlight Mountain Resort
10901 County Rd. 117, Glenwood Springs,
970-945-7491, 800-445-7931;
www.sunlightmtn.com
Triple, two double chairlifts; surface tow; patrol, school, rentals; cafeteria, bar; nursery. 67 runs; longest run 2 1/2 miles; vertical drop 2,010 feet. Snowmobiling half-day rates. Late November-early April, daily. Also cross-country touring center, 10 miles.

### White River National Forest
Ninth and Grand, Glenwood Springs,
970-945-2521; www.fs.fed.us/r2/whiteriver
More than 2,500,000 acres in the heart of the Colorado Rocky Mountains. Recreation at 70 developed sites with boat ramps, picnicking, campgrounds and observation points; Holy Cross, Flat Tops, Eagles Nest, Maroon Bells-Snowmass, Raggeds, Collegiate Peaks and Hunter-Frying Pan wildernesses. (Check with local ranger for information before entering wildernesses or any backcountry areas.) Many streams and lakes with trout fishing; large deer and elk populations. Dillon, Green Mountain and Ruedi reservoirs.

## SPECIAL EVENTS

### Garfield County Fair & Rodeo
Garfield County Fairgrounds,
1001 Railroad Ave., Rifle, 970-625-2514
Mid-August.

### Strawberry Days Festival
Sayre Park, Glenwood Springs,
970-945-6589;
www.strawberrydaysfestival.com
Arts and crafts fair, rodeo, parade. Third weekend in June.

## HOTELS

### ★Best Western Antlers
171 W. Sixth St., Glenwood Springs,
970-945-8535, 800-626-0609;
www.bestwestern.com

99 rooms. Complimentary continental breakfast. Pool. **$**

### ★Hot Springs Lodge
415 E. Sixth St., Glenwood Springs,
970-945-6571, 800-537-7946;
www.hotspringspool.com

107 rooms. Complimentary continental breakfast. Airport transportation available. Pool. **$**

## RESTAURANTS
### ★★Florindo's
721 Grand Ave., Glenwood Springs,
970-945-1245

Italian menu. Dinner. Bar. Children's menu. Casual attire. **$$**

### ★Los Desperados
55 Mel Rey Rd., Glenwood Springs,
970-945-6878

Mexican menu. Lunch, dinner. Bar. Children's menu. Casual attire. Outdoor seating. **$**

### ★★River's Restaurant
2525 S. Grand Ave., Glenwood Springs,
970-928-8813;
www.theriversrestaurant.com

American menu. Dinner, Sunday brunch. Bar. Children's menu. Casual attire. Outdoor seating. **$$**

# GOLDEN

Not surprisingly, Golden was founded during Colorado's gold rush. A mere 15 miles from downtown Denver, Golden has done a good job preserving its small town charm.

Information: Greater Golden Chamber of Commerce, 1010 Washington Ave., 303-279-3113, 800-590-3113; www.goldencochamber.org

## WHAT TO SEE AND DO

### Armory Building
13th and Arapahoe Streets, Golden,
303-270-3113

This is the largest cobblestone building in the United States (circa 1913). Approximately 3,000 wagon loads of cobblestones were used in the construction. The rocks are from Clear Creek and the quartz from Golden Gate Canyon.

### Astor House Hotel Museum
822 12th St., Golden, 303-278-3557;
www.astorhousemuseum.org

The first stone hotel west of the Mississippi, the Astor House was built in 1867. Period furnishings. Self-guided and guided tours (reservations required). Tuesday-Saturday 10 a.m.-4:30 p.m.

### Colorado Railroad Museum
17155 W. Fourth Ave., Golden,
303-279-4591, 800-365-6263;
www.crrm.org

This 1880s-style railroad depot houses memorabilia and an operating model railroad. More than 50 historic locomotives and cars from Colorado railroads are displayed outside. Daily 9 a.m.-5 p.m.

### Colorado School of Mines
1500 Illinois St., Golden,
303-273-3000, 800-446-9488;
www.mines.edu

World-renowned institution devoted exclusively to education of mineral, energy and material engineers and applied scientists. Tours of campus.

### Coors Brewery Tour
13th and Ford Streets, Golden,
303-277-2337, 866-812-2337;
www.coors.com

For a fun, free factory tour, visit Coors Brewing Company—the nation's third largest brewer—to see how beer is made. The 40-minute walking tour reviews the malting, brewing and packaging processes and ends with a free sampling in the hospitality room (proper ID required). Visitors under 18 must be accompanied by an adult. Monday-Saturday 10 a.m.-4 p.m.

**135**

**COLORADO**

★
★
★
★

### Golden Gate Canyon State Park
Crawford Gulch Rd., Golden,
303-582-3707;
www.parks.state.co.us/goldengatecanyon
On 12,000 acres. Nature and hiking trails,
cross-country skiing, snowshoeing, biking,
horseback riding, ice skating, picnicking,
camping. Visitor center. Panorama Point
Overlook provides a 100-mile view of the
Continental Divide. Daily.

### Golden Pioneer Museum
923 10th St., Golden, 303-278-7151;
www.goldenpioneermuseum.com
This museum houses more than 4,000 items
dating from Golden's days as the territorial capital, including household articles,
clothing, furniture, mining, military and
ranching equipment. Monday-Saturday
10 a.m.-4:30 p.m.; Memorial Day-Labor
Day: Sunday 11 a.m.-5 p.m.

### Heritage Square
18301 W. Colfax Ave., Golden,
303-279-2789; www.heritagesquare.info
Heritage Square family entertainment park
is reminiscent of an 1870s Colorado mining town with its Old West streetscapes and
Victorian facades. In addition to specialty
shops, restaurants, museums and theater,
there are amusement rides, water slide,
70-foot bungee tower, go-karts and a miniature golf course. Heritage Square is also
home to Colorado's longest Alpine slide.
Winter: Monday-Saturday 10 a.m.-5 p.m.,
Sunday noon-5 p.m.; summer: Monday-
Saturday 10 a.m.-8 p.m., Sunday noon-
8 p.m.)

### Lariat Trail
Golden, also known as Lookout Mountain
Rd., trail begins west of Sixth Ave. at 19th St.,
720-971-9649; www.lariatloop.org
Leads to Denver Mountain Parks. Lookout
Mountain (five miles west off Hwy. 6) is
the nearest peak.

### Buffalo Bill Grave and Museum
987-1/2 Lookout Mountain Rd.,
Golden, 303-526-0747;
www.buffalobill.org

Lookout Mountain is the final resting place
of the man who virtually defined the spirit
of the Wild West: William F. "Buffalo
Bill" Cody, whose life included stints as
a cattle driver, fur trapper, gold miner,
Pony Express rider and scout for the U.S.
cavalry. He became world famous with his
traveling Buffalo Bill's Wild West Show.
At the Buffalo Bill Grave and Museum,
Cody still draws crowds who come to see
the museum's western artifacts collection,
take advantage of the beautiful hilltop
vistas and pay homage to this legendary
Western hero. May-October: daily 9 a.m.-
5 p.m.; November-April: Tuesday-Sunday
9 a.m.-4 p.m.

## SPECIAL EVENTS
### Buffalo Bill Days
Golden, 303-279-8141;
www.buffalobilldays.com
Held in honor of "Buffalo Bill" Cody, this
event features a parade, golf tournament,
children's rides and games, car show, food
and arts and crafts. July.

## HOTELS
### ★La Quinta Inn
3301 Youngfield Service Rd., Golden,
303-279-5565, 800-642-4271;
www.laquinta.com
129 rooms. Complimentary continental
breakfast. Pets accepted. Pool. $

### ★★★Marriott Denver West
1717 Denver West Blvd., Golden,
303-279-9100, 888-238-1803;
www.marriott.com
Rooms at this hotel feature new Revive
bedding and high speed Internet access.
The renovated health club is stocked with
cutting-edge equipment. The sports bar has
37 flat screen high-def TVs. This hotel is
non-smoking.
307 rooms. Restaurant, bar. $

### ★★Table Mountain Inn
1310 Washington Ave., Golden,
303-277-9898, 800-762-9898;
www.tablemountaininn.com

**136**

COLORADO

74 rooms. Restaurant, bar. Airport transportation available. **$**

## RESTAURANTS

### ★★Chart House
25908 Genesee Trail Rd., Golden,
303-526-9813; www.chart-house.com
American menu. Dinner. Bar. Children's menu. **$$**

### ★★Simms Landing
11911 W. Sixth Ave., Golden,
303-237-0465;
www.simmslandingrestaurant.com

Seafood menu. Lunch, dinner, Sunday brunch. Bar. Children's menu. Business casual attire. Reservations recommended. Outdoor seating. **$$**

### ★★Table Mountain Inn
1310 Washington Ave., Golden,
303-216-8040; www.tablemountaininn.com
Southwestern menu. Breakfast, lunch, dinner, Sunday brunch. Bar. Children's menu. Outdoor seating. **$$**

# GRANBY

The Arapaho National Recreation Area, developed by the Department of Interior as part of the Colorado-Big Thompson Reclamation Project, is northeast of Granby. Several national forests, lakes and big-game hunting grounds are within easy reach. Two ski areas are also nearby.

Information: Greater Granby Area Chamber of Commerce, 970-887-2311, 800-325-1661; www.granbychamber.com

## WHAT TO SEE AND DO

### Arapaho National Recreation Area
9 Ten Mile Dr., Granby, 970-887-4100;
www.fs.fed.us/r2/arnf
The area includes Shadow Mountain and several lakes. Boating, fishing, hunting, camping, picnicking, horseback riding. Daily.

### Budget Tackle
255 E. Agate, Granby, 970-887-9344
Rent ice-fishing equipment, get advice on techniques and request directions to the best places to fish.

### Grand Adventure Balloon Tours
127 Fourth St., Granby, 970-887-1340;
www.grandadventureballoon.com
Take a sunrise hot air balloon flight over the Rockies from the Winter Park/Fraser Valley area.

### SilverCreek Ski Area
1000 Village Rd., Granby
Two triple, double chairlifts; Pomalift; patrol, school, rentals, snowmaking; concession, cafeteria, bar; nursery; day-lodge.

22 runs; longest run 1 1/2 miles; vertical drop 1,000 feet. December-mid-April. Snowboarding, sleigh rides. Health club.

## SPECIALITY LODGINGS

### C Lazy U Ranch
3640 Hwy. 125, Granby, 970-887-3344;
www.clazyu.com
Since the 1940s, C Lazy U Ranch has offered families a taste of life on a Western ranch. Enjoy the beautiful Colorado countryside—there are no televisions or telephones here to distract you. The horsemanship program is the centerpiece of the ranch—upon arrival, you're matched with a horse for the duration of your stay. The guest rooms are decorated with a distinctively Western décor, and nearly all have fireplaces. Meals are served family style and there's a fireside sing-a-long afterward. 40 rooms. Closed mid-February-mid-May, early October-mid-December. Complimentary full breakfast. High-speed wireless Internet access. Two bars. Children's activity center. Airport transportation available. **$**

**Drowsy Water Ranch**
County Rd. 219, Granby,
970-725-3456, 800-845-2292;
www.drowsywater.com
17 rooms. Closed mid-September-May.
Children's activity center. Pool. **$$**

## RESTAURANTS
**★Longbranch & Schatzi's Pizza**
165 E. Agate Ave., Granby, 970-887-2209
German menu. Lunch, dinner. Closed early
April-mid-May and early November-mid-
December. Bar. Children's menu. Casual
attire. Reservations recommended. **$$**

# GRAND JUNCTION

Grand Junction's name stems from its location at the junction of the Colorado and Gunnison
rivers. The altitude and warm climate combine to provide a rich agricultural area, which
produces peaches, pears and grapes for the local wine industry. The city serves as a trade
and tourist center for western Colorado and eastern Utah, as well as a gateway to two
national parks, six national forests and seven million acres of public land.
Information: Visitor & Convention Bureau, 740 Horizon Dr., 800-962-2547;
www.visitgrandjunction.com

## WHAT TO SEE AND DO
**Adventure Bound River Expeditions**
2392 H. Rd., Grand Junction,
970-245-5428, 800-423-4668;
www.raft-colorado.com
Two-to five-day whitewater rafting trips on
the Colorado, Green and Yampa rivers.

**Cross Orchards Historic Farm**
3073 F Rd., Grand Junction, 970-434-9814;
www.wcmuseum.org/crossorchards.htm
Costumed guides interpret the social and
agricultural heritage of western Colorado.
Restored buildings and equipment on display; narrow gauge railroad exhibit and country store. Demonstrations, special events.
May-October: Tuesday-Saturday 9 a.m.-
4 p.m.

**Museum of Western Colorado**
462 Ute Ave., Grand Junction,
970-242-0971, 888-488-3466;
www.wcmuseum.org
Features exhibits on regional, social and
natural history of the Western Slope, plus
a collection of small weapons and wildlife
exhibits. Tuesday-Saturday 10 a.m.-3 p.m.
Tours by appointment.

**Rabbit Valley Trail through Time**
2815 H. Rd., Grand Junction,
970-244-3000;
www.co.blm.gov/mcnca/ttt.htm

This 1 1/2-mile self-guided walking trail
takes you through a paleontologically significant area where you can see fossilized
flora and fauna from the Jurassic Age. No
pets allowed. Daily.

**Riggs Hill**
S. Broadway and Meadows Way,
Grand Junction, 970-241-9210
A 3/4-mile, self-guided walking trail in an
area where bones of the Brachiosaurus dino-
saur were discovered in 1900. Daily.

## SPECIAL EVENTS
**Colorado Mountain Winefest**
2785 Hwy. 50, Grand Junction,
970-464-0111, 800-704-3667;
www.coloradowinefest.com
Wine tastings, outdoor events. Late
September.

**Colorado Stampede**
Grand Junction
Rodeo. Third week in June.

## HOTELS
**★Best Western Sandman Motel**
708 Horizon Dr., Grand Junction,
970-243-4150; www.bestwestern.com
80 rooms. Airport transportation available.
Pets accepted. Pool. **$**

138

COLORADO

## ★★Doubletree Hotel Grand Junction
743 Horizon Dr., Grand Junction,
970-241-8888; www.doubletree.com
273 rooms. Restaurant, bar. Airport transportation available. Pool. Tennis. **$**

## ★★Grand Vista Hotel
2790 Crossroads Blvd., Grand Junction,
970-241-8411, 800-800-7796;
www.grandvistahotel.com
158 rooms. Restaurant, bar. Airport transportation available. Pets. Swim. **$**

## ★★Holiday Inn
755 Horizon Dr., Grand Junction, 81506,
970-243-6790, 888-489-9796;
www.holiday-inn.com
292 rooms. High-speed Internet access. Restaurant, bar. Airport transportation available. Pets. Exercise. Swim. **$**

## RESTAURANTS
### ★★Far East Restaurant
1530 North Ave., Grand Junction, 81501,
970-242-8131
Chinese, American menu. Lunch, dinner. Bar. Children's menu. **$**

### ★Starvin' Arvin's
752 Horizon Dr.,
Grand Junction, 81506
American menu. Breakfast, lunch, dinner. Bar. Children's menu. **$**

### ★★Winery Restaurant
620 Main St.,
Grand Junction, 81501,
970-242-4100
American menu. Dinner. Bar. **$$**

# GRAND LAKE
Grand Lake is on the northern shore of the largest glacial lake in Colorado. As one of the state's oldest resort villages, Grand Lake boasts the world's highest yacht club, a full range of water recreation and horseback riding and pack trips on mountain trails. Grand Lake is at the terminus of Trail Ridge Road at the west entrance to Rocky Mountain National Park.
Information: Grand Lake Area Chamber of Commerce, West Portal Rd. and Hwy. 34, 970-627-3402, 800-531-1019; www.grandlakechamber.com

## SPECIAL EVENTS
### Buffalo Barbecue & Western Week Celebration
Grand Lake, 970-627-3402
Parade, food; Spirit Lake Mountain Man rendezvous. Third week in July.

### Lipton Cup Sailing Regatta
Grand Lake, 970-627-3402;
www.grandlakechamber.com
Early August.

### Rocky Mountain Repertory Theatre
Community Building, Town Square,
Grand Lake,
970-627-3421, 970-627-5087;
www.rockymountainrep.com
Three musicals change nightly, Monday-Saturday. Reservations advised. Late June-late August.

### Winter Carnival
Grand Lake, 970-627-3372;
www.grandlakechamber.com
Ice skating, snowmobiling, snow sculptures, ice-fishing derby, ice-golf tournament. February.

## SPECIALTY LODGINGS
### Spirit Mountain Ranch Bed & Breakfast
3863 County Rd. 41, Grand Lake,
970-887-3551; www.spiritmtnranch.com
4 rooms. Children over 10 years only. Complimentary full breakfast. **$$**

## RESTAURANTS
### ★★★Caroline's Cuisine
9921 Hwy. 34, Grand Lake,
970-627-8125, 800-627-9636;
www.sodaspringsranch.com

**COLORADO**

At this cozy restaurant, large windows offer views of either the mountain or the hills, and the bistro-style menu includes steak frites and roasted duck.
French, American menu. Dinner. Closed two weeks in April and two weeks in November. Bar. Children's menu. Outdoor seating. **$$**

★**E. G.'s Garden Grill**
1000 Grand Ave., Grand Lake,
970-627-8404; www.egscountryinn.com
American menu. Lunch, dinner. Bar. Children's menu. Outdoor seating. **$$**

# GREELEY

Horace Greeley conceived of "Union Colony" as a Utopian agricultural settlement similar to the successful experiment at Oneida, New York. The town was founded by Nathan Meeker, agricultural editor of Greeley's *New York Tribune*. Thanks to irrigation, the region today is rich and fertile and sustains a thriving community.
Information: Greeley Convention & Visitors Bureau, 902 Seventh Ave.,
970-352-3567, 800-449-3866; www.greeleycvb.com

## WHAT TO SEE AND DO

**COLORADO**

**Centennial Village**
1475 A St., Greeley, 970-350-9220
Restored buildings with period furnishing show the growth of Greeley and Weld County from 1860 to 1920. Tours, lectures, special events. April-October, Tuesday-Sunday.

**Fort Vasquez**
13412 Hwy. 85, Greeley, 970-785-2832;
www.coloradohistory.org
This reconstructed adobe fur trading post of the 1830s contains exhibits of Colorado's fur trading and trapping industries, the Plains Indians and archaeology of the fort. Wednesday-Saturday, Labor Day-Memorial Day, 9:30 a.m.-4:30 p.m. Sunday afternoons; Memorial Day-Labor Day, Monday-Saturday 9:30 a.m.-4:30 p.m. Sunday afternoons.

**Meeker Home**
1324 Ninth Ave., Greeley, 970-350-9220
The 1870 house of city founder Nathan Meeker contains many of his belongings, as well as other historical mementos. May-September, Wednesday-Friday 1 p.m.-4 p.m.

## WHAT TO SEE AND DO

**Great Sand Dunes Four-Wheel Drive Tour**
5400 Hwy. 150, Great Sand Dunes
National Monument, 719-378-2222
This 12-mile, two-hour round-trip tour through the Great Sand Dunes National Monument features spectacular scenery and includes stops for short hikes on the dunes. May-October, daily.

**University of Northern Colorado**
1862 10th Ave., Greeley, 970-351-2097;
www.unco.edu
Established in 1889; 10,800 students. On the 236-acre campus is the James A. Michener Library, Colorado's largest university library. Collection includes materials owned by Michener while he was writing the book *Centennial*.

**Mariani Art Gallery**
1819 Eighth Ave., Greeley, 970-351-2184
Features faculty, student and special exhibitions. Multipurpose University Center.

## SPECIAL EVENTS

**Greeley Independence Stampede**
600 N. 14th Ave., Greeley,
970-356-2855, 800-982-2855;
www.greeleystampede.org
This week-long celebration includes nightly country and western concerts by top-name entertainers and culminates in a rodeo. Also includes a bull fighting event, demolition derby and carnival. Fees vary per event. Late June-early July.

## SPECIALTY LODGINGS

**Sod Buster Inn**
1221 Ninth Ave., Greeley,
970-392-1221, 866-501-8667;
www.thesodbusterinn.com
10 rooms. Complimentary full breakfast.

# GUNNISON

With 2,000 miles of trout-fishing streams and Colorado's largest lake within easy driving range, Gunnison has long been noted as an excellent fishing center.
Information: Gunnison Country Chamber of Commerce, 500 E. Tomichi Ave., 970-641-150; www.visitgunnison.com

## WHAT TO SEE AND DO

**Alpine Tunnel**
500 E. Tomichi Ave., Gunnison, 36 miles northeast via Hwy. 50
Completed in 1881 and abandoned in 1910, this railroad tunnel—nearly 12,000 feet above sea level—is 1,771 feet long. July-October.

**Curecanti National Recreation Area**
102 Elk Creek, Gunnison, 970-641-2337; www.nps.gov/cure
This area includes Blue Mesa, Morrow Point and Crystal reservoirs. Elk Creek Marinas, Inc., offers boat tours on Morrow Point Lake (Memorial Day-Labor Day, daily; 970-641-0402 for reservations). Blue Mesa Lake has water-skiing, windsurfing, fishing, boating; picnicking, camping. The Elk Creek visitor center is 16 miles west (mid-April-October, daily).

**Gunnison National Forest**
216 N. Colorado St., Gunnison, 970-641-0471
This forest contains 27 peaks. Activities include fishing, hiking, picnicking, camping. Includes West Elk Wilderness and portions of the Maroon Bells-Snowmass, Collegiate Peaks, la Garita and Raggeds wilderness areas.

**Taylor Park Reservoir**
216 N. Colorado St., Gunnison, 970-641-2922

The road runs through this 20-mile canyon. Fishing, boating, hunting, camping. Memorial Day-September, daily.

## SPECIAL EVENTS

**Cattlemen's Days, Rodeo and County Fair**
275 S. Spruce, Gunnison, 970-641-4160; www.visitgunnison.com
The oldest rodeo in Colorado. Mid-July.

## HOTELS

★★**Best Western Vista Inn**
733 E. Hwy. 24, Gunnison,
970-641-1131, 800-641-1131;
www.bestwestern.com/tomichivillageinn
49 rooms. Restaurant. Airport transportation available. Pool. **$**

★**Holiday Inn Express**
910 E. Tomichi Ave., Gunnison,
970-641-1288, 888-465-4329;
www.holiday-inn.com
108 rooms. Complimentary continental breakfast. Airport transportation available. Pool. **$**

## RESTAURANTS

★★**Trough**
37550 Hwy. 50, Gunnison, 970-641-3724
American menu. Dinner. Bar. Children's menu. Casual attire. **$$**

**141**

**COLORADO**

★
★
★
★

# KEYSTONE

This tiny town is best known for its skiing and scenic setting, so strap on your sticks and enjoy.

Information: keystone.snow.com

## WHAT TO SEE AND DO

### Keystone Resort Ski Area

1254 Soda Ridge Rd., Keystone,
800-344-8878; ww.keystone.snow.com

Four ski mountains (Arapahoe Basin, Keystone Mountain, North Peak and the Outback). Patrol, school, rentals. Snowmaking at Keystone, North Peak and the Outback. Late October-early May. Cross-country skiing, night skiing, ice skating, snowmobiling and sleigh rides. Shuttle bus service. Combination and half-day ski rates; package plans. Summer activities include boating, rafting and gondola rides, plus golf, tennis, horseback riding, bicycling and jeep riding.

## HOTELS

### ★★★Keystone Lodge

22101 Hwy. 6, Keystone,
970-496-3000, 888-455-7625;
www.keystonelodge.rockresorts.com

Keystone Lodge is a perfect Rocky Mountain getaway, thanks to a variety of activities, comfortable accommodations and enjoyable dining. The guest rooms and suites are the picture of mountain chic, with large windows framing unfor-gettable views of snow-capped peaks and the Snake River. You'll never be at a loss for something to do, with an on-site ice skating rink, BMW driving tours, nearby skiing and golf and a complete fitness center. After an action-packed day, the Avanyu Spa offers a variety of soothing treatments. The dining is superb, from the elegant French dining at Champeaux to the prime cuts Bighorn Steakhouse. 152 rooms. Pool. $$$

## SPECIALTY LODGINGS

### Ski Tip Lodge

764 Montezuma Rd., Keystone,
877-753-9786; www.skitiplodge.com

11 rooms. Complimentary full breakfast. Restaurant, bar. Tennis. $

## RESTAURANTS

### ★★★Ski Tip Lodge

764 Montezuma Rd., Keystone,
800-354-4386; www.skitiplodge.com

This charming bed and breakfast has been served American regional cuisine for more than 50 years.

Dinner. Bar. Children's menu. $$$

# LAKEWOOD

Lakewood is a suburban community west of Denver.

Information: West Chamber Serving Jefferson County, 1667 Cole Blvd., 303-233-5555; www.lakewood.org

## WHAT TO SEE AND DO

### Bear Creek Lake Park

15600 W. Morrison Rd., Morrison,
303-697-6159

Approximately 2,600 acres. Water-skiing school, fishing, boating; hiking, bicycle trails, picnicking, camping. Archery. View of downtown Denver from Mount Carbon. Daily.

### Colorado Mills

14500 W. Colfax Ave., Lakewood,
303-384-3000; www.coloradomills.com

This brand-new 1.2 million-square-foot state-of-the-art retail and entertainment complex is just 10 minutes from downtown Denver, and brings a vast array of value-oriented stores, restaurants and entertainment venues together. Movie theaters, shops, restaurants, an inter-active play area for kids and a 40,000 square-foot ESPN X Games Skatepark for older kids form the core of the entertainment center. Monday-Saturday 10 a.m.-9:00 p.m., Sunday 11 a.m.-6 p.m.

COLORADO

### Crown Hill Park

W. 26th Ave., and Kipling St., Lakewood,
303-271-5925

This 242-acre nature preserve includes Crown Hill Lake and a wildlife pond. Fishing, hiking, bicycle, bridle trails. Daily.

### Lakewood's Heritage Center

801 Yarrow St., Lakewood, 303-987-7850

This 127-acre park includes nature, art and historical exhibits in. Turn-of-the-century farm; one-room schoolhouse; vintage farm machinery; Barn Gallery with permanent and changing exhibits, interpretive displays. Lectures, workshops. visitor center. Tuesday-Saturday 10 a.m.-4 p.m.

## HOTELS

### ★Hampton Inn

3605 S. Wadsworth Blvd., Lakewood,
303-989-6900, 800-426-7866;
www.hamptoninn.com

150 rooms. Complimentary continental breakfast. Pool. **$**

### ★★Holiday Inn

7390 W. Hampden Ave., Lakewood,
303-980-9200, 888-565-6159;
www.holiday-inn.com

188 rooms. Restaurant, bar. Pets accepted. Pool. **$**

### ★★★Sheraton Denver West Hotel

360 Union Blvd., Lakewood,
303-987-2000, 800-325-3535;
www.sheraton.com

Adjacent to the Denver Federal Center, this hotel is a perfect launching pad to explore nearby attractions, including Coors Brewery and Red Rocks Concert Amphitheater. The 10,000-square foot health club includes a heated indoor lap pool and the spa offers a variety of relaxing treatments. The rooms are warm and cozy with deep maroons and traditional décor. And even dogs get the Sheraton Sweet Sleeper beds.

242 rooms. Business center. **$$**

## RESTAURANTS

### ★★★240 Union

240 Union Blvd., Lakewood, 303-989-3562;
www.240union.com

This contemporary American grille with a large open kitchen is known for having some of the best seafood in the Denver area. Other favorites include wood-fired oven pizzas, New York strip steak with forest mushrooms and short ribs with garlic mashed potatoes. The wine list features a number of good selection, and desserts like key lime pie and chocolate mousse are worthwhile temptations.

American menu. Lunch, dinner. Bar. Business casual attire. Reservations recommended. **$$**

### ★Casa Bonita of Denver

6715 W. Colfax Ave., Lakewood,
303-232-5115;
www.casabonitadenver.com

Mexican menu. Lunch, dinner. Bar. Children's menu. Casual attire. **$$**

**143**

COLORADO

# LEADVILLE

Located just below the timberline, Leadville's high altitude contributes to its reputation for excellent skiing, cool summers and beautiful fall colors. First a rich gold camp, then an even richer silver camp, the town boasts a lusty, brawling past in which millionaires were made and destroyed in a single day, a barrel of whiskey could net $1,500 and thousands of dollars could be won and lost in a card game in the town's saloons and smoky gambling halls.

Leadville's lively history is intertwined with the lives of Horace Tabor and his two wives, Augusta and Elizabeth Doe, whose rags-to-riches-to-rags story is the basis of the American opera *The Ballad of Baby Doe*. The "unsinkable" Molly Brown (from *Titanic* fame) made her fortune here, as did David May, Charles Boettcher, Charles Dow and Meyer Guggenheim.

Until 1950, Leadville was a decaying mining town. However, a burst of civic enthusiasm has led to many attractions that date back to the town's glory days, including several museums and a Victorian downtown area.

Information: Greater Leadville Area Chamber of Commerce, 809 Harrison Ave., 719-486-3900, 888-532-3845; www.leadvilleusa.com

## WHAT TO SEE AND DO

### Earth Runs Silver
Fox Theater, 115 West Sixth St., Leadville, 719-486-3900
Video presentation featuring Leadville's legendary mining camp with music and narration. Daily.

### Healy House-Dexter Cabin
912 Harrison Ave., Leadville, 719-486-0487; www.coloradohistory.org
The restored Healy House, built in 1878, contains many fine Victorian-era furnishings. Dexter Cabin, built by early mining millionaire James V. Dexter to entertain wealthy gentlemen, looks like an ordinary two-room miner's cabin from the outside but is surprisingly luxurious. Memorial Day-Labor Day, daily.

### Heritage Museum and Gallery
Ninth St. and Harrison Ave., Leadville, 719-486-1878
Learn all about the local history at this museum including Victorian costumes, memorabilia of mining days and changing exhibits of American art. Mid-May-October, daily.

### Leadville, Colorado & Southern Railroad Train Tour
326 E. Seventh St., Leadville, 719-486-3936, 866-386-3936; www.leadville-train.com
Depart from the old depot for a 23-mile round-trip scenic ride following the headwaters of the Arkansas River through the Rocky Mountains. Memorial Day-October, daily.

### National Mining Hall of Fame and Museum
120 W. Ninth St., Leadville, 719-486-1229; www.mininghalloffame.org
Dedicated to those who have made significant contributions to the industry. Includes history and technology exhibits of the mining industry. May-October, daily; rest of year, Monday-Friday.

### Ski Cooper
Hwy. 24, Leadville, 800-707-6114; www.skicooper.com
Triple, double chairlift; Pomalift, T-bar; patrol, school, rentals; snowcat tours; cafeteria, nursery; 26 runs; longest run 1 1/2 miles; vertical drop 1,200 feet. Groomed cross-country skiing (15 miles). Late November-early April, daily.

### Tabor Opera House
308 Harrison Ave., Leadville, 719-486-8409; www.taboroperahouse.net
Now a museum, this 1879 theater was host to the Metropolitan Opera, the Chicago Symphony and most of the famous actors and actresses of the period. Their photos line the corridors. Many of the original furnishings, scenery and the dressing areas are still in use and on display. Summer shows. Memorial Day-September, daily.

### The Matchless Mine
E. Seventh St., Leadville, 719-486-1899; www.matchlessmine.com
When Horace Tabor died in 1899, his last words to his wife were "hold on to the Matchless," which produced as much as $100,000 a month in its bonanza days. Faithful to his wish and ever hopeful, the once fabulously rich Baby Doe lived on in poverty in the little cabin next to the mine for 36 years, where she was found frozen to death in 1935. The cabin is now a museum. June-Labor Day, daily.

## SPECIAL EVENTS
### Boom Days & Burro Race
Leadville, 719-486-3900, 888-532-3845; www.leadville.com/boomdays

**144**

**COLORADO**

Celebrates the town's 1880s Old West heritage with mining skill competitions, gunslingers, a parade and the 21-mile International Pack Burro Race. Early August.

### Crystal Carnival Weekend
Harrison Ave., Leadville, 719-486-0739; www.leadvilleusa.com
This event does not actually include a carnival. Instead, it features a skijoring competition in which dogs draw a person on skis over a snowy obstacle course. First full weekend of March.

### Victorian Home Tour and Brunch
Leadville, 888-532-3845
Locals and visitors dress in Victorian fashions and tour the town's historic Victorian homes decorated brightly and cheerfully for Christmas. First Saturday in December.

## SPECIALTY LODGINGS
### Ice Palace Inn Bed & Breakfast
813 Spruce St., Leadville, 719-486-8272, 800-754-2840; www.icepalaceinn.com
5 rooms. Complimentary full breakfast. **$**

### The Leadville Country Inn
127 E. Eighth St., Leadville, 719-966-4770; www.leadvillebednbreakfast.com
This stately 15-room Victorian mansion was built in the 1800s and has been an inn since 1999.
9 rooms. Complimentary full breakfast. Pets. **$$**

## RESTAURANTS
### ★★★Tennessee Pass Cookhouse
1892 CO 25, Leadville, 719-486-8114; www.tennesseepass.com
This ski-oriented dining room serves one prix fixe meal nightly with entrées ordered 24 hours in advance.
American menu. Lunch, dinner. Reservations recommended. **$$$**

# LONGMONT
Considered one of the top small communities in the country, Longmont has found its own limelight outside the shadow of Boulder, its better-known neighbor.
Information: Chamber of Commerce, 528 Main St., 303-776-5295; www.longmontchamber.org

## WHAT TO SEE AND DO
### Longmont Museum
400 Quail Rd., Longmont, 303-651-8374; www.ci.longmont.co.us/museum
Changing and special exhibits on art, history, space and science; permanent exhibits on the history of Longmont and the St. Vrain Valley. Tuesday-Saturday, Sunday afternoons.

## SPECIAL EVENTS
### Boulder County Fair and Rodeo
Longmont, 303-441-3927
Fairgrounds. Nine days in early August.

### Rhythm on the River
Roger's Grove, Hover St. and Boston Ave., Longmont, 303-776-5295; www.ci.longmont.co.us/rotr
This annual festival honors Roger Jones, who preserved this riverside grove for generations to enjoy. Activities include music, an art show and children's activities. Early July.

## HOTELS
### ★★Radisson Hotel
1900 Ken Pratt Blvd., Longmont, 303-776-2000, 888-201-1718; www.radisson.com

★
★
★
★
★

210 rooms. High-speed Internet access, wireless Internet access. Restaurant, two bars. Pets accepted. Pool. **$**

# LOVELAND

In recent years, more than 300,000 Valentines have been re-mailed annually by the Loveland post office, stamped in red with the "Sweetheart Town's" cachet, a different valentine verse each year.

Information: Visitor Center/Chamber of Commerce, 5400 Stone Creek Circle, 970-667-6311, 800-258-1278; www.loveland.org

## WHAT TO SEE AND DO

### Boyd Lake State Park

3720 N. Country Rd., Loveland, 970-669-1739; www.parks.state.co.us/parks/boydlake
Swimming, water-skiing, fishing, boating; picnicking, camping. Daily.

## SPECIAL EVENTS

### Larimer County Fair and Rodeo

The Ranch, Crossroads Blvd. and Fairgrounds Ave., Loveland, 970-619-4000; www.larimercountyfair.org
The fair includes a carnival, parade, PRCA rodeo and other activities. Mid-August.

## SPECIALTY LODGINGS

### Cattail Creek Inn Bed & Breakfast

2665 Abarr Dr., Loveland, 970-667-7600; www.cattailcreekinn.com
Located on the Cattail Creek Golf Course, this luxury inn offers views of Lake Loveland and the Rocky Mountains. The open guest rooms have cherry woodwork and ceiling fans. Delicious breakfasts include dishes like Belgian pecan waffles with sautéed peaches. 8 rooms. Children over 14 years only. Complimentary full breakfast. **$**

### Sylvan Dale Guest Ranch

2939 N. County Rd. 31 D, Loveland, 970-667-3915, 877-667-3999; www.sylvandale.com
This dude ranch, owned and operated by the Jessup family, was established in the 1920s and is still a working cattle and horse ranch. Located in a river valley at the mouth of Colorado's Big Thompson Canyon, the ranch has more than 3,000 acres to enjoy, with elevations ranging up to 7,500 feet. 23 rooms. Complimentary full breakfast. Restaurant (public by reservation). Children's activity center. Airport transportation available. Pool. **$**

# LYONS

In the foothills of the Rocky Mountains, this small town is known for the beautiful red cliffs that surround it.

Information: Chamber of Commerce, 303-823-5215, 877-596-6726; www.lyons-colorado.com

## SPECIAL EVENTS

### Good Old Days Celebration

350 Broadway Ave., Lyons, 303-823-5215
Parade, flea market, craft fair, food. Last weekend in June.

## SPECIALTY LODGINGS

### Peaceful Valley Ranch

475 Peaceful Valley Rd., Lyons, 303-747-2881, 800-955-6343; www.peacefulvalley.com
52 rooms. Restaurant. Children's activity center. Airport transportation available. **$$**

# RESTAURANTS

## ★Andrea's Homestead Cafe
216 E. Main St., Lyons, 303-823-5000;
www.andreashomesteadcafe.com
German menu. Breakfast, lunch, dinner. Closed Wednesday. Bar. Children's menu. Casual attire. Reservations recommended. **$$**

## ★★★Black Bear Inn
42 E. Main St., Lyons, 303-823-6812;
www.blackbearinn.com
Since 1977, owners Hand and Annalies Wyppler have welcomed guests to their cozy Alpine-style restaurant with hearty dishes such as roasted duck and pork schnitzel.
American menu. Lunch, dinner. Closed Monday-Tuesday; also January-mid-February. Bar. Outdoor seating. **$$$**

## ★★★La Chaumiere
Hwy. 36, Lyons, 303-823-6521;
www.lachaumiere-restaurant.com
This charming French restaurant offers friendly service and a simple but delicious menu of French cuisine. The menu changes with the seasons, but you might see filet mignon with red wine sauce, and stuffed quail with wild mushrooms and a port wine demi-glaze. One mainstay is the chef's award-winning Maryland crab soup. The tranquil mountain setting adds to the relaxing atmosphere.
French menu. Dinner. Closed Monday. Children's menu. **$$**

# MANITOU SPRINGS

Nestled at the foot of Pikes Peak, only seven miles west of downtown Colorado Springs, Manitou Springs is one of the state's definitive—and most accessible—mountain communities. The many mineral springs gave nearby Colorado Springs its name. The natives, attributing supernatural powers to the waters (Manitou is an American Indian word for "Great Spirit"), once marked off the surrounding area as a sanctuary. Today, the town is a National Historic District and a popular tourist resort. Manitou Avenue has many artists' studios, restaurants and boutiques.
Information: Chamber of Commerce, 354 Manitou Ave., 719-685-5089, 800-642-2567; www.manitousprings.org

## WHAT TO SEE AND DO

### Cave of the Winds
Cave of the Winds Rd., Manitou Springs, 719-685-5444; www.caveofthewinds.com
This fascinating 45-minute guided tour through underground passageways filled with beautiful stalactites, stalagmites and flowstone formations created millions of years ago leaves every 15 minutes and includes a laser light show with music. Summer, 9 a.m.-9 p.m., Winter, 10 a.m.-5 p.m.

### Iron Springs Chateau
444 Ruxton Ave., Manitou Springs, 719-685-5104
Dinner theater featuring a traditional "olio" show. Named for the mineral-rich water beneath the ground. Monday-Saturday.

### Manitou Cliff Dwellings Museum
Hwy. 24 W, Manitou Springs, 719-685-5242, 800-354-9971; www.cliffdwellingsmuseum.com
See the architecture of the cliff-dwelling natives, A.D. 1100-1300. American Indian dancing (June-August). Museum March-November, daily.

### Miramont Castle Museum
9 Capitol Hill Ave., Manitou Springs, 719-685-1011; www.miramontcastle.org
A 46-room, four-story Victorian house (circa 1895) featuring nine styles of architecture, miniatures and doll collection, tea room, soda fountain, gardens. Tuesday-Sunday.

## HOTELS

### ★Best Value Inn
481 Manitou Ave., Manitou Springs,
719-685-5492, 888-315-2378;
www.villamotel.com
47 rooms. Pool. $

### ★★★The Cliff House at Pikes Peak
306 Canon Ave., Manitou Springs,
719-685-3000, 888-212-7000;
www.thecliffhouse.com
Built in 1873—before Colorado was even
a state—this hotel has retained every
charming detail of the Victorian age,
while adding modern details. Each room
is different and may include a gas fireplace, steam shower and towel warmers.
Galleries, shops restaurants and museums
surround the hotel, and bicycles are available for rent. The dining room and wine
cellar repeatedly win national awards.
55 rooms. Complimentary full breakfast.
High-speed wireless Internet access. Res-
taurant. $$$

### ★★★Red Crags Bed & Breakfast Inn
302 El Paso Blvd., Manitou Springs,
719-685-1920, 800-721-2248;
www.redcrags.com
Housed in an 1884 mansion that was
originally built as a clinic, this charming
and elegant inn, surrounded by the Rocky
Mountains, has high ceilings, hardwood
floors and beautiful antiques. In-room
fireplaces provide a romantic atmosphere.
All rooms also have plasma TVs.
8 rooms. Children over 10 years only. Com-
plimentary full breakfast. $$

### ★★★Rockledge Country Inn
328 El Paso Blvd., Manitou Springs,
719-685-4515, 888-685-4515;
www.rockledgeinn.com
Situated atop a hill and surrounded by
lush juniper and pine trees, the Rockledge
Country Inn is located at the foot of Pikes
Peak and has a beautiful view of the Rocky
Mountains. Built in 1912, the inn is built in
an Arts and Crafts style. The living room
has leather couches, a marble fireplace and
a grand piano. And there's plenty on hand

here, from bike rentals to hiking trails to
croquet.
5 rooms. Children over 8 permitted. Complimentary full breakfast. Wireless Internet
access. $$

## RESTAURANTS

### ★★★Briarhurst Manor
404 Manitou Ave., Manitou Springs,
719-685-1864, 877-685-1448;
www.briarhurst.com
Located in a pink sandstone Tudor manor
house built in 1876 by the founder of
Manitou Springs, this elegant fine-din-
ing restaurant's kitchen is headed up by
executive chef Lawrence "Chip" Johnson,
who uses homegrown vegetables and herbs
in his recipes. Menu items include arti-
san cheeses, crusted lamb chops, Sicilian
pheasant and black hollow wild boar. The
dessert sampler is the perfect ending to a
delicious meal.
American menu. Dinner. Closed Monday-
Tuesday in January-March. Bar. Children's
menu. Business casual attire. Reservations
recommended. Outdoor seating. Credit
cards accepted. $$$

### ★★★The Cliff House Dining Room
306 Canon Ave., Manitou Springs,
719-685-3000, 888-212-7000;
www.thecliffhouse.com
Located in the historic Cliff House hotel,
this elegant dining room serves up new
American cooking presented with flair.
Look for dishes like Rocky Mountain red
trout almondine, or vanilla-marinated pork
tenderloin. The ingredients in each dish are
fresh and local, and the restaurant has more
than 700 bottles of wine to accompany
them.
American menu. Breakfast, lunch, dinner. $$

### ★★★Craftwood Inn
404 El Paso Blvd., Manitou Springs,
719-685-9000; www.craftwood.com
This romantic restaurant located in a 1912
Tudor manor house serves Southwestern-
influenced cuisine. The focus in on steaks,
elk, pheasant, venison, quail and seafood.
When in season, the kitchen also uses

**148**

COLORADO

Colorado vegetables and produce. Dining here is an adventure. Dishes include antelope with Porcini mushroom sauce, and Colorado blue cheese and pheasant with smoked Gouda and baked in a phyllo crust.

American menu. Dinner. Bar. Outdoor seating. $$$

★★**Mission Bell Inn**

178 Crystal Park Rd., Manitou Springs, 719-685-9089; www.missionbellinn.com

Mexican menu. Dinner. Closed first three weeks of January; Monday and Tuesday in winter. Children's menu. Casual attire. Outdoor seating. $$

★★**Stage Coach Inn**

702 Manitou Ave., Manitou Springs, 719-685-9400; www.stagecoachinn.com

American menu. Lunch, dinner. Bar. Children's menu. Casual attire. Reservations recommended (summer). Outdoor seating. $$

# MESA VERDE NATIONAL PARK

In the far southwest corner of Colorado exists the largest—and arguably the most interesting—archaeological preserve in the nation. Mesa Verde National Park, with 52,000 acres encompassing 4,000 known archaeological sites, is a treasure trove of ancestral Pueblo cultural artifacts, including the magnificent Anasazi cliff dwellings. Constructed in the 13th century, these huge, elaborate stone villages built into the canyon walls are spellbinding. To fully appreciate their significance, first take a walk through the park's Chapin Mesa Museum for a historical overview. A visit to the actual sites can be physically challenging but is well worth the effort. Several of the sites can be explored year-round, free of charge; others require tickets for ranger-guided tours in summer months only. Tour tickets can be purchased at the parks Far View Visitor Center. Daily.

Information: Mesa Verde, eight miles east of Cortez, 36 miles west of Durango on Hwy. 160 to park entrance, then 15 miles south to visitor center, 970-529-4465; www.nps.gov/meve

**149**

COLORADO

# WHAT TO SEE AND DO

## Cliff Dwelling Tours

Mesa Verde National Park, 970-529-4465

The cliff dwellings can be entered only while rangers are on duty. During the summer, five cliff dwellings may be visited at specific hours. During the winter there are trips to Spruce Tree House only, weather permitting. Obtain daily tickets for Cliff Palace, Balcony House and Long House tours at Far View Visitor Center. Balcony House tours are limited to 50 people, Cliff Palace tours are limited to the first 60 and Long House tours are limited to 40 people.

## Mesa Top Loop and Cliff Palace Loop

Mesa Verde National Park, enter at crossroads near museum, 970-529-4465

Two six-mile, self-guided loops afford visits to 10 excavated mesa-top sites illustrating 700 years of architectural development; views of 20 to 30 cliff dwellings from canyon rim vantage points. Daily; closed during heavy snowfalls.

## Museum

Mesa Verde National Park, 21 miles south of park entrance, 970-529-4465

Learn the story of the Mesa Verde people though arts, crafts, industries. Daily.

## Park Point Fire Lookout

Mesa Verde National Park, halfway between the park entrance and headquarters, 970-529-4465

From an elevation of 8,572 feet, enjoy spectacular views of the entire Four Corners area

★
★
★
★
★

of Colorado, Arizona, New Mexico and Utah. The access road is closed in winter.

150 rooms. Closed late October-mid-April. Restaurant, bar. Pets accepted. **$**

## HOTELS
**★★Far View Lodge in Mesa Verde**
1 Navajo Hill, Mesa Verde National Park,
866-875-8456;
www.nationalparkreservations.com/
mesaverde.htm

# MONTE VISTA
Located in the heart of the high-altitude San Luis Valley, Monte Vista means "mountain view" in Spanish.
Information: Monte Vista Chamber of Commerce, 1035 Park Ave., 719-852-2731, 800-562-7085; www.monte-vista.org

## WHAT TO SEE AND DO
**Monte Vista National Wildlife Refuge**
9383 El Rancho Lane, Alamosa,
719-589-4021; www.fws.gov/alamosa
Created as a nesting, migration and wintering habitat for waterfowl and other migratory birds. Marked visitor tour road.

## SPECIAL EVENTS
**Monte Vista Crane Festival**
Ski-Hi Park, 2345 Sherman Ave.,
Monte Vista, 719-852-2731;
www.cranefest.com
Tours of refuge to view cranes and other wildlife. Arts, crafts, workshops. Mid-March.

**Ski-Hi Stampede**
Ski-Hi Park, 2345 Sherman Ave.,
Monte Vista, 719-852-2055;
www.skihistampede.com

Rodeo, carnival, arts and crafts show, street parade, barbecue, Western dances. Last weekend in July.

## HOTELS
**★★Best Western Movie Manor**
2830 W. Hwy. 160, Monte Vista,
719-852-5921, 800-771-9468;
www.bestwestern.com
59 rooms. Restaurant, bar. Pets accepted. **$**

## SPECIALTY LODGINGS
**Pecosa Inn**
1519 Grand Ave., Monte Vista,
719-852-0612, 888-732-6724;
www.pecosainn.com
44 rooms. Complimentary continental breakfast. Pets accepted. Pool. **$**

# MONTROSE
Montrose is a trading center for a rich mining, agricultural and recreational area in the Uncompahgre Valley. Several fishing areas are nearby, which includes the Gunnison River east of town and Buckhorn Lakes southeast.
Information: Montrose Chamber of Commerce, 1519 E. Main St., 970-249-5000, 800-923-5515; www.montrosechamber.com

## WHAT TO SEE AND DO
**Black Canyon of the Gunnison National Monument**
102 Elk Creek, Gunnison, 970-641-2337;
www.nps.gov/blca

Within this monument, 12 of the most spectacular miles of the rugged gorge of the Gunnison River slice down to a maximum depth of 2,660 feet. At one point, the river channel is only 40 feet wide. The narrowest width between the north and south rims at the top is 1,100 feet. The combination of dark, weathered rock and lack of sunlight due to the narrowness of the canyon give the monument its name. The spectacular scenery includes Pion trees—some more than 800 years old. There are scenic drives along South Rim (the road is plowed to Gunnison Point in winter) and North Rim (approximately May-October). There are also hiking areas and concessions (June-Labor Day). The visitor center is located at Gunnison Point on the south rim. A descent into the canyon requires a free hiking permit from the visitor center. Cross-country skiing is open in winter from Gunnison Point to High Point.

### Montrose County Historical Museum
In Depot Building, 21 N. Rio Grande, Montrose, 970-249-2085
Collections of antique farm machinery; archaeological artifacts; pioneer cabin with family items; tool collection; early electrical equipment; Montrose newspapers 1896-1940. May-September, daily.

### Scenic Drive, Owl Creek Pass
Montrose, 23 miles south on Hwy. 550 to the left-hand turnoff for Owl Creek Pass, marked by a U.S. Forest Service sign, then east seven miles along Cow Creek to Debbie's Park
A scene with Debbie Reynolds from *How the West Was Won* was filmed in the meadow here. Go up the Owl Creek Pass (at 10,114 feet). Fifteen miles from the pass is Silver Jack Reservoir, an area with good fishing and scenic hiking trails. About 20 miles north, the road joins Highway 50 at Cimarron.

## HOTELS
### ★★Best Western Red Arrow
1702 E. Main St., Montrose, 970-249-9641, 800-468-9323; www.bestwestern.com/redarrow
59 rooms. Restaurant. Airport transportation available. Pets accepted. **$**

## RESTAURANTS
### ★Whole Enchilada
44 S. Grand Ave., Montrose, 970-249-1881
Mexican menu. Lunch, dinner. Closed Sunday. Bar. Casual attire. Outdoor seating. **$**

# MORRISON
This tiny town has played a big role in paleontologists' search for dinosaur bones. In the late 19th century, scientists found fossil remains of a Stegosaurus and an Apatosaurus in and around Morrison, and recent discoveries include preserved adult Stegosaurus tracks.
Information: www.town.morrison.co.us

## WHAT TO SEE AND DO
### Red Rocks Park and Amphitheater
18300 W. Alameda Rkwy., Morrison, 720-865-2494; www.redrocksonline.com
Red Rocks Amphitheater is located in the majestic 816-acre Red Rocks Park, 15 miles west of Denver. Two 300-foot sandstone monoliths serve as stadium walls for this open-air arena. During the summer months, the 8,000-seat amphitheater, with its perfect acoustical conditions, awe-inspiring beauty and panoramic view of Denver, serves as a stunning stage for performers ranging from chart-topping rock bands to world-renowned symphony orchestras.

## RESTAURANTS
### ★★★The Fort
19192 Hwy. 8, Morrison, 303-697-4771; www.thefort.com
Sam Arnold's popular, kitschy restaurant has been serving buffalo steaks for 30 years. The menu also features other game, such as elk chops, as well as beef and seafood. The adobe recreation of the historic Bent's Fort is reason enough to check out this restaurant.

**151**

COLORADO

American menu. Dinner. Bar. Children's menu. Business casual attire. Reservations recommended. Outdoor seating. **$$$**

# OURAY

Ouray's location in a natural basin surrounded by majestic 12,000-to 14,000-foot peaks of the San Juan Mountains has made it a nice spot for visitors. Ouray, named for a Ute chief, is reached by the magnificent Million Dollar Highway section of the San Juan Skyway, which was blasted from sheer cliff walls high above the Uncompahgre River.
**Information: Ouray Chamber Resort Association, 970-325-4746, 800-228-1876; www.ouraycolorado.com**

## WHAT TO SEE AND DO

### Bachelor-Syracuse Mine Tour
**1222 County Rd. 14, Ouray,**
**970-325-0220, 888-227-4585;**
**www.bachelorsyracusemine.com**
This mine has been in continuous operation since 1884. Guided tours are aboard a mine train that advances 3,350 feet horizontally into Gold Hill (mine temperature 47°F) where you can see mining equipment, visit work areas and learn how explosives are used. Gold panning. Late May-September, daily.

### Bear Creek Falls
**1230 Main, Ouray, 970-325-4746**
An observational point lets you take in the 227-foot falls.

### Box Canon Falls Park
**Hwy. 550, Ouray, 970-325-7080**
Canyon Creek has cut a natural canyon 20 feet wide, 400 feet deep. Take the stairs and a suspended bridge to the floor of the canyon, where you can see the thundering falls. Daily.

### Hot Springs Pool
**Ouray City Park, 1200 Main, Ouray,**
**970-325-7073**
Outdoor, million-gallon pool fed by natural mineral hot springs (sulphur-free). Bathhouse; spa. Daily)

## SPECIAL EVENTS

### Artists' Alpine Holiday & Festival
**476 Main St., Ouray, 970-325-4746**

Each year, artists from across the country come to Ouray to enter their work into this juried art show. One week in mid-August.

### Imogene Pass Mountain Marathon
**100 Fifth St., Ouray, 970-728-0251;**
**www.imogenerun.com**
The 18-mile course, which follows an old mining trail, starts at Ouray's 7,800-foot elevation, crosses over Imogene Pass (13,114 feet) and ends at Main Street, Telluride (8,800 feet).

## HOTELS

### ★Box Canyon Lodge & Hot Spring
**45 Third Ave., Ouray,**
**970-325-4981, 800-327-5080;**
**www.boxcanyonouray.com**
38 rooms. Pool. **$**

### ★Comfort Inn
**191 Fifth Ave., Ouray,**
**970-325-7203, 800-438-5713;**
**www.ouraycomfortinn.com**
33 rooms. Complimentary continental breakfast. Whirlpool. Pets accepted. **$**

### ★★★St. Elmo Hotel
**426 Main St., Ouray, 970-325-4951;**
**www.stelmohotel.com**
The guest rooms at this restored 1898 hotel are individually decorated in Victorian style and feature period antiques. Enjoy a wine and cheese social hour every afternoon in the parlor and a full breakfast every morning in the sun room.

**152**

**COLORADO**

9 rooms. Complimentary continental breakfast. Restaurant. Whirlpool. $

## SPECIALTY LODGINGS
### China Clipper Bed Breakfast Inn
525 Second St., Ouray,
970-325-0565, 800-315-0565;
www.chinaclipperinn.com
Each guest room has a view of the magnificent San Juan Mountains. Winter guests receive half-price coupons to the nearby million-gallon natural Hot Springs Pool. 12 rooms. Children over 15 years only. Complimentary continental breakfast. Whirlpool. $

## RESTAURANTS
### ★★Bon Ton
426 Main St., Ouray, 970-325-4951;
www.stelmohotel.com
American, Italian menu. Dinner. Bar. Children's menu. Casual attire. Outdoor seating. $$$

### ★Buen Tiempo
515 Main St., Ouray, 970-325-4544;
www.stelmohotel.com
Mexican menu. Lunch, dinner. Bar. Children's menu. Casual attire. Outdoor seating. $$

# PAGOSA SPRINGS
People come here for the remarkable mineral springs. The town is surrounded by the San Juan National Forest, and deer and elk hunting are popular activities.
Information: Pagosa Springs Chamber of Commerce, 402 San Juan St., 970-264-2360, 800-252-2204; www.pagosa-springs.com

## WHAT TO SEE AND DO
### Chimney Rock Archaeological Area
180 N. Pagosa Blvd., Pagosa Springs,
970-883-5359; www.chimneyrockco.org
This area features twin pinnacles, held sacred by the Anasazi. The Fire Tower offers a spectacular view of ruins. Four guided scheduled tours daily.

### Fred Harman Art Museum
85 Harman Park Dr., Pagosa Springs,
970-731-5785;
www.harmanartmuseum.com
See original paintings by Fred Harman—best known for his famous Red Ryder and Little Beaver comic strip. Rodeo, movie and Western memorabilia. Late May-early October, daily; rest of year, Monday-Friday.

### Rocky Mountain Wildlife Park
4821 Hwy. 84, Pagosa Springs,
970-264-5546;
www.alldurango.com/wildlife
Exhibits animals indigenous to the area, plus wildlife museum and photography displays. Summer, 9 a.m.-6 p.m., Winter, noon-4 p.m.

### Wolf Creek Pass
Pagosa Springs, 20 miles northeast on Hwys. 160 and 84
(10,857 feet) Take a scenic drive across the Continental Divide. The eastern approach is through the Rio Grande National Forest, the western approach through the San Juan National Forest. The best time to drive through is September, when you'll see spectacular views of the aspens changing color. Drive takes approximately one hour.

### Treasure Mountain
Pagosa Springs
Begin at the Wolf Creek Pass, just east of summit marked where Continental Divide Trail winds southward and connects with the Treasure Mountain Trail. Legend states that in 1790, 300 men mined five million dollars in gold and melted it into bars, but were forced to leave it behind. The gold has never been found.

### Wolf Creek Ski Area
Pagosa Springs, 20 miles northeast of Hwy. 160 and Hwy. 84, 970-264-5639;
www.wolfcreekski.com

COLORADO

Two triple, two double chairlifts; Poma-lift; patrol, school, rentals; cafeteria, Restaurant, bar, day lodge; 50 runs; longest run two miles; vertical drop 1,604 feet. Shuttle bus service. Early November-April, daily.

## HOTELS

### ★★Best Value High Country Lodge
3821 E. Hwy. 160, Pagosa Springs, 800-862-3707; www.highcountrylodge.com 35 rooms. Complimentary continental breakfast. Restaurant. Whirlpool. Pets accepted. **$**

### ★★Pagosa Lodge
3505 W. Hwy. 160, Pagosa Springs, 970-731-4141, 800-523-7704; www.pagosalodge.com 101 rooms. Restaurant, bar. Airport transportation available. Pool. **$**

## RESTAURANTS

### ★★Tequila's
439 San Juan St., Pagosa Springs, 970-264-9989 Mexican menu. Lunch, dinner. Children's menu. Casual attire. Outdoor seating. **$**

# PUEBLO

Pueblo began as a crossroad for Native Americans, Spaniards and fur traders. When the Rio Grande Railroad reached here in 1872, Pueblo was the leading center for steel and coal production west of the Mississippi. Today, Pueblo is a major transportation and industrial center—more than half of all goods manufactured in Colorado are produced in Pueblo.
Information: Chamber of Commerce, 302 N. Santa Fe Ave., 719-542-1704, 800-233-3446; www.pueblo.org

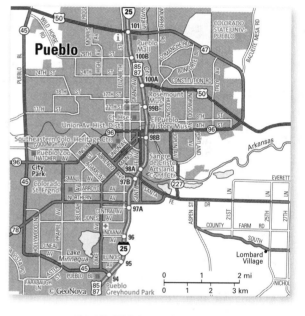

## WHAT TO SEE AND DO

### Mineral Palace Park
1500 N. Santa Fe, Pueblo
In addition to a pool, this park has a rose garden and green house. Also here is the Pueblo Art Guild Gallery, which showcases the work of local artists. Saturday-Sunday; closed December-February.

### El Pueblo Museum
301 N. Union, Pueblo, 719-583-0453; www.coloradohistory.org
Check out this full-size replica of Old Fort Pueblo, which served as a base for fur traders and other settlers from 1842 to 1855. Daily.

### Fred E. Weisbrod Aircraft Museum
Pueblo Memorial Airport, 31001 Magnuson Ave., Pueblo, 719-948-9219; www.pwam.org
This outdoor museum features static aircraft display. Adjacent is the B-24 Aircraft Memorial Museum, with indoor displays of the history of the B-24 bomber. Guided tours. Daily.

### Lake Pueblo State Park
640 Pueblo Reservoir Rd., Pueblo, 719-561-9320; www.parks.state.co.us/Parks/lakepueblo

Swimming, water-skiing, boating, hiking, camping. Daily.

### Rosemount Victorian House Museum
419 W. 14th St., Pueblo, 719-545-5290;
www.rosemount.org
This 37-room mansion contains original Victorian furnishings and the McClelland Collection of world curiosities. Tuesday-Sunday; closed in January.

### San Isabel National Forest
2840 Kachina Dr., Pueblo, 719-553-1400
On 1,109,782 acres, this forest offers camping and two winter sports areas: Monarch and Ski Cooper. In the southern part of the forest is the Spanish Peaks National Natural Landmark. Collegiate Peaks, Mount Massive and Holy Cross Wilderness areas are also within the forest, as well as four wilderness study areas. Colorado's highest peak, Mount Elbert (14,433 feet), is within the forest south of Leadville.

### Sangre de Cristo Arts and Conference Center
210 N. Santa Fe Ave., Pueblo,
719-295-7200; www.sdc-arts.org
The four art galleries here include the Francis King Collection of Western Art on permanent display. Children's museum, workshops, dance studios, theater. Monday-Saturday.

## SPECIAL EVENTS
### Colorado State Fair
Fairgrounds, 1001 Beulah Ave.,
Pueblo, 719-561-8484, 800-876-4567;
www.coloradostatefair.com
Rodeo, grandstand and amphitheater entertainment, agricultural and technological displays, arts and crafts, carnival. August-September.

## HOTELS
### ★La Quinta Inn & Suites
4801 N. Elizabeth St., Pueblo,
719-542-3500; www.laquinta.com
101 rooms. Complimentary continental breakfast. High-speed Internet access. Airport transportation available. Pets accepted. Pool. $

### ★★★Marriott Pueblo Convention Center
110 W. First St., Pueblo,
719-542-3200, 800-228-9290;
www.marriott.com
This hotel is connected to the convention center downtown and is surrounded by beautiful landscaping. Guest rooms feature modern furnishings and include microwaves and ergonomic desk chairs. The restaurant offers western fare. This hotel is non-smoking.
164 rooms. High-speed Internet access. Restaurant, bar. Pets accepted. Pool. Business center. $$

## SPECIALTY LODGINGS
### Abriendo Inn
300 W. Abriendo Ave., Pueblo,
719-544-2703; www.abriendoinn.com
Located just south of downtown, this inn is decorated with antiques and period furniture. Wake up to a gourmet breakfast and enjoy refreshments in the afternoon. Relax on the large front porch that overlooks the lovely residential area surrounding the inn or soak in your in-room whirlpool.
10 rooms. Wireless Internet access. $

## RESTAURANTS
### ★★Giacomo's Ristorante
910 Hwy. 50 W., Pueblo City,
719-546-0949
Italian menu. Lunch, dinner. Bar. Children's menu. Casual attire. Reservations recommended. Outdoor seating. $$

### ★★★La Renaissance
217 E. Routt Ave., Pueblo, 719-543-6367;
www.larenaissancerestaurant.com
This award-winning restaurant was originally built in 1886 as a Presbyterian church and still includes the pews and stained-glass windows. It's an interesting atmosphere for dining, and the food is superb, from lobster tail to prime rib.
American menu. Dinner. Closed Sunday-Monday. Bar. Casual attire. Reservations recommended. $$

**155**

**COLORADO**

★
★
★
★

**★The Laughing Crow**
5200 Nature Center Rd., Pueblo,
719-549-2009
American, Mexican menu. Breakfast, lunch, dinner. Children's menu. Casual attire. Reservations recommended. Outdoor seating. **$**

---

## ROCKY MOUNTAIN NATIONAL PARK

Straddling the Continental Divide, the 415-square-mile park contains a staggering profusion of peaks, upland meadows, sheer canyons, glacial streams and lakes. Dominating the scene is Longs Peak, with its east face towering 14,255 feet above sea level. The park's forests and meadows provide sanctuary for more than 750 varieties of wildflowers, 260 species of birds and such indigenous mammals as deer, wapiti (American elk), bighorn sheep and beaver. There are five campgrounds, two of which take reservations from May to early September. Some attractions are not accessible during the winter months.
Information: Rocky Mountain National Park, 970-586-1206.

---

# SALIDA

On the eastern slope of the Rocky Mountains, Salida is surrounded by San Isabel National Forest. A pleasant climate makes it ideal for recreational activities throughout the year, including river rafting, fishing, mountain biking, hiking and hunting.
Information: Heart of the Rockies Chamber of Commerce, 406 W. U.S. 50, 719-539-2068, 877-772-5432; www.salidachamber.org

## WHAT TO SEE AND DO

### Angel of Shavano
Salida
Every spring the snow melts on the 14, 239-foot slopes of Mount Shavano leaving an outline called "the Angel."

### Arkansas Headwaters State Recreation Area
307 W. Sackett, Salida, 719-539-7289; www.parks.State.co.us/Parks/arkansasheadwaters
An outstanding waterway cuts its way through rugged canyons for 148 miles, from Leadville to Pueblo. One of the world's premier waterways for kayaking and whitewater rafting. Fishing, boating, hiking, bridle trails, picnicking, camping. Daily.

### Jeep tours
Chamber of Commerce, Salida, 719-539-2068
Outfitters offer half-hour, half-day and full-day trail rides. Fishing, hunting, photography and pack trips. Contact Chamber of Commerce for details.

### Monarch Scenic Tram
Chamber of Commerce, 406 W. Rainbow Blvd., Salida, 719-539-4789, 888-996-7669;
This trip to deck and observatory at 12,000 feet offer panoramic views of Rocky Mountains. May-September, daily.

### Monarch Ski & Snowboard Area
1 Powder Place, Monarch, 719-539-3573, 888-996-7669; www.skimonarch.com
Four double chairlifts; patrol, school, rentals; 63 runs; longest run one mile; vertical drop 1,170 feet. Multiday, half-day rates. Mid-November-mid-April, daily. Cross-country skiing.

**Mountain Spirit Winery**
16150 County Rd. 220, Salida,
719-539-1175, 888-679-4637;
www.mountainspiritwinery.com
Family-operated boutique winery. Five acres
with apple orchard, homestead. Tours, tastings. Memorial Day-Labor Day, weekends.

**Salida Museum**
406 Hwy. 50, Salida, 719-539-7483
Museum features mineral display, American Indian artifacts, early pioneer household display, mining and railroad display.
Late May-early September, daily.

**Tenderfoot Drive**
Salida, west on Hwy. 291
This spiral drive encircling Mount Tenderfoot offers view of the surrounding mountain area and the upper Arkansas Valley.

## SPECIAL EVENTS
**Artwalk**
Downtown Historic District, 406 W.
Rainbow Blvd., Salida, 877-772-5432;
www.salidaartwalk.org
Local artists, craftspeople and entertainers
display artwork to celebrate Colorado's largest historic district. Last weekend in June.

**Christmas Mountain USA**
406 W. Rainbow Blvd., Salida,
719-539-2068
This three-day event kicks off the holiday
season. More than 3,500 lights outline
a 700-foot Christmas tree on Tenderfoot
Mountain. Parade. Day after Thanksgiving.

**FIBArk River International Whitewater Boat Race**
240 N. F St., Salida, 719-539-6918;
www.fibark.com
International experts comPetse in a 26-mile
kayak race. Other events include slalom,
raft, foot and bicycle races. Father's Day
weekend.

**New Old-Fashioned Chaffee County Fair**
10165 County Rd. 120, Poncha Springs,
719-539-6151
This annual event features a rodeo, live entertainment, arts and crafts, food, a beer garden,
livestock auctions, tractor-pull contests and
much more. Late July-early August.

## SPECIALTY LODGINGS
**Tudor Rose Bed & Breakfast**
6720 County Rd. 104, Salida,
719-539-2002, 800-379-0889;
www.thetudorrose.com
6 rooms. Children over 10 years only. Complimentary full breakfast. Whirlpool. **$**

## RESTAURANTS
★★**Country Bounty**
413 W. Hwy. 50, Salida, 719-539-3546;
www.countrybounty.net
American menu. Breakfast, lunch, dinner.
Children's menu. Casual attire. **$**

★**Windmill**
720 E. Rainbow Blvd., Salida,
719-539-3594
American menu. Lunch, dinner. Bar. Children's menu. Casual attire. **$**

# SILVERTON
Situated in the San Juan Mountains, Silverton is nicknamed "the mining town that never
quits." The last mine in Silverton closed in 1991. Since then, tourists have discovered the
natural beauty, historic ghost towns and many recreational opportunities of the area.
Information: Silverton Chamber of Commerce, Hwy. 550 and Hwy. 110, 970-387-5654,
800-752-4494; www.silverton.org

## WHAT TO SEE AND DO
**Circle Jeep Tour**
414 Greene St., Silverton,
970-387-5654, 800-752-4494

Take in the history of the area (including
information on mines and ghost towns) on
a jeep tour.

**157**

**COLORADO**

### Old Hundred Gold Mine Tour
721 County Rd. 4 A, Silverton,
970-387-5444, 800-872-3009;
www.minetour.com
Learn all about the methods of hardrock mining. This guided one-hour tour of an underground mine offers view of the equipment and crystal pockets. Memorial Day-September, daily.

### Red Mountain Pass
Silverton, Hwy. 550 between Ouray and Silverton
Stretching through the towering San Juan Mountains, the 23-mile stretch of Highway 550 between Ouray and Silverton passes through some of Colorado's wildest country. The road rises to 11,075 feet to cross the Red Mountain Pass, a favorite spot for hikers, rock climbers, mountain bikers and backcountry ski enthusiasts. Along the way you'll see numerous gorges and falls, as well as abandoned log cabins and mining equipment.

### San Juan County Historical Society Museum
1315 Snowden, Silverton
Located in an old three-story jail, this museum showcases mining and railroad artifacts from Silverton's early days. Memorial Day-mid-October, daily.

## SPECIAL EVENTS
### Great Western Rocky Mountain Brass Band Concerts
Silverton, 800-752-4494;
www.silvertoncolorado.com
Nationally recognized musicians—and Silverton's own brass band—perform concerts throughout the weekend. Mid-August.

## HOTELS
### ★★Wyman Hotel
1371 Greene St., Silverton,
970-387-5372, 800-609-7845;
www.thewyman.com
17 rooms. Closed late March-early May, mid-October-mid-December. Complimentary continental breakfast. Restaurant. Pets accepted. $

## SPECIALTY LODGINGS
### Alma House Bed and Breakfast
220 E. 10th St., Silverton,
970-387-5336, 800-267-5336;
www.innoftherockies.com
9 rooms. Whirlpool. $

# SNOWMASS VILLAGE
Snowmass Village, only eight miles from Aspen, is best known as the location of Snowmass Ski Area, a popular winter resort. (The village is located at the base of the ski area.) There's also much to do in summer, including swimming (there are 50 outdoor heated pools and hot tubs), rafting, hiking, horseback riding, 18-hole golf, tennis, hot air balloon rides and free outdoor concerts. The village includes more than 20 restaurants. A free shuttle bus runs throughout the village.
Information: Snowmass Resort Association, 104 A Gateway Center, 970-923-2000, 800-766-9627; www.snowmassvillage.com

## WHAT TO SEE AND DO
### Bicycle trips and Jeep trips
105 Snowmass Village Mall,
Snowmass Village, 970-923-4544
Throughout the Snowmass/Aspen area. Transportation and equipment provided. June-September.

### Snowmass Ski Area
40 Carriage Way, Snowmass Village,
970-923-1220;
www.aspensnowmass.com
Seven quad, two triple, six double chairlifts; two platter pulls; patrol, school, rentals, snowmaking; restaurants, bar, nursery.

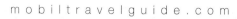

91 runs; longest run five miles, vertical drop 4,406 feet. Cross-country skiing (50 miles). Shuttle bus service from Aspen. Late November-mid-April, daily.

## HOTELS

### ★★Stonebridge Inn
300 Carriage Way, Snowmass Village, 970-923-2420, 800-213-3214; www.stonebridgeinn.com
92 rooms. Closed mid-April-May. Complimentary continental breakfast. Restaurant. Airport transportation available. $$

### ★★Wildwood Lodge
100 Elbert Lane, Snowmass Village, 970-923-3520, 800-837-4255; www.wildwood-lodge.com
140 rooms. Closed early April-May. Complimentary continental breakfast. Restaurant. Children's activity center. Airport transportation available. Pets accepted. Pool. $$

### ★★★Silvertree Hotel Snowmass Village
100 Elbert Lane, Snowmass Village, 970-923-3520, 800-837-4255; www.silvertreehotel.com
This year-round mountain resort offers ski in/ski out access, two heated pools and a fitness center with steam room and massage services. Family-style suites are available. 260 rooms. Restaurant. Children's activity center. Airport transportation available. Pets accepted. Business center. $$$

### ★★★Snowmass Club
0239 Snowmass Club Circle, Snowmass Village, 970-923-5600, 800-525-0710; www.snowmassclub.com
This year-round resort is located in the Elk Mountain range area and offers one-, two- and three-bedroom villas with daily maid service. All of the villas have full kitchens and high speed Internet access, and most feature a fireplace, deck with barbecue grill and laundry. The 19,000-square-foot health club includes four pools, spa services and dozens of fitness classes. (There are also private residences here.) Brother's Grille serves everything from barbecue to New York style cuisine.
55 rooms. Restaurant. Children's activity center. Spa. Airport transportation available. Golf. Tennis. Business center. $$$$

## RESTAURANTS

### ★★★Krabloonik
4250 Divide Rd., Snowmass Village, 970-923-3953; www.krabloonik.com
Celebrate the dog days of winter at this log restaurant with ski-in access and large picture windows framing the mountain views. More than 200 sled dogs live in the kennel next door—take a sled ride after a lunch of wild mushroom soup, fresh baked bread and smoked meat from the on-site smokehouse. (No lunch during summer.) At night, the sunken fire pit keeps everyone warm and toasty.
American, seafood menu. Lunch, dinner. Closed mid-April-May, October-Thanksgiving. Children's menu. Casual attire. Reservations recommended. $$$

### ★★★Sage
239 Snowmass Circle, Snowmass Village, 970-923-0923
Located in the Snowmass Club, this restaurant offers simple classics with fresh ingredients. In the summer, the patio is a lovely spot for lunch, thanks to unobstructed views of mount Daly.
American menu. Breakfast, lunch, dinner. Bar. Children's menu. Valet parking. Outdoor seating. $$$

# STEAMBOAT SPRINGS

In 1913, Carl Howelsen, a Norwegian, introduced ski jumping here. Since then, 10 national ski-jumping records have been set on Steamboat Springs's Howelsen Hill. The area has produced 47 winter Olympians (hence the nickname). Summer activities include camping, fishing, hot air ballooning, horseback riding, hiking, bicycling, river rafting, canoeing and

★
★
★
★
★

llama trekking. One of the largest elk herds in North America ranges near the town. There are more than 100 natural hot springs in the area.

Information: Steamboat Ski Resort Corporation, 2365 Mt. Werner Circle, 970-879-6111, 800-922-2722; www.steamboat.com

## WHAT TO SEE AND DO

### Howelsen Hill Ski Complex
245 Howelsen Pkwy., Steamboat Springs, 970-879-8499

International ski/jump complex includes a double chairlift, Pomalift, rope tow, five ski jumping hills; patrol; ice skating, snowboarding. Evening skiing available. December-March, daily.

### Routt National Forest
925 Weiss Dr., Steamboat Springs, 970-879-1722

Includes the 139,898-acre Mount Zirkel Wilderness. Fishing, hunting, winter sports area, hiking, picnicking, camping.

### Steamboat
2305 Mount Werner Circle, Steamboat Springs, 970-879-6111, 800-922-2722; www.steamboat.com

High-speed gondola; four high-speed quad (two covered), quad, six triple, seven double chairlifts; two surface tows; patrol, school, rentals, snowmaking; cafeterias, restaurants, bars, nursery; 142 runs; longest run more than three miles; vertical drop 3,668 feet. Snowboarding. Cross-country skiing (14 miles). Multiday, half-day rates. Late November-early April, daily. Gondola also operates mid-June-mid-September. Daily; fee.

### Steamboat Health & Recreation Association
136 Lincoln Ave., Steamboat Springs, 970-879-1828; www.sshra.org

Three hot pools fed by 103 F mineral water. Lap pool, saunas, exercise classes, massage, weight room, tennis courts (summer). Daily.

### Steamboat Lake State Park
61855 Routt County Rd. 129, Steamboat Springs, 970-879-3922; parks.state.co.us/Parks/steamboatlake

Swimming, water-skiing, fishing, boating, picnicking, camping. Daily.

### Strawberry Park Natural Hot Springs
44200 County Rd. 36, Steamboat Springs, 970-879-0342; www.strawberryhotsprings.com

Mineral springs feed four pools (water cooled from 160 F to 105 F). Changing area, picnicking, camping, cabins. Daily.

### Tread of Pioneers Museum
800 Oak St., Steamboat Springs, 970-879-2214; www.treadofpioneers.org

Check out the permanent ski exhibit tracing the evolution of skiing. Also: Victorian house with period furnishings, and pioneer and cattle-ranching artifacts. Fall/spring, Tuesday-Saturday; summer/winter, Monday-Saturday.

## SPECIAL EVENTS

### Cowboy Roundup Days
Steamboat Springs

Rodeos, parade, entertainment. July 4 weekend.

### Rocky Mountain Mustang Round-Up
Steamboat Springs, 970-879-0880; www.steamboatchamber.com

Car fanatics will enjoy this parade of more than 350 Ford Mustangs. Timed driving event. Mid-June.

### Winter Carnival
Steamboat Springs

Snow and ski competitions, parade. Early February.

## HOTELS

### ★★Ptarmigan Inn
2304 Apres Ski Way, Steamboat Springs, 970-879-1730, 800-538-7519; www.steamboat-lodging.com

77 rooms. Closed early April-late May. Restaurant, bar. Pets accepted. Pool. **$**

### ★Fairfield Inn By Marriott

3200 S. Lincoln Ave., Steamboat Springs,
970-870-9000, 800-325-3535;
www.fairfieldinn.com
66 rooms. **$**

### ★Hampton Inn & Suites

725 S. Lincoln Ave., Steamboat Springs,
970-871-8900; www.hamptoninn.com
40 rooms. **$**

### ★★★Sheraton Steamboat Springs Resort And Conference Center

2200 Village Inn Court, Steamboat Springs,
970-879-8000, 800-325-3535;
www.starwoodhotels.com
This hotel is a great choice for families and business travelers—it's the only conference hotel in the area with ski in/ski out access. After a day on the slopes, enjoy the rooftop hot tubs or get a massage at the spa. The rooms are elegant and comfortable with the Sweet Sleeper beds. Ask for a slope view room. The resort has boutiques and an art gallery.
317 rooms. Closed mid-April-May, fall season. Restaurant, bar. Children's activity center. Spa. Golf. **$$**

### ★★★The Steamboat Grand Resort Hotel

2300 Mount Werner Circle,
Steamboat Springs,
970-871-5500, 877-366-2628;
www.steamboatgrand.com
The accommodations here range from studios to private residences with alder cabinets and granite countertops. The spa offers a wide variety of treatments, from hot stone massage to herbal hibernation body wraps, and the fitness center has lots of equipment but, more important, a eucalyptus steam room, perfect after a day on the slopes. The Cabin restaurant has an extensive wine list and serves Midwestern beef aged at least 30 days in controlled cellars and native Colorado game.
327 rooms. Restaurant, bar. **$$$**

# SPECIALTY LODGINGS

### The Home Ranch

54880 Rou County Rd. 129, Clark,
970-879-1780; www.homeranch.com
The Home Ranch makes everyone feel at home. Situated in the Elk River Valley with the majestic Rocky Mountains in the distance, the ranch is only 18 miles from Steamboat Springs and offers an authentic guest ranch experience. Activities are plentiful, with more than 12 miles of snow-covered trails for snowshoeing and cross-country skiing in winter, and mountain biking and hiking in summer. But horsemanship is the focus here. Cattle-working and stockmanship lessons are offered in addition to general riding. The Western-style rooms in the main lodge are convenient to the pool and dining room or for more privacy, there are eight cabins. The family-style meals in the restaurant are memorable. After dinner, listen to the sounds of the Ranch Hand Band.
8 rooms. Closed late October-mid-December, late March-late May. Restaurant. Children's activity center. Airport transportation available. **$$$**

### Vista Verde Guest And Ski Ranch

31100 Seehouse Rd., Steamboat Springs,
970-879-3858, 800-526-7433;
www.vistaverde.com
Situated on 500 acres in the Rocky Mountains, this wonderful ranch is fun for the whole family. The cozy accommodations range from lodge rooms to private cabins and feature furnishings handcrafted by the ranch's very own woodworker. There are plenty of activities on the property, from backcountry skiing and sleigh rides to fly fishing, hot air ballooning and hiking, though horseback riding is the most popular activity at the ranch (instruction is available for both kids and adults). Afterward, feast on gourmet meals in the rustic dining room.
12 rooms. Closed late September-late December, late March-early June. Restaurant. Children's activity center. Airport transportation available. **$$$**

## RESTAURANTS

### ★★Antares
57 1/2 Eighth St., Steamboat Springs,
970-879-9939
American menu. Dinner. Closed mid-April-
early June. Bar. Children's menu. Casual
attire. **$$$**

### ★★★L'Apogee
911 Lincoln Ave., Steamboat Springs,
970-879-1919; www.lapogee.com
Housed in a former saddlery store, L'Apogee
has become local favorite. The interesting
American menu features favorites like dry-
aged New York strip steak and filet mignon,
as well as less traditional dishes such as
marinated and baked tofu served with shi-
take mushrooms and bok choy. The large
wine cellar is filled with many reasonably
priced choices from around the world.
American menu. Dinner. Bar. Children's
menu. Casual attire. Outdoor seating. **$$$**

### ★★La Montana
2500 Village Dr., Steamboat Springs,
970-879-5800; www.la-montana.com
Southwestern, Mexican menu. Dinner.
Closed mid-April-early June. Bar.
Children's menu. Casual attire. Outdoor
seating. **$$**

### ★★Ore House at the Pine Grove
1465 Pine Grove Rd., Steamboat Springs,
970-879-1190, 800-280-8310;
www.orehouseatthepinegrove.com
American menu. Dinner. Closed mid-
April-mid-May 15. Bar. Children's menu.
Casual attire. Outdoor seating. **$$$**

### ★Tugboat Grill & Pub
1860 Mt Werner Rd., Steamboat Springs,
970-879-7070
American menu. Lunch, dinner. Closed
mid-April-early June. Bar. Children's
menu. Casual attire. Outdoor seating. **$**

### ★Winona's Deli-Bakery
617 Lincoln Ave., Steamboat Springs,
970-879-2483
American menu. Breakfast, lunch.
Children's menu. Casual attire. Outdoor
seating. **$**

# STERLING
Sterling is known as the "City of Living Trees" because of the unique carved trees found
throughout town.
Information: Logan County Chamber of Commerce, 109 N. Front St.,
970-522-5070, 800-522-5070; www.sterlingcolo.com

## WHAT TO SEE AND DO
### Overland Trail Museum
210533 County Rd. 26.5, Sterling,
970-522-3895
This village of seven buildings includes collections of American Indian artifacts, cattle
brands, farm machinery, archaeological and
paleontological exhibits, one-room schoolhouse, fire engine and more. Park and picnic area. April-October, daily; rest of year,
Tuesday-Saturday.

## HOTELS
### ★Best Western Sundowner
125 Overland Trail St., Sterling,
970-522-6265; www.bestwestern.com
58 rooms. Complimentary continental
breakfast. Pets accepted. **$**

### ★★Ramada
22140 E. Hwy. 6, Sterling,
970-522-2625, 800-272-6232;
www.ramada.com
100 rooms. Restaurant, bar. Whirlpool. Pets
accepted. **$**

## SPECIALTY LODGINGS
### Pioneer Trails Lodge
47490 Weld County Rd. 155, Stoneham,
970-735-2426;
www.bbonline.com/co/elkecho

This large log bed and breakfast offers guest rooms with a quiet atmosphere. Watch over 500 head of elk and a small buffalo herd from the deck.
4 rooms. Complimentary full breakfast. **$**

## RESTAURANTS
**★T. J. Bummer's**
203 Broadway, Sterling, 970-522-8397
American menu. Breakfast, lunch, dinner. Closed holidays. Children's menu. **$$**

# TELLURIDE
Gray granite and red sandstone mountains surround this mining town named for the tellurium ore containing precious metals found in the area. Telluride, proud of its bonanza past, has not changed its façade. Because of its remoteness and small size, Telluride is a favorite getaway spot for celebrities. Summer activities include fly-fishing, mountain biking, river rafting, hiking, Jeep trips, horseback riding and camping, as well as many annual events and festivals from May to October.
Information: Telluride Visitor Services, 666 W. Colorado Ave., 970-728-4431, 888-605-2578; www.telluride.com

## WHAT TO SEE AND DO
### Bear Creek Trail
South end of Pine St., Telluride
This two-mile canyon walk features a view of a tiered waterfall. May-October.

### Bridal Veil Falls
Telluride, 2 1/2 miles east on Hwy. 145
See the highest waterfall in Colorado.

### Telluride Gondola
Aspen and San Juan, Telluride
Passengers are transported from downtown Telluride to Mount Village. Early June-early October and late November-mid-April, daily.

### Telluride Historical Museum
201 W. Gregory Ave., Telluride, 970-728-3344; www.telluridemuseum.org
Built in 1893 as the community hospital, this historic building houses artifacts, historic photos and exhibits that show what Telluride was like in its Wild West days. Tuesday-Saturday 11 a.m.-5 p.m. sunday 1-5 p.m.

### Telluride Ski Resort
565 Mountain Village Blvd., Telluride, 800-778-8581; www.tellurideskiresort.com
Three-stage gondola; 7 quad, two triple, two double chairlifts; 2 surface lift; patrol, school, rentals; restaurants, nursery. 92 runs; longest run 4 1/2 miles; vertical drop 3,530 feet. Thanksgiving-early April, daily. Cross-country skiing, heliskiing, ice skating, snowmobiling, sleigh rides. Shuttle bus service and two in-town chairlifts.

## SPECIAL EVENTS
### Balloon Festival
Colorado Ave., Telluride, 970-728-4769; www.tellurideballoonfestival.com
See the balloons launch in the morning, or come in the evening to see them lined up on Colorado Avenue. Early June.

### Jazz Celebration
Telluride, 81435, Town Park, 970-728-7009; www.telluridejazz.com
After the daytime concerts with the San Juan Mountains as a backdrop, several of the musicians can be found in the Main Street saloons mingling with visitors and fans. Early August.

### Mountain Film Festival
109 E. Colorado Ave., Telluride, 970-728-4123; www.mountainfilm.org
In addition to showing films, the Mountain Film Festival is a unique conglomeration of filmmakers, authors, political activists and other thinkers who host seminars and symposiums throughout the weekend. These high-brow hosts discuss with the public the films shown and how they relate to the festival's theme. Late May.

**163**

**COLORADO**

### Telluride Bluegrass Festival
Telluride;
www.bluegrass.com/telluride
Thousands of music lovers come to Telluride for what many agree is the nation's premier bluegrass festival. The festival draws top bluegrass and folk performers. But the best part might be the spontaneous jams that break out in the wee hours at local drinking spots. The festival includes amateur competitions and workshops, and is a favorite destination for campers seeking high-spirited fun in a natural setting. Mid-June.

## HOTELS
### ★★★Hotel Columbia
300 W. San Juan Ave., Telluride,
970-728-0660, 800-201-9505;
www.columbiatelluride.com
Situated on the San Miguel River at the base of the Telluride Ski resort, this hotel feels more like a small inn, with only 21 Victorian-style rooms, each with a gas fireplace. (Columbia is the original name for Telluride.) Spring for the penthouse—it has a steam shower and two-person jetted tub surrounded by windows overlooking the mountains and river.
21 rooms. Restaurant, bar. Fitness room. Pets accepted. **$$**

### ★★★Wyndham Peaks Resort & Golden Door Spa
136 Country Club Dr., Telluride,
866-282-4557, 800-789-2220;
www.thepeaksresort.com
This is the perfect home for outdoor enthusiasts who like to rough it a bit outdoors—and live it up indoors. Situated on top of the mountain, the Wyndham Peaks Resort is a skier's heaven with ski-in/ski-out access and a ski valet who will warm and tune your equipment. The guest rooms and suites are cocoons of luxury, with huge picture windows with plantation shutters, fluffy duvets and glass-enclosed showers with separate tubs. Suites boast leather furniture and stone fireplaces. The centerpiece of this first-class resort is the Golden Door Spa, an outpost of the legendary California destination spa featuring a variety of restorative treatments. There's even a doggie spa

for your pooch. If you're here in summer, challenge yourself on one of the country's highest golf courses.
174 rooms. Closed mid-April-mid-May, mid-October-mid-November. Restaurant, bar. Children's activity center. Spa. Ski in/ski out. Airport transportation available. Pets accepted. **$$$**

### ★★★New Sheridan Hotel
231 W. Colorado Ave., Telluride,
970-728-4351, 800-200-1891;
www.newsheridan.com
Built in 1891, this hotel is located in the heart of Telluride. Many of the elegant guest rooms feature mountain views and separate sitting rooms. Warm up with a hearty gourmet breakfast and then relax in the afternoon with a complimentary glass of Pine Ridge wine at the New Sheridan Bar.
32 rooms. Closed mid-April-mid-May. Complimentary continental breakfast. Restaurant. Whirlpool. **$$**

## SPECIALTY LODGINGS
### The San Sophia Inn and Condominiums
330 W. Pacific Ave., Telluride,
970-728-3001, 800-537-4781;
www.sansophia.com
The interior of this romantic inn is Victorian-meets-Southwestern, with stained and etched glass and period furnishings. You can choose to stay in a standard guest room or in one of the private residences. After a day on the slopes—there's ski in/ski out access—the Gazebo-covered hot tub with views of Bear Creek beckons. You won't go hungry here, from the treats (like Rocky Mountain toffee) handed out at check-in to the full breakfast to the cocktail hour, where you can sample wines from around the world and nibble on appetizers such as brie and red grape quesadillas.
16 rooms. Closed April, November. Children over 9 years only. Complimentary full breakfast. Whirlpool. **$**

## RESTAURANTS
### ★★★Allred's
2 Coonskin Ridge, Telluride, 970-728-7474;
www.allredsrestaurant.com

**COLORADO**

At more than 10,000 feet above sea level, Allred's offers mountain views to complement the delicious culinary creations. The menu is made up of regional Colorado cuisine with international accents such as free-range chicken breast with creamy polenta, Manchengo, spinach and roasted peppers and elk shortloin with summer squash and braised figs. If you're looking for a special treat, reserve the Chef's Table (for four to six guests), where you'll be treated to a five-course, chef-prepared menu with the option to pair wines with each course. American menu. Dinner. Closed mid-April-mid-June, late September-mid-December. Bar. Children's menu. Casual attire. Reservations recommended. **$$$**

★★★**Cosmopolitan**
300 W. San Juan, Telluride, 970-728-1292; www.cosmotelluride.com

Housed in the luxurious Hotel Columbia, Cosmopolitan is an elegant restaurant where fresh ingredients and flavors from around the world are blended together to create an innovative contemporary American menu. Dishes, which change on a weekly basis, have included creations like crispy Asian short rib roll with kim chee, black bean sauce and mango sauce and a pesto grilled vegetable open calzone with goat cheese, parmesan and basil. French, American menu. Dinner. Closed mid-April-mid-May and the last week in October. Bar. Children's menu. Casual attire. Reservations recommended. **$$**

★★**Floradora**
103 W. Colorado Ave., Telluride, 970-728-8884
Southwestern, American menu. Lunch, dinner. Bar. Children's menu. **$$**

# VAIL

Built to resemble a Bavarian village, Vail is the world's largest single-mountain ski resort. Known for having vast and varied terrain for every skill level of skier or snowboarder, Vail often tops ski resort lists and gets rave reviews for its legendary powder. Summer has also emerged as a prime recreation season on Vail Mountain, with mountain biking the sport of choice. Today, ski conglomerate Vail Resorts owns numerous ski resorts in Colorado, including Beaver Creek, Breckenridge and Arapahoe Basin, and many passes work at all the properties.

Information: Vail Valley Tourism & Convention Bureau, 100 E. Meadow Dr., 970-476-1000, 800-525-3875; www.vail.com

## WHAT TO SEE AND DO

### Colorado Ski Museum & Ski Hall of Fame
In Vail Village Transportation Center, 231 S. Frontage Rd. E., Vail, 970-476-1876; www.skimuseum.net
Learn everything you ever wanted to know about skiing. The museum traces the history of skiing in Colorado for more than 120 years. Memorial Day-late September and late November-mid April, Tuesday-Sunday.

### Gerald R. Ford Amphitheater Vilar Pavilion/Betty Ford Alpine Gardens
Ford Park and the Betty Ford Alpine Gardens, Vail, 970-845-8497, 888-920-2797; www.vvf.org

Enjoy top-notch entertainment under Vail's crystal-clear, starlit skies at this open-air theater surrounded by the Betty Ford Alpine Gardens—a public botanical garden with more than 500 varieties of wildflowers and alpine plants. Performances throughout the summer normally include classical music, rock and roll, jazz, ballet, contemporary dance and children's theater. June-August.

### Vail Ski Resort
137 Benchmark Rd., Avon, 970-476-9090, 800-503-8748; www.vail.com
Gondola; 14 high-speed quad, seven fixed-grip quad, three triple, five double chairlifts; ten surface lifts; patrol,

school, rentals, snowmaking; cafeterias, restaurants, bars, nursery. Longest run four miles; vertical drop 3,450 feet. Late November-mid-April, daily. Cross-country trails, rentals November-April; ice skating, snowmobiling, sleigh rides. Gondola and Vista Bahn June-August, daily; May and September, weekends.

## SPECIAL EVENTS

### Taste of Vail

Vail, 970-926-5665; www.tasteofvail.com
This unique food festival combines tastings, competitions and cooking seminars. Sample premium desserts, or watch the annual bartender mix-off. Listen to winemakers talk about their craft—and then taste the fruits of their labor. Or learn something new. Past demonstrations have explained how to pair wine with Japanese cuisine. Early April.

## HOTELS

### ★★Hotel Gasthof Gramshammer

231 E. Gore Creek Dr., Vail,
970-476-5626, 800-610-7374;
www.pepis.com
34 rooms. Closed mid April-June. Complimentary continental breakfast. High-speed Internet access. Restaurant, bar. **$**

### ★★Lion Square Lodge

660 W. Lionshead Place, Vail,
970-476-2281, 800-525-1943;
www.lionsquare.com
108 rooms. Restaurant. Children's activity center. Pool. **$$**

### ★★★The Lodge At Vail

174 E. Gore Creek Dr., Vail,
970-476-5011, 877-528-7625;
www.rockresorts.com
This lodge perfectly marries the charm of an alpine inn with the amenities of a world-class resort. The individually decorated rooms are the ideal blend between Western style and European elegance. Located at the base of Vail Mountain, the lift—as well as boutiques and shops of Vail Village—are just steps away. Mickey's Piano Bar is a great spot for a drink.

145 rooms. High-speed wireless Internet access. Restaurant, bar. Children. Whirlpool. Ski in/ski out. Pool. **$$$**

### ★★★Marriott Vail Mountain Resort

715 W. Lionshead Circle, Vail,
970-476-4444, 800-648-0720;
www.marriott.com
This newly renovated hotel is in a great location at the base of Vail Mountain near the lift and many boutiques and restaurants. The rustic guest rooms contain wood furnishings and marble and granite baths. Privately-owned condos are also available. The new Golden Leaf Spa offers body wraps and massages. The full-service retail shop has rental equipment. This hotel is non-smoking.
347 rooms. Restaurant, bar. Spa. Exercise. **$$**

### ★Savory Inn

2405 Elliott Rd., Vail,
970-476-1304, 866-728-6794;
www.savoryinn.com
12 rooms. Closed mid-April-mid-May. Complimentary full breakfast. Whirlpool. **$$**

### ★★Sitzmark Lodge

183 Gore Creek Dr., Vail,
970-476-5001, 888-476-5001;
www.sitzmarklodge.com
35 rooms. Complimentary continental breakfast. Wireless Internet access. Restaurant, bar. Ski in/ski out. Swim. **$**

### ★★★Sonnenalp Resort of Vail

20 Vail Rd., Vail,
970-476-5656, 800-654-8312;
www.sonnenalp.com
This charming family-owned and operated resort recalls the Bavarian countryside. Located in Vail Village within walking distance of the ski lift, it's a natural choice for winter sports lovers while the 18-hole championship golf course and European-style makes it a treasure any time of the year. A variety of restaurants—from contemporary American to ski favorites such as fondue at the Swiss Chalet—promise to keep your stomach happy. The King's Club fireside lounge

COLORADO

is perfect for live entertainment après ski, serving everything from burgers to caviar.

127 rooms, all suites. High-speed Internet access. Restaurant, bar. Spa. **$$$**

### ★★★Vail Cascade Resort & Spa
1300 Westhaven Dr., Vail,
970-476-7111, 800-282-4183;
www.vailcascade.com

Located on Gore Creek at the base of Vail Mountain, this European-style alpine village contains a combination of standard guest rooms, condominiums and private residences. This huge property boasts the largest athletic facility in the Vail Valley, a shopping arcade, two movie theaters, a beauty shop, two outdoor pools and five whirlpools. Camp Cascade keeps kids entertained throughout the day.

292 rooms. Restaurant, bar. Children's activity center. Spa. Ski in/ski out. Exercise. **$$**

### ★★Vail Mountain Lodge & Spa
352 E. Meadow Dr., Vail,
970-476-0700, 866-476-0700;
www.vailmountainlodge.com

28 rooms. Complimentary full breakfast. High-speed Internet access. Restaurant, bar. Spa. Whirlpool. **$$**

### ★★Vail's Mountain Haus
292 E. Meadow Dr., Vail,
970-476-2434, 800-237-0922;
www.mountainhaus.com

75 rooms. Complimentary continental breakfast. High-speed Internet access. Restaurant, bar. Spa. Pool. **$$$**

## SPECIALTY LODGINGS
### Galatyn Lodge
365 Vail Valley Dr., Vail,
970-479-2419, 800-943-7322;
www.vail.net/galatyn
15 rooms. **$$**

## RESTAURANTS
### ★Blu's
193 E. Gore Creek Dr., Vail,
970-476-3113;
www.blusrestaurant.com

American menu. Breakfast, lunch, dinner. Bar. Children's menu. Casual attire. Outdoor seating. **$$**

### ★★Golden Eagle Inn
118 Beaver Creek Place, Vail,
970-949-1940

American menu. Lunch, dinner. Bar. Children's menu. Casual attire. Outdoor seating. **$$**

### ★★Lancelot Restaurant
201 E. Gore Creek Dr., Vail, 970-476-5828;
www.lancelotinn.com

Seafood, steak menu. Lunch, dinner. Closed April-Memorial Day weekend. Bar. Casual attire. Reservations recommended. Valet parking. Outdoor seating. **$$$**

### ★★★Left Bank
183 Gore Creek Dr., Vail, 970-476-3696;
www.leftbankvail.com

As the name suggests, this restaurant serves classic French cuisine in a friendly, casual atmosphere in the heart of the Village. The restaurant serves all the classics—from escargot to steak au poivre. Start off with a Kir Royale.

French, Mediterranean menu. Dinner. Closed Wednesday; two weeks in March-April and two weeks in fall. Bar. Casual attire. Reservations recommended. **$$$**

### ★★Montauk Seafood Grill
549 W. Lionshead Circle, Vail,
970-476-2601;
www.montaukseafoodgrill.com

Seafood menu. Dinner. Casual attire. Reservations recommended. **$$$**

### ★★★Restaurant Kelly Liken
12 Vail Rd., Vail, 970-479-0175;
www.kellyliken.com

The warm burgundy and champagne colors, custom-made furniture, slate and glass tile floors and hand-blown glass chandelier create an elegant and romantic atmosphere. And Kelly Liken is *the* chef in Vail. Liken uses a majority of locally produced and cultivated products for the seasonal American menu, including elk carpaccio, potato-crusted trout and Colorado lamb.

**167**

**COLORADO**

★
★
★
★
★

American menu. Dinner. Closed mid-April-mid-May. Bar. Children's menu. Business casual attire. Reservations recommended. Valet parking. $$$

### ★★★Sweet Basil
193 E. Gore Creek Dr., Vail, 970-476-0125; www.sweetbasil-vail.com
This contemporary American restaurant has been a local favorite since it opened in 1977. Understated modern décor with cherry wood accents and colorful artwork provides a comfortable setting in which to enjoy the inventive menu. The culinary adventure begins with starters like Dungeness crab and avocado salad and inside-out French onion soup with gruyere, white cheddar and caramelized onions. Entrées might include pumpkin-crusted New England sea scallops, grilled Niman Ranch pork chop with sweet potato pie, and dry-aged, Kansas City strip steak with Colorado russet potato puree. An award-winning wine list complements all menu selections, and a number of desserts provide the perfect ending.

American menu. Lunch, dinner, brunch. Bar. Business casual attire. Reservations recommended. Outdoor seating. $$$$

### ★★★The Wildflower
174 Gore Creek Dr., Vail, 877-528-7625; www.lodgeatvail.com
If you're searching for a memorable dining experience, head to the Wildflower, a beautiful restaurant located inside the Lodge at Vail. Filled with baskets of wildflowers and massive floral arrangements, the room boasts wonderful views and tables lined with country-style floral linens. The restaurant features a delicious and innovative selection of seafood, poultry and game (Nebraska ostrich), accented with global flavors like lemongrass, curry and chilies, and incorporating local fruits and vegetables, including herbs grown in the Wildflower's garden. An extensive and reasonably priced wine list concentrates on Italy and matches the distinctive menu.

American menu. Lunch, dinner. Closed Monday. Bar. Business casual attire. Reservations recommended. Outdoor seating. $$$$

**COLORADO**

# WINTER PARK
Winter Park is located in the Arapaho National Forest on the western slope of Berthoud Pass, one of the nation's highest and oldest ski areas. It is an easy 90-minute drive from Denver, or a two-hour ride on the popular weekend Ski Train. In addition to its many winter activities, Winter Park is gaining a reputation as a year-round recreational area with dozens of activities available during the spring, summer and fall.

Winter Park, Granby and Hot Sulphur Springs are part of the Sulphur Ranger District of the Arapho and Roosevelt national forests.

Information: Winter Park/Fraser Valley Chamber of Commerce, 800-903-7275; www.winterpark-info.com

## WHAT TO SEE AND DO
### Devil's Thumb Ranch
3530 County Rd. 83,
Tabernash, 800-933-4339;
www.devilsthumbranch.com
Set on 3,700 acres at the foot of the Continental Divide, Devils Thumb Ranch is a year-round resort with an abundance of activities in every season. In summer, visitors enjoy fly fishing, horseback riding, river rafting, hiking, bird/nature walks and inflatable kayaking.

Winter brings opportunities for cross-country skiing, sleigh rides, winter horseback riding, ice skating and snowshoeing.

### Dogsled rides
Fraser, 970-726-8326;
www.dogsledrides.com/winterpark
Thirty-minute, one-hour and two-hour rides on a sled pulled by eight Siberian and Alaskan huskies. Guides give talks on wildlife, trees and mountains.

### Fraser River Trail

Winter Park, one mile southeast off
Hwy. 40, 970-726-4118

This wide, flat, five-mile trail runs between the Winter Park Resort and the towns of Winter Park and Fraser, and is a haven for walkers, bikers and in-line skaters who want to enjoy the scenery without worrying about crosswalks or traffic lights. The route between Winter Park and Fraser has picnic tables.

### Monarch Stables and Wagon Rides

1400 County Rd. 5, Fraser, 970-726-5376

Horse-drawn wagon rides, playground, Petsting zoo, pony rides, volleyball and horseshoes.

### Pole Creek Golf Club

6827 County Rd. 51, Tabernash,
970-887-9195, 800-511-5076;
www.polecreekgolf.com

The *Rocky Mountain News* ranked this 27-hole course the best mountain golf course. It is also the only nationally ranked course open to the public.

### Winter Park Resort

239 Winter Park Dr., Winter Park,
970-726-5514, 800-979-0332;
www.skiwinterpark.com

In winter, skiers make full use of the resort's eight high-speed quad, five triple and seven double chairlifts, and 143 runs—longest is five miles, vertical drop 2,610 feet. Patrol, school, equipment rentals and snowmaking; cafeterias, restaurants and bars. NASTAR and coin-operated racecourses. Mid-November-mid-April, daily.

In summer, the Zephyr Express chairlift takes mountain bikers and their bikes to the top of a summit where they can access the resort's 50-mile network of interconnected trails. Colorado's longest Alpine Slide takes riders on heavy-duty plastic sleds equipped with hand-held brakes 3,030 feet down the side of a mountain. Also available are an outdoor climbing wall, bungee jumping,

disc golf (18 holes that wrap around the top of Winter Park Mountain) and miniature golf.

## HOTELS

### ★★Gasthaus Eichler Hotel

78786 Hwy. 40, Winter Park,
970-726-5133, 800-543-3899;
www.gasthauseichler.com

15 rooms. Restaurant, bar. Whirlpool. **$$**

## RESTAURANTS

### ★★Deno's Mountain Bistro

78911 Hwy. 40, Winter Park,
970-726-5332;
www.denosmountainbistro.com

American menu. Lunch, dinner. Bar. Children's menu. Casual attire. Outdoor seating. **$**

### ★★Dezeley's

78786 Hwy. 40, Winter Park, 970-726-5133;
www.gasthauseichler.com

German, American menu. Breakfast, lunch, dinner. Bar. Children's menu. Casual attire. Outdoor seating. **$$**

### ★★★Dining Room at Sunspot

239 Winter Park Dr., Winter Park,
970-726-1446

The upscale dining room at the Winter Park Ski Resort can be reached only by chairlift—and it's worth the trip. The restaurant has the feel of a mountain lodge, built with logs from Grand County. The windows are eight feet high, so you have magnificent views of the Continental Divide. It is a glorious setting to enjoy the satisfying American menu.

American menu. Lunch, dinner. Closed May-October. Bar. Children's menu. Reservations recommended. **$$$**

### ★★Randi's Irish Saloon

78521 Hwy. 40, Winter Park, 970-726-1172

Irish menu. Breakfast, lunch, dinner. Bar. Children's menu. Outdoor seating. **$**

**169**

**COLORADO**

★

★

★

# NEVADA

THERE'S MORE TO NEVADA THAN LAS VEGAS AND GAMBLING. NEVADA ALSO HAS A RICH HISTORY, magnificent scenery and some of the wildest desert country on the continent. You'll find large mountain peaks and beautiful lakes, including Lake Tahoe. Ghost towns hint at the early days of fabulous gold and silver streaks that made millionaires overnight.

Nevada became part of U.S. territory after the Mexican-American War in 1846. It became a state in 1864 (for a while, it was part of Utah). Gold was found along the Carson River in Dayton Valley in May of 1850. A decade later, the fabulous Comstock Lode (silver and gold ore) was discovered. The gold rush was on, and Virginia City mushroomed into a town of 20,000.

Unregulated gambling (called "gaming" here) was common in these early mining towns but was outlawed in 1909. It was legalized in 1931, when construction on the Hoover Dam began and there was a population boom. This was also the same year residency requirements for obtaining a divorce were relaxed. The government owns much of the land in Nevada, and the area about one hour northwest of Las Vegas has been the site of much nuclear testing.

**NEVADA**

Las Vegas keeps reinventing itself. These days, it's perhaps known for some of the best dining in the country as much as it is for gambling. You'll also find some of the best shopping and spas.

Information: www.travelnevada.com

## ★ SPOTLIGHT

★ Nevada is the largest gold-producing state in the nation.

★ The federal government owns 87 percent of the land in Nevada.

## SCENIC NEVADA

This tour from Reno, which can be accomplished over one or two days, combines the scenic beauty and recreational opportunities of Lake Tahoe with historic sites from Nevada's mining days. From Reno, go south on Highway 395 to Highway 431 (the Mount Rose Scenic Byway), which heads west and southwest as it climbs to an 8,911-foot pass and then drops down to Lake Tahoe, providing splendid panoramic views of the lake. Continue on Highway 431 to Highway 28 and Incline Village, a good base from which to enjoy the beach, swimming, fishing and the spectacular views at Lake Tahoe Nevada State Park. The beach at the park's Sand Harbor section is delightful—and also very popular. If you're looking for a little more seclusion, opt for Memorial Point and Hidden Beach. Those visiting from late July through August might want to experience the Lake Tahoe Shakespeare Festival, with shows at an outdoor theater at Sand Harbor. Also in Incline Village is the Ponderosa Ranch, a Western theme park where the popular television series *Bonanza* was filmed from 1959 to 1973.

From Incline Village, continue south on Highway 28 along Lake Tahoe's eastern shore, and then take Highway 50 east to Carson City. Part of the Lake Tahoe Scenic Byway, this route offers panoramic views of the lake and nearby mountains. Carson City, Nevada's capital, is roughly the halfway point of this tour and is a good spot to spend the night. Founded in 1858, Carson City features numerous historic sites, including the handsome state capitol, built in 1871, with a dome of silver. Attractions also include the 1864 Bowers Mansion, built of granite and furnished with many original pieces; the Warren Engine Company No. 1 Fire Museum, where you'll see a variety of historic firefighting equipment; and the Nevada State Railroad Museum, with three steam locomotives and numerous freight and passenger cars.

Now head northeast on Highway 50 to Highway 341, which you follow north to picturesque Virginia City, a historic mining town that had its heyday in the 1870s. Beautifully restored, Virginia City today offers a glimpse into its opulent and sometimes wicked past with historic buildings, a mine and a working steam train. To see the epitome of 19th-century extravagance, stop at the Castle, an 1868 Victorian mansion known for its marble fireplaces, crystal chandeliers and silver doorknobs. Other attractions include Piper's Opera House, which hosted the major stars of the late 1800s, and the Mackay Mansion, built in 1860 as the headquarters of mining magnate John Mackay. To return to Reno, take Highway 341 north to Highway 395 north. Approximately 100 miles.

# BOULDER CITY

A mere 20 miles from Las Vegas, Boulder City is also a world away from the bright lights of Sin City. This quiet town is a haven for visitors seeking thrills outside the walls of casinos. Its proximity to Lake Mead National Recreation Area makes it a perfect spot to rest after a day of fishing, swimming, hiking and sightseeing in one of the Southwest's most beautiful playgrounds.
Information: www.bcnv.org

## WHAT TO SEE AND DO
### Lake Mead National Recreation Area
601 Nevada Hwy., Boulder City,
702-293-8906; www.nps.gov/lame
Lake Mead was formed with the 1935 completion of the Hoover Dam. Located 30 miles from the strip, visitors come here for boating and fishing. You can catch trout, bass and bluegill. Several marinas around the lake and on neighboring Lake Mojave offer rentals: everything from kayaks to houseboats that sleep up to 14 people (because of the great demand for the latter, call six months prior to your visit). Hikers can take in the desert basins, steep canyons, rainbow-hued rocks and wildlife including bighorn sheep in the recreation area surrounding the lake. Open 24 hours; visitors center 8:30 a.m.-4:30 p.m.

### Hoover Dam
Hwy. 93, Boulder City,
702-494-2517, 866-730-9097
It took 6.6 million tons of concrete—enough to pave a highway between New York and San Francisco—to stop the mighty Colorado River at Hoover Dam, which was completed in 1935 and is now a National Historic Landmark. Check out the visitor center where you can watch a short film that tells the story of the dam's construction in Black Canyon. An elevator plunges 500 feet down the canyon wall, depositing passengers in a tunnel that

leads to the power plant and its eight enormous generators. The observation deck takes in both sides of the dam, including Lake Mead and the Colorado River. Parking. Daily 9 a.m.-6 p.m.

Paddlewheelers take you on a 90-minute sightseeing cruise to the Hoover Dam. Breakfast and dinner cruises available. Daily.

**Lake Mead Cruises**
Lake Mead Marina, 480 Lakeshore Rd., Boulder City, 702-293-6180; www.lakemeadcruises.com

# CARSON CITY
The state capital is situated near the edge of the forested eastern slope of the Sierra Nevada in Eagle Valley. A Ranger District office of the Humboldt-Toiyabe National Forest is located here.
Information: Carson City Convention and Visitors Bureau, 1900 S. Carson St., 775-687-7410, 800-638-2321; www.carson-city.org

## WHAT TO SEE AND DO

### Bowers Mansion
4005 Old Hwy. 395, Washoe Valley, 775-849-0201
The Bowers, Nevada's first millionaires, built this $200,000 granite house with the profits from a gold and silver mine. Half-hour guided tours of 16 rooms with many original furnishings. Memorial Day-Labor Day, daily 11 a.m.- 4:30 p.m.

### Children's Museum of Northern Nevada
813 N. Carson St., Carson City, 775-884-2226; www.cmnn.org
This excellent kids' museum provides 8,000 square feet of education and playground-style fun. A grocery store, arts and crafts station, and a walk-in kaleidoscope are among the permanent exhibits. Daily 10 a.m.-4:30 p.m.

### Nevada State Museum
600 N. Carson St., Carson City, 775-687-4810
Former U.S. Mint. Exhibits of Nevada's natural history and anthropology; life-size displays of Nevada ghost town and American Indian camp. A 300-foot mine tunnel with displays runs beneath the building. Daily 8:30 a.m.-4:30 p.m.

### Nevada State Railroad Museum
2180 S. Carson St., Carson City, 775-687-6953; www.nsrm-friends.org
This museum houses more than 600 pieces of railroad equipment. It also exhibits 50 freight and passenger cars, as well as five steam locomotives that once belonged to the Virginia and Truckee railroad. Also houses pictorial history gallery and arti-

## MINING AND MONEY IN CARSON CITY

A walking tour of Carson City offers a good viewpoint for investigating the heady days of the Old West's 19th-century mining boom. Start at the Nevada State Museum (600 N. Carson St.), which served as a U.S. Mint from 1870 to 1895 and pressed more than $50 million in coinage during that span. Opened as a museum a half-century after the mint closed, the building houses a collection of archaeological finds, dioramas, Indian baskets and an antique and operational coin press.

Next, head two blocks north on Carson Street to the Children's Museum of Northern Nevada (813 N. Carson St), the area's best attraction for kids. You'll pass through Carson City's primary casino district in the vicinity of Spear and Telegraph streets. The casinos house the majority of the restaurants in downtown Carson City, so this is a good opportunity to grab a bite to eat. Continuing south on Carson Street for three blocks, the quarried sandstone Nevada State Capitol (just east of the intersection of Carson and Second streets) is the cornerstone of a beautifully landscaped plaza that is also home to the state's supreme court, legislative building and library and archives building.

Just southeast of the capitol plaza on Stewart Street is the Warren Engine Company No. 1 Museum (777 S. Stewart St.), with exhibits, photographs and memorabilia detailing the oldest continuously operating firefighting company in the West. From here, it is just a block north on Stewart Street to Fifth Street; take Fifth west to Nevada Street and walk three blocks north to King Street, on which you'll want to go west once again. At 449 West King Street is the Brewery Arts Center, a showcase for the work of local artists in the former Carson Brewing Company building, which was built in 1864 and is currently on the National Historic Register. The Arts Center is in the heart of Carson City's most historic neighborhood.

facts of the famed Bonanza Road. Daily 8:30 a.m.-4:30 p.m.

**State Capitol**
101 N. Carson St., Carson City, 775-684-5700
Large Classical Revival structure with Doric columns and a silver dome. Houses portraits of past Nevada governors. Self-guided tours. Daily 8 a.m.-5 p.m.

**State Library Building**
100 N. Stewart, Carson City, 775-684-3360
Files of Nevada newspapers and books about the state. Monday-Friday 8 a.m.-5 p.m.

**Warren Engine Company No. 1 Fire Museum**
777 S. Stewart St., Carson City, 775-887-2210

See the old photographs, antique fire-fighting equipment, the state's first fire truck (restored), an 1847 four-wheel cart and more. Children under 18 must be accompanied by an adult.

## SPECIAL EVENTS
**Nevada Day Celebration**
Carson St., and Hwy. 50 E., Carson City, 775-882-2600, 866-683-2948; www.nevadaday.com
Commemorates Nevada's admission to the Union. Grand Ball, parades, exhibits. Four days in late October.

## HOTELS
★**Hardman House Park Inn**
917 N. Carson St., Carson City, 775-882-7744, 800-626-0793
62 rooms. **$**

## RESTAURANTS
**★★Adele's**
1112 N. Carson St., Carson City,
775-882-3353;
www.adelesrestaurantandlounge.com

American menu. Lunch, dinner, late-night. Closed Sunday. Bar. Business casual attire. Valet parking. Outdoor seating. **$$**

# CRYSTAL BAY
On the California-Nevada state line, Crystal Bay sits on the north rim of Lake Tahoe, overlooking its namesake bay. (Swim from one state to another at Cal-Neva Resort's pool.)

## HOTELS
**★★Cal Neva**
2 Stateline Rd., Crystal Bay,
800-233-5551, 800-225-6382;
www.calnevaresort.com
220 rooms. Restaurant, bar. Casino. Tennis. **$**

**★★Tahoe Biltmore Lodge and Casino**
5 Hwy. 28, Crystal Bay,
775-831-0660, 800-245-8667;
www.tahoebiltmore.com
92 rooms. Complimentary full breakfast. Two restaurants, bar. Casino. Pets accepted. Pool. **$**

# ELKO
On the Humboldt River, Elko is the center of a large ranching area. Originally a stopping point for wagon trains headed for the West Coast, its main sources of revenue today include tourism, gold mining and gaming.
Information: Elko Chamber of Commerce, 1405 Idaho St., 775-738-7135, 800-428-7143; www.elkonevada.com

## WHAT TO SEE AND DO
**Northeastern Nevada Museum**
1515 Idaho St., Elko, 775-738-3418;
www.museum-elko.us
Three galleries feature art, historical, American Indian and nature exhibits of the area. See pioneer vehicles and an original 1860 Pony Express cabin. Tuesday-Saturday, 9 a.m.- 5 p.m., Sunday, 1-5 p.m.

## SPECIAL EVENTS
**County Fair and Livestock Show**
13th and Cedar Streets, Elko,
775-738-7135
Horse racing. Four days on Labor Day weekend.

**Cowboy Poetry Gathering**
501 Railroad St., Elko, 775-738-7135
Working cowboys and cowgirls participate in storytelling verse. Demonstrations; music. Last full week in January.

**National Basque Festival**
Basque House at Golf Course Rd. and Cedar St., Elko, 775-738-7135
Contests in weightlifting, sheep hooking and other skills of mountaineers; dancing, feast. Weekend early in July.

## HOTELS
**★★High Desert Inn**
3015 E. Idaho St., Elko, 89801,
775-738-8425, 888-394-8303
170 rooms. Restaurant, bar. Airport transportation available. Pets accepted. Pool. **$**

**★★Red Lion**
2065 E. Idaho St., Elko,
775-738-2111, 800-733-5466;
www.redlion.com
223 rooms. Restaurant, bar. Airport transportation available. Casino. Pets accepted. **$**

# ELY

Although founded in 1868 as a silver mining camp, Ely's growth began in 1906 with the arrival of the Nevada Northern Railroad, which facilitated the development, in 1907, of large-scale copper mining. Gold and silver are still mined in Ely. The seat of White Pine County, it is the shopping and recreational center of a vast ranching and mining area. The city is surrounded by mountains and offers winter skiing, deer hunting and trout fishing. Its high elevation provides a cool, sunny climate.

Information: White Pine Chamber of Commerce, 636 Aultman St., 775-289-8877; www.whitepinechamber.com

## WHAT TO SEE AND DO

### Nevada Northern Railway Museum
1100 Ave. A, Ely, 866-407-8326;
www.nevadanorthernrailway.net
Located in the historic Nevada Northern Railway Depot.

### Ward Charcoal Ovens State Historic Park
Hwy. 6/50/93 and Cave Valley Rd., Ely,
775-728-4460;
www.parks.nv.gov/ww.htm
Includes six stone beehive charcoal ovens used during the 1870 mining boom.

### White Pine Public Museum
2000 Aultman St., Ely,
775-289-4710
See a 1905 stagecoach, as well as early-day relics and mementos; mineral display. Daily.

## SPECIAL EVENTS

### Pony Express Days
Hwy. 50 and Pony Express Trail,
Ely, 775-289-8877
Pari-mutuel betting. Last two weekends in August.

## HOTELS

### ★★Ramada Inn & Copper Queen Casino
805 Great Basin Blvd., Ely,
775-289-4884, 800-851-9526;
www.ramada.com
65 rooms. Complimentary continental breakfast. Restaurant, bar. Airport transportation available. Casino. Pets accepted. **$**

# FALLON

Fallon is one of the westernmost cities on what is often called "the Loneliest Road in America," a segment of Route 50 that runs through Nevada and is known for its relative seclusion.

Information: Fallon Chamber of Commerce, 85 N. Taylor St., 775-423-2544; www.fallonchamber.com

## WHAT TO SEE AND DO

### Lahontan State Recreation Area
16799 Lahontan Dam, Fallon,
775-867-3500;
www.parks.nv.gov/lah.htm
Approximately 30,000 acres with a 16-mile-long reservoir. Water sports, fishing, boating (launching, ramps), picnicking, camping.

## SPECIAL EVENTS

### All Indian Rodeo
65 S. Maine St., Fallon, 775-423-2544

Rodeo events, parade, powwow, American Indian dances, arts, games. Third weekend in July.

### Fallon Air Show
Fallon Naval Air Station,
4755 Pasture Rd., Fallon, 775-426-2880;
www.fallon.navy.mil
Military exhibition flying, civilian aerobatics, aircraft displays; Blue Angels Demonstration Team. Ground events and static displays of vintage and modern aircraft. Late spring-early summer.

## HOTELS

★**Comfort Inn**
1830 W. Williams Ave., Fallon,
775-423-5554, 877-424-6423;
www.comfortinn.com
82 rooms. Complimentary continental breakfast. Pets accepted. **$**

★**Super 8**
855 W. Williams Ave., Fallon,
775-423-6031; www.super8.com
75 rooms. Restaurant, bar. Casino. Pets accepted. **$**

## GREAT BASIN NATIONAL PARK

Established as a national park in 1986, Great Basin consists of 77,092 acres of diverse scenic, ecologic and geologic attractions. It includes Lehman Caves (formerly Lehman Caves National Monument), Wheeler Peak, the park's only glacier and Lexington Arch, a natural limestone arch more than six stories tall.

Of particular interest is Lehman Caves, a large limestone solution cavern. The cave contains numerous limestone formations, including shields and helictites.

The 12-mile Wheeler Peak Scenic Drive reaches to the 10,000-foot elevation mark of Wheeler Peak. From there, you can hike to the summit. Backcountry hiking and camping are permitted. The Lexington Arch is located at the south end of the park. Camping is allowed at three campgrounds located along the Wheeler Peak Scenic Drive: the Wheeler Peak Campground, the Upper Lehman Creek Campground and the Lower Lehman Campground. Baker Creek Campground is located approximately five miles from park headquarters. Picnic facilities are available near park headquarters.

Information: Five miles west of Baker on Hwy. 488, 775-234-7331; www.nps.gov/grba

# HENDERSON

The fastest growing city in Nevada, Henderson has become the third-largest city in the state, thanks to its proximity to Las Vegas. Many of the area's swankiest resorts are actually in Henderson.

Information: Henderson Chamber of Commerce, 590 S. Boulder Hwy., 702-565-8951; www.hendersonchamber.com

## WHAT TO SEE AND DO

**Clark County Heritage Museum**
1830 S. Boulder Hwy., Henderson,
702-455-7955; www.co.clark.nv.us
Learn all about the history of southern Nevada. You'll see replicas of Native American dwellings, historic houses and businesses from the early 20th century, a ghost town, vintage automobiles, 1932 train depot, old photos of the Strip and more. A detailed timeline charts the region's evolution from prehistoric times. Daily 9 a.m.-4:30 p.m.

**Ethel M. Chocolates Factory & Cactus Garden**
2 Cactus Garden Dr., Henderson,
702-458-2655, 800-471-0352;
www.ethelm.com
Take the self-guided tour of this factory, where everything from chewy caramels to crunchy nut clusters roll off the assembly line. Daily 8:30 a.m.-7 p.m.

## Galleria at Sunset
1300 W. Sunset Rd., Henderson,
702-434-0202; www.galleriaatsunset.com
This mall has 140 shops and restaurants.
There is also find a free rock climbing wall.
Monday-Saturday 10 a.m.-9 p.m., Sunday
11 a.m.-7 p.m.

## MonteLago Village
1600 Lake Las Vegas, Henderson,
702-564-4700, 866-564-4799;
www.montelagovillage.com
Escape to this charming development reminiscent of a centuries-old seaside village.
About 35 unique shops and restaurants
line the cobblestone streets of MonteLago,
which borders the Ritz-Carlton Las Vegas.
Retailers offer everything from fine art and
custom-made jewelry to women's apparel
and handcrafted home furnishings.

## Reflection Bay Golf Club
1600 Lake Las Vegas Pkwy., Henderson,
702-564-1600, 877-698-4653;
www.lakelasvegas.com
Designed by golf great Jack Nicklaus, the
public, par-72 resort course follows the
rugged desert contours with the final holes
along the shore of the 320-acre man-made
Lake Las Vegas. Arroyo-meets-grass flora,
maddening bunkers and interesting (and
frustrating) water features make the course
memorable. Afterward, kick back at the
Mediterranean-style clubhouse with patio
dining under a colonnade. Winter 7 a.m.-
dusk, summer 6:30 a.m.-dusk.

## Rio Secco Golf Club
2851 Grand Hills Dr., Henderson,
702-777-2400; www.riosecco.net
Rio Secco is an expensive course, but its
variety makes it well worth playing. The
course is essentially divided into thirds,
with six holes in small canyons, six on plateaus with views of the local skyline and
six reminiscent of the Nevada desert. The
course is more than 7,300 yards long, so be
prepared to swing for the fences. Number
9 is a long par-five with bunkers surrounding the green. Make the turn facing the city
and count yourself lucky if you've played

8 and 9 (back-to-back par-fives measuring
1,150 yards combined) at one or two over.

# SPECIAL EVENTS
## Heritage Days
590 S. Boulder Hwy., Henderson,
702-565-8951
This annual festival is one of the largest in
Henderson. It lasts nine days and features
food, a carnival, appraisal fair and more.
Late April.

# HOTELS
## ★★Sunset Station Hotel
1301 W. Sunset Rd., Henderson,
702-547-7777, 888-786-7389;
www.sunsetstation.com
457 rooms. High-speed wireless Internet
access. Seven restaurants, four bars. Airport transportation available. Casino. **$**

## ★★★Green Valley Ranch Resort and Spa
2300 Paseo Verde Pkwy., Henderson,
702-617-7777, 866-782-9487;
www.greenvalleyranchresort.com
The Mediterranean-style Green Valley
Ranch Resort and Spa is a peaceful escape,
but there's still plenty of action when the
mood strikes. The elegant rooms come with
in-room martini bars. There are seven restaurants, and the Whiskey Bar is a great spot to
gather with friends. The Whiskey also has a
large patio, which goes out to a pool, café and
amphitheater used for live concerts. The spa
has a dizzying array of treatments, including
20 different kinds of massage therapies.
490 rooms. High-speed wireless Internet
access. Seven restaurants, four bars. Spa.
Beach. Airport transportation available.
Pets accepted. **$$$**

## ★★★★The Ritz-Carlton Lake Las Vegas
1610 Lake Las Vegas Pkwy.,
Henderson, 702-567-4700;
www.ritzcarlton.com
Exchange the over-the-top glitz of the Las
Vegas strip for the serenity of the Mediter-
ranean-inspired Ritz-Carlton on Lake Las
Vegas. A 35-minute ride from the Strip, the
resort is nestled in a valley surrounded by
low-lying desert mountains. A replica of

**177**

**NEVADA**

★
★
★
★
★

Florence's Ponte Vecchio extends across the 320-acre lake, and singing gondoliers take guests on a romantic trip under the bridge. After playing the tables at the nearby MonteLago Village Resort, wind down with a massage in one of 22 treatment rooms at the resort spa or a round of golf on one of two championship golf courses. Guests can dine at the Medici Cafe and Terrace, which overlooks the resort's Florentine gardens or have a cocktail in the Firenze Lobby Lounge. 349 rooms. High-speed wireless Internet access. Restaurant, bar. Spa. Pets accepted. Golf. Tennis. Business Center. **$$**

## SPAS

**★★★★The Spa at Ritz-Carlton Lake Las Vegas**
1610 Lake Las Vegas Pkwy., Henderson, 702-567-4700, 800-241-3333; www.ritzcarlton.com

This Mediterranean-influenced, 30,000-square-foot facility is a sanctuary from the hot desert sun. Treatment rooms are luxurious and spacious—several have outdoor terraces that overlook the lake, and some are designed exclusively for couples. The La Culla treatment includes an array of body and facial treatments, accompanied by music and other sounds and aromatherapy. The signature facial uses an exclusive marine concentrate. The spa facilities include a complete fitness center, movement studio for yoga and pilates, full service salon and a boutique. Nutritional and wellness counseling, physician-directed cosmetic dermatology and extensive recreations programs and activities are available.

# INCLINE VILLAGE

Swanky and affluent, Incline Village sits on the north rim of Lake Tahoe. It derives its name from the Great Incline Tramway built by loggers in 1878, but today, the town is primarily a haven for those seeking outdoor fun.

Information: Lake Tahoe Incline Village/Crystal Bay Visitors Bureau, 969 Tahoe Blvd., 775-832-4440; www.gotahoe.com

NEVADA

## WHAT TO SEE AND DO

**Diamond Peak Ski Resort**
1210 Ski Way, Incline Village, 775-832-1177; www.diamondpeak.com
Three quads, three double chairlifts; patrol, school, rentals, snowmaking. Thirty runs; longest run approximately 2 1/2 miles; vertical drop 1,840 feet. Mid-December-mid-April, daily.

**Lake Tahoe Nevada State Park**
2005 Hwy. 28, Incline Village, 775-831-0494; www.parks.nv.gov/lt.htm
Approximately 14,200 acres on the eastern shore of beautiful Lake Tahoe. Gently sloping sandy beach, swimming, fishing, boating (ramp), hiking, mountain biking, cross-country skiing. No camping. Daily.

## SPECIAL EVENTS

**Lake Tahoe Chautauqua**
Sand Harbor State Park, Hwy. 28, Incline Village, 800-747-4697; www.tahoechautauqua.com
This annual two-day event features costumed speakers who portray historical characters. Held at Sand Harbor, past Lake Tahoe Chautauquas have had such themes as the American Revolution and Lewis and Clark. The proceedings are interactive: the audience is encouraged to wear period clothing and ask questions of the speakers. Late June.

**Lake Tahoe Shakespeare Festival**
Sand Harbor State Park, 948 Incline Way, Incline Village, 775-832-1616, 800-747-4697; www.laketahoeshakespeare.com

This event has grown into one of the premiere Shakespeare festivals in the West. The troupe performs nightly from mid-July to late August in a natural amphitheater on the waters edge at Sand Harbor. A food court serves tasty fare from several outstanding local eateries, as well as beer and wine. Mid-July-late August.

**Lake Tahoe Winter Games Festival**
Diamond Peak Ski Resort,
1210 Ski Way, Incline Village,
775-832-1177
Early March.

# LAS VEGAS

Plan a visit to Vegas these days and you'll still see "world wonders," glitzy showgirls and plenty of dice throwing. But today's version of Las Vegas is more haute. The kitsch has been toned down a bit and world-class spas, more refined accommodations and some of the country's best restaurants have moved in. In the last few years, Las Vegas has morphed into one of the top cities for dining in the country.

You'll still hear plenty of ding, ding, ding all day long. But today it's as much about the pool—as in which resort has the best one—championship golf and Cirque du Soleil.

## HOTELS
### ★★★Hyatt Regency Lake Tahoe Resort & Casino
1111 Country Club Dr., Incline Village,
775-832-1234; www.hyatt.com
This resort is a top pick for rustic, luxury accommodations on the North Shore of Lake Tahoe. It's not on a mountain but the resort will shuttle you to the slopes. Spa services are offered through the fitness center. The hotel also houses a small but charming old-style casino, a private hotel beach and a destination restaurant with arguably one of the best dining views of the lake.
422 rooms. Four restaurants, bar. Children's activity center. Spa. Casino. $$

179

NEVADA

Check out one of the best aquariums (at Mandalay) and browse the collections at the Guggenheim Museum.

And bring your hiking shoes! You'll find numerous canyons, valleys and man-made lakes around the city. Enjoy spectacular scenery and a wide range of recreational activities, including hiking, swimming, fishing, biking, boating, horseback riding, rock climbing, camping and whitewater rafting.

Information: Las Vegas Convention/Visitors Authority, Convention Center, 3150 Paradise Rd., 702-892-0711; www.lasvegas24hours.com

# WHAT TO SEE AND DO

## Folies Bergere

Tropicana Hotel & Casino,
3801 Las Vegas Blvd. S., Las Vegas,
702-739-2222, 888-826-8767;
www.tropicanalv.com

This daring cabaret show debuted on the Strip in 1959 and has been packing in audiences ever since, making it Sin City's longest-running production show. The 90-minute extravaganza features vocalists, acrobats, adagio artists, a juggler and show-girls. All-ages shows (no nudity) are held weekdays at 7:30 p.m. Monday, Wednesday, Thursday, and Saturday at 7:30 p.m. and 10 p.m.; Tuesday and Friday 8:30 p.m.

## Mystere by Cirque du Soleil

Treasure Island, 3300 Las Vegas Blvd. S.,
Las Vegas, 702-894-7722, 800-392-1999;
www.treasureisland.com

Cirque du Soleil has taken up permanent residence at Treasure Island with *Mystere*. Monday-Wednesday, Saturday 7:30 and 9:30 p.m., Sunday 4:30 and 7 p.m.

## O by Cirque du Soleil

Bellagio, 3600 Las Vegas Blvd. S.,
Las Vegas, 702-693-7722, 888-488-7111;
www.bellagiolasvegas.com

The inventive French Canadian troop Cirque du Soleil takes their acrobatic choreography to the pool in a theater built specifically for the aquatic show. Wednesday-Sunday 7:30 p.m. and 10:30 p.m.; closed Monday-Tuesday.

## A Permanent Tribute to Heroes

New York-New York Hotel and Casino,
3790 Las Vegas Blvd. S., Las Vegas,
800-689-1797; www.nynyhotelcasino.com

This memorial of September 11, 2001, includes display cases showing some of the thousands of T-shirts, notes and other mementos left by mourning tourists in the months following the terror attacks.

## Adventuredome

Circus Circus Hotel & Casino,
2880 Las Vegas Blvd. S., Las Vegas,
702-794-3939, 866-634-8894;
www.adventuredome.com

Escape the heat at the country's largest indoor theme park, where you'll find more than 15 exciting rides, including the Canyon Blaster, a double-loop, double-corkscrew roller coaster, and the Rim Runner, which includes a slide down a 60-foot waterfall. A carnival midway and clown shows add to the fun. Monday-Thursday 10 a.m.-6 p.m; Friday-Saturday to midnight; Sunday to 8 p.m.

## Air Play

Tropicana Hotel & Casino,
3801 Las Vegas Blvd. S., Las Vegas,
702-739-2222; www.tropicanalv.com

Step inside the Tropicana to glimpse a performance by acrobats, aerialists, jugglers and singers to a variety of music. The 20-minute show takes place just under the famous Tiffany glass ceiling on a stage that was set up atop a bank of slot machines. Daily at 11 a.m., 1 p.m., 3 p.m., 5 p.m., 7 p.m., and 9 p.m.

## Art Encounter

3979 Spring Mountain Rd.,
Las Vegas, 702-227-0220, 800-395-2996;
www.artencounter.com

More than 100 artists display oils, watercolors, jewelry, pottery, sculpture and more in a wide variety of styles. Tuesday-Friday 10 a.m.-6 p.m., Saturday and Monday noon-5 p.m.

## Badlands Golf Club

9119 Alta Dr., Las Vegas, 702-363-0754;
www.badlandsgc.com

Designed by Chi Chi Rodriguez and Johnny Miller. Badlands is an example of an increasing trend of three sets of nine holes, offering different combinations of courses. The three nines (Diablo, Desperado and Outlaw) are markedly different. The Outlaw course is more forgiving than the other two, which are the usual tournament 18.

## Bali Hai Golf Club

5160 Las Vegas Blvd. S., Las Vegas,
888-427-6678; www.balihaigolfclub.com

The white sand bunkers here complement the traditional architecture of the clubhouse, which contains Cili, an exclusive

**180**

**NEVADA**

Vegas eatery. The signature hole is the 16th, a par-three with an island green.

### Bellagio Casino
Bellagio, 3600 Las Vegas Blvd. S.,
Las Vegas, 702-693-7111, 888-987-3456;
www.bellagiolasvegas.com
Where other Vegas casinos cram in the tables and pour on the flash, Bellagio makes a more soothing pitch for your money. Tables are well spaced and slot machines ding at lower volume levels. Daily, 24 hours.

### Bellagio Conservatory and Botanical Gardens
Bellagio,
3600 Las Vegas Blvd. S., Las Vegas,
702-693-7111, 888-987-3456;
www.bellagiolasvegas.com
Take a leisurely stroll through the 90,000-square-foot conservatory at the Bellagio to see thousands of gorgeous plants and colorful blooms, including orchids and other exotics that are painstakingly maintained by 140 horticulturists. Daily, 24 hours.

### Bellagio Gallery of Fine Art
Bellagio, 3600 Las Vegas Blvd. S.,
Las Vegas, 702-693-7871, 877-957-9777;
www.bellagiolasvegas.com
The Bellagio Gallery of Fine Art mounts rotating exhibitions on subjects ranging from Faberge eggs to Calder mobiles to Andy Warhol's celebrity silkscreens. Daily 9 a.m.-9 p.m.

### Bonnie Springs Old Nevada
1 Gunfighter Lane, Blue Diamond,
702-875-4191; www.bonniesprings.com
Experience what life was like in the Wild West at this replica of a mining town complete with stagecoaches, saloons, simulated gunfights and more. Summer: daily 10:30 a.m.-6 p.m.; winter: daily 10:30 a.m.-5 p.m.

### Boulevard Mall
3528 S. Maryland Pkwy., Las Vegas,
702-732-8949; www.blvdmall.com
Shop at the more than 150 stores including Macy's, Victoria's Secret and Gap.

Monday-Saturday 10 a.m.-9 p.m., Sunday 11 a.m.-6 p.m.

### Broadacres Swap Meet
2930 Las Vegas Blvd. N.,
Las Vegas, 702-642-3777;
www.broadacresswapmeet.com
Up to 1,000 vendors hawk new and merchandise that's priced to *sell*. Friday 6:30 a.m.-12:30 p.m., Saturday-Sunday 6:30 a.m.-2 p.m.

### Coney Island Emporium
New York-New York Hotel and Casino,
3790 Las Vegas Blvd. S., Las Vegas,
702-736-4100;
www.coneyislandemporium.com
This 32,000-square-foot emporium is a replica of the famed Coney Island in New York and includes more than 20 midway-style games and more than hundreds of arcade games. Kids will enjoy laser tag, bumper cars (which are bright yellow cabs) and racing in Daytona-style driving stimulators. Sunday-Thursday 8 a.m.-midnight, Friday-Saturday 8-2 a.m.

### Cottonwood Valley
Las Vegas, on State Rte. 160,
at about mile marker 17
Pedal your way across the desert in one of the most popular cycling areas in the Las Vegas Valley. Several trails snake their way through the rugged but beautiful terrain. Trail maps are available at kiosks in the area.

### Creative Cooking School
7385 W. Sahara Ave., Las Vegas,
702-562-3900;
www.creativecookingschool.com
The city's first cooking school, opened by chef-author Catherine Margles, offers demonstrations and hands-on lessons. Also includes children's classes.

### Danny Gans Show
Mirage Hotel and Casino,
3400 Las Vegas Blvd. S., Las Vegas,
702-792-7777, 800-963-9634;
www.mirage.com

This singer-impressionist never disappoints with his dead-on mimicking of your favorite tunes, making his award-winning show one of the hottest on the Strip. Tuesday-Wednesday, Friday-Saturday 8 p.m.

### Desert Fox Tours
6265 Dean Martin Rd., Las Vegas,
702-361-0676;
www.vegashummertours.com
If you're the adventurous type, go off-road in a Hummer and see the desert in all its rugged glory. Various tours last from three to six hours and take you to Red Rock National Conservation Area, the Valley of Fire, or a gold mine and ghost town.

### Miracle Mile Shops
Aladdin Resort & Casino,
3663 Las Vegas Blvd. S., Las Vegas,
702-866-0710, 888-800-8284;
www.desertpassage.com
Modeled after a North African bazaar with Moroccan archways, mosaic tiles and fountain courtyards, this circular center includes 130 shops and 14 restaurants. Sunday-Thursday 10 a.m.-11 p.m., Friday-Saturday 10 a.m.-midnight.

### Desert Pines Golf Club
3415 E. Bonanza Rd., Las Vegas,
888-427-6678; www.waltersgolf.com
Desert Pines strives to emulate the seaside designs found in the Carolinas. Pine trees line most of the narrow fairways, and several ponds can increase a score in short order. The Desert Pines golf center is comprehensive, even offering target areas shaped like famous holes such as the 17th island green at Sawgrass and the second hole at Pinehurst.

### Eiffel Tower Experience
Paris Las Vegas, 3655 Las Vegas Blvd. S., Las Vegas, 877-603-4386;
www.parislasvegas.com
See this 50-story half-scale replica of the Eiffel Tower. A glass elevator whisks tourists to 460 feet for panoramic views of the mountain-ringed valley by day and the neon canyon by night. The 11th-floor restaurant

Eiffel Tower serves classic French food. Daily 10-1 a.m.

### Fantastic Indoor Swap Meet
1717 S. Decatur Blvd., Las Vegas,
702-877-0087;
www.fantasticindoorswapmeet.com
Locals flock to this giant indoor swap meet in search of bargains. The 700 shops are packed with merchandise, from car accessories to toys to perfume. Friday-Sunday 10 a.m.-6 p.m.

### Fashion Show Mall
3200 Las Vegas Blvd. S., Las Vegas,
702-784-7000;
www.thefashionshow.com
Most of the nation's major department stores anchor the vast two-story Fashion Show Mall. Monday-Saturday 10 a.m.-9 p.m., Sunday 11 a.m.-7 p.m.

### Flamingo Wildlife Habitat
Flamingo Las Vegas,
3555 Las Vegas Blvd. S., Las Vegas,
702-733-3111; www.flamingolv.com
Walk through this 1 1/2-acre birdhouse and you'll see Chilean flamingos, crowned cranes, swans, African penguins, pheasants, quail and more. Daily, 24 hours.

### Floyd Lamb Park
9200 Tule Springs Rd., Las Vegas,
702-229-6297
This pleasant 2,000-acre park has four small fishing lakes, tree-shaded picnic areas with tables and grills, a walking/bicycle path, volleyball courts and horseshoe pits. No overnight camping.

### Flyaway Indoor Skydiving
200 Convention Center Dr., Las Vegas,
702-731-4768, 877-545-8093;
www.flyawayindoorskydiving.com
This vertical wind tunnel simulates the freefall experience of skydiving. The column of air is 12 feet across and up to 22 feet high, with vertical airspeeds of up to 120 mph. Your experience begins with a 20-minute training class and a 15-minute equipment preparation and concludes

NEVADA

with a three-minute flight session. Daily 10 a.m.-7 p.m.

### Forum Shops at Caesars Palace
Caesars Palace, 3500 Las Vegas Blvd. S., Las Vegas, 702-893-4800; www.forumshops.com
With piazzas, fountains and an ever-changing (painted) sky overhead, the Forum Shops offers a taste of Rome. Time your visit to catch one of the hourly shows at the Festival Fountain, where the statues of Bacchus, Venus, Apollo and Mars come to life in an animatronic bacchanal (there's also a similar show at the other end of the mall involving Atlas). Stores scale toward luxury retailers like Gucci and Fendi, but also include Gap, FAO Schwarz and Niketown. Several good restaurants include Wolfgang Puck's Spago and Chinois. Sunday-Thursday10 a.m.-11 p.m., Friday-Saturday 10 a.m.-midnight.

### Fountains of Bellagio
Bellagio, 3600 Las Vegas Blvd. S., Las Vegas, 702-693-7111; www.bellagiolasvegas.com
A Busby Berkeley chorus line with water cannons subbing for gams, the Fountains of the Bellagio perform daily to a roster of tunes ranging from campy to operatic. The razzle-dazzle really roils after dark, when 4,500 lights dramatize the 1,000-nozzle, 27-million-gallon performances. Crowds tend to stake out spots along the wall ringing the hotel-fronting lake several minutes before every evening show. It goes off every 15 minutes between 8 p.m. and midnight and every half hour before 8 p.m. Monday-Friday 3 p.m.-midnight; Saturday-Sunday noon-midnight.

### Fremont Street Experience
425 Fremont St., Las Vegas, 702-678-5600; www.vegasexperience.com
This light and sound show broadcast on a 90-foot-high canopy over a 4 1/2-block stretch of Fremont Street was built in 1995. Embedded with 12 million lights and 218 speakers, the overhead show synchronizes music and colored-light-derived images in six-minute shows. Each computerized performance per night is different, keying off various musical styles from calypso to disco to country-western. Hourly shows dusk to midnight.

### Gamblers General Store
800 S. Main St., Las Vegas, 702-382-9903, 800-322-2447; www.gamblersgeneralstore.com
Wares range from portable poker chip sets and playing cards to roulette wheels, slot machines and raffle drums—all shippable. Daily 9 a.m.-5 p.m.

### GameWorks Las Vegas
3785 Las Vegas Blvd. S., Las Vegas, 702-432-4263; www.gameworks.com
Over 300 video and virtual reality games as well as a 75-foot climbing wall entertain the clan, while the adults-only bar offers pool tables and live music. The kitchen serves casual fare. Sunday-Thursday 10 a.m.-midnight; Friday-Saturday 10-1 a.m.

### Grand Canal Shoppes at the Venetian
The Venetian Resort Hotel Casino, 3355 Las Vegas Blvd. S., Las Vegas, 702-414-4500, 877-883-6423; www.venetian.com
A 1,200-foot-long replica of the Grand Canal bisects the Grand Canal Shoppes. Venetian bridges, arches and arcades dress up the mall, where you can scoop up Burberry and Jimmy Choos. Stop at Il Prato or Ripa de Monte for Venetian paper goods, carnival masks and Murano glass. Grab at bite at the food court or in one of the full-service restaurants, many with patio seating. Sunday-Thursday10 a.m.-11 p.m., Friday-Saturday 10 a.m.-midnight.

### Guggenheim Hermitage Museum
The Venetian, 3355 Las Vegas Blvd. S., Las Vegas, 702-414-2440; www.guggenheimlasvegas.org
A venue for rotating exhibitions, the Guggenheim Hermitage is actually managed by a trio of museums, including the New York Guggenheim, Russia's Hermitage and the Kunsthistorisches Museum in Vienna. Daily 9:30 a.m.-8:30 p.m.

**183**

**NEVADA**

### Hard Rock Memorabilia Tour
Hard Rock Hotel Casino,
4455 Paradise Rd., Las Vegas,
800-473-7625;
www.hardrockhotel.com
This is the largest exhibition of rock memorabilia ever assembled in one place. Shuttles depart from the Harley-Davidson Cafe, Fashion Show Mall and Caesars Palace between 10 a.m. and 7 p.m. daily.

### Imperial Palace Auto Collection
Imperial Palace Hotel & Casino,
3535 Las Vegas Blvd.,
Las Vegas, 702-794-3174;
www.autocollections.com
The Auto Collection housed on the fifth floor of the parking lot at Imperial Palace showcases some 170 plus vintage cars (some of which are for sale). Models range from historic autos to muscle cars and late-model luxury brands thrown in. See a 1962 red Alfa Romeo Spider, 1954 Chevy Bel Air convertible and 1929 Duesenberg sedan. Also: vintage car parts and jukeboxes. Daily 9:30 a.m.-9:30 p.m.

### King Tut's Tomb and Museum
Luxor Hotel and Casino,
3900 Las Vegas Blvd. S., Las Vegas,
888-777-0188; www.luxor.com
Explore an exact replica of King Tut's tomb and see hundreds of reproductions of eye-popping treasures found in the original. 15-minute self-guided tour. Daily 10 a.m.-11 p.m.

### Lance Burton: Master Magician
Monte Carlo Resort and Casino,
3770 Las Vegas Blvd. S., Las Vegas,
702-730-7160, 877-386-8224;
www.lanceburton.com
Since 1996, this world-champion magician has been mesmerizing audiences five nights a week with impressive illusions that defy logic. Smoke effects, pyrotechnics and even a live bird named Elvis make up this entertaining 90-minute spectacle. To perform his sleight-of-hand tricks, Burton often enlists the help of kids on stage. Tuesday-Saturday 7 p.m. and 10 p.m.

### Las Vegas 51s
Cashman Fields, 850 Las Vegas Blvd. N.,
Las Vegas, 702-798-7825;
www.lv51.com
A farm team of the L.A. Dodgers, the 51s play at Cashman Field, which seats more than 9,000 fans.

### Las Vegas Art Museum
Sahara West Library/Fine Arts Museum,
9600 W. Sahara Ave., Las Vegas,
702-360-8000;
www.lasvegasartmuseum.org
An affiliate of the Smithsonian, this museum serves primarily as a venue for traveling shows. Tuesday-Saturday 10 a.m.-5 p.m., Sunday 1 p.m.-5 p.m.

### Las Vegas Convention Center
3150 Paradise Rd., Las Vegas,
702-892-0711;
www.lasvegas24hours.com
This facility occupies 3.2-million-square feet, making it the largest single-level convention center in the country.

### Las Vegas Harley-Davidson/Buell
2605 S. Eastern Ave., Las Vegas,
702-431-8500, 877-571-7174;
www.lvhd.com
This Harley dealership ranks as the world's largest. Either buy one of the flashy two-wheelers or rent one. The dealership offers shuttle service from some area hotels. Monday-Friday 9 a.m.-7 p.m., Saturday 9 a.m.-6 p.m., Sunday 10 a.m.-5 p.m.

### Las Vegas Mini Gran Prix
1401 N. Rainbow Blvd., Las Vegas,
702-259-7000; www.lvmgp.com
Three tracks feature go-karts, sprint carts and Grand Prix cars, so take your pick. The smallest of drivers maneuver kiddie carts around the fourth track. There's also a large arcade and amusement rides, including a roller coaster and a 90-foot slide. Sunday-Thursday 10 a.m.-10 p.m.; Friday-Saturday to 11 p.m.

**184**

**NEVADA**

### Las Vegas Motor Speedway
**7000 Las Vegas Blvd. N., Las Vegas,**
**800-644-4444; www.lvms.com**
Competitive events occur most weekends and include short-track programs as well as motocross, dragway and marquee races like NASCAR Nextel Cup races. Also includes a driving school with classes such as the popular Richard Petty Driving Experience and CART Driving 101.

### Las Vegas Natural History Museum
**900 Las Vegas Blvd. N., Las Vegas,**
**702-384-3466; www.lvnhm.org**
Exhibits focus on wildlife and plants from Africa and other parts of the world, as well as Nevada's Mojave Desert. Kids will love the Dinosaur Gallery and Marine Life, a 3,000-gallon reef tank where shark feedings take place several times a week at 2 p.m. Daily 9 a.m.-4 p.m.

### Las Vegas Outlet Center
**7400 Las Vegas Blvd. S., Las Vegas,**
**702-896-5599; www.premiumoutlets.com**
This outlet mall now boasts 155 shops and two food courts (with plans to expand) and includes Tommy Hilfiger, Calvin Klein and Bose. Monday-Saturday 10 a.m.-9 p.m., Sunday 10 a.m.-8 p.m.

### Las Vegas Ski and Snowboard Resort
**Hwy. 156, Las Vegas, 702-385-2754;**
**www.skilasvegas.com**
Choose from 11 different ski runs at this alpine resort, just 45 minutes from the city in the Spring Mountain Range, in Mount Charleston's Lee Canyon. A half-pipe and terrain park challenge snowboarders. Thanksgiving-Easter, daily 9 a.m.-4 p.m.

### Las Vegas Soaring Center
**23600 S. Las Vegas Blvd., Jean,**
**702-874-1010; www.soaringcenter.net**
Soar above the desert in a towplane or sailplane. Daily 10 a.m.-dusk.

### Laser Quest
**7361 W. Lake Mead Blvd.,**
**Las Vegas, 702-243-8881;**
**www.laserquest.com**
People of all ages come to play, snake through labyrinths and use laser pistols to take their best shots and tag other players wearing vests with laser-sensitive targets. Shots can even be ricocheted off mirrored reflecting paper hanging from the walls. Tuesday-Thursday 6-9 p.m., Friday 4-11 p.m., Saturday noon-11 p.m., Sunday noon-6 p.m.

### Le Boulevard District
**Paris Las Vegas, 3655 Las Vegas Blvd. S.,**
**Las Vegas, 877-603-4386;**
**www.parislasvegas.com**
Go on a French-style spending spree in this 31,500-square-foot shopping district that transports you overseas to the City of Light. The cobblestone streets and winding alleyways will make you feel like you're in Paris. Buy French wines, cheese and treats at La Cave.

### Left of Center Art Gallery and Studio
**2207 W. Gowan, North Las Vegas,**
**702-647-7378**
Local and national artists display artwork that typically touches on social issues at this 3,6000-square-foot gallery in an industrial part of town. Resident artists also present workshops and gallery talks and teach classes. Tuesday-Friday 1-6 p.m., Saturday 10 a.m.-2 p.m.

### Lion Habitat
**MGM Grand, 3799 Las Vegas Blvd. S.,**
**Las Vegas, 702-891-1111;**
**www.mgmgrand.com**
During the day, you can see lions up close at the sky-lit habitat surrounded by waterfalls, Acacia trees and a pond at the MGM. There's even a see-through tunnel that allows you to see the lions' pad above and below. Feline expert Keith Evans trucks up to six big cats daily to the Strip from his ranch 12 miles away. Daily 11 a.m.-10 p.m.

### Madame Tussaud's Las Vegas
**The Venetian Resort Hotel Casino,**
**3377 Las Vegas Blvd. S., Las Vegas,**
**702-862-7800; www.venetian.com**

**185**

**NEVADA**

See more than 100 wax figures of celebrities, from Barbara Streisand to Harrison Ford. Daily; varies by season.

### Manhattan Express
**New York-New York,**
**3790 Las Vegas Blvd. S., Las Vegas,**
**702-740-6969; www.nynyhotelcasino.com**
Looping around the faux Big Apple skyline, New York-New York's Manhattan Express roller coaster looks tame enough from street level. But buckled into one of its yellow cab cars, its a streaker, climbing 16 stories, dropping 12 and reaching 67 miles per hour through somersaults, barrel rolls and a twisting dive. Sunday-Thursday 11 a.m.-11 p.m., Friday-Saturday 10:30 a.m. to midnight.

### Masquerade Show in the Sky
**Rio All-Suite Hotel and Casino,**
**3700 W., Flamingo Rd., Las Vegas,**
**702-777-7776, 866-746-7671;**
**www.playrio.com**
This unique and exciting show is modeled after Brazil's Carnivale. The show features state-of-the-art floats suspended from the ceiling that parade above the casino floor. Performers wear exotic masks and colorful costumes. Audience members can take part in the parade and ride a float and wear a costume. Thursday-Monday at 3 p.m., 4 p.m., 5 p.m., 6:30 p.m., 7:30 p.m., 8:30 p.m., and 9:30 p.m.

### Neon Museum
**Third and Fremont Streets,**
**Las Vegas, 702-387-6366;**
**www.neonmuseum.org**

In an effort to preserve the outrageous neon signs for which the city is famed, this museum currently consists of 10 vintage ads, refurbished and remounted in two outdoor galleries located on the Third Street cul-de-sac and the intersection of Fremont Street and Las Vegas Boulevard. The neon signs, including Dots Flowers (from 1949) and the Nevada Motel (1950) almost seem quaint beside today's more elaborately evolved wattage. Daily, 24 hours.

### Neonopolis
**450 Fremont St., Las Vegas, 702-477-0470;**
**www.neonopolis.com**
This three-story, 200,000-square-foot entertainment complex has upped the ante on non-gaming activities for families. Take in one of the latest Hollywood flicks at the 14-screen Crown Theatre multiplex, dine in one of the casual restaurants and go bowling afterward. As the name suggests, you'll also see lots of cool neon signs. Sunday-Thursday 11 a.m.-9 p.m., Friday-Saturday 11 a.m.-10 p.m.

### Nevada State Museum and Historical Society
**Lorenzi Park, 700 Twin Lakes Dr.,**
**Las Vegas, 702-486-5205**
The Nevada State Museum and Historical Society delivers a mix of natural and human history. Prehistory galleries mount a reconstructed Columbian mammoth and Pacific horse as well as an ichthyosaur fossil. Regional coverage includes gangster Bugsy Siegel's involvement in the Flamingo hotel. Though the museum primarily draws school groups, its sylvan lakeside setting in Lorenzi Park offers an incentive to visit. Daily 9 a.m.-5 p.m.

### Nevada Test Site History Center
**755 E. Flamingo Rd., Las Vegas,**
**702-794-5161; www.ntshf.org**
At this center, learn more about the role this site played in strengthening the country's defense and increase your overall knowledge of the U.S. nuclear testing program, from 1950 to the present. You'll see exhibits on Camp Desert Rock, experiments done to try building a nuclear rocket for manned flight to Mars, as well as other interesting topics. Monday-Saturday 9 a.m., Sunday 1 p.m.-5 p.m.

### Painted Desert Golf Club
**5555 Painted Mirage Rd., Las Vegas,**
**702-645-2570; www.painteddesertgc.com**
Painted Desert is one of the older desert-style golf courses in Vegas and it makes a deliberate effort to be playable to almost everyone, even on a bad day. The course

is meticulously maintained. Eight of the nine par-fours measure less than 400 yards, so if your approach shots are good, you have a nice chance of making some birdies while enjoying the course's namesake feature.

### Red Rock Canyon National Conservation Area

**1000 Scenic Dr., Las Vegas, 702-515-5350**
As the days wear on in Vegas and the trilling of slot machines wears you down, head to the red-rock boulders and pinnacles that form the western view from Strip hotel windows. Although it's only 10 miles from the city limits, Red Rock Canyon feels far away. The 13-mile-loop through the conservation area on a one-way road takes you to its most entertaining features, including several trailhead stops for day hikes and an almost certain photo opportunity with the assertive wild burros who thrive here. Thirty miles of Mojave Desert trails take hikers deep into the petrified sand dunes, past ancient pictographs and mysterious waterfalls. Scenic drive: winter 6 a.m.-5 p.m., spring and fall to 7 p.m., summer to 8 p.m.; visitor center, winter 8 a.m.-4:30 p.m., summer to 5:30 p.m.

### Red Rooster Antique Mall

**1109 Western Ave., Las Vegas, 702-382-5253**
Housed in a former soda pop bottling plant, this is the oldest antique mall in town. Goods constantly change, but regulars check the warehouse-sized space frequently for old signs, vintage Vegas memorabilia and 50s modern furniture. You'll find more than 50 antique and collectible dealers here. Daily 10 a.m.-6 p.m.

### Rhodes Ranch Golf Club

**20 Rhodes Ranch Pkwy., Las Vegas, 702-740-4114; www.rhodesranch.com**
Tucked into the southwest corner of the Las Vegas Valley, the Ted Robinson-designed Rhodes Ranch course is the center of a 1,500-acre planned community. Open to the public, the well-groomed 162-acre course spreads over multiple elevations with city, plateau and mountain views plus ample water features. Course management claims three of Robinson's best par-threes. Winter 7 a.m.-dusk, summer 6 a.m.-dusk.

### Royal Links Golf Club

**5995 E. Vegas Valley Dr., Las Vegas, 702-450-8123, 888-427-6678; www.royallinksgolfclub.com**
Royal Links does its best to create the atmosphere of a traditional Scottish or Irish golf links. Each hole was inspired by one on which the British Open is contested each year. Hole designs were taken from Royal Troon, Prestwick and Royal Birkdale, among others. The club suggests that you let the caddies on staff carry your bag to get the full experience of British Isles golf right here in the states.

### Scenic Airlines

**2705 Airport Dr., North Las Vegas, 702-638-3300, 800-634-6801; www.scenicairlines.com**
Board one of this company's twin-engine planes for a birds-eye view of the glorious Grand Canyon. More than 20 different tours are offered, ranging from one hour to three days of sightseeing. Depending on which tour you choose, you'll also see other popular natural attractions, such as Bryce Canyon, the Hoover Dam, Lake Mead, Monument Valley and the Valley of Fire. On some tours, you'll also spend some time exploring on foot or in a boat. Plane wings are up high, so no aerial views are obstructed, and oversized panoramic windows give you an even better look at what's down below.

### Shadow Creek Golf Club

**5400 Losee Rd., North Las Vegas, 866-260-0069; www.shadowcreek.com**
Probably the most exclusive course in town—a tee time here will cost you $500 and you might find yourself playing behind George Clooney or Michael Jordan. The views of the surrounding mountains are breathtaking. (Since it's so pricey, the course isn't crowded.) Pine trees make for an interesting site in the Nevada desert, as do crystal clear lagoons and streams along

**NEVADA**

holes like the signature 15th, which runs toward the mountains.

### Shark Reef at Mandalay Bay
Mandalay Bay Resort and Casino, 3950 Las Vegas Blvd. S., Las Vegas, 702-632-4555; www.mandalaybay.com
This aquarium houses more than 2,000 animals, including the great hammerhead shark, the only one in a closed-system aquarium in the world. Its residence is a 1.6-million-gallon tank, the third largest in North America. Other remarkable exhibits include five of the 12 golden crocodiles in captivity in the world as well as an Asian water monitor and green sea turtles, all of which are endangered species. Daily 10 a.m.-11 p.m., last admission at 10 p.m.

### Siena Golf Club
10575 Siena Monte Ave., Las Vegas, 702-341-9200, 888-689-6469; www.sienagolfclub.com
Sienna has a lot of bunkers. The sand is nearly omnipresent, but it's only a problem on the back nine, which features doglegs and blind shots that stand in contrast to the long, straight holes of the front side. Siena is more of a risk-reward course than it is a course for playing target golf. You could go for an adventurous shot in many places, but by the end of the day, the sand traps may have you thinking twice before you play such brazen golf.

### Sirens of TI
Treasure Island, 3300 Las Vegas Blvd. S., Las Vegas, 702-894-7111; www.treasureisland.com
The sailors of the *HMS Britannia* challenge pirates offloading their stolen booty from the *Hispaniola* in this animatronic spectacle staged outside Treasure Island. The show has recently been updated, bringing new innovations in lighting and pyrotechnics and adding a sexy new twist. Women now battle it out with the renegade pirates in a more adult interpretation of this popular attraction. Join the crowds that cluster around the ships well before show time for best viewing. Daily at 7 p.m., 8:30 p.m., 10 p.m. and 11:30 p.m.

### Southern Nevada Zoological-Botanical Park
1775 N. Rancho Dr., Las Vegas, 702-647-4685; www.lasvegaszoo.org
This park, with 150 species of animals and plants, is home to the last family of Barbary Apes in this country and the very rare Bali Mynah birds. You'll also see endangered cats, chimpanzees, eagles, emus, ostriches, venomous reptiles native to southern Nevada and wallabies. Those interested in botany will appreciate the endangered cycads and rare bamboos. Half-day and full-day eco-desert tours are also available. Daily 9 a.m.-5 p.m.

### Speed—The Ride
NASCAR Cafe, Sahara Hotel & Casino, 2535 Las Vegas Blvd. S., Las Vegas, 702-737-2111; www.saharavegas.com/thrills
This 70-mph thrill ride begins inside the NASCAR Cafe and propels you over its first hill with electromagnetic force. It then travels through a loop and shoots up a 224-foot tower before dropping backward down the same track. Sunday-Thursday 10 a.m.-midnight, Friday-Saturday to 1 a.m.

### Sports Book at the Mirage Hotel and Casino
Mirage Hotel and Casino, 3400 Las Vegas Blvd. S., Las Vegas, 702-791-7111; www.mirage.com
Most casinos have one, but sports books are shrinking in newer hotels. The Mirage boasts a 10,000-square-foot sports betting palace. Big events, including the Super Bowl, the Kentucky Derby and the NBA Finals, are predictably jammed. Daily.

### Sports Hall of Fame
Las Vegas Club Casino and Hotel, 18 E. Fremont St., Las Vegas, 702-385-1664, 800-634-6532; www.vegasclubcasino.net
Hardcore sports fans won't want to miss a visit to this championship attraction, which is packed with memorabilia connected to some of the sports world's biggest names. The all-star collection includes Michael Jordan's

autographed University of North Carolina basketball jersey, 10 autographed NFL footballs, prized photos of boxing greats such as Muhammad Ali and Joe Louis and many more noteworthy items. The hotel showcases all the memorabilia in the long hallways that connect its two towers. Daily, 24 hours.

### Stallion Mountain Country Club
5500 E. Flamingo Rd., Las Vegas,
702-450-8077;
www.stallionmountaincc.com
A private 54-hole facility, Stallion Mountain follows the lead of several other courses in the area and gives its three tracks the names Secretariat, Man O War and Citation, after the legendary Triple Crown winning thoroughbreds. Secretariat is the course to play if you have to choose just one. It plays at the foot of Sunrise Mountain, and each hole has a name that suggests something about the tracks layout (including Forced Carry and Entrapment). The course is fairly difficult and pricey.

### Star Trek: The Experience
Las Vegas Hilton, 3000 Paradise Rd.,
Las Vegas, 702-697-8717, 888-462-6535;
www.startrekexp.com
Trekkies will love this sci-fi immersion. Get beamed up to the Starship *Enterprise*. The 22-minute tour Turbo-lifts you to the Shuttlebay to board a four-minute sound-and-motion simulator ride through space. Disembark at the History of the Future Museum filled with props and costumes from the various Star Trek series. Quarks, the canteen based on the café aboard *Deep Space Nine*, gives you your fill of "hamborgers" and glop on a stick. Daily 11 a.m.-11 p.m.

### Stratosphere Tower Thrill Rides
Stratosphere Hotel and Casino,
2900 Las Vegas Blvd. S., Las Vegas,
702-380-7777, 800-998-6937;
www.stratospherehotel.com
Go 1,149 feet to the top of the tallest freestanding building west of the Mississippi and then get tossed 160 feet at 45 mph. Or ride the X-Scream and let a mechanical arm dangle you off the side like a cruel see-saw. The roller coaster is much tamer, but will give

you some of the best aerial views of Vegas. Sunday-Thursday 10-1 a.m., Friday-Saturday 10-2 a.m.

### Sundance Helicopter Tours
5596 Haven St., Las Vegas, 800-653-1881;
www.helicoptour.com
Take a seat in one of Sundance's choppers for a breathtaking, birds-eye view of the majestic Grand Canyon. On some of the more expensive tours, you'll descend below the canyon rim and even land for a scenic boat ride along the Colorado River, followed by a picnic lunch and champagne toasts. For a lot less money, you can fly over the Strip to see the city's trump card from high above the nonstop action.

### Sunset Park
2601 E. Sunset Rd., Las Vegas,
702-455-8200
When you feel like getting out of those windowless casinos, head to this 320-acre park. Shoot some hoops on one of the basketball courts, play a round of disk golf, get in a game of tennis or volleyball, go swimming and much more. The park has ample picnic facilities. Daily 7 a.m.-11 p.m.

### The Secret Garden of Siegfried & Roy
Mirage Hotel and Casino,
3400 Las Vegas Blvd. S., Las Vegas,
702-791-7111;
www.miragehabitat.com
Besides stunningly beautiful royal white tigers, you'll see an Asian elephant, a black panther, heterozygous tigers, a snow leopard, white lions and more wild creatures. Use one of the free listening wands to learn about each animal from the famed duo themselves. Also visit the 2.5-million-gallon Dolphin Habitat, where Atlantic bottlenose dolphins will charm you with their playfulness. Daily 10 a.m.-7 p.m.

### Tournament Players Club at The Canyons
9851 Canyon Run Dr.,
Las Vegas, 702-256-2000;
www.tpc.com/canyons
Co-designed by PGA legend Raymond Floyd, the Canyons features short fairways

**NEVADA**

and rough that's consistent but tough. The course hosts the Las Vegas Senior Classic on the PGA's Champions Tour each year. There are fairway bunkers on many holes to penalize golfers for hitting errant tee shots, and the greens make it challenging to get your approach shots close enough to have consistent birdie opportunities. It's a difficult course, but one that shouldn't be missed.

### University of Nevada, Las Vegas
4505 S. Maryland Pkwy.,
Las Vegas, 702-895-3011;
www.unlv.edu
Established in 1957; 19,500 students. Campus tours arranged in advance. On campus is the Artemus W. Ham Concert Hall. This 1,900-seat theater features the Charles Vanda Master Series of symphony, opera and ballet. Jazz and popular music concerts are also performed here.

### Marjorie Barrick Museum of Natural History
4505 S. Maryland Pkwy., Las Vegas,
702-895-3381;
www.hrc.nevada.edu/museum
Exhibits of the biology, geology and archaeology of the Las Vegas area, including live desert animals. Monday-Friday 8 a.m.-4:45 p.m., Saturday 10 a.m.-2 p.m.

### Thomas & Mack Center
4505 S. Maryland Pkwy., Las Vegas,
702-895-3761; www.unlvtickets.com
This 18,500-seat events center features concerts, ice shows, rodeos and sporting events.

### UNLV Performing Arts Center
University of Nevada Las Vegas,
4505 S. Maryland Pkwy., Las Vegas,
702-895-2787; www.pac.unlv.edu
Performers as diverse as Herbie Hancock, Yo-Yo Ma, the Shanghai Ballet, Regina Carter and Andre Watts have all played here. In addition to classical musicians, jazz players and world dance troops, the center hosts lectures by visiting authors such as John Irving and journalists such as Cokie

Roberts. The UNLV departments of theater and performing arts also mount shows on the several stages here.

### UNLV Sports
Las Vegas, 702-739-3267;
www.unlvrebels.cstv.com
A perennial contender in the NCAA's basketball tourney each March, the Runnin Rebels' basketball team is the oldest team in a town that lacks deep roots. Football games come with pageantry from marching bands to tailgating parties. Basketball, November-March; football, August-November.

### Xeriscape
4505 S. Maryland Pkwy., Las Vegas,
702-895-1421
This 1 1/2-acre garden proves that a landscape featuring desert plants can be a real eye-pleaser. You'll get lost in the serene setting as you wander the many paved pathways and cross over the wooden bridges scattered across the grounds. Many of the plants are indigenous to North America's four desert regions, while others were introduced from Australia, the Mediterranean, Mexico and South America. Daily, 24 hours.

### Via Bellagio
Bellagio, 3600 Las Vegas Blvd. S.,
Las Vegas, 702-693-7111;
www.bellagiolasvegas.com
The sky-lit Via Bellagio provides fittingly luxe surroundings for high-end designer shops, including Giorgio Armani, Gucci, Prada, Chanel, Yves Saint Laurent and Hermes and Fred Leighton. Daily 11 a.m.-midnight.

## SPECIAL EVENTS
### Boxing at Caesars Palace
Caesars Palace, 3570 Las Vegas Blvd. S.,
Las Vegas, 702-731-7110, 877-427-7243;
www.caesarspalace.com
Nowhere is the sport of boxing cheered more vigorously than in Las Vegas, where bouts are often sponsored by Caesars Palace. Key title match-ups range from featherweight to heavyweight. Major boxing event weekends tend to flood Las Vegas with Saturday

**190**

**NEVADA**

night visitors, making both beds and tickets hard to come by without advance planning.

## Michelin Championship at Las Vegas (Las Vegas Invitational)

Tournament Players Club at Summerlin, 1700 Village Center Cir., Las Vegas, 702-873-1010;
www.pgatour.com/tournaments/r047/index.html
Host of the PGA event since 1992, the Tournament Players' Club at Summerlin was designed by architect Bobby Weed with input from player/consultant Fuzzy Zoeller. In addition to offering elevation changes and a variety of challenges, the course was built to accommodate spectators with natural amphitheaters and clear sightlines to the tees. October.

## National Finals Rodeo

Thomas & Mack Center, 4505 S. Maryland Pkwy., Las Vegas, 719-593-8840, 888-388-3267;
www.prorodeo.com
For 10sw days in December, the Old West rides into Las Vegas with a round up of events, including bull riding, calf roping, barrel racing and steer wrestling. Only the top 15 money winners per event on the Professional Rodeo Cowboys Association competitive circuit earn the right to compete in this championship event, vying for millions in prize money. For a novelty act, this rodeo is one of the most sought-after tickets in Vegas. Ten days in early December.

## World Series of Poker

Las Vegas, 702-382-1600;
www.worldseriesofpoker.com
The number of competitors in this tournament has increased dramatically from fewer than 100 in the early days to more than 7,000 in recent years. The prize money has climbed proportionately to $20 million, more than $7.5 million of which the champion pocketed in 2005. A wide variety of games are played, and anyone age 21 or older can enter the competition, which continues for five suspenseful, nerve-wracking weeks. May-July.

# HOTELS

## ★★Alexis Park All-Suite Resort

375 E. Harmon Ave., Las Vegas, 702-796-3300, 800-582-2228;
www.alexispark.com
495 rooms, all suites. High-speed Internet access. Restaurant, bar. Spa. $

## ★★★Bally's Las Vegas

3645 Las Vegas Blvd., Las Vegas, 877-603-4390; www.ballyslv.com
A neon-lit tunnel ushers you from the heart of the Strip into Bally's. At more than 500 square feet each, the rooms are spacious and comfortable. The pool and spa are small compared to newer hotels, but Bally's is a good value in a prime location for those who still equate Vegas with showgirls.
2,814 rooms. High-speed Internet access. Eleven restaurants, five bars. Spa. Casino. Tennis. $$

## ★★★★Bellagio

3600 Las Vegas Blvd. S., Las Vegas, 702-693-7111, 888-987-6667;
www.bellagiolasvegas.com
A fantastic casino is only the beginning at this all-encompassing hotel, with a beautifully landscaped pool, arcade of fine shopping and celebrity-chef restaurants. Visitors will gaze with awe at the exotic botanical gardens and magnificent hand-blown glass flowers by renowned artist Dale Chihuly in the lobby. Of course, the star of the show is the eight-acre man-made lake, where the popular fountain and light show takes place every half-hour. The Bellagio is also home to Cirque du Soleil's O, a mesmerizing aquatic performance. The rooms have luxurious fabrics and Italian marble. The only downside here is that you have to go through the casino to get everywhere. But then again, that's the point.
3,933 rooms. High-speed Internet access, wireless Internet access. Twelve restaurants, 5 bars. Spa. Casino. $$

## ★★★Caesars Palace

3570 Las Vegas Blvd. S., Las Vegas, 702-731-7110, 866-227-5938;
www.caesarspalace.com

★

★

★

★

★

★

The Roman-themed Caesars was the Strip's first mega-resort when it opened in 1966, and it remains one of the top hotels, mostly because it's always changing and challenging competitors to keep up. The hotel's swimming deck, modeled on Pompeii, surrounds the three pools. The lavish rooms have couches and marble bathrooms and a variety of suites are offered, some with high ceilings and whirlpool tubs. Prepare to spend at the Forum Shops.
2,500 rooms. High-speed Internet access, wireless Internet access. Ten restaurants, eight bars. Spa. Airport transportation available. Casino. **$$**

### ★★Clarion Hotel
325 E. Flamingo Rd., Las Vegas,
702-732-9100, 800-424-6423;
www.choicehotels.com
150 rooms. Restaurant, bar. Pool. **$**

### ★★Courtyard Las Vegas Convention Center
3275 Paradise Rd., Las Vegas,
702-791-3600, 800-661-1064;
www.courtyard.com
149 rooms. High-speed Internet access. Restaurant. **$$**

### ★★Embassy Suites Hotel Las Vegas
4315 Swenson St., Las Vegas,
702-795-2800, 800-362-2779;
www.embassysuites.com
220 rooms, all suites. High-speed Internet access. Restaurant, bar. Pool. **$$**

### ★Fairfield Inn
3850 Paradise Rd., Las Vegas,
702-791-0899, 800-228-2800;
www.fairfieldinn.com
129 rooms. Wireless Internet access. Pool. **$**

### ★Fiesta Rancho Station Casino Hotel
2400 N. Rancho Dr., Las Vegas,
702-631-7000, 888-899-7770;
www.fiestacasino.com
100 rooms. High-speed Internet access. Five restaurants, two bars. Casino. Pool. **$**

### ★★Fitzgeralds Hotel Casino
301 Fremont St., Las Vegas,
702-388-2400, 800-274-5825;
www.fitzgeraldslasvegas.com
638 rooms. High-speed Internet access. Three restaurants, two bars. Casino. **$**

### ★★Flamingo Las Vegas
3555 Las Vegas Blvd. S., Las Vegas,
702-733-3111, 888-902-9929;
www.lv-flamingo.com
3,642 rooms. High-speed Internet access, wireless Internet access. Seven restaurants, seven bars. Spa. Airport transportation available. Casino. Pets accepted. **$$**

### ★★★★Four Seasons Hotel Las Vegas
3960 Las Vegas Blvd. S., Las Vegas,
702-632-5000, 877-632-5000;
www.fourseasons.com
The Four Seasons Hotel is a palatial refuge in glittering Las Vegas. Located on the southern tip of the Strip on the top floors of the Mandalay Bay Resort tower, it's close to the action but also provides a welcome respite when you need it. The sumptuous rooms at this non-gaming hotel have floor-to-ceiling windows overlooking the city. The glorious pool is a lush oasis with its swaying palm trees and attentive poolside service. The sublime spa offers innovated treatments. Steak lovers will enjoy Charlie Palmer Steak, while the sun-filled Verandah offers a casual dining alternative.
424 rooms. High-speed Internet access. Two restaurants, bar. Spa. **$$$**

### ★★★Golden Nugget Hotel And Casino
129 E. Fremont St., Las Vegas,
702-385-7111, 800-846-5336;
www.goldennugget.com
This downtown hotel is the best of the bunch. You get Strip-style amenities, including a cabana-ringed pool with a 200,00-gallon shark tank and full-service spa, at discount prices, since everything is cheaper downtown, including the gambling minimums. Still, the Nugget upholds elegant standards with a marble-trimmed lobby just off raucous Fremont Street, and the rooms are comfortable and modern. The International

NEVADA

Beer Bar pours 40 foreign brands, while Zax serves an eclectic menu that includes everything from sushi to tostadas.
1,907 rooms. High-speed wireless Internet access. Five restaurants, four bars. Spa. Casino. **$$**

### ★★★Hard Rock Hotel Casino
**4455 Paradise Rd., Las Vegas,**
**702-693-4415, 800-473-7625;**
**www.hardrockhotel.com**
A youthful party atmosphere prevails in the memorabilia-strewn complex. About a mile off the Strip, Hard Rock generates its own fun, particularly when a big act is booked at the Joint concert hall. That's when the swim-up blackjack tables by the pool really fill up and it's harder to nab at table at Nobu, the celebrated sushi spot. Rooms feature French doors that open to views of the Strip or mountains (try to get one facing the city), Bose stereos and bathrooms with stainless-steel sinks. Simon Kitchen and Bar—the chef has won *Iron Chef*—is a great spot for dining.
641 rooms. High-speed wireless internet access. Five restaurants, two bars. Spa. Casino. **$$**

### ★★★Harrah's Hotel and Casino Las Vegas
**3475 Las Vegas Blvd. S., Las Vegas,**
**800-214-9110; www.harrahs.com**
The gaming powerhouse Harrah's runs this Strip hotel, where the emphasis is on the casino. The carnival theme spills out to an outdoor plaza that features entertainers, trinket vendors and snack booths. Spacious but rather bland rooms are lodged in a 35-story tower behind the gaming floor, although guests spend most of their time at the many tables, Olympic-size swimming pool, boutique spa and seven eateries. Entertainer Rita Rudner performs at the showroom here.
2,526 rooms. High-speed Internet access. Seven restaurants, four bars. Spa. Casino. **$**

### ★★★JW Marriott Las Vegas Resort & Spa
**221 N. Rampart Blvd., Las Vegas,**
**702-869-7777, 877-869-8777;**
**www.marriott.com**

Fifteen minutes from the Strip, the JW Marriott Las Vegas Resort offers a tranquil alternative to the neon lights. Set on 50 acres of lush tropical gardens against the backdrop of the Red Rock Mountains, this resort is lavish and comfortable. Guest rooms include marble-paved entries, premium bedding and oversized bathrooms. The shimmering pool is an inviting spot to enjoy the warm weather, while eight championship courses lure golfers away from their lounge chairs. The deluxe European-style spa is the perfect retreat, while those who prefer blackjack to body treatments head for a nearby casino.
536 rooms. High-speed Internet access. Restaurant, bar. Spa. Pool. **$$$$**

### ★La Quinta Inn
**3970 Paradise Rd., Las Vegas,**
**702-796-9000, 800-531-5900;**
**www.laquinta.com**
251 rooms. Complimentary continental breakfast. Airport transportation available. Pets accepted. **$**

### ★★Las Vegas Club Hotel
**18 E. Fremont St., Las Vegas,**
**702-385-1664, 800-634-6532;**
**www.playlv.com**
408 rooms. Restaurant, bar. Casino. **$**

### ★★★Las Vegas Hilton
**3000 Paradise Rd., Las Vegas,**
**702-732-5111, 888-732-7117;**
**www.lvhilton.com**
This popular, family-friendly Las Vegas destination is adjacent to the Convention Center. Set on 80 lushly landscaped acres, this 30-story hotel has more than a dozen restaurants, a spa and an enormous sports book. The theater—everyone from Barry Manilow to Tony Bennett plays here—is one of the old great showrooms.
3,000 rooms. High-speed Internet access. Fifteen restaurants, nine bars. Spa. Casino. Tennis. **$$**

### ★★★Luxor Hotel and Casino
**3900 Las Vegas Blvd. S., Las Vegas,**
**702-262-4444, 888-777-0188;**
**www.luxor.com**

**NEVADA**

★
★
★
★
★

This big, shiny Vegas wonder certainly stands out on the Strip. Supposedly the light beam on top of the pyramid can be seen from outer space. "Inclinators" transport you to your room in the main tower where you'll find an Egyptian motif and a sloping wall, a constant reminder that you are, in fact, staying in a pyramid. Rooms in the tower next door are newer and don't require inclinators. King Tutankhamuns Tomb and Museum, a replica of the King Tut's tomb, is a lot of fun. Kids will love the arcade floor.

4,407 rooms. Restaurant, bar. Spa. Casino. **$**

### ★★Main Street Station
200 N. Main St., Las Vegas,
702-387-1896, 800-465-0711;
www.mainstreetcasino.com

406 rooms. High-speed Internet access, wireless Internet access. Two restaurants, two bars. Airport transportation available. Casino. **$**

### ★★★Mandalay Bay Resort and Casino
3950 Las Vegas Blvd. S., Las Vegas,
702-632-7777, 877-632-7800;
www.mandalaybay.com

Even in over-the-top Las Vegas, Mandalay Bay exceeds expectations. Located at the southern end of the Strip, this all-encompassing resort has rooms with a tropical flavor, and the casino is a paradise of lush foliage and flowing water. The resort is known for its Shark Reef aquarium. There's also a variety of entertainment, from live music to Broadway-style shows, as well as 13 restaurants. The more affordable, but still luxurious, rooms in the main hotel have comfortable beds and slate bathrooms.

3,215 rooms. Thirteen restaurants, bar. Spa. Beach. Casino. **$$**

### ★★★Marriott Suites Las Vegas
325 Convention Center Dr., Las Vegas,
702-650-2000, 800-228-9290;
www.marriott.com

Adjacent to the Las Vegas Convention Center and near the famous Las Vegas Strip, this is a good choice for business travelers. Rooms feature multiple data ports and workstations.

And after a long day of conventions, you can hit the pool or fitness center.

278 rooms, all suites. Restaurant, bar. Airport transportation available. **$**

### ★★★MGM Grand Hotel and Casino
3799 Las Vegas Blvd. S., Las Vegas,
702-891-7777, 888-646-1203;
www.mgmgrand.com

The largest hotel on the Strip (and perhaps the world—this place is *huge*), the MGM Grand virtually pulses with Las Vegas energy. The Art Deco rooms are nice—but you're not likely to ever be in them, as there's so much to see and do here. In the casino, lions roam about a glassed-in habitat with waterfalls. The outdoor pool includes a current-fed river and the spa specializes in cutting-edge treatments. MGM eateries Coyote Cafe, NobHill and Craftsteak are some of the best in the city. Big-name headliners like Cher and David Copperfield often play the MGM, and the French act *Le Femme* updates the showgirl revue. The party crowd crows for the dance club Studio 54 and the lounge Tabu. For a more luxurious experience, check into the ultra-chic Skylofts at MGM Grand (a boutique hotel-within-the-hotel offering contemporary, full-service lofts perched on the top levels of the building) or the Signature at MGM Grand (modern junior suites with their own separate entrance).

5,018 rooms. High-speed wireless Internet access. Nineteen restaurants, seven bars. Children's activity center. Spa. Airport transportation available. Casino. **$$**

### ★★★Mirage Hotel and Casino
3400 Las Vegas Blvd. S., Las Vegas,
702-791-7111, 800-456-4564;
www.mirage.com

The Strip-side volcano—which erupts every hour at night—marks the Mirage and its exotic theme. A huge aquarium serves as the backdrop for the registration desk, the route to room elevators passes through a cascade of jungle foliage and a lavish pool deck is ringed by towering palms. Though Sigfield and Roy are no longer here, you can see their animals in the garden. The elegant and cheerful rooms feature spacious, marble-trimmed baths. 3,323 rooms. High-speed Internet access. Ten restaurants, three bars. Spa. Casino. **$**

### ★★★Monte Carlo Resort and Casino
3770 Las Vegas Blvd. S., Las Vegas, 702-730-7777, 888-529-4828; www.montecarlo.com

Modeled on the sophisticated European republic of Monaco, this resort on the Strip is relatively toned down in comparison to its neighbor Bellagio. Its quiet opulence, with marble floors underfoot and chandeliers above, is its chief asset and a significant contrast to the party set. But the Monte Carlo couldn't claim a piece of Strip real estate without its considerable amenities: four pools, including a lazy river and a wave pool, a luxurious spa and seven eateries. Standard rooms are bright and attractively furnished in cherry wood and Italian marble and granite. Crowd-pleasing magician Lance Burton is the house entertainer. 3,002 rooms. High-speed Internet access. Four restaurants, bar. Spa. Indoor pool. Casino. Tennis. Business center. **$$**

### ★★★New York-New York Hotel and Casino
3790 Las Vegas Blvd. S., Las Vegas, 800-689-1797, 866-815-4365; www.nynyhotelcasino.com

With its Manhattan skyline façade, New York-New York does a cheerful imitation of the Big Apple. The main-floor casino mimics Central Park with trees, bridges and brooks, while Coney Island beckons guests with carnival games and the thrilling Manhattan Express roller coaster. Even the rooms are cramped—another ode to the city that never sleeps? The pool is a relatively straightforward affair relative to others on the strip. Il Fornaio does fine Italian. 2,034 rooms. High-speed Internet access. Eight restaurants, two bars. Spa. Airport transportation available. Casino. **$**

### ★★Orleans Hotel and Casino
4500 W. Tropicana Ave., Las Vegas, 702-365-7111, 800-675-3267

1,886 rooms. High-speed Internet access. Restaurant, bar. Children's activity center. Spa. Casino. **$$**

### ★★Palace Station Hotel
2411 W. Sahara Ave., Las Vegas, 702-367-2411, 800-634-3101; www.palacestation.com

1,021 rooms. Restaurant, bar. Casino. **$**

### ★★★The Palms
4321 W. Flamingo Rd., Las Vegas, 702-942-7777, 866-942-7777; www.palms.com

It's like a party in the lobby of this boutique hotel. The rooftop Ghost Bar and the swanky 9 restaurant attract a lively crowd. The pool is also a scene, and there's 95,000-square-feet of gaming action. For a little quiet, there's a 14-screen movie theater. The inviting rooms have supremely comfortable beds, although the hotel is known for its suites, from the 1960s-style bachelor and bachelorette rooms to the *Real World*: *Las Vegas* residence. 710 rooms. High-speed Internet access, wireless Internet access. 8 restaurants, bar. Spa. Outdoor pool, whirlpool. Business center. Casino. **$$$**

### ★★★Paris Las Vegas
3655 Las Vegas Blvd. S., Las Vegas, 877-603-4386; www.parislasvegas.com

A half-scale model of the Eiffel Tower is the landmark attraction at Paris Las Vegas. There's also the "Arc de Triomphe" and costumed landscape painters fronting the Strip-side pavilion. The scene continues inside, where three legs of the Eiffel rest in the casino and a cobblestone street winds its way through the shopping arcade. Rooms underscore the theme with French fabrics and custom furniture. Request a Strip view to see the dancing Bellagio fountains across the street. Most of the restaurants here are French, including the charming Mon Ami Gabi, which features outdoor dining on a terrace overlooking the Las Vegas Boulevard. 2,916 rooms. Restaurants, bar. Casino. **$$**

**NEVADA**

★
★
★
★
★

### ★★★Planet Hollywood Resort & Casino
3667 Las Vegas Blvd. S., Las Vegas,
702-785-5555, 866-919-7472;
www.planethollywood.com

This resort may have a Los Angeles theme, but the experience is pure Las Vegas. The glitzy, nightclub-like casino features 100,000 square feet of gaming space with more than 90 gaming tables, 2,800 slots and poker room with daily tournaments. It may not be Rodeo Drive but the Miracle Mile offers 170 shops. Mandara Spa can undo the stress of an all-night gambling spree with its selection of relaxing massages, facials, aroma stone therapies and body wraps. After a busy day, guests retire to luxurious rooms fit for a movie star that feature deluxe amenities like marble baths with separate showers and tubs and 27-inch televisions. For a night away from the gambling table, guests can take in a show like *Stomp Out Loud.*

2,567 rooms. High-speed Internet access, wireless Internet access. Six restaurants, four bars. Spa. Casino. **$$**

### ★★★Red Rock Casino, Resort and Spa
11011 W. Charleston Blvd., Las Vegas,
702-797-7777, 866-767-7773;
www.redrocklasvegas.com

An upbeat, contemporary retreat off the Strip, this resort and casino offers an upscale casino experience away from the crowds. Rooms are crisp and modern with flat-screen TVs, iPod stations and luxury linens. The 10 different restaurants serve up everything from fresh oysters to Mexican cuisine. The adventure spa offers a unique opportunity to get outdoors and experience the Red Rock country beyond Las Vegas, with hiking, rock climbing, horseback riding and more.

828 rooms. Pets accepted; some restrictions, fee. High-speed wireless Internet access. Nine restaurants, four bars. Children's activity center. Spa. Airport transportation available. Casino. **$$**

### ★★★Rio All-Suite Hotel and Casino
3700 W. Flamingo Rd., Las Vegas,
866-746-7671; www.playrio.com

The all-suite Rio furnishes spacious rooms with sitting areas and floor-to-ceiling views of the Strip. There are better rooms in Vegas, but if you want a celebratory atmosphere, this is it. A carnival parades above the casino floor seven times a day. Rosemary's restaurant is acclaimed by local gourmets. You won't find waterfalls and Roman statues out by the pool, but there are four of them to choose from.

2,522 rooms, all suites. High-speed Internet access. Thirteen restaurants, five bars. Spa. Casino. Swim. Golf. **$$$**

### ★★St. Tropez All-Suite Hotel
455 E. Harmon Ave., Las Vegas,
702-369-5400, 800-666-5400;
www.sttropezlasvegas.com

149 rooms, all suites. Complimentary continental breakfast. High-speed Internet access. Restaurant, bar. Fitness room. Outdoor pool, whirlpool. Airport transportation available. Pool. **$**

### ★★Sahara Hotel & Casino
2535 Las Vegas Blvd. S., Las Vegas,
702-737-2654, 866-382-8884;
www.saharavegas.com

1,720 rooms. High-speed Internet access. Five restaurants, four bars. Casino. Pool. **$**

### ★★Santa Fe Station Hotel
4949 N. Rancho Dr., Las Vegas,
702-658-4900, 866-767-7771;
www.stationcasinos.com

200 rooms. Twelve restaurants, four bars. Whirlpool. Casino. **$**

### ★★Silverton Hotel Casino
3333 Blue Diamond Rd., Las Vegas,
702-263-7777, 866-946-4373;
www.silvertoncasino.com

300 rooms. Two restaurants, three bars. Casino. Pool. **$**

### ★★★Treasure Island
3300 Las Vegas Blvd. S., Las Vegas,
702-894-7111, 800-288-7206;
www.treasureisland.com

Treasure Island's South Seas pirate theme makes it appealing for families. The sinking of a British frigate in the "Sirens of TI" show outside the hotel draws crowds here every night (as does Cirque du Soleil's show *Mystere*). The hotel has modern, urban décor. Done in beige and gold hues, the spacious guest rooms provide a tranquil respite from the theme of the place. The pool has a tropical theme with tiki accents and outdoor dining. 2,665 rooms. High-speed wireless Internet access. Eight restaurants, four bars. Spa. Casino. **$$**

### ★★★★★The Tower Suites at Wynn Las Vegas
**3131 Las Vegas Blvd. S., Las Vegas, 702-770-7100, 877-321-9966; www.wynnlasvegas.com**
As if the regular guest rooms at the ultra-posh resort on Las Vegas's famed Strip weren't luxurious enough, the 50-story Wynn features refined, apartment-like suites located in their own tower that raise the bar for luxury resorts. Upon arrival, guests are whisked up in private elevators to the suites, which overlook either the city lights or the Wynn Country Club—the only golf course on the Strip. With a private gated entrance to the Tower and Suites, priority access to high-stakes tables and slots in the 111,000-square-foot casino, and access to an exclusive pool—where servers will clean your sunglasses for you—guests are given the star treatment. Ranging in size from 640 to nearly 2,000 square feet, the rooms are spacious and have the feel of an intimate residence. Tranquil and refined, the suites feature replicas of artwork from Steve Wynn's impressive art collection, floor-to-ceiling windows covered by sleek, electronic draperies and 42-inch flat-screen LCD televisions. Marble baths feature bubble-jet tubs, enclosed showers, two sinks and a vanity and 13-inch LCD televisions. A restful night's sleep is guaranteed on the signature Wynn bed, with fluffy pillow-top mattresses and ultra-soft, 320-count European linens. Tableau, the restaurant in the Tower and Suites turns out impeccable American cuisine. (Dinner is served to all hotel guests but breakfast and lunch are reserved for suites-only customers).

653 rooms. High-speed Internet access. Restaurant, bar. Spa. Casino. Golf. Pool. **$$$$**

### ★★★★The Venetian Resort Hotel Casino
**3355 Las Vegas Blvd. S., Las Vegas, 702-414-1000, 877-883-6423; www.venetian.com**
From the masterfully re-created Venetian landmark buildings to the frescoed ceilings and gilded details, the Venetian faithfully re-creates the splendor that is Venice in the heart of the Las Vegas Strip. Guests walk down winding alleys and glide past ornate architecture in gondolas. From the moment you enter through the Doge's Palace and walk through the lobby to the casino with its frescoes, you'll be impressed. The suites are large and luxurious, with sunken living rooms and walk-in closets. Some of the biggest names in American cuisine operate award-winning restaurants here, including Lutece. The Venetian's Guggenheim showcases rotating exhibits while the Canyon Ranch Spa offers the same pampering treatments as the famed spa in Arizona. The Grand Canal Shoppes is a who's who of designers, from Chanel to Jimmy Choo.
4,027 rooms, all suites. Nineteen restaurants, six bars. Spa. Casino. Pool. **$$**

### ★★★The Westin Casuarina Hotel & Spa
**160 E. Flamingo Rd., Las Vegas, 702-836-5900, 866-837-4215; www.westin.com**
Comfortable accommodations with numerous business amenities, a large casino and an ideal location near the Strip and convention center make the Westin an ideal destination for both corporate and leisure travelers. This hotel caters to the modern traveler in both its look and feel, and the rooms and suites show off a stylish contemporary design. Westin signature amenities, including the comfortable Heavenly Bed and soothing Heavenly Bath, are among the many plusses of a visit to this hotel. The hotel's own Starbucks is a perk.
826 rooms. Restaurant, bar. Spa. Casino. Pets accepted. **$**

### ★★★★Wynn Las Vegas

3131 Las Vegas Blvd. S., Las Vegas,
702-770-7100, 888-320-9966;
www.wynnlasvegas.com

You won't find any world wonders or replicas here. This is the haute version of Las Vegas. The rooms, with deep orange walls, impressive art work and richly appointed couches, are decorated to make you feel like you're staying in someone's apartment in London or Manhattan. Here you can open the drapes with the push of a button and soak in the tub while watching the flat screen LCD in the bathroom. On the main level there are two spacious pools, a European-style bathing pool and the Cabana Bar, where you can play poolside blackjack in season. (Guests of the suites enjoy two quieter pools.) Then there's the championship golf course and the boutiques. Shops include Manolo Blahnik, Dior, Louis Vuitton, de la Renta. There's even a Ferrari dealership, and some of the most revered chefs, including Daniel Boulud, have opened restaurants here.

2,716 rooms. 18 restaurants, bars. Spa. Casino. Pool. **$$$$**

## RESTAURANTS

### ★★★★★Alex

3131 Las Vegas Blvd. S., Las Vegas,
702-248-3463, 888-352-3463;
www.wynnlasvegas.com

Famed chef Alessandro Stratta has brought his sumptuous French cuisine to this stunning restaurant at the Wynn, which has a grand hour-glass-shaped staircase, chandeliers and mahogany furniture. The artfully presented dishes might include Robiola cheese agnolotti with black truffles and aged Parmigiano or the Dover Sole with a potato crust, artichokes and tomato confit. Desserts by Pastry Chef Jenifer Witte are just as imaginative and special. Request one of two private seating areas overlooking a private courtyard, or reserve the popular chef's table.

French menu. Dinner. Closed Monday. Bar. Reservations recommended. Valet parking. Outdoor seating. **$$$$**

### ★★★Alize

4321 W. Flamingo Rd., Las Vegas,
702-951-7000; www.alizelv.com

This refined French restaurant is located on the top floor of the Palms Casino Resort. Diners will enjoy a 280-degree view through the floor-to-ceiling windows as they indulge in the French creations of chef/owner André Rochat. Dishes include pan-seared Muscovy duck with peach and foie gras tart, and grilled milk-fed veal chop with artichoke, morel and Gruyère cannelloni. The two-story-high wine tower provides plenty of choices for the perfect dinner pairing. A jacket isn't required but jeans are discouraged.

French menu. Dinner. Bar. Business casual attire. Reservations recommended. Valet parking. **$$$**

### ★★All American Bar & Grille

Rio Hotel & Casino, 3700 W. Flamingo Rd.,
Las Vegas, 702-777-7923;
www.harrahs.com

American menu. Lunch, dinner. Bar. Casual attire. Valet parking. **$$$**

### ★★America

3790 Las Vegas Blvd. S., Las Vegas,
702-740-6451; www.nynyhotelcasino.com

American menu. Breakfast, lunch, dinner, late-night. **$$**

### ★★★AquaKnox

3355 S. Las Vegas Blvd. S., Las Vegas,
702-414-3772; www.venetian.com

The Venetian's Restaurant Row offers an eatery to satisfy every culinary craving, with AquaKnox, sibling to the popular Dallas eatery, positioned to please seafood-seeking diners. A raw bar is stocked with oysters and stone crab claws. Other offerings include caviar, grilled lobster with drawn herb butter and butternut squash soup with duck confit. The exhibition kitchen provides a bustling focal point for the sleek dining room, which also includes a water-encased walk-in wine cellar.

Seafood menu. Dinner. Bar. Casual attire. Reservations recommended. Valet parking. **$$$**

## ★★★★Aureole

3950 Las Vegas Blvd. S., Las Vegas, 89119, 702-632-7401;
www.aureolerestaurant.com

A branch of chef Charlie Palmer's New York original, Aureole wows patrons with its centerpiece four-story wine tower. Be sure to order a bottle just to see the catsuit-clad climber, suspended by ropes, locate your vintage. The extensive wine list complements Palmers seasonal contemporary American cuisine typified by dishes such as Peking duck with foie gras ravioli and roast pheasant with sweet potato gnocchi. The modern but romantic room with encircling booths sets the stage for event dining at Mandalay Bay.

American menu. Dinner. Bar. Reservations recommended. Valet parking. $$$

## ★★★Bartolotta Ristorante Di Mare

3131 Las Vegas Blvd. S., Las Vegas, 702-248-3463, 888-352-3463;
www.wynnlasvegas.com

Guests will feel like they've escaped to Italy when visiting Bartolotta. The dining room is a grand, two-story space with enchanting views of the lake through floor-to-ceiling windows and magnificent frescos. Chef Paul Bartolotta, whose previous efforts earned him a nod from the James Beard Foundation, insists that all seafood be flown in fresh from Europe and Italy the day before. Appetizers include regional favorites like tiny clams with garlic white wine and warm seafood salad. Don't miss such stunners as the seafood risotto and linguine with clams in a white wine garlic sauce.

Italian, seafood menu. Lunch, dinner. Bar. Business casual attire. Reservations recommended. Valet parking. Outdoor seating. $$$$

## ★★Blue Agave

4321 W. Flamingo Rd., Las Vegas, 702-942-7777;
www.thepalmslasvegas.com

Latin American menu. Lunch, dinner. Bar. Casual attire. Valet parking. $$

## ★★★Bouchon

3355 Las Vegas Blvd. S., Las Vegas, 702-414-6200; www.frenchlaundry.com

Star chef Thomas Keller has brought delicious French bistro fare—"bouchon" describes a particular style of French café—to this sophisticated restaurant in the Venezia Tower of the Venetian Resort Hotel Casino. The beautiful interior by famed designer Adam D. Tihany, sets a romantic mood with an impressive French pewter bar, colorful mosaic flooring, deep blue velvet banquettes, antique light fixtures and truly gorgeous hand-painted mural. The restaurant is open for breakfast and dinner, and offers classic bistro dishes such as steak frites, roasted chicken, pot de crème and profiteroles.

French bistro menu. Lunch, dinner. Bar. Business casual attire. Jacket required. Reservations recommended. Valet parking. Outdoor seating. $$$

## ★★★★Bradley Ogden

3570 Las Vegas Blvd. S., Las Vegas, 877-346-4642; www.caesarspalace.com

Bradley Ogden's eponymous restaurant at Caesars Palace—his first outside of California—is a sure bet. Although this modern Las Vegas location is a world away from the farms and ranches Ogden depends on when preparing his innovative take on American cuisine, no expense is spared in bringing it all in. Dishes include oak-grilled lamb rack with fava bean and cumin spaetzel, and hot and cold foie gras with kumquats.

American menu. Dinner. Bar. Business casual attire. Reservations recommended. Valet parking. $$$$

## ★Buffet at Bellagio

3600 Las Vegas Blvd. S., Las Vegas, 702-693-7111; www.bellagiolasvegas.com

American menu. Breakfast, lunch, dinner. Bar. Children's menu. Casual attire. $$

## ★★Buzio's

3700 W. Flamingo Rd., Las Vegas, 702-777-7923; www.playrio.com

NEVASA

★
★
★
★
★
★

American, Seafood menu. Dinner. Bar. Casual attire. Outdoor seating. **$$$**

### ★Cathay House
5300 W. Spring Mountain Rd.,
Las Vegas, 702-876-3838;
www.cathayhouse.com
Chinese menu. Lunch, dinner. Bar. Casual attire. **$$**

### ★★★Chinois
3500 Las Vegas Blvd. S., Las Vegas,
702-737-9700; www.wolfgangpuck.com
This spin-off of chef Wolfgang Puck's acclaimed Chinois in Santa Monica features similar Asian-fusion fare in the Forum Shops at Caesars Palace. The broad menu includes sushi and sashimi, dim sum, wok-fried meat and vegetable recipes such as kung pao chicken, and Asian noodle dishes such as pad Thai.
Asian menu. Lunch, dinner. Bar. Children's menu. Casual attire. Valet parking. **$$$**

### ★★★Commander's Palace
3663 S. Las Vegas Blvd., Las Vegas,
702-892-8272;
www.commanderspalace.com
Straight from the Garden District, this New Orleans favorite imported many of the people behind the original restaurant's success, including manager Brad Brennan of the famed Brennan restaurant clan, which owns Commander's. With palms in the corners, tufted silk on the ceiling and linen topping the tables, the restaurant evokes the gracious style of the Crescent City, while its pecan-crusted fish, turtle soup and bread pudding send your taste buds south. Check out the Dixieland jazz brunch on Sundays.
Cajun/Creole menu. Breakfast, lunch, dinner, late-night, Sunday brunch. Bar. Casual attire. Outdoor seating. **$$$**

### ★★★The Country Club
3131 Las Vegas Blvd. S., Las Vegas,
702-248-3463, 888-352-3463;
www.wynnlasvegas.com
Executive Chef Rene Lenger brings his culinary talents from New York City to the Wynn at this hideaway overlooking the championship golf course. He knows the desires of a steak lover and his menu does not disappoint. Lenger compliments the superb cuts of meat with tasty appetizers such as jumbo lump crab cake, Maine lobster bisque and green and white asparagus salad with prosciutto di Parma and lemon aioli. Sides include truffle cream spinach and buttermilk onion rings. Several fish dishes are also offered.
Steak menu. Breakfast, lunch, dinner. Bar. Business casual attire. Reservations recommended. Valet parking. Outdoor seating. **$$$$**

### ★★Corsa Cucina
3131 Las Vegas Blvd. S., Las Vegas,
702-248-3463, 888-352-3463;
www.wynnlasvegas.com
Italian menu. Dinner. Bar. Business casual attire. Reservations recommended. Valet parking. **$$$**

### ★★★Craftsteak
3799 Las Vegas Blvd. S., Las Vegas,
702-891-7318; www.mgmgrand.com
After earning the James Beard Foundation's 2002 best new restaurant nod for Craft in New York, chef Tom Colicchio—you might know him as a judge on Bravo's *Top Chef*—spun off this version in the MGM Grand. With an emphasis on top-shelf ingredients from boutique farms and artisanal producers, the a la carte menu incorporates fish, shellfish, poultry, veal, lamb and pork as well as steak. A raw bar, generous salads and a roster of veggies supplement the main items. Many dishes are served in small skillets or pots that facilitate sharing. The handsome room features generous circular booths and open sightlines for spotting celebrities who frequently dine here.
Steak menu. Dinner. Bar. Casual attire. Reservations recommended. **$$$$**

### ★★★Daniel Boulud Brasserie
3131 Las Vegas Blvd. S., Las Vegas,
702-248-3463, 888-352-3463;
www.wynnlasvegas.com

**200**

NEVADA

Daniel Boulud Brasserie provides diners with a modern and romantic dining experience. The room is divided into intimate sections with antique farmhouse windows and a kitchen that is encased in dark, tinted glass. Chef Daniel Boulud and Chef Philippe Rispoli provide a diverse menu including a selection of dishes for two, a la carte items and a prix fixe menu. A selection of recipes including cheeses and seafood are prepared in the restaurant's brick oven. Specialty dishes include the steak au poivre, wild mushroom paté with homemade pickles and a roasted chicken with tarragon jus. The cocoa-crusted profiteroles with rocky road ice cream and bittersweet chocolate are heavenly.

American, French menu. Dinner. Bar. Business casual attire. Reservations recommended. Valet parking. Outdoor seating. **$$$$**

### ★★★Delmonico Steakhouse
3355 Las Vegas Blvd. S., Las Vegas, 702-414-3737; www.emerils.com
Exuberant New Orleans chef Emeril Lagasse is behind this meat-centric dining room in the Venetian Resort Hotel and Casino, a sequel to the Crescent City original. Luxe appointments—a baby grand piano, French doors, and linen-topped tables—make a seductive affair of indulgence. All the steakhouse standards make the menu, along with specialties such as Creole-marinated rack of lamb, chateaubriand for two and charred sirloin.

Cajun/Creole menu. Lunch, dinner. Bar. Casual attire. Reservations recommended. **$$$**

### ★★Embers
3535 Las Vegas Blvd. S., Las Vegas, 702-731-3311; www.imperialpalace.com
Steak menu. Dinner. Bar. Casual attire. **$$**

### ★★★Emeril's New Orleans Fish House
3799 Las Vegas Blvd. S., Las Vegas, 702-891-7374; www.mgmgrand.com
Big Easy chef Emeril Lagasse runs this Louisiana kitchen at the MGM Grand. Wrought-iron gates, a stone courtyard and French doors evoke historic New Orleans. But the star is the bold food for which the gregarious chef is renowned. Creole-spiced lobster, pecan-roasted redfish and cedar plank steak typify Emeril's big flavors. Finish off with the swoon-worthy banana cream pie.

Seafood, Cajun menu. Lunch, dinner. Bar. Casual attire. Reservations recommended. Valet parking. **$$**

### ★★★Empress Court
3570 Las Vegas Blvd. S., Las Vegas, 877-346-4642; www.caesarspalace.com
Overlooking the Roman pool deck at Caesars Palace, Empress Court prepares a range of dishes from Malaysia, Thailand, Indonesia and China. Fresh and saltwater tanks are stocked with cod, crab and lobster. For a splurge, opt for the multi-course, fixed-price meals for two. Rare indulgences such as abalone and the attention of knowledgeable servers justify the up-market prices.

Chinese menu. Dinner. Closed Monday-Tuesday. Bar. Jacket required. Reservations recommended. Valet parking. **$$$**

### ★★Ferraro's
5900 W. Flamingo Rd., Las Vegas, 702-364-5300; www.ferraroslasvegas.com
Italian menu. Lunch, dinner. Bar. Children's menu. Casual attire. **$$$**

### ★★★Fiamma Trattoria & Bar
3799 Las Vegas Blvd. S., Las Vegas, 702-891-7600;
www.mgmgrand.com
With a fun, vibrant atmosphere, Fiamma Trattoria & Bar in the MGM Grand is a good choice for those looking for a night out with friends. The setting is contemporary Italian, and the décor is warm, with rich, dark wood floors, modern furniture and copper-toned lighting. The Italian cuisine features such specialties as raviolinio, brasato and branzino.

Italian menu. Dinner. Bar. Business casual attire. Reservations recommended. Valet parking. **$$$**

### ★★Fiore Steakhouse
3700 W. Flamingo Rd., Las Vegas, 702-777-7702; www.harrahs.com

**NEVADA**

Steak menu. Dinner. Bar. Business casual attire. Reservations recommended. Valet parking. $$$

### ★★Garduno's
4321 W. Flamingo Rd., Las Vegas, 702-942-7777; www.thepalmslasvegas.com
Mexican menu. Lunch, dinner, Sunday brunch. Bar. Children's menu. Casual attire. Outdoor seating. $$$

### ★★Hamada of Japan
365 E. Flamingo Rd., Las Vegas, 702-733-3005; www.hamadaofjapan.com
Japanese menu. Lunch, dinner. Bar. Casual attire. Valet parking. $$$

### ★★Il Fornaio
3790 Las Vegas Blvd. S., Las Vegas, 702-650-6500; www.ilfornaio.com
Italian menu. Breakfast, lunch, dinner. Bar. Casual attire. Valet parking. $$$

### ★★★Jasmine
3600 S. Las Vegas Blvd., Las Vegas, 702-693-8166; www.bellagiolasvegas.com
No expense was spared when enticing famed Chef Philip Lo to create a new restaurant for the Bellagio. Lo, renowned for his contemporary takes on traditional Cantonese and Szechuan dishes, does not disappoint, providing such favorites as Imperial Peking duck and caramelized pork tenderloin with pineapples and bell pepper. The décor is not the traditional take on a Chinese restaurant, but rather an exploration of Victorian Hong Kong with such touches as high ceilings, chintz curtains, crystal chandeliers and windows that overlook the famed Bellagio fountains.
Chinese menu. Dinner, late-night. Bar. Casual attire. Reservations recommended. $$$

### ★★★★★Joël Robuchon at the Mansion
3799 Las Vegas Blvd. S., Las Vegas, 702-891-7925; www.mgmgrand.com
Foodies everywhere salivated when they heard of Joel Robuchon's arrival in Sin City. His first of three restaurants in North America, Joel Robuchon at the Mansion, located in the MGM Grand, is a super-luxe temple of haute cuisine, showcasing the signature cooking style that earned Robuchon his reputation as one of the world's greatest chefs. The menu, which reflects simplicity and a respect for fine ingredients, includes signatures dishes like crispy amadai snapper with pistachio oil, truffled langoustine ravioli with diced cabbage and scallops in a ginger bouillon with baby leeks. Additional highlights include the bread cart (which showcases nearly two dozen different kinds of breads baked fresh daily) and a petit four cart with fanciful confections. The intimate Art Deco space features has 17-foot ceilings and features cream-colored walls, black lacquered furniture and a black-and-white tiled entrance lit by a stunning crystal chandelier. The knowledgeable and graceful staff almost seems invisible. You'll remember a meal here for years to come.
French menu. Dinner. Bar. Children's menu. Jacket required. Reservations recommended. Valet parking. Outdoor seating. $$$$

### ★★★L'Atelier de Joël Robuchon
3799 Las Vegas Blvd. S., Las Vegas, 702-891-7358; www.mgmgrand.com
Las Vegas is synonymous with show-stopping performances, but where can you watch a world-famous French chef work his magic? L'Atelier de Joël Robuchon at the MGM Grand lets diners do just that. The legendary chef's casual counterpart to his more formal restaurant (also inside the MGM Grand) offers a unique approach to fine dining where you can grab a seat at the counter and prepare to be dazzled by the food and the show. Expect anything and everything: steak tartar and miniature lamb chops are the chef's signature dishes. Friendly, knowledgeable service complements the spirited atmosphere.
French menu. Dinner. $$

### ★★★Le Cirque
3600 Las Vegas Blvd. S., Las Vegas, 877-234-6358; www.bellagiolasvegas.com

★
★
★
★
★

The iconic New York restaurant has made it to Las Vegas at the Bellagio. Like its New York City outpost, this Le Cirque is a shining jewel of a restaurant, awash in bold colors and warm fabrics, with a bright, silk-tented ceiling that brings a festive big-top feel to the sumptuous dining room. The show-stopping French fare includes braised rabbit with Reisling and fava beans, and the Le Cirque lobster salad with black truffle dressing.

French menu. Dinner, late-night. Bar. Reservations recommended. Valet parking. $$$

### ★★★Lillie's Noodle House
129 E. Fremont St., Las Vegas,
702-385-7111; www.goldennugget.com

Presenting traditional Cantonese and Szechwan favorites, Lillie's, with its tranquil and refined atmosphere, is a nice break from the onslaught of sights and sounds that is Las Vegas. Specialties include Mongolian beef and stir-fried lobster.

Chinese, pan-Asian menu. Dinner. Bar. Casual attire. Reservations recommended. $$$

### ★★★Luxor Steakhouse
3900 S. Las Vegas Blvd., Las Vegas,
702-262-4772; www.luxor.com

World-class cuisine is served in a luxurious, cherry wood dining room. Start with the roasted Valley foie gras or Maryland crab cake before cutting into the mouth-watering aged prime beef, fillet mignon or Maine lobster.

French menu. Dinner. Closed Tuesday-Wednesday. Bar. Casual attire. Reservations recommended. $$$

### ★★Mayflower Cuisinier
4750 W. Sahara Ave., Las Vegas,
702-870-8432;
www.mayflowercuisinier.com

Chinese menu. Lunch, dinner. Closed Sunday. Bar. Outdoor seating. $$

### ★★★★Michael Mina
3600 Las Vegas Blvd. S., Las Vegas,
877-234-6358;
www.bellagiolasvegas.com

This luxurious, contemporary dining room bathed creamy neutral tones and golden light is just past the botanical gardens at the Bellagio. The menu here is in the care of a talented group of chefs trained and transported from San Francisco, who create innovate seafood dishes with California ingredients. The menu is extensive and offers la carte selections in addition to a pair of five-course tasting menus, one vegetarian and one seasonal. Classic dishes include savory black mussel soufflé with saffron and Chardonnay cream and Maine lobster pot pie. The wine list focuses on American producers and contains some gems from small vineyards.

Seafood menu. Dinner, late-night. Bar. Reservations recommended. Valet parking. $$$

### ★★Ming's Table
3475 Las Vegas Blvd. S., Las Vegas,
800-214-9110;
www.harrahs.com

Asian menu. Lunch, dinner. Bar. Casual attire. Reservations recommended. $$$

### ★★★★Mix Restaurant
3950 Las Vegas Blvd., Las Vegas,
702-632-9500;
www.mandalaybay.com

It was only a matter of time before culinary mastermind Alain Ducasse took his place on the Strip. And in classic Ducasse style, the result is nothing less than grand. Located on the 64th floor of the hotel at Mandalay Bay, Mix is something of a futuristic fantasy. The light and airy, Patrick Jouin-designed interior features a 24-foot, $500,000 Champagne-bubble chandelier consisting of more than 15,000 glass spheres, massive floor-to-ceiling windows that offer spectacular 360-degree views of Las Vegas, and tables with white faux leather-covered chairs. The staff inside the $2-million open kitchen turns out Ducasse's classic French cuisine, but with a contemporary twist. Dishes include duck foie gras with date-apricot chutney and beef tenderloin Rossini with potato galette and black

**NEVADA**

truffle sauce. The extensive wine collection, consisting of approximately 7,000 bottles, lines an entire wall at the dining room's entrance.

French, American menu. Dinner. Bar. Business casual attire. Reservations recommended. Valet parking. **$$$**

### ★★★NobHill
3799 S. Las Vegas Blvd., Las Vegas,
702-891-7337; www.mgmgrand.com
Chef Michael Mina of San Francisco and teamed with hot designer Tony Chi to create a snug city-by-the-Bay-inspired eatery in Sin City's MGM Grand. Named for the ritzy San Fran enclave, NobHill conjures California cuisine with its fresh-baked sourdough bread, organic produce, natural meats, locally-caught sand dabs and a heaping raw bar. Don't miss the whipped potatoes, which come in a chorus of flavors from leek to cheese. Glass-walled booths oppose the bar, which dispenses the applause-worthy house Cable Car martini.

American menu. Dinner. Bar. Casual attire. Reservations recommended. Valet parking. **$$$**

### ★★★Nobu
4455 Paradise Rd., Las Vegas,
702-693-5000; www.hardrockhotel.com
The Zen-like decor of Nobu at the Hard Rock Hotel, with its bamboo-lined walls and seaweed-toned banquettes, brings a sense of calm to the otherwise frenetic pace of Las Vegas. This mini-empire, which began with the original Nobu in New York's Tribeca, is known for spicy sashimi and creative dishes like miso-marinated black cod.

Japanese menu. Dinner. Bar. Jacket required. Reservations recommended. Valet parking. **$$**

### ★★★Okada
3131 Las Vegas Blvd. S., Las Vegas,
702-248-3463, 888-352-3463;
www.wynnlasvegas.com
Steve Wynn commissioned architectural firm Hirsch Bedner to create a contemporary Japanese design—clean lines, Japanese characters and traditional gardens—for his new restaurant, Okada. The design is a metaphor for chef Masa Ishizawa's modern take on Japanese cuisine with a French flair. Signature dishes include red miso bouillabaisse, braised *Kurobuta* short ribs with fingerling potatoes and organic chicken with ginger-caramel broth. There's also sushi and shashimi and a selection of marinated vegetables, fish and poultry bites that are grilled over Japanese charcoal in a process known as *robatayaki*.

Japanese menu. Dinner. Bar. Business casual attire. Reservations recommended. Valet parking. Outdoor seating. **$$$$**

### ★★Olives
3600 S. Las Vegas Blvd., Las Vegas,
877-234-6358; www.bellagiolasvegas.com
Italian, Mediterranean menu. Lunch, dinner, late-night. Bar. Casual attire. Outdoor seating. **$$$**

### ★★Osteria del Circo
3600 S. Las Vegas Blvd., Las Vegas,
702-693-8150; www.osteriadelcirco.com
Italian menu. Lunch, dinner. Bar. Casual attire. **$$**

### ★★★The Palm
3500 Las Vegas Blvd. S., Las Vegas,
702-732-7256; www.thepalm.com
A destination eatery in the Forum Shops at Caesars Palace, the Palm steakhouse is a branch of the New York power eatery. The woody surroundings lend a clubby feel to the dining room that specializes in healthy portions of meat supplemented by la carte vegetables and potatoes. Lunches of salads, pastas and the house burger make this a more affordable midday option. Local notables like mayor Oscar Goodman and tennis pro Andre Agassi have been spotted dining here, as have many others; celebrity cartoon caricatures adorn the walls.

Steak menu. Lunch, dinner, late-night. Bar. Business casual attire. Reservations recommended. **$$**

### ★★Pearl
3799 Las Vegas Blvd. S., Las Vegas,
702-891-7380; www.mgmgrand.com
Chinese menu. Dinner. **$$$**

### ★★★★Picasso
3600 Las Vegas Blvd. S., Las Vegas,
877-234-6358; www.bellagiolasvegas.com
Considered by many to be the most popular of Las Vegas restaurants, Picasso impresses with its ambience and food. Gold and red surround the dining room like holiday wrapping paper, drawing attention to authentic oil paintings and ceramics of the master artist. Chef Julian Serrano's French-Mediterranean cuisine more than competes for similar accolades. The prix-fixe menu changes daily, but certain favorites may be available, including poached oysters, roasted ruby red shrimp or sautéed center cut filet of swordfish, all of which are artfully presented.
French, Spanish menu. Dinner, late-night. Closed Tuesday. Bar. Jacket recommended. Reservations recommended. Valet parking. Outdoor seating. **$$$$**

### ★★Pinot Brasserie
3355 S. Las Vegas Blvd., Las Vegas,
702-414-8888; www.patinagroup.com
California bistro, French menu. Breakfast, lunch, dinner. Bar. Business casual attire. Reservations recommended. Valet parking. Outdoor seating. **$$$**

### ★★Postrio
3377 Las Vegas Blvd. S., Las Vegas,
702-796-1110; www.wolfgangpuck.com
American menu. Lunch, dinner. Bar. Children's menu. Business casual attire. Reservations recommended. Valet parking. **$$**

### ★★★Prime
3600 Las Vegas Blvd. S., Las Vegas,
877-234-6358; www.bellagiolasvegas.com
Modeled after a 1930s speakeasy, Prime—with its plush drapery and powder blue marble—sets the stage for famed chef Jean-Georges Vongerichten's modern steakhouse. The aged steaks are nice, but order the veal chop with kumquat-pineapple chutney and caramelized cauliflower, or the seared tuna au poivre with wasabi-mashed potatoes. Sides include gingered sweet potatoes, truffled mashed potatoes and roasted root vegetables. Prime manages one of the most impressive wine collections in the city, focusing on hearty reds from California and Bordeaux.
Steak menu. Dinner, late-night. Bar. Reservations recommended. Valet parking. **$$$**

### ★★Red 8
3131 Las Vegas Blvd. S., Las Vegas,
702-248-3463, 888-352-3463;
www.wynnlasvegas.com
Chinese menu. Lunch, dinner. Bar. Casual attire. Valet parking. **$$$**

### ★★★★Restaurant Guy Savoy
3570 Las Vegas Blvd. S., Las Vegas,
877-346-4642; www.caesarspalace.com
Perfect for a romantic dinner or a night out with friends, Restaurant Guy Savoy offers a fine-dining experience in a chic atmosphere with dark wood lattice, dramatic high ceilings and contemporary art. The creative French cuisine includes specialties such as artichoke black truffle soup, crispy sea bass with delicate spices and butter-roasted veal sweetbreads. Restaurant Guy Savoy is located in Caesar's Palace on the second floor of the Augustus Tower.
French menu. Dinner. Closed Monday-Tuesday. Bar. Business casual attire. Reservations recommended. Valet parking. **$$$$**

### ★Sam Woo BBQ
4215 Spring Mountain Rd., Las Vegas,
702-368-7628
Chinese menu. Breakfast, lunch, dinner. Casual attire. **$**

### ★★Samba Brazilian Steakhouse
3400 Las Vegas Blvd. S., Las Vegas,
866-339-4566; www.mirage.com
Latin American menu. Dinner. Reservations recommended. **$$$**

### ★★Shanghai Lilly
3950 Las Vegas Blvd. S., Las Vegas,

★
★
★
★
★

702-632-7409; www.mandalaybay.com
Shanghai Lilly's upscale Chinese cuisine is dished up on Limoges china and strikes a refined note in the often party-hearty Mandalay Bay Resort and Casino. Despite its location near the gaming floor, the elegant restaurant designed by the celebrated Tony Chi does its best to conjure tranquility. A water wall leads guests into the dining room, where three-story ceilings create a grand stage, while sheer curtain-draped booths serve those seeking intimacy. Cantonese, Szechwan and Hong Kong specialties feature authentic indulgences like braised sharks fin, abalone with sea cucumber, lobster sashimi and Peking duck.
Chinese menu. Dinner. **$$**

### ★★★Shintaro
3600 Las Vegas Blvd. S., Las Vegas,
877-234-6358; www.bellagiolasvegas.com
If you want an authentic Japanese experience, look no further than Shintaro at the Bellagio. The dining room is a blend of Asian and Californian influences, resulting in a sleek, modern design with natural stone floors and wide-ranging views of the famous fountains. Under chef Joel Versola, Shintaro offers both an a la carte menu and a prix fixe menu for his contemporary Pan-Asian dishes, including authentic teriyaki and tempura. There's also a fresh Sushi bar, which features an awe-inspiring jellyfish-filled tank. For those who want a more interactive experience with the cooking staff, Shintaro offers *teppanyaki*, where master chefs prepare full-course meals tableside.
Japanese menu. Dinner. Bar. Reservations recommended. Outdoor seating. **$$$**

### ★★★Smith & Wollensky
3767 Las Vegas Blvd. S., Las Vegas,
702-862-4100;
www.smithandwollensky.com
This Las Vegas outpost of the growing Manhattan-based chain re-creates the atmosphere of the original, right down to the chalkboards listing daily specials.

Steak menu. Lunch, dinner. Bar. Casual attire. Valet parking. **$$$**

### ★Spice Market Buffet
3667 Las Vegas Blvd. S., Las Vegas,
702-785-5555; www.planethollywood.com
International menu. Breakfast, lunch, dinner, brunch. **$$**

### ★★The Steak House
2880 Las Vegas Blvd. S., Las Vegas,
702-794-3767; www.circuscircus.com
Steak menu. Dinner, Sunday brunch. Bar. Valet parking. **$$$**

### ★★★SW Steakhouse
3131 Las Vegas Blvd. S., Las Vegas,
702-248-3463, 888-352-3463;
www.wynnlasvegas.com
European sophistication comes to the traditional steakhouse, thanks to award-winning Chef David Walzog at the Wynn Las Vegas. The entrance and ambiance is as grand as the menu. Guests descend on a winding escalator that leads to a foyer filled with plush couches and a captivating bar. The menu offers both traditional cuts of beef such as bone-in ribeye, New York strip and veal chop, as well as creative dishes such as wild French sea bass, lobster bouillabaisse and roast duck breast l'orange.
Steak menu. Dinner. Bar. Business casual attire. Reservations recommended. Valet parking. Outdoor seating. **$$$$**

### ★★★Tableau
3131 Las Vegas Blvd. S., Las Vegas,
702-248-3463, 888-352-3463;
www.wynnlasvegas.com
This signature restaurant at the Wynn, with its atrium setting highlighting poolside views, features the American cuisine of chef Mark LoRusso. Start with the Dungeness crab ravioli or Hamachi carpaccio before digging into Colorado rack of lamb with goat cheese soufflé or the organic roasted chicken with corn pudding and summer truffles. The chef's tasting menu (available in a fantastic vegetarian version) changes often. Don't miss Sunday brunch, when you can indulge in blueberry

**206**

**NEVADA**

and lemon ricotta pancakes or Kobe short ribs and eggs.

American menu. Breakfast, lunch, dinner. Bar. Casual attire. Reservations recommended. Valet parking. Outdoor seating. **$$$$**

### ★★★Tao
3355 Las Vegas Blvd., Las Vegas,
702-388-8338; www.taorestaurant.com

This super-swanky fusion restaurant is massive. Occupying 40,000 square feet, Tao attracts visitors who want to dine, party or chill out—or all of the above. The focal point is the 20-foot-high Buddha that towers above the infinity pool. This is a place to come with a group. Chef Sam Hazen's menu is meant for sharing. While you can order a fresh and traditional selection of sushi and sashimi, the focus here is on new interpretations of old favorites. Seaweed salad is replaced by mango and truffle salad with wasabi caviar, egg rolls give way to spicy lobster rolls with black caviar. Other highlights include grilled rare yellowfin tuna, Hoisin chicken for two and the 12-ounce grilled Kobe ribeye with yuzu cilantro butter.

Pan-Asian menu. Dinner. Bar. Business casual attire. Reservations recommended. Valet parking. **$$$**

### ★★★Top of the World
2000 Las Vegas Blvd. S., Las Vegas,
702-380-7711;
www.stratospherehotel.com

Located atop the Stratosphere Hotel Tower, the circular room revolves once every 80 minutes, offering 360-degree nighttime views of Vegas. Few scenery-centric restaurants push the culinary envelope, and Top of the World is no exception, though it does a nice job with steaks and continental classics like lobster bisque. The mini chocolate stratosphere, which serves two, is a decadent dessert.

American menu. Lunch, dinner. Bar. Reservations recommended. Valet parking. **$$$**

### ★★★Valentino
3355 Las Vegas Blvd., S., Las Vegas,
702-414-3000; www.valentinolv.com

Restaurateur Piero Selvaggio's restaurant, Valentino, is a Vegas replica of his Angelino original. Chef Luciano Pellegrini hails from Italy, where he learned to create the authentic, rustic fare that makes the intimate Valentino a worthy destination. The bilingual menu includes classic a la carte choices such as carpaccio and lasagna, as well as several seasonal five-course tasting menus that delve into delicacies like quail paired with foie gras and oysters accented with caviar. The vast 24,000-bottle wine cellar also distinguishes it among the numerous dining venues at the Venetian.

Italian menu. Dinner, late-night. Bar. Casual attire. Reservations recommended. **$$$$**

### ★★★The Verandah
3960 Las Vegas Blvd. S., Las Vegas,
702-632-5000; www.fourseasons.com

Discreetly hidden just off the Las Vegas Strip, the Four Seasons Hotel houses this equally discreet restaurant and patio. Overlooking the palm-flanked pool, the Verandah serves as the hotel's all-day restaurant, serving breakfast, lunch, dinner and afternoon tea in a casual but stylish setting. Selections are eclectic and include ahi sashimi, crab Napoleon, seared salmon and beef tenderloin with foie gras sauce.

American menu. Breakfast, lunch, dinner. Bar. Casual attire. Outdoor seating. **$$$**

### ★★Viva Mercados
3553 S. Rainbow, Las Vegas,
702-871-8826; www.vivamercadoslv.com

Mexican menu. Lunch, dinner. Bar. Children's menu. Casual attire. Reservations recommended. **$**

### ★★VooDoo Steck & Lounge
3700 W. Flamingo Rd., Las Vegas,
702-777-7923; www.harrahs.com

American, Cajun/Creole menu. Dinner. Bar. Business casual attire. Reservations recommended. Valet parking. **$$$$**

### ★★★Wing Lei
3131 Las Vegas Blvd. S., Las Vegas,
702-248-3463, 888-352-3463;

East meets West at chef Richard Chen's restaurant at the Wynn. While at the acclaimed Shanghai Terrace restaurant in Chicago, Chen helped create the concept of reverse fusion in which Western ingredients are used to create traditional Chinese dishes. Signature favorites include pan-seared crab cake, lobster dan dan noodle, steamed stuffed poussin and braised veal shank. The restaurant offers an a la carte menu, five-course Peking duck prix fixe menu and a chef's Signature Menu. This is a popular group restaurant and fills up quickly, so make reservations well in advance.
Chinese menu. Dinner. Bar. Children's menu. Business casual attire. Reservations recommended. Valet parking. **$$$$**

### ★★Wolfgang Puck Cafe

3799 Las Vegas Blvd. S., Las Vegas,
702-891-3000; www.mgmgrand.com
International menu. Lunch, dinner. Bar. **$$**

## SPAS

### ★★★The Bathhouse at THEHotel

3950 Las Vegas Blvd. S., Las Vegas,
702-632-7777; www.mandalaybay.com
This spa consistently delivers the unexpected. The Bathhouse at THEHotel at Mandalay Bay Resort has attracted international accolades for its striking interior. The entranceway's gray slate walls and marble floors establish instant, understated drama. The 12 treatment rooms include a redwood sauna, a eucalyptus steam room, several cold and hot plunge pools and a coed relaxation area. The exhaustive spa menu is as creative as it is endless, with everything from massage to reflexology, facials and body treatments. Ingredients in the intensely fresh herbal skincare line the spa uses, Eminence Organics of Hungary, are so fragrant you can almost taste the apple, grape and lime extracts. **$$**

### ★★★★Canyon Ranch SpaClub at the Venetian

3355 Las Vegas Blvd. S., Las Vegas,
702-414-3606, 877-220-2688;

For years, Canyon Ranch has been the gold standard in the spa industry, known for its innovative approach to healthy living. The focus here is on fitness, nutrition and stress management. This 65,000-square-foot facility has the largest fitness center on the Las Vegas Strip and includes cutting-edge fitness classes, state-of-the-art equipment and a 40-foot rock-climbing wall. After a vigorous workout, reward yourself with one of the spa's massages (from neuromuscular therapy to Thai) or body treatments. There's also a full-service salon. **$$**

### ★★★QUA Baths and Spa

3570 Las Vegas Blvd. S., Las Vegas,
702-731-7110; www.harrahs.com/qua
It's hard to believe people come to Las Vegas to relax, but the QUA Baths and Spa at Caesars Palace offer a transcendent experience. Roman baths are the focal point (they call it "social spa-ing"), but Vichy showers, chakra balancing, couples rituals and an Arctic Ice Room where snowflakes fall from the ceiling, are what set the spa apart. Treatments range from practical to sensual, and water's healing properties are worked into many of the spa's services. The facility features an incredible 51 treatment rooms, including 35 massage suites, seven facial rooms, a Men's Zone plus Barber Spa, two hydrotherapy tubs and his and hers tea lounges, so you'll never get wound up waiting to unwind. **$$**

### ★★★★The Spa at Four Seasons Hotel Las Vegas

3960 Las Vegas Blvd. S., Las Vegas,
702-632-5000, 800-819-5053;
www.fourseasons.com
A Buddhist goddess greets visitors at this Asian-inspired spa. Try the 80-minute JAMU massage, which blends Hindu, Chinese and European styles and techniques (including acupressure and skin rolling) with essential oils to work out every last kink. Other treatments include Balinese foot washes, aromatherapy scalp massages and reflexology. There are a variety of herbal wraps, salt glows and European facials. **$$**

**208**

**NEVADA**

### ★★★★Spa Bellagio at Bellagio
**3600 Las Vegas Blvd. S., Las Vegas,**
**702-693-7472, 888-987-3456;**
**www.bellagio.com**

This Roman-style spa is the height of luxury, even in over-the-top Las Vegas. The facility includes a redwood sauna, eucalyptus steam room and cold plunge pools. The staff attends to your every whim. You'll feel pampered as you sip a latte served in Bernadaud china that fits perfectly into the armrest of a pedicure chair. Try a lemon-ginger stone or deluxe scalp massage. Hot toe voodoo can be added to any massage and is a wonderfully relaxing treatment in which warm stones are placed between your toes to re-energize tired feet. The lemon-ginger scrub is another fantastic treatment for rough skin. Facials target common problems, such as sun damage, dehydration and wrinkles, and eye and lip treatments can be added to these services. Hydrotherapy services include thalasso seaweed baths, revitalizing mineral baths and aromatic Moor mud baths. **$$**

### ★★★The Spa at Red Rock
**11011 W. Charleston Blvd., Las Vegas,**
**702-797-7777; www.redrocklasvegas.com**
While not turning its back totally on Las Vegas's neon strip, the Spa at Red Rock instead looks out and up to the commanding sandstone cliffs that give their name to the Red Rock Casino, Resort and Spa.

There are 20 treatments rooms and several al fresco private cabanas where you can experience everything from massage to Champagne pedicures. The Adventure Spa (a spa within a spa) offers indoor rock climbing, rafting down the Colorado River below Hoover Dam, mountain biking over wild horse trails in the high desert or a hiking up to bubbling hot springs. **$$**

### ★★★★The Spa at the Wynn Las Vegas
**3131 Las Vegas Blvd. S., Las Vegas,**
**702-770-3900, 877-321-9966;**
**www.wynnlasvegas.com**
A soothing atmosphere with shades of cream and gold, decadent treatments and luxurious, well-appointed amenities will make this spa your new reason for return trips to Las Vegas. Available exclusively to guests of the resort, the spa focuses on providing individualized treatments. Whether you opt for a facial, massage or hydrotherapy, the staff will make you feel as if this tranquil sanctuary were created exclusively for you. Slip into a velvety robe and slippers and relax in the lounge area until you're swept away to one of the 45 garden-themed treatment rooms. The signature Good Luck Ritual includes a customized massage along with a lemon verbena and peppermint foot treatment, moisturizing hand therapy and stimulating scalp treatment. The Anakiri facial is a bioenergetic treatment customized to all skin types, while the brown sugar body treatment uses a light, warming massage with sugar-infused formulas to nourish skin. **$$**

# LAUGHLIN

This resort community offers a pleasant change of pace from the glitz of Las Vegas. In many ways, it resembles Las Vegas in its earlier days. Hotels and casinos line the Colorado River, and some provide ferry service to and from parking facilities on the Arizona side. Laughlin offers other diversions such as fishing, waterskiing and swimming in nearby Lake Mohave.
**Information: Laughlin Visitor Information Center, 1555 Casino Dr., 702-298-3321, 800-452-8445;**
**www.visitlaughlin.com**

## SPECIAL EVENTS

**Laughlin River Days**

Hwy. 95 and Colorado River, Laughlin,
702-298-2214; www.superstockracing.com
APBA Powerboat racing on a 1 1/2-mile
course. Early June.

## HOTELS

**★★★Aquarius Casino Resort**

1900 S. Casino Dr., Laughlin,
702-298-5111, 888-662-5825;
www.aquariuscasinoresort.com
The largest resort on the Colorado River, this
enormous property offers activities for every
member of the family. Visitors will enjoy the
2,000-seat showroom, 3,300-seat outdoor
amphitheater and 60,000-square-foot casino.
1,912 rooms. Restaurant, bar. Spa. Airport
transportation available. Casino. Tennis. **$**

**★★Don Laughlin's Riverside Resort**

1650 Casino Dr., Laughlin,
702-298-2535, 800-227-3849;
www.riversideresort.com

1,404 rooms. Restaurant, bar. Airport
transportation available. Casino. Movie
theaters. **$**

**★★★Golden Nugget**

2300 S. Casino Dr., Laughlin,
702-298-7111, 800-955-7278;
www.goldennugget.com/laughlin
This resort is like a tropical paradise in the
desert. A jungle theme is carried from the
rain-forest-inspired lobby to the tropical
themed rooms. Tarzan's Night Club completes the illusion.
300 rooms. Restaurant, bar. Outdoor pool.
Airport transportation available. Casino.
Pool. **$**

**★★River Palms**

2700 S. Casino Dr., Laughlin,
800-835-7904; www.rvrpalm.com
1,003 rooms. Restaurant, bar. Spa. Airport transportation available. **$**

# MINDEN

This small town is located just minutes from beautiful Lake Tahoe.
Information: www.townofminden.com

## HOTELS

**★★Carson Valley Inn Hotel Casino**

1627 US 395 N., Minden,
775-782-9711, 800-321-6983;
www.cvinn.com

152 rooms. Restaurant, bar. Children's activity center. Casino. **$**

# PRIMM

Forty miles south of Las Vegas, Primm is primarily a gaming destination, especially for
gamers from Southern California on their way to Las Vegas.

## WHAT TO SEE AND DO

**Fashion Outlets of Las Vegas**

I-15 S., Primm, 702-874-1400;
www.fashionoutletlasvegas.com
Located about 30 miles south of Las Vegas,
the nearly 100 retailers here include Burberry,
Coach, Kenneth Cole New York, Polo Ralph
Lauren Factory Store and Versace. The mall

offers daily shuttle service from the MGM
Grand Hotel and Casino. 10 a.m.-3 p.m.

## HOTELS

**★★Primm Valley Resort & Casino**

31900 S. Las Vegas Blvd., Primm,
702-386-7867, 860-386-7867
624 rooms. Two restaurants, two bars.
Casino. Pool. **$**

# RENO

Reno, "the biggest little city in the world," is renowned as a gambling and vacation center. Between the steep slopes of the Sierra and the low eastern hills, Reno spills across the Truckee Meadows. The neon lights of the nightclubs, gambling casinos and bars give it a glitter that belies its quiet acres of fine houses, churches and schools. The surrounding area is popular for sailing, boating, horseback riding and deer and duck hunting. The downtown Riverwalk along the Truckee's banks is loaded with coffee shops, art galleries, chic eateries, eclectic boutiques, antique stores, salons and theaters.

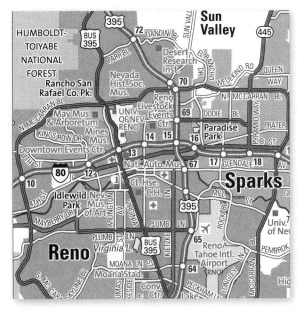

Information: Chamber of Commerce, 1 E First St., 775-337-3030; www.reno-sparkschamber.org

## WHAT TO SEE AND DO

### Animal Ark
Reno, 775-970-3111; www.animalark.org
Tucked in the forested hills north of Reno, Animal Ark is not a zoo, but a sanctuary for animals that cannot be returned to the wild. Many were disabled or orphaned, and others were unwanted exotic pets. The residents include big cats (tigers, snow leopards and cougars), gray wolves, black bears and a few reptiles and birds. Each has a name and is presented as an "ambassador" for its species. April-October Tuesday-Sunday 10 a.m.-4:30 p.m.

### Fleischmann Planetarium and Science Center
1650 N. Virginia St., Reno, 775-784-4811; www.planetarium.unr.edu
This facility projects public shows on the inside of its 30-foot dome. The museum here also houses all four of the meteorites that have landed in Nevada (including a massive specimen that weighs more than a ton) and scales rigged to reflect the gravity on Jupiter or a neutron star. On cloud-less Friday nights, guests can peer through telescopes with members of the Astronomical Society of Nevada.

### Great Basin Adventure
Rancho San Rafael Regional Park, 1595 N. Sierra., Reno, 775-785-4064; www.maycenter.com
Part of the Wilbur D. May Center in Rancho San Rafael Regional Park, Great Basin Adventure consists of several attractions designed to educate and entertain kids. At Wilbur's Farm, pint-sized visitors can take a pony ride or explore the 1.5-acre petting zoo. Guests can pan for gold at a replica mine building, with faux mine shafts that double as slides and displays on minerals and the area's mining history. Tuesday-Saturday 10 a.m.-5 p.m., Sunday noon-5 p.m.

### Humboldt-Toiyabe National Forest
1200 Franklin Way, Sparks, 775-331-6444; www.fs.fed.us/1-4htnf
At 6.3 million acres, this is the largest national forest in the lower 48 states. It extends across Nevada from the Califor-

NEVADA

★
★
★
★
★

nia border in a scattershot pattern, comprising 10 ranger districts that encompass meadows, mountains, deserts and canyons. Just northwest of the Reno city limits, Peavine Mountain is crisscrossed by a number of old mining roads now reserved for hikers and mountain bikers. Other Humboldt-Toiyabe highlights include scenic Lamoille Canyon and the Ruby Mountains, southeast of Elko; the rugged, isolated Toiyabe Range, near the geographical center of Nevada; and Boundary Peak, the state's highest point at 13,143 feet, southeast of Reno on the California-Nevada border.

### Meadowood Mall
5000 Meadowood Mall Circle, Reno, 775-827-8451
The most contemporary shopping center in the region, this is actually the city's most-visited tourist attraction.

### Mount Rose Ski Area
22222 Mt. Rose Hwy., Reno, 775-849-0704, 800-754-7673; www.mtrose.com
Of all the ski resorts in the Reno-Tahoe area, Mount Rose has the highest base elevation (a precipitous 7,900 feet above sea level), making it the best bet for late-season skiing. Eight lifts, including two six-person, high-speed chairlifts, take skiers and snowboarders to the 9,700-foot summit, to 1,200 acres of terrain nearly evenly split among skill levels (20 percent beginner, 30 percent intermediate and 40 percent advanced) and a pair of snowboarding parks. Located northwest of Lake Tahoe, Mount Rose is also known for its excellent beginners' program. There are no on-mountain accommodations. Mid-November-mid-April, daily.

### National Automobile Museum (The Harrah Collection)
10 Lake St. S., Reno, 775-333-9300; www.automuseum.org
The brainchild of car collector and gaming titan Bill Harrah, this excellent facility covers more than a century of automotive history in detail. Four galleries house the museum's collection of more than 200 cars: The first details the late 19th and early 20th century (complete with a blacksmith's shop, the garage of the day); the second covers 1914 to 1931; the third, 1932 to 1954; and the fourth, 1954 to modern day. The Masterpiece Circle Gallery in the fourth gallery also accommodates temporary themed exhibits on subjects ranging from Porsches to pickup trucks. The oldest car in the museum dates from 1892, and there are a number of collector's trophies (such as the 1949 Mercury Coupe driven by James Dean in *Rebel Without a Cause*) and one-of-a-kind oddities (the steam-powered 1977 Steamin Demon). Monday-Saturday 9:30 a.m.-5:30 p.m., Sunday 10 a.m.-4 p.m.

### Nevada Historical Society Museum
1650 N. Virginia St., Reno, 775-688-1190
Founded in 1904, this is Nevada's oldest museum and one of its best. On permanent display is "Nevada: Prisms and Perspectives," which examines the Silver State's five biggest historical stories: the Native American perspective, the mining boom, the neon-lit story of gaming, transportation and the "Federal Presence," since the federal government owns 87 percent of Nevada's land. Monday-Saturday 10 a.m.-5 p.m.

### Nevada Museum of Art
160 W. Liberty St., Reno, 775-329-3333; www.nevadaart.org
The only nationally accredited art museum in the entire state, the Nevada Museum of Art would be a top-notch facility no matter where it was located. Perhaps the most distinctive architectural specimen in all of artsy Reno, the curved, sweeping structure is a work of art in and of itself: modern (it opened in 2003) and monolithic (60,000 square feet), evoking the image of the legendary Black Rock of the Nevada desert. The collection housed within is equally impressive, broken into five different themes: contemporary art, contemporary landscape photography (one of the best of its kind anywhere), regional art, American art from 1900 to 1945, and the E. L.

NEVADA

Weigand Collection, American art with a work ethic theme. Tuesday-Wednesday, Friday-Sunday 10 a.m.-5 p.m., Thursday 10 a.m.-8 p.m.

### Reno Arch
Virginia St., downtown Reno
In 1926, Reno commemorated the completion of the first transcontinental highway in North America, which ran through the city en route to San Francisco, with an arch that traverses Virginia Street downtown. Three years later, locals adopted the tagline, "the biggest little city in the world" and added it to the landmark. The arch has since been replaced twice, in 1964 and in 1987, but remains one of the most photographed structures in the United States.

### Reno-Sparks Theater Coalition
528 W. First St., Reno, 775-786-2278;
www.theatercoalition.org
Consisting of more than 20 separate companies in the Reno-Sparks area, this organization is a cooperative effort to market a varied slate of theater, dance and other performing arts. Member troupes range from the avant-garde to the kid-friendly, and the Coalition puts together an up-to-date events schedule for all of them.

### Sierra Safari Zoo
10200 N. Virginia St., Reno, 775-677-1101;
www.sierrasafarizoo.com
The largest zoo in Nevada, Sierra Safari is home to 150 representatives of more than 40 species. The majority of the animals were selected for the rugged Reno climate, including a Siberian tiger and a number of other felines, but there are also tropical birds, a few reptiles and a number of primates. A petting zoo and a picnic area are on-site. April-October, daily 10 a.m.-5 p.m.

### University of Nevada, Reno
1664 N. Virginia St., Reno, 775-784-1110;
www.unr.edu
Established in 1874; 12,000 students. The campus covers 200 acres on a plateau overlooking the Truckee Meadows, in the shadow of the Sierra Nevada Mountains. Opened in Elko, it was moved to Reno and reopened in 1885. Tours of campus.

### W. M. Keck Earth Sciences and Engineering Museum
Mackay School of Mines Building, 1664 N. Virginia St., Reno, 775-784-4528;
www.mines.unr.edu/museum
Located in the Mackay School of Mines Building, the Keck Museum focuses on the state's mining history. The collection of specimens originated from Nevada's most renowned mining districts—the Comstock Lode, Tonopah and Goldfield—but exotic minerals from all over the world share the space. Rounding out the museum are displays of fossils, vintage mining equipment and a collection of fine silver donated by the family of mining tycoon John Mackay. Monday-Friday 9 a.m.-4 p.m.

## SPECIAL EVENTS
### Artown Festival
Reno, 775-322-1538;
www.renoisartown.com
Held annually in July (with a newer holiday counterpart in November and December), Reno's Artown Festival is a month-long extravaganza that includes more than 200 events and exhibitions and 1,000 artists in all—making it the largest arts festival in the United States. Not surprisingly, it has won its fair share of national acclaim since it launched in 1996. The artists span the disciplines of ballet, opera, theater, film and the visual arts. There are flamenco dancers, comedy troupes and internationally-known performers of all stripes, not to mention myriad gallery openings and historical tours. Multiple downtown venues host various aspects of the festival: Wingfield Park is the setting of an outdoor film every week; Rollin on the River is a weekly concert series. Mondays are family nights, with entertainment ranging from science experiments to storytelling. July.

### Eldorado Great Italian Festival
Fourth and Virginia Streets, Reno,

**213**

**NEVADA**

775-786-5700, 800-648-5966;
www.eldoradoreno.com
Put on by the Eldorado Hotel and Casino, the two-day event includes several buffets, a farmers market and live entertainment, but the contests are the real attractions, including a spaghetti sauce cook-off, gelato-eating contest for kids and a grape-stomping competition. Early October.

### Eldorado's Great BBQ, Brew and Blues
Fourth and Virginia Streets, Reno, 775-786-5700, 800-648-5966;
www.eldoradoreno.com
This street fair focuses on the three staples in its name: tangy barbecue, ice-cold beer and a pair of stages featuring nonstop blues. The participating breweries hail from Nevada, California and Oregon. Only those 21 years old and over are admitted. Last weekend in June.

### Hot August Nights
Reno, 775-356-1956;
www.hotaugustnights.net
This retro event pays homage to the 1950s and '60s. Highlights include a series of concerts by nostalgia acts (past performers have included Chuck Berry, the Turtles, and Jan and Dean) and a classic car parade. There are street dances and sock hops, and casinos get in on the action by awarding a classic car or two to a few lucky winners. Early August.

### National Championship Air Races
Reno Stead Field, 4895 Texas Ave., Reno, 775-972-6663; www.airrace.org
Races (classes include Biplane, Formula One, Unlimited, Jet, Sport and T-6), demonstrations and fly-bys. Four days in mid-September.

### Nevada Opera
Pioneer Center for the Performing Arts, 100 S. Virginia St., Reno, 775-786-4046;
www.nevadaopera.com
Founded in 1967 and having survived a tumultuous financial era in the late 1990s, the Nevada Opera stages several noteworthy operas each year in its fall/spring calendar. Recent productions have included *La Traviata* and *Aida*.

### Nevada State Fair
1350 N. Wells Ave., Reno, 775-688-5767;
www.nevadastatefair.org
A Reno area tradition since 1874, the Nevada State Fair features rodeo events, livestock competitions and a carnival midway. The event also includes a kid-oriented science festival, an aerial motorcycle stunt show and contests for the best homemade pies, cookies and salsa. Late August.

### Reno Basque Festival
Wingfield Park, Reno, 775-762-3577
Basques from northern Spain and southern France immigrated to Nevada's Great Basin in the early 20th century to herd sheep, and they have been a visible part of the Reno community ever since. The Reno Basque Festival started in 1959 with the goal of preserving Basque culture in the United States. Today, it's one of the largest events of its kind in the country, kicked off by a parade that snakes around downtown before coming to a stop at Wingfield Park along the Truckee River. From there, the festival takes over, with food, dancing, singing and athletic competitions. Basque cuisine available for sampling includes sheepherder bread, Basque beans, lamb stew and other hearty staples, and there's also a market. Crowds gather for the traditional games: soka tira (a Basque tug-of-war), woodcutting and weightlifting. Late July.

### Reno Film Festival
528 W. First St., Reno, 775-334-6707;
www.renofilmfestival.com
Drawing a handful of celebrities to downtown Reno every November, this film festival consists of Hollywood productions, independent features, world premieres and retrospective revivals. Screenings are shown at various downtown venues (casinos, museums and theaters), and there are also a number of film-related workshops, demonstrations and lectures. Early November.

### Reno Jazz Festival
Reno, 775-784-4046

**214**

**NEVADA**

Held on the University of Nevada at Reno campus since 1963, this three-day event is one of the biggest of its kind, drawing hundreds of school bands (junior high to college) from Nevada, California, Oregon, Idaho and Washington. The top bands and soloists play at a concluding encore performance, and the first two nights are highlighted by sets from nationally known jazz names. Late April.

### Reno Philharmonic Orchestra

925 Riverside Dr., Reno, 775-323-6393;
www.renophilharmonic.com

Reno's symphony orchestra plays a September-to-April Master Classics Series (as well as a July 4th pops concert) at a number of venues in town, with Pioneer Center for the Performing Arts serving as its home stage. The orchestra plays works from composers such as Mozart, Beethoven, Copland and Gershwin. A free one-hour lecture is given immediately before each concert.

### Reno Rodeo

Reno Livestock Events Center,
1350 N. Wells Ave., Reno,
775-329-3877, 800-225-2277;
www.renorodeo.com

Known as the wildest, richest rodeo in the west—with a total purse in excess of $1 million—the Reno Rodeo has been a big event since its inaugural year in 1919. Includes bull riding, barrel racing and roping events. Late June.

## HOTELS

### ★★★Atlantis Casino Resort

3800 S. Virginia St., Reno,
775-825-4700, 800-723-6500;
www.atlantiscasino.com

Located about three miles south of downtown, Atlantis is among Reno's top resorts, with several smoke-free gaming areas in the glass-enclosed casinos, a top-notch business center and a dizzying array of rooms. A highlight is the excellent spa, which offers a variety of treatments using Ahava and Dermalogica products. The Sky Terrace has sushi and oyster bars.

973 rooms. Restaurant, bar. Spa. Airport transportation available. Casino. Pets accepted. **$**

### ★★Best Western Airport Plaza Hotel

1981 Terminal Way, Reno,
775-348-6370, 800-648-3525;
www.bestwestern.com

269 rooms. Restaurant, bar. Airport transportation available. Casino. **$**

### ★★★Eldorado Hotel and Casino

345 N. Virginia St., Reno, 800-879-8879;
www.eldoradoreno.com

Of the casinos in downtown Reno, Eldorado attracts the youngest crowd, thanks to its myriad nightspots which include a microbrewery with live rock and blues, a martini/piano bar and BuBinga, a popular dance club with DJs and live bands. Eldorado has some of the best-looking hotel rooms in town. The casino boasts the best poker room and is known for its generous comps, earned through Club Eldorado.

817 rooms. Ten restaurants, bar. Airport transportation available. Casino. **$**

### ★★★Harrah's Hotel Reno

219 N. Center St., Reno, 775-786-3232;
www.harrahs.com

Located downtown next to the Reno Arch, Harrah's Reno is one of the glitziest casinos in the city, a distinction it has held since opening in the early 1960s. The casino is immense and diverse, featuring 1,300 slot machines, table games of all kinds and a sports book. Accommodations come in the form of nearly 1,000 sleek hotel rooms, ranging from standard rooms to skyline suites. There are seven restaurants, including the renowned Steak House at Harrah's Reno. Entertainers work the crowd onstage at Sammy's Showroom, named after Sammy Davis, Jr., who performed here 40 times.

928 rooms. Seven restaurants, bar. Airport transportation available. Casino. Pets accepted. **$**

### ★La Quinta Inn

4001 Market St., Reno,
775-348-6100, 800-531-5900;

www.laquinta.com
130 rooms. Complimentary continental breakfast. Airport transportation available. Pets accepted. **$**

### ★★★Peppermill Hotel and Casino Reno
2707 S. Virginia St., Reno,
775-826-2121, 800-648-6992;
www.peppermillreno.com
Consistently ranked as one of the best casinos in the city, Peppermill's flagship resort is a fixture in the entertainment district near the airport, about two miles south of downtown. The slick property features 2,000 slot machines, the full spectrum of table gaming, poker, sports betting and nightly live entertainment in the swanky cabaret and the more intimate piano lounge. In addition to seven restaurants, the resort boasts a dozen nightspots, including Oceano, with large aquariums, and the domed-shape Romanza.
1,070 rooms. Seven restaurants, bars. Airport transportation available. Casino. Pool. **$**

### ★★★Siena Hotel Spa Casino
1 S. Lake St., Reno,
775-327-4362, 877-743-6233;
www.sienareno.com
Designed to resemble a Tuscan village, this comprehensive resort, located along the banks of the Truckee River, includes a 23,000-square-foot casino and a full-service spa with a variety of treatments. The bright and comfortable rooms include custom fabrics reflecting the Sun-drenched palette of Tuscany and have views of the mountains or river. Among the three restaurants, Lexie's offers view of the water.
214 rooms. Three restaurants, bars. Spa. Casino. **$**

### ★★★Silver Legacy Resort Casino Reno
407 N. Virginia St., Reno,
775-325-7401, 800-687-7733;
www.silverlegacyreno.com
This Victorian-themed resort has a steel and brass dome and a façade designed to resemble 1890s storefronts. Beyond the gaming—2,000 slots, table games, sports book and a keno lounge—there's a comedy club and a rum bar with dueling pianos. And the showroom attracts big-name entertainers.
1,720 rooms. Restaurant, bar. Airport transportation available. Pool. **$**

## RESTAURANTS

### ★★Bricks Restaurant and Wine Bar
1695 S. Virginia St., Reno, 775-786-2277
American menu. Lunch, dinner. Closed Sunday. Bar. **$$**

### ★★Famous Murphy's
3127 S. Virginia St., Reno, 775-827-4111;
www.famousmurphys.com
Seafood, steak menu. Lunch, dinner. Closed Sunday. Bar. Children's menu. **$$**

### ★★Palais de Jade
960 W. Moana Lane, Reno, 775-827-5233
Chinese menu. Lunch, dinner. Bar. **$$**

### ★★Rapscallion
1555 S. Wells Ave., Reno, 775-323-1211,
877-932-3700; www.rapscallion.com
Seafood menu. Dinner, Sunday brunch. Bar. Outdoor seating. **$$**

### ★★Washoe Grill
4201 W. Fourth St., Reno, 775-786-1323;
www.washoesteakhouse.com
Seafood, steak menu. Dinner. Bar. **$$$**

# SOUTH LAKE TAHOE

With more than 300 sunny days a year and a mountain playground to make any outdoor enthusiast grin, this small town on Lake Tahoe has plenty to offer.
Information: www.tahoeinfo.com

## WHAT TO SEE AND DO
**Factory Stores at the Y**
Hwys. 50 and 89, South Lake Tahoe;
www.shopthe-y.com
This small group of factory stores includes Adidas and Izod. Daily 10 a.m.-6 p.m.

## SPECIAL EVENTS

### Valhalla Winter Microbrew Festival

Horizon Casino, 50 Hwy. 50,
South Lake Tahoe, 530-542-4166

Held at the Horizon Casino, this annual fundraiser for the Valhalla Arts and Music Festival gives attendees the chance to sample 120 microbrews from Nevada and northern California. Mid-February.

# SPARKS

In the Truckee Meadows of northern Nevada, Sparks is close to Reno. Its desert climate makes it a perfect destination if you want to recreate outdoors and enjoy some of Reno's high-stakes fun.

Information: www.ci.sparks.nv.us

## WHAT TO SEE AND DO

### Sparks Heritage Museum

820 Victorian Ave., Sparks, 775-355-1144

Housed in a former courthouse, the museums exhibits detail Sparks' progression from a train depot to a mining hub to a municipality of more than 80,000 people. Highlights include a vintage model train set and a pump-powered antique player piano. Tuesday-Friday 11 a.m.-4 p.m., Saturday-Sunday 1-4 p.m.

### Wild Island Family Adventure Park

250 Wild Island Court, Sparks,
775-359-2927; www.wildisland.com

Primarily known as a summer water park, Wild Island is now a year-round facility with the 2003 addition of Coconut Bowl, a state-of-the-art 20-lane bowling alley, and the surprisingly chic Smokin' Marlin Grill. The water park is huge, with a wave pool, tubing river and myriad slides. Hours vary by attraction and season.

## SPECIAL EVENTS

### Best of the West Rib Cook-off

John Ascuaga's Nugget Casino Resort,
1100 Nugget Ave., Sparks, 775-356-3428;
www.nuggetribcookoff.com

Nearly 300,000 barbecue lovers flock to this annual event. In recent years, about 150,000 pounds of ribs have been consumed at this five-day cook-off where two dozen of the West's most revered barbecue pros (all of whom are invited) compete for the first-prize trophy. There is also a lineup of live entertainment on numerous outdoor stages. Labor Day weekend.

### Sparks Hometowne Farmers Market

Victorian Square, Sparks, 775-353-2291

Every Thursday evening between June and August, more than 100 vendors gather and offer everything from rhubarb to pastries to tacos. Also includes cooking demonstrations, kids' area, and home and garden vendors.

## HOTELS

### ★★★John Ascuaga's Nugget

1100 Nugget Ave., Sparks,
775-356-3300, 800-648-1177;
www.janugget.com

An anchor in downtown Sparks, the Nugget has been one of the top resorts in the Reno area since opening in 1955. It's a few miles outside of downtown Reno, but right on the doorstep of Victorian Square, the site of numerous special events. The casino is loaded with all of the standards: slots, table games, poker room and sports book. The Celebrity Showroom is the place to go for fabulous entertainment. The hotel itself is a landmark, with a pair of 29-story towers flanking the casino, and a slate of amenities that includes everything from an arcade to a wedding chapel.

1,407 rooms. Eight restaurants, bars. Airport transportation available. Casino. Exercise. Pool. $

★
★
★
★
★

# STATELINE

This area is best known for its famous high-rise casino/hotels, cabarets and fine dining, but as an integral part of Tahoe's "south shore," it is also appreciated for its spectacular natural beauty. Alpine beaches and Sierra forests afford visitors an endless variety of year-round recreation. There are several excellent public golf courses in the area.

## HOTELS

### ★Horizon Casino Resort
50 Hwy. 50, Stateline,
775-588-6211, 800-648-3322;
www.horizoncasino.com
539 rooms. Restaurant, bar. Casino. Exercise. Pool. $

### ★★Lakeside Inn and Casino
168 Hwy. 50, Stateline,
775-588-7777, 800-624-7980;
www.lakesideinn.com
124 rooms. Restaurant, bar. Casino. Pool. $

### ★★★Harrah's Lake Tahoe
15 Hwy. 50, Stateline,
775-588-6611, 800-427-7247;
www.harrahstahoe.com
This property offers 18,000 square feet of function space and plenty of recreation options for leisure visitors. Shop at the Galleria, swim in the glass-domed pool and, of course, hit the casino.
532 rooms. Restaurant, bar. Casino. Pets accepted. Pool. $

### ★★★Harvey's Lake Tahoe
Stateline Ave., Stateline,
775-588-2411, 800-427-8397;
www.harveys.com
Most rooms at this resort, the first built in South Lake Tahoe, have a view of Lake Tahoe or the Sierra Nevada mountains. The resort offers a variety of ski packages in winter and the outdoor arena draws top music guests (including Beyonce and Diana Krall) in summer.
740 rooms. Restaurant, bar. Airport transportation available. Casino. Pool. $

## RESTAURANTS

### ★★Chart House
392 Kingsbury Grade, Stateline,
775-588-6276; www.chart-house.com
American menu. Dinner. Bar. Children's menu. Outdoor seating. $$$

### ★★★Friday's Station Steak & Seafood Grill
15 Hwy. 50, Stateline, 775-588-6611;
www.harrahs.com
The view of the lake from this restaurant, located on the 18th floor, is truly breathtaking. Several steak and seafood combos are offered, such as filet mignon and Alaskan King crab or blackened shrimp.
Seafood, steak menu. Dinner. Bar. $$$

### ★★★Sage Room
Hwy. 50, Stateline, 775-588-2411;
www.harrahs.com
Since 1947, the Sage Room Steak House has been world-renowned for its old Western ambience and fine cuisine. Dine among the works of Russell and Remington while enjoying traditional steak house dining highlighted by tableside flambe service. Top off your meal with the Sage Room's famous bananas Foster.
American menu. Dinner. Bar. Valet parking. $$$

### ★★★Summit
15 Hwy. 50, Stateline, 775-588-6611;
www.harrahs.com
Located on the 16th and 17th floors of Harrah's, this restaurant has stunning views and sophisticated cuisine. Try the filet mignon with truffled parsnip purée or pistachio-encrusted rack of lamb.
American menu. Dinner. Bar. Valet parking. $$$$

# TONOPAH

In the hills of the San Antonio Mountains, Tonopah is located about halfway between Reno and Las Vegas. Visitors will enjoy roaming Tonopah's historic streets, taking in the scenic vistas and exploring nearby ghost towns.

Information: Chamber of Commerce, 301 Brougher St., 775-482-3558; www.tonopahnevada.com

## WHAT TO SEE AND DO

### Mining Museum and Park

520 McCulloch, Tonopah, 775-482-9274

If you're into rock collecting, this historic mining park has a rich variety of minerals. Daily.

## HOTELS

### ★Best Western Hi-Desert Inn

320 Main St., Tonopah,
775-482-3511, 877-286-2208;
www.bestwestern.com

89 rooms. Complimentary full breakfast. Pets accepted. **$**

### ★★Station House Hotel and Casino

1137 S. Main St., Tonopah,
775-482-9777, 866-611-9777;
www.tonopahstation.com

75 rooms. Restaurant, bar. Casino. Pets accepted. **$**

# VIRGINIA CITY

Nevada's most famous mining town once had a population of about 35,000 people and was one of the richest cities in North America. Its dazzling career coincided with the life of the Comstock Lode, which yielded more than $1 billion worth of silver and gold. In the 1870s, Virginia City had four banks, six churches, 110 saloons, an opera house, numerous theaters and the only elevator between Chicago and San Francisco. Great fortunes, including those of Hearst and Mackay, were founded here.

Virginia City is perched on the side of Mount Davidson, where a diagonal slit marks the Comstock Lode. The site is beautiful and the air is so clear that the blue and purple masses of the Stillwater Range can be seen 120 miles away. Visitors can tour mines and old mansions, some of which have been restored (Easter week, Memorial Day-October, daily); visit several museums and saloons (Daily); stroll through the local shops; and ride on the steam-powered V&T Railroad (May-September).

Information: Chamber of Commerce, 86 South C. St., 775-847-7500; www.virginiacity-nv.org

## WHAT TO SEE AND DO

### The Castle

70 South B. St., Virginia City

Built by Robert N. Graves, a mine superintendent of the Empire Mine, the building was patterned after a castle in Normandy, France. Filled with international riches and original furnishings. Memorial Day weekend-October; daily.

# WINNEMUCCA

Originally called French Ford, the town was renamed for the last great chief of the Paiutes, who ruled the area. Winnemucca was first settled by a Frenchman who set up a trading post. Many Basques live here.

Information: Winnemucca visitors Authority, 50 W. Winnemucca Blvd., 775-623-5071; www.winnemucca.nv.us

**NEVADA**

## WHAT TO SEE AND DO

### Humboldt Museum

175 W. Jungo Rd., Winnemucca,
775-623-2912

Historical museum features American Indian artifacts; pioneers' home items; antique auto display; old country store and more. Monday-Friday, also Saturday afternoons.

## HOTELS

### ★Best Western Gold Country Inn

921 W. Winnemucca Blvd., Winnemucca,
775-623-6999, 800-346-5306;
www.bestwestern.com

71 rooms. Airport transportation available. Pets accepted **$**

### ★Days Inn

511 W. Winnemucca Blvd., Winnemucca,
775-623-3661, 800-329-7466;
www.daysinn.com

50 rooms. Pets accepted. Pool. **$**

### ★★Red Lion

741 W. Winnemucca Blvd., Winnemucca,
775-623-2565, 800-733-5466;
www.redlion.com

105 rooms. Restaurant, bar. Airport transportation available. Casino. Pets accepted. Pool. **$**

## RESTAURANTS

### ★Ormachea's

180 Melarky St., Winnemucca,
775-623-3455

Basque, American menu. Dinner. Closed Monday. Bar. Children's menu. **$$**

**220**

NEVADA

# NEW MEXICO

NEW MEXICO IS A LAND OF CONTRASTS. ITS HISTORY DATES BACK FAR BEFORE THE FIRST Spanish explorers arrived in 1540 in search of gold. One day you might be on a Native American reservation, the next you may be taking in the many art galleries and restaurants in Santa Fe.

New Mexico was first occupied by Native Americans and had been a territory of Spain and then Mexico before becoming a state in 1912. Today, it still has the highest percentage of Hispanic Americans and the second highest population of Native Americans, making for a unique culture.

The landscape ranges from desert in the south to forest and mountain country with clear streams and snow in the north. The Sangre Cristo Mountains (Blood of Christ) run north and south along the east side of the Rio Grand in the north. There are many national parks in New Mexico and several reservations, which are popular with tourists. The government built the Los Alamos Research Center during World War 11, where the atomic bomb was developed and which was first detonated in the desert in 1954. Experiments near Roswell caused some people to believe that a UFO landed here after headlines reported that a "flying disk" was found. The government said this was a research balloon, but this hasn't stopped speculation of a cover up, although this has never been proven. There are atomic museums in Albuquerque. The capital, Santa Fe, has a large artistic community. There are many art galleries and museums, including one honoring Georgia O'Keefe.

Information: www.newmexico.org

 **SPOTLIGHT**

★ One out of four workers in New Mexico works directly for the federal government.

★ Santa Fe, at 7,000 feet, is the highest capital in the U.S.

## ALAMOGORDO

Alamogordo is a popular tourist destination because of its proximity to Mescalero Apache Indian Reservation, Lincoln National Forest and White Sands National Monument. A branch of New Mexico State University is located here. Surrounded by desert and mountains, the first atomic bomb was set off nearby.

Information: Chamber of Commerce, 1301 N. White Sands Blvd., 505-437-6120, 888-843-3441; www.alamogordo.com

### WHAT TO SEE AND DO

**Alameda Park Zoo**
1321 N. White Sands Blvd., Alamogordo, 505-439-4290
Built in 1898, this is the oldest zoo in the Southwest. It has 300 native and exotic animals. Daily 9 a.m.-5 p.m.

**Lincoln National Forest**
3496 Hwy. 82, Alamogordo, 505-434-7200; www.fs.fed.us/r3/lincoln
This forest is known as the birthplace of Smokey Bear. Fishing, hunting, picnicking, camping, wild cave tours and winter

sports in the Sacramento, Capitan and Guadalupe mountains. Backpack in the White Mountain Capitan Wildernesses. Camping.

### New Mexico Museum of Space History
Hwy. 2001, Alamogordo,
505-437-2840, 877-333-6589;
www.nmspacemuseum.org
This museum features space-related artifacts and exhibits and an IMAX theater. Daily 9 a.m.-5 p.m.

### Oliver Lee State Park
409 Dog Canyon Rd., Alamogordo,
505-437-8284
Mountain climbers, photographers and history buffs will enjoy this state park, the site of at least five major battles. The box canyon is protected by a 2,000-foot bluff. Also includes Frenchy's Place, a substantial rock house with miles of stone fence. Hiking, camping. Visitor center, museum, tours of restored Lee Ranch House.

### Three Rivers Petroglyph Site
County Rd. B-30, Three Rivers,
505-525-4300
Twenty thousand rock carvings were made here between A.D. 900-1400 by the Jornada Branch of the Mogollon Indian Culture; semi desert terrain; interpretive signs; reconstructed prehistoric village; six picnic sites; tent and trailer sites.

### Toy Train Depot
1991 N. White Sands Blvd.,
Alamogordo, 888-207-3564;
www.toytraindepot.homestead.com
More than 1,200 feet of model railroad track and hundreds of model and toy trains are on display in this five-room, 100-year-old train depot. Also a two-mile outdoor miniature railroad track.

## SPECIAL EVENTS
### Trinity Site Tour
1301 N. White Sands Blvd., Alamogordo,
505-437-6120, 888-843-3441
Visit the site of the first A-bomb explosion, open to the public twice a year. First Saturday in April and October, 9 a.m.-2 p.m.

## HOTELS
### ★Best Western Desert Aire Hotel
1021 S. White Sands Blvd.,
Alamogordo, 505-437-2110;
www.bestwestern.com
92 rooms. Complimentary continental breakfast. Pets accepted. **$**

## WHITE SANDS NATIONAL MONUMENT
These shifting, dazzling white dunes are a challenge to plants and animals. Here, lizards and mice are white like the sand, helping them blend in with the background. (Similarly, mice are black in the black lava area only a few miles north.)

Plants elongate their stems up to 30 feet so that they can keep their leaves and flowers above the sand. When the sands recede, the plants are sometimes left on elevated pillars of hardened gypsum bound together by their roots. Even an ancient two-wheeled Spanish cart was laid bare when the sands shifted.

Beach sand is usually silica, but White Sands National Monument sand is gypsum, from which plaster of paris is made. Dunes often rise to 60 feet; White Sands is the largest gypsum dune field in the world.

White Sands National Monument encloses 143,732 acres of this remarkable area. The visitor center has exhibits concerning the dunes and how they were formed. Daily. Evening programs and guided nature walks in the dunes area are conducted Memorial Day-mid-August. Picnic area with shaded tables and grills (no water); primitive backpackers' campsite (by permit only).

Information: Hwy. 70, Alamogordo, 505-679-2599; www.nps.gov/whsa

## THE NATIVE AMERICAN INFLUENCE

Native Americans occupied New Mexico for centuries before the arrival of Europeans. The exploring Spaniards called them Pueblo Indians because their tightly clustered communities were not unlike Spanish pueblos, or villages. The Apache and Navajo, who arrived in New Mexico after the Pueblo people, were semi-nomadic wanderers. The Navajo eventually adopted many of the Pueblo ways, although their society is less structured than the Pueblo. The main Navajo reservation straddles New Mexico and Arizona. The Apache, living closer to the Plains Indians, remained more nomadic.

The 19 Pueblo groups have close-knit communal societies and cultures, even though they speak six different languages. Their pueblos are unique places to visit. In centuries-old dwellings, craftspeople make and sell a variety of wares. The religious ceremonies, which include many dances and songs, are quite striking and not to be missed.

Tourists are welcome at all reservations in New Mexico on most days, although there are various restrictions. Since the religious ceremonies are sacred, photography is generally prohibited. This may also be true of certain sacred areas of the pueblo (in a few cases, the entire pueblo). Sometimes permission to photograph or draw is needed and fees may be required. The ancient culture and traditions of these people hold great meaning; visitors should be as respectful of them as they would be of their own. Questions should be directed to the pueblo governor or representative at the tribal office.

More can be learned about New Mexico's Native Americans and their origins at the many museums and sites in Santa Fe, the visitor center at Bandelier National Monument and the Indian Pueblo Cultural Center.

# ALBUQUERQUE

In 1706, Don Francisco Cuervo y Valdes, then governor of New Mexico, moved 30 families from Bernalillo to a spot some 15 miles south on the Rio Grande where the pasturage was better.

Catholic missionaries began to build churches in the area and inadvertently brought diseases that afflicted the Pueblo Indians. The settlers fought with the American Indians for many years, but Albuquerque now celebrates the cultural heritage of groups like the Pueblo, the Anasazi and other tribes. By 1790, the population had grown to almost 6,000 (a very large town for New Mexico at the time). Today, Albuquerque is the largest city in New Mexico.

Albuquerque was an important U.S. military outpost from 1846 to 1870. In 1880, when a landowner near the Old Town refused to sell, the Santa Fe Railroad chose a route two miles east, forming a new town called New Albuquerque. It wasn't long before the new town had enveloped what is still called "Old Town," now a popular tourist shopping area.

Surrounded by mountains, Albuquerque continues to grow. The largest industry is Sandia National Laboratories, a laboratory engaged in solar and nuclear research and the testing and development of nuclear weapons.

Dry air and plenty of sunshine (more than 75 percent of the time) have earned Albuquerque a reputation as a health center. Adding to that reputation is the Lovelace Medical Center (similar to the Mayo Clinic in Rochester, Minnesota), which gave the first United

States astronauts their qualifying examinations. The University of New Mexico is also located in Albuquerque.

Local attractions such as the annual Albuquerque Balloon Fiesta and several nearby vineyards make it a place for all to visit and enjoy. The culture is an active one and the people of Albuquerque enjoy as many outdoor activities as they can fit into their schedules.

Information: Convention & Visitors Bureau, 20 First Plaza N.W., 505-842-9918, 800-284-2282; www.abqcvb.org

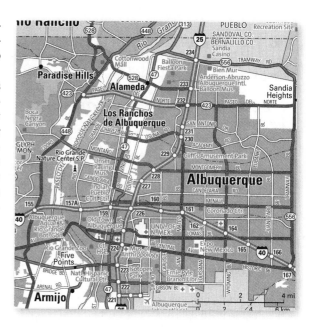

## WHAT TO SEE AND DO

### Albuquerque Biological Park
903 Tenth St. S.W., Albuquerque, 505-764-6200; www.cabq.gov/biopark
This biological park consists of the Albuquerque Aquarium, the Rio Grande Botanic Garden and the Rio Grande Zoo. The aquarium features a shark tank, eel tunnel and shrimp boat. The botanic garden displays formal walled gardens and a glass conservatory. The zoo exhibits include koalas, polar bears, sea lions and shows. Daily 9 a.m.-5 p.m., until 6 p.m. in summer.

### Albuquerque Little Theatre
224 San Pasquale Ave. S.W., Albuquerque, 505-242-4750; www.swpc.com
This historic community theater troupe stages Broadway productions. September-May.

### Albuquerque Museum
2000 Mountain Rd. N.W., Albuquerque, 505-243-7255; www.albuquerquemuseum.com
Located in a solar-heated building across from the New Mexico Museum of Natural History and Science, this museum showcases regional art and history. Tuesday-Sunday 9 a.m.-5 p.m.

### Cibola National Forest
2113 Osuna Rd. N.E., Albuquerque, 505-346-3900; www.fs.fed.us/r3/cibola
This forest has more than 1.5 million acres and stretches throughout central New Mexico. The park includes Mount Taylor (11,301 feet), several mountain ranges and four wilderness areas: Sandia Mountain (where you'll see bighorn sheep), Manzano Mountain, Apache Kid and Withington. Scenic drives.

### Coronado State Monument
485 Kuaua Rd., Bernalillo, 505-867-5351
Coronado is said to have camped near this excavated pueblo in 1540 on his famous quest for the seven golden cities of Cibola. Reconstructed, painted kiva; visitor center devoted to Southwestern culture and the Spanish influence on the area. Wednesday-Monday 8:30 a.m.-4:30 p.m.

### Indian Pueblo Cultural Center

2401 12th St. N.W., Albuquerque,
505-843-7270, 866-855-7902;
www.indianpueblo.org

Owned and operated by the 19 pueblos of New Mexico, exhibits in the museum tell the story of the Pueblo culture. The gallery showcases handcrafted art; American Indian dance and craft demonstrations (weekends). Restaurant. Daily.

### National Atomic Museum

1905 Mountain Rd. N.W.,
Albuquerque, 505-245-2137;
www.atomicmuseum.com

This nuclear energy science center, the nation's only such museum, features exhibits depicting the history of the atomic age, including the Manhattan Project, the Cold War and the development of nuclear medicine. See replicas of Little Boy and Fat Man, the world's first two atomic weapons deployed in Japan in World War II, as well as B-52 and B-29 aircraft. Guided tours and audiovisual presentations are offered. Daily 9 a.m.-5 p.m.

### New Mexico Museum of Natural History and Science

1801 Mountain Rd. N.W.,
Albuquerque, 505-841-2800;
www.museums.state.nm.us/nmmnh

Those interested in dinosaurs, fossils and volcanoes will love this museum, with exhibits on botany, geology, paleontology and zoology. The LodeStar Astronomy Center gives museum-goers a view of the heavens in its observatory. Daily 9 a.m.-5 p.m.

### Old Town

Old Town and Romero Roads,
Albuquerque

The original settlement is one block north of Central Avenue, the city's main street, at Rio Grande Boulevard. Old Town Plaza retains a lovely Spanish flavor with many interesting shops and restaurants.

### Petroglyph National Monument

6001 Unser Blvd., Albuquerque,
505-899-0205; www.nps.gov/petr

This park contains concentrated groups of rock drawings experts believe ancestors of the Pueblo carved on lava formations. Three hiking trails wind along the 17-mile escarpment. Daily 8 a.m.-5 p.m.

### Rio Grande Nature Center State Park

2901 Candelaria Rd., N.W., Albuquerque,
505-344-7240;
www.emnrd.state.nm.us/prd/RGNC.htm

The highlight here is a glass-enclosed observation room overlooking a three-acre pond that is home to birds and other wildlife; interpretive displays on the wildlife of the bosque (cottonwood groves) along the Rio Grande; two miles of nature trails. Guided hikes, hands-on activities. Daily 8 a.m.-5 p.m.

### Rio Grande Zoo

903 Tenth St. S.W., Albuquerque,
505-764-6200; www.cabq.gov/biopark/zoo

More than 1,200 exotic animals; rain forest, reptile house, white tigers and more. Daily 9 a.m.-5 p.m., until 6 p.m. weekends in summer.

### Sandia Peak Tramway Ski Area

Albuquerque, in Cibola National Forest,
Crest Scenic Byway, Sandia Mountains,
505-856-7325; www.sandiapeak.com

Four double chairlifts, surface lift; patrol, school, rentals, snowmaking. Aerial tramway on the west side of the mountain meets lifts at the top. Longest run is more than 2 1/2 miles; vertical drop 1,700 feet. Mid-December-March, daily. Chairlift also operates July-Labor Day. Friday-Sunday.

### Sandia Peak Aerial Tramway

Albuquerque, five miles northeast of city limits via I-25 and Tramway Rd.,
505-856-7325

The tram travels almost three miles up the west slope of the Sandia Mountains to 10,378 feet, with amazing 11,000-square-mile views. Hiking trail; restaurant at summit and Mexican grill at base. Memorial Day-Labor Day: daily 9 a.m.-9 p.m., shorter hours rest of year; closed

**NEW MEXICO**

two weeks in April and two weeks in October.

### Telephone Pioneer Museum
110 Fourth St. NW., Albuquerque,
505-842-2937
Displays trace the development of the telephone from 1876 to the present. More than 400 types of telephones, plus switchboards, early equipment and old telephone directories. Monday-Friday 10 a.m.-2 p.m.; weekends by appointment.

### University of New Mexico
Central Ave. and University Blvd.,
Albuquerque,
505-277-1989, 800-225-5866;
www.unm.edu
Established 1889; 25,000 students. This campus has both Spanish and Pueblo architectural influences. It is one of the largest universities in the Southwest.

### Fine Arts Center, Univeristy of New Mexico
Central Ave., Albuquerque, 505-277-4001
Houses the University Art Museum, which features more than 23,000 pieces in its collection. Tuesday-Friday 9 a.m.-4 p.m., Sunday 1-4 p.m.; the Fine Arts Library, which contains the Southwest Music Archives; the Rodey Theatre; and Popejoy Hall, home of the New Mexico Symphony Orchestra and host of the Best of Broadway International Theatre seasons of plays, dance and music.

### Jonson Gallery
1909 Las Lomas N.E., Albuquerque,
505-277-4967
This gallery, owned by the University of New Mexico and part of its art museums, houses the archives and work of modernist painter Raymond Jonson (1891-1982) and a few works by his contemporaries. Tuesday-Friday 10 a.m.-4 p.m.

### Maxwell Museum of Anthropology
Anthropology Building, University Blvd. and M. L. King Jr. Blvd., Albuquerque,
505-277-4405
Permanent and changing exhibits of early man and American Indian cultures with an emphasis on the Southwest. Tuesday-Friday 9 a.m.-4 p.m., Saturday 10 a.m.-4 p.m.

### Museum of Geology and Institute of Meteoritics Meteorite Museum
Northrop Hall, 200 Yale Blvd. N.E., Albuquerque, 505-277-4204
The Museum of Geology contains numerous samples of ancient plants, minerals, rocks and animals, while the meteorite museum has a major collection of more than 550 meteorites. Monday-Friday 7:30 a.m.-4:30 p.m.

## SPECIAL EVENTS

### Albuquerque International Balloon Fiesta
Balloon Fiesta Park, North Albuquerque,
505-821-1000, 888-422-7277;
www.aibf.org
As many as 100,000 people attend this annual event, the largest of its kind in the world. Attendees can catch their own balloon rides from Rainbow Ryders, Inc. (505-823-1111). First Saturday in October through the following Sunday.

### Founders Day
Old Town, Albuquerque, 505-768-3556
Celebrates the city's founding in 1706 with traditional New Mexican festivities. Late April.

### Musical Theater Southwest
2401 Ross S.E., Albuquerque,
505-265-9119;
www.musicaltheatresw.com
This troupe produces five Broadway-style musicals each season at the historic Hiland Theater in the Frank A. Peloso Performing Arts Center.

### New Mexico Arts & Crafts Fair
Expo New Mexico State Fairgrounds,
Central and San Pedro Boulevards,
Albuquerque, 505-884-9043;
www.nmartsandcraftsfair.org
Exhibits and demonstrations by more than 200 craftsworkers representing Spanish, American Indian and other North American cultures. Artists sell their

wares, which range from paintings to sculpture to jewelry. Last weekend in June.

## New Mexico State Fair

Expo New Mexico State Fairgrounds, Central and San Pedro Boulevards, Albuquerque, 505-265-3976

Horse shows and racing, rodeo, midway, flea market; entertainment. September.

## New Mexico Symphony Orchestra

University of New Mexico, Popejoy Hall, 4407 Menaul Blvd., Albuquerque, 505-881-9590, 800-251-6676; www.nmso.org

September-May.

## Santa Ana Feast Day

Santa Ana and Taos Pueblos, Albuquerque, www.santaana.org

Corn dance. Late July.

## Taos Pueblo Dances

Taos Pueblo, Albuquerque, 505-758-1028; www.taospueblo.com

Several American Indian dances are held throughout the year. For a schedule of annual dances, contact the pueblo.

# HOTELS

## ★★Best Western Rio Grande Inn

1015 Rio Grande Blvd. N.W., Albuquerque, 505-843-9500, 800-959-4726; www.riograndeinn.com

40 rooms. Restaurant, bar. $

## ★★Courtyard Albuquerque Airport

1920 S. Yale Blvd., Albuquerque, 505-843-6600, 800-321-2211; www.marriott.com

150 rooms. High-speed wireless Internet access. Restaurant, bar. Airport transportation available. Airport. Pool. $

## ★★Doubletree Hotel

201 Marquette N.W., Albuquerque, 505-247-3344; www.albuquerque.doubletree.com

295 rooms. High-speed Internet access. Restaurant, bar. Pool. Business Center. $$

## ★★Holiday Inn

2020 Menaul N.E., Albuquerque, 505-884-2511; www.holiday-inn.com

360 rooms. Restaurant, bar. Airport transportation available. Pets accepted. Pool. Fitness center. $

## ★Homewood Suites By Hilton Albuquerque

7101 Arvada Ave. N.E., Albuquerque, 505-881-7300; www.homewood-suites.com

151 rooms, all suites. $

## ★★★Hilton Albuquerque

1901 University N.E., Albuquerque, 505-884-2500, 800-274-6835; www.hilton.com

With its arched doorways, Indian rugs and local art, this hotel on 14 acres near the university fits right in. Guests will enjoy the indoor and outdoor heated pools, sauna and lighted tennis courts. Accommodations feature sliding glass doors and balconies with great view of the high desert.

263 rooms. High-speed Internet access. Two restaurants, bar. Pool. Fitness center. Business Center. $

## ★★★Hotel Albuquerque at Old Town

800 Rio Grande Blvd. N.W., Albuquerque, 505-843-6300, 800-237-2133; www.buynewmexico.com

With its large, open lobby and tiled floors, this property offers a casual yet elegant environment. Located in historic Old Town across from the New Mexico Museum of Natural History, it is close to more than 200 specialty stores. All guest rooms feature furniture made by local artists.

188 rooms. High-speed Internet access. Two restaurants, bar. Pets accepted. Pool. Business center. $

★

★

★

★

★

### ★★★Hyatt Regency Albuquerque

330 Tijeras N.W., Albuquerque,
505-842-1234, 800-233-1234;
www.hyatt.com

Adjacent to the convention center, this 22-story tower is centrally located near Old Town and the Rio Grande Zoo and is only five miles from the airport. One of the city's newest high-rise hotels, the property offers a health club, sauna and outdoor pool. Business rooms include separate work areas and dual line phones. All rooms have a warm Southwestern décor and views of the city or mountains.

395 rooms. High-speed Internet access. Restaurant, two bars. Fitness center. Pool. Business center. **$$**

## SPECIALTY LODGINGS

### Casas De Suenos Old Town Bed and Breakfast Inn

310 Rio Grande Blvd. S.W., Albuquerque,
505-247-4560, 800-655-7002;
www.casasdesuenos.com

Situated in the valley of the Sandia Mountains just three blocks from the Historic Old Town Area, this inn features the art of local talents. Beautiful guest rooms offer private baths, private entrances, televisions and VCRs. Enjoy a full breakfast in the sunny garden room featuring such dishes as Southwestern frittatas.

21 rooms. Complimentary full breakfast. High-speed wireless Internet access. Pets accepted. **$**

### Hacienda Antigua B&B

6708 Tierra Dr. N.W., Albuquerque,
505-345-5399, 800-201-2986;
www.haciendaantigua.com

Built on the famous El Camino Real, this 200-year-old adobe inn is conveniently located in the North Valley area. The warm property features traditional kiva fireplaces and antique furnishings in the guest rooms.

8 rooms. Complimentary full breakfast. Pets accepted. Pool. **$$**

### Mauger B&B Inn

701 Roma Ave. N.W., Albuquerque,
505-242-8755, 800-719-9189;
www.maugerbb.com

This warm bed and breakfast is centrally located near the business district and Old Town. The suites in this restored Queen Anne house include fresh flowers, antique furniture, private baths and data ports.

10 rooms. Complimentary full breakfast. Pets accepted. **$**

## RESTAURANTS

### ★66 Diner

1405 Central Ave. N.E., Albuquerque,
505-247-1421; www.66diner.com

American, Southwestern menu. Breakfast, lunch, dinner. Children's menu. Casual attire. **$**

### ★★Antiquity

112 Romero St. N.W., Albuquerque,
505-247-3545

American, Southwestern menu. Dinner. Casual attire. Reservations recommended. **$$**

### ★★★Artichoke Cafe

424 Central St., Albuquerque,
505-243-0200; www.artichokecafe.com

This pleasant eatery, which has tables set with beautiful fresh flowers, serves a mix of French, Italian and creative American cuisine. Dishes include steamed artichokes with three dipping sauces, or house-made pumpkin ravioli and scallops wrapped in proscuitto.

American menu. Lunch, dinner. Casual attire. Reservations recommended. **$$**

### ★★Barry's Oasis

4451 Osuna, Albuquerque,
505-884-2324;
www.barrysoasis.com

Mediterranean menu. Lunch, dinner. Casual attire. Reservations recommended. **$**

**228**

NEW MEXICO

### ★Christy Mae's
1400 San Pedro N.E., Albuquerque,
505-255-4740; www.christymaes.com
American menu. Lunch, dinner. Closed
Sunday. Children's menu. Casual attire. **$**

### ★Cooperage
7220 Lomas Blvd. N.E., Albuquerque,
505-255-1657
American menu. Lunch, dinner. Bar.
Casual attire. **$$**

### ★Garduno's of Mexico
10551 Montgomery N.E., Albuquerque,
505-298-5000
Mexican meu. Lunch, dinner, Sunday-
brunch. Bar. Children's menu. Casual attire.
Outdoor seating. **$$**

### ★★High Noon
425 San Felipe St. N.W.,
Albuquerque, 505-765-1455;
www.999dine.com
Southwestern, steak menu. Lunch, dinner.
Bar. Children's menu. Casual attire. **$$**

### ★La Hacienda Dining Room
302 San Felipe N.W., Albuquerque,
505-243-3131
Southwestern menu. Lunch, dinner. Bar.
Children's menu. Casual attire. Outdoor
seating. **$$**

### ★★★Le Cafe Miche
1431 Wyoming Blvd. N.E.,
Albuquerque, 505-299-6088;
www.cafemiche.com
Although the French country cuisine
served here is a bit old-fashioned—think
veal Orloff and chicken cordon bleu—this
romantic, candlelit restaurant remains a
favorite, especially with the attentive service and welcoming ambience.
French menu. Lunch, dinner. Casual attire.
Reservations recommended. **$$**

### ★Mr. K
5001 Central Ave. N.E., Albuquerque,
505-265-8859
Chinese menu. Lunch, dinner. Casual
attire. **$**

### ★★★Scalo Nob Hill
3500 Central Ave. S.E.,
Albuquerque, 505-255-8782;
www.scalonobhill.com
Chef Enrique Guerrero has taken over the
kitchen of this northern Italian grill with
dining areas on several levels. He's already
brought back favorites such as chicken
cooked under a brick.
American menu. Lunch, dinner. Closed
Monday. Bar. Casual attire. Reservations
recommended. Outdoor seating. **$$**

### ★★Trombino's Bistro Italiano
5415 Academy Blvd. N.E., Albuquerque,
505-821-5974
Italian menu. Lunch, dinner, brunch. Closed
Super Bowl Sunday. Bar. Children's
menu. **$$**

**NEW MEXICO**

# ANGEL FIRE
This is a family resort area high in the Sangre de Cristo Mountains of northern New Mexico.
Information: Chamber of Commerce, 505-377-6661, 800-446-8117;
www.angelfirechamber.org

## WHAT TO SEE AND DO

**Angel Fire Ski Resort**
10 Miller Lane, Angel Fire,
575-377-6401, 800-633-7463;
www.angelfireresort.com
Resort has two high-speed quad, three double chairlifts; patrol, school, rentals; 70 runs, longest run more than three miles; vertical drop 2,077 feet. Thanksgiving-March, daily. Nordic center, snowmobiling. Summer resort includes fishing, boating, 18-hole golf, tennis, mountain biking, riding stables. Conference center all year.

**Cimarron Canyon State Park**
29519 Hwy. 64, Eagle Nest, 505-377-6271
This region of high mountains and deep canyons has scenic 200-foot palisades; winding mountain stream has excellent trout fishing; state wildlife area. Hiking, rock climbing, wildlife viewing, winter sports, camping. Daily.

**Eagle Nest Lake**
Hwy. 64, Angel Fire,
www.eaglenestlake.org
This 2,200-acre lake offers year-round fishing for rainbow trout and Kokonee salmon (fishing license required).

**Vietnam Veterans State Park Memorial**
Hwy. 64, Angel Fire,
505-377-6900;
www.angelfirememorial.com
This beautiful, gracefully designed building stands on a hillside overlooking Moreno Valley and the Sangre de Cristo Mountains. Chapel. Daily.

# 230 ARTESIA

Artesia was named for the vast underground water supplies that once rushed up through drilled wells and are now used to irrigate the area's farmland. The first underground school in the United States, Abo Elementary School, was built here for safety from the radiation effects of fallout. Artesia is also the home of the Federal Law Enforcement Training Center. The area offers wild turkey, deer, bear and upland game for hunting enthusiasts.
Information: Chamber of Commerce, 107 N. First St., 505-746-2744, 800-658-6251; www.artesiachamber.com

## WHAT TO SEE AND DO

**Historical Museum and Art Center**
503 and 505 W. Richardson Ave., Artesia,
505-748-2390
Pioneer and American Indian artifacts; changing art exhibits. Tuesday-Saturday.

## HOTELS

**★★Best Western Pecos Inn Motel**
2209 W. Main St., Artesia, 505-748-3324;
www.bestwestern.com
81 rooms. Restaurant, bar. Pool. $

**Heritage Inn**
209 W. Main St., Artesia,
505-748-2552, 866-207-0222;
www.artesiaheritageinn.com
11 rooms. Complimentary continental breakfast. Wireless Internet access. Pets accepted. $

## RESTAURANTS

**★★La Fonda**
310 W. Main St., Artesia, 505-746-9377
Mexican menu. Lunch, dinner. Casual attire. $

# AZTEC

Aztec is the seat of San Juan County, a fruit-growing and cattle-grazing area. This town is filled with history. Architectural and historic commentary for walking tours may be obtained at the Aztec Museum.

Information: Chamber of Commerce, 110 N. Ash, 505-334-9551; www.aztecnm.com

## WHAT TO SEE AND DO

### Aztec Museum and Pioneer Village
125 N. Main, Aztec, 505-334-9829

The main museum here houses authentic pioneer artifacts, including mineral and fossil displays, household items, farm and ranch tools and American Indian artifacts. Also includes the Oil Field Museum with 1920s cable tool oil rig, oil well pumping unit and more. Also here is Pioneer Village, which features 12 reconstructed buildings, including doctor's and sheriff's offices, blacksmith shop and foundry, pioneer cabin (1880), general store and post office, original Aztec jail and church. Monday-Saturday.

### Aztec Ruins National Monument
Aztec Ruins Rd., Aztec, 505-334-6174;
www.nps.gov/azru

These are actually ancient Pueblo ruins, dating back to the 11th to 13th centuries that were misnamed by early settlers in the 1800s. The partially excavated pueblo contains nearly 450 rooms, with its plaza dominated by the Great Kiva (48 feet in diameter). Instructive museum; interpretive programs in summer. Self-guided tours; trail guide available at visitor center for the 1/4-mile trail. Daily.

### Navajo Lake State Park
Aztec, 18 miles east via Hwy. 173,
505-632-2278;
www.emnrd.state.nm.us/ PRD/navajo.htm

Surrounded by sandstone mesas and stands of pinon and juniper, the reservoir extends 35 miles upstream into Colorado, totaling 15,000 surface acres of water. Daily.

### Pine River Site
Aztec

Swimming, waterskiing, fishing (panfish, catfish, bass, salmon and trout), boating (ramps, rentals, marina); picnicking (fireplaces), camping. Visitor center with interpretive displays.

### San Juan River Recreation Area
Aztec, Below the dam

Fishing (trout); camping.

### Sims Mesa Site
Aztec, East side

Boat ramp; camping.

## HOTELS

### ★Step Back Inn
123 W. Aztec Blvd., Aztec,
505-334-1200, 800-334-1255

39 rooms. Complimentary continental breakfast. $

# BERNALILLO

Located in the Rio Grande Valley, midway between Santa Fe and Albuquerque, Bernalillo is an area rich in history. Camino del Pueblo, the city's main street, is part of the famed Route 66.

Information: 243 Camino del Pueblo, 505-867-8687, 800-252-0191

## SPECIALTY LODGINGS

### La Hacienda Grande
21 Barros Rd., Bernalillo,
505-867-1887, 800-353-1887;
www.lahaciendagrande.com

This bed and breakfast, a Spanish hacienda built in the 1750s, has cathedral ceilings, an open-air center courtyard, a kiva-warmed sitting room and brick kitchen.

6 rooms. Complimentary full breakfast. Pets accepted. **$**

## RESTAURANTS

**★★★Prairie Star**
288 Prairie Star Rd., Bernalillo,
505-867-3327; www.santaanagolf.com
This casual fine-dining restaurant in the Santa Ana Golf Club specializes in game and has stunning views of the Sandias.

American menu. Dinner. Closed Monday. Bar. Children's menu. Casual attire. Reservations recommended. Outdoor seating. **$$**

**★Range Café and Bakery**
925 Camino del Pueblo, Bernalillo,
505-867-1700; www.rangecafe.com
Southwestern menu. Breakfast, lunch, dinner. Bar. Children's menu. Casual attire. **$$**

# CAPITAN

Capitan, a village in Lincoln County, is known as the birthplace of Smokey the Bear. In 1950, a badly burned bear was rescued from a large forest fire in the Capitan Mountains. The bear was named Smokey and was used as the mascot for the U.S. Forest Service. He was sent to the National Zoo in Washington. DC, where he spent 26 years. After he died, he was returned here and buried in Smokey Bear Historical State Park.
Information: www.villageofcapitan.com

## WHAT TO SEE AND DO

**Smokey Bear Historical State Park**
118 Smokey Bear Blvd., (Hwy. 380),
Capitan, 505-354-2748
Commemorates the history and development of the national symbol of forest fire prevention. The original Smokey, who was orphaned by a fire raging in the Lincoln National Forests, is buried here within sight of the mountain where he was found. Fire prevention exhibit, film. Daily.

**Smokey Bear Museum**
102 Smokey Bear Blvd., Capitan,
505-354-2298

Features 1950s memorabilia of famed firefighting bear, whose real-life counterpart was found in the nearby Capitan Mountains. Daily.

## HOTELS

**★Smokey Bear Motel**
316 Smokey Bear Blvd., Capitan,
505-354-2257, 800-766-5392;
www.smokeybearmotel.com
9 rooms. **$**

232

**NEW MEXICO**

# CARLSBAD

On the lovely Pecos River, Carlsbad is an excellent place to get out and explore, thanks to nearby Carlsbad Caverns and the Guadalupe Mountains national parks.
Information: Convention & Visitors Bureau, 302 S. Canal, 505-887-6516, 800-221-1224; www.carlsbadchamber.com

## WHAT TO SEE AND DO

### Carlsbad Museum & Art Center
Halagueno Park, 418 W. Fox St., Carlsbad, 505-887-0276; www.nmculture.org
Showcases Pueblo pottery, art and meteorite remains; pioneer and Apache relics; bird carvings by Jack Drake; mineral exhibits and more. Summer: Monday-Saturday 10 a.m.-6 p.m.; winter: Monday-Saturday 10 a.m.-5 p.m.

### Lake Carlsbad Water Recreation Area
Carlsbad, Off Green St. on the Pecos River, 575-887-2702
Swimming, water sports, fishing, boating; tennis, golf, picnic area.

### Living Desert Zoo and Gardens State Park
1504 Miehls Dr., Carlsbad, 505-887-5516; www.emnrd.state.nm.us/PRD/livingdesert.htm
This 1,100-acre park is an indoor/outdoor living museum of the Chihuahuan Desert's plants and animals. The Desert Arboretum has an extensive cactus collection and the zoo has more than 60 animal species native to the region, including mountain lions, bear, wolf, elk, bison and an extensive aviary. Summer: daily 8 a.m.-8 p.m.; winter: daily 9 a.m.-5 p.m.

### Sitting Bull Falls
Carlsbad, 11 miles northwest on Hwy. 285 to Hwy. 137, then 30 miles southwest, in Lincoln National Forest, 505-885-4181, 800-221-122

## CARLSBAD CAVERNS NATIONAL PARK

One of the largest and most remarkable in the world, this cavern extends approximately 30 miles and is as deep as 1,037 feet below the surface. It was once known as Bat Cave because of the spectacular bat flights, still a daily occurrence at sunset during the warmer months.

Cowboy and guano miner Jim White first explored and guided people through the caverns in the early 1900s, later working for the National Park Service as the Chief Park Ranger. Carlsbad Cave National Monument was established in 1923 and in 1930 the area was enlarged and designated a national park. The park contains 46,755 acres and more than 80 caves. Carlsbad Cavern was formed by the dissolving action of acidic water in the Tansill and Capitan limestones of the Permian age. When an uplift drained the cavern, mineral-laden water dripping from the ceiling formed the stalactites and stalagmites.

The main cavern has two self-guided routes, a Ranger-guided Kings Palace tour and several "off-trail" trips. The "Cavern Guide," an audio tour rented at the visitor center, enhances self-guided tours with interpretations of the caverns, interviews and historic re-creations. Tours are also available in two backcountry caves: Slaughter Canyon Cave and Spider Cave. All guided tours require reservations.

Bat flight programs are held each evening during the summer at the cavern entrance amphitheater.
Information: 727A Carlsbad Caverns Hwy., Carlsbad, 505-785-2232; www.nps.gov/cave

## HOTELS

**★★Best Western Stevens Inn**
1829 S. Canal St., Carlsbad, 505-887-2851;
www.bestwestern.com
220 rooms. Complimentary full breakfast.
Restaurant, bar. Pets accepted. Pool. **$**

**★★Holiday Inn**
2210 W. Pierce, Carlsbad,
505-234-1252, 888-465-4329;
www.holiday-inn.com
100 rooms. Complimentary full breakfast.
Restaurant, bar. Pool. **$**

# CEDAR CREST

Twenty miles outside of Albuquerque, Cedar Crest is a small town off of Highway 40.
Information: 12480 N. Hwy 14B-163, Cedar Crest; www.eastmountainchamber.com

### WHAT TO SEE AND DO

**Museum of Archaeology and Material Culture**
22 Calvary Rd., Cedar Crest,
505-281-2005
Highlights 12,000 years of American
Indian history and archaeological artifacts. Turquoise mining exhibit. Open May
1-November 1, daily noon-7 p.m.

### SPECIALTY LODGINGS

**Elaine's, A Bed & Breakfast**
72 Showline Rd., Cedar Crest,
505-281-2467, 800-821-3092;
www.elainesbnb.com
Set in a beautiful log cabin within easy distance of golfing, hiking, skiing, bird watching and more.
5 rooms. **$**

# CERRILLOS

"Little Hills" in Spanish, Cerillos is one of this region's traditional villages. Thanks to its
preserved historic buildings, visitors can imagine the Wild West as they stroll the town's
tree-lined streets.
Information: www.newmexico.org

### WHAT TO SEE AND DO

**Broken Saddle Riding Company**
56 Vicksville Rd., Cerrillos, 505-424-7774;
www.brokensaddle.com
Explore the high desert backcountry
surrounding the historic mining town of
Cerrillos on smooth riding Missouri Foxtrot-
ers and Tennessee Walkers. Broken Saddle
Riding Company offers morning, afternoon
and sunset rides catering to all riding levels
and private rides by appointment. Excursions
can include any number of scenic and historic areas surrounding the town of Cerrillos,
including old mining areas, ghost towns and
beautifully scenic desert terrain. Monthly full-
moon rides are also offered. By appointment.

**Cerrillos Turquoise Mining Museum**
17 Waldo St., Cerrillos, 505-438-3008
Celebrates the mining legacy of this area
with a collection of mineral samples that
are breathtaking. Daily.

### SPECIALTY LODGINGS

**High Feather Ranch Bed & Breakfast**
29 High Feather Ranch, Cerrillos,
505-424-1333, 800-757-4410;
www.highfeatherranch-bnb.com
This architecturally stunning ranch on 65
private acres features luxurious accommodations and a full gourmet breakfast.
3 rooms. **$$**

## CHACO CULTURE NATIONAL HISTORICAL PARK

From A.D. 900 to 1150, Chaco Canyon was a major center of Anasazi culture. A prehistoric roadway system, which included stairways carved into sandstone cliffs, extends for hundreds of miles in all directions. Ancient roads up to 30 feet wide represent the most developed and extensive road network of this period north of Central America. Researchers speculate that Chaco Canyon was the center of a vast, complex and interdependent civilization in the American Southwest.

There are five self-guided trails with tours conducted Memorial Day-Labor Day, as well as evening campfire programs in summer. Visitor center has museum. Daily. Camping.

Information: Nageezi, from Hwy. 44, 25 miles south on country road 7900; three miles south of Nageezi Trading Post; from I-40, 60 miles north of Thoreau on Hwy. 57. Check road conditions locally; may be extremely difficult when wet; www.nps.gov/chcu

# CHAMA

Like many of New Mexico's towns, Chama began in the mid-1800s, when explorers discovered gold and silver in the surrounding hills and streams. The precious metals ran out, but the area's natural beauty is prize enough: Chama sits at the base of the Cumbres Pass in the San Juan Mountains.

Information: www.chamanewmexico.com

## WHAT TO SEE AND DO

### Cumbres & Toltec Scenic Railroad, New Mexico Express

500 S. Terrace Ave., Chama, 888-286-2737; www.cumbrestoltec.com

Take a round-trip excursion to Osier, Colorado on an 1880s narrow-gauge steam railroad. The route passes through backwoods country and features spectacular mountain scenery. Memorial Day-mid-October, daily. Trips to Antonito, Colorado, are also available with van return. Reservations advised.

### El Vado Lake State Park

Chama, 15 miles south on Hwy. 84 to Tierra Amarilla, then 13 miles southwest on Hwy. 112, 575-588-7247; www.emnrd.state.nm.us/PRD/elvado.htm

This park features an irrigation lake with fishing, ice fishing, boating (dock, ramps); hiking trail connects to Heron Lake, picnicking, playground, camping. Daily.

### Heron Lake State Park

640 Hwy. 95, Chama, 505-588-7470; www.emnrd.state.nm.us/PRD/heron.htm

This region, with tall ponderosa pines, offers swimming, fishing (trout, salmon), ice fishing, boating (ramp, dock); hiking, winter sports, picnicking, camping. Daily.

# CIMARRON

This historic Southwestern town was part of Lucien B. Maxwell's land holdings on the Santa Fe Trail. The St. James Hotel (1872), where Buffalo Bill Cody held his Wild West Shows, old jail (1872) and several other historic buildings still stand.

Information: Chamber of Commerce, 505-376-2417, 888-376-2417; www.cimarronnm.com

## WHAT TO SEE AND DO

**Philmont Scout Ranch**

17 Deer Run Rd., Cimarron, 575-376-2281;
www.scouting.org/philmont

A 138,000-acre camp for some 20,000 Boy Scouts. Villa Philmonte, former summer home of ranch's benefactor, offers tours (mid-June-mid-August, daily; rest of year, call for schedule; fee). Ernest Thompson Seton Memorial Library and Philmont Museum includes several thousand drawings, paintings and American Indian artifacts (Monday-Friday). Kit Carson Museum (seven miles south of headquarters; mid-June-August, daily). Camp also has buffalo, deer, elk, bear and antelope.

## SPECIAL EVENTS

**Cimarron Days**

Village Park Hwy. 64, Cimarron,
505-376-2417;
www.cimarronnm.com/cimarron_days.htm
Crafts, entertainment. Labor Day weekend.

**Maverick Club Rodeo**

Maverick Club Arena, Cimarron,
505-376-2417

Rodeo for working cowboys. Parade, dance. July 4.

## SPECIALTY LODGINGS

**Casa Del Gavilan**

Hwy. 21 S, Cimarron,
505-376-2246, 800-428-4526;
www.casadelgavilan.com

Nestled in the Sangre de Cristo Mountains, this Southwestern adobe built in 1912 is away from it all. Relax in the library or on the porch while sipping tea or wine. Or go hiking in the trails behind the inn.

5 rooms. Complimentary full breakfast. **$**

# CLOUDCROFT

Cloudcroft has one of the highest golf courses in North America, but this is also a recreation area for non-golfers. It is located at the crest of the Sacramento Mountains in the Lincoln National Forest, among fir, spruce, pine and aspen trees. The area is popular with writers, photographers and artists. Several art schools conduct summer workshops here. There are also many miles of horseback trails through the mountains and skiing, snowmobiling and skating in winter. Several campgrounds are located in the surrounding forest. During the day temperatures seldom reach 80° F and nights are always crisp and cool.

Information: Chamber of Commerce, 505-682-2733, 866-874-4447; www.cloudcroft.net

## WHAT TO SEE AND DO

**Sacramento Mountains Historical Museum**

1000 Hwy. 82, Cloudcroft, 505-682-2932

Exhibits depict life from 1880 to 1910 in the Sacramento Mountains area. Monday, Tuesday, Friday-Sunday.

**Ski Cloudcroft**

1 Corona Place, Cloudcroft, 575-682-2333

Double chairlift, beginner tows; patrol, school, rentals, snowmaking, lodge, snack bar, cafeteria, restaurant. Vertical drop 700 feet. Mid-December-mid-March, daily. Snowboarding. Elevations of 8,350-9,050 feet.

## HOTELS

**★★★The Lodge Resort and Spa**

1 Corona Place, Cloudcroft,
505-682-2566, 800-395-6343;
www.thelodgeresort.com

This historic 1899 building is surrounded by 215,000 acres of the Lincoln National Forest and features a challenging golf course, full-service spa and lawn games including croquet, horseshoes and volleyball. Individually appointed rooms are decorated with antiques.

61 rooms. High-speed Internet access. Restaurant, bar. Children's activity center. Spa. Pets accepted. Pool. Golf. Business Center. **$$**

# CLOVIS

A mid-sized city in eastern New Mexico, Clovis calls itself the gateway to the Land of Enchantment.

Information: Chamber of Commerce, 105 E. Grand Ave., 575-763-3435, 800-261-7656; www.clovisnm.org

## WHAT TO SEE AND DO

### Clovis Depot Model Train Museum

221 W. First St., Clovis,
505-762-0066, 888-762-0064;
www.clovisdepot.com

Built in 1907 by the Atchison, Topeka and Santa Fe Railway, the Depot has been restored to its condition in the 1950s era, and features working model train layouts, railroad memorabilia, historical displays and an operating telegraph station. Real train operations along one of the busiest rail lines in the U.S. can be viewed from platform.

### Hillcrest Park and Zoo

Sycamore and 10th, Clovis, 575-769-7873
Second-largest zoo in New Mexico with more than 500 animals, most of which are exhibited in natural environments. Informational programs. Also includes a park with amusement rides, outdoor and indoor swimming pool, golf course, picnic areas and sunken garden.

## SPECIAL EVENTS

### Pioneer Days & PRCA Rodeo

1002 W. McDonald, Clovis,
575-763-3435
Parade, Little Buckaroo Rodeo. First week in June.

## RESTAURANTS

### ★Guadalajara Cafe

916 L Casillas St., Clovis,
505-769-9965
Mexican menu. Lunch, dinner. Closed Sunday. Children's menu. Casual attire. Outdoor seating. $

### ★Leal's Mexican Food

3100 E. Mabry Dr., Clovis,
505-763-4075
Mexican menu. Lunch, dinner. Children's menu. Casual attire. $$

**237**

# CORRALES

Part of the Albuquerque metro area, Corrales grew up as an agricultural center and it's striving to preserve its rural lifestyle in the midst of the area's growth. It is home to Rancho de Corrales, a bar that locals claim is haunted.

Information: 4324 Corrales Rd., 505-897-0502; www.corrales-nm.org

## SPECIALTY LODGINGS

### Chocolate Turtle Bed And Breakfast

1098 W. Meadowlark,
Corrales,
505-898-1800, 877-298-1800;
www.chocolateturtleblo.com

Situated on 1 1/2 acres, guests can relish the beautiful view of the mountains, while enjoying the homemade chocolates and gourmet breakfasts.
4 rooms. Children over 6 years only. Complimentary full breakfast. $

# DEMING

The old Butterfield Trail, route of an early stagecoach line to California, passed about 12 miles north of here; there is a marker on Highway 180. Hunting enthusiasts will find deer, antelope, ibex, bear and blue quail plentiful in the surrounding mountains.

Information: Chamber of Commerce, 800 E. Pine St., 505-546-2674, 800-848-4955; www.cityofdeming.org

## WHAT TO SEE AND DO

### Deming-Luna Mimbres Museum
301 S. Silver St., Deming, 505-546-2382
See mining, military, ranching, railroad, American Indian and Hispanic artifacts of the Southwest. Includes Mimbres pottery, Indian baskets, chuckwagon with equipment, quilt room gems and minerals and more. Musical center; art gallery. Daily.

### Rock hunting
Deming Gem and Mineral Society,
Raymond Reed Blvd.,
Southwestern NM Fair Grounds,
Deming, 505-546-2674
Check out the jasper, onyx, nodules and many other types of semiprecious stones found in the area.

### Rockhound State Park
Hwy. 143, Deming, 575-546-6182;
www.emnrd.state.nm.us/prd/Rockhound.htm
This 1,000-acre park is on the rugged western slope of the Little Florida Mountains and has an abundance of agate, geodes and other semiprecious stones for collectors (limit 15 lbs). Display of polished stones. Hiking, picnicking, playground, camping Daily.

## SPECIAL EVENTS

### Old West Gun Show
Fairgrounds, 800 E. Pine, Deming,
800-848-4955

Western artifacts, jewelry, military equipment, guns, ammunition. Third weekends in Febrauary and August.

### Rockhound Roundup
Fairgrounds, 3115 S. Belen, Deming,
800-848-4955
Guided field trips for agate, geodes, candy rock, marble and honey onyx attract more than 6,000 participants. Auctions; exhibitions; demonstrations. Mid-March.

### Southwestern New Mexico State Fair
Deming, Done Ana country Fairgrounds,
505-524-8602;
www.snmstatefair.com
Livestock shows, midway, parade. Early-mid-October.

## HOTELS

### ★★Holiday Inn
I-10 E., Deming, 505-546-2661,
888-465-4329;
www.holiday-inn.com
120 rooms. Restaurant. Airport transportation available. Pets accepted. Pool. $

## ★ DULCE

This small town is the headquarters of the Jicarilla Apache Reservation. Folks who believe in UFOs and extra terrestrials contend that Dulce houses an underground hub, populated by aliens. Information: 800-477-0149; www.chamavalley.com

## WHAT TO SEE AND DO

### Jicarilla Apache Indian Reservation
Seneca Dr., Dulce, 505-759-3242;
www.jicarillaonline.com
The Jicarilla Apaches came from a group that migrated from southwestern Canada several centuries ago. The reservation is at an elevation of 6,500-8,500 feet and has excellent fishing and boating.

## SPECIAL EVENTS

### Little Beaver Roundup
Dulce, Jicarilla Apache Indian Reservation,
505-759-3242
Parade, rodeo, dances, arts and crafts, carnival, 62-mile pony express race; baseball tournament; archery. Mid-July.

## EL MORRO NATIONAL MONUMENT (INSCRIPTION ROCK)

The towering cliff that served as the guest book of New Mexico is located here on the ancient trail taken by the conquistadores from Santa Fe to Zuni. Don Juan de Oate carved his name here in 1605; scores of other Spaniards and Americans added their names to the cliff at later dates. The rock is pale buff Zuni sandstone. The cliff, 200 feet high, has pueblo ruins on its top and pre-Columbian petroglyphs. Visitor center and museum. Daily. Trail, picnic facilities. Primitive camping). Information: El Morro National Monument, from I-40, 43 miles southwest of Grants off Hwy. 53, 505-783-4226; www.nps.gov/elmo

# ESPAÑOLA

First settled 700 years ago by the Pueblo, then by Don Juan de Oate in 1598, Española was claimed by the United States in 1846. Española is situated between Taos and Santa Fe, Information: Española Valley Chamber of Commerce, 710 Pasco de Onate, 505-753-2831; www.espanolanmchamber.com

## WHAT TO SEE AND DO

### Florence Hawley Ellis Museum of Anthropology
Mile Post 224, Hwy. 84, Española, 505-685-4333, 877-804-4678
Exhibits of American Indian/Spanish history. Memorial Day-Labor Day, Tuesday-Sunday; closed December; rest of year, Tuesday-Saturday.

### Ruth Hall Museum of Paleontology
Mile Post 224, US-84, Española, 505-685-4333, 877-804-4678
Exhibits on Triassic animals, Coelophysis, New Mexico state fossil. Memorial Day-Labor Day, Tuesday-Sunday; rest of year, Tuesday-Saturday.

## SPECIAL EVENTS

### Fiesta del Valle de Española
Española
Celebrates the establishment of New Mexico's first Spanish settlement in 1598. Torch relay, vespers, candlelight procession, street dancing, arts and crafts, food, entertainment, parade. Second week in July.

### Sainte Claire Feast Day
Santa Clara Pueblo, Española, 505-753-7326
Dancing, food, market. Mid-August.

### San Juan Feast Day
Española, San Juan Pueblo, 505-852-4400, 800-793-4955
Dancing, food, carnival. Late June.

### Tri-cultural Arts Festival
Northern New Mexico Community College, 921 Paseo de Onte Rd., Española
Features local artisans and their works, including potters, weavers, woodworkers, photographers, painters, singers and dancers. Usually first weekend in October.

### White Water Race
Española, 800-222-7238
Canoe, kayak and raft experts challenge 14 miles of white water below Pilar. Mother's Day.

## HOTELS

### ★★★Rancho De San Juan Country Inn
Hwy. 285, Española, 505-753-6818; www.ranchodesanjuan.com
Situated between Taos and Santa Fe, this inn offers many tranquil spots in its 225 scenic acres. Designed in the Spanish tradition, the décor is both rustic and refined with wildflower-filled courtyards, exposed

NEW MEXICO

beams, tile floors and Southwestern art and antiques. Rooms features views of the colorful mountain and river-valley. The elegant rooms are adorned with local art and warmed by wood burning fireplaces; the bathrooms have granite countertops and marble showers. The award-winning restaurant is a gem.

17 rooms. Children over 12 years only. Complimentary full breakfast. Restaurant. $$

## RESTAURANTS

★★El Paragua
603 Santa Cruz Rd., Española,
505-753-3211, 800-929-8226;
www.elparagua.com
Southwestern menu. Lunch, dinner. Bar. Children's menu. Casual attire. Reservations recommended. $$

★★★Rancho de San Juan
Hwy. 285, Española, 505-753-6818;
www.ranchodesanjuan.com
The elegant, cheerful dining room of this inn overlooks the Ojo Caliente River Valley and the Jemez Mountains. The tranquil setting is the perfect backdrop for chef/owner John H. Johnson's Southwest-inspired, international cuisine, including such dishes as roast coriander quail and coconut-crusted white shrimp. Each dish on the daily-changing prix fixe menu is artistically prepared and as stunning as the patio sunsets.

International menu. Dinner. Closed Sunday-Monday; also January. Bar. Casual attire. Reservations recommended. Outdoor seating. $$$

# FARMINGTON

The Navajos call it Totah, the meeting place at the convergence of three rivers in the colorful land of the Navajo, Ute, Apache and Pueblo. Once the home of the ancient Anasazi, Farmington is now the largest city in the Four Corners area and supplies much of the energy to the Southwest. From Farmington, visitors may explore Mesa Verde, Chaco Canyon and the Salmon and Aztec ruins. You can enjoy some of the best year-round fishing in the state at Navajo Lake State Park and in the San Juan River. And there are many shops offering traditional American Indian crafts in the immediate area—baskets, jewelry, pottery, rugs and sand paintings. Obtain a list of local art galleries and trading posts at the Convention and Visitors Bureau.

Information: Visitors Burea, 3041 E. Main St., 505-326-7602, 800-448-1240; www.farmingtonnm.org

## WHAT TO SEE AND DO

Bisti Badlands
Hwy. 371, Farmington,
505-599-8900
A federally protected wilderness area of strange geologic formations; large petrified logs and other fossils are scattered among numerous scenic landforms. No vehicles permitted beyond boundary.

Four Corners Monument
Navajo Reservation, Farmington, 64 miles northwest via Hwy. 64, Hwy. 504, Hwy. 160,
928-871-6647
Only point in the country common to four states: Arizona, Colorado, New Mexico and Utah.

## SPECIAL EVENTS

Black River Traders
Lions Wilderness Park Amphitheater,
Pion Hills and College, Farmington,
505-326-7602
Historical drama about the Southwest's multicultural heritage presented in an outdoor amphitheater. Contact Convention and Visitors Bureau for schedule. Mid-June-mid-August.

Connie Mack World Series Baseball Tournament
Ricketts Park, 1101 Fairgrounds Rd., Farmington
Seventeen-game series hosting teams from all over the U.S. and Puerto Rico. August.

### Farmington Invitational Balloon Rally
3041 E. Main, Farmington, 800-448-1240
Hare and hound races; competitions. Memorial Day weekend.

### San Juan County Fair
41 Rd. 5568, Farmington
Parade; rodeo; fiddlers' contest; chili cook-off; exhibits. Mid-late August.

### Totah Festival
200 W. Arrington, Farmington
Fine arts juried show. Rug auction; pow-wow. Labor Day weekend.

## HOTELS
### ★★Best Western Inn & Suites
700 Scott Ave., Farmington, 505-327-5221; www.bestwestern.com
192 rooms. Complimentary full breakfast. Restaurant, bar. Pets accepted. Pool. Business center. $

### ★Comfort Inn
555 Scott Ave., Farmington, 505-325-2626, 800-341-1495; www.comfortinn.com

60 rooms. Complimentary continental breakfast. High-speed Internet access. Pets accepted. Pool. Business center. $

## SPECIALTY LODGINGS
### Casa Blanca
505 E. La Plata St., Farmington, 505-327-6503, 800-550-6503; www.4cornersbandb.com
This mission-style house built in the 1950s features manicured lawns and gardens on a bluff overlooking Farmington and the San Juan River. Rooms have hand-crafted furniture, Navajo rugs and Guatemalan textiles.
4 rooms. Complimentary full breakfast. Airport transportation available. $

## RESTAURANTS
### ★Clancy's Pub
2703 E. 20th St., Farmington, 505-325-8176; www.clancys.net
Mexican, American menu. Lunch, dinner. Bar. Children's menu. Casual attire. Outdoor seating. $

**241**

## GRANTS
More than half of the known domestic reserves of uranium ore are found in this area. About four miles east, I-40 (Hwy. 66) crosses one of the most recent lava flows in the continental United States. Indian pottery has been found under the lava, which first flowed about four million years ago from Mount Taylor to the north. Lava also flowed less than 1,100 years ago from fissures that, today, are near the highway. The lava is sharp and hard; heavy shoes are advisable for walking on it.
Information: Chamber of Commerce, 100 N. Iron St., 505-287-4802, 800-748-2142; www.grants.org

## WHAT TO SEE AND DO
### Casamero Pueblo Ruins
Grants, 505-761-8700
The Chacoan Anasazi between A.D. 1000 and 1125 occupied Casamero Pueblo as a community building that served a number of nearby farmsteads. It was used for social and religious activities aimed at uniting individual families into a cohesive community. Casamero is included on the World Heritage List.

### El Malpais National Monument and National Conservation Area
11000 Ice Cave Rd., Grants, 505-783-4774; www.nps.gov/elma
These two areas total 376,000 acres of volcanic formations and sandstone canyons. Monument features splatter cones and a 17-mile-long system of lava tubes. Conservation area, which surrounds the monument, includes La Ventana Natural Arch, one of the state's largest freestanding natural

arches; Cebolla and West Malpais wildernesses; and numerous Anasazi ruins. The Sandstone Bluffs Overlook, off Hwy. 117, offers an excellent view of the lava-filled valley and surrounding area. Facilities include hiking, bicycling, scenic drives, primitive camping (acquire Backcountry Permit at information center or ranger station). Lava is rough; caution is advised. Most of the lava tubes are accessible only by hiking trails; check with the information center in Grants before attempting any hikes. Monument, conservation area, daily. Information center and visitor facility on Hwy. 117 Daily.

### Ice Cave and Bandera Volcano
Grants, Hwy. 53, 28 miles southwest, 888-423-2283; www.icecaves.com

See example of volcanic activity and hike on lava trails. The ice cave is part of a collapsed lava tube. The temperature never rises above 31° degrees, but reflected sunlight creates beautiful scenery. A historic trading post displays and sells artifacts and American Indian artwork. daily 8 a.m.-one hour before sunset.

### New Mexico Mining Museum
100 N. Iron Ave., Grants, 505-287-4802, 800-748-2142

Only underground uranium mining museum in the world. Indian artifacts and relics; native mineral display. Monday-Saturday.

## HOTELS
### ★★Best Western Inn & Suites
1501 E. Santa Fe Ave., Grants, 505-287-7901, 800-528-1234; www.bestwestern.com

126 rooms. Complimentary full breakfast. High-speed Internet access. Restaurant, bar. **$**

# JEMEZ SPRINGS
Nestled among red rock mesas, the village is named for its hot springs.
Information: www.jemezsprings.org

## WHAT TO SEE AND DO
### Jemez State Monument
18160 State Rd. 4, Jemez Springs, 505-829-3530

Stabilized Spanish mission built in 1621 by Franciscan missionaries next to a prehistoric pueblo. Self-guided bilingual trail. Visitor center has anthropology and archaeology exhibits. Picnicking. Daily.

## SPECIALTY LODGINGS
### Canon Del Rio Riverside Inn
16445 Hwy. 4, Jemez Springs, 505-829-3262; www.canondelrio.com

Located near the village of Jemez Springs, the beauty of this five-acre property is the natural landscaping. The guest rooms all have an Native American tribal name and motif. A fine art gallery is located on the premises.

8 rooms. Closed January. Complimentary full breakfast. Whirlpool. Children 12 and older. **$**

### Jemez Mountain Inn
Hwy. 4, Jemez Springs, 505-829-3926, 888-819-1075; www.jemezmtninn.com

Located within walking distance of local restaurants, sights and attractions, this completely remodeled turn-of-the-20th century inn has six individually decorated rooms.

6 rooms. **$**

# LAS CRUCES

In 1830 a group of people from Taos were traveling on the Spanish highway El Camino Real. They camped here and were massacred by the Apache. They were buried under a field of crosses; hence the name Las Cruces ("the crosses"). Situated in the vast farming area of the fertile lower Rio Grande Valley, this region is especially noted for its homegrown green chiles. There are ghost mining towns, extinct volcanoes, frontier forts, mountains and pecan orchards in the area.

Information: Convention & Visitors Bureau, 211 N. Water St., 575-541-2444, 800-343-7827; www.lascrucescvb.org

## THE WILD WEST

This two- to three-day tour from Las Cruces offers a combination of scenic wonders, hiking and fishing opportunities and a glimpse into the old West. From Las Cruces, head northeast on Hwy. 70 to White Sands National Monument, a seemingly endless expanse of sparkling white gypsum dunes. You'll drive past the dunes along a 16-mile scenic drive, which also provides access to the monument's four hiking trails. Or just take off on foot into the dunes, where kids will have endless hours of fun sliding down the mountains of sand on plastic saucers (available at the monument's gift shop). Visiting the monument is best either early or late in the day, when the dunes display mysterious and often surreal shadows.

Continue northeast on Hwy. 70 to Alamogordo, a good spot to spend the night. Attractions here include the Space Center, where you can test your skills as a pilot in a Space Shuttle simulator, explore the International Space Hall of Fame and visit the Toy Train Depot, which has a fascinating collection of toy trains, some dating from the 1800s. About 12 miles south of Alamogordo via Hwy. 54 is Oliver Lee Memorial State Park, with a short, pleasant nature trail along a shaded stream, plus a rugged hiking trail that climbs up the side of a mountain and offers spectacular views. The park also includes the ruins of a pioneer cabin and a museum that tells the story of the site's violent past.

From Alamogordo, go north on Hwy. 54 to Tularosa, where you can visit Tularosa Vineyards. Then head east on Hwy. 70 up into the Sacramento Mountains to the resort community of Ruidoso, whose name (Spanish for "noisy") comes from the babbling Ruidoso Creek. Surrounded by the Lincoln National Forest, this picturesque town is a good base for hiking. Head east out of Ruidoso Downs to Hondo and then turn back to the northwest on Hwy. 380, which leads to Lincoln. This genuine Wild West town, which is preserved as a state monument, was the site of a jail break by famed outlaw Billy the Kid. Continue west on Hwy. 380 to the town of Capitan for a visit to Smokey Bear Historical State Park, with exhibits and the grave of the orphaned bear cub who was found in a forest fire near here and became a symbol of forest fire prevention. Leaving Capitan, drive west on Hwy. 380 to the town of Carrizozo and cross Hwy. 54. Continue four miles to Valley of Fires National Recreation Site, where a short trail provides close-up views of numerous jet-black lava formations. Return to Carrizozo and head south on Hwy. 54 to the turnoff to Three Rivers Petroglyph Site, one of the best places in the Southwest to see prehistoric rock art. An easy trail meanders along a hillside where there are thousands of images, ranging from geometric patterns to handprints to a variety of animals (some pierced by arrows or spears) created by the Mogollon people at least 1,000 years ago. To return to Las Cruces, take Hwy. 54 south through Tularosa and Alamogordo; turn southwest on Hwy. 70. Approximately 349 miles.

## WHAT TO SEE AND DO

### Branigan Cultural Center
501 N. Main St., Las Cruces, 505-541-2155; www.las-cruces.org
Located at the north end of the Downtown Mall, this complex includes the Las Cruces Museum of Fine Art & Culture and the Bicentennial Log Cabin Museum.

### New Mexico Farm and Ranch Heritage Museum
4100 Dripping Springs Rd., Las Cruces, 505-522-4100; www.frhm.org
Interactive 47-acre museum that brings to life Mexico's 3,000-year history and farming and ranching life. Hands-on exhibits including plowing, blacksmithing and cow-milking. Outdoor animal and plant life. Monday-Saturday 9 a.m.-5 p.m., Sunday noon -5 p.m.

### New Mexico State University
University Ave, Las Cruces, 505-646-0111, 800-662-6678; www.nmsu.edu
Established in 1888; 15,500 students. The 950-acre campus includes a history museum (Tuesday-Sunday), art gallery and an 18-hole public golf course.

### White Sands Missile Range
Las Cruces, 20 miles east on Hwy. 70, 505-678-1134; www.wsmr.army.mil
The range (where missiles are tested) is closed to the public but visitors are welcome at the outdoor missile park and museum. Missile Park daily 8 a.m.-4 p.m.; Museum Monday-Friday 8 a.m.-4:30 p.m.

## SPECIAL EVENTS

### Whole Enchilada Fiesta
Downtown Mall, Main and Las Cruces Streets, Las Cruces, 505-526-1938; www.enchiladafiesta.com
Street dancing, entertainment, parade, crafts, food including world's largest enchilada. Last weekend in September.

## HOTELS

### ★★Best Western Mesilla Valley Inn
901 Avenida De Mesilla, Las Cruces, 505-524-8603, 800-327-3314; www.mesillavalleyinn.com
160 rooms. Restaurant, bar. Pets accepted. Pool. $

### ★Fairfield Inn
2101 Summit Ct, Las Cruces, 505-522-6840; www.fairfieldinn.com

NEW MEXICO

78 rooms. Complimentary continental breakfast. High-speed Internet access. Pool. **$**

### ★★★Meson De Mesilla B&B Inn
1803 Avenida Demesilla, Mesilla,
505-525-9212; www.mesondemesilla.com
This delightful hotel offers a tranquil and romantic setting. Individually decorated rooms feature Southwestern-style antiques and balconies with mountain views. A cocktail lounge features an extensive wine selection and the restaurant offers a fresh, seasonal menu of European-inspired dishes such as rack of lamb, chateaubriand and seared duck breast.
15 rooms. Complimentary full breakfast. Restaurant, bar. Pets accepted. Pool. **$**

### ★★★Hotel Encanto de Las Cruces
705 S. Telshor Blvd., Las Cruces,
575-522-4300; www.sterlinghotels.com
This hotel is minutes from New Mexico State University, Las Cruces International Airport, White Sands Missile Range and Historic Old Mesilla. Activities such as golfing, bowling, horse-back riding and fishing are nearby. All of the guest rooms feature a warm Southwestern style.
203 rooms. High-speed Internet access. Restaurant, bar. Pets accepted. Pool. **$$**

### ★★Ramada Palms de Las Cruces
201 E. University Ave., Las Cruces,
505-526-4411; www.ramada.com
114 rooms. Restaurant, bar. Airport transportation available. Pets accepted. **$**

## SPECIALTY LODGINGS
### Lundeen Inn of the Arts
618 S. Alameda Blvd., Las Cruces,
505-526-3326, 888-526-3326;
www.innofthearts.com
This 100-year old inn includes a pair of two-story guest houses connected by a great room with dark wood floors, a tin ceiling, antique furniture and an impressive art collection.
7 rooms. Complimentary full breakfast. Pets accepted. **$**

## RESTAURANTS
### ★★★Meson de Mesilla
1803 Avenida de Mesilla, Las Cruces,
505-525-9212; www.mesondemesilla.com
This romantic restaurant in an adobe-style bed and breakfast combines continental cuisine with Italian and Southwestern accents for an unusual and delicious menu.
French menu. Dinner. Closed Monday. Bar. Casual attire. Reservations recommended. **$$$**

# LAS VEGAS
Las Vegas was once a stopover on the old Santa Fe Trail. The town prospered as a shipping point and after the arrival of the railroad in 1879 it began an active period of building and rebuilding. There are 918 historic buildings (1846-1938) here as a result. Las Vegas is home to New Mexico Highlands University and Armand Hammer United World College of the American West.
Information: Las Vegas-San Miguel Chamber of Commerce, 701 Grand Ave., 505-425-8631, 800-832-5947; www.lasvegasnewmexico.com

## WHAT TO SEE AND DO
### City of Las Vegas Museum and Rough Riders' Memorial Collection
Municipal Building, 727 Grand Ave.,
Las Vegas, 505-454-1401
See artifacts and memorabilia from Spanish-American War and turn-of-the-century northern New Mexico life. May-October, daily; November-April, Monday-Friday.

### Las Vegas National Wildlife Refuge
Storrie Project, Las Vegas, two miles east via Hwy. 104, then four miles south via Hwy. 281, 505-425-3581
See all kinds of wildlife, including migratory water fowl. Nature trails. Daily; some areas Monday-Friday.

**Storrie Lake State Park**
Las Vegas, four miles north on Hwy. 518,
505-425-7278;
www.emnrd.state.nm.us/PRD/storrielake.htm
Swimming, waterskiing, fishing, boating, windsurfing, picnicking, playground, camping. Daily.

## HOTELS
★Comfort Inn
2500 N. Grand Ave., Las Vegas,
505-425-1100, 877-424-6423;
www.comfortinn.com

101 rooms. Complimentary continental breakfast. Pets accepted. Pool. Business center. $

★★Plaza Hotel
230 Plaza, Las Vegas,
505-425-3591, 800-328-1882;
www.plazahotel-nm.com
36 rooms. Complimentary continental breakfast. High-speed wireless Internet access. Restaurant, bar. Pets accepted. Business center. $

# LINCOLN
This small town, only about 60 miles west of Roswell, was once the home of Billy the Kid.
Information: www.ruidosonow.com

## SPECIALTY LODGINGS
Casa de Patron Bed and Breakfast Inn
Hwy. 380 E., Lincoln,
505-653-4676; www.casapatron.com
This inn, built in 1860, was the home of Juan Patron, the youngest Speaker of the House

in the Territorial Legislature. Legendary figures such as Billy the Kid and Pat Garrett are said to have spent the night here. 7 rooms. Complimentary continental breakfast. $

**246**

# LOS ALAMOS
Nestled on high mesas between the Rio Grande Valley floor and the Jemez Mountain peaks, Los Alamos offers spectacular views and outdoor activities. The city was originally the site of a boys' school. It was acquired by the government in 1942 to develop the first atomic bomb. In 1967, the city property was turned over to Los Alamos County. The scientific laboratory, where research continues, remains a classified installation.
Information: Los Alamos County Chamber of Commerce, 109 Central Park Square,
505-662-8105, 800-444-0707; www.losalamoschamber.com

## WHAT TO SEE AND DO
Bradbury Science Museum
15th St. and Central Ave., Los Alamos,
505-667-4444; www.lanl.gov
Displays artifacts relating to the history of the laboratory and the atomic bomb. Exhibits on modern nuclear weapons, life sciences, materials sciences, computers, particle accelerators, geothermal, fusion and fission energy sources. Daily.

Los Alamos Historical Museum
Fuller Lodge Cultural Center,
1921 Juniper, Los Alamos,
505-662-6272; www.losalamoshistory.org

See artifacts, photos, other material tracing local history from prehistoric to present times; exhibit on the Manhattan Project. Daily.

Fuller Lodge Art Center and Gallery
2132 Central Ave., Los Alamos,
505-662-9331; www.artfulnm.org
A historic log building provides is the setting for changing exhibits featuring arts and crafts of northern New Mexico. Monday-Saturday.

Pajarito Mountain Ski Area
Camp May Rd., Los Alamos, 505-662-5725;
www.skipajarito.com

Despite being a small resort (280 acres), Pajarito offers some excellent and challenging terrain, making it a well-kept secret for local ski buffs. Friday-Sunday, 9 a.m.-4 p.m.; closed Monday-Thursday.

## HOTELS
### ★Best Western Hilltop House Hotel
400 Trinity Dr., Los Alamos,
505-662-2441, 800-462-0936;
www.bestwestern.com

92 rooms. Complimentary full breakfast. High-speed Internet access. Bar. Pets accepted. Pool. $

## SPECIALTY LODGINGS
### Ashley Hotel & Suites
2175 Trinity Dr., Los Alamos,
505-662-7211, 800-745-9910;
www.zshkeyhotelandsuites.com
115 rooms. Complimentary full breakfast. High-speed wireless Internet access. Pets accepted. $

## BANDELIER NATIONAL MONUMENT

A major portion of this 32,000-acre area is designated wilderness. The most accessible part is in Frijoles Canyon, which features cave dwellings carved from the soft volcanic turf and houses built out from the cliffs. There's also a great circular pueblo ruin (Tyuonyi) on the floor of the canyon. These houses and caves were occupied from about AD 1150-1550. The depletion of resources forced the residents to abandon the area. Some of the modern pueblos along the Rio Grande are related to the prehistoric Anasazi people of the canyon and the surrounding mesa country. There is a paved one-mile self-guided trail to walk and view these sites. The monument is named after Adolph Bandelier, ethnologist and author of the novel, *The Delight Makers*, which used Frijoles Canyon as its locale.

There are 70 miles of trails (free permits required for overnight trips; no pets allowed on the trails. Visitor center with exhibits depicting the culture of the pueblo region, ranger-guided tours (summer), campfire programs (Memorial Day-Labor Day). Campground (March-November, daily)

Information: Los Alamos, six miles southwest on Hwy. 502, then six miles southeast on Hwy. 4 to turnoff sign; 505-672-0343; www.nps.gov/band

## RATON
Raton is at the southern foot of famous Raton Pass, on the original Santa Fe Trail (the main road to Denver, now I-25). The road over the pass is a masterpiece of engineering and the view from several points is magnificent.
Information: Chamber & Economic Development Council, 100 Clayton Rd., 505-445-3689, 800-638-6161; www.raton.info

## WHAT TO SEE AND DO
### Sugarite Canyon State Park
Sugarite Canyon, Raton, 575-445-5607;
www.emnrd.state.nm.us/PRD/sugarite.htm
This park contains 3,500 acres on the New Mexico side and offers fishing, ice fishing, boating (oars or electric motors only) and tubing; cross-country skiing, ice skating, riding trails (no rentals); picnicking, camping. Visitor center.

May-September, daily; rest of year by appointment.

## HOTELS
### ★★Best Western Sands
300 Clayton Rd., Raton,
505-445-2737, 800-518-2581;
www.bestwestern.com
50 rooms. Restaurant. Pets accepted. Pool. $

# RED RIVER

This was a gold mining boom town with a population of 3,000 in the early days of the twentieth century. Today it is a summer vacation and winter ski center. Trout fishing, hunting (deer, elk and small game), snowmobiling, horseback riding and backpacking are all popular.

Information: Chamber of Commerce, Main St., 575-754-2366, 800-348-6444; www.redrivernewmex.com

## WHAT TO SEE AND DO

### Red River Ski Area

400 Pioneer Rd., Red River,505-754-2223

Two triple, three double chairlifts, surface tow; patrol, school, rentals; snowmaking. Fifty-seven runs, longest run more than 2 1/2 miles; vertical drop 1,600 feet. Thanksgiving-late March, daily. Chairlift also operates Memorial Day-Labor Day. Daily.

## SPECIAL EVENTS

### Enchanted Circle Century Bike Tour

100 E. Main, Red River

Nearly 1,000 cyclists participate in a 100-mile tour around the Enchanted Circle (Red River, Angel Fire, Taos, Questa). September.

### Mardi Gras in the Mountains

Red River

Ski slope parades, Cajun food. February.

## HOTELS

### ★★Alpine Lodge

417 W. Main, Red River, 575-754-2952, 800-252-2333; www.thealpinelodge.com 45 rooms. Restaurant, bar. **$**

### ★Best Western River's Edge

301 W. River St., Red River, 505-754-1766, 877-600-9990; www.bestwestern.com 30 rooms. Pets accepted. **$**

## RESTAURANTS

### ★★Sundance

401 E. High St., Red River, 505-754-2971; www.rednvernm.com/sundance Mexican menu. Dinner. Closed April-mid-May. Children's menu. **$**

**248**

★
★
★
★
★

# ROSWELL

Did a UFO crash here in 1947? That has been the question for decades. The government maintains that materials recovered were from a top-secret research balloon. UFO proponents believe it was wreckage of an alien spacecraft and that the military has been covering it up. You decide.

Information: Chamber of Commerce, 131 W. Second St., 505-623-5695; www.roswellnm.org

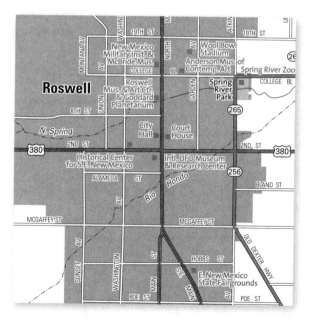

# WHAT TO SEE AND DO

## Bitter Lake National Wildlife Refuge
4065 Bitter Lakes Rd., Roswell,
505-622-6755;
www.fws.gov/southwest/refuges/newmex/
bitterlake
Wildlife observation, auto tour. Daily.

## Bottomless Lakes State Park
Roswell, 10 miles east on Hwy. 380, then
six miles south on Hwy. 409,
575-624-6058;
www.emnrd.state.nm.us/PRD/bottomless.
htm
Bordered by high red bluffs, seven small
lakes were formed when circulating underground water formed caverns that collapsed
into sinkholes. Headquarters at Cottonwood
Lake has displays and a network of trails.
Beach and swimming at Lea Lake only;
some lakes have fishing (trout), paddleboat
rentals; picnicking, camping. Daily.

## Dexter National Fish Hatchery and Technology Center
7116 Hatchery Rd., Roswell,
505-734-5910
This facility is the U.S. Fish and Wildlife
Service's primary center for the study and
culture of endangered fish species of the
American Southwest. Daily. Visitor center
April-October, daily.

## Historical Center for Southeast New Mexico
200 N. Lea, Roswell,
505-622-8333
See turn-of-the-century furnishings, communications exhibits and more; research
library and archives. Daily, afternoons; Friday, by appointment.

## International UFO Museum & Research Center
114 N. Main St., Roswell,
505-625-9495, 800-822-3545;
www.iufomrc.org
Check out the exhibits here on various
aspects of UFO phenomena; video viewing
room. Daily 9 a.m.-5 p.m.

## New Mexico Military Institute
101 W. College Blvd., Roswell,
575-622-6250, 800-421-5376;
www.nmmi.edu
Established in 1891; 1,000 cadets. State-
supported high school and junior college. Alumni Memorial Chapel, near the
entrance, has beautiful windows. Also
here is the General Douglas L. McBride
Military Museum with an interpretation of
20th-century American military history.
Tuesday-Friday. Occasional marching formations and parades. Tours.

## Roswell Museum and Art Center
100 W. 11th St., Roswell, 575-624-6744;
www.roswellmuseum.org
Southwest arts collection including Georgia
O'Keeffe, Peter Hurd, Henriette Wyeth;
Native American, Mexican-American and
western arts. Dr., Robert H. Goddard's
early liquid-fueled rocketry experiments.
Monday-Saturday, also Sunday and holiday
afternoons.

## Spring River Park & Zoo
1306 E. College Blvd., Roswell,
505-624-6760
Zoo and children's zoo area; small lake
with fishing for children 11 and under only;
miniature train; antique wooden-horse carousel. Picnicking, playground. Daily.

# SPECIAL EVENTS

## Eastern New Mexico State Fair and Rodeo
Fair Park, 2500 N. Main St., Roswell,
505-623-9411; www.enmsf.com
The oldest and second largest fair in New
Mexico, with rodeos, carnival, demoli-
tion derby, antique tractor shows and pulls,
motorcross shows and other entertainment.
September-October.

## UFO Encounters Festival
International UFO Museum & Research
Center, 114 Main St., Roswell,
505-625-9495; www.iufomrc.org
UFO Expo trade show, alien chase, alien
parade, costume contest, guest speeches.
July 4 weekend.

**249**

**NEW MEXICO**

## HOTELS

**★★Best Western Sally Port Inn & Suites**
2000 N. Main St., Roswell, 505-622-6430;
www.bestwestern.com
124 rooms. Complimentary continental breakfast. High-speed Internet access. Restaurant, bar. Pool. **$**

**★Ramada**
2803 W. Second St., Roswell,
505-623-9440, 800-272-6232;
www.ramada.com

58 rooms. Complimentary continental breakfast. Pets accepted. Pool. **$**

## RESTAURANTS

**★El Toro Bravo**
102 S. Main St., Roswell, 505-622-9280
Mexican menu. Lunch, dinner. Children's menu. Casual attire. **$**

# RUIDOSO

This resort town in the Sierra Blanca Mountains, surrounded by the trees of the Lincoln National Forests, has seen spectacular growth. It is a year-round resort with skiing in winter and fishing and horseback riding in summer. If you're planning to visit in the summer, secure confirmed reservations before leaving home. The forested mountain slopes and streams are idyllic, the air is clear and cool and there are many interesting things to do.
Information: Ruidoso Valley Chamber of Commerce, 720 Sudderth Dr.,
505-257-7395, 877-784-3676; www.ruidoso.net

## WHAT TO SEE AND DO

**Hubbard Museum of the American West**
841 Hwy. 70 W., Ruidoso Downs,
575-378-4142
Western-themed exhibits relating to horses and pioneer life. Daily.

**Lincoln State Monument**
Ruidoso, 30 miles east on Hwy. 70, then
10 miles northwest on Hwy. 380
Lincoln was the site of the infamous Lincoln County War and a hangout of Billy the Kid. Several properties have been restored, including the Old Lincoln County Courthouse and the mercantile store of John Tunstall. Guided tours (summer, reservations required). Daily

**Old Dowlin Mill**
Sudderth 641, Ruidoso, 505-257-2811
A 20-foot waterwheel still drives a mill more than 100 years old.

**Ski Apache Resort**
Hwy. 532, Ruidoso, 505-464-3600;
www.skiapache.com
Resort has four-passenger gondola; two quad, five triple, one double chairlift; surface lift; patrol, school, rentals. Fifty-five

runs, longest run more than two miles; vertical drop 1,800 feet. Thanksgiving-Easter, daily.

**The Spencer Theater for the Performing Arts**
108 Spencer Rd., Airport Hwy. 220, Alto,
575-336-4800, 888-818-7872;
www.spencertheater.com
This stunning $22 million structure was created from 450 tons of Spanish limestone; breathtaking blown glass installations by Seattle artist Dale Chihuly are inside. Tours Tuesday, Thursday.

## SPECIAL EVENTS

**Aspenfest**
Ruidoso, 505-257-7395, 877-784-3676;
www.ruidosonow.com/aspenfest
Includes motorcycle convention, official state chili cook-off, arts and crafts. Early October.

**Horse racing**
Ruidoso Downs, 1461 Hwy. 70 W.,
505-378-4431;
www.ruidosodownsracing.com
Thoroughbred and quarter horse racing; pari-mutuel betting. Home of All-American Futurity, the world's richest quarter horse

NEW MEXICO

race (Labor Day); All-American Derby and All-American Gold Cup. Thursday-Sunday and holidays. Early May-Labor Day.

### Ruidoso Art Festival

Paradise Canyon Rd. and Sudderth, Ruidoso, 505-257-7395;
www.ruidosonow.com/artfestival
More than 125 artists exhibits displaying painting, drawings, photography, glass, porcelain, woodwork, jewelry, pottery and sculpture. Last full weekend in July.

### Smokey Bear Stampede

8 Fifth St., Ruidoso
Fireworks, music festival, parade, dances, barbecue. Early July.

## HOTELS

### ★Swiss Chalet Inn

1451 Mechem Dr., Ruidoso, 505-258-3333;
www.sciruidoso.com
82 rooms. Complimentary continental breakfast Bar. Pets accepted. Pool. **$**

# SANTA FE

This picturesque city, the oldest capital in the United States, is set at the base of the Sangre de Cristo Mountains. A few miles south, these mountains taper down from a height of 13,000 feet to a rolling plain, marking the end of the North American Rockies. Because of the altitude, the climate is cool and bracing. There's much to do and see here all year.

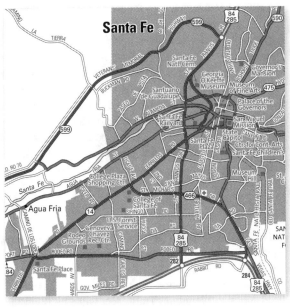

Don Pedro de Peralta, who laid out the plaza and built the Palace of the Governors in 1610, founded Santa Fe. In 1680, the Pueblo revolted and drove the Spanish out. In 1692, led by General Don Diego de Vargas, the Spanish made a peaceful re-entry. Mexico gained its independence from Spain in 1821. The opening of the Santa Fe Trail followed this. In 1846, General Stephen Watts Kearny led U.S. troops into the town without resistance and hoisted the American flag. During the Civil War, Confederate forces occupied the town for two weeks before they were driven out.

In addition to its own attractions, Santa Fe is also the center of a colorful area, which can be reached by car. It is in the midst of the Pueblo country. The Pueblo, farmers for centuries, are also extremely gifted crafts workers and painters. Their pottery, basketry and jewelry are especially beautiful. At various times during the year, especially on the saint's day of their particular pueblo, they present dramatic ceremonial dances. Visitors are usually welcome.
Information: Convention & Visitors Bureau, 505-955-6200, 800-777-2489; www.santafe.org

★ SANTA FE'S PALACE OF THE GOVERNORS, BUILT IN 1610, IS ONE OF THE OLDEST PUBLIC BUILDINGS IN AMERICA.

★ SANTE FE IS THE OLDEST STATE CAPITAL IN THE COUNTRY.

**SPOT★ LIGHT**

# SANTA FE'S ART AND ARCHITECTURE

Every visitor's exploration of Santa Fe begins at the Plaza, plotted when the town was built in 1610. A square block planted with trees and grass, it's a great place to take in the city. Lining the Plaza on the east, south and west are art galleries, Native American jewelry shops, boutiques and restaurants. Facing the Plaza on the north is the Palace of the Governors, the first stop on your walking tour. Sheltered along the porch that spans the front of the block-long, pueblo-style building, you'll find dozens of craft and art vendors from nearby pueblos.

One block west along Palace Avenue, the Museum of Fine Arts was built in 1917 and represents the Pueblo Revival style of architecture, also called Santa Fe style. Continue west on Palace another block, turning north on Grant Avenue one block, then west on Johnson Street one block. Stop inside the relatively new Georgia O'Keeffe Museum to see the world's largest collection of her work.

Next, head to the Catron Building, which forms the east wall of the Plaza. Inside this building are several art galleries and stores. At the building's southern end, anchoring the southeast corner of the Plaza, is La Fonda, the oldest hotel in Santa Fe. The lobby's art is worth a look and the rooftop bar is a favorite gathering place. From the plaza, walk south two blocks on Old Santa Fe Trail to Loretto Chapel. Now walk east on Water Street one block to Cathedral Place, turning left (north) on Cathedral one block to the magnificent St. Francis Cathedral, built over several years in the later 1800s. Directly across the street, see the Institute of American Indian Arts Museum. Back on Palace, Sena Plaza is on the north side of the street. Inside the lovely, flower-filled courtyard, you'll find a 19th-century hacienda filled with art galleries, shops and a restaurant.

## WHAT TO SEE AND DO

### Atalaya Mountain Hiking Trail

St. John's College,
1160 Camino Cruz Blanca, Santa Fe

The Atalaya Mountain Trail, accessible from the parking lot at St. Johns College, is one of the most popular and easily accessible hiking trails in Santa Fe. Hikers have the option of taking the longer route (Trail 174), which is approximately seven miles round-trip, or parking further up near the Ponderosa Ridge development and doing a 4.6-mile loop (Trail 170). Both trails eventually join and take you toward the top of Atalaya Mountain, a 9,121-foot peak. The first few miles of the trail are relatively easy, but it becomes increasingly steep and strenuous as you near the summit, which offers great views of the Rio Grande valley and the city below.

### Canyon Road Tour

Many artists live on this thoroughfare and there is no better way to savor the unique character of Santa Fe than to travel along its narrow, picturesque old streets, which includes the famous Camino del Monte Sol. Stop in the Cristo Rey Church, the largest adobe structure in the U.S., with beautiful ancient stone reredos (altar screens). Monday-Friday.

### Museum of Indian Arts and Culture

710 Camino Lejo, Santa Fe, 505-476-1250;
www.indianartsandculture.org

When the Spanish arrived in the Southwest in the 16th century they found many sprawling towns and villages, which they referred to as pueblos, a name that is still used to identify Indian communities here. The Museum of Indian Arts and Culture houses an extensive collection of historic and contemporary Pueblo art from through-out the Southwest. The highlight is an excellent interpretive section where you can encounter Pueblo cultures from the view-point and narrative of modern-day natives and exhibit designers. The museum itself is housed in a large, adobe-style building that blends architecturally into the surroundings and also houses many outstanding examples of Pueblo textiles, pottery, jewelry, contem-porary paintings and other rotating exhibits. Tuesday-Sunday 10 a.m.-5 p.m.

### Wheelwright Museum
704 Camino Lejo, Santa Fe,
505-982-4636, 800-607-4636;
www.wheelwright.org
Founded in 1937 by Mary Cabot Wheel-wright and Navajo singer/medicine man Hastiin Klah to help preserve Navajo art and traditions, the Wheelwright now devotes itself to hosting major exhibits of Native American artists from tribes throughout North America. The Case Trading Post in the basement sells pottery, jewelry, tex-tiles, books, prints and other gift items. Monday-Saturday 10 a.m.-5 p.m., Sunday 1-5 p.m.

### Cathedral of St. Francis
Santa Fe Plaza, 231 Cathedral Place,
Santa Fe, 505-982-5619
This French Romanesque cathedral was built in 1869 under the direction of Arch-bishop Jean-Baptiste Lamy, the first arch-bishop of Sante Fe (the novel *Death Comes for the Archbishop* is based on his life). Also here is La Conquistadora Chapel, said to be the country's oldest Marian shrine. Daily 8 a.m.-5:45 p.m., except during mass. Tours in summer.

### College of Santa Fe
1600 St., Michael's Dr., Santa Fe,
505-473-6133, 800-456-2673;
www.csf.edu
Established in 1947; 1,400 students. Includes the Greer Garson Theatre Cen-ter, Garson Communications Center and Fogelson Library.

### Cross of the Martyrs
Paseo de la Loma, Santa Fe, 505-983-2567
This large, hilltop cross weighs 76 tons, stands 25 feet tall and honors the memory of more than 20 Franciscan priests and numer-ous Spanish colonists who were killed during the 1680 Pueblo Revolt against Spanish dominion. Dedicated in 1920, this cross shouldn't be confused with the newer one at nearby Fort Marcy Park. Vistas from the old cross include those of the Sangre de Cristos mountain range immediately north-east, the Jemez about 40 miles west and the Sandias, 50 miles south near Albuquerque.

### El Rancho de las Golondrinas
334 Los Pinos Rd., Santa Fe,
505-471-2261; www.golondrinas.org
This living history museum is set in a 200-acre rural valley and depicts Spanish Colo-nial life in New Mexico from 1700-1900. It was once a stop on the Camino Real and is one of the most historic ranches in the South-west. Original colonial buildings date from the 18th century. Special festivals offer visi-tors a glimpse of the music, dance, clothing, crafts and celebrations of Spanish Colonial New Mexico. June-September: Wednesday-Sunday 10 a.m.-4 p.m.

### Federal Court House
Federal Place and Paseo De Peralta,
Santa Fe
A monument to American frontiersman Kit Carson stands in front of the courthouse.

### Georgia O'Keeffe Museum
217 Johnson St., Santa Fe, 505-946-1000;
www.okeeffemuseum.org
One of the most important American art-ists of the 20th century, Georgia O'Keefe lived and worked at Ghost Ranch near Abiqui for much of her career, drawing inspiration from the colors and forms of the surrounding desert environment. This museum houses the world's largest perma-nent collection of her artwork and is also dedicated to the study of American Mod-ernism, displaying special exhibits of many of her contemporaries. November-June:

★
★
★
★
★

Monday-Tuesday, Thursday, Saturday-Sunday 10 a.m.-5 p.m., Friday 10 a.m.-8 p.m.; daily rest of year.

### Hyde Memorial State Park
740 Hyde Park Rd., Santa Fe,
505-983-7175;
www.emnrd.state.nm.us/PRD/Hyde.htm
Perched 8,500 feet up in the Sangre de Cristo Mountains near the Santa Fe Ski Basin, this state park serves as a base camp for backpackers and skiers in the Santa Fe National Forests. Cross-country skiing, rentals, picnicking, camping. Daily.

### Hyde Park hiking/biking trails
Santa Fe, eight miles northeast via Hyde Park Road
One of the closest hiking opportunities to Santa Fe is available in the Hyde Park area on the road to the ski basin. From the Hyde Park parking lot, you can access a loop covering three different trails offering easy hiking that's popular with dog walkers and locals on weekends. The loop consists of switchbacks, moderate grades and creek crossings and has good views of the mixed conifer forest. If you come during the fall, you can view the spectacularly colorful changing of the Aspen leaves. Start with the common trailhead at the far side of the parking lot. Look for the Borrego Trail (150), Bear Wallow Trail (182) and Winsor Trail (254) markings. A loop covering all three is about four miles long.

### Institute of American Indian Arts Museum
108 Cathedral Place, Santa Fe,
505-983-8900; www.iaiancad.org
The Institute of American Indian Arts, established in 1962, runs a college in south Santa Fe in addition to a museum just off the Plaza. The museum is the only one in the country dedicated solely to collecting and exhibiting contemporary Native American art, much of it produced by the staff and faculty of the college. June-September: daily 9 a.m.-5 p.m.; October-May: daily 10 a.m.-5 p.m.

### Kokopelli Rafting Adventures
551 W. Cordova Rd., Santa Fe,
505-983-3734, 800-879-9035;
www.kokopelliraft.com
Kokopelli Rafting offers a full range of whitewater rafting trips to the Rio Grande and Rio Chama rivers, as well as sea kayaking trips to Cochiti and Abiqui lakes and Big Bend National Park in Texas. Excursions include half-day, full-day, overnight and two- to eight-day wilderness expeditions. Transportation from Santa Fe included. April-September.

### Las Cosas School of Cooking
DeVargas Center, 181 Paseo de Peralta,
Santa Fe, 877-229-7184;
www.lascosascooking.com
Located within a beautiful store stocked with gourmet kitchen tools and elegant tableware, this cooking center offers hands-on culinary education experiences that fill a morning or evening. Taught by school director John Vollertsen and chefs from New Mexico's leading restaurants, the classes cover a wide range of topics. Classes usually at 10 a.m. and 6 p.m.

### Lensic Performing Arts Center
211 W. San Francisco St., Santa Fe,
505-988-1234; www.lensic.com
The Lensic Theater is one of Santa Fe's historical and architectural gems, reopened after a full restoration in 2001. The structure was first built in 1931 in a Moorish/Spanish Renaissance style and has always been Santa Fe's premiere theater space, having played host to celebrities such as Roy Rogers and Judy Garland over the years. Since reopening, it has provided a constantly changing schedule of theater, symphony and performing arts events.

### Loretto Chapel
207 Old Santa Fe Trail, Santa Fe,
505-982-0092; www.lorettochapel.com
Modeled after St. Chapelle cathedral in Paris, this chapel built in 1873 was the first Gothic building built west of the Mississippi. The chapel itself is not particularly impressive, but what draws countless tourists is the miraculous

★

★

★

★

★

stairway, a two-story spiral wooden staircase built without any nails or central supports that seems to defy engineering logic. Summer: Monday-Saturday 9 a.m.-6 p.m., Sunday 10:30 a.m.-5 p.m.; winter: Monday-Saturday 9 a.m.-5 p.m., Sunday 10:30 a.m.-5 p.m.

## Museum of Fine Arts
107 W. Palace Ave., Santa Fe,
505-476-5072;
www.museumofnewmexico.org
Designed by Isaac Hamilton Rapp in 1917, the museum is one of Santa Fe's earliest Pueblo revival structures and its oldest art museum. It contains more than 20,000 holdings, with an emphasis on southwest regional art and the artists of Santa Fe and Taos from the early 20th century. The St. Francis Auditorium inside the museum also presents lectures, musical events, plays and various other performances. Free admission on Friday evenings. Tuesday-Sunday 10 a.m.-5 p.m., Friday 5-8 p.m.

## Museum of International Folk Art
706 Camino Lejo, Santa Fe, 505-476-1200;
www.moifa.org
The Museum of International Folk Art, first opened in 1953, contains more than 130,000 objects, billing itself as the world's largest folk museum dedicated to the study of traditional cultural art. Much of the massive collection was acquired when the late Italian immigrant, architect/designer Alexander Girard donated his 106,000-object collection of toys, figurines, figurative ceramics, miniatures and religious/ceremonial art that he had collected from more than 100 countries around the world. This is a rich museum experience and can easily take several hours to explore. Two museum shops offer a wide variety of folk-oriented books, clothing and jewelry to choose from. Tuesday-Sunday 10 a.m.-5 p.m.

## Museum of Spanish Colonial Art
150 Camino Lejo, Santa Fe, 505-982-2226;
www.spanishcolonial.org
This small museum, housed in a building designed in 1930 by famous local architect John Gaw Meem, holds some 3,000 objects showcasing traditional Hispanic art in New Mexico dating from conquest to present day. The collection includes many early works in wood, tin and other local materials, as well as numerous works by contemporary New Mexican artists. The galleries are open Tuesday-Sunday 10 a.m.-5 p.m.

## Oldest House
De Vargas St and Old Santa Fe Trail, Santa Fe
It is believed that Native Americans built this structure more than 800 years ago.

## Palace of the Governors
105 Palace Ave., Santa Fe, 505-476-5100;
www.palaceofthegovernors.org
Built in 1610, this is the oldest public building in continuous use in the U.S. It was the seat of government in New Mexico for more than 300 years. Lew Wallace, governor of the territory (1878-1881), wrote part of *Ben Hur* here in 1880. It is now a major museum of Southwestern history. The Palace, Museum of Fine Arts, Museum of Indian Arts and Culture, Museum of International Folk Art and state monuments all make up the Museum of New Mexico. Free admission Friday evenings. Tours Monday-Saturday 10:15 a.m.-noon. Tuesday-Sunday 10 a.m.-5 p.m., Friday 5-8 p.m.

## Plaza
100 Old Santa Fe Trail, Santa Fe
The Santa Fe Plaza, steeped in a rich history, has been a focal point for commerce and social activities in Santa Fe since the early 17th century. The area is marked by a central tree-lined park surrounded by some of Santa Fe's most important historical landmarks, many of which hail from Spanish colonial times. The most important landmark is the Palace of the Governors. Native American artists from nearby Pueblos sell handmade artwork in front of the Palace and various museums, shops and dining establishments surround the Plaza, making it the top tourist destination in Santa Fe. Numerous festivals and activities are held throughout the year.

**255**

**NEW MEXICO**

★
★
★
★
★
★

### San Ildefonso Pueblo

Santa Fe, 16 miles north on Hwy. 84, 285, then six miles west. on Hwy. 502, 505-455-2273

This pueblo is famous for its beautiful surroundings and its black, red and polychrome pottery made famous by Maria Poveka Martinez. Daily; closed winter weekends; visitors must register at the visitor center. Various festivals take place here throughout the year. The circular structure with the staircase leading up to its rim is a *kiva*, or ceremonial chamber. There are two shops in the pueblo plaza and a tribal museum adjoins the governor's office.

### San Miguel Mission

401 Old Santa Fe Trail, Santa Fe, 505-983-3974

Built in the early 1600s, this is the oldest church in the U.S. still in use. Construction was overseen by Fray Alonso de Benavidez, along with a group of Tlaxcala Indians from Mexico who did most of the work. The original adobe still remains beneath the stucco walls and the interior has been restored along with Santa Fe's oldest wooden reredos (altar screen). Church services are still held on Sundays. Sunday 1-4:30 p.m.; summer: Monday-Saturday 9 a.m.-4:30 p.m.; winter: Monday-Saturday 10 a.m.-4 p.m.

### Santa Fe Children's Museum

1050 Old Pecos Trail, Santa Fe, 505-989-8359; www.santafechildrensmuseum.org

The hands-on exhibits invite kids to make magnetic structures, route water streams, create paintings, illustrate cartoon movies, discover plants on a greenhouse scavenger hunt, scale an 18-foot-high climbing wall, use an old-fashioned pitcher pump and weave beads and fabric on a loom. Local artists and scientists make appearances. Wednesday-Saturday 10 a.m.-5 p.m., Sunday noon-5 p.m.

### Santa Fe National Forest

1474 Rodeo Rd., Santa Fe, 505-438-7840; www.fs.fed.us/r3/sfe

This forest covers more than 1.5 million acres. Fishing is excellent in the Pecos and Jemez rivers and tributary streams and hiking trails are close to unusual geologic formations. You'll find hot springs in the Jemez Mountains. Four wilderness areas within the forest total more than 300,000 acres. Campgrounds are provided by the Forest Service at more than 40 locations.

### Santa Fe Fashion Outlets

8380 Cerrillos Rd., Santa Fe, 505-474-4000

This is New Mexico's only outlet center. More than 40 stores include Bose, Brooks Brothers and more. Daily

### Santa Fe Rafting Company

1000 Cerrillos Rd., Santa Fe, 505-988-4914, 888-988-4914; www.santaferafting.com

The Rio Grande and Rio Chama rivers north of Santa Fe provide excellent opportunities for river running and white water rafting. Santa Fe Rafting Company offers several rafting trips including half-day, full-day and multi-day camping excursions, some of which include a boxed lunch. The biggest rapids are found on their Taos Box full-day trip, open to anyone over age 12. All trips include roundtrip transportation from Santa Fe. April-September.

### Santa Fe School of Cooking

116 W. San Francisco St., Santa Fe, 505-983-4511, 800-982-4688; www.santafeschoolofcooking.com

Sign up for classes offered several times weekly in traditional and contemporary Southwestern cuisine. Culinary tours involve classes with nationally renowned chefs with trips to local farms and wineries.

### Santa Fe Southern Railway

410 S. Guadalupe St., Santa Fe, 505-989-8600, 888-989-8600; www.sfsr.com

Several scenic train rides in restored vintage cars are offered to the public, following the original high desert route to and from Lamy. The rides range from short scenic roundtrips to longer outings that include picnics, barbecues and various holiday-themed events, such as the Halloween Highball Train and New Years Eve Party Train. The start of the route is housed in the old Santa Fe Depot, where you can view vintage railcars and shop for gifts and memorabilia in the original mission-style train depot.

### Santa Fe Trail Museum
614 Maxwell Ave., Springer,
505-483-2682
The Santa Fe Trail Museum displays artifacts and exhibits about pioneer life on and around the trail from 1880-1949. Open daily 9 a.m.-4 p.m., summer only.

### Santuario de Guadalupe
100 Guadalupe St., Santa Fe,
505-988-2027
Built in 1781, the oldest shrine in America dedicated to Our Lady of Guadalupe has been converted into an art and history museum specializing in religious art and iconography. The holdings include a large collection of Northern New Mexican santos (carved wooden saints) and paintings in the Italian Renaissance and Mexican baroque styles. A famous rendering of Our Lady of Guadalupe by renowned Mexican artist Jose de Alzibar is also on display. November-April: Monday-Friday 9 a.m.-4 p.m.; May-October: Monday-Saturday 9 a.m.-4 p.m.

### Sena Plaza and Prince Plaza
Washington and E. Palace Avenues,
Santa Fe
Both plazas include small shops and old houses, built behind portals and around central patios.

### Shidoni Bronze Foundry and Gallery
1508 Bishop's Lodge Rd., Santa Fe,
505-988-8001; www.shidoni.com
A fantastic resource for art collectors and sculptors, Shidoni consists of a bronze foundry, art gallery and outdoor sculpture garden set in an eight-acre apple orchard. Artists from around the country come to work at Shidoni's 14,000-square-foot foundry, open to the general public for self-guided tours. Explore the lovely sculpture garden during daylight hours or shop for works of bronze and metal in the adjacent gallery. Gallery Monday-Saturday 9 a.m.-5 p.m. Foundry Monday-Friday noon-1 p.m., Saturday 9 a.m.-5 p.m.

### Shona Sol Sculpture Garden
Turquoise Trail, Hwy. 14,
Santa Fe, 505-473-5611
See exhibits of some of the world's finest stone sculptors, whose work is also shown around the world. Open weekends 10 a.m.-6 p.m.

### Ski Santa Fe
2209 Brothers Rd., Santa Fe,
505-982-4429; www.skisantafe.com
World-class skiing and snowboarding in the majestic Sangre de Cristo Mountains is only a 20-minute drive from the downtown Santa Fe Plaza. Ski Santa Fe is a family-owned resort catering to skiers and snowboarders of all levels. In addition to great views of the city, the 12,075-foot summit offers six lifts and 67 runs (20 percent easy, 40 percent more difficult, 40 percent most difficult), with a total of 660 acres of terrain. The longest run is three miles and the mountain offers a vertical drop of 1,725 feet. The average yearly snowfall is 225 inches. A PSIA-certified ski school offers group and private lessons for adults and children and there are restaurants, rental shops and a clothing boutique on site. The Chipmunk Corner offers activities and lessons for children ages 4-9. Late November-early April, daily.

### State Capitol
Old Santa Fe Trail at Paseo de Peralta,
Santa Fe, 505-986-4589
This round building, in modified Territorial style, is intended to resemble a Zia Sunday symbol. Mid-May-August: Monday-Saturday 8 a.m.-7 p.m.; September-mid-May: Monday-Friday 8 a.m.-7 p.m.

**257**

**NEW MEXICO**

### Ten Thousand Waves
3451, Hyde Park Rd., Santa Fe,
505-982-9304;
www.tenthousandwaves.com

This exquisite Japanese-themed spa and bathhouse is a genuine treat. Located in a unique Zen-like setting in the Sangre de Cristo Mountains, Ten Thousand Waves offers soothing hot tubs, massages, facials, herbal wraps and other spa treatments. Includes coed public hot tubs (where clothing is optional before 8:15 p.m.), a women-only tub, secluded private tubs and large private tubs that can accommodate up to 20. All the tubs are clean and chlorine-free and amenities such as kimonos, towels, sandals, lotion and lockers provided for you. Be sure to call ahead for reservations, especially for massage services. Daily.

### Turquoise Trail
South from Santa Fe on I-25, Hwy. 14
south toward Madrid;
www.turquoisetrail.org

Undeniably the most interesting path between Albuquerque and Santa Fe, this poetically named route is the 50-mile reach of New Mexico 14 that parallels I-25 north from I-40, and is a National Scenic Byway. Cutting a course along the backside of the Sandias just north of Albuquerque, the trail winds through a rolling countryside of sumptuous, cactus-lined hills populated by tiny burgs. Along the way, watch for crumbling rock houses, ancient family cemeteries and long-abandoned ranch houses and barns. Stops include the town of Golden, where the first discovery of gold west of the Mississippi was made and where a silver boom once employed more than 1,200 workers and Madrid (pronounced MAD-rid), once rich in coal mines but today the refuge of artists whose galleries and shops have become lucrative businesses. The wonderful Mine Shaft Tavern offers burgers, buffalo steaks and cold beer, along with live entertainment on weekends.

## SPECIAL EVENTS
### Christmas Eve Canyon Road Walk
Santa Fe Plaza, Canyon Rd.,
Santa Fe, 800-777-2489

This major Santa Fe tradition is not to be missed. Adorned with thousands of *farolitos* (paper bag lanterns), the streets and homes around Canyon Road play host to a unique and colorful festival each Christmas Eve. Thousands of pedestrians stroll up and down the streets while singing Christmas carols, lighting bonfires and enjoying hot apple cider. December 24.

### Eight Northern Pueblos Arts & Crafts Show
San Juan Pueblo, Santa Fe, 505-747-1593;
www.eightnorthernpueblos.com

This annual festival features traditional and contemporary American Indian art at more than 500 booths. Approximately 1,500 artists attend and have their work judged for prizes before being displayed for sale. Third weekend in July.

### Fiesta at Santo Domingo Pueblo
Santo Domingo Pueblo, Santa Fe,
505-465-2214

This is probably the largest and most famous of the Rio Grande pueblo fiestas. Includes a corn dance. Early August.

### Indian Market
Santa Fe Plaza, Santa Fe, 505-983-5220;
www.swaia.org/indianmrkt.html

Buyers and collectors from all over the world come to the largest and oldest American Indian arts show and market in the world. More than 1,200 artists from 100 North American tribes participate in the show, with around 600 outdoor booths set up in the middle of the ancient Santa Fe Plaza. The market is a great opportunity to meet the artists and buy directly. Numerous outdoor booths sell food. The event draws an estimated 100,000 visitors to Santa Fe during the weekend. Late August.

### International Folk Art Market
Milner Plaza, Camino Lejo, Santa Fe,
505-476-1189; www.folkartmarket.org

**258**

NEW MEXICO

This new two-day event brings together 75 master folk artists from Bangladesh to Zimbabwe in a celebration of color, music and cuisine. Includes everything from textiles to woodblock prints to ceramics and sculptures. In addition to shopping for works to take home, visitors can attend demonstrations and lectures, tour local folk art collections, bid on works at an auction and participate in children's activities. Mid-July.

### Invitational Antique Indian Art Show
Sweeney Center, 201 W. Marcy,
Santa Fe
This large show attracts dealers, collectors and museum curators. Includes pre-1935 items. Two days in mid-August.

### Mountain Man Rendezvous and Festival
105 W. Palace Ave., Santa Fe,
505-955-6200
Costumed mountain men ride into town on horseback for the Museum of New Mexico's annual buffalo roast, part of a large gathering of trappers and traders from the pre-1840 wilderness. Participants sell primitive equipment, tools and trinkets and compete in period survival skills such as knife and tomahawk throwing, muzzleloader rifle shooting and cannon firing. Early August.

### Santa Fe Chamber Music Festival
St. Francis Auditorium,
Museum of Fine Arts and the Lensic
Performing Arts Center, Santa Fe,
505-983-2075, 888-221-9836;
www.sfcmf.org
Since the first season of the festival in 1973, this artistic tradition has grown into a major event consisting of more than 80 performances, open rehearsals, concert previews and roundtable discussions with composers and musicians during the annual summer season. Performances are frequently heard on National Public Radio. July-August.

### Santa Fe Fiesta
Santa Fe Plaza, Santa Fe,
505-988-7575

This ancient folk festival dating back to 1712 features historical pageantry, religious observances, arts and crafts shows and street dancing. It also celebrates the reconquest of Santa Fe by Don Diego de Vargas in 1692. First weekend in September.

### Santa Fe Opera
Hwys. 84/285, Santa Fe,
505-986-5900, 800-280-4654;
www.santafeopera.org
Founded in 1957, this opera company presents one of the world's most famous and respected opera festivals each summer. The company stages five works per season, including two classics, a lesser-known work by a well-known composer, a Richard Strauss offering and a world premiere or new American staging. What's more, the Santa Fe Opera performs in a gorgeous hilltop amphitheater. Designed by Polshek & Partners of New York, who refurbished Carnegie Hall in Manhattan, the Opera incorporates bold, swooping lines with excellent sight lines and is known for superb acoustics. Backstage tours early July-late August: Monday-Saturday at 1 p.m. Performances begin between 8 p.m. and 9 p.m.

### Santa Fe Pro Musica
Lensic Performing Arts Center,
211 W. San Francisco St., Santa Fe,
505-988-4640, 800-960-6680;
www.santafepromusica.com
This chamber orchestra and ensemble performs classical and contemporary music. A performance of *Messiah* takes place during Christmas season. Mozart Festival in Febrauary. September-May.

### Rodeo de Santa Fe
Santa Fe Rodeo Grounds,
2801 W. Rodeo Rd., Santa Fe,
505-471-4300; www.rodeodesantafe.org
The Santa Fe Rodeo offers the chance to see real cowboys and bucking broncos in action. Various professional competitions and public exhibitions are put on during the brief summer season. Rodeo events generally happen during evening and weekend matinee hours.

A downtown rodeo parade takes place in mid-June at the start of the season.

### Santa Fe Stages
Lensic Performing Arts Center, Santa Fe, 505-982-6680; www.santafestages.org
With presentations offered primarily at the wonderfully renovated, historic Lensic Performing Arts Center, Santa Fe Stages hosts a season of dance, music and theater with national appeal. The season typically begins before Memorial Day and ends in late September and may offer Irish folk dance, classical ballet, opera, jazz, drama, comedy and cabaret shows. Late May-late September.

### Santa Fe Symphony and Chorus
Lensic Performing Arts Center, 211 W. San Francisco St., Santa Fe, 505-983-1414, 800-480-1319; www.sf-symphony.org
Santa Fe's orchestral company presents works in classical and jazz music, as well as specialty programs that may include the music of Spain and Mexico. The season generally runs from early October through Memorial Day, with matinée and evening performances at the Lensic Performing Arts Center. Early October-late May.

### Santa Fe Wine and Chile Fiesta
551 W. Cordova Rd., Santa Fe, 505-438-8060; www.santafewineandchile.org
Begun in 1991, this wildly popular festival honoring the best in food and drink brings in some 2,000 appreciative fans from around the state and across the country. Roughly 30 local restaurants and 90 wineries from around the globe team up with a half-dozen or so of America's top celebrity chefs and cookbook authors to present a culinary extravaganza in a variety of venues around town. Includes wine seminars, cooking demonstrations, special vintners lunches and dinners and the gastronomic circus called the Grand Tasting, staged in mammoth tents on the Santa Fe Opera grounds. Late September.

### Spanish Market
Museum of Spanish Colonial Art, 750 Camino Lejo, Santa Fe, 505-982-2226; www.spanishmarket.org
The rich and colorful Hispanic art traditions of Northern New Mexico are celebrated twice a year during Spanish Market, the oldest and largest exhibition and sale of traditional Hispanic art in the U.S. The smaller winter market in December is held indoors in the Sweeney Convention Center (201 W. Marcy St), while the larger summer market occupies the entire Santa Fe Plaza for one weekend in July. As many as 300 vendors sell and display santos (carved saints), hide paintings, textiles, furniture, jewelry, tinwork, basketry, pottery, bonework and other locally produced handicrafts reflecting the unique and deeply religious traditional art that still flourishes in this part of New Mexico. Sponsored by the Spanish Colonial Arts Society. December and late July.

### Spring Corn Dances
Santa Fe, Cochiti, San Felipe, Santo Domingo and other pueblos, 505-843-7270
Races, contests. Late May-early June.

### St. Anthony's Feast-Comanche Dance
San Clara Pueblo, Santa Fe, 505-843-7270
Mid-June.

### Tesuque Pueblo Flea Market
Hwy. 84/285, Santa Fe, 505-995-7767; www.tesuquepueblofleamarket.com
You'll find hundreds of vendors offering antiques, gems, jewelry, pottery, rugs and folk art, all at very competitive prices, at this flea market. Plan on devoting a couple of hours to browse all the various treasures and myriad of vendor booths stretching for several acres.

### Zozobra Festival
Fort Marcy Park, 490 Washington Ave., Santa Fe, 87501; www.zozobra.com

260

NEW MEXICO

Each year on the Thursday before Labor Day, the Kiwanis Club of Santa Fe hosts the burning of Zozobra, a 50-foot effigy of Old Man Gloom, whose passing is designed to dispel the hardships and travails of the previous year. Zozobra started in 1924 as part of the Fiesta's celebration when a local artist conceived a ritual based on a Yaqui Indian celebration from Mexico. Over the years, Zozobra caught on and the crowd sizes have grown, making it Santa Fe's largest and most colorful festival. Lasting for several hours, as many as 60,000 visitors crowd into a large grassy field in Fort Marcy Park to listen to live bands, watch spectacular fireworks displays and cheer the ritual burning. The celebration continues through the Labor Day weekend with booths and activities set up in the nearby plaza. Thursday before Labor Day.

# HOTELS

### ★★★Bishop's Lodge
1297 Bishop's Lodge Rd., Santa Fe,
505-983-6377, 800-419-0492;
www.bishopslodge.com
This lodge is a Santa Fe treasure. The historic resort dates back to 1918 and its beloved chapel, listed on the National Register of Historic Places, remains a popular site for weddings. This resort is vintage chic, with rooms decorated either in an old Sante Fe style or with more modern décor. The Sha-Nah spa is influenced by Native American traditions—each treatment begins with a soothing drumming and blessing. Modern American cuisine is the focus at the lodge's restaurant.
88 rooms. Restaurant, bar. Children's activity center. Spa. Pets accepted. Tennis. **$$$**

### ★Comfort Inn Santa Fe
4312 Cerrillos Rd., Santa Fe,
505-474-7330, 877-424-6423;
www.comfortinn.com
83 rooms. Complimentary continental breakfast. High-speed wireless Internet access. Pets accepted. Pool. **$**

### ★★★Eldorado Hotel
309 W. San Francisco St., Santa Fe,
505-988-4455, 800-955-4455;
www.eldoradohotel.com
The Pueblo Revival-style building is one of Santa Fe's largest and most important landmarks. Its lobby and interiors are lavishly decorated with an extensive collection of original Southwest art. Rooms have private balconies and kiva fireplaces. The lobby lounge is a great spot for snacking, people watching and enjoying live entertainment. Sunday brunch is a local favorite.
219 rooms. High-speed Internet access. Two restaurants, bar. Pets accepted. Pool. Business center. **$$$**

### ★★Galisteo Inn
9 La Vega, Galisteo, 866-404-8200;
www.galisteoinn.com
11 rooms. Children over 10 years only. Complimentary continental breakfast. Restaurant, bar. Pool. **$$**

### ★★★Hilton Santa Fe
100 Sandoval St., Santa Fe,
505-986-2811, 800-336-3676;
www.hiltonofsantafe.com
Located just two blocks from the historic Plaza, this hotel is in a 380-year-old family estate, and takes up an entire city block. The hotel has the city's largest pool. Guest rooms feature locally hand-crafted furnishings.
157 rooms. Three restaurants, bar. Airport transportation available. Pets accepted. **$$**

### ★★Hotel Plaza Real
125 Washington Ave., Santa Fe,
505-988-4900, 877-901-7666;
www.sterlinghotels.com
56 rooms. Restaurant, bar. Pets accepted. **$$**

### ★★Hotel Santa Fe
1501 Paseo De Peralta, Santa Fe,
800-825-9876; www.hotelsantafe.com
129 rooms. Restaurant, bar. Airport transportation available. Pets accepted. Pool. **$$**

**261**

## ★★Hotel St. Francis

210 Don Gaspar Ave., Santa Fe,
505-983-5700, 800-529-5700;
www.hotelstfrancis.com
82 rooms. Restaurant, two bars. **$$**

## ★★★Hyatt Regency Tamaya Resort and Spa

1300 Tamaya Trail, Santa Ana Peublo,
505-867-1234, 800-554-9288;
www.tamaya.hyatt.com
Located on 500 acres of unspoiled desert, the Hyatt Regency Tamaya Resort & Spa has striking views of the Sandia Mountains. The property blends right in with its Pueblo-style buildings and open-air courtyards and includes punches of turquoise and bright oranges throughout the public and private spaces. Golf, tennis and hot air ballooning are among the activities available at this family-friendly resort, where programs for kids are available. The restaurants are a showcase of Southwestern flavors, offering sophisticated takes on local favorites.
350 rooms. High-speed Internet access. Five restaurants, two bars. Children's activity center. Spa. Airport transportation available. Pets accepted. **$$**

## ★★★Inn And Spa at Loretto

211 Old Santa Fe Trail, Santa Fe,
505-988-5531, 800-727-5531;
www.hotelloretto.com
Built in 1975, this boutique hotel, which rests at the end of the Sante Fe Trail, is a re-creation of an ancient adobe. Rooms feature a charming Southwestern motif with hand-carved furniture and Native American art. The property includes a heated pool and 12 specialty stores, including many art galleries.
135 rooms. Restaurant, bar. Spa. Fitness room. Pool. **$$**

## ★★★★Inn of the Anasazi

113 Washington Ave., Santa Fe,
505-988-3030;
www.innoftheanasazi.com
Located just off the historic Plaza, the inn was designed to resemble the traditional dwellings of the Anasazi. Enormous hand-crafted doors open to a world of authentic artwork, carvings and textiles synonymous with the Southwest. The lobby sets a sense of place for arriving guests with its rough-hewn tables, leather furnishings, unique objects and huge cactus plants in terra-cotta pots. The region's integrity is maintained in the guest rooms, where fireplaces and four-poster beds rest under ceilings of vigas and latillas and bathrooms are stocked with toiletries made locally with native cedar extract. The restaurant earns praise for honoring the areas culinary heritage.
57 rooms. Restaurant, bar. Pets accepted. Fitness room. **$$$**

## ★★★Inn of the Governors

101 W. Alameda, Santa Fe,
800-234-4534;
www.innofthegovernors.com
Discerning travelers know this inn as one of Santa Fe's best. First-rate service and amenities are the draw, and guests are treated to a complimentary full breakfast each morning, a friendly and helpful concierge and a heated outdoor pool with poolside service. Rooms are decorated Southwestern style and feature handcrafted furniture, Spanish artwork, fireplaces and French doors that open to a patio. Amenities include wireless Internet, feather pillows, down comforters and plush towels and robes. The rustic Del Charro Saloon, a popular gathering place for locals and tourists alike, offers cocktails and a full bar menu, including what many say are the best burgers in town.
100 rooms. Complimentary full breakfast. Restaurant, bar. Pool. **$$**

## ★★★La Posada De Santa Fe

330 E. Palace Ave., Santa Fe,
505-986-0000, 866-331-7625;
www.rockresorts.com
Nestled on six lush acres, La Posada effortlessly blends past and present. The original Staab House, dating to 1870, is the focal point of the resort. The lovely rooms and suites are scattered throughout the gardens in a village setting. Rich

★

★

★

★

★

colors mix with Spanish colonial and old-world style and every amenity has been added. The fantastic Avanyu Spa features Native American-themed treatments using local ingredients. Fuego Restaurant is a standout for its innovative food with Spanish and Mexican inflections, while the historic Staab House is an inviting setting for American classics.
157 rooms. Restaurant, bar. Spa. Fitness room. Pool. **$$$**

### ★La Quinta Inn
4298 Cerrillos Road, Santa Fe,
505-471-1142; www.laquinta.com
130 rooms. Complimentary continental breakfast. Pets accepted. Pool. **$**

### ★★★Sunrise Springs
242 Los Pinos Rd., Santa Fe,
505-471-3600, 800-955-0028;
www.sunrisesprings.com
Get your chakras in order at Santa Fe's Zen-chic Sunrise Springs. This eco-conscious resort proves that it's easy being green with biodynamic gardens, organic produce and locally harvested spa products. It's all about peace and tranquility at this 70-acre property, where trickling ponds provide background music for meditation and yoga. Sunrise Springs takes its cues from the East for its activity menu, offering tai chi, Raku ceramics and yoga, as well as traditional tea ceremonies in its authentic Japanese tea house, but the guestrooms and casitas are definitively Southwestern. The spa, the centerpiece of the resort, blends ancient traditions with native therapies in its treatments.
56 rooms. Spa. Restaurant. **$$**

## SPECIALTY LODGINGS

### Adobe Abode
202 Chapelle St., Santa Fe, 505-983-3133;
www.adobeabode.com
Built in 1905 as officer quarters for Fort Marcy, this property offers guests a unique stay in one of the finely decorated rooms. Visitors will enjoy the complimentary sherry and Santa Fe cookies in the afternoon.
6 rooms. Complimentary full breakfast. **$**

### Casa Pueblo Inn
138 Park Ave., Santa Fe,
505-986-9610, 800-955-4455;
www.casapueblo.com
32 rooms. Complimentary continental breakfast. Pets accepted. **$$**

### Dancing Ground of the Sun
711 Paseo De Peralta, Santa Fe,
505-986-9797, 800-745-9910;
www.dancingground.com
21 rooms. Complimentary continental breakfast. Pets accepted. **$$**

### El Farolito Bed & Breakfast
514 Galisteo St., Santa Fe,
505-988-1631, 888-634-8782;
www.farolito.com
8 rooms. **$$**

### El Rey Inn
1862 Cerrillos Rd., Santa Fe,
505-982-1931, 800-521-1349;
www.elreyinnsantafe.com
About two miles from downtown, this adobe-style inn (1936) is well kept, with a cozy atmosphere and friendly staff.
86 rooms. Complimentary continental breakfast. Swim. **$**

### Guadalupe Inn
604 Agua Fria St., Santa Fe, 505-989-7422;
www.guadalupeinn.com
This is a quiet inn offering rooms with unique décor. Local artists display their work in the rooms and many pieces are for sale.
12 rooms. Complimentary full breakfast. **$**

### Inn of the Turquoise Bear
342 E. Buena Vista, Santa Fe,
505-983-0798, 800-396-4104;
www.turquoisebear.com
10 rooms. Complimentary continental breakfast. Pets accepted. **$$$**

### Inn on the Alameda
303 E. Alameda, Santa Fe,
505-984-2121, 888-984-2121;
www.inn-alameda.com
Tucked unassumingly behind adobe walls near the start of Canyon Road, this inn

**NEW MEXICO**

offers all the comforts of a luxury hotel, but has the quiet elegance of a smaller bed and breakfast with lovely gardens and sheltered courtyards.

69 rooms. Complimentary continental breakfast. Bar. Two whirlpools. Pets accepted. **$$**

### Inn on the Paseo

630 Paseo de Peralta, Santa Fe,
505-984-8200, 800-457-9045;
www.innonthepaseo.com

Located on the Paseo de Peralta in the heart of downtown Santa Fe, this recently renovated inn offers a relaxing Southwest experience. Guest rooms feature down comforters, patchwork quilts and private baths. The breakfast buffet is served on the Sunday deck.

18 rooms. Complimentary full breakfast. **$**

### Water Street Inn

427 W. Water St., Santa Fe,
505-984-1193, 800-646-6752;
www.waterstreetinn.com

Located just two blocks from Santa Fe's historic Plaza, this inn features Southwestern décor with art and photography lining its walls. Spacious brick-floored guest rooms have private baths, cable TV with VCRs and decks/patios. The courtyard offers a sundeck with great views.

12 rooms. Complimentary continental breakfast. Whirlpool. Pets accepted. **$$**

★ # RESTAURANTS

### ★★Amaya at Hotel Santa Fe

1501 Paseo de Peralta, Santa Fe,
800-825-9876; www.hotelsantafe.com

Southwestern menu. Breakfast, lunch, dinner. Bar. Children's menu. Casual attire. Outdoor seating. **$$$**

### ★★★The Anasazi

113 Washington Ave., Santa Fe,
505-988-3236; www.innoftheanasazi.com

The creators of the memorable cuisine at this Plaza mainstay like to point out that the Navajo definition of Anasazi has come to embody an ancient wisdom that is "synonymous with the art of living

harmoniously and peacefully with our environment." That philosophy is translated in the petroglyph-inspired art on the walls of this dining favorite. Executive chef Tom Kerpon devotes himself to inventive uses of locally grown, organic products in dishes such as grilled basil-marinated opah with green chile risotto, buffalo osso bucco and grilled corn, tortilla and lime soup.

Southwestern menu. Breakfast, lunch, dinner, Sunday brunch. Bar. Children's menu. Casual attire. Valet parking. **$$$**

### ★★Andiamo

322 Garfield, Santa Fe, 505-995-9595;
www.andiamoonline.com

Italian menu. Dinner. Children's menu. Casual attire. Outdoor seating. **$$**

### ★★★Blue Heron

242 Los Pinos Rd., Santa Fe,
505-471-3600, 800-955-0028;
www.sunrisesprings.com

Housed at the unique, eco-friendly Sunrise Springs resort, this restaurant is equally green, serving only fresh, organic ingredients, many of them picked daily in the onsite gardens. Dishes are straightforward and delicious, from the grilled basil salmon with brown rice to the chile-rubbed filet mignon with goat cheese chile rileno. The wine list features organic wines and fine sakes.

Southwestern menu. Brunch, lunch, dinner. **$$**

### ★Blue Corn Cafe

133 Water St., Santa Fe, 505-984-1800;
www.bluecorncafe.com

Southwestern menu. Lunch, dinner. Bar. Children's menu. Casual attire. Outdoor seating. **$$**

### ★★Cafe Paris

31 Burro Alley, Santa Fe, 505-986-1688;
www.cafeparisnm.com

French menu. Breakfast, lunch, dinner. Closed Monday. Casual attire. Reservations recommended. Outdoor seating. **$$**

### ★★Cafe Pasqual's
121 Don Gaspar, Santa Fe, 505-983-9340;
www.pasquals.com
Southwestern menu. Breakfast, lunch, dinner. Children's menu. Casual attire. Reservations recommended. **$$$**

### ★★Celebrations
613 Canyon Rd., Santa Fe, 505-989-8904
American menu. Breakfast, lunch, dinner, Sunday brunch. Children's menu. Casual attire. Reservations recommended. Outdoor seating. **$$**

### ★Chow's Cuisine Bistro
720 St., Michaels Dr., Santa Fe,
505-471-7120; www.mychows.com
Chinese menu. Lunch, dinner. Closed Sunday. Casual attire. **$$**

### ★★★The Compound Restaurant
653 Canyon Rd., Santa Fe, 505-982-4353;
www.compoundrestaurant.com
The setting of this landmark restaurant is casual yet elegant, with minimalist décor, neutral tones and white-clothed tables. Patios surrounded by flower gardens and a marble fountain make for a relaxing outdoor dining experience. The Contemporary American menu features specialties such as grilled beef tenderloin and tuna tartar topped with Osetra caviar and preserved lemon. The warm bittersweet liquid chocolate cake is a star dessert. Guests can also choose from an extensive wine list, featuring rare and French wines. American menu. Lunch, dinner. Bar. Business casual attire. Reservations recommended. Outdoor seating. **$$**

### ★★★Coyote Cafe
132 W. Water St., Santa Fe, 505-983-1615;
www.coyotecafe.com
Famed cookbook author and Southwestern cuisine pioneer Mark Miller has enjoyed nothing but success at this super-cool restaurant decorated with folk art located just a block off the Plaza. Although the menu changes seasonally, regulars know they'll find a whimsical mingling of the cuisines of New Mexico, Mexico, Cuba and Spain. Look for chile-glazed beef short ribs with

corn dumplings, pecan wood-roasted quail and halibut in a mango-habaero blend. The rooftop Cantina is a festive spot.
Southwestern menu. Dinner. Bar. Children's menu. Casual attire. Reservations recommended. Outdoor seating. **$$$**

### ★★El Farol
808 Canyon Rd., Santa Fe, 505-983-9912;
www.elfarolsf.com
Spanish menu. Lunch, dinner. Bar. Casual attire. Reservations recommended. Outdoor seating. **$$$**

### ★★El Meson—La Cocina de Espana
213 Washington Ave., Santa Fe,
505-983-6756; www.elmeson-santafe.com
Spanish, tapas menu. Dinner. Closed Sunday-Monday. Bar. Children's menu. Casual attire. **$$**

### ★★Gabriel's
4 Banana Lane, Santa Fe, 505-455-7000;
www.restauranteur.com/gabriels
Southwestern menu. Lunch, dinner. Closed Late November-late December. Bar. Casual attire. Reservations recommended. Outdoor seating. **$$**

### ★★★★Geronimo
724 Canyon Rd., Santa Fe, 505-982-1500;
www.geronimorestaurant.com
Housed in a restored 250-year-old landmark adobe building, Geronimo (the name of the restaurant is an ode to the hacienda's original owner, Geronimo Lopez) offers robust southwestern-spiked global fusion fare in a stunning and cozy space. Owners Cliff Skoglund and Chris Harvey treat each guest like family. The interior is like a Georgia O'Keeffe painting come to life, with its wood-burning cove-style fireplace, tall chocolate-and-garnet-leather seating and local Native American-style artwork decorating the walls. The food is remarkable, fusing the distinct culinary influences of Asia, the Southwest and the Mediterranean. Vibrant flavors, bright colors and top-notch seasonal and regional ingredients come together in such dishes as Maryland soft-shell tempura crabs with soba noodle

and asian pear salad, or mesquite-grilled New York strip steak with French onion tart and polenta fries with green pepper corn and mustard sauce. When it's warm outside, sit on the patio for prime Canyon Road people watching.

International menu. Lunch, dinner, Sunday brunch. Bar. Casual attire. Reservations recommended. Valet parking. Outdoor seating. **$$$**

### ★★Il Piatto
95 W. Marcy St., Santa Fe, 505-984-1091; www.ilpiattorestaurant.com
Italian menu. Lunch, dinner. Bar. Children's menu. Casual attire. Reservations recommended. Outdoor seating. **$$**

### ★★India Palace
227 Don Gaspar Ave., Santa Fe, 505-986-5859; www.indiapalace.com
Indian menu. Lunch, dinner. Children's menu. Casual attire. Outdoor seating. **$$**

### ★★★Julian's
221 Shelby St., Santa Fe, 505-988-2355; www.juliansofsantafe.com
Officially called Julian's Cucina d'Italia, this bistro has long been a favorite for romantic dining in a neighborhood cluster of high-end shops and galleries. Two fireplaces warm the old adobe room, where owner-executive chef Wayne Gustafson treats guest to creative versions of authentic dishes, such as the antipasto of oysters baked with Parmesan and the pasta shells stuffed with snails, prosciutto, garlic butter and pesto. Signature entrées include osso bucco Milanese with saffron risotto and shrimp sauteed with tomatoes and graced with fresh basil and mascarpone.

Italian menu. Dinner. Bar. Casual attire. Outdoor seating. **$$$**

### ★★★Las Fuentes at Bishop's Lodge
1297 Bishop's Lodge Rd., Santa Fe, 505-983-6377, 800-419-0492; www.bishopslodge.com
Executive chef Alfonso Ramirez brings an explosion of Nuevo Latino cuisine to the Bishop's Lodge at this inviting restaurant. Favorite dishes include seared plantain-crusted salmon with fennel and chipotle juice and swordfish marinated with chile guajillo. Spa cuisine choices include gazpacho with roasted cumin seeds and Cuban black bean soup.

American, Southwestern menu. Breakfast, lunch, dinner, Sunday brunch. Bar. Children's menu. Outdoor seating. **$$$**

### ★★Maria's New Mexican Kitchen
555 W. Cordova Rd., Santa Fe, 505-983-7929; www.marias-santafe.com
Southwestern menu. Lunch, dinner. Bar. Children's menu. Casual attire. Reservations recommended. Outdoor seating. **$$**

### ★★★The Old House Restaurant
309 W. San Francisco St., Santa Fe, 505-988-4455, 800-955-4455; www.eldoradohotel.com
Chef Charles Kassels is known for introducing unexpected flavors in otherwise everyday items. Witness his roasted pork tenderloin, accompanied by sweet potatoes puréed with oranges that he's preserved for nine days, duck confit and foie gras in puff pastry with pistachios and cherry-celery compote and soup with lobster tempura and osetra caviar. Take a moment to look up and take in the candlelit stucco room, which is adorned with Mexican folk art and bold, oversized paintings and is part of one of the city's oldest buildings.

Southwestern menu. Dinner. Bar. Business casual attire. Reservations recommended. Valet parking. **$$$**

### ★★Ore House on the Plaza
50 Lincoln Ave., Santa Fe, 505-983-8687; www.orehouseontheplaza.com
Southwestern, steak menu. Lunch, dinner. Bar. Children's menu. Casual attire. Outdoor seating. **$$**

### ★★Osteria d'Assisi
58 S. Federal Place, Santa Fe, 505-986-5858; www.osteriadassisi.net
Italian menu. Lunch, dinner. Bar. Children's menu. Casual attire. Reservations recommended. Outdoor seating. **$$$**

**266**

**NEW MEXICO**

### ★★The Pink Adobe
406 Old Santa Fe Trail,
Santa Fe, 87501,
505-983-7712;
www.thepinkadobe.com
Southwestern menu. Lunch, dinner. Bar. Children's menu. Casual attire. Reservations recommended. Outdoor seating. **$$$**

### ★Plaza
54 Lincoln Ave., Santa Fe, 505-982-1664;
Southwestern menu. Breakfast, lunch, dinner. Children's menu. Casual attire. **$$**

### ★★Pranzo Italian Grill
540 Montezuma, Santa Fe,
505-984-2645;
www.pranzosantafe.com
Italian menu. Lunch, dinner, late-night. Bar. Children's menu. Casual attire. Reservations recommended. **$$**

### ★★Ristra
548 Agua Fria St., Santa Fe,
505-982-8608;
www.ristrarestaurant.com
French, Southwestern menu. Dinner. Casual attire. Reservations recommended. Outdoor seating. **$$$**

### ★★San Marcos Cafe
3877 NM 14, Santa Fe,
505-471-9298
Southwestern menu. Breakfast, lunch. **$**

### ★★★Santacafe
231 Washington Ave., Santa Fe,
505-984-1788;
www.santacafe.com
Situated a block from the Plaza in the restored Padre Gallegos House, Santacafe offers simple but exquisite dishes such as a salad of blood oranges and grapefruit with fennel and celeriac remoullade, shrimp-spinach dumplings in a tahini sauce, filet mignon with persillade and green chile mashed potatoes and roasted free-range chicken with quinoa and a cranberry-chipotle chuntey. Patio dining in warmer weather is divine.

American, Pan-Asian, Southwestern menu. Lunch, dinner, Sunday brunch. Bar. Children's menu. Casual attire. Reservations recommended. Outdoor seating. **$$$**

### ★The Shed
113 1/2 E. Palace Ave., Santa Fe,
505-982-9030; www.sfshed.com
Southwestern menu. Lunch, dinner. Closed Sunday. Bar. Children's menu. Casual attire. Reservations recommended. Outdoor seating. **$$**

### ★★Shohko-Cafe
321 Johnson St., Santa Fe,
505-982-9708
Japanese menu. Lunch, dinner. Casual attire. Reservations recommended. **$$**

### ★Steaksmith at El Gancho
104 B Old Las Vegas Hwy.,
Santa Fe, 505-988-3333;
www.santafesteaksmith.com
Steak menu. Dinner. Bar. Children's menu. Casual attire. **$$$**

### ★★Tomasita's
500 S. Guadalupe, Santa Fe,
505-983-5721
Southwestern menu. Lunch, dinner. Closed Sunday. Bar. Children's menu. Casual attire. Outdoor seating. **$$**

### ★★★Trattoria Nostrani
304 Johnson St., Santa Fe,
505-983-3800;
www.trattorianostrani.com
Guests can dine in one of four semiprivate dining rooms at Trattoria Nostrani, a northern Italian restaurant housed in an 1883 territorial-style house. The casual yet elegant interior retains much of its historical ambience, with tin ceilings and adobe archways. Tempting entrées include filet mignon with Tuscan vegetable ragu and fried potatoes; stuffed chicken with sweet Italian sausage, Fontina and Asiago; and ravioli with black pepper and Pecorino Toscano. More than 400 wines are offered

★
★
★
★
★

on the extensive European wine list and a knowledgeable staff will assist in selecting the perfect one.

Italian menu. Dinner. Closed Sunday. Casual attire. Reservations recommended. **$$$**

★★**Vanessie of Santa Fe**
434 W. San Francisco St., Santa Fe, 505-982-9966; www.vanessiesantafe.com
American menu. Dinner. Bar. Casual attire. Reservations recommended. **$$**

# SANTA ROSA

In grama-grass country on the Pecos River, Santa Rosa has several natural and man-made lakes. Information: Santa Rosa Chamber of Commerce, 141 S. Fifth St., 505-472-3404; www.santarosanm.org

## WHAT TO SEE AND DO

### Billy the Kid Museum
1435 E. Sumner Ave., Fort Sumner, 575-355-2380; www.billythekidmuseumfortsumner.com
Contains 60,000 items, including relics of the Old West, Billy the Kid and Old Fort Sumner. Summer, daily 8.30 a.m.-5 p.m.; winter, Monday-Saturday 8:30 a.m.-5 p.m.

### Blue Hole
Blue Hole Rd., Santa Rosa
This clear blue lake in a rock setting is fed by natural artesian spring; scuba diving.

### Fort Sumner State Monument
RR 1, Fort Sumner, 505-355-2573
Original site of the Bosque Redondo, where the U.S. Army held thousands of Navajo and Mescalero Apache captive from 1863-1868. The military established Fort Sumner to oversee the containment. Visitor center has exhibits relating to the period. Monday, Wednesday-Sunday.

### Grzelachowski Territorial House
Santa Rosa
Billy the Kid visited this store and mercantile built in 1800 frequently. Grzelachowski had a major role in the Civil War battle at Glorieta Pass. Daily, mid-morning-early evening.

### Puerta de Luna
Santa Rosa, 10 miles south on Hwy. 91, 505-472-3763

Founded in approximately 1862, this Spanish-American town of 250 people holds to old customs in living and working.

### Santa Rosa Dam and Lake
Hwy. 91, Santa Rosa, 505-472-3115
An irrigation pool is often available for recreation. Fishing, boating; nature trails; camping. Daily.

### Sumner Lake State Park
Santa Rosa, three miles east on Hwys. 54/66, then 32 miles south on Hwy. 84, near Fort Sumner, 575-355-2541
An irrigation dam created this 4,500-surface-acre reservoir. Swimming, fishing (bass, crappie, channel catfish); camping. Daily.

## SPECIAL EVENTS

### Old Fort Days
Santa Rosa, Fort Sumner, downtown and County Fairgrounds
Parade, rodeo, bank robbery, barbecue, contests, exhibits. Second week in June.

### Santa Rosa Day Celebration
Santa Rosa
Sports events, contests, exhibits. Memorial Day weekend.

## HOTELS

★**Best Western Adobe Inn**
1501 Historic Rte 66 St., Santa Rosa, 505-472-3446; www.bestwestern.com
58 rooms. Complimentary continental breakfast. High-speed Internet access. Pets accepted. Pool. **$**

**268**

**NEW MEXICO**

# SILVER CITY

The rich gold and silver ores in the foothills of the Mogollon Mountains are running low, but copper mining has now become important to the economy. Cattle ranching thrives on the plains. The forested mountain slopes to the north are the habitat of turkey, deer, elk and bear and the streams and lakes provide excellent trout fishing.

Information: Chamber of Commerce, 201 N. Hudson, 505-538-3785, 800-548-9378; www.silvercity.org

## WHAT TO SEE AND DO

### Gila National Forest
Silver City, surrounds town on all borders except on the southeast, 505-388-8201; www.fs.fed.us/r3/gila
The Gila National Forest covers about three million acres. Blue Range Wilderness and Aldo Leopold Wilderness are in its borders. Hunting, backpacking, horseback riding. Also includes several lakes (Quemado, Roberts, Snow) for fishing, boating and camping.

### Gila Cliff Dwellings National Monument
Silver City, 44 miles north on Hwy. 15, 505-536-9461; www.nps.gov/gicl
More than 40 rooms in six caves are accessible by a one-mile hiking trail. The Mogollon circa 1300 occupied the caves. Self-guided tour; camping. Forest naturalists conduct programs Memorial Day-Labor Day. Ruins and visitor center Daily.

### Phelps Dodge Copper Mine
Silver City, seven miles northeast on Hwy. 15, 505-538-5331
This historic mining town is home to forts and other historic buildings.

### Silver City Museum
312 W. Broadway, Silver City, 505-538-5921, 877-777-7947; www.silvercitymuseum.org
This museum is located in the restored 1881 house of H. B. Ailman, owner of a rich silver mine. Includes Victorian antiques and furnishings; artifacts; memorabilia from mining town of Tyrone. Tuesday-Sunday.

### Western New Mexico University Museum
In Fleming Hall, 1000 College Ave., Silver City, 575-538-6386
This museum depicts the contribution of American Indian, Hispanic, African American and European cultures to the history of region; largest display of Membres pottery in the nation; photography, archive and mineral collections. Daily.

## SPECIAL EVENTS

### Frontier Days
Silver City
Parade, dances, exhibits, food. Western dress desired. July 4.

## HOTELS

### ★Comfort Inn
1060 E. Hwy. 180, Silver City, 505-534-1883; www.comfortinn.com
92 rooms. $

### ★★Copper Manor Motel
710 Silver Heights Blvd., Silver City, 505-538-5392
68 rooms. Complimentary continental breakfast. Restaurant. Pets accepted. Pool. $

## RESTAURANTS

### ★★Buckhorn Saloon and Opera House
32 Main St., Pinos Altos, 505-538-9911
Steak menu. Dinner. Closed Sunday. Bar. Casual attire. Reservations recommended. $$

# SOCORRO

Socorro is located in the Rio Grande Valley. Originally a Piro Indian town, Socorro had a Franciscan mission as early as 1598. It is the home of a very large astronomy observatory (where parts of the movie *Contact* with Jodie Foster were filmed).

Information: Socorro County Chamber of Commerce, 101 Plaza, 505-835-0424; www.socorro-nm.com

★
★
★
★
★

## WHAT TO SEE AND DO

### Mineral Museum
801 Leroy Place, Socorro, 505-835-5140
See more than 12,000 mineral specimens from around the world. Free rockhounding and prospecting information. Monday-Saturday.

### National Radio Astronomy Observatory
1003 Lopez Ville Rd., Socorro, 505-835-7000; www.nrao.edu
The main component here is the VLA (Very Large Array), a radio telescope that consists of 27 separate antennas situated along three arms of railroad track. The VLA is used to investigate all kinds of astronomical topics. Self-guided walking tour of grounds and visitor center. Daily.

### Old San Miguel Mission
403 El Camino Real N.W., Socorro, 505-835-1620; www.sdc.org/smiguel

This restored 17th-century mission has carved ceiling beams and corbels and walls are five feet thick. Daily. Artifacts on display in church office (building south of church). Monday-Friday.

## HOTELS

### ★Best Western Socorro
1100 California N.E., Socorro, 575-838-0556; www.bestwestern.com
120 rooms. Complimentary continental breakfast. Pets accepted. Pool. $

### ★Econo Lodge Socorro
713 California St. N.W., Socorro, 505-835-1500, 877-424-6423; www.econolodge.com
40 rooms. Complimentary continental breakfast. Restaurant. Pets accepted. Pool. $

## SALINAS PUEBLO MISSIONS NATIONAL MONUMENT

This monument was established to explore European-American Indian contact and the resultant cultural changes. The stabilized ruins of the massive 17th-century missions are basically unaltered, preserving the original design and construction. All three units are open and feature wayside exhibits, trails and picnic areas. Monument Headquarters, one block west of Hwy. 55 on Hwy. 60 in Mountainair, has an audiovisual presentation and an exhibit depicting the Salinas story. There are three units of this monuent:

*Gran Quivira.* The massive walls of the 17th-century San Buenaventura Mission (begun in 1659 but never completed) are here, as well as "San Isidro" Church (circa 1639) and 21 pueblo mounds, two of which have been excavated. A self-guided trail and museum/visitor center combine to vividly portray Native American life over the past 1,000 years. Various factors led to the desertion of the pueblo and the mission around 1671. Tompiro Indians occupied this and the Ab site. 25 miles southeast of Mountainair on Hwy. 55, 505-847-2770.

*Ab.* Contains ruins of the mission church of San Gregorio de Ab (circa 1622), built by Native Americans under the direction of Franciscan priests. This is the only early church in New Mexico with 40-foot buttressed curtain walls—a style typical of medieval European architecture. The pueblo adjacent to the church was abandoned around 1673 because of drought, disease and Apache uprisings. The Ab and others from the Salinas jurisdiction eventually moved south with the Spanish to El Paso del Norte, where they established the pueblo of Ysleta del Sur and other towns still in existence today. There are self-guided trails throughout the mission compound and pueblo mounds. Nine miles west of Mountainair on Hwy. 60, then 3/4 mile north on Hwy. 513, 505-847-2400.

*Quarai.* Encompasses the ruins of the Mission de la Pursima Concepcin de Cuarac, other Spanish structures and unexcavated American Indian mounds, all built of red sandstone. Built about 1630, it was abandoned along with the pueblo about 1677, most likely for the same reasons. Unlike the other two, Tiwa-speaking people occupied this site. Much of the history is related to the Spanish-Indian cultural conflict. The church ruins have been excavated and it is the most complete church in the monument. The visitor center has a museum and interpretive displays. Eight miles north of Mountainair on Hwy. 55, then one mile west on a county road from Punta.

Information: Socorro, approximately 75 miles southeast of Albuquerque via I-40, Hwy. 337, 55; 505-847-2290; www.nps.gov/sapu

# TAOS

As early as 1615, a handful of Spanish colonists settled in this area. In 1617 a church was built. After the Pueblo Rebellion of 1680, the town was a farming center plagued by Apache raids and disagreements with the Taos Indians and the government of Santa Fe. The first artists came in 1898; since then it has flourished as an art colony. Many people come here for the clear air, magnificent surroundings and exciting and congenial atmosphere.

Taos is actually three towns: the Spanish-American settlement into which Anglos have infiltrated, which is Taos proper; Taos Pueblo, two and a half miles north; and Ranchos de Taos, four miles south. Many farming communities and fishing resorts can be found in the surrounding mountains. Taos Ski Valley, 19 miles northeast, is a popular spot for winter sports. The town has a few famous residents, including Julia Roberts, Val Kilmer and Donald Rumsfeld.

Information: Taos County Chamber of Commerce, 1139 Paseo Del Pueblo Sur, 505-758-3873, 800-732-8267; www.taos.org

## WHAT TO SEE AND DO

### Carson National Forest
208 Cruz Alta Rd., Taos, 575-758-6200; www.fs.fed.us/r3/carson/
This forest occupies 11/2 million acres and includes Wheeler Peak, New Mexico's highest mountain at 13,161 feet. Lots of small mountain lakes and streams provide good fishing. There's also hunting, hiking, winter sports, picnicking, camping. Daily.

### Ernest L. Blumenschein Home
222 Ledoux St., Taos,
505-758-0505;
www.taosmuseums.org/blumenschein.php
This restored adobe house includes furnishings and exhibits of paintings by the Blumenschein family and other early Taos artists. May-October: daily 9 a.m.-5 p.m.; call for winter hours. Combination tickets to seven Taos museums available.

### Fort Burgwin Research Center
6580 Hwy. 518, Taos, 505-758-8322
The First Dragoons of the U.S. Calvary (1852-1860) occupied this restored fort. Summer lecture series, music and theater performances. Operated by Southern Methodist University. Schedule varies.

### Governor Bent House Museum and Gallery
117 Bent St., Taos, 505-758-2376;
www.laplaza.org/art/museums_bent.php3

Visit the home of New Mexico's first American territorial governor (and the scene of his death in 1847). Includes Bent family possessions, American Indian artifacts, western American art. Summer: daily 9 a.m.-5 p.m.; winter: daily 10 a.m.-4 p.m.

### Hacienda de los Martinez
708 Ranchitos Rd., Taos, 505-758-0505; www.taoshistoricmuseums.com
Contains early Spanish Colonial hacienda with period furnishings; 21 rooms, two large patios. Early Taos, Spanish culture exhibits. Used as a fortress during raids. Living museum demonstrations. Summer: daily 9 a.m.-5 p.m., call for winter hours. Combination tickets to seven Taos museums available.

### Harwood Museum of Art
238 Ledoux St., Taos, 505-758-9826; www.harwoodmuseum.org
Founded in 1923, this museum features paintings, drawings, prints, sculptures and photographs by artists of Taos from 1800 to the present. Tuesday-Saturday 10 a.m.-5 p.m., Sunday noon-5 p.m.; Closed Monday. Combination tickets to seven Taos museums available.

### Kit Carson Home and Museum
113 Kit Carson Rd., Taos, 505-758-4945; www.kitcarsonhome.com
Restored 1825 home of the famous frontiersman with artifacts, including a gun exhibit. Summer: daily 9 a.m.-5 p.m., call for winter hours.

### Kit Carson Park
211 Paseo del Pueblo Norte, Taos, 505-758-8234
This 25-acre park includes bicycle/walking path, picnic tables, playground and sand volleyball pit. No camping. The graves of Kit Carson and his family are also here. Daily.

### Orilla Verde Recreation Area
Hwy. 570 and Hwy. 68, Taos, 505-758-8851
This park runs along the banks of the Rio Grande, offering some of the finest trout fishing in the state; whitewater rafting through deep chasm north of park. Hiking, picnicking. Spectacular views. Daily.

### Ranchos de Taos
60 Ranchos Plaza Rd., Taos, 505-758-2754
This adobe-housed farming and ranching center has one of the most beautiful churches in the Southwest—the San Francisco de Asis Church. Its huge buttresses and twin bell towers only suggest the beauty of its interior. Monday-Saturday 9 a.m.-4 p.m.

### Rio Grande Gorge Bridge
Taos, 12 miles northwest on Hwy. 64
This bridge is 650 feet above the Rio Grande; observation platforms, picnic and parking areas.

### Sipapu Ski & Summer Resort
Hwy. 518, three miles west of Tres Ritos, 800-587-2240; www.sipapunm.com
Area has two triple chairlifts, two Poma-lifts; patrol, school, rentals, snowmaking; 39 runs, the longest two miles; vertical drop 1,055 feet. Mid-December-March, daily. Cross-country skiing on forest roads and trails. Snowboarding.

### Taos Pueblo
Taos, 505-758-1028; www.taospueblo.com
With a full-time population of 150, this is one of the most famous Native American pueblos and has been continuously inhabited for more than 1,000 years. Within the pueblo is a double apartment house. The north and south buildings, separated by a river, are five stories tall and form a unique communal dwelling. Small buildings and corrals are scattered around these impressive architectural masterpieces. The residents here live without modern utilities such as electricity and plumbing and get their drinking water from the river. The people are independent, conservative and devout in their religious observances. Fees are charged for parking and photography permits. Photographs of individual Native

Americans may be taken only with their consent. Daily 8 a.m.-4 p.m.; closed for special occasions in spring.

### Taos Ski Valley
103A Suton Place, Taos Ski Valley, 866-968-7386; www.skitaos.org
Area has 12 chairlifts, two surface lifts; patrol, school, rentals; cafeteria, restaurants, bar; nursery, lodges. Longest run more than four miles; vertical drop 2,612 feet. November-April, daily.

## SPECIAL EVENTS
### Annual Pow-Wow
Taos Pueblo, Taos, 505-758-1028; www.taospueblopowwow.com
Intertribal dancers from throughout U.S., Canada and Mexico participate in this competition. Second weekend in July.

### Chamber Music Festival
145 Paseo del Pueblo, Taos, 505-776-2388; www.taosschoolofmusic.com
Mid-June-early August.

### Fiestas de Taos
Taos Plaza, Taos, 505-741-0909; www.fiestasdetaos.com
This traditional festival honoring the patron saints of Taos includes a candlelight procession, parade, crafts, food and entertainment. Late July.

### San Geronimo Eve Sundown Dance
Taos Pueblo, Taos, 505-758-1028
See a traditional men's dance, which is followed the next day by San Geronimo Feast Day, with intertribal dancing, trade fair, pole climb, footraces. Last weekend in September.

### Spring Arts Festival
Taos, 505-758-3873, 800-732-8267; www.taoschamber.com
This three-week festival celebrates the visual, performing and literary arts. May.

### Taos Arts Festival
Taos, 505-758-1028; www.taosguide.com

Arts and crafts exhibitions, music, plays, poetry readings. Mid-September-early October.

### Taos Pueblo Dances
Taos Pueblo, Albuquerque, 505-758-1028; www.taospueblo.com
Several Native American dances are held throughout the year. For a schedule of annual dances, contact the pueblo.

### Taos Pueblo Deer or *Matachines* Dance
Taos Pueblo, Taos, 505-758-1028
Symbolic animal dance or ancient Montezuma dance. December 25.

### Taos Rodeo
County Fairgrounds, 502 Los Pandos, Taos, 800-732-8267
Late June or early July.

### Yuletide in Taos
Taos, 800-732-8267
'The celebration includes area *farolito* (paper bag lantern) tours, food and craft fairs, art events and dance performances. Late November-late December.

## HOTELS
### ★Comfort Inn
1500 Paseo Del Pueblo Sur, Taos, 505-751-1555; www.comfortinn.com
60 rooms. Complimentary continental breakfast. Pool. $

### ★★★El Monte Sagrado
317 Kit Carson Rd., Taos, 505-758-3502, 800-828-8264; www.elmontesagrado.com
El Monte Sagrado speaks to the naturalist in all travelers. This unique resort, tucked away in magical Taos, celebrates the natural beauty of New Mexico while highlighting its rich Native American heritage. The themed guestrooms and suites, which proudly display local and international artwork, are seductive retreats. Taos, well known for its world-class skiing, is a year-round playground, offering everything from rock climbing and fly fishing to llama trekking

**273**

**NEW MEXICO**

★
★
★
★
★

and mountain biking. Closer to home, El Monte Sagrado features a world-class spa, with a focus on renewal of body and mind. The award-winning De La Tierra restaurant is a feast for the eyes and the palate.
36 rooms. Spa. Pool. Fitness room. **$$$$**

### ★Hampton Inn
1515 Paseo Del Pueblo Sur, Taos,
505-737-5700; www.hamptoninn.com
71 rooms. Complimentary continental breakfast. Pool. **$**

### ★★★The Historic Taos Inn
125 Paseo Del Pueblo Norte, Taos,
505-758-2233, 888-518-8267;
www.taosinn.com
This historic inn offers a comfortable Old West atmosphere and modern amenities. Guests will enjoy the outdoor heated pool and greenhouse whirlpool. The unique guest rooms feature Southwestern décor and many offer kiva fireplaces. Be sure to dine at the acclaimed Doc Martin's Restaurant.
36 rooms. Restaurant, bar. Pool. **$**

### ★★★Sagebrush Inn
1508 Paseo Del Pueblo Sur., Taos,
505-758-2254, 800-428-3626;
www.sagebrushinn.com
Built in 1929, this 100-room adobe inn houses a large collection of paintings, Native American rugs and other regional art. The most recent addition, an 18,000-square-foot conference center, features hand-hewn vigas and fireplaces. Visitors will enjoy the outdoor pool and two whirlpools. Guest rooms feature have hand-made furniture.
100 rooms. Complimentary full breakfast. Restaurant, bar. Pets accepted. Pool. **$**

## SPECIALTY LODGINGS

### Adobe and Stars Inn
584 Hwy. 150, Taos,
505-776-2776, 800-211-7076;
www.taosadobe.com
Located near the Historic Taos Plaza and the Taos Ski Valley, this Southwestern inn offers panoramic views of the Sangre de Christo Mountains. Guest rooms feature

kiva fireplaces, private baths with terra-cotta tile and ceiling fans.
8 rooms. Complimentary full breakfast. Pets accepted. **$**

### Austing Haus B&B
1282 Hwy. 150, Taos Ski Valley,
505-776-2649, 800-748-2932;
www.austinghaus.net
This newly remodeled inn was constructed of oak-pegged heavy timbers with beams exposed inside and out.
45 rooms. Closed mid-April-mid-May. Complimentary continental breakfast. Restaurant. Whirlpool. Pets accepted. **$**

### Casa de las Chimeneas
405 Cordoba Rd., Taos,
505-758-4777, 877-758-4777;
www.visit-taos.com
True to its Spanish name (the House of Chimneys), all guest rooms in this bed and breakfast have kiva fireplaces as well as brass and wooden beds, private entrances and baths, down pillows and electric blankets or down comforters. Guests will enjoy the inn's formal gardens and courtyards, fountains and whirlpool.
9 rooms. Complimentary full breakfast. **$$**

### Casa Europa Inn
840 Upper Ranchitos, Taos,
505-758-9798, 888-758-9798;
www.casaeuropanm.com
Set on six acres of land, this 17th-century Pueblo-style inn offers a soothing experience with its beautiful views. The flowered courtyards feature a fountain, as well as a sauna and whirlpool. The spacious guest rooms offer private bathrooms, desks and fans.
7 rooms. Complimentary full breakfast. **$**

### Hacienda Del Sol
109 Mabel Dodge Lane, Taos,
505-758-0287, 866-333-4459;
www.taoshaciendadelsol.com
This inn consists of three adobe buildings set on 1.2 acres overlooking the Taos Mountains. The romantic guest rooms

feature thick adobe walls, original artwork and corner fireplaces.
11 rooms. Complimentary full breakfast. **$$**

### Inn on La Loma Plaza
315 Ranchitos Rd., Taos,
505-758-1717, 800-530-3040;
www.vacationtaos.com
This restored historic inn offers mountain views and spacious gardens. Visitors will enjoy the large whirlpool and can take advantage of complimentary spa, tennis and health club privileges nearby. Guest rooms feature private baths, fireplaces, phones, televisions, robes and slippers.
7 rooms. Complimentary full breakfast. Pool. **$**

### La Posada De Taos
309 Juanita Lane, Taos,
505-758-8164, 800-645-4803;
www.laposadadetaos.com
6 rooms. Complimentary full breakfast. **$**

### Salsa Del Salto Bed & Breakfast Inn
543 Hwy. 150, Anoyo Seco,
505-776-2422, 800-530-3097;
www.bandbtaos.com
With the inn conveniently located close to Taos Ski Valley and Taos, guests will have the option of skiing or shopping. After a game of tennis, you can enjoy the mountain and sunset view from the whirlpool.
10 rooms. Children over 6 years only. Complimentary full breakfast. Tennis. **$**

### San Geronimo Lodge
1101 Witt Rd., Taos,
505-751-3776, 800-894-4119;
www.sangeronimolodge.com
18 rooms. Complimentary full breakfast. Pool. Pets accepted. **$**

### Touchstone Inn & Spa
110 Mabel Dodge Lane, Taos,
505-758-0192, 800-758-0192;
www.touchstoneinn.com
This quiet, historic bed and breakfast is nestled among the trees on the edge of Taos Pueblo Lands.

10 rooms. Complimentary full breakfast. No children under 12. **$**

## RESTAURANTS

### ★★Apple Tree
123 Bent St., Taos, 505-758-1900;
www.appletreerestaurant.com
American, Southwestern menu. Lunch, dinner, Sunday brunch. Children's menu. Business casual attire. Reservations recommended. Outdoor seating. **$$**

### ★★★De La Tierra
317 Kit Carson Rd., Taos,
505-758-3502, 800-828-8267;
www.elmontesagrado.com
From its one-of-a-kind décor to its sensational cuisine, De la Tierra, tucked inside Taos' striking El Monte Sagrado resort, practically begs for special occasions. Towering ceilings capped by an enormous wrought iron chandelier, high-backed, tapestry-covered chairs and soft, golden lighting make this dining room pure seduction. Chef Ruben Tanuz's signature style puts a Southwestern spin on an internationally influenced menu. Everything from mustard-crusted elk, rack of lamb with sage bread pudding, grilled salmon with spinach enchiladas, and molasses marinated grilled quail is given his unique stamp.
Southwestern/American menu. Breakfast, lunch, dinner. **$$$**

### ★★★Doc Martin's
125 Paseo Del Pueblo, Taos,
505-758-1977; www.taosinn.com
Chef Zippy White serves organic Southwestern in an adobe setting. Specialties include chipotle shrimp on corn cake and Southwestern lacquered duck. The wine list is one of the best in the area.
American, Southwestern menu. Breakfast, lunch, dinner, Sunday brunch. Bar. Children's menu. Casual attire. Reservations recommended. Outdoor seating. **$$$**

### ★★★Lambert's of Taos
309 Paseo Del Pueblo Sur, Taos,
505-758-1009;
www.lambertsoftaos.com

**NEW MEXICO**

Zeke and Tima Lambert came to Taos years ago on their honeymoon and never left. This restaurant serves contemporary cuisine. The produce is local when possible and all the sauces are made from scratch. Dishes include grilled lamb tenderloin with warm lentil salad and New Mexico feta cheese or filet of beef on potato cake with grilled spinach and horseradish cream. The extensive wine list is primarily from California.
American menu. Dinner. Bar. Children's menu. Casual attire. Reservations recommended. Outdoor seating. **$$$**

★**Michael's Kitchen and Bakery**
304 N. Pueblo Rd., Taos, 505-758-4178; www.michaelskitchen.com
Mexican, American menu. Breakfast, lunch, dinner. Closed November. Children's menu. **$**

★★**Ogelvie's Taos Bar and Grille**
103 E. Plaza, Taos, 505-758-8866; www.ogelvies.com
American, Southwestern menu. Lunch, dinner. Bar. Children's menu. Casual attire. Outdoor seating. **$$**

★★★**Old Blinking Light**
Mile Marker One, Ski Valley Rd., Taos, 505-776-8787; www.oldblinkinglight.com
American, Southwestern menu. Dinner. Bar. Children's menu. Casual attire. Outdoor seating. **$$**

★★**Stakeout Grill and Bar**
101 Stakeout Dr., Taos, 505-758-2042; www.stakeoutrestaurant.com
Seafood, steak menu. Dinner. Closed November. Bar. Children's menu. Casual attire. Outdoor seating. May-October. **$$**

# TRUTH OR CONSEQUENCES

Formerly called Hot Springs, for the warm mineral springs, the town changed its name in 1950 to celebrate the tenth anniversary of Ralph Edwards' radio program, "Truth or Consequences."

In the early 1500s, the Spanish Conquistadores came through this area and legends of lost Spanish gold mines and treasures in the Caballo Mountains persist today. There are numerous ghost towns and old mining camps in the area.

Information: Truth or Consequences/Sierra County Chamber of Commerce, 400 W. Fourth St., 575-894-3536; www.truthorconsequencesnm.net

## WHAT TO SEE AND DO

**Caballo Lake State Park**
Truth or Consequences, 18 miles south on I-25, 575-743-3942; www.emnrd.state.nm.us/prd/caballo.htm
The Caballo Mountains form a backdrop for this lake. Swimming, windsurfing, waterskiing, fishing, boating (ramp); hiking, picnicking, playground, camping. Daily.

**Geronimo Springs Museum**
211 Main St., Truth or Consequences, 505-894-6600; www.geronimospringsmuseum.com
See exhibits of Mimbres pottery, fossils and photographs, as well as articles on local history. Gift shop. (Monday-Saturday.)

## HOTELS

★**Best Western Hot Springs Motor Inn**
2270 N. Date St., Truth or Consequences, 505-894-6665; www.bestwestern.com
40 rooms. Pets accepted. Pool. **$**

★★★**Quality Inn**
401 Hwy. 195, Elephant Butte, 575-744-5431; www.elephantbutteinn.com
47 rooms. Complimentary continental breakfast. Restaurant, bar. Pets accepted. Pool. **$**

## RESTAURANTS

★★**Los Arcos Steak House**
1400 N. Date St., Truth or Consequences, 505-894-6200
American menu. Dinner. Bar. Children's menu. Casual attire. Outdoor seating. **$$**

★
★
★
★
★

# TUCUMCARI

Tucumcari is a convenient stopping point between Amarillo, Texas and Albuquerque. Tucumcari Mountain (4,957 feet) is to the south.

Information: Tucumcari/Quay County Chamber of Commerce, 404 W. Rte. 66, 575-461-1694; www.tucumcarinm.com

## WHAT TO SEE AND DO

### Tucumcari Historical Museum
416 S. Adams St., Tucumcari, 575-461-4201

See Western Americana, Native American artifacts, gems, minerals, rocks, fossils and more. Summer, Monday-Saturday, 8 a.m.-6 p.m.; Winter, Monday-Friday 8 a.m.-5 p.m.

## SPECIAL EVENTS

### Route 66 Festival
404 W. Tumcari Blvd., Tucumcari

Rodeo, car show, parade, arts and crafts, entertainment. July.

## HOTELS

### ★Comfort Inn
2800 E. Tucumcari Blvd., Tucumcari, 505-461-4094, 877-424-6423; www.comfortinn.com

59 rooms. Complimentary continental breakfast. Pet. Swim. **$**

### ★★Holiday Inn
2624 S. Adams St., Tucumcari, 505-461-3333, 888-465-4329; www.holiday-inn.com

100 rooms. Complimentary full breakfast. Restaurant, bar. Pool. **$**

# ZUNI PUEBLO

Thirty-nine miles south of Gallup, via Hwy. 602 and west on Hwy. 53, is one of Coronado's "Seven Cities of Cibola." Fray Marcos de Niza reported that these cities were built of gold. When looking down on the Zuni pueblo from a distant hilltop at sunset, it does seem to have a golden glow.

The people here make beautiful jewelry, beadwork and pottery. They also have a furniture and woodworking center with colorful and uniquely painted and carved items. Ashiwi Awan Museum and Heritage Center displays historical photos and exhibits. The pueblo, built mainly of stone, is one story high. The old Zuni mission church has been restored and its interior painted with murals of Zuni traditional figures. A tribal permit is required for photography; certain rules must be observed.

★
★
★
★
★

# UTAH

UTAH'S NATURAL DIVERSITY HAS MADE IT A STATE OF MAGNIFICENT BEAUTY, WITH MORE than 3,000 lakes, miles of mountains, acres of forests and large expanses of desert. In northern Utah, the grandeur of the Wasatch Range, one of the most rugged mountain ranges in the United States, cuts across the state north to south. The Uinta Range, capped by the white peaks of ancient glaciers, is the only major North American range that runs east to west. In the western third of the state is the Great Basin. Lake Bonneville extended over much of western Utah leaving behind the Great Salt Lake, Utah Lake and Sevier Lake. To the east and west extends the Red Plateau. This red rock country, renowned for its brilliant coloring and fantastic rock formations, is home to one of the largest concentrations of national parks and monuments. Utah is definitely the place for those who love the western outdoors and can appreciate the awesome accomplishments of the pioneers who developed it.

This natural diversity created an environment inhospitable to early settlers. Although various groups explored much of the state, it took the determination and perseverance of a band of religious fugitives, members of the Church of Jesus Christ of Latter-Day Saints, to settle the land permanently.

**278**

Brigham Young, leader of the Mormons, once remarked, "If there is a place on this earth that nobody else wants, that's the place I am hunting for." On July 24, 1847, on entering the forbidding land surrounding the Great Salt Lake, Young exclaimed, "This is the place!" The determined settlers immediately began to plow the unfriendly soil and build dams for irrigation. During 1847, as many as 1,637 Mormons came to Utah, and by the time the rail-road made its way here, more than 6,000 had settled in the state. Before his death in 1877, 30 years after entering the Salt Lake Valley, Brigham Young had directed the founding of more than 350 communities.

The LDS church undoubtedly had the greatest influence on the state, developing towns in an orderly fashion with wide streets, planting straight rows of poplar trees to provide wind breaks and introducing irrigation throughout the desert regions. But the church members were not the only settlers. In the latter part of the 19th century, the West's fabled pioneer era erupted. The gold rush of 1849-1850 sent gold seekers pouring through Utah on their way to California. The arrival of the Pony Express in Salt Lake City in 1860 brought more immigrants, and when the mining boom hit the state in the 1870s and 1880s, Utah's mining towns appeared almost over-night. In 1900, the population was 277,000. It now stands at more than 1.7 million, with more than 75 percent living within 50 miles of Salt Lake City. The LDS church con-tinues to play an important role, and close to 60 percent of the state's population are members.

**Information: www.utah.com**

 **SPOTLIGHT**

★ Rainbow Bridge, nature's abstract sculpture carved of solid sandstone, is the world's largest natural-rock span. It stands 275 feet wide and 209 feet high.

★ Kanab is known as Utah's Little Hollywood because a large number of motion pictures are filmed in the area.

# ALTA

Founded around silver mines in the 1870s, Alta was notorious for constant shoot-outs in its 26 saloons. With the opening of Utah's first ski resort in 1937, the town became the center of a noted resort. Unusual wildflowers are found in Albion Basin.
Information: 801-742-3522; www.townofalta.com

## WHAT TO SEE AND DO

### Alta Ski Area
Hwy. 210, Alta, 801-359-1078;
www.alta.com
Two quad, two triple, three double chairlifts; four rope tows; patrol, school, rentals, snowmaking. Longest run 3.5 miles, vertical drop 2,020 feet. Half-day rates. No snowboarding. Mid-November-April, daily.

## HOTELS

### ★Alta Lodge
10230 State Rd. 210, Alta,
801-742-3500, 800-707-2582;
www.altalodge.com
57 rooms. Closed mid-late October, May. Wireless Internet access. Restaurant, bar. Children's activity center. Whirlpool. Ski in/ski out. Tennis. Skiing. **$**

### ★★★Alta's Rustler Lodge
10380 Hwy. 210, Alta,
801-742-2200, 888-532-2582;
www.rustlerlodge.com
With its ski in/ski out access to all of Alta's lift base facilities and a full-service ski shop on site, the Rustler Lodge is all about the slopes. A complimentary shuttle takes guests wherever they want to go in Alta and Snowbird. The new business center offers high-speed and wireless Internet access for those who need to get some work done between runs. The lodge also has a steam room and offers manicures, pedicures and other spa treatments. A children's programs will keep kids occupied. 85 rooms. Closed May-October. Restaurant, bar. Ski in/ski out. Exercise. Pool. Skiing. **$$$**

★
★
★
★
★

## ARCHES NATIONAL PARK

This natural landscape of giant stone arches, pinnacles, spires, fins and windows was once the bed of an ancient sea. Over time, erosion laid bare the skeletal structure of the earth, making this 114-square-mile area a spectacular outdoor museum. This wilderness, which contains the greatest density of natural arches in the world, was named a national monument in 1929 and a national park in 1971. More than 2,000 arches have been cataloged, ranging in size from three feet wide to the 105-foot-high, 306-foot-wide Landscape Arch. The arches, other rock formations and views of the Colorado River canyon (with the peaks of the LaSal Mountains in the distance) can be reached by car, but hiking is the best way to explore. Petroglyphs from the primitive peoples who roamed this section of Utah from A.D. 700-1200 can be seen at the Delicate Arch trailhead.

Hiking, rock climbing or camping in isolated sections should not be undertaken unless first reported to a park ranger at the visitor center (check locally for hours). Twenty-four miles of paved roads are open year-round. Graded and dirt roads should not be attempted in wet weather. Devils Garden Campground, 18 miles north of the visitor center off Hwy. 191, provides 52 individual and two group campsites (year-round; fee; water available only March-mid-October).
Information: Five miles northwest of Moab on Hwy. 191 to paved entrance road. 435-719-2299; www.nps.gov/arch

# BEAVER

The seat of Beaver County, this town is a national historic district with more than 200 houses of varied architectural styles and periods. Butch Cassidy was born here in 1866.
Information: Beaver County Travel Council, 405 Main St., 435-438-5438; www.beaverutah.net

## SPECIAL EVENTS

### Pioneer Day Celebration and Parade
Beaver, 435-438-5438
Features a parade, entertainment and horse racing, along with other events. Late July.

## HOTELS

### ★Best Western Butch Cassidy Inn
161 S Main St., Beaver, 84713,
435-438-2438, 800-780-7234;
www.bestwestern.com
35 rooms. Complimentary continental breakfast. High-speed Internet access. Pets accepted. Pool. $

### ★Quality Inn
781 W. 1800 S., Beaver, 435-438-5426;
www.qualityinn.com
52 rooms. Pets accepted. Pool. $

# BLANDING

The city is a gateway to hunting and fishing grounds and national monuments. The sites can be explored by jeep or horseback along the many trails, or by boat through the waters of Glen Canyon National Recreation Area. A Pueblo ruin, inhabited between A.D. 800 and A.D. 1200, is now a state park within the city limits.
Information: San Juan County Visitor Center, 117 S. Main St., Monticello, 435-587-3235, 800-574-4386; www.southeastutah.org

## WHAT TO SEE AND DO

### Edge of the Cedars State Park
660 W. 400 North, Blanding, 435-678-2238;
www.utah.com/stateparks/
edge_of_cedars.htm
This park sits on the site of a pre-Columbian Pueblo Indian ruin. You'll find excavated remnants of ancient dwellings and ceremonial chambers fashioned by the ancient Pueblo people, as well as artifacts and pictographs. Visitor center. Daily; hours vary by season.

### Glen Canyon National Recreation Area/Lake Powell
Blanding, four miles south on Hwy. 191, then 85 miles west on Hwy. 95 and Hwy. 276; 928-608-6200; www.nps.gov/glca

More than 1.2 million acres of recreational bliss, Glen Canyon National Recreation Area is an ideal place for backcountry exploration or fun in Lake Powell.

### Hovenweep National Monument
Blanding, 970-562-4282;
www.nps.gov/hove
The monument consists of six units of prehistoric ruins; the best preserved are the remains of pueblos (small cliff dwellings) and towers at Square Tower. Self-guided trail; park ranger on duty; visitor center. Daily 8 a.m.-5 p.m.

## NATURAL BRIDGES NATIONAL MONUMENT

This 7,439-acre area of fantastically eroded and colorful terrain was made a national monument in 1908. It features three natural bridges (formed through erosion by water), all with Hopi names. Sipapu, a 268-foot span, and Kachina, a 204-foot span, are both in White Canyon, a major tributary gorge of the Colorado River. Owachomo, a 180-foot span, is near Armstrong Canyon, which joins White Canyon. Sipapu is the second-largest natural bridge in the world. From 2,000 to 650 years ago, the ancestral Puebloan people lived in this area, leaving behind cliff dwelling ruins and pictographs that visitors can view today. The major attraction is Bridge View Drive, a nine-mile-loop road open daily from early morning to 30 minutes past sunset, providing views of the three bridges from rim overlooks. There are also hiking trails to each bridge within the canyon.

The park also has a visitor center (Daily 8 a.m.-5 p.m.) and primitive campground with 13 tent and trailer sites (all year). Car and passenger ferry service across Lake Powell is available.

Information: Blanding, four miles south on Hwy. 191, then 36 miles west on Hwy. 95, then four miles north on Hwy. 275, 435-692-1234; www.nps.gov/nabr

# BLUFF

Bluff's dramatic location between the sandstone cliffs along the San Juan River, its Anasazi ruins among the canyon walls and its Mormon pioneer past all combine to make it an interesting stop along scenic Highway 163 between the Grand Canyon and Mesa Verde national parks.
Information: San Juan County Visitor Center, 117 S Main St., Monticello, 435-587-3235, 800-574-4386; www.bluffutah.org

## WHAT TO SEE AND DO

### Tours of the Big Country
Hwy. 191, Bluff, 435-672-2281
Naturalist-guided walking and four-wheel-drive tours include trips to Monument Valley, the Navajo Reservation and more. Also includes llama rentals. Half-day, full-day and overnight trips. Year-round.

### Wild Rivers Expeditions
101 Main St., Bluff, 800-422-7654; www.riversandruins.com
This tour company, in business since 1957, arranges fun and educational single-day and multi-day trips on the archaeologically rich San Juan River, framed by dramatic red rock formations and fossil beds. Licensed guides, many of whom are archaeologists, geologists or of Navajo descent, conduct the tours, interpreting the native ruins and rock art found along the journey. Reserve well in advance. March-mid-November.

## SPECIAL EVENTS

### Utah Navajo Fair
Bluff, 435-651-3755
Traditional song and dance, food, crafts, and a rodeo. Mid-September.

# BRIGHAM CITY

Renamed for Brigham Young in 1877, when he made his last public address here, this community, situated at the base of the towering Wasatch Mountains, was first known as

Box Elder because of the many trees of that type that grew in the area. Main Street, which runs through the center of this city, is still lined with these leafy trees.
Information: Chamber of Commerce, 6 N. Main St., 435-723-3931; www.bcareachamber.com, www.brighamcity.utah.gov

## WHAT TO SEE AND DO

### Brigham City Museum-Gallery
24 N. 300 W. Brigham City, 435-723-6769
Displays include furniture, clothing, books, photographs and documents reflecting the history of the Brigham City area since 1851. Also showcases rotating art exhibits. Tuesday-Friday 11 a.m.-6 p.m., Saturday 1-5 p.m.

### Golden Spike National Historic Site
Brigham City, 32 miles west via Hwys. 13 and 83, 435-471-2209; www.nps.gov/gosp
This is the site where America's first transcontinental railroad was completed when the Central Pacific and Union Pacific lines met on May 10, 1869. At the visitor center, you'll find movies and exhibits. Daily 9 a.m.-5 p.m. There's also a self-guided auto tour along the old railroad bed. The summer interpretive program includes presentations and operating replicas of steam locomotives May-early October, daily.

### Tabernacle
251 S. Main St., Brigham City, 435-723-5376
The Box Elder tabernacle, one of the most architecturally interesting buildings in Utah, has been in continuous use since 1881. Gutted by fire and rebuilt in the late 1890s, it was restored in the late 1980s. Guided tours are given in the summer months.

## SPECIAL EVENTS

### Driving of the Golden Spike
Brigham City, 435-471-2209
The reenactment of the driving of the golden spike (the ceremonial nail driven to mark the completion or a railroad) takes place at the site where the Central Pacific and Union Pacific railroads met in 1869. Locomotive replicas are used. Mid-May.

### Peach Days Celebration
Brigham City
Parade, arts and crafts, carnival, car show, entertainment. First weekend after Labor Day.

## HOTELS

### ★Crystal Inn, A Rodeway Inn
480 Westland Dr., Brigham City, 435-723-0440, 877-462-7978; www.crystalinns.com
30 rooms. Pets accepted. **$**

282

UTAH

# BRYCE CANYON NATIONAL PARK

Bryce Canyon is a 56-square-mile area of colorful, fantastic cliffs created by millions of years of erosion. Towering rocks worn to odd, sculptured shapes stand grouped in striking sequences. The Paiute, who once lived nearby, called this "the place where red rocks stand like men in a bowl-shaped canyon." Although termed a canyon, Bryce is actually a series of "breaks" in 12 large amphitheaters—some plunging as deep as 1,000 feet into the multicolored limestone. The formations appear to change color as the sunlight strikes from different angles and seem incandescent in the late afternoon. The famous Pink Cliffs were carved from the Claron Formation; shades of red, orange, white, gray, purple, brown and soft yellow appear in the strata. The park road follows 17 miles along the eastern edge of the Paunsaugunt Plateau, where the natural amphitheaters are spread out below. Plateaus covered with evergreens and valleys filled with sagebrush stretch into the distance.

The visitor center at the entrance station has information about the park, including orientation shows, geologic displays and detailed maps. The park is open 24 hours a day year-round; in winter, the park road is open to most viewpoints. Lodging is also available from April to October.

Information: Panguitch, seven miles south on Hwy. 89, then 17 miles S.E., on Hwy. 12 to Hwy. 63, three miles to entrance; 435-834-5322; www.nps.gov/brca

## WHAT TO DO AND SEE
### Camping
Bryce Canyon
Camping is available at the North Campground (year-round), east of park headquarters; Sunset Campground, two miles south of park headquarters. Fourteen-day limit at both sites; fireplaces, picnic tables, restrooms, water available. April-October.

## HOTELS
★★**Best Western Ruby's Inn**
1000 Hwy. 63, Bryce Canyon, 435-834-5341, 866-866-6616; www.rubysinn.com
368 rooms. Restaurant. Pets accepted. Pool. **$**

## RESTAURANTS
★**Foster's Steak House**
1150 Hwy. 12, Bryce, 435-834-5227; www.fostersmotel.com
Steak menu. Breakfast, lunch, dinner. Children's menu. Casual attire. **$$**

UTAH

★
★
★
★
★

# CEDAR CITY
In 1852, Cedar City produced the first iron made west of the Mississippi. The blast furnace operation was not successful, however and stock-raising soon overshadowed it. A branch line of the Union Pacific entered the region in 1923 and helped develop the area. Now a tourist center because of its proximity to Bryce Canyon and Zion national parks, Cedar City takes pride in its abundant natural wonders. Streams and lakes have rainbow trout and the Markagunt Plateau provides deer and mountain lion hunting. Headquarters and a Ranger District office of the Dixie National Forest are located here.

Information: Chamber of Commerce, 581 N. Main St., 84720, 435-586-4484; www.cedarcity.org

## WHAT TO SEE AND DO
### Dixie National Forest
82 N. and 100 E. Cedar City, 435-865-3700; www.fs.fed.us/dxnf
This two-million-acre forest provides opportunities for camping, fishing, hiking, mountain biking and winter sports. Daily.

### Iron Mission State Park
635 N. Main, Cedar City, 435-586-9290; www.stateparks.utah.gov/parks/iron-mission

The museum at the park is dedicated to the first pioneer iron foundry west of the Rockies and features an extensive collection of horse-drawn vehicles and wagons from Utah pioneer days. Daily.

### Southern Utah University
351 W. Center, Cedar City, 435-586-5432; www.suu.edu
Established in 1897; 7,000 students. Braithwaite Fine Arts Gallery, Monday-Saturday.

## SPECIAL EVENTS
### Renaissance Fair
City Park, Cedar City; www.umrf.net
Entertainment, food and games, all in the style of the Renaissance. Held in conjunction with opening of Utah Shakespearean Festival. Early July.

### Utah Shakespearean Festival
Southern Utah University Campus,
351 W. Center St., Cedar City,
435-586-7880; www.bard.org
Shakespeare is presented on an outdoor stage (a replica of 16th-century Tiring House) and 750-seat indoor facility. Monday-Saturday evenings; pre-play activities. Children over five years only; babysitting at festival grounds. Late June-early October.

### Utah Summer Games
351 W. Center St., Cedar City,
435-865-8421; www.utahsummergames.org

Olympic-style athletic events for amateur athletes. June.

## HOTELS
### ★Abbey Inn
940 W. 200 N. Cedar City,
435-586-9966, 800-325-5411;
www.abbeyinncedar.com
81 rooms. Complimentary full breakfast. Airport transportation available. Pool. **$**

### ★Best Western Town and Country Inn
189 N. Main, Cedar City,
435-586-9900, 800-493-0062;
www.bwtowncountry.com
157 rooms. Pool. **$**

## CEDAR BREAKS NATIONAL MONUMENT
Cedar Breaks National Monument's major formation is a spectacular, multicolored, natural amphitheater created by the same forces that sculpted Utah's other rock formations. The amphitheater, shaped like an enormous coliseum, is 2,000 feet deep and more than three miles in diameter. It is carved out of the Markagunt Plateau and is surrounded by Dixie National Forest. Cedar Breaks, at an elevation of more than 10,000 feet, was established as a national monument in 1933. It derives its name from the surrounding cedar trees; "breaks" means "badlands." Although similar to Bryce Canyon National Park, the formations here are fewer but more vivid and varied in color. Young lava beds, resulting from small volcanic eruptions and cracks in the earth's surface, surround the Breaks area. The heavy forests include bristlecone pines, one of the oldest trees on the earth. As soon as the snow melts, wildflowers bloom profusely and continue to bloom throughout the summer.

Rim Drive, a five-mile scenic road through the Cedar Breaks High Country, provides views of the monument's formations from four different overlooks. The area is open late May to mid-October, weather permitting. Point Supreme Campground, two miles north of south entrance, provides 30 tent and trailer sites (mid-June-mid-September). The visitor center offers geological exhibits (June-mid-October, daily); interpretive activities (mid-June-Labor Day).

Information: Cedar City, 23 miles east of Cedar City via Hwy. 14, 435-586-0787; www.nps.gov/cebr

# FILLMORE

Fillmore, the seat of Millard County and Utah's territorial capital until 1856, is today a trading center for the surrounding farm and livestock region. It is a popular hunting and fishing area.

Information: City of Fillmore, 75 W. Center, 435-743-5233; www.millardcounty.com

## WHAT TO SEE AND DO

### Territorial Statehouse State Park

50 W. Capitol Ave., Fillmore, 435-743-5316; www.utah.com/stateparks/ territorial_house.htm

Utah's first territorial capitol, built in the 1850s of red sandstone, is now a museum with an extensive collection of pioneer furnishings, American Indian artifacts and early documents. There's also a lovely rose garden. Monday-Saturday.

## HOTELS

### ★★Best Western Paradise Inn And Resort

905 N. Main, Fillmore, 435-743-6895; www.bestwestern.com

78 rooms. Restaurant. Pets accepted. Pool. $

# GARDEN CITY

This small resort town on the western shore of Bear Lake offers many water-based activities.

Information: Bear Lake Convention & Visitors Bureau, 208-945-2333, 800-448-2327; www.bearlake.org

## WHAT TO SEE AND DO

### Bear Lake

Garden City

Covering 71,000 acres on the border of Utah and Idaho, this body of water is the state's second-largest freshwater lake. Approximately 20 miles long and 200 feet deep, it offers good fishing for mackinaw, rainbow trout and the rare Bonneville Cisco. Boat rentals at several resorts.

### Bear Lake State Park

1030 N. Bear Lake Rd., Garden City, 435-946-3343; www.utah.com/stateparks/bear_lake.htm

Three park areas include State Marina on west shore of lake, Rendezvous Beach on south shore and Eastside area on east shore. Swimming, beach, waterskiing, fishing, ice fishing, boating (ramp, dock), sailing; hiking, mountain biking, cross-country skiing, snowmobiling, picnicking, tent and trailer sites. Visitor center. Daily.

### Beaver Mountain Ski Area

40000 E. Hwy. 89, Garden City, 435-753-0921; www.skithebeav.com

Three double chairlifts, two surface lifts; patrol, school, rentals; day lodge, cafeteria. Twenty-two runs; vertical drop 1,600 feet. Half-day rates. December-early April, daily.

# GREEN RIVER

This tiny town (fewer than 1,000 people live here) in eastern Utah is named for the river that winds through much of Utah (and the town itself).

Information: Green River Travel Council, 885 E. Main St., 435-564-3526

## WHAT TO SEE AND DO

### Goblin Valley State Park

450 S. Green River Blvd., Green River, 435-564-3633; www.utah.com/stateparks/goblin_valley.htm

This mile-wide basin is filled with intricately eroded sandstone formations. Hiking, camping. Daily.

**John Wesley Powell River History Museum**
1765 E. Main St., Green River,
435-564-3427; www.jwprhm.com
This 20,000-square-foot museum sits on the banks of the Green River and contains exhibits exploring the geology and geography of area; auditorium with 20-minute multi-media presentation; river runner Hall of Fame. Green River Visitor Center. Daily.

## HOTELS
★**Best Western River Terrace Motel**
1740 E. Main St., Green River,
435-564-3401; www.bestwestern.com
50 rooms. Pool. **$**

★**Holiday Inn Express**
1845 E. Main St., Green River,
435-564-4439; www.hiexpress.com
60 rooms. Pets accepted. **$**

## RESTAURANTS
★**Tamarisk**
870 E. Main St., Green River,
435-564-8109
American menu. Breakfast, lunch, dinner. Children's menu. Casual attire. **$**

# HEBER CITY

Located in a fertile, mountain-ringed valley, Heber City is the bedroom community for Orem, Provo, Park City and Salt Lake City. Unusual crater mineral springs, called hot pots, are located four miles west near Midway. Mount Timpanogos, one of the most impressive mountains in the state, is to the southwest in the Wasatch Range.
Information: Heber Valley Chamber of Commerce, 475 N. Main St., 435-654-3666; www.hebervalleycc.org

## WHAT TO SEE AND DO
**Heber Valley Railroad**
450 S. 600 W., Heber City,
435-654-5601, 800-888-7499;
www.herbervalleyrr.org
A 100-year-old steam-powered excursion train takes passengers through the farmlands of Heber Valley, along the shore of Deer Creek Lake and into Provo Canyon on various one-hour to four-hour trips. Restored coaches and open-air cars. Special trips some Friday, Saturday evenings. Reservations required. May-mid-October, Tuesday-Sunday; mid-October-November, schedule varies; December-April, Monday-Saturday.

**Wasatch Mountain State Park**
Heber City, two miles northwest
off Hwy. 224, 435-654-1791;
stateparks.utah.gov/parks/wasatch
This park occupies approximately 25,000 acres in Heber Valley and offers fishing, hiking, 36-hole golf, snowmobiling, cross-country skiing, picnicking and camping. Visitor center. Daily.

## SPECIAL EVENTS
**Wasatch County Fair**
2843 S. Daniels Rd., Heber City
Parades, exhibits, country market, livestock shows, rodeos, dancing. First weekend in August.

## HOTELS
★**Holiday Inn Express**
1268 S. Main St., Heber City,
435-654-9990, 800-465-4329;
www.holiday-inn.com
75 rooms. Pool. **$**

## SPECIALTY LODGINGS
**The Sundowner Inn B&B**
425 Moulton Lane, Heber City,
435-654-4200, 866-455-4200;
www.thesundownerinn.com
9 rooms. Complimentary full breakfast. **$$**

## TIMPANOGOS CAVE NATIONAL MONUMENT

Timpanogos Cave National Monument consists of three small, beautifully decorated underground chambers within limestone beds. The cave entrance is on the northern slope of Mount Timpanogos. A filigree of colorful crystal formations covers much of the cave's interior, where stalactites and stalagmites are common. But what makes Timpanogos unique is its large number of helictites—formations that appear to defy gravity as they grow outward from the walls of the cave. The temperature in Timpanogos Cave is a constant 45° F, and the interior is electrically lighted.

The cave's headquarters are located on Hwy. 92, eight miles east of American Fork. There is picnicking at Swinging Bridge Picnic Area, 1/4 mile from the headquarters. The cave entrance is 1 1/2 miles from headquarters via a paved trail with a vertical rise of 1,065 feet. Allow three to five hours for a guided tour. Tours limited to 20 people (late May-early September, daily). Purchase tickets in advance by calling 801-756-5238 or stopping at the visitor center.

Information: Heber City, 26 miles south of Salt Lake City on I-15, then 10 miles east on Hwy. 92, 801-756-5238; www.nps.gov/tica

# KANAB

Since 1922, more than 200 Hollywood productions have used the sand dunes, canyons and lakes surrounding Kanab as their settings. Some movie-set towns can still be seen. Kanab is within a 1 1/2-hour drive from the north rim of the Grand Canyon, Zion and Bryce Canyon national parks, Cedar Breaks and Pipe Spring national monuments and Glen Canyon National Recreation Area.

Information: Kane County Office of Tourism, 78 S. 100 E., 435-644-5033, 800-733-5263; www.kaneutah.com

## WHAT TO SEE AND DO

**Coral Pink Sand Dunes State Park**
Yellowjacket and Hancock Roads, Kanab, 435-648-2800;
stateparks.utah.gov/parks/coral-pink
Includes six square miles of very colorful, windswept sandhills. Hiking, picnicking, tent and trailer sites. Off-highway vehicles allowed; exploring, photography. Daily.

## RESTAURANTS

**★Houston's Trail's End**
32 E. Center St., Kanab, 435-644-2488;
www.houstons.net
American menu. Breakfast, lunch, dinner. Closed mid-December-mid-March. Children's menu. Casual attire. **$**

## HOTELS

**★★Parry Lodge**
89 E. Center St., Kanab,
435-644-2601, 888-289-1722;
www.parrylodge.com
89 rooms. Complimentary full breakfast. Restaurant. Pets accepted. Pool. **$**

# LAKE POWELL

Lake Powell is the second largest man-made lake in the United States, with more than 1,900 miles of shoreline. The lake is named for John Wesley Powell, the one-armed explorer who, in 1869, successfully navigated the Colorado River through Glen Canyon and the Grand Canyon, and later became director of the U.S. Geological Survey.
Information: www.lakepowell.com

## WHAT TO SEE AND DO

### Boat trips on Lake Powell
Bullfrog Marina, Hwy. 276, Lake Powell, 435-684-3010; www.lakepowell.com
Trips include the Canyon Explorer tour (2 1/2 hours) and the half-day and all-day Rainbow Bridge tours. (Due to the current level of the lake, these tours involve a 1 1/4-mile hike to see the monument.) Visitors can also take wilderness float trips and rent houseboats and powerboats. Reservations are advised. Daily.

### Glen Canyon National Recreation Area (Bullfrog Marina)
Hwy. 276, Lake Powell, 435-684-3010
Additional access and recreational activities avail at Hite Marina, north end of lake. This boasts more than one million acres with year-round recreation area, includ-

ing swimming, fishing, boating, boat tours and trips, boat rentals; picnicking, camping, tent and trailer sites, lodgings. April-October, daily.

### Lake Powell Ferry
Bullfrog Marina on Hwy. 276, Lake Powell, 435-538-1030
Instead of driving 130 miles around the lake, take this three-mile boat trip between Bullfrog and Hall's Crossing. Daily; reduced hours in winter.

UTAH

## RAINBOW BRIDGE NATIONAL MONUMENT

Rainbow Bridge, which rises from the eastern shore of Lake Powell, is the largest natural rock bridge in the world. It was named a national monument in 1910. This natural bridge stands 290 feet tall, spans 275 feet, and stretches 33 feet wide at the top. One of the seven natural wonders of the world, Rainbow Bridge is higher than the nation's capitol dome and nearly as long as a football field. The monument is predominantly salmon pink in color, modified by streaks of iron oxide and manganese. In the light of the late afternoon sunday, the bridge is a brilliant sight. American Indians consider the area a sacred place; legend holds that the bridge is a rainbow turned to stone.

The easiest way to reach Rainbow Bridge is a half-day round-trip boat ride across Lake Powell from Page, Arizona, or a full-day round-trip boat ride from Bullfrog and Halls Crossing marinas. The bridge also can be reached on foot or horseback via the Rainbow Trail through the Navajo Indian Reservation. Fuel and camp supplies are available at Dangling Rope Marina, accessible by boat only, 10 miles south down lake.
Information: Rainbow Bridge National Monument, 928-608-6200; www.nps.gov/rabr

# LOGAN

Situated in the center of beautiful Cache Valley, Logan is surrounded by snowcapped mountains and is home to Utah State University.
Information: City of Logan, 255 N. Main, 435-716-9000; www.loganutah.org

## WHAT TO SEE AND DO

### Daughters of the Utah Pioneers Museum
160 N. Main, Logan, 435-752-5139
Exhibits depict Utah's past. Monday-Friday.

### Hyrum State Park
405 W. 300 S. Logan, 435-245-6866;
stateparks.utah.gov/parks/hyrum
A 450-acre reservoir with beach swimming, waterskiing, fishing, ice fishing, boating (ramp, dock), sailing; picnicking, camping. Year-round.

### Mormon Tabernacle
50 N. Main St., Logan, 435-755-5598
A gray limestone example of an early Mormon building. Genealogy library. Monday-Friday.

### Mormon Temple
175 N. 300 E. Logan, 435-752-3611
The site for this massive, castellated limestone structure was chosen by Brigham Young, who broke ground here in 1877. Grounds are open all year, but the temple is closed to the general public.

### Utah State University
Logan, 435-797-1000; www.usu.edu
Established in 1888; 20,100 students. On campus is the Nora Eccles Harrison Museum of Art. Monday-Friday.

### Wasatch-Cache National Forest, Logan Canyon
1500 E. Hwy. 89, Logan, 435-755-3620;
www.fs.fed.us/r4/wcnf
This national forest offers fishing, backcountry trails, hunting, winter sports, picnicking and camping. Daily.

### Willow Park Zoo
419 W. 700 S. Logan, 435-716-9265
This small but attractive zoo has shady grounds and especially good bird-watching of migratory species, with more than 100 captive species and 80 species of wild birds visiting and nesting at the zoo. Daily 9 a.m.-dusk.

## SPECIAL EVENTS

### Cache County Fair
400 S. 500 W., Logan
Rodeo, horse races, exhibits. Early August.

### Utah Festival Opera Company
59 S. 100 W., Logan
July-August.

## HOTELS

### ★★Best Western Baugh Motel
153 S. Main St., Logan,
435-752-5220, 800-462-4154;
www.bestwestern.com
76 rooms. Complimentary continental breakfast. Restaurant. Pool. $

### ★Comfort Inn
447 N. Main St., Logan,
435-752-9141, 866-537-6459;
www.choicehotels.com
83 rooms. Complimentary continental breakfast. Exercise. Pool. $

## SPECIALTY LODGINGS

### The Anniversary Inn
169 E. Center St., Logan,
435-752-3443, 800-324-4152;
www.anniversaryinn.com
Each room or suite at this charming inn has its own theme, from the Pyramids of Egypt to Aphrodite's Court to Lost in Space. Most have jetted tubs, and some have fireplaces and big-screen TVs.
20 rooms. No children allowed. Whirlpool. $$

## RESTAURANTS

### ★Bluebird
19 N. Main St., Logan, 435-752-3155
American menu. Lunch, dinner. Closed Sunday. Children's menu. Casual attire. $

★
★
★
★
★

**★The Copper Mill**
55 N. Main St., Logan,
435-752-0647
American menu. Lunch, dinner. **$**

**★★Le Nonne**
129 N. Main St., Logan, 435-752-9577
Italian menu. Lunch, dinner. Closed Monday. **$$**

# MIDWAY

This town recalls its Swiss roots with Swiss architecture and an annual festival that celebrates the town's heritage. Less than an hour's drive from Salt Lake, Midway is near Wasatch Mountain State Park.
Information: 75 N. 100 W., 435-654-3227; www.midwaycityut.org

## SPECIAL EVENTS
### Swiss Days
Midway Town Square;
www.midwayswissdays.com
Old country games, activities, costumes. Friday and Saturday before Labor Day.

## HOTELS
### ★★★The Blue Boar Inn
1235 Warm Springs Rd., Midway,
435-654-1400, 888-650-1400;
www.theblueboarinn.com
The blissful quiet of this remote location is perfect for visitors who want to get away from it all, yet stay in relatively close proximity to the slopes and nightlife of the ski resorts of Deer Valley, the Canyons and Sundance. During summer months, nearby fly-fishing and 54 holes of golf entertain guests. Decorated in a unique Austrian-influenced style, the guest rooms feature amusing themes inspired by famous authors and poets. From the handmade willow bed of the Robert Frost to the English cottage-style of the William Butler Yeats and the exotic flavor of the Rudyard Kipling, each room attempts to capture its namesake's distinctive personality. While the chandeliers are crafted of antlers and the furnishings are indicative of the region, the restaurant is a showpiece of fresh American cuisine.
14 rooms. Complimentary full breakfast. Restaurant, bar. Business center. **$$**

### ★★★Homestead Resort
700 N. Homestead Dr., Midway,
435-654-1102, 888-327-7220;
www.homesteadresort.com
Surrounded by lush gardens and the Wasatch Mountains, this historic country resort on 200 acres welcomes guests with Western hospitality. Quaint cottages make up the majority of the accommodations, which include traditional and historic rooms, executive suites and condos that accommodate large groups. Amenities include an Aveda spa, adventure center with billiards, board games, video library and more, championship golf course and a crater in which guests can float in the crystal-clear, 90-plus-degree mineral waters. The resort also rents cross-country skis and snowshoes and provides transportation to nearby Deer Valley's Jordanelle Express Gondola.
142 rooms. Restaurant, bar. Children's activity center. Spa. Golf. Tennis. Business center. **$$**

### ★★★Inn on the Creek
375 Rainbow Lane, Midway,
435-654-0892, 800-654-0892;
www.innoncreek.com
Picturesque landscaping and hot springs surround this luxurious full-service inn. Located at the base of the Wasatch Mountains in Heber Valley, the inn is near popular ski resorts and golf courses. Guests can choose from rooms in the main inn or luxury chalets. All are spacious and tastefully decorated, and most rooms feature fireplaces and balconies or private decks. The spa offers a variety of services, including massages, facials, pedicures and manicures. The inn's restaurant, which serves American-French cuisine, utilizes garden vegetables and herbs, and has an extensive wine selection.
40 rooms. Restaurant, bar. **$$**

# RESTAURANTS

### ★★★Simon's Fine Dining
700 N. Homestead Dr., Midway,
435-654-1102, 800-327-7220;
www.homesteadresort.com
Dine on delicious western cuisine in an elegant country setting, either inside the dining room by the fireplace or outside on the deck, with beautiful views of the valley. American menu. Dinner, Sunday brunch. Closed Monday-Tuesday. Bar. Children's menu. Casual attire. Outdoor seating. **$$**

### ★★★The Blue Boar Inn Restaurant
1235 Warm Springs Rd., Midway,
435-654-1400, 888-650-1400;
www.theblueboarinn.com
Well worth the 20-minute drive from Park City, this charming Tyrolean chalet offers some of the best New American cuisine in Utah. The menu changes periodically to capture the best produce and fresh seafood available, but you might see entrées like grilled Copper River salmon or broiled range-fed veal chop with rustic French bread, creamed spinach and morels. American menu. Lunch, dinner, Sunday brunch. Bar. Casual attire. Outdoor seating. **$$$**

# MOAB

The first attempt to settle this valley was made in 1855, but Moab, named after an isolated area in the Bible, was not permanently settled until 1880. Situated on the Colorado River at the foot of the LaSal Mountains, Moab was a sleepy agricultural town until after World War II, when uranium and oil exploration made it boom. Today, tourism and moviemaking help make it a thriving community. Headquarters for Canyonlands and Arches national parks are located here.
Information: Moab Area Travel Council, 435-259-8825, 800-635-6622;
www.discovermoab.com

## WHAT TO SEE AND DO

### Adrift Adventures
378 N. Main St., Moab,
435-259-8594, 800-874-4483;
www.adrift.net
Oar, paddle and motorized trips available; one to seven days. Jeep tours and horseback rides are also offered. Early April-late October.

### Canyon Voyages Adventure Co
211 N. Main St., Moab,
435-259-6007, 800-733-6007;
www.canyonvoyages.com
Kayaking, whitewater rafting, canoeing, biking or four-wheel drive tours. Early April-October.

### Canyonlands By Night
1861 S. Hwy. 191, Moab,
435-259-2628, 800-394-9978;
www.canyonlandsbynight.com

This two-hour boat trip with sound-and-light presentation highlights the history of area. April-mid-October, daily, leaves at sundown, weather permitting. Reservations required.

### Canyonlands Field Institute
1320 S. Hwy. 191, Moab,
435-259-7750, 800-860-5262;
www.canyonlandsfieldinst.org
Adult and family-oriented educational seminars and trips feature geology, natural and cultural history, endangered species and Southwestern literature. Many programs use Canyonlands and Arches national parks as outdoor classrooms. Monday-Friday.

### Dan O'Laurie Canyon Country Museum
118 E. Center St., Moab, 435-259-7985
See exhibits on local history, archaeology, geology, uranium and minerals of the area. Walking tour information. Summer: Monday-Friday 10-6 p.m.; Saturday-Sunday

**UTAH**

★
★
★
★

noon-6 p.m. winter: Monday-Friday 10-3 p.m., Saturday-Sunday noon-5 p.m.

### Dead Horse Point State Park
313 State Rd., Moab,
435-259-2614, 800-322-3770;
stateparks.utah.gov/parks/dead-horse
This island mesa offers views of the LaSal Mountains, Canyonlands National Park and the Colorado River. Visitor center, museum. Daily.

### Hole N' the Rock
11037 S. Hwy. 191, Moab, 435-686-2250;
www.moab-utah.com/holeintheroc
See a 5,000-square-foot home carved into huge sandstone rock. Picnic area with stone tables and benches. Tours. Daily 8 a.m.-dusk.

### Manti-LaSal National Forest, LaSal Division
599 W. Price River Dr., Price,
435-637-2817;
www.fs.fed.us/r4/mantilasal
The land here is similar in color and beauty to some parts of the Grand Canyon, and also includes high mountains nearing 13,000 feet, as well as pine and spruce forests. Swimming, fishing; hiking, hunting.

### Pack Creek Ranch trail rides
LaSal Mountain Loop Rd., Moab,
435-259-5505;
www.packcreekranch.com
Go horseback riding through the foothills of the La Sal Mountains. Guided tours for small groups; reservations required. March-October; upon availability.

### Redtail Aviation Scenic Air Tours
N. Hwy. 191, Moab,
435-259-7421, 800-842-9251;
www.moab-utah.com/redtail
Offers flights over Canyonlands National Park and various other tours. All-year.

### Rim tours
1233 S. Hwy. 191, Moab,
435-259-5223, 800-626-7335;
www.rimtours.com

Guided mountain bike tours in canyon country and the Colorado Rockies. Vehicle support for camping tours. Daily and overnight trips; combination bicycle/river trips available.

### Sheri Griffith River Expeditions
2231 S. Hwy. 191 Moab,
435-259-8229, 800-332-2439;
www.griffithexp.com
Take your pick: oarboats, motorized rafts, paddleboats or inflatable kayaks; one- to five-day trips; instruction available. May-October.

### Tex's Riverways
691 N. 500 W. Moab, 435-259-5101;
www.texsriverways.com
Flatwater canoe trips, four to 10 days. Confluence pick-ups available, jet boat cruises. March-October.

### Tag-A-Long Expeditions
452 N. Main St., Moab,
435-259-8946, 800-453-3292;
www.tagalong.com
Choose from one- to seven-day whitewater rafting trips on the Green and Colorado rivers; jetboat trips on the Colorado River; and jetboat trips and four-wheel-drive tours into Canyonlands National Park. Winter four-wheel-drive tours, November-February. One-day jetboat trips with cultural performing arts programs are offered part of the year as well. April-mid-October.

## SPECIAL EVENTS

### Butch Cassidy Days PRCA Rodeo
Moab, 800-635-6622
Second weekend in June.

### Jeep Safari
Moab, 435-259-7625
This event, sponsored by Red Rock Four Wheelers, offers 30 different trails. Easter week and weekend.

### Moab Music Festival
58 E. 300 S. Moab,
435-259-7003;
www.moabmusicfest.org

This festival features classical music performed in natural settings throughout southeastern Utah. First two weeks in September.

## HOTELS

### ★★Best Western Canyonlands Inn
16 S. Main St., Moab, 435-259-5167;
www.bestwestern.com
77 rooms. Complimentary continental breakfast. Pool. **$**

### ★★Best Western Greenwell Inn
105 S. Main St., Moab, 435-259-6151;
www.bestwestern.com
72 rooms. Pool. Fitness center. **$**

### ★Bowen Motel
169 N. Main St., Moab,
435-259-7132, 800-874-5439;
www.bowenmotel.com
40 rooms. Complimentary continental breakfast. Pets accepted. Pool. **$**

### ★★★Sorrel River Ranch Resort
Hwy. 128, Moab,
435-259-4642, 877-359-2715;
www.sorrelriver.com
Set amid a dramatic landscape of red rock formations, this full-service resort is just 30 minutes from Arches National Park. Many of the Western-themed guest rooms, all of which have kitchenettes, overlook the Colorado River. Family loft suites are also avai lable. Fireplaces and jetted hydrother-apy tubs are found in the deluxe suites. The resort offers horseback tours, tennis and a spa. After an activity-filled day, enjoy an upscale meal at the River Grill.
59 rooms. High-speed Internet access. Restaurant. Children's activity center. Spa. Tennis. **$$**

## SPECIALTY LODGINGS

### Pack Creek Ranch
Pack Creek Ranch Rd.,
Moab, 435-259-5505;
www.packcreekranch.com
This complex of widely spaced, rustic cabins is 15 miles from downtown in a spec-tacular setting. The ranch is set in a valley with the LaSal Mountains on one side and the red rocks of Moab on the other. All the cabins have a full kitchen and a large sitting area with a rock fireplace. With no TVs or phones, you might actually relax.
11 rooms. Pets accepted. Pool. **$$**

### Sunflower Hill Bed and Breakfast
185 N. 300 E. Moab,
435-259-2974, 800-662-2786;
www.sunflowerhill.com
12 rooms. Children over 10 years only. Whirlpool. **$**

## RESTAURANTS

### ★★Center Cafe
60 N. 100 W., Moab, 435-259-4295;
www.centercafemoab.com
International menu. Dinner. Business casual attire. Outdoor seating. **$$**

### ★Moab Brewery
686 S. Main St., Moab, 435-259-6333;
www.themoabbrewery.com
American menu. Lunch, dinner. **$$**

### ★★Slickrock Cafe
5 N. Main St., Moab, 435-259-8004;
www.slickrockcafe.com
American menu. Breakfast, lunch, dinner. **$**

**293**

UTAH

## MOAB AND BEYOND

This three- to four-day tour out of Moab includes magnificent vistas, unique rock formations and the upper reaches of Lake Powell. From Moab, head south on Hwy. 191 to Hwy. 211; follow 211 west to Newspaper Rock, a huge sandstone panel with petroglyphs that are up to 1,500 years old. Prehistoric peoples such as the Fremonts and Ancestral Puebloans, as well as the Utes, Navajo and European-American settlers left images etched into this wall of stone. From Newspaper Rock, it is an easy drive west on Hwy. 211 to the Needles District of Canyonlands National Park. You probably visited the Island in the Sky District of Canyonlands during your stay in Moab, but this section of the park offers a different perspective. Although best explored by mountain bike or in a high-clearance four-wheel-drive vehicle, there are several roadside viewpoints from which you can see the district's namesake red-and-white-striped rock pinnacles and other formations. Several easy hikes offer additional views.

Retrace your route back to Hwy. 191 and continue south to Hwy. 95, where you will head west to Natural Bridges National Monument. This easy-to-explore monument has a scenic drive with overlooks that offer views of three awe-inspiring natural stone bridges and some 700-year-old Ancestral Puebloan cliff dwellings. There is also prehistoric rock art and a demonstration of how solar energy is used to produce the monument's electricity. The viewpoints are short walks from parking areas. You can also hike to all three of the natural bridges, which were created over millions of years as water cut through solid rock.

Returning to Hwy. 95, head northwest to the Hite Crossing section of Glen Canyon National Recreation Area. Encompassing the northern end of Lake Powell, this is one of the least developed (and least crowded) sections of the recreation area. Hite Crossing has scenic views, boat rentals and plenty of available lodging (including houseboats).

From Hite, continue northwest on Hwy. 95 across rock-studded terrain to Hanksville; head north on Hwy. 24 to the turnoff to Goblin Valley State Park. This delightful little park is a fantasyland where whimsical stone goblins seem to be frozen in mid-dance. From Goblin Valley, return to Hwy. 24 and continue north to I-70. Head east to the community of Green River, where you'll find several motels. Here you'll discover Green River State Park, a good spot for a picnic under the Russian olive and cottonwood trees along the river, or perhaps a round of golf at the park's nine-hole championship course. Nearby, the John Wesley Powell River History Museum tells the incredible story of explorer Powell, a one-armed Civil War veteran who did what was considered impossible when he charted the Green and Colorado rivers in the late 1800s. From Green River continue east on I-70 to Hwy. 191, which leads south back to Moab. Approximately 448 miles.

★

★

★

★

★

## CANYONLANDS NATIONAL PARK

Set aside by Congress in 1964 as a national park, this 337,570-acre area is largely undeveloped and includes spectacular rock formations, canyons, arches, ancestral Puebloan ruins and more. Road conditions vary; primary access roads are paved and maintained, while others are safe only for high-clearance four-wheel-drive vehicles.

Island in the Sky, North District, south and west of Dead Horse Point State Park, has Grand View Point, Upheaval Dome and Green River Overlook. This section is accessible by passenger car via Hwy. 313 and by four-wheel-drive vehicles and mountain bikes on dirt roads.

Needles, South District, has hiking trails and four-wheel-drive roads to Angel Arch, Chesler Park and the confluence of the Green and Colorado rivers. You'll also see prehistoric ruins and rock art here. This section is accessible by passenger car via Hwy. 211, by four-wheel-drive vehicle on dirt roads and by mountain bike.

Maze, West District, is accessible by hiking or by four-wheel-drive vehicles using unimproved roads. The most remote and least-visited section of the park, this area received its name from the many mazelike canyons. Horseshoe Canyon, a separate unit of the park nearby, is accessible via Hwy. 24 and 30 miles of two-wheel-drive dirt road. Roads are usually passable only in mid-March through mid-November.

Canyonlands is excellent for calm-water and whitewater trips down the Green and Colorado rivers. Permits are required for private and commercial trips.

Campgrounds, with tent sites, are located at Island in the Sky and at Needles; water is available only at Needles. Visitor centers are in each district and are open daily.

Information: Canyonlands National Park, 2282 S. West Resource Blvd., Moab, 435-719-2313; www.nps.gov/cany

# MONTICELLO

The highest county seat in Utah (San Juan County), Monticello was named for Thomas Jefferson's Virginia home. On the east slope of the Abajo Mountains, the elevation makes for delightful weather.

Information: San Juan County Visitor Center, 232 S. Main St., 435-587-3235, 800-574-4386; www.monticelloutah.org

## WHAT TO SEE AND DO

**Canyon Rims Recreation Area**
82 E. Dogwood St., Monticello;
www.blm.gov/utah/moab/canyon_rims.html
Two overlooks (Anticline and Needles) into Canyonlands National Park are located here, as are well as two campgrounds (Wind Whistle and Hatch).

**Manti-La Sal National Forest, La Sal Division**
62 E. 100 N. Monticello, 435-587-2041;
www.fs.fed.us/r4/mantilasal
The forest land of this division ranges from red rock canyons to high alpine terrain. Ancient ruins and rock art contrast with pine and spruce forests and aspen-dotted meadows. Fishing; hiking, snowmobiling, cross-country skiing, hunting, camping.

## SPECIAL EVENTS

**Monticello Pioneer Days**
Monticello; www.sanjuancounty.info
Parade, booths, food, games, sports. Weekend nearest July 24.

**San Juan County Fair & Rodeo**
Monticello, 360-378-4310;
www.sanjuancountyfair.org
Second weekend in August.

## HOTELS
★**Best Western Wayside Motor Inn**
197 E. Central Ave., Monticello,
435-587-2261; www.bestwestern.com
37 rooms. Complimentary continental breakfast. Pets accepted. Pool. **$**

UTAH

# NEPHI

Named for Mormon prophets who share the same name, Nephi is about 85 miles south of Salt Lake City.

Information: Juab Travel Council, 4 S. Main, 435-623-5203, 800-748-4361; www.juabtravel.com

## WHAT TO SEE AND DO

**Yuba State Park**

Nephi, 435-758-2611;
stateparks.utah.gov/parks/yuba
Waterskiing and walleyed pike fishing are
the big attractions of this lake, as are sandy
beaches. Daily.

## SPECIAL EVENTS

**Ute Stampede Rodeo**

795 S. Main St., Nephi, 435-623-5608;
www.utestampederodeo.com
Three-day festival featuring Western and
Mammoth parades, carnival, PRCA rodeo,
contests, arts and crafts, concessions.
Second weekend in July.

## HOTELS

**★Best Western Paradise Inn Of Nephi**

1025 S. Main, Nephi, 435-623-0624;
www.bestwestern.com
40 rooms. Complimentary continental
breakfast. Pets accepted. Pool. **$**

# OGDEN

Brigham Young laid out the
streets of Ogden, the fourth-
largest city in Utah, in traditional Mormon geometrical
style: broad, straight and bordered by poplar, box elder,
elm and cottonwood trees. In
1846, Miles Goodyear, the
first white settler, built a cabin
and trading post here, which
he sold to the Mormons a year
later. During the last 30 years
of the 19th century, Ogden
was an outfitting center for
trappers and hunters heading
north. Its saloons and gambling halls were typical of a
frontier town, and there was
considerable friction between

the Mormons and the "gentiles." With the coming of the railroad, Ogden became one of
the few cities in Utah whose inhabitants were not primarily Mormons.

Today, Ogden is a commercial and industrial center. Hill Air Force Base is nearby.
Mount Ben Lomond, north of the city in the Wasatch Range, was the inspiration for the
logo of Paramount Pictures.

Information: Convention & Visitors Bureau, 2501 Wall Ave., 866-867-8824;
www.ogdencvb.org

## WHAT TO SEE AND DO

**Daughters of Utah Pioneers Museum
and Relic Hall**

2148 Grant Ave., Ogden, 801-621-4891;
www.dupinternational.org
See old handicrafts, household items and
portraits of those who came to Utah prior
to the railroad of 1869. This is also the site
of Miles Goodyear's cabin, the first permanent house built in Utah. Mid-May-mid-
September, Monday-Saturday.

**296**

**UTAH**

### Eccles Community Art Center

2580 Jefferson Ave., Ogden,
801-392-6935;
www.ogden4arts.org
This 19th-century castle-like mansion hosts changing art exhibits. It also has a dance studio and outdoor sculpture and floral garden. Monday-Saturday.

### Fort Buenaventura State Park

2450 A. Ave., Ogden, 801-399-8099;
www.utah.com/stateparks/
buenaventura.htm
The exciting era of mountain men is brought to life on this 32-acre site, where Miles Goodyear built the Ogden's first settlement in 1846. The fort has been reconstructed according to archaeological and historical research. No nails have been used in building the stockade; wooden pegs and mortise and tenon joints hold the structure together. April-November.

### George S. Eccles Dinosaur Park

1544 E. Park Blvd., Ogden,
801-393-3466;
www.dinosaurpark.org
This outdoor display contains more than 100 life-size reproductions of dinosaurs and other prehistoric creatures. There's also an educational building with a working paleontological lab, as well as fossil and reptile displays. Daily; closed November-March.

### Hill Aerospace Museum

7961 Wardleigh Rd., Hill AFB 84056,
801-777-6868;
www.hill.af.mil
More than 55 aircraft on display here, including the SR-71 "Blackbird" reconnaissance plane and B-52 bomber. Helicopters, jet engines, missiles, uniforms and other memorabilia are also featured. Daily.

### Nordic Valley

3567 Nordic Valley Way, Eden,
801-745-3511
Two chairlifts; patrol, school, rentals. Longest run 1 1/2 miles, vertical drop 1,000 feet. December-April, daily.

### Pine View Reservoir

Ogden, nine miles east on Hwy. 39 in Ogden Canyon in Wasatch-Cache National Forest, 801-625-5306;
www.fs.fed.us/r4/wcnf/recreation/
pineview.shtml

### Union Station—the Utah State Railroad Museum

2501 Wall Ave., Ogden, 801-393-9886
See some of the world's largest locomotives. The Browning-Kimball Car Museum and Browning Firearms Museum are also here (John Browning was the inventor of the automatic rifle), plus a 500-seat theater for musical and dramatic productions, art gallery and restaurant. Visitors Bureau for northern Utah is located here. Monday-Saturday. 10 a.m.-5 p.m.

### Weber State University

3750 Harrison Blvd., Ogden, 801-626-6000;
weber.edu
Established in 1889; 17,000 students. On campus is the Layton P. Ott Planetarium with Foucault pendulum; shows Wednesday; no shows summer. The Stewart Bell Tower, with 183-bell electronic carillon, also offers performances. Daily. Campus tours.

### Willard Bay State Park

Ogden, 435-734-9494;
stateparks.utah.gov/parks/willard-bay
This park features a 9,900-acre lake. Swimming, fishing, boating (ramps), sailing; picnicking, tent and trailer sites. Daily.

## SPECIAL EVENTS

### Pioneer Days

Ogden Pioneer Stadium,
1875 Monroe Blvd., Ogden
Rodeo, concerts, vintage car shows, fireworks, chili cook-off. Monday-Saturday evenings. Mid-late July.

### Utah Symphony Pops Concert

Lindquist Fountain/Plaza,
1875 Monroe Blvd., Ogden
Music enhanced by fireworks display. Late July.

**297**

**UTAH**

## HOTELS

### ★Best Western High Country Inn
1335 W. 12th St., Ogden,
801-394-9474, 800-594-8979;
www.bestwestern.com
109 rooms. Pets accepted. Pool. **$**

### ★Comfort Suites Ogden
2250 S. 1200 W. Ogden, Ogden,
801-621-2545;
www.ogdencomfortsuites.com
40 rooms. **$**

### ★Hampton Inn & Suites
2401 Washington Blvd., Ogden,
801-394-9400; www.hamptoninn.com
135 rooms. **$**

### ★★Marriott
247 24th St., Ogden,
801-627-1190, 888-825-3163;
www.marriott.com
292 rooms. High-speed Internet access.
Restaurant, bar. Pool. Business center. **$**

## SPECIALTY LODGINGS

### Alaskan Inn
435 Ogden Canyon Rd., Ogden,
801-621-8600; www.alaskaninn.com
12 rooms. **$$**

# PARK CITY

Soldiers struck silver here in 1868, starting one of the nation's largest silver mining camps, which reached a population of 10,000 before declining to a near ghost town when the silver market collapsed. Since then, however, Park City has been revived as a four-season resort with skiing, snowboarding, golf, tennis, water sports and mountain biking.
Information: Park City Chamber/Visitors Bureau, 1826 Olympic Pkwy., 435-658-9616, 800-453-1360; www.parkcityinfo.com

UTAH

## WHAT TO SEE AND DO

### Brighton Ski Resort
12601 E. Big Cottonwood Canyon Rd.,
Brighton, 801-532-4731, 800-873-5512;
www.skibrighton.com

### Canyons
4000 The Canyons Resort Dr.,
Park City, 435-649-5400;
www.thecanyons.com
Sixteen high-speed quad, triple, double chairlifts; gondola; patrol, school, rentals; restaurant, cafeteria, bar, lodge. 155 trails. Winter lift daily 9 a.m.-4 p.m. Thanksgiving-April, daily.

### Deer Valley Resort
2250 Deer Valley Dr. S, Park City,
435-649-1000, 800-424-3337
Eight high-speed quad, eight triple, two double chairlifts; rental, patrol, school, snowmaking; restaurants, lounge, lodge, nursery. Approximately 1,750 skiable acres. Vertical drop 3,000 feet. No Snowboarding.

December-mid-April, daily. Summer activities include mountain biking, hiking, horseback riding and scenic chairlift rides.

### Egyptian Theatre
328 Main St., Park City, 435-649-9371;
www.egyptiantheatrecompany.org
Originally built in 1926 as a silent movie and vaudeville house, this is now a year-round performing arts center with a full semiprofessional theater season. Thursday-Saturday; some performances other days.

### Tanger Factory Outlet
6699 N Landmark Dr., Park City,
435-645-7078, 866-665-8681;
www.tangeroutlet.com
The more than 45 outlet stores here include Gap, Nike and Eddie Bauer. Daily.

### Kimball Art Center
638 Park Ave., Park City, 435-649-8882;
www.kimball-art.org

Exhibits in various media by local and regional artists. Gallery, Monday, Wednesday-Friday 10 a.m.-5 p.m, Saturday-Sunday noon-5 p.m.)

### Park City Mountain Resort
1310 Lowell Ave., Park City,
435-649-8111, 800-222-7275;
www.pcski.com
Gondola; 2 quad, four double, five triple, four 6-passenger chairlifts; patrol, school, rentals, snowmaking; restaurants, cafeteria, bar. Approximately 3,300 acres; 104 trails; 750 acres of open-bowl skiing. Lighted snowboarding. Mid-November-mid-April, daily. Alpine slide, children's park, miniature golf in summer.

### Rockport State Park
9040 N Hwy. 302, Peoa, 435-336-2241;
stateparks.utah.gov/parks/rockport
This 1,000-acre park along east side of Rockport Lake offers great opportunities for viewing wildlife, including bald eagles (winter) and golden eagles. Swimming, waterskiing, sailboarding, fishing, boating; cross-country ski trail (six miles), camping, tent and trailer sites. Daily.

### Solitude Mountain Resort
12000 Big Cottonwood Canyon, Solitude,
801-534-1400; www.skisolitude.com

### Utah Winter Sports Park
3000 Bear Hollow Dr., Park City,
435-658-4200; www.olyparks.com
Recreational ski jumping is available at this $25-million park built for 2002 Olympic Winter Games. Lessons are offered, followed by two-hour jumping session. Olympic bobsled and luge track (high-speed rides available). Wednesday-Sunday.

### White Pine Touring Center
1790 Bonanza Dr., Park City,
435-649-8710;
www.whitepinetouring.com
Groomed cross-country trails (12 miles), school, rentals; guided tours. November-April, daily. Summer mountain biking; rentals.

## SPECIAL EVENTS
### Art Festival
Main St., Park City
Open-air market featuring work of more than 200 visual artists. Also street entertainment. First weekend in August.

### Sundance Film Festival
Park City, events held throughout city;
www.sundance.org/festival
This 10-day festival for independent filmmakers attracts lots of celebrities. Workshops, screenings and special events. Mid-January.

## HOTELS
### ★★★The Canyons Grand Summit Resort Hotel
4000 The Canyons Resort Dr., Park City,
435-615-8040, 866-604-4171;
www.thecanyons.com
This lovely mountain lodge, one of three at the Canyons Resort, is set at the foot of Park City's ski slopes. Guest rooms, most of which have balconies and fireplaces, have excellent views of the mountains and the valley below. If you need a break from skiing, check out the resort's Village Shops, where regularly scheduled concerts and other events are held. Summer brings warm-weather activities like horseback riding, hiking and fly-fishing, and the gondola remains open for scenic rides.
358 rooms. High-speed wireless Internet access. Two restaurants, two bars. Children's activity center. Spa. Ski in/ski out. Pool. $$$$

### ★★★Chateaux at Silver Lake
7815 E. Royal St., Park City,
435-658-9500, 888-976-2732;
www.chateaux-deervalley.com
Situated in the heart of Deer Valley Resort's Silver Lake Village, the Chateaux at Silver Lake offers guests a comfortable stay in an elegant and picturesque setting. Rooms are decorated with custom-designed furniture and feature pillow-top mattresses and feather beds, gas fireplaces and wet bars. Onsite amenities include a full-service spa, heated covered parking, free

local shuttle service and winter sports equipment rentals.

95 rooms. High-speed wireless Internet access. Restaurant, bar. Spa. Airport transportation available. Pool. Business center. **$$$$**

### ★★★Club Lespri Boutique Inn & Spa
1765 Sidewinder Dr., Park City,
435-645-9696; www.clublespri.com

This is one of the area's most intimate spa destinations, with only 10 suites, all of which feature fireplaces, hand carved furniture, custom beds, oversize tubs and full kitchens.

10 rooms, all suites. Restaurant, bar. Spa. Whirlpool. Airport transportation available. **$$$**

### ★★★Goldener Hirsch Inn
7570 Royal St. E. Park City,
435-649-7770, 800-252-3373;
www.goldenerhirschinn.com

Warm and inviting, this exceptional ski resort blends the services of a large hotel with the charm of a bed and breakfast. The romantic guest rooms and suites have warm colors and hand painted furniture. All-day dining and après-ski service are available at the hotel's Austrian-themed restaurant.

20 rooms. Closed mid-April-early June, early October-early December. Complimentary full breakfast. High-speed Internet access, wireless Internet access. Restaurant, bar. Whirlpool. Ski in/ski out. Airport transportation available. **$$$$**

### ★Holiday Inn Express
1501 W. Ute Blvd., Park City,
435-658-1600, 888-465-4329;
www.hiexpress.com

76 rooms. High-speed wireless Internet access. Airport transportation available. Pool. **$**

### ★★★Hotel Park City
2001 Park Ave., Park City,
435-200-2000, 888-999-0098;
www.hotelparkcity.com

This all-suite resort pampers its guests. The amenities are top-notch, from triple-headed showers and jetted tubs to Bose audio systems and Bulgari bath products. The suites have a residential air about them with cozy fireplaces, spacious sitting areas and traditional alpine-style furnishings. Set at the base of the Wasatch Mountains, this hotel has a scenic location that is ideal for skiers. Those who prefer a less rigorous route can visit the comprehensive spa. The charming Western-style restaurant wins raves for its mountain views and its delicious cuisine.

100 rooms, all suites. High-speed wireless Internet access. Two restaurants, bar. Spa. Ski in/ski out. Airport transportation available. Golf. Skiing. **$$**

### ★★★Marriott
1895 Sidewinder Dr., Park City,
435-649-2900, 800-234-9003;
www.marriott.com

This newly renovated hotel is located a mile from downtown Park City and the historic Main Street. Take the complimentary shuttle to Utah Olympic Park, Outlet Stores and old Main Street. Starbucks fans will find a coffee kiosk in the lobby, and the hotel also rents ski equipment in winter and bicycles in summer. This hotel is non-smoking.

198 rooms. High-speed Internet access. Restaurant, bar. Pets accpted. Pool. Business center. **$$**

### ★★★★★Stein Eriksen Lodge
7700 Stein Way, Park City,
435-649-3700, 800-453-1302;
www.steinlodge.com

Nestled mid-mountain at Utah's Deer Valley ski resort, this Scandinavian masterpiece enjoys a magnificent alpine setting. The resort offers visitors unparalleled levels of service. Heated sidewalks and walkways will keep you toasty, while the ski valet service will take care of all your needs on the slopes. The dining is outstanding, and the Sunday Jazz Brunch and Skiers Lunch Buffet are local sensations. The blazing fireplace and inviting ambience of the Troll Hallen Lounge make it a cozy spot for après-ski or light fare. Guests rest weary muscles at the spa, work out at the well-equipped fitness center or unwind in the year-round outdoor heated pool. Rooms are all distinctive but all feature jetted tubs; suites have gourmet kitchens, stone fireplaces and master bedrooms.

175 rooms. High-speed wireless Internet access. Restaurant, bar. Children's activity center. Spa. Outdoor pool, whirlpool. Ski in/ski out. Airport transportation available. Fitness center. Business center. **$$$$**

## SPECIALTY LODGINGS

### Silver King Hotel

1485 Empire Ave., Park City,
435-649-5500, 800-331-8652;
www.silverkinghotel.com

66 rooms, all suites. High-speed wireless Internet access. Ski in/ski out. Pool. **$$$**

### Washington School Inn

543 Park Ave., Park City,
435-649-3800, 800-824-1672;
www.washingtonschoolinn.com

Built in 1889, this historic stone schoolhouse is charming and well appointed with turn-of-the-century country décor and modern amenities.

15 rooms. Children over 8 years only. Complimentary full breakfast. High-speed wireless Internet access. Whirlpool. Airport transportation available. **$$**

### Woodside Inn B&B

1469 Woodside Ave., Park City,
435-649-3494, 888-241-5890;
www.woodsideinn.com

6 rooms. Complimentary full breakfast. High-speed wireless Internet access. Airport transportation available. **$$**

## RESTAURANTS

### ★★★The Cabin

4000 The Canyons Resort Dr.,
Park City, 435-615-8060;
www.thecanyons.com

This upscale restaurant with rustic décor and a friendly staff at the Canyons Grand Summit Hotel serves an eclectic Western menu, including buffalo tenderloin, lamb osso bucco and the signature crispy trout.

American menu. Breakfast, lunch, dinner. Bar. Children's menu. Casual attire. Reservations recommended. Valet parking. **$$$**

### ★★Chez Betty

1637 Short Line Rd., Park City,
435-649-8181; www.chezbetty.com

American menu. Dinner. Closed Tuesday-Wednesday. Casual attire. Outdoor seating. **$$$**

### ★★★Chimayo

368 Main St., Park City, 435-649-6222;
www.chimayorestaurant.com

Park City's most stylish come to this restaurant to sample Southwestern cuisine. Dishes include scallops wrapped in wild boar bacon and served with a tortilla tomato casserole with salsa verde, and trout fajitas. A fireplace at one end of the dining room enhances the warm colorful atmosphere.

Southwestern menu. Dinner. Children's menu. Casual attire. Reservations recommended. **$$$**

### ★★★★The Glitretind

7700 Stein Way, Park City, 435-645-6455;
www.steinlodge.com

The celebrated Stein Ericksen Lodge claims not only the most impressive of views of the Wasatch Mountains, but one of the most lauded restaurants in Utah as well. Executive Chef Zane Holmquist prepares delicious New American cuisine. Try the scallop and lobster burger or the loin of organic Utah lamb with white. The wine selection is also impressive. Managed by Sommelier Cara Schwindt, the selection houses more than 350 types of wine that total more than 8,000 bottles. The restaurant also provides a wide selection of dessert and after dinner drinks, including a wide range of single malt scotch, bourbon, Cognac and brandy.

American menu. Breakfast, lunch, dinner, late-night, Sunday brunch. Bar. Children's menu. Business casual attire. Reservations recommended. Valet parking. Outdoor seating. **$$$**

### ★★★Grappa

151 Main St., Park City, 435-645-0636;
www.grapparestaurant.com

Located in a former boarding house on Park City's historic Main Street, this upscale restaurant offers dining on three levels. Many of the dishes feature just-picked herbs and flowers from the adjacent gardens, such as the polenta and herb-crusted rainbow trout served over mushroom risotto.

Italian menu. Dinner. Closed one month in spring and fall. Children's menu. Casual attire. Reservations recommended. Outdoor seating. **$$$**

**★★Kampai**
586 Main St., Park City, 435-649-0655;
www.latituderg.com
Sushi menu. Lunch, dinner. Casual attire. Reservations recommended. **$$**

**★★★★Riverhorse on Main**
540 Main St., Park City, 435-649-3536;
www.riverhorsegroup.com
Even ski bunnies (and bums) must eat, and when they do, they come to Riverhorse on Main, a bustling, happening scene. Located in the renovated historic Masonic Hall on Main Street, this modern restaurant, with dark woods, soft candlelight and fresh flowers offers lots of fun Asian-inspired eats such as chicken satay, shrimp potstickers, crispy duck salad, macadamia-crusted

halibut, grilled lobster tail and charred rack of lamb. While the dress code is informal, reservations are a must.
American menu. Dinner. Children's menu. Business casual attire. Reservations recommended. Outdoor seating. **$$$**

## SPAS
**★★★★The Spa at Stein Erikson Lodge**
7700 Stein Way, Park City, 435-649-6475;
www.steinlodge.com
The Spa at Stein Eriksen Lodge was designed to appeal to guests needing remedies for sore and tired muscles after skiing or those affected by the resort's high altitude. All spa services grant complimentary use of the fitness center, steam room, sauna, whirlpool, and relaxation room. Aromatic and exhilarating treatments refresh and renew at this European-style spa, where Vichy showers and kurs are de rigueur. The extensive massage menu includes Swedish, deep tissue, aromatic, stone, reflexology, and a special massage for mothers-to-be. In-room massages are available for additional privacy. **$$**

# PAYSON
Payson sits at the foot of the Wasatch Mountains, near Utah Lake. Mormons first settled the area after spending a night on the banks of Peteneet Creek.
Information: Chamber of Commerce, 439 W. Utah Ave., 801-465-5200; www.payson.org

## WHAT TO SEE AND DO
**Mount Nebo Scenic Loop Drive**
Payson
This 45-mile drive around the eastern shoulder of towering Mount Nebo (elevation 11,877 feet) is one of the most thrilling in Utah. Mount Nebo's three peaks are the highest in the Wasatch range. The road travels south through Payson and Santaquin canyons and then climbs 9,000 feet up Mount Nebo, offering a view of Devil's Kitchen, a brilliantly colored canyon. (This section of the drive is not recommended for those who dislike heights.) The forest road continues south to Hwy. 132; take Hwy. 132 east to Nephi, and then drive north on I-15 back to Payson.

**Peteetneet Cultural Museum and Arts Center**
10 N. 600 East, Payson, 801-465-5265;
peteetneetacademy.org
Named after Ute leader Chief Peteetneet, the center and museum (also called the Peteetneet Academy) is housed in a historic Victorian-style building, which includes an art gallery, photography exhibit, blacksmith shop and visitor's center. Open Monday-Friday 10 a.m.-4 p.m.

## SPECIAL EVENTS
**Golden Onion Days**
Payson; www.payson.org
Includes community theater presentations, 5K and 10K runs, horse races, demolition

derby, parade, fireworks and picnic. Labor Day weekend.

## HOTELS

★**Cherry Lane Motel**
240 E. 100 N. Payson, 801-465-2582
10 rooms. **$**

★**Comfort Inn**
830 N. Main St., Payson, 801-465-4861;
www.comfortinn.com

62 rooms. Complimentary continental breakfast. Pets accepted. Pool. **$**

## RESTAURANTS

★**Dalton's Fine Dining**
20 S. 100 W. Payson, 801-465-9182
American menu. Lunch, dinner. Closed Sunday. **$**

# PRICE

Price, the seat of Carbon County, bases its prosperity on coal. More than 30 mine properties are within 30 miles. Several parks are located here.
Information: Carbon County Chamber of Commerce, 81 N. 200 E., 435-637-2788; www.pricecityutah.com

## WHAT TO SEE AND DO

### Cleveland-Lloyd Dinosaur Quarry
125 S. 600 W. Price, 435-636-3600;
www.blm.gov/utah/price/quarry.htm
Since 1928, more than 12,000 dinosaur bones, representing at least 70 different animals, have been excavated on this site. Visitor center, nature trail, picnic area. Memorial Day-Labor Day, daily; Easter-Memorial Day, weekends only.

### College of Eastern Utah Prehistoric Museum
155 E. Main St., Price,
435-613-5060, 800-817-9949;
museum.ceu.edu
This museum includes dinosaur displays and archaeology exhibits. Memorial Day-Labor Day, daily; rest of year, Monday-Saturday.

### Geology tours
90 N. 100 E., Price
Self-guided tours of Nine Mile Canyon, San Rafael Desert, Cleveland-Lloyd Dinosaur Quarry, Little Grand Canyon and more. Maps available at Castle Country Travel Region or Castle Country Regional Information Center, 155 E Main, 800-842-0784.

### Manti-La Sal National Forest, Manti Division
599 W. Price River Dr., Price,
435-637-2817;
www.fs.fed.us/r4/mantilasal

This 1,327,631-acre area offers scenic mountain drives, riding trails, campsites, winter sports and deer and elk hunting. Joe's Valley Reservoir on Hwy. 29 and Electric Lake on Hwy. 31 have fishing and boating. Areas of geologic interest, developed as a result of massive landslides, are near Ephraim.

### Price Canyon Recreation Area
Price, 15 miles north on Hwy. 6, then three miles west on unnumbered road.
435-636-3600;
www.blm.gov/utah/price/pricerec.htm
Scenic overlooks, hiking, picnicking, camping. Roads have steep grades. May-mid-October, daily.

### Scofield State Park
Hwy. 6 and Hwy. 96, Price, 435-448-9449
(summer), 435-687-2491 (winter);
stateparks.utah.gov/parks/scofield
Utah's highest state park has a 2,800-acre lake that lies at an altitude of 7,616 feet. Fishing, boating (docks, ramps), ice fishing; camping; snowmobiling; cross-country skiing in winter. May-October.

## HOTELS

★**Best Western Carriage House Inn**
590 E. Main St., Price,
435-637-5660, 800-937-8376;
www.bestwestern.com

40. rooms. Complimentary continental breakfast. Pool. **$**

**★★Holiday Inn**
838 Westwood Blvd., Price,
435-637-8880, 888-465-4329;

www.holiday-inn.com
151 rooms. High-speed Internet access. Restaurant, bar. Pool. **$**

# PROVIDENCE

Very close to Logan (about a mile away), Providence is located where Spring Creek meets the Logan River. The small town was named by leaders of the LDS church, who found its location providential.
Information: www.providence-city.com

## SPECIALTY LODGINGS
**Providence Inn**
10 S. Main, Providence,
435-752-3432, 800-480-4943;
www.providenceinn.com
This historic bed and breakfast has rooms decorated in various periods: Early

American, Victorian a nd Georgian. Built in 1869, the structure has been accurately restored. A hearty breakfast is provided. 17 rooms. **$$**

# PROVO

Provo received its name from French-Canadian trapper Etienne Provost, who arrived in the area in 1825. But it wasn't until 1849 that the first permanent settlement, begun by a party of Mormons, was established. The Mormon settlers erected Fort Utah as their first building, and despite famine, drought, hard winters and the constant danger of attack, they persisted and the settlement grew. Today, Provo is the seat of Utah County and the state's third-largest city. An important educational and commercial center, Provo's largest employer is Brigham Young University.

Provo lies in the middle of a lush, green valley: to the north stands 12,008-foot Mount Timpanogos; to the south is the perpendicular face of the Wasatch Range; to the east Provo Peak rises 11,054 feet; and to the west lies Utah Lake, backed by more mountains. Provo is the headquarters of the Uinta National Forest, and many good fishing, boating, camping and hiking spots are nearby.
Information Utah County Visitors Center, 111 S. University Ave., 801-851-2100, 800-222-8824; www.utahvalley.org/cvb

## WHAT TO SEE AND DO

### Brigham Young University
Provo, 801-422-4636; www.byu.edu
Established 1875; 27,000 students. Founded by Brigham Young and operated by the Church of Jesus Christ of Latter-day Saints. This is one of the world's largest church-related institutions of higher learning, with students from every state and more than 90 foreign countries. One-hour, free guided tours arranged at Hosting Center Monday-Friday; also by appointment.

### Earth Science Museum
1683 North Canyon Rd., Provo, 801-422-3680; cpms.byu.edu
Geological collection, extensive series of minerals and fossils.

### Harris Fine Arts Center
HFAC Campus Dr., Provo,
801-422-7664;
www.cfac.byu.edu
Includes periodic displays of rare instruments and music collection. Concert, theater performances.

### Monte L. Bean Life Science Museum
645 E. 1430 N. Provo, 801-442-5051;
www.mlbean.byu.edu
Exhibits and collections of insects, fish, amphibians, reptiles, birds, animals and plants.

### Museum of Art
North Campus Drive, Provo, 801-442-8287; moa.byu.edu
Exhibits from the BYU Permanent Collection; traveling exhibits.

### Museum of Peoples and Cultures
105 Allen Hall, Provo, 801-422-0020;
mpc.byu.edu
Material from South America, the Near East and the southwestern United States.

### Pioneer Museum
500 W. 500 N. Provo, 801-852-6609
This museum includes an outstanding collection of Utah pioneer relics and Western art. Pioneer Village.

### Uinta National Forest
88 W. and 100 N. Provo, 801-342-5100;
www.fs.fed.us/r4/uinta
Scenic drives through the forest give an unsurpassed view of colorful landscapes, canyons and waterfalls. Stream and lake fishing; hunting for deer and elk, camping, picnicking. Reservations accepted.

### Utah Lake State Park
4400 W. Center St., Provo, 801-375-0731;
stateparks.utah.gov/parks/utah-lake
The park is situated on the eastern shore of Utah Lake, a 150-square-mile, freshwater remnant of ancient Lake Bonneville that created the Great Salt Lake. Fishing, boating (ramp, dock); ice skating; roller skating; picnicking, play area, camping. Visitor center. Daily.

## SPECIAL EVENTS

### Freedom Festival
4626 N. 300 W., Provo, 801-818-1776;
www.freedomfestival.org
Bazaar, carnival, parades. Early July.

## HOTELS

### ★Best Western Cottontree Inn
2230 N. University Pkwy., Provo,
801-373-7044, 800-662-6886;
www.bestwestern.com
80 rooms. Complimentary continental breakfast. Pool. $

### ★★Courtyard Provo
1600 N. Freedom Blvd., Provo,
801-373-2222; www.marriott.com
100 rooms. High-speed Internet access. Restaurant, bar. Pool. $

### ★Fairfield Inn
1515 S. University Ave., Provo,
801-377-950; www.marriott.com
72 rooms. Complimentary continental breakfast. Pool. $

### ★★★Marriott Provo Hotel And Conference Center
101 W. 100 N. Provo,
801-377-4700, 800-777-7144;
www.marriott.com

Nearby attractions include two shopping malls, as well as the Seven Peaks Water Park and Ice Rink, where the ice hockey competition and practices for the 2002 Winter Olympics were held. The comfortable rooms feature views of the Wasatch Mountains. This hotel is non-smoking. 330 rooms. Restaurant, bar. Airport transportation available. Pool. Business center. **$$**

## RESTAURANTS

★★**Bombay House**
463 N. University Ave., Provo,
801-373-6677; www.bombayhouse.com

Indian menu. Dinner. Closed Sunday. Casual attire. **$**

★**Joe Vera's Mexican Restaurant**
250 W. Center St., Provo, 801-375-6714
Mexican menu. Lunch, dinner. Closed Sunday. Children's menu. Casual attire. **$$**

# RICHFIELD

Located in the center of Sevier Valley in south central Utah, Richfield has become the commercial hub of the region. Today, some of the world's best beef is raised in and shipped from this area.
Information: Chamber of Commerce, 435-896-4241; www.richfieldcity.com

## WHAT TO SEE AND DO

**Big Rock Candy Mountain**
Richfield, 25 miles south on Hwy. 89, in Marysvale Canyon, 435-896-4241
Burl Ives popularized this multicolored mountain in a song.

**Fishlake National Forest**
115 E. and 900 N. Richfield, 435-896-9233; www.fs.fed.us/r4/fishlake
This 1,424,000-acre forest offers fishing, hunting, hiking, picnicking and camping. It is named for the biggest lake in the forest area. Fish Lake (33 miles southeast, via Hwy. 119 and Hwy. 24, then seven miles northeast on Hwy. 25) offers high-altitude angling on a six-mile-long lake covering 2,600 acres.

## HOTELS

★**Days Inn**
333 N. Main, Richfield,
435-896-6476, 888-275-8513;
www.daysinn.com
51 rooms. Restaurant. Pets accepted. Pool. **$**

★**Quality Inn**
540 S. Main St., Richfield,
435-896-5465, 800-228-5151;
www.qualityinn.com
79 rooms. Pool. **$**

## CAPITOL REEF NATIONAL PARK

Capitol Reef, at an elevation ranging from 3,900 to 8,800 feet, is composed of red sandstone cliffs capped with domes of white sandstone. It was named Capitol Reef because the rocks formed a natural barrier to pioneer travel and the white sandstone domes resemble that of the U.S. Capitol.

Located in the heart of Utah's slickrock country, the park is actually a 100-mile section of the Waterpocket Fold, an upthrust of sedimentary rock created during the formation of the Rocky Mountains. Pockets in the rocks collect thousands of gallons of water each time it rains. From A.D. 700-1350, this 378-square-mile area was the home of an ancient people who grew corn along the Fremont River. Petroglyphs can be seen on some of the sandstone walls. A schoolhouse, farmhouse and orchards, established by early Mormon settlers, are open to the public in season.

The park can be approached from either the east or the west via Hwy. 24, a paved road. There is a visitor center on this road about seven miles from the west boundary and eight miles from the east (Daily). A 25-mile round-trip scenic drive, some parts unpaved, starts from this point. There are evening programs and guided walks Memorial Day-Labor Day. Three campgrounds are available: Fruita, approximately one mile south off Hwy. 24, provides 70 tent and trailer sites year-round; Cedar Mesa, 23 miles south off Hwy. 24, and Cathedral, 28 miles north off Hwy. 24, offer five primitive sites with access depending on the weather. Information: Torrey, 10 miles east of Richfield on Hwy. 119, then 65 miles southeast on Hwy. 24, 435-425-3791; www.nps.gov/care

# ROOSEVELT

Roosevelt, in the geographical center of Utah's "dinosaur land," was named after Theodore Roosevelt, who once camped on the banks of a nearby river. Nine Mile Canyon, with its American Indian petroglyphs, can be reached from here. A Ranger District office of the Ashley National Forest is located in the town.
Information: Chamber of Commerce, 50 E. 200 S., Roosevelt, 435-722-4598

## HOTELS
★Best Western Inn
2203 E. Hwy. 40, Roosevelt, 435-722-4644;
www.bestwestern.com

40 rooms. High-speed Internet access. Pool. $

# SALINA

Mormon settlers established this town in the mid-1800s and named their settlement after the abundant salt deposits nearby. Salina's biggest claim to fame is the annual pageant, performed by hundreds of members of the LDS church.

## SPECIAL EVENTS
Mormon Miracle Pageant
4 N. 100 E., Manti,
435-835-3000, 800-255-8860;
www.mormonmiracle.org
A cast of more than 600 portray events from the Book of Mormon. Early-mid-June.

## HOTELS
★Best Western Shaheen Motel
1225 S. State St., Salina, 435-529-7455;
www.bestwestern.com
40 rooms. Complimentary continental breakfast. Pool. $

# SALT LAKE CITY

Salt Lake City, with its 10-acre blocks, 132-foot-wide, tree-lined streets and mountains rising to the east and west, is one of the most beautifully planned cities in the country.

On a hill at the north end of State Street stands Utah's classic capitol building. Three blocks south is Temple Square, with the famed Mormon Temple and Tabernacle. The adjacent block houses the headquarters of the Church of Jesus Christ of Latter-Day Saints, whose members are commonly called Mormons.

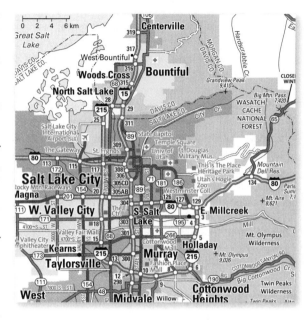

Once a desert wilderness, Salt Lake City was built by Mormon settlers who sought refuge from religious persecution. Followers of Brigham Young arrived and named their new territory "Deseret." In the early days, the Mormons began a variety of experiments in farming, industry and society, many of which were highly successful. Today, Salt Lake City is an industrious, businesslike city, a center for electronics, steel, missiles and a hundred other enterprises.

West of the city is the enormous Great Salt Lake, stretching 48 miles one way and 90 miles the other. It is less than 35 feet deep and between 15 and 20 percent salt—almost five times as salty as the ocean. You can't sink in the water—instead you'll just bob up and down. The lake is what remains of ancient Lake Bonneville, once 145 miles wide, 350 miles long and 1,000 feet deep. As Lake Bonneville's water evaporated over thousands of years, a large expanse of perfectly flat, solid salt was left. Today, the Bonneville Salt Flats stretch west almost to Nevada.

Salt Lake City was laid out in grid fashion, with Temple Square at the center. Most street names are coordinates on this grid: Fourth South Street is four blocks south of Temple Square, Seventh East is seven blocks east. These are written as 400 South and 700 East.

Information: Convention & Visitors Bureau, 90 S. West Temple, 801-521-2822; www.saltlake.org

**308**

**UTAH**

★
★
★
★
★

## SPOT★ LIGHT

★ THE FIRST KENTUCKY FRIED CHICKEN FRANCHISE WAS OPENED IN SALT LAKE CITY.

★ SALT LAKE CITY WAS FOUNDED IN 1847 BY MORMON PIONEERS.

★ THE CITY HOSTED THE WINTER OLYMPICS IN 2002.

## SALT LAKE CITY'S MORMON HERITAGE

The centerpiece of downtown Salt Lake City is Temple Square, the city block bordered by three streets named Temple West, North and South and Main Street on the east side. Utah's top tourist attraction, Temple Square is the hub for the Church of Jesus Christ of the Latter-Day Saints, where guests are invited to join a free guided tour that offers a glimpse of several architectural and cultural landmarks, including the Mormon Tabernacle, the Museum of Church History and Art and the

Joseph Smith Memorial Building. (Tours start at the flagpole every few minutes.) If your timing is right, you can also take in a film, choir rehearsal or organ recital here.

From Temple Square, head east on South Temple to a pair of historic homes, the Lion House (63 East South Temple) and the Beehive House (67 East South Temple). No tours are available of the Lion House, which served as Brigham Young's home during the mid-19th century, but there is a restaurant on the lower level that is a good spot for a lunch break. Next door, the Beehive House, another former Young residence and a National Historic Landmark, offers free tours every day. Just east of these houses on South Temple is Eagle Gate (at the intersection of State Street), an impressive arch capped by a two-ton sculpture of an eagle with a 20-foot wingspan.

South of Eagle Gate on the east side of State Street are two of Salt Lake City's standout cultural facilities: the Hansen Planetarium (15 South State Street) and the Social Hall Heritage Museum (39 South State Street). The former features daily star shows and a free space museum with hands-on exhibits. The latter includes remnants of Utah's first public building and the West's first theater. From the museum, it's best to reverse course and walk north on State Street, passing under Eagle Gate. Just beyond North Temple, hop on the paths that run through the lush City Creek Park and head north to the adjoining Memory Grove Park. From here, it's only a two-block walk west to the Utah State Capitol (just north of the intersection of State Street and 300 North Street), an exemplary Renaissance Revival-style structure built from Utah granite in 1915. The building is open to the public daily and guided tours are offered on weekdays.

Two blocks west of the State Capitol is the Pioneer Memorial Museum (300 North Main Street), a majestic replica of the original Salt Lake Theater (demolished in 1928) with 38 rooms of relics from the area's past, including photographs, vehicles, dolls, and weapons. The museum is on the eastern edge of one of the city's oldest neighborhoods, the tree-lined Marmalade District (between 300 and 500 North Streets to the north and south and Center and Quince Streets to the east and west), a good place to meander and gaze at historic homes.

## WHAT TO SEE AND DO
### Brigham Young Monument
**Salt Lake City, Main and S. Temple Streets**
This statue honoring the church leader was first seen at the Chicago World's Fair in 1893.

### Clark Planetarium
**110 S. 400 W., Salt Lake City,**
**801-456-7827;**
**www.hansenplanetarium.net**
The Hansen Dome Theatre and the Imax Theatre are the two main attractions here.

Daily. Free exhibits include images from the Hubble Space telescope and a fully functioning weather station.

### Council Hall
**300 N. State St., Salt Lake City,**
**801-538-1900**
Council Hall was once the meeting place of territorial legislature and city hall for 30 years. It was dismantled and then reconstructed in 1963 at its present location. Visitor information center and office; memorabilia. Daily.

### Governor's Mansion
603 E. S. Temple St., Salt Lake City,
801-538-1005
Built by Thomas Kearns, a wealthy Utah senator in the early 1900s, this mansion is the official residence of Utah's governor. It was painstakingly restored after a fire in 1993. President Theodore Roosevelt, a personal friend of Senator Kerns, dined here often. Tours. June-September, Tuesday and Thursday 2-4 p.m.

### InnsBrook Tours
Salt Lake City, 801-534-1001;
www.saltlakecitytours.org
This is the best way to see all the famous sites in Salt Lake City. Pick-up begins at 9:15 a.m., and then you're off to see landmarks like the Mormon Tabernacle, the Salt Lake Temple and the Olympic Stadium and Village. Daily.

### Lagoon Amusement Park, Pioneer Village and Water Park
Salt Lake City, 17 miles north on I-15,
800-748-5246; www.lagoonpark.com
Besides fun rides and water slides, the village includes a re-creation of a 19th-century Utah town with stagecoach and steam-engine train rides. Camping, picnicking. Memorial Day-August, daily; mid-April-late May and September, Saturday-Sunday only.

### Liberty Park
1300 South St., Salt Lake City,
801-972-7800
This 100-acre park is Salt Lake's largest. Go for a run, grab a game of tennis or enjoy a picnic. Paddleboats are available in summer, and there's a playground for kids. Park daily 7 a.m.-10 p.m. Aviary daily 9 a.m-6 p.m; November-March: daily 9 a.m.-4:30 p.m.

### Lion House
63 E. South Temple, Salt Lake City,
801-363-5466
Lion House was home to Brigham Young's family. Today it houses a restaurant. Next door is another residence, Beehive House, which is open to the public for tours. Monday-Saturday 11 a.m.-8 p.m.

### Maurice Abravanel Concert Hall
123 W. South Temple, Salt Lake City,
801-355-2787;
www.maurice-abravanel.com
Home to the Utah Symphony, this building is adorned with more than 12,000 square feet of 24-karat gold leaf and a mile of brass railing. It has been rated one of the best halls in the U.S. for acoustics. Free tours by appointment. The symphony has performances most weekends.

### Park City Mountain Resort
1310 Lowell Ave., Park City,
435-649-8111, 800-331-3178;
www.pcski.com

### Pioneer Memorial Museum
300 N. Main St., Salt Lake City,
801-532-6479;
www.dupinternational.org
This extensive collection of pioneer relics includes a carriage house, with exhibits relating to transportation, including Brigham Young's wagon and Pony Express items. One-hour guided tours by appointment. Monday-Saturday 9 a.m.-5 p.m.; June-August, also Sunday 1-5 p.m.

### Moki Mac River Expeditions
6006 S. 1300 E. Salt Lake City,
801-268-6667, 800-284-7280;
www.mokimac.com
Offers one- to 14-day whitewater and canoeing trips on the Green and Colorado rivers.

### Salt Lake Art Center
20 S. West Temple, Salt Lake City,
801-328-4201; www.slartcenter.org
Changing exhibits feature photographs, paintings, ceramics and sculptures. The school hosts lectures and shows films. Tuesday-Thursday, Saturday 11 a.m.-6 p.m. Friday 11 a.m.-9 p.m.

## Solitude Resort

12000 Big Cottonwood Canyon,
Salt Lake City, 801-534-1400;
www.skisolitude.com

Three quad, one triple, four double chair-lifts; racecourse, patrol, school, rentals. Longest run 3 1/2 miles, vertical drop 2,047 feet. November-April, daily. Cross-country center.

## Temple Square

Main and W. Temple Steets,
Salt Lake City,
801-240-1245, 800-537-9703

This 10-acre square is owned by the Church of Jesus Christ of Latter-Day Saints. Two visitor's centers provides information, exhibits and guided tours; 1/2- to 1-hour; daily, every 10 minutes.

## Assembly Hall

500 W. North Temple, Salt Lake City,
801-240-3318

(1880) Victorian gothic congregation hall. Tours daily.

## Family History Library

35 N.W., Temple, Salt Lake City,
801-240-2584, 800-346-6044

This genealogical library is the largest such facility in the world. Monday 8 a.m.-5 p.m., Tuesday-Saturday 8 a.m.-9 p.m.

## Museum of Church History and Art

45 N. West Temple St., Salt Lake City,
801-240-4615

Exhibits of Latter-Day Saints church history from 1820 to present. Monday-Friday 9 a.m.-9 p.m., Saturday-Sunday 10 a.m.-7 p.m.

## Seagull Monument

Temple Square and State Street,
Salt Lake City, 801-521-2822

The monument commemorates what many church members call the "Miracle of the Gulls." Seagulls saved the first crops ever planted here in 1848 from crickets that were devouring entire fields.

## Tabernacle

50 W. North Temple, Salt Lake City,
801-240-4872

The self-supporting roof, an elongated dome, is 250 feet long and 150 feet wide. The tabernacle organ has 11,623 pipes, ranging from 5/8 inch to 32 feet in length. The world-famous Tabernacle Choir may be heard at rehearsal (Thursday 8 p.m.) or at broadcast time (Sunday 9:30 a.m., be seated by 9:15 a.m.). Organ recitals Monday-Saturday noon, Sunday afternoon.

## Temple

50 W. North Temple, Salt Lake City,
801-240-4872

Used for sacred ordinances, such as baptisms and marriages. Closed to non-Mormons.

## This Is the Place Heritage Park

2601 Sunnyside Ave., Salt Lake City,
801-582-1847; www.thisistheplace.org

This historic park is located at the mouth of Emigration Canyon, where Mormon pioneers first entered the valley, and includes Old Deseret Pioneer Village and This Is the Place Monument (1947), commemorating Brigham Young's words upon first seeing the Salt Lake City site. Hundreds of people depict pioneer life. Admission to the monument and visitor's center, which includes an audio presentation and murals of the Mormon migration, is free. Monument and grounds, daily, dawn-dusk. Visitor center Monday-Saturday 9 a.m.-6 p.m. Village late May-early September: Monday-Saturday 10 a.m.-6 p.m.

## Trolley Square

600 S. 700 East St., Salt Lake City,
801-521-9877

This 10-acre complex of trolley barns has been converted into an entertainment/shopping/dining center. Daily.

**311**

**UTAH**

★
★
★
★

### University of Utah
201 S. Presidents Dr., Salt Lake City,
801-581-7200; www.utah.edu
Established in 1850. On campus is the J. Willard Marriott Library. Named for the hotel magnate, this library includes a vast Western Americana collection. Monday-Thursday 7 a.m.-midnight, Friday 7 a.m.-8 p.m., Saturday 9 a.m.-8 p.m., Sunday 10 a.m.-midnight; closed holidays, also July 24.

### Pioneer Theatre Company
300 S. 1400 E. Salt Lake City,
801-581-6961; www.pioneertheatre.org
Two auditoriums host dramas, musicals, comedies. Mid-September-mid-May.

### Red Butte Garden and Arboretum
300 Wakara Way, Salt Lake City,
801-581-4747; www.redbuttegarden.org
Includes more than 9,000 trees on 150 acres, representing 350 species; conservatory. Self-guided tours. Special events in summer. Daily.

### Utah Museum of Fine Arts
410 Campus Center Dr.,
Salt Lake City, 801-581-7332;
www.umfa.utah.org
Representations of artistic styles from Egyptian antiquities to contemporary American paintings; 19th-century French and American paintings and furniture. Tuesday-Friday 10 a.m.-5 p.m., Saturday-Sunday 11 a.m.-5 p.m.

### Utah Museum of Natural History
1390 E. Presidents Circle, Salt Lake City,
801-581-6927; www.umnh.utah.edu
Shows exhibits of the Earth's natural wonders and honors Utah's native cultures. Monday-Saturday 9:30 a.m.-5:30 p.m., Sunday noon-5 p.m.; closed July 24.

### Utah Jazz (NBA)
301 W. South Temple, Salt Lake City,
801-325-2500; www.nba.com/jazz
Professional basketball team.

### Utah Opera Company
123 W. South Temple,
Salt Lake City, 801-533-5626;
www.utahopera.org
Grand opera. October-May.

### Utah Starzz (WNBA)
301 W. South Temple,
Salt Lake City, 801-355-3865;
www.utah.com/sports/starzz.htm
Women's professional basketball team.

### Wasatch-Cache National Forest
125 S. State St., Salt Lake City,
801-466-6411; www.fs.fed.us/r4/wcnf
This wilderness area has alpine lakes, rugged peaks and several canyons. Fishing, boating, deer and elk hunting, winter sports and camping.

### Wheeler Historic Farm
6351 S. 900 E. St., Salt Lake City,
801-264-2241; www.wheelerfarm.com
This living history farm on 75 acres depicts rural life from 1890 to 1918, and includes a farmhouse, farm buildings, animals, crops and hay rides. Tour. Visitors can feed the animals, gather eggs and milk cows. There is a small fee for various activities and events. Monday-Saturday dawn to dusk.

### ZCMI (Zion's Co-operative Mercantile Institution) Center
Main and South Temple, Salt Lake City
A department store established in 1868 by Brigham Young anchors this 85-store, enclosed downtown shopping mall. Monday-Saturday.

## SPECIAL EVENTS
### Utah Arts Festival
230 S. 500 W., Salt Lake City,
801-322-2428; www.uaf.org
This four-day festival featuring visual, performing and culinary artists, draws more than 80,000 people every year. Last week in June.

312

UTAH

# HOTELS

## ★Days Inn
1900 W. North Temple, Salt Lake City,
801-539-8538, 800-329-7466;
www.daysinn.com
110 rooms. Complimentary continental breakfast. Airport transportation available. Pets accepted. Pool. **$**

## ★★Embassy Suites
110 W. 600 S., Salt Lake City,
801-359-7800; www.hilton.com
241 rooms, all suites. Complimentary full breakfast. High-speed Internet access. Restaurant, bar. Pool. **$**

## ★★★★The Grand America Hotel
555 S. Main St., Salt Lake City,
801-258-6000, 800-621-4505;
www.grandamerica.com
Set against the beautiful backdrop of the Wasatch Mountains, the Grand America is a tribute to the glory of old-world Europe. This esteemed hotel is the pinnacle of refinement. The guest rooms are classically French, with plush carpets, luxurious fabrics, fine art and Richelieu furniture. The world-class spa is a sanctuary and includes a full-service salon. Both the indoor and outdoor pools are spectacular.
775 rooms. High-speed Internet access. Restaurant, two bars. Spa. Airport transportation available. **$$$**

## ★★Hilton Salt Lake City Airport
5151 Wiley Post Way, Salt Lake City,
801-539-1515, 800-999-3736;
www.hilton.com
278 rooms. High-speed Internet access. Restaurant, bar. Airport transportation available. Pets accepted. Pool. Business center. **$**

## ★★★Hilton Salt Lake City Center
255 S.W., Temple, Salt Lake City,
801-328-2000; www.hilton.com
Located in the heart of downtown, this large hotel offers spacious and very nicely appointed rooms and friendly service.
499 rooms. High-speed Internet access. Two restaurants, bar. Spa. Airport transportation available. Pets accepted. **$**

## ★★★Hotel Monaco Salt Lake City
15 W. 200 S. Salt Lake City,
801-595-0000, 877-294-9710;
www.hotelmonaco.com
The Hotel Monaco stands out for its haute décor and personalized services. Located in the heart of downtown Salt Lake City, this refurbished 14-story landmark hotel makes an instant impression with its vibrant lobby featuring velvet furnishings. The rooms are equally delightful with beds swathed in Frette linens. Tall rooms are available with eight-foot beds and heightened showerheads. Amenities include coffeemakers with Starbucks coffee, yoga programs (grab a mat from the basket and flip on the Yoga channel) and gourmet mini-bars. If all you're missing is a travel companion, you can adopt a goldfish during your stay. Pets are also welcome.
225 rooms. High-speed wireless Internet access. Restaurant, bar. Airport transportation available. Pets accepted. **$**

## ★★★Little America Hotel
500 S. Main St., Salt Lake City,
801-596-5700, 800-453-9450;
www.littleamerica.com/slc
This elegant hotel offers a variety of accommodations. Rooms in the tower are decorated in rich French brocade fabrics and English wool carpets, and offer large parlor areas with views of the city. There's also a separate dressing area and bathroom with an oval shaped tub. Garden rooms are also spacious and have private entrances. There's a large indoor pool, salon and barber shop.
850 rooms. High-speed Internet access. Two restaurants, bar. Airport transportation available. **$**

## ★★★Marriott Salt Lake City Downtown
75 S. West Temple, Salt Lake City,
801-531-0800; www.marriott.com
Located across from the Salt Palace Convention Center, this hotel caters to business travelers and is close to the airport and major ski resorts. Everything is on hand here, including a heated pool, fitness center and a Starbucks.

**313**

UTAH

★

★

★

☆

☆

515 rooms. High-speed Internet access. Restaurant, bar. Business center. **$$**

### ★★★Marriott Salt Lake City-City Center
220 S. State St., Salt Lake City,
801-961-8700, 866-961-8700;
www.marriott.com

Situated adjacent to the Gallivan Center, which hosts concerts in summer and skating in winter, this hotel is within walking distance to numerous restaurants and shops. The contemporary and comfortable guest rooms are decorated in a relaxing palette, and feature down comforters, large marble baths and views of either the city or the mountains. The hotel's restaurant, Piastra, serves up continental cuisine in a sophisticated setting.

359 rooms. High-speed Internet access. Restaurant, bar. **$**

### ★★Peery Hotel
110 W. Broadway, Salt Lake City,
801-521-4300, 800-331-0073;
www.peeryhotel.com

73 rooms. High-speed wireless Internet access. Restaurant, bar. **$**

### ★★★Radisson Hotel Salt Lake City Downtown
215 W. S. Temple, Salt Lake City,
801-531-7500, 800-333-3333;
www.radisson.com

Located downtown next to the Salt Palace Convention Center, this hotel completed a $5 million renovation in 2006 and added new luxury beds. All rooms have spacious work areas with Herman Miller-designed ergonomic chairs and complimentary high speed Internet. There's also an indoor pool, fitness center, sauna and whirlpool.

381 rooms. Restaurant, bar. Airport transportation available. **$**

## SPECIALTY LODGINGS
### Armstrong Mansion
667 E. 100 S., Salt Lake City,
801-531-1333, 800-708-1333;
www.armstrongmansion.com

This bed and breakfast built in 1893 is tastefully decorated with antiques and carved wood.

16 rooms. Complimentary full breakfast. **$$**

## RESTAURANTS
### ★★Baci Trattoria
134 W. Pierpont Ave., Salt Lake City,
801-328-1500; www.gastronomyinc.com

Italian menu. Lunch, dinner. Closed Sunday. Children's menu. Casual attire. Reservations recommended. Outdoor seating. **$$$**

### ★★★Bambara
202 S. Main St., Salt Lake City,
801-363-5454; www.bambara-slc.com

This chic New American bistro housed in a former bank serves up creations such as seared halibut with basil mashed potatoes and tomato pine nut truffle vinaigrette, and house made tagliattelle and organic English peas, shaved truffle and wild mushroom-thyme cream sauce.

American menu. Breakfast, lunch, dinner. Children's menu. Business casual attire. Reservations recommended. Valet parking. **$$$**

### ★★Creekside at Solitude
12000 Big Cottonwood Canyon,
Solitude, 801-536-5787;
www.skisolitude.com

American menu. Dinner, Saturday-Sunday brunch. Closed May, late September-mid-November. Bar. Casual attire. Outdoor seating. **$$**

### ★★★Fresco Italian Cafe
1513 S. 1500 E., Salt Lake City,
801-486-1300; www.frescoitaliancafe.com

A winding brick walkway lined with flowers leads the way to this charming neighborhood bistro, where you'll find a fireplace in winter and al fresco dining during the summer. Guests will enjoy the fresh and authentic flavors of Italy in dishes such as the chef's nightly risotto and delicious herb gnocchi.

Italian menu. Dinner. Casual attire. Reservations recommended. Outdoor seating. **$$**

### ★★★La Caille
9565 S. Wasatch Blvd., Little Cottonwood Canyon, 801-942-1751; www.lacaille.com
This impressive country French chateau is surrounded by beautiful gardens populated by peacocks, llamas, ducks and a host of other exotic creatures. Inside, the friendly staff is dressed in 18th-century costumes and the menu features innovative fare such as Champagne ravioli.
French menu. Dinner, brunch. Bar. Children's menu. Casual attire. Reservations recommended. Valet parking. Outdoor seating. $$$

### ★★★Log Haven
6451 E. Millcreek Canyon Rd.,
Salt Lake City, 801-272-8255;
www.log-haven.com
This rustic log mansion is one of Utah's most innovative and elegant restaurants. The fresh specialties change daily, but you might see fire-grilled corn soup or jumbo lump crab cakes. The restaurant also has an extensive wine list.
International menu. Di nner. Bar. Business casual attire. Reservations recommended. Outdoor seating. $$$

### ★★Market Street Broiler
260 S. 1300 E., Salt Lake City,
801-583-8808; www.gastronomyinc.com
Seafood menu. Lunch, dinner. Children's menu. Casual attire. Outdoor seating. $$

### ★★Market Street Grill
48 W. Market St., Salt Lake City,
801-322-4668; www.gastronomyinc.com
Seafood menu. Breakfast, lunch, dinner, Sunday brunch. Closed Labor Day. Children's menu. Casual attire. Valet parking. $$

### ★★★Metropolitan
173 W. Broadway, Salt Lake City,
801-364-3472; www.themetropolitan.com
This contemporary and whimsical restaurant specializes in "hand crafted New American cuisine." Indulge your inner kid with the TV dinner: a choice between fish and chips or wild boar ribs with peas and carrots and peach crisp. End with a sno-cone in a variety of flavors including spicy chocolate and cherry limeade.
American menu. Dinner, late-night. Closed Sunday. Bar. Business casual attire. Reservations recommended. Valet parking. $$$

### ★★Mikado at Cottonwood
6572 S. Big Cottonwood Canyon Rd.,
Salt Lake City, 801-947-9800;
www.latituderg.com
Sushi menu. Lunch, dinner. Children's menu. Casual attire. Reservations recommended. Outdoor seating. $$

### ★★★The New Yorker
60 W. Market St., Salt Lake City,
801-363-0166;
www.gastronomyinc.com
Recognized as one of Salt Lake's best dining spots since 1978, this elegant restaurant serves excellent traditional fare. Appetizers (including fruit, cheese and seafood) are offered as guests arrive.
Steak menu. Lunch, dinner. Closed Sunday. Bar. Reservations recommended. Valet parking. $$$

### ★★Rino's
2302 Parleys Way, Salt Lake City,
801-484-0901;
www.rinositalianrestaurant.com
Italian menu. Dinner. Casual attire. Reservations recommended. Outdoor seating. $$

### ★Rio Grande Cafe
270 S. Rio Grande St., Salt Lake City,
801-364-3302
Southwestern menu. Lunch, dinner. Bar. Children's menu. Casual attire. Outdoor seating. $

### ★Squatters Pub Brewery
147 W. Broadway, Salt Lake City,
801-363-2739;
www.squatters.com
American menu. Lunch, dinner, late-night, brunch. Bar. Children's menu. Casual attire. Outdoor seating. $$

**315**

**UTAH**

★
★
★
★
★

**★★Tucci's Cucina Italia**
515 S. 700 E., Salt Lake City,
801-533-9111
Italian menu. Lunch, dinner, brunch. Children's menu. Casual attire. Reservations recommended. Outdoor seating. **$$**

**★★★Tuscany**
2832 E. 6200 S., Salt Lake City,
801-277-9919;
www.tuscanyslc.com
This tremendously popular place maintains a high quality of service and offers authentic Tuscan fare while incorporating modern American culinary trends. One of the most popular items on the menu is the hardwood grilled double cut pork chop with scallion mashed potatoes.
Italian menu. Lunch, dinner, Sunday brunch. Bar. Casual attire. Reservations recommended. Valet parking. Outdoor seating. **$$$**

# SNOWBIRD

In 1971, a Texas oil man recognized the potential of Little Cottonwood Canyon in the Wasatch National Forest and developed the area as a ski resort. Once home to thriving mining communities, the resort village of Snowbird, 29 miles east of Salt Lake City, now offers year-round recreational activities. With an average of 500 inches of snowfall annually, Snowbird claims to have the world's best powder.
Information: www.snowbird.com

## WHAT TO SEE AND DO
**Snowbird Ski and Summer Resort**
Hwy. 210, Snowbird,
801-933-2222, 800-232-9542;
www.snowbird.com
Includes 89 runs on 2,500 acres; 27 percent beginner, 38 percent intermediate, 35 percent advanced/expert. Elevations of 7,800 to 11,000 feet. Six double chairlifts, four high-speed quads, 125-passenger aerial tram. Patrol, school, rentals. Four lodges. Night skiing Wednesday, Friday. Heli-skiing, halfpipe. Snowboarding, snowshoeing, ice skating. Mid-November-early May, daily. Summer activities include rock climbing, hiking, mountain biking, tennis, tram rides and concerts.

## SPECIAL EVENTS
**Utah Symphony**
7350 S. Wasatch Blvd., Snowbird,
801-533-5626, 888-355-2787;
www.utahsymphony.org
Snowbird Ski and Summer Resort is the summer home of the orchestra. Several Sunday afternoon concerts. July-August.

## HOTELS
**★★Lodge at Snowbird**
Little Cottonwood Canyon, Snowbird,
801-933-2222, 800-232-9542;
www.snowbird.com
125 rooms. Restaurant, bar. Children's activity center. Airport transportation available. **$$**

**★★Cliff Lodge & Spa**
Little Cotton Canyon, Snowbird,
801-933-2222, 800-232-9542;
www.snowbird.com
511 rooms. 12 restaurants, bar. Ski in/ski out. **$$$**

## RESTAURANTS
**★★Steak Pit**
Snowbird Center, Snowbird,
801-933-2260;
www.snowbird.com
Steak menu. Dinner. Children's menu. Casual attire. Valet parking. **$$**

# SPRINGDALE

This small village is right outside Zion National Park.
Information: www.zionpark.com

## HOTELS

**★Cliffrose Lodge and Gardens**
281 Zion Park Blvd.,
Springdale,
435-772-3234, 800-243-8824;
www.cliffroselodge.com
40 rooms. Pool. **$**

**★★Flanigan's Inn and Deep Canyon Spa**
450 Zion Park Blvd.,
Springdale,
435-772-3244, 800-765-7787;
www.flanigans.com
36 rooms. Restaurant, bar. Spa. Pool. **$**

## SPECIALTY LODGINGS

**Novel House Inn**
73 Paradise Rd., Springdale,
435-772-3650, 800-711-8400;
www.novelhouse.com
This literary-themed bed and breakfast is set among the towering sandstone cliffs of Zion National Park. It is secluded but within walking distance of shops and restaurants. Complimentary breakfast and afternoon tea are served in the dining room with a view of West Temple Mountain.
10 rooms. No children allowed. Complimentary full breakfast. Whirlpool. **$**

# ST. GEORGE

Extending themselves to this hot, arid corner of southwest Utah, members of the LDS church built their first temple here and struggled to survive by growing cotton. With determination and persistence, members of the church constructed the temple. Hundreds of tons of rocks were pounded into the mud until a stable foundation could be laid. Mormons from the north worked 40-day missions, and southern church members gave one day's labor out of every 10 until the temple was complete. The workers quarried 17,000 tons of rock by hand. A team of ox hauled the stones to the construction site, and for seven straight days, timber was hauled more than 80 miles from Mount Trumbull to build the structure. Made of red sandstone plastered to a gleaming white, the Mormon temple is not only the town's landmark, but also a beacon for passing aircraft.

In St. George, warm summers are balanced by mild winters, and the village is fast becoming a retirement destination. The seat of Washington County, St. George is the closest town of its size to Zion National Park.
Information: St. Geoge Area Chamber of Commerce, 97 E. St. George Blvd., 435-628-1658; www.stgeorgechamber.com

**317**

**UTAH**

★
★
★
★
★

## WHAT TO SEE AND DO

**Brigham Young Winter Home**
67 W. 200 N., St. George, 435-673-5181
Brigham Young spent the last four winters of his life in this two-story adobe house, which still includes period furnishings. Daily.

**Pine Valley Chapel**
St. George, 30 miles north via Hwy. 18,
435-634-5747
Ebenezer Bryce, a shipbuilder by trade, built this white-framed chapel, which is still in use, in 1868 as an upside-down ship. The walls were completed on the ground, then raised and joined with wooden pegs and rawhide. Memorial Day-Labor Day, daily.

**St. George Temple**
250 E. 400 S., St. George, 435-673-3533
This red sandstone structure was built between 1863-1876 with local materials and resembles a colonial New England church. Daily.

**Temple Visitor Center**
490 S 300 E., St. George, 435-673-5181
A guided tour of the center explains local history and beliefs of the Latter-Day Saints; audiovisual program. Daily.

## HOTELS

### ★Best Western Coral Hills
125 E. St. George Blvd., St. George,
435-673-4844, 800-542-7733;
www.coralhills.com
98 rooms. Complimentary continental breakfast. High-speed wireless Internet access. Airport transportation available. **$**

### ★Comfort Inn
1239 S. Main St., St. George,
435-673-7000, 800-428-0754;
www.comfortsuites.net
122 rooms. Complimentary continental breakfast. High-speed wireless Internet access. Airport transportation available. Pets accepted. **$**

### ★★Holiday Inn
850 S. Bluff St., St. George,
435-628-4235, 800-457-9800;
www.histgeorgeutah.com
164 rooms. High-speed Internet access. Restaurant. Airport transportation available. Pets accepted. Business center. **$**

## SPECIALTY LODGINGS

### Green Gate Village
76 W. Tabernacle St., St. George,
435-628-6999, 800-350-6999;
www.greengatevillage.com
Situated in the historic district of St. George, these elegantly restored pioneer houses are perfect for those who want nostalgic charm with modern conveniences. 14 rooms. Complimentary full breakfast. Pool. **$**

# SUNDANCE

This popular ski resort was purchased by Robert Redford in 1968 and is named after the role Redford played in the film *Butch Cassidy and the Sundance Kid*. The popular Sundance Film Festival, held 30 miles north in Park City is one of the largest independent film festivals in the world.

## WHAT TO SEE AND DO

### Sundance Ski Area
North Fork Provo Canyon, Sundance,
801-225-4107, 800-892-1600;
www.sundanceresort.com
Three chairlifts, rope tow; patrol, school, rentals; warming hut, restaurants. Longest run two miles, vertical drop 2,150 feet. Cross-country trails. Late November-April, daily.

## HOTELS

### ★★★Sundance Resort
N. Fork Provo Canyon, Sundance,
801-225-4107, 800-892-1600;
www.sundanceresort.com
This resort offers standard rooms, studios and cottages, all of which, like the resort itself, are intended to blend with the surrounding landscape. All of the rooms feature natural wood and Native American accents; most have fireplaces and private decks. The resort also offers fine dining and endless recreation, from artist workshops to nature programs. The general store is so popular that a mail-order catalog has been designed. A fabulous spa completes the well-rounded experience available at this unique resort. 110 rooms. Two restaurants, bar. Children's activity center. Fitness room. Spa. Ski. **$$$**

## RESTAURANTS

### ★★Foundry Grill
N. Fork Provo Canyon, Sundance,
801-223-4220, 800-892-1600;
www.sundanceresort.com
American menu. Breakfast, lunch, dinner, Sunday brunch. Bar. Outdoor seating. **$$**

### ★★★The Tree Room
N. Fork Provo Canyon, Sundance,
801-223-4200, 800-892-1600;
www.sundanceresort.com
Located at the base of the Sundance ski lift, this restaurant's two-story windows offer stunning views of the rugged mountains and surrounding wilderness. The upscale-yet-casual room is filled with beautiful displays of Native American dolls and pottery. The sophisticated new American cuisine includes wild game, steaks and seafood,

prepared with herbs and vegetables from the resort's own organic gardens.

American menu. Dinner. Bar. Reservations recommended. $$$

# VERNAL

This is the county seat of Uintah County in northeastern Utah, which boasts oil, natural gas and many mineral deposits. Vernal is in an area of ancient geologic interest. Nearby are beautiful canyons, striking rock formations and majestic peaks.
Information: Dinosaurland Travel Board, 55 E. Main St., 435-789-1352, 800-477-5558; www.dinoland.com

## WHAT TO SEE AND DO

### Ashley National Forest
355 N. Vernal Ave., Vernal, 435-789-1181;
www.fs.fed.us/r4/ashley
The Uinta Mountains run through the heart of this nearly 1 1/2 million-acre forest. Red Canyon, Kings Peak and Sheep Creek Geological Area are also here. Swimming, fishing, boating (ramps, marinas), whitewater rafting, canoeing; hiking and nature trails, cross-country skiing, snowmobiling, improved or back-country campgrounds. Visitor centers.

### Daughters of Utah Pioneers Museum
500 W. 186 S. Vernal, 435-789-0352;
www.dupinternational.org
This museum contains relics and artifacts dating from before 1847, when pioneers first settled in Utah. Includes period furniture, quilts, clothing, dolls, early medical instruments and more. June-weekend before Labor Day, Monday-Saturday.

### Flaming Gorge Dam and National Recreation Area
Vernal, 42 miles north on Hwy. 191, in Ashley National Forest, 435-784-3445;
www.utah.com/nationalsites/
flaming_gorge.htm
The area surrounds 91-mile-long Flaming Gorge Reservoir and 502-foot-high Flaming Gorge Dam. Fishing on reservoir and river (all year), marinas, boat ramps, water-skiing; lodges, campgrounds. River rafting below dam. Visitor centers at dam and Red Canyon (on secondary paved road three miles off Hwy. 44).

### Ouray National Wildlife Refuge
Vernal, 30 miles southwest on Hwy. 88, 435-545-2522; www.fws.gov/ouray

The desert scenery here includes waterfowl nesting marshes. Daily.

### Red Fleet State Park
8750 N. Hwy. 191, Vernal, 435-789-4432;
stateparks.utah.gov/parks/red-fleet
This scenic lake is highlighted by red rock formations, and you can see several hundred well-preserved dinosaur tracks. Boating, swimming, fishing; camping. Daily.

### Hatch River Expeditions
55 E. Main St., Vernal, 800-856-8966;
www.hatchriverexpeditions.com
Guided whitewater trips on the Green and Yampa rivers.

### Steinaker State Park
4335 N. Hwy. 191, Vernal, 435-789-4432;
stateparks.utah.gov/parks/steinaker
This state park encompasses approximately 2,200 acres on the west shore of Steinaker Reservoir. Swimming, waterskiing, fishing, boating; picnicking, tent and trailer sites. April-November; fishing all year.

### Utah Field House of Natural History and Dinosaur Gardens
496 E. Main St., Vernal, 435-789-3799;
stateparks.utah.gov/parks/field-house
Guarded outside by three life-size cement dinosaurs, this museum has exhibits of fossils, archaeology, life zones, geology and fluorescent minerals of the region. The adjacent Dinosaur Gardens contain 18 life-size model dinosaurs in natural surroundings. Daily.

### Western Heritage Museum
28 E. 200 S., Vernal, 435-789-7399
Relive the town's outlaw past at this museum that houses lots of local memorabilia and

**319**

**UTAH**

★
★
★
★
★

artifacts of the ancient people of Utah. Monday-Saturday.

## HOTELS
**★★Best Western Dinosaur Inn**
251 E. Main St., Vernal, 435-789-2660;
www.bestwestern.com
60 rooms. Restaurant, bar. **$**

**★The Sage Motel**
54 W. Main St., Vernal, 800-760-1442;
www.vernalmotels.com
26 rooms. Pets accepted. **$**

## SPECIALTY LODGINGS
**Hills House**
675 W. 3300 N., Vernal, 435-789-0700
4 rooms. **$**

**Landmark Inn Bed & Breakfast**
288 E. 100 S., Vernal,
435-781-1800, 888-738-1800;
www.landmark-inn.com
10 rooms. **$**

## RESTAURANT
**★7-11 Ranch**
77 E. Main St., Vernal, 435-789-1170
American menu. Breakfast, lunch, dinner. Closed Sunday. Children's menu. **$**

### DINOSAUR NATIONAL MONUMENT/UTAH ENTRANCE

On August 17, 1909, paleontologist Earl Douglass discovered dinosaur bones in this area, including several nearly complete skeletons. Since then, this location has revealed more skeletons, skulls and bones of Jurassic-period dinosaurs than any other dig in the world. Utah's Dinosaur Quarry section can be entered from the junction of Hwy. 40 and Hwy. 149, north of Jensen, 13 miles east of Vernal. Approximately seven miles north on Hwy. 149 is the fossil exhibit. Another five miles north is Green River Campground, with 90 tent and trailer sites available mid-May to mid-September. A smaller campground, Rainbow Park, provides a small number of tent sites from May to November. Lodore, Deerlodge and Echo Park campgrounds are available in Colorado.

The dinosaur site comprises only 80 acres of this 325-square-mile park, which lies at the border of Utah and Colorado. The backcountry section, most of which is in Colorado, is a land of fantastic and deeply eroded canyons of the Green and Yampa rivers. Access to this backcountry section is via the Harpers Corner Road, starting at monument headquarters on Hwy. 40, two miles east of Dinosaur, Colorado. At Harpers Corner, the end of this 32-mile surfaced road, a one-mile foot trail leads to a promontory overlooking the Green and Yampa rivers, more than 2,500 feet below. The entire area was named a national monument in 1915.

Some areas of the monument are closed from approximately mid-November to mid-April because of snow.

Information: 4545 E. U.S. 40, Vernal, 435-374-3000; www.nps.gov/dino

## WHAT TO SEE AND DO
**River rafting**
Dinosaur National Monument,
435-781-7700

Go rafting down the Green and Yampa rivers. Get an advanced permit from National Park Service or with concession-operated guided float trips.

# ZION NATIONAL PARK

The spectacular canyons and enormous rock formations in this 147,551-acre national park are the result of powerful upheavals of the earth and erosion by flowing water and frost. Considered the grandfather of Utah's national parks, Zion is one of the nation's oldest national parks and one of the state's wildest, with large sections virtually inaccessible. The Virgin River runs through the interior of the park, and Zion Canyon, with its deep, narrow chasm and multicolored vertical walls, cuts through the middle, with smaller canyons branching from it like fingers. A paved roadway following the bottom of Zion Canyon is surrounded by massive rock formations in awe-inspiring colors that change with the light. The formations, described as temples, cathedrals and thrones, rise to great heights, the loftiest reaching 8,726 feet. The canyon road runs seven miles to the Temple of Sinawava, a natural amphitheater surrounded by cliffs. Another route, an extension of Hwy. 9, cuts through the park in an east-west direction, taking visitors through the mile-long Zion-Mount Carmel Tunnel, and then descends through a series of switchbacks with viewpoints above Pine Creek Canyon.

Zion's main visitor center, open daily, is near the south entrance. Check here for maps, information about the park and schedules of naturalist activities and evening programs. Each evening in spring through fall, park naturalists give illustrated talks on the natural and human history of the area. Pets must be kept on leash and are not permitted on trails. The park is open year-round.
Information: 435-772-3256; www.nps.gov/zion

## WHAT TO DO AND SEE

### Bicycling
**Zion**
Biking is permitted on roads in park, except through Zion-Mt. Carmel Tunnel.

### Escorted horseback trips
**Zion, 435-772-3967**
Special guide service may be obtained for other trips not regularly scheduled. Contact Bryce/Zion Trail Rides at Zion Lodge. March-October, daily.

### Park trails
**Zion, 435-772-3256**
Trails lead to otherwise inaccessible areas: the Narrows ( walls of this canyon are 2,000 feet high and as little as 50 feet apart at the stream), the Hanging Gardens of Zion, Weeping Rock, the Emerald Pools. Trails range from 1/2-mile trips to day-long treks, some requiring great stamina. Trails in less-traveled areas should not be undertaken without first obtaining information from a park ranger. Backcountry permits required for travel through the Virgin River Narrows and other canyons, and on all overnight trips.

### Zion Nature Center
**Zion, adjacent to South Campground, 435-772-2356**
Kids between the ages of 6-12 can sign up for the junior ranger program. Memorial Day-Labor Day, Monday-Friday.

# INDEX

**322**

**INDEX**

**327**

**INDEX**

**328**

**329**

**INDEX**

**331**

**INDEX**

★
★
★
★

**332**

**INDEX**

**333**

**INDEX**

**334**

**INDEX**

★

★

★

★

**335**

**INDEX**

★

★

★

☆

☆

**336**

**337**

**INDEX**

★

★

★

✦

✦

**338**

**339**

**INDEX**

★
★
★
★
★

**341**

**INDEX**

★
★
★
★
★

**342**

INDEX

**343**

**INDEX**

★

★

★

☆

☆

**U**

U.S. Air Force Academy (Colorado Springs, CO), *103*

U.S. Olympic Training Center (Colorado Springs, CO), *103*

UFO Encounters Festival (Roswell, NM), *249*

Uinta National Forest (Provo, UT), *305*

Ullr Fest & World Cup Freestyle (Breckenridge, CO), *95*

Union Station—the Utah State Railroad Museum (Ogden, UT), *297*

University of Arizona (Tucson, AZ), *67*

University of Colorado (Boulder, CO), *91*

University of Colorado Museum (Boulder, CO), *91*

University of Denver (Denver, CO), *115*

University of Nevada, Las Vegas (Las Vegas, NV), *190*

University of Nevada, Reno (Reno, NV), *213*

University of New Mexico (Albuquerque, NM), *226*

University of Northern Colorado (Greeley, CO), *140*

University of Utah (Salt Lake City, UT), *312*

UNLV Performing Arts Center (Las Vegas, NV), *190*

UNLV Sports (Las Vegas, NV), *190*

Utah Arts Festival (Salt Lake City, UT), *312*

Utah Festival Opera Company (Logan, UT), *289*

Utah Field House of Natural History and Dinosaur Gardens (Vernal, UT), *319*

Utah Jazz (NBA) (Salt Lake City, UT), *312*

Utah Lake State Park (Provo, UT), *305*

Utah Museum of Fine Arts (Salt Lake City, UT), *312*

Utah Museum of Natural History (Salt Lake City, UT), *312*

Utah Navajo Fair (Bluff, UT), *281*

Utah Opera Company (Salt Lake City, UT), *312*

Utah Shakespearean Festival (Cedar City, UT), *284*

Utah Starzz (WNBA) (Salt Lake City, UT), *312*

Utah State University (Logan, UT), *289*

Utah Summer Games (Cedar City, UT), *284*

Utah Symphony (Snowbird, UT), *316*

Utah Symphony Pops Concert (Ogden, UT), *297*

Utah Winter Sports Park (Park City, UT), *299*

Ute Mountain Round-Up Rodeo (Cortez, CO), *107*

Ute Mountain Tribal Park (Cortez, CO), *107*

Ute Stampede Rodeo (Nephi, UT), *296*

**V**

Vail Cascade Resort & Spa (Vail, CO), *167*

Vail Mountain Lodge & Spa (Vail, CO), *167*

Vail Ski Resort (Avon, CO), *165*

Vail's Mountain Haus (Vail, CO), *167*

Valentino (Las Vegas, NV), *207*

Valhalla Winter Microbrew Festival (South Lake Tahoe, NV), *217*

Vanessie of Santa Fe (Santa Fe, NM), *268*

Vans Skatepark (Phoenix, AZ), *33*

Verde Valley Fair (Cottonwood, AZ), *8*

Veteran's Memorial Rally (Cripple Creek, CO), *109*

Via Bellagio (Las Vegas, NV), *190*

Victor (Cripple Creek, CO), *109*

Victor Hotel (Victor, CO), *110*

Victorian Home Tour and Brunch (Leadville, CO), *145*

Vietnam Veterans State Park Memorial (Angel Fire, NM), *230*

Village Tavern (Scottsdale, AZ), *53*

Vincent Guerithault on Camelback (Phoenix, AZ), *37*

Vista Ridge Golf Club (Erie, CO), *91*

Vista Verde Guest And Ski Ranch (Steamboat Springs, CO), *161*

Viva Mercados (Las Vegas, NV), *207*

VooDoo Steck & Lounge (Las Vegas, NV), *207*

**W**

W. M. Keck Earth Sciences and Engineering Museum (Reno, NV), *213*

Walnut Canyon National Monument (Flagstaff, AZ), *11*

Ward Charcoal Ovens State Historic Park (Ely, NV), *175*

Warren Engine Company No. 1 Fire Museum (Carson City, NV), *173*

Wasatch County Fair (Heber City, UT), *286*

Wasatch Mountain State Park (Heber City, UT), *286*

Wasatch-Cache National Forest (Salt Lake City, UT), *312*

Wasatch-Cache National Forest, Logan Canyon (Logan, UT), *289*

Washington Park (Denver, CO), *115*

Washington School Inn (Park City, UT), *301*

Washoe Grill (Reno, NV), *216*

Water Street Inn (Santa Fe, NM), *264*

Waterworld Safari (Glendale, AZ), *13*

Wazee Supper Club (Denver, CO), *121*

Weber State University (Ogden, UT), *297*

Wellshire Inn (Denver, CO), *121*

West Beaver Creek Lodge (Avon, CO), *87*

West Valley Invitational American Indian Arts Festival (Litchfield Park, AZ), *21*

Western Heritage Museum (Vernal, UT), *319*

Western New Mexico University Museum (Silver City, NM), *269*

Westward Look Resort (Tucson, AZ), *69*

WestWorld of Scottsdale (Scottsdale, AZ), *44*

Wheeler Historic Farm (Salt Lake City, UT), *312*

Wheelwright Museum (Santa Fe, NM), *253*

White Pine Public Museum (Ely, NV), *175*

White Pine Touring Center (Park City, UT), *299*

White River National Forest (Glenwood Springs, CO), *134*

White Sands Missile Range (Las Cruces, NM), *244*

**345**

**INDEX**

**346**

**INDEX**

# NOTES

★
★
★
★
★

# NOTES

# NOTES

★
★
★
★
★

# NOTES

350

INDEX

★
★
★
★
★

# NOTES

★
★
★
★
★

# NOTES

★
★
★
★
★

# NOTES

★
★
★
★
★

# NOTES

354

INDEX

# NOTES

★
★
★
★
★

# NOTES

INDEX

★
★
★
★
★

# NOTES

★
★
★
★
★

# NOTES

# NOTES

★
★
★
★
★

# NOTES

★
★
★
★
★

# NOTES

★
★
★
★
★

# NOTES

★
★
★
★
★

# NOTES

363

INDEX

★
★
★
★
★

# NOTES

★

★

★

★

★

# NOTES

365

INDEX

# NOTES

★

★

★

★

★

# NOTES

★
★
★
★
★

# NOTES

★

★

★

★

★

# NOTES

★
★
★
★
★

# NOTES

370

INDEX

★
★
★
★
★

# NOTES

★

★

★

★

★

# NOTES

INDEX

★
★
★
★
★

# NOTES

★
★
★
★
★

# NOTES

★
★
★
★
★

# NOTES

★
★
★
★
★

# NOTES

★

★

★

★

★

# NOTES

★
★
★
★
★

# NOTES

378

INDEX

★
★
★
★
★

# NOTES

★
★
★
★
★

# NOTES

★
★
★
★
★

# NOTES

★
★
★
★
★

# NOTES

382

INDEX

★
★
★
★
★

# NOTES

# NOTES

★
★
★
★
★

# NOTES

★
★
★
★
★

# NOTES

★

★

★

★

★

# NOTES

★
★
★
★
★

# NOTES

★

★ ★

★ ★ ★

★ ★ ★ ★

★ ★ ★ ★ ★

# NOTES

389

INDEX

★
★
★
★
★

# NOTES

★
★
★
★
★

# NOTES

# NOTES

392

INDEX

★
★
★
★
★

# NOTES

★
★
★
★
★

# NOTES

★

★ ★

★ ★ ★

★ ★ ★ ★

★ ★ ★ ★ ★

# NOTES

★
★
★
★
★

# NOTES

396

INDEX

★
★
★
★
★

# NOTES

★
★
★
★
★

# NOTES

398

INDEX

★

★

★

★

★

# NOTES

★
★
★
★
★

# NOTES

**400**

INDEX

★
★
★
★
★